ON THE PSYCHOBIOLOGY OF PERSONALITY:

ESSAYS IN HONOR OF MARVIN ZUCKERMAN

Related books:

H. NYBORG (ED.)
The Scientific Study of Human Nature: Tribute to Hans J. Eysenck

H. NYBORG (ED.)
The Scientific Study of General Intelligence: Tribute to Authur R. Jensen

Related journals – Sample copies available online from
http://www.elsevier.com

Personality and Individual Differences
Intelligence
Journal of Personality Research
Developmental Review
Cognitive Development
Infant Behavior Development
Journal of Adolescence
Psychology of Sport and Exercise
Addictive Behaviors

We would like to acknowledge Frances Hodes as the designer of the images used on the front cover. The images depict the four faces representing the four temperaments of antiquity (choleric, melancholic, sanguine, and phlegmatic) and it was initially designed to advertise the Third ISSID Conference where Marvin Zuckerman gave the Presidential Address.

We would like to thank ISSID allowing us to use the images on the cover.

ON THE PSYCHOBIOLOGY OF PERSONALITY:

ESSAYS IN HONOR OF MARVIN ZUCKERMAN

EDITED BY

ROBERT M. STELMACK

University of Ottawa, Ottawa, Canada

2004

ELSEVIER

Amsterdam – Boston – Heidelberg – London – New York – Oxford
Paris – San Diego – San Francisco – Singapore – Sydney – Tokyo

ELSEVIER B.V.
Radarweg 29
P.O. Box 211
1000 AE Amsterdam
The Netherlands

ELSEVIER Inc.
525 B Street, Suite 1900
San Diego
CA 92101-4495
USA

ELSEVIER Ltd
The Boulevard, Langford Lane, Kidlington
Oxford OX5 1GB
UK

ELSEVIER Ltd
84 Theobalds Road
London
WC1X 8RR
UK

First edition 2004

Library of Congress Cataloging in Publication Data
A catalog record is available from the Library of Congress.

British Library Cataloguing in Publication Data
A catalogue record is available from the British Library.

ISBN: 0-08-044209-9

♾ The paper used in this publication meets the requirements of ANSI/NISO Z39.48-1992 (Permanence of Paper). Printed in The Netherlands.

Contents

Contributors

Alois Angleitner	Department of Psychology, University of Bielefeld, Bielefeld, Germany
Samuel A. Ball	Yale University School of Medicine, New Haven, CT, USA
Michael T. Bardo	Center for Prevention Research, University of Kentucky, Lexington, KY, USA
Ernest S. Barratt	Psychiatry and Behavioral Science Department, University of Texas Medical Branch, Galveston, TX, USA
P. Gordon Bazana	Assessment Strategies, Ottawa, Ontario, Canada
Burkhard Brocke	Department of Psychology, Dresden University of Technology, Dresden, Germany
Vilfredo De Pascalis	Department of Psychology, University of Rome "La Sapienza," Rome, Italy
Lewis Donohew	Department of Communication, University of Kentucky, Lexington, KY, USA
Sybil B. G. Eysenck	Department of Psychology, Institute of Psychiatry, University of London, UK
Adrian Furnham	Department of Psychology, University College, University of London, UK
Montserrat Gomà-i-Freixanet	Department of Health Psychology, Autonomous University of Barcelona, Barcelona, Spain
Richard J. Haier	Department of Pediatrics, University of California at Irvine, Irvine, CA, USA
Juergen Hennig	Department of Psychology, University of Giessen, Giessen, Germany
Andrew M. Johnson	Faculty of Health Sciences, University of Western Ontario, London, Ontario, Canada

Jeffrey Joireman	Department of Psychology, University of Washington, Pulman, WA, USA
Magdalena Kaczmarek	Warsaw School of Social Psychology, Warsaw, Poland
Britt af Klinteberg	Department of Psychology, Stockholm University, Stockholm, Sweden
Lars von Knorring	Department of Neuroscience, University of Uppsala, Uppsala, Sweden
D. Michael Kuhlman	Department of Psychology, University of Delaware, Newark, DE, USA
Gerald Matthews	Department of Psychology, University of Cincinnati, Cincinnati, OH, USA
F. Gerard Moeller	Psychiatry and Behavioral Science Department, University of Texas Health Science Center, Houston, TX, USA
Petra Netter	Department of Psychology, University of Giessen, Giessen, Germany
Lars Oreland	Department of Neuroscience, University of Uppsala, Uppsala, Sweden
Luis F. Orozco-Cabal	Psychiatry and Behavioral Science Department, University of Texas Medical Branch, Galveston, TX, USA
Alan D. Pickering	Goldsmiths College, University of London, UK
Thomas Rammsayer	Department of Psychology, University of Goettingen, Goettingen, Germany
Rainer Riemann	Institute of Psychology, Fredrich-Schiller University, Jena, Germany
Paul Schmitz	Institute of Psychology, University of Bonn, Bonn, Germany
Frank Spinath	Department of Psychology, University of Bielefeld, Bielefeld, Germany
Jerome Siegel	Department of Psychology, University of Delaware, Newark, DE, USA and Warsaw School of Social Psychology, Warsaw, Poland
Robert M. Stelmack	School of Psychology, University of Ottawa, Ottawa, Ontario, Canada
Jan Strelau	Warsaw School of Social Psychology, Warsaw, Poland

P. A. Vernon Department of Psychology, University of Western Ontario, London, Ontario, Canada

Rick S. Zimmerman Research Department of Communication, University of Kentucky, Lexington, KY, USA

Foreword

During the past 50 years, there has been remarkable progress in the understanding of individual differences in personality. There now is considerable agreement that lengthy lists of personality trait terms can be reliably referred to a small number of independent, descriptive factors, notably sociability, emotional stability, impulsiveness, sensation seeking, openness to experience, conscientiousness, and agreeableness. Although there is some debate on which of these personality factors are fundamental, this psychometric work constitutes an important foundation for defining and structuring personality characteristics into a rational classification schema. The heritability of personality factors was also convincingly demonstrated in several large-scale identical twin and adoption studies. Determining the genetic architecture that serves individual differences in personality is now an important research objective. Moreover, this work strongly suggests that constitutional factors, under the influence of genetic mechanisms, contribute substantially to the expression of personality traits. In this respect, too, significant progress has been made in revealing the psychological processes and physiological mechanisms that mediate individual differences in personality. Throughout this span of inquiry, Marvin Zuckerman was an important contributor and an inspiring catalyst for a broad range of scientific research on the nature of personality.

In recognition of his outstanding productive scholarship, colleagues of Professor Zuckerman at the University of Delaware initiated a plan to honor his academic career and his retirement from the University with a symposium on personality at the University of Delaware and with the dedication of a book of essays contributed by colleagues, collaborators and experts in the field of personality. I was invited by his colleagues to organize and edit this book and I was pleased to do so.

Marvin Zuckerman is a well-established, renowned leader in research and writing on the social and biological bases of personality. In particular, he is a leading authority on the biological bases of sensation seeking and fundamental personality dispositions and on the manifestation of these dispositions in social behavior and in psychopathology. His major books *Sensation seeking: Beyond the optimal level of arousal* (1979), *Psychobiology of Personality* (1991), and *Behavioral expressions and biosocial bases of sensation seeking* (1994) are well known, required reading by students and researchers in this field. His personal research contributions and commentary exploited the full range of methods and models in psychological and physiological research, from the identification of fundamental personality traits through factor analysis, social behavior, psychopathology, psychophysiology, biochemical assays to molecular genetics. During the course of this interdisciplinary work, he collaborated and communed with leading authorities in those fields. These colleagues have committed to contribute essays in this tribute to Professor Zuckerman.

The title of this book, *On the psychobiology of personality: Essays in honor of Marvin Zuckerman*, mirrors the title of his first major work and marks the scope of this book. An important objective of the text is to encompass the broad range of research in personality that provided the context for Zuckerman's work and that also highlights his own contribution to progress in this field. The contributors to this volume were encouraged to address issues within their area of expertise that were resolved, to discuss issues that are unresolved, and to make an informed statement on current knowledge in their research domain. Thus, the text is intended to provide a succinct and state-of-the-art analysis of our current understanding of personality. The text offers both reflections on issues in personality research and technical reviews and research reports. By this approach, it is hoped that the text will constitute a useful resource and reference guide for students of personality. In addition, the text will serve as a catalyst for future research in the area, in much the same way that the contributions of Marvin Zuckerman served as a catalyst for work by a host of research scientists.

The book is organized in five parts. Part I provides brief historical perspectives on the biological bases of personality. Part II treats the identification and structure of fundamental personality traits and Part III deals with personality and social behavior. The fourth part is presented in two sections, psychophysiological analyses and biochemical analyses. The fifth section, an epilogue, contains a postscript on personality and it also includes an autobiography by our protagonist, Marvin Zuckerman.

1. Part I

A framework for understanding the psychobiology of personality is developed in the first section by introducing influential concepts and by identifying significant developments and issues. The text begins with a chapter by Ernest Barratt, who is a pioneer in personality research and noted for his work on impulsiveness, and by his colleagues Luis Orozco-Cabal and Gerard Moeller. This chapter provides a historical perspective on current challenges to research on impulsivity and sensation seeking. In the second chapter, Robert Stelmack discusses the role of the arousal construct in understanding the personality dimensions of extraversion, and sensation seeking. The arousal construct is of significant heuristic value as an explanatory construct in several theories of personality, including Zuckerman's theory of sensation seeking and Eysenck's theory of extraversion. This introductory section closes with a chapter by Jan Strelau and Magdalena Kaczmarek who provide an international, East European perspective, in a chapter on sensation seeking research that was conducted at the University of Warsaw.

2. Part II

The second section includes chapters that are germane to the identification and structure of fundamental personality factors. A rigorous, independent, personality classification scheme that receives broad endorsement from the academic community is an essential criterion for advancing the empirical analysis of personality. The contribution of Zuckerman to the development of a Five-Factor Model (FFM) of personality is outlined in essays by his colleague and co-author Mike Kulhman and by Jeffrey Joireman. They also detail the construction of the Zuckerman-Kuhlman Personality Questionnaire (ZKPQ) and chart the validity studies that have established authenticity of the test. Paul Schmitz describes his work on the confirmatory factor analysis of the German version of the ZKPQ and the validation studies that he conducted with the test. The chapter by Alois Angleitner and his colleagues, Frank Spinath and Rainer Riemann, report on their study of the psychometric properties of the ZKPQ and its relation to the FFM. They also present a behavioral genetic analysis of genetic and environmental influences on the ZKPQ scales and facets. In her chapter, Sybil Eysenck discusses issues and developments that define the place of impulsiveness and venturesomeness in Eysenck's well-known typology of personality.

As Zuckerman (1991) noted, the stability of personality across the life span and the heritability of personality factors are two criteria that are important in determining that personality factors are fundamental. The former topic is addressed by Gordon Bazana and Robert Stelmack who present a detailed meta-analysis of studies that examine the test-retest reliability of the FFM at different age intervals. They present a strong case that personality factors are stable across the life span. The genetic basis of substance abuse and the mediating effects of sensation seeking are treated by Andrew Johnson and Tony Vernon. There is good evidence of the genetic and physiological basis of individual differences in sensation seeking. They argue that the latent trait purported to underlie alcohol, tobacco, and drug abuse is a sensation seeking dimension similar to that originally conceptualized by Zuckerman.

3. Part III

The development of a fundamental personality typology is not an end in itself. Rather, it is a rational means to describe, and subsequently, to understand human behavior and to reveal the social and biological determinants of that behavior. The third section of the text includes chapters on a broad range of social activities and life experiences that illustrate the pervasive expression of personality differences in our daily lives. How personality dispositions are linked to the selection of leisure activities is discussed by Adrian Furnham, and Monserrat Gomà i Freixanet reviews research on the role of sensation seeking in participation in physical risk sports.

Individual differences in personality are also implicated in the development of personality disorders, substance abuse, and psychopathology. These are vital personal and social subjects. Lewis Donohew, and his colleagues Michael Bardo and Rick Zimmerman, make the case that sensation seeking and impulsive decision-making play significant roles in attention and persuasion. They show that these traits must be taken into account in programs that aim to discourage individuals from engaging in risky activities such as unprotected sex or that promote health and safety such as anti-smoking campaigns and safety in the work place.

Marvin Zuckerman is a leader in research on the role that personality, especially sensation seeking, plays in alcohol and drug abuse. Sam Ball, a former student with Zuckerman, pursued this line of research. In his chapter, he suggests that impulsivity, novelty seeking and sensation seeking may be direct risk factors for substance use and that a personality profile, such as low-agreeableness and high-aggression/hostility, may be a risk factor for personality disorders that have substance abuse as an important behavioral expression. The assessment of normal personality dimensions may also assist in identifying individuals who are at risk of substance abuse and to whom prevention efforts are directed.

4. Part IV — A

The idea that personality characteristics are determined, in part, by differences in physical constitution has persisted for more than 2000 years, as can be seen in the writings of ancient Greek physicians Hippocrates and Galen. However, the identification of the psychological processes and physiological systems that serve individual differences in personality remains a modern problem, one that is a focal interest in Zuckerman's scholarly work. Psychophysiological recording and psychopharmacological manipulation and measurement are two of the major methodical approaches that are used to probe the biological bases of personality and that are treated in this text.

Psychophysiological methods include non-invasive recording procedures, such as the electroencephalogram and positron emission tomography (PET) that monitor central nervous system activity and electrodermal and cardiac recording techniques that monitor autonomic nervous system activity. In the fourth section of the text, Vilfredo De Pascalis reviews the voluminous literature on the psychophysiology of extraversion. He makes a strong case for the view that introverts are more reactive to sensory stimulation than extraverts, an effect that can contribute to the reserve and reticence that is characteristic of introversion.

In a thoughtful analysis, Gerry Matthews applies the three levels of explanation of cognitive science — biological, symbol processing, and knowledge — to order the many correlates of neuroticism. He concludes that neuroticism does not seem to correspond with any single brain process, and similarly, that the trait has multiple correlates at the symbol processing and knowledge levels of explanation.

The search for psychophysiological correlates of sensation seeking has proven to be an arduous task with little to show for considerable effort. In his chapter, Burkhard Brocke has seized on one robust effect, augmenting-reducing, for the focus of his analysis. In response to increasing levels of stimulus intensity, high-sensation seekers exhibit an increase in event-related potential amplitude, whereas low-sensation seekers show little change or even decrease in response amplitude. In an attempt to explicate this effect, Brocke reviews the literature and describes his own recent work in the context of a four-level research program on Zuckerman's multilevel approach.

Richard Haier is a pioneer in brain imaging research, having presented the first positron emission tomography (PET) study in 1985. Because brain imaging, both PET and magnetic resonance imaging, are costly procedures, the application of these techniques to personality research is quite limited. In his chapter, Haier reviews the literature and critiques the studies on these promising procedures.

The section closes with a chapter by Jerome Siegel on the physiological bases of sensation seeking that were revealed through his work with animals using direct brain recording procedures. Siegel is a long-time colleague of Marvin Zuckerman at the University of Delaware, with their association dating to the 1970s. Using animal models of sensation seeking, Siegel and his colleagues showed that the augmenting-reducing of event-related potentials was mediated by cortical processes. His recent work probes the physiological bases of augmenting-reducing effect further with manipulation of the neurotransmitter excitatory amino acid.

5. Part IV — B

Biochemical methods are comprised of a wide range of procedures that monitor the effects of drugs on behavior and of advanced technologies that are used to assay hormones, neurotransmitters, and biochemical by-products of nervous system activity. The application of these procedures to probe the psychobiology of personality is considered in the final section of the text.

The role of hormones in the expression and maintenance of personality characteristics is outlined in the chapter by Petra Netter. She presents an introduction to the hormonal regulating feedback systems, mechanisms of hormone action, and rhythmic variations of hormones. The chapter is a comprehensive review of personality and individual variation in cortisol, notably in depression and anxiety; testosterone, notably its role in aggression; and the catecholamines, and adrenaline, and their role in anxiety.

Juergen Hennig also provides an introduction to the neurotransmitters, serotonin and noradrenaline and presents a comprehensive review of their contribution to individual differences in personality. He reports that a cluster of traits, impulsivity, aggression and depression, are salient correlates of the serotonergic transmitter system and demonstrates the close relationship between noradrenaline and depression.

In his chapter, Thomas Rammsayer considers the neurotransmitter dopamine as a determinant of individual differences in extraversion. He provides converging evidence from behavioral and biochemical research that endorses a functional relation between extraversion and dopaminergic mechanisms in the brain. Dopamingergic responsiveness is higher in introverts than extraverts. This view is based on observation of peripheral physiological responses mediated by the tuberoinfundibular tuberohypophysial dopamine systems and by behavioral responses that are mediated by mesostriatal and mesolimbocortical dopamine systems.

Britt af Klinteberg, Lars von Knorring and Lars Oreland address evidence and issues in the neurobiological bases of impulsiveness. They present a comprehensive review of the psychology of impulsiveness as it is expressed in both normal and pathological behavior. Low levels of monoamine oxidase is characteristic of alcoholics and cigarette smokers and has also been linked to sensation seeking.

Alan Pickering examines the hypothesis put forth by Zuckerman that impulsive antisocial sensation seeking reflects individual differences in a behavioral approach system (BAS) that is mediated by dopaminergic mechanisms. From studies that employed tasks that indexed the BAS, he concludes that extraversion rather than impulsive antisocial sensation seeking is associated with BAS-related task performance. He also proposes that variation in impulsive antisocial sensation seeking traits might relate to variation in the functioning of the hippocampal system and related structures.

6. Epilogue

In the epilogue, I have written a brief postscript on the psychobiology of personality and its portents. In addition, I have received permission to reprint an autobiography of Marvin Zuckerman that was recently published in the *Journal of Personality Assessment*. It is a wonderful story that provides all of the themes and threads that have been woven into this text that honors him.

Acknowledgments

To begin, I would like to thank Roger Kobak at the University of Delaware for initiating this project and for inviting me to serve as editor of this volume. It has been a privilege for me to coordinate this tribute to Marvin Zuckerman in recognition of his more than 50 years of scholarly work on personality and individual differences. All of the contributors are indebted to him for the leadership and encouragement that he has provided. I would like to personally acknowledge Marvin for his counsel over the past 20 years, beginning with a meeting in Los Angeles where Marvin, Ernie Barratt and I initiated a plan that culminated in establishing the International Society for the Study of Individual Differences (ISSID) and continuing with discussion and debate during sabbatical leaves in England and at every ISSID conference.

Many thanks are extended to the contributors to this volume who took up the cause to celebrate Marvin with enthusiasm and dedication. I gratefully acknowledge Fiona Barron and the staff at Elsevier for endorsing the publication of this project. I would also like to thank Laura Kealey for her assistance with the citation and reference lists. And finally, I would like to thank my wife Carole for her support during this project and for the many hours that she devoted to editing the text.

Robert M. Stelmack
University of Ottawa
Ottawa, Canada

Part I

Historical Perspectives on the Biological Bases of Personality

Chapter 1

Impulsivity and Sensation Seeking: A Historical Perspective on Current Challenges

E. Barratt, L. F. Orozco-Cabal and F. G. Moeller

1. Introduction

Nowhere is the challenge of defining and measuring personality constructs more obvious than in a historical review of impulsivity and sensation seeking. Debates about these traits have revolved around their level of complexity, their relationship with other traits, and their relationship with each other. Examples of specific questions posed in these debates include: (1) Do impulsivity and sensation seeking have subdimensions? If so, what are they? (2) Do impulsivity and sensation seeking combine to define a superfactor? (3) How do these two traits relate to other higher-order personality constructs that have been identified in more encompassing personality models? (4) How do different measures of these traits as defined within different disciplines or subdisciplines relate to each other? For example, how do phenomenal self measures, e.g. self-report questionnaires, relate to behavioral measures involving delay of reward? What relative value do these discipline specific measures have as predictors of impulse-control disorders? Although both impulsivity and sensation seeking have a relatively long history within the general context of personality research, these debates have not been resolved. These questions per se will not be broached in depth in this chapter but, rather, general observations that currently preclude their being answered will be reviewed briefly and selected general suggestions for their resolution will be outlined.

The major goal of this chapter is to review the current pragmatic status of these two personality constructs at the cusp between past and future research. From the viewpoint of better understanding persons and achieving a more promising future for societies and individuals, is the current status of these two personality traits all there is? The answer is no if different approaches can be used to inter-relate data from the different disciplines that study persons from molecular biology to social interactions. An alternative strategy for defining and measuring personality dimensions in general and impulsivity and sensation

On the Psychobiology of Personality
Edited by R. M. Stelmack

ISBN: 0-08-044209-9

seeking in particular must be found. The strategies proposed for new approaches are not meant to be the only approaches nor ones that will endure beyond a limited time frame. Most scientific methodologies are usually modified over time. The more basic the problems addressed by the methodologies, the longer will be their influence.

This chapter will not chronicle in depth the history of impulsivity and sensation seeking research and their role in clinical and social decision-making. The history of the study of both traits has been well documented in other sources. Reviews of both theoretical and applied impulsivity research include: (1) McCown and De Simone (1993); this source not only provides a historical overview but also defines important terms (e.g. impulsivity and impulses); this review is part of a book (McCown & De Simone 1993) whose chapters cover a wide range of theoretical and clinical approaches to understanding impulsivity; (2) Webster and Jackson (1997); the first five chapters review different approaches to impulsivity ranging across clinical, social psychology, sociological, legal, "cybernautical" perspectives; this book is more oriented toward social applications, especially forensic considerations; and (3) Evenden (1999); this article in an issue of *Psychopharmacology* is an overview of varieties of impulsivity. It is an excellent overview contrasting the theory and development of self-report measures of impulsivity with behavioral measures that are primarily based on learning theory principles. The article reviews a wide range of impulsivity research especially with lower animals.

Reviews of sensation seeking research include: (1) Zuckerman (1979); this book contains a historical review by the author whose pioneering research on sensation seeking has made his name almost synonymous with the study of this trait; and (2) Zuckerman (1991); chapter one provides an overview from a broader perspective of how sensation seeking and other personality traits are related to more encompassing personality theories; the difficulties in classifying personality traits are made obvious in this chapter.

The current chapter is divided into four parts: (1) Why are impulsivity and sensation seeking important personality traits? (2) Why is there confusion about defining and measuring impulsivity and sensation seeking? (3) What challenges and potential solutions confront researchers in defining these traits? (4) The future: selective alternative approaches.

2. Why are Impulsivity and Sensation Seeking Important Personality Traits?

Impulsivity and sensation seeking are implicated in a broad range of psychopathologies and social problems that are part of a wide spectrum of impulse control disorders. For example, in the *Diagnostic and Statistical Manual of Mental Disorders* (4th ed., Text Revision) (DSM-IV-TR; American Psychiatric Association 2000), impulsivity is implicated in attention deficit hyperactivity disorder, conduct disorders, antisocial personality disorders, borderline personality disorder, substance abuse, aggression (intermittent explosive disorder), mood disorders, (especially mania), and eating disorders (especially binge eating). If this list is translated into the context of social problems that currently plague human kind, the basis for the importance of impulsivity is obvious. Sensation seeking has also been related to a wide range of psychopathologies and social problems including for example delinquency (Greene *et al.* 2000), aggression (Joireman *et al.* 2003), and antisocial and borderline personality disorders (DSM IV-TR). Zuckerman and Neeb (1979) in an early study relating the Sensation Seeking Scale (SSS) to psychopathology found that the SSS was related primarily to a spectrum of sociopathic disorders.

Lessons learned in reviewing the relation of impulsivity and sensation seeking to clinical disorders include: (1) both traits are multidimensional; (2) different sub-dimensions of both traits relate to different impulse control disorders; (3) the two traits often interact with each other and with other personality traits in their involvement with selected psychopathologies.

Why do impulsivity and sensation seeking relate to a wide range of impulse-control disorders and social adjustment problems? It is proposed that not only are these traits multidimensional but they can also be characterized by a wide range of biological, behavioral, cognitive, and social/environment constructs and measurements. The substratum of the impulsivity and sensation seeking measures within these four categories of constructs have common variance with the substrates of the psychopathological and social disorders listed above and provide the bases for the relationships of the two personality traits to these disorders.

3. Why is There Confusion About Defining and Measuring Impulsivity and Sensation Seeking?

After reviewing "a number of different approaches to analyzing impulsivity ranging from the study of human personality traits, through psychiatric symptoms to animal behavior," Evenden (1999: 358) noted that "even though almost all authors are in agreement that impulsivity is multifactorial, there is little agreement as to what these factors are even within a single field of research such as human personality traits." It is proposed here that the main reason for lack of agreement on measuring impulsivity and sensation seeking lies within two contexts: First, the lack of general agreement on an encompassing personality model which can allow for the synthesis of data ranging from molecular biology measures to measures of social/pathological disorders; most models establish a structure of personality based on self-report measures or interview data even though they may have originally been conceived as personality measurements of biologically based constructs. For example, Zuckerman (1979) developed the SSS based on biological and behavioral research data related to an optimal level of arousal. Cloninger (1986) and his colleagues (Cloninger *et al.* 1993, 1994) started with biological data when developing the Temperament and Character Inventory. This test contains a novelty seeking trait which is similar to sensation seeking. Actually, most self-report measures of impulsivity and sensation seeking (as well as measures of other personality traits) were developed primarily within the context of phenomenal self data, primarily self-report measures. Parenthetically, this discussion is not meant to be a criticism of the use of self-report or phenomenal data to measure personality traits but rather, as will be discussed, an appeal to consider both the strengths and weaknesses of self-reports. Once a self-report measure is developed there is a tendency to forget the origins of its conception.

The second context leading to confusion is the complexity of impulsivity and sensation seeking as constructs. Both are multidimensional and involve multidisciplinary approaches and can be measured using a wide range of techniques. As noted, self-report measures are one common technique used in human personality level research. The value of this approach is evident in the everyday aphorism that the "best way to find out what a person is thinking is to ask him/her." Asking persons to assess their thoughts and behaviors is a legitimate technique for arriving at one view of their personality (Damasio 1999). But often, as Rorer and Widiger (1983) noted two decades ago, "trying to understand personality and to measure personality structure is another matter. We have tried to use assessment (individual difference) models that are inappropriate to the task" (p. 433). Personality models must be broader in their scope than those based on one or a few techniques as will be discussed.

As noted, laboratory techniques from many disciplines have been used to define and measure impulsivity beyond self-report and interview phenomenal self data. For example, impulsivity has been measured by variations of the continuous performance task (Dougherty *et al.* 2003), gambling or risk-taking tasks (Bechara *et al.* 1994), and delay of reward (Rachlin *et al.* 1991). The latter tasks involve intolerance to reward delay and have been included in studies of both impulsivity and sensation seeking.

Electrophysiological recordings have also played an important role in understanding the possible neurological substrates of impulsivity and sensation seeking. Event-related potentials (ERPs) reflect electrophysiological activity of cortical neurons evoked by well-defined stimuli and regulated by the psychophysiological state of the organism (Coles & Rugg 1995; Stelmack & Houlihan 1995). Combined behavioral and electrophysiological measures suggest that high-impulsive subjects in contrast to low-impulsive subjects process information in the central nervous system less efficiently (Barratt 1993; Barratt *et al.* 1981; Barratt & Patton 1983). Dickman (1993) arrived at the same conclusion about information processing from his research using verbal learning paradigms.

In addition, neurochemical, cognitive, and combinations of tasks in the four categories mentioned above have also been used to measure impulsivity and sensation seeking but no model has encompassed all of these measures. Further, it has been rare that the behavioral, biological, and cognitive measures per se have been used to assess impulsivity and sensation seeking. They are usually listed as correlates of the personality dimensions that were defined by self-report questionnaires.

4. Challenges and Potential Solutions to Defining and Measuring Impulsivity and Sensation Seeking

As discussed, research on impulsivity and sensation seeking is multidisciplinary, as evidenced in an overview of relevant work. Both constructs are implicated in a variety of psychopathologies within DSM-IV-TR. Further, as noted, this resulted in different disciplines using discipline-specific techniques to measure these traits. An important challenge is to develop a discipline neutral personality model that allows data to be synthesized across disciplines in order to define and measure personality constructs. This is not a new problem (Hyland 1985). Nor are suggestions for broaching it new, but it is a problem that still lacks a solution. Parenthetically, Davidson (2003) also suggested that psychophysiology should pursue new "synthesizing" approaches rather than becoming "technique bound" which indicates that this problem is broader than the study of personality.

How can a model that encompasses the wide range of human characteristics be developed? Duke (1986) proposed developing a science of personality to achieve this goal, but this approach did not catch-on. Biopsychosocial models have been proposed implicitly or explicitly for many years without gaining anything near universal acceptance. One reason for new hope is that times have changed. New techniques are available that were not present even a decade ago. Kluckhon and Murray (1949) noted "we have failed to produce a 'personality' system which invites unanimous assent" (p. 3). They noted, further, the limitations in understanding of brain correlates of cognition: "Since we know next to nothing about the electrical field of forces which constitute the physical aspect of the stream of consciousness, the best terminology available for conceptualizing each pattern of regnant processes is that which has been derived from introspection" (p. 9). Five decades later, we have made unbelievable advances in the study of the nervous system as evidenced in research using event-related potentials, magnetoencephalography, functional magnetic resonance imaging, and molecular genetics. However, we still do not have a universally accepted model of personality encompassing cognition and biology. How do we proceed with developing a model?

In the mid 1970s, one of the co-authors (ESB) was faced with the problem of integrating data from different disciplines including biological, behavioral, self-report, and social data. He had been exposed to system theory models, as described by Weiss (1969), von Bertalanffy (1968) and Ashby (1960). He was especially impressed with Ashby's closed systems model for a brain that interrelates behavior, brain functioning, the environment, and motivation. He was also impressed with Lazare's (1973) discussion of "hidden conceptual models in psychiatry" in which Lazare reviewed four models of psychiatric practice: the medical (biological); the behavioral; the social (environmental/milieu); and the psychological (cognitive). Within a broad context of systems models, Barratt asked "what are the minimal number of categories of constructs and measurements necessary to describe a person and how can they be described in a general systems model?" He wedded Ashby's and Lazare's models into a general systems personality model (Barratt 1985; Barratt & Patton 1983; Barratt & Slaughter 1998) and included four categories of basic concepts and measurements that describe humans: biological, behavioral, social/environmental, and cognitive variables. The system was a closed feedback system. Most systems of human personality dimensions or brain functions are open systems, the logic being that human beings are exposed to a wide range of environmental influences and a closed system would result in endless oscillatory (negative) feedback. He defended a closed system on several grounds including Lewin's (1935) concept of life space (Métraux 1981). Because he included the environment as one category of constructs, life space could be argued to be part of a closed system that would avoid feedback oscillation. Parenthetically, the current emerging discipline of social cognitive neuroscience (Ochsner & Lieberman 2001) includes the same four basic categories of human characteristics that were included in this early model.

How does Barratt's model help resolve the multidisciplinary turf issues in defining and measuring impulsivity and sensation seeking? As noted, impulsivity and sensation seeking are multi-dimensional as defined by self-report questionnaires (Eysenck & Eysenck 1977; Patton *et al.* 1995; Zuckerman 1979). For example, the Barratt Impulsiveness Scale (BIS-11; Patton *et al.* 1995) has three independent subdimensions: *attention* or the ability to focus

Four Categories of Constructs from General Systems Theory Personality Model

Barratt Impulsivity Scale Sub-dimensions

	BIOLOGICAL	COGNITIVE	BEHAVIORAL	ENVIRONMENTAL
NON-PLANNING	• ERNs • Reward/ Punishment sensitivity	• Time Zone Scale	• Social inappropriate behaviors • Trails A & B. • Mazes	• Social Stimuli as contextual cues
ATTENTION	• Arousal physiological correlates • Short-latency ERPs • P300 complex	• Time Judgment • Continuous performance tasks • Change detection paradigms	• Wisconsin Card Sorting • Stroop • Continuous Performance Tasks	• Amount & type of information to be processed
MOTOR	• Contingence Negative Variation • LRPs • ERNs (conflict detection)	• Motor "plans"	• Pursuit-Rotor • Paced Timing • Go/NoGo • Reading • Reaction times	• Warning signals • Pre-response cues
TOTAL SCORE	• Dopamine • Serotonin • Norepinephrine • Genetic • Grapheme-Phoneme linkages		• Commission Errors on continuous performance tasks	

Figure 1: Multidimensional characterization of impulsivity. Entries in the matrix are "examples" and are in some instances speculative.

and be vigilant; *non-planning*, living for the moment; *motor* or acting without thinking. The three subdimensions combine to provide a total impulsivity score.

As a heuristic exercise, we define impulsivity by interrelating the four categories of constructs and measurements from the general systems model with the four measures from the BIS-11 in a matrix (Figure 1). We then search for patterns across the matrix based on our theories about each BIS-11 dimension. For example, we have used a wide range of "timing and rhythm" (e.g. paced tapping and pursuit rotor) behavioral tasks in our research because early research indicated that subjects with high levels of impulsivity were more variable in performing fine perceptual motor tasks. We hypothesized that motor impulsivity was a timing and rhythm sub-dimension (Barratt 1983).

Reviewing the laboratory behavioral measures of impulsivity across the matrix led to identifying the etiological basis of motor impulsivity as "the processing of sequential information related to performance on fine perceptual-motor tasks." We could have done this without the use of the model but using the model forced us to consider how other measures (e.g. biological) might overlap with other sub-dimensions of impulsivity. As noted, this is a discipline neutral heuristic model that allows one to interrelate data from the molecular to the social. Although we used this model to study impulsivity, it can also be used to assess sensation seeking and other personality constructs.

This is a brief review of one alternative approach. Within this approach, biological and behavioral measures are not considered correlates of personality traits defined by self-report questionnaires. Rather, all measures included in the matrix (Figure 1) are potential measures of personality traits. This is a shift from the more traditional approaches within individual differences research.

5. The Future

5.1. Introduction: The Challenge for the Future

As Rorer and Widiger (1983) earlier challenged the individual difference approach to measuring personality, the challenge to us seems obvious. Scientists must agree on a general systematic approach to interrelating data from the molecular to the social and also use selected common measurements across studies. One method for modeling was suggested here, a heuristic working type model but one that is discipline neutral. We should also explore at both the theoretical and applied levels new approaches to use within our models. Marks-Tarlow's (1993) suggestion that impulsivity is a system in chaos is not a familiar concept to most personality theorists but one that has promise. Finn's (2002) use of assessment devices as a basis for significant interpersonal encounters in therapy could possibly lead to impulsivity and sensation seeking questionnaires being developed to extend their usefulness to therapeutic interventions. New approaches need to be explored.

Our research group is currently working on establishing the role of impulsivity in a spectrum of impulse-control disorders using the general approach discussed above. In this research we consider impulsivity and sensation seeking to be different personality dimensions. Impulsivity can be combined with sensation seeking tendencies just as it can be combined with aggression or the drive to eat and related binge eating behaviors. Both impulsivity and sensation seeking have been related to psychopathological and social problems (e.g. substance abuse) but both play different roles in these personal and social disorders. When impulsivity is combined with sensation seeking, the resulting behaviors involve a higher probability of being at risk for harm than when sensation seeking alone influences the behaviors (Zuckerman & Kuhlman 2000).

5.2. Consciousness and Impulsivity/Sensation Seeking

To illustrate another possible construct that has not been explored in depth in impulsivity and sensation seeking research, the potential role of *consciousness* in motor impulsivity research will be reviewed. Both impulsivity and sensation seeking raise general questions about the control of behaviors and thoughts. To what extent do persons have control of their behavior at any given moment? Is this control conscious? This, of course, is a relevant social question, especially in a forensic context (Barratt & Felthous 2003). A key construct in research related to behavioral control is consciousness that we think will play a more pivotal role in future research on impulsivity and sensation seeking. The following brief review of the role of consciousness in motor impulsivity will illustrate integration of cognitive, behavioral (both clinical and laboratory), and biological measures.

In the DSM-IV-TR, it is stated for selected impulse-control disorders (e.g. intermittent explosive disorder) that "the individual feels an increasing sense of tension or arousal before committing the act and then experiences pleasure, gratification, or relief at the time of committing the act" (p. 663). It is also noted that "regret, self-reproach, or guilt" may follow the act (p. 663). Damasio (1999) in discussing feelings noted that "perhaps the most startling idea in this book is that, in the end, consciousness begins as a feeling, a special kind of feeling, to be sure, but a feeling nonetheless" (p. 312). Question: is the "tension" described in the DSM-IV-TR for selected impulse control disorders a "feeling"? When we were studying aggression among inmates in prison (Barratt *et al.* 1997), we often asked them "why do you continue to commit aggressive acts since the outcome for you is not desirable . . . you will be moved to less desirable living conditions and you will less likely be considered for early parole." The inmates who committed the impulsive aggressive acts noted that "we can't help it, we just do it." Further, many of them noted that following the aggressive act, they felt "guilty" and "swore not to do it again." The inmates who committed primarily premeditated aggressive acts did not in general report these feelings. In contrast, the inmates who committed impulsive aggressive acts when their aggression was being controlled by medication (phenytoin) would say that "we still experience anger and a feeling to hit and yell at someone but we don't." Do these observations involve conscious awareness of impulsive tendencies? The feeling of guilt following an impulsive aggressive act was also commonly reported.

In a factor analytic study aimed at noting whether persons could classify their behaviors as impulsive or aggressive (Barratt *et al.* 1999), we demonstrated that non-clinical subjects could describe their aggressive behaviors in terms of impulsive and premeditated acts. Further, items on the impulsive aggressive factor were characterized by "lack of control, guilt feelings following the act, and thought confusion". Their "general" feelings on the day the act occurred defined a separate dimension from impulsive or premeditated aggression. Items that defined general feelings included: the day the act occurred I was having a bad day in general; I was feeling more aggressive than usual the day act occurred; I was in a good mood before the act occurred (negative factor loading).

Damasio (1999) proposes that consciousness consists of "simple and complex kinds" (p. 16). He describes the simplest kind as core consciousness which is a "sense about one moment — now — and one place — here" (p. 16). He proposes that "sense of self" comes from a complex form of consciousness called "extended consciousness." He further notes that knowing that we feel an emotion, "feeling that feeling, occurs only *after* we build the second-order representations necessary for core consciousness" (Damasio 1999: 280).

Orozco-Cabal (2000) also noted that one can be "aware that one is aware of" phenomena that are not within the limits of the physical world. To the extent that humans can be "aware of awareness" suggests that they can potentially control plans for executing behavior. This would assume that the nervous system could, for example, use serial and parallel processing of information with an objective goal of making accurate predictions about events in our surroundings in order to anticipate and conform our behaviors to the coping demands of society (Llinás, 2001; Morin 1986; Young 1978). This would assure that sensory-motor programs could be configured in the brain and reviewed before hand without physically performing them. This would be similar to writing a script and rehearsing it before the play begins in a self-recreated space. What brain functions relate to this process? Parenthetically, an important observation by Brunia and van Boxtel (2000) related to this discussion is that it is "impossible to exclusively discuss motor processes without taking into account the related perception" (p. 507). Their observation emphasizes the need to integrate across different categories of techniques.

5.3. A Conceptual Brain Model for Motor Preparation and Consciousness

Let us briefly review a conceptual neural model that could sub-serve motor preparation and consciousness. Direct current scalp recordings of the brain's electrical activity during self-initiated acts in human subjects have shown that conscious intention to act is preceded by a preparatory phase (Libet 1985). Preparation for a motor response correlates with the appearance of a progressive negative shift of the electrical potential over the vertex. These ERPs are labeled readiness potentials (RP) or *Bereitschaftspotentials* (Kornhuber & Deecke 1965). Negativity is initially bilateral and symmetrical with maximal amplitude over the vertex electrodes suggesting activation of the underlying supplementary motor cortex and basal ganglia circuitry; this activity then lateralizes shortly before muscle activation towards the primary motor cortical area contralateral to the side of the limb that performs the movement (Brunia & van Boxtel 2000; Deecke 1987; Praamstra *et al.* 1996). The first symmetrical component of the RP is believed to correspond to automatic activation of premotor structures by generated inputs or drives originating in the limbic system. The next asymmetrical component of the RP has been proposed to indicate the possible role of a motor plan for the engagement of the motor system for movement. Libet (1985) provided data that they interpret as a "conscious urge" to make a movement. This urge occurs 150–200 ms before the onset of muscular activity in self-initiated movements.

What is known about the function of premotor areas in motor programming? In humans, the supplementary motor area is located in superior-lateral and medial aspects of the frontal lobe rostral to the precentral gyrus (Broadman's area 6). Because of its particular anatomical localization and functional connectivity, the supplementary motor area has been hypothesized to serve as the context for the integration of incoming external signals with our intentions and motives for action (Wiesendanger 1993). Embryologically related to the anterior cingulate cortex, it has been proposed that the supplementary motor area is part of a medial system loop which includes the ventral striatopallidal system, anterior cingulate cortex, somatosensory cortex (linkage between sensation and action), open cortico-thalamo-cortical loops, nucleus reticularis thalami, nucleus ventralis lateralis pars oralis, striatum and internal division of the globus pallidus. Structures within this extensive loop interconnect via excitatory pathways through the ventral thalamus creating a positive feedback circuitry (Brunia & van Boxtel 2000; Goldberg 1985).

The medial loop system is involved in processing of sequential information related to motor programming. Activity within the loop has been suggested to be responsible for generating a series of short temporal sequences of alternative plans of action (Coterill 2001; Goldberg 1985). Efferent copies of such plans travel to other premotor and sensory areas in the brain where they are integrated (e.g. eyes-hand movement coordination) and contrasted with afferent information to determine the appropriateness of the movement sequence and its rate of progression (Flanagan & Johansson 2003; Guillery 2003).

All of the above is a logically coherent model from a neuroanatomical and physiological viewpoint and shows how cognitive, biological, and behavioral constructs can be integrated in a discipline neutral model. But how could this neural model relate to consciousness and motor impulsivity? Pursuing answers to that question is part of our current research.

5.4. Lateralized Readiness Potentials and Impulsivity/Sensation Seeking

As part of studying biological constructs related to impulsivity we have been measuring lateralized readiness potentials (LRP) in subjects with high and low levels of impulsivity as defined by self-report questionnaire measures. LRPs are ERPs that are recorded "over motor areas of the cortex . . . and occur before the movement itself" (Coles *et al.* 1995: 97). They are normally "larger over scalp sites that are contra-lateral to the side of the body that is to be moved . . . and may be useful in monitoring covert aspects of motor preparation (Coles *et al.* 1995: 97).

High-impulsive subjects have lower LRP amplitudes compared to those of low-impulsive subjects in a non-clinical group (Barratt *et al.* 2002; Barratt unpublished data). One possible interpretation of these findings is that impulsivity is related to an increased tendency within the conceptual nervous system model outlined above to act as a closed system, partially inactivating the modulatory effect on motor programming exerted by afferent input and attentional systems. This would be consistent with our hypothesis that processing of sequential information related to performance on fine motor tasks is related to motor impulsivity. The basal ganglia and prefrontal cortex circuitry have rich inter-connections that could be related to motor impulsivity in terms of processing sequential information as described above. It has often been conjectured that impulsivity is clinically related to frontal lobe activity. Within the context of this chapter, LRPs could be considered not only as correlates of self-report measures of impulsivity, but also as potential measures per se of impulsivity which when added to other measures give an overall index of impulsivity.

6. Summary

In summary, this chapter suggests that research on impulsivity and sensation seeking is hindered by: (1) the lack of an encompassing personality model which can allow the synthesis of data from molecular biology measures to measures of social/pathological disorders; and (2) the lack of integration of multidisciplinary measures into prediction indices. One possible solution to these challenges was described as an example of one potential approach. Whatever approach is used, the obstacles hindering research on impulsivity and sensation seeking must be overcome for the field to advance beyond the groundbreaking work of the last 50 years.

Acknowledgments

This work was supported by a grant from the Health Foundation, Rogosin Institute, New York Hospital, Cornell Medical Center.

References

Ashby, W. (1960). *Design for a brain*. New York: Wiley.

American Psychiatric Association (2000). *Diagnostic and statistical manual of mental disorders* (4th ed., Text Revision). Washington, DC: American Psychiatric Association.

Barratt, E. S. (1983). The biological basis of impulsiveness: The significance of timing and rhythm disorders. *Personality and Individual Differences*, *4*, 381–391.

Barratt, E. S. (1985). Impulsiveness defined within a systems model of personality. In: C. Spielberger, & J. Butcher (Eds), *Advances in personality assessment* (Vol. 5). Hillsdale, NJ: Lawrence-Erlbaum.

Barratt, E. S. (1993). Impulsivity: Integrating cognitive, behavioral, biological, and environmental data. In: W. G. McCown, J. L. Johnson, & M. B. Shure (Eds), *The impulsive client: Theory, research, and treatment* (pp. 39–56). Washington, DC: American Psychological Association.

Barratt, E. S., & Felthous, A. R. (2003). Impulsive vs. premeditated aggression: Implications for mens rea decisions. *Behavioral Science and The Law*, *21*, 619–630.

Barratt, E. S., Mishalanie, J., Matthews, S., & Moeller, F. G. (2002). Lateralized readiness potential and impulsivity. Poster presentation at Cognitive Neuroscience Society, Ninth Annual Meeting, San Francisco.

Barratt, E. S., Patton, J., Olsson, N. G., & Zuker, G. (1981). Impulsivity and paced tapping. *Journal of Motor Behavior*, *13*, 286–300.

Barratt, E. S., & Patton, J. (1983). Impulsivity: Cognitive, behavioral, and psychophysiological correlates. In: M. Zuckerman (Ed.), *Biological bases of sensation seeking, impulsivity and anxiety* (pp. 77–116). Hillsdale, NJ: Erlbaum.

Barratt, E. S., & Slaughter, L. (1998). Defining, measuring, and predicting impulsive aggression: A heuristic model. *Behavioral Sciences and The Law*, *16*, 285–302.

Barratt, E. S., Stanford, M. S., Dowdy, L., Liebman, M. J., & Kent, T. A. (1999). Impulsive and premeditated aggression: A factor analysis of self-reported acts. *Psychiatric Research*, *86*, 163–173.

Barratt, E. S., Stanford, M. S., Kent, T. A., & Felthous, A. (1997). Neuropsychological and cognitive psychophysiological substrates of impulsive aggression. *Biological Psychiatry*, *41*, 1045–1061.

Bechara, A., Damasio, A. R., Damasio, H., & Anderson, S. W. (1994). Insensitivity to future consequences following damage to human prefrontal cortex. *Cognition*, *50*, 7–15.

von Bertalanffy, L. (1968). *General systems theory*. New York: G. Braziller.

Brunia, C. H. M., & van Boxtel, G. J. M. (2000). Motor preparation. In: J. T. Cacioppo, L. G. Tassinary, & G. G. Bertson (Eds), *Handbook of psychophysiology* (2nd ed., pp. 507–532). New York: Cambridge University Press.

Cloninger, C. R. (1986). A unified biosocial theory of personality and its role in the development of anxiety states. *Psychiatric Developments*, *3*, 167–226.

Cloninger, C. R., Przybeck, T. R., Svrakic, D. M., & Wetzel, R. D. (1994). *The Temperament and Character Inventory (TCI): A guide to its development and use*. St. Louis, MO: Center for Psychobiology of Personality.

Cloninger, C. R., Svrakic, D. M., & Przybeck, T. R. (1993). A psychobiological model of temperament and character. *Archives of General Psychiatry*, *50*, 975–990.

Coles, M. G. H., & Rugg, M. D. (1995). Event-related brain potentials: An introduction. In: M. D. Rugg, & M. G. H.Coles (Eds), *Electrophysiology of mind* (pp. 1–26). New York: Oxford University Press.

Coles, M. G. H., Smid, H. G. O. M., Scheffers, M. K., & Otten, L. J. (1995). Mental chronometry and the study of human information processing. In: M. D.Rugg, & M. G. H. Coles (Eds), *Electrophysiology of mind* (pp. 86–131). New York: Oxford University Press.

Coterill, R. M. J. (2001). Cooperation of the basal ganglia, cerebellum, sensory cerebrum and hippocampus: Possible implications for cognition, consciousness, intelligence and creativity. *Progress in Neurobiology*, *64*, 1–33.

Damasio, A. (1999). *The feeling of what happens*. New York: Harcourt Brace.

Davidson, R. J. (2003). Affective neuroscience and psychophysiology: Toward a synthesis. *Psychophysiology*, *40*, 655–665.

Deecke, L. (1987). Bereitschaftspotential as an indicator of movement preparation in supplementary motor area and motor cortex. In Ciba Foundation Symposium No. 132. *Motor Areas of the cerebral cortex*. Chichester, UK: Wiley.

Dickman, S. J. (1993). Impulsivity and information processing. In: W. G. McCown, J. L. Johnson, & M. B. Shure (Eds), *The impulsive client: Theory, research, and treatment* (pp. 151–184). Washington, DC: American Psychological Association.

Dougherty, D. M., Mathias, C. W., & Marsh, D. M. (2003). Laboratory measures of impulsivity. In: E. F. Coccaro (Ed.), *Aggression: Assessment and treatment* (pp. 247–265). New York: Marcel Decker Publishers.

Duke, M. P. (1986). Personality science: A proposal. *Journal of Personality and Social Psychology*, *50*, 382–385.

Evenden, J. L. (1999). Varieties of impulsivity. *Psychopharmacology*, *146*, 348–361.

Eysenck, S. B. G., & Eysenck, H. J. (1977). The place of impulsiveness in a dimensional system of personality description. *British Journal of Social and Clinical Psychology*, *16*, 57–68.

Finn, S. E. (2002). Obstacles to practicing psychological assessment. *SPA Exchange*, *15*, 1–3.

Flanagan, J. R., & Johansson, R. S. (2003). Action plans used in action observation. *Nature*, *424*, 769–771.

Greene, K., Kromar, M., Walters, L. H., Rubin, D. L., & Jerold, H. L. (2000). Targeting adolescent risk-taking behaviors: The contributions of ego centrism and sensation seeking. *Journal of Adolescence*, *23*, 439–461.

Goldberg, G. (1985). Supplementary motor area structures and functions: Review and hypotheses. *The Behavioral and Brain Sciences*, *8*, 567–616.

Guillery, R. W. (2003). Branching thalamic afferents link action and perception. *Journal of Neurophysiology*, *90*, 539–548.

Hyland, M. E. (1985). Do person variables exist in different ways? *American Psychologist*, *40*, 1003–1010.

Joireman, J., Anderson, J., & Strathman, A. (2003). The aggression paradox: Understanding links among aggression, sensation seeking, and the consideration of future consequences. *Journal of Personality and Social Psychology*, *84*, 1287–1302.

Kluckhon, C., & Murray, H. A. (1949). *Personality in nature, society and culture*. New York: Alfred A. Knopf.

Kornhuber, H. H., & Deecke, L. (1965). Hirnpotentiänderungen bei Willkürbewegungen und passiven Bewegungen des menschen: Bereitschaftspotential und reafferente Potentiale. *Pflügers Archives*, *284*, 1–17.

Lazare, A. (1973). Hidden conceptual models in clinical psychiatry. *New England Journal of Medicine*, *288*, 345–350.

Lewin, K. (1935). *A dynamic theory of personality*. New York: McGraw Hill.

Libet, B. (1985). Unconscious cerebral initiative and the role of conscious will in voluntary action. *The Behavioral and Brain Sciences*, *8*, 529–566.

Marks-Tarlow, T. (1993). A new look at impulsivity: Hidden order beneath apparent chaos? In: W. G. McCown, J. L. Johnson, & M. B. Shure (Eds), *The impulsive client: Theory, research, and treatment* (pp. 119–130). Washington, DC: American Psychological Association.

McCown, W. G., & De Simone, P. (1993). Impulses, impulsivity, and impulsive behaviors: A historical review of a contemporary issue. In: W. G. McCown, J. L. Johnson, & M. S. Shure (Eds), *The impulsive client: Theory, research, and treatment* (pp. 3–22). Washington, DC: American Psychological Association.

Métraux, A. (1981). *Kurt-Lewin-werkausgabe. Band 1: Wissenschafts theorie 1*. Bern, Switzerland: Verlag Hans Huber.

Morin, E. (1986). *El metodo*. Madrid, Spain: Catedra.

Ochsner, K., & Lieberman, M. (2001). The emergence of social cognitive neuroscience. *American Psychologist, 56*, 717–734.

Orozco-Cabal, L. F. (2000). Sobre la naturaleza humana; explicación y comprensión de la conciencia. *Revista Colombiana de Psiquiatría, 29*, 375–384.

Patton, J. H., Stanford, M. S., & Barratt, E. S. (1995). Factor structure of the Barratt Impulsiveness Scale. *Journal of Clinical Psychology, 51*, 768–774.

Praamstra, P., Stegeman, D. F., Horstink, M. W. I. M., & Cools, A. R. (1996). Dipole source analysis suggests selective modulation of the supplementary motor area contribution to the readiness potential. *Electroencephalography and Clinical Neurophysiology, 98*, 468–477.

Rachlin, H., Raineri, A., & Cross, D. (1991). Subjective probability and delay. *Journal of the Experimental Analysis of Behaviour, 55*, 233–244.

Rorer, L. G., & Widiger, T. A. (1983). Personality structure and assessment. *Annual Review of Psychology*. Palo Alto, CA: Annual Reviews.

Stelmack, R. M., & Houlihan, M. (1995). Event-related potentials, personality, and intelligence. Concepts, issues, and evidence. In: D. H. Saklofske, & M. Zeidner (Eds), *International Handbook of Personality and Intelligence* (pp. 349–365). New York: Plenum Press.

Webster, C. D., & Jackson, M. A. (1997). *Impulsivity: Theory, assessment, and treatment*. New York: Guilford Press.

Weiss, P. (1969). The living system: Determinism stratified. In: A. Koestler, & J. R. Smythies (Eds), *Beyond reductionism* (pp. 3–55). New York: Macmillan.

Wiesendanger, M. (1993). The riddle of supplementary motor area function. In: N. Mano, I. Hamada, & M. R. DeLong (Eds), *Role of the cerebellum and basal ganglia in voluntary movement* (pp. 253–266). Amsterdam: Elsevier.

Young, J. Z. (1978). *Programs of the brain*. Oxford, UK: Oxford University Press.

Zuckerman, M. (1979). *Sensation seeking: Beyond the optimal level of arousal*. Hillsdale, NJ: Lawrence Erlbaum.

Zuckerman, M. (1991). *Psychobiology of personality*. New York: Cambridge University Press.

Zuckerman, M., & Kuhlman, D. M. (2000). Personality and risk-taking: Common biosocial factors. *Journal of Personality, 68*, 999–1029.

Zuckerman, M., & Neeb, M. (1979). Sensation seeking and psychopathology. *Psychiatry Research, 1*, 255–264.

Chapter 2

On Personality and Arousal: A Historical Perspective on Eysenck and Zuckerman

R. M. Stelmack

1. Introduction

Elizabeth Duffy (1904–1970) was an emeritus professor at the University of North Carolina who made significant, seminal contributions to the areas of emotion and motivation in 40 years of research activity. Her early writings were influenced by the work of W. B. Cannon (1915) who is largely responsible for elaborating the principle of homeostasis. An important tenet in this work is that the body functions to maintain an optimal state of physiological activity. With respect to motivation and emotion, Cannon's research also advanced the idea that aversive physical and emotional stimuli that disrupt homeostasis elicit generalized sympathetic nervous system activity, manifest as fight or flight responses.

Duffy's work on physiological arousal and behavior in children revealed a continuity of energy mobilization in emotional and motivated behavior. The generalized activation of the sympathetic nervous system was often as evident under conditions of high motivation as it was in the emotional states that Cannon explored, with differences being a matter of degree. Duffy pioneered the application of psychophysiological methods to study the degree of physiological activation of different individuals in different situations. Despite the continuity with Cannon's work, the concept of activation that she explicated, especially in her later writing, bore little resemblance to the undifferentiated activation of the sympathetic nervous system that Cannon described in 1915. In her view, "the description of behavior at a given moment requires the consideration of two basic aspects: (a) *direction*, approach or withdrawal with respect to persons, things, ideas, or any aspect of the environment; and (b) *activation*, *arousal*, or *intensity*" (Duffy 1972: 577). Activation was a term that she came to regard as synonymous with arousal, intensity, energy mobilization, and drive. Arousal eventually emerged as a concept that incorporated all of those terms. In this sense, arousal became a unifying concept, bringing diverse areas of physiological research into common focus. In terms of physiological activity, however, arousal was not conceived as a unitary

On the Psychobiology of Personality
Edited by R. M. Stelmack

ISBN: 0-08-044209-9

construct, a fact for which she and other arousal advocates, such as Malmo, were harshly but mistakenly criticized.

"Activation is both general and specific . . . . Changes constantly occur in the physiological functioning of the organism as it lives and meets, as best it can, the demands of the situations in which it finds itself . . . . Any change in the situation to which the organism is responding might be expected to cause, to some degree, a change in one or more of the systems of the organism. The same statement might be made in regard to any change in an attitude or a set for a particular kind of action . . . . The number of different patterns of physiological response employed by an organism must, then, be staggering in number" (Duffy 1972: 578). "Some systems operate in an antagonistic fashion to maintain homeostasis. Different situations, or interpretations of situations, may require maximal activity in different parts of the organism to secure an effective response" (Duffy 1972: 580).

As early as 1934, Duffy proposed that a continuum of psychological states could be understood in terms of their correspondence to a continuum of energy mobilization. This view of arousal was widely shared, notably by Lindsley (1951) and by Malmo (1959). In this view, arousal (activation) was conceived as a dimension that described a continuum of neurophysiological states, ranging from deep sleep at the low end of the continuum to excited states at the high end. In this period, research on the reticular formation marked an important advance in the neurophysiology of arousal. It had been established that low-amplitude, high-frequency EEG activity was associated with wakefulness and attention, while high-amplitude, low-frequency EEG activity was associated with sleep and drowsiness (Jasper 1949). Moruzzi and Magoun (1949) demonstrated that these indices of arousal were modulated by activity in the ascending reticular activation system (ARAS). In pursuing the functional significance of this system, it was proposed that the relation between the state of arousal along this sleep/excited continuum and performance was described by an inverted-U shaped curve (Hebb 1949, 1955). Although this conception of arousal emphasized the important role that the ARAS could play in mediating a wide range of neuropsychological states along the arousal continuum, all of these luminaries of arousal theory acknowledged the complex relations between the physiological systems, the neuropsychological states that they supported, and the behavior that was expressed.

The term ubiquitous is certainly an adjective that fits the concept of arousal, i.e. existing or being everywhere. For example, Duffy stated that "almost any physiological response might be considered an indicator (rough or refined) of the degree of activation" (1972: 580). The use of multiple psychophysiological recording methods was also encouraged, again, with a view to identifying systems and response patterns that corresponded to specific phenomena along the arousal continuum and with their interaction with environmental conditions and individual differences in behavior. Another influential writer, D. O. Hebb, shared Duffy's view. In describing his version of arousal, Hebb conceptualized the motivational and psychological implications that stemmed from the ARAS. In his view, arousal (drive) was likened to an "energizer but not a guide" . . . and functionally "efficient learning is only possible in the waking, alert responsive animal, in which the level of arousal is high." He was clear in stating that the nervous system that he conceptualized was a working simplification to facilitate research. "There is reason to think that the arousal system may not be homogeneous, but may consist of a number of subsystems with distinctive functions."

He noted that the "Olds and Milner (1954) study, reporting 'reward' by direct intracranial stimulation, is not easy to fit into the notion of a single, homogeneous system .... and it may be reasonably anticipated that arousal will eventually be found to vary qualitatively as well as quantitatively" (Hebb 1955: 249).

In his widely cited review, Malmo (1959: 374) also acknowledged the difficulty "in defending the position that the ARAS is a unitary intensity-mediating mechanism, because the ARAS does not appear to be a homogeneous anatomical system." Although he did not rule out a unitary function for the ARAS, despite the distinctive functional anatomy within it, neither did he argue forcefully for this conception. Low intercorrelations between psychophysiological indices of the arousal construct, e.g. palmar skin conductance, heart rate, muscle potentials, EEG desynchronization, which were observed under some conditions, were also widely invoked as evidence against the validity of a unitary arousal construct (Elliot 1964; Lacey 1967). Moderate intra-individual correlations to mild stimulation did provide some support for the view that the low inter-individual correlations are due to individual response specificity, i.e. a disposition to respond more intensely with one autonomic response, e.g. palmar skin conductance, than another, e.g. heart rate (Duffy 1962; Elliot 1964). Debates on this issue were also hindered by understating the fact that the response measures employed in the salient analyses differed markedly, both qualitatively and temporally. For example, Malmo and his colleagues had a preference for measuring arousal level by electromyographic recordings taken over a period of minutes during a tracking task, whereas Lacey focused on cardiac response measures that developed within seconds of simple physical stimulation. In any case, it can be argued that the low intercorrelations of measures presumed to measure the arousal construct, an effect observed from the beginning of multiple psychophysiological recordings, do not invalidate the concept of arousal, but only the notion that it is unidimensional (Kaplan 1964).

Johnson and Anderson, in the 1990 handbook *Principles of Psychophysiology* (p. 223), state that "the classic Lacey (1967) paper is viewed by most as the death knell for the naive line of research testing the simplified form of activation that predicts parallel incremental relations among response systems." In fact, the evidence was perfectly consistent with the arousal concept, and indeed, much of the evidence cited was provided by advocates of the arousal concept. Nevertheless, the legacy of this Lacey paper is a dismissal of the arousal construct because it was not unitary.

The basic objectives of the research enterprise envisioned and practiced by the early activation scholars, i.e. identifying patterns of physiological activity specific to neuropsychological states and psychological phenomena, continued with an ever-growing battery of psychophysiological response measures of increased refinement and reliability and with the support of a rapidly expanding neuroscience. Psychophysiological indices of arousal, e.g. EEG, cardiac and electrodermal measures, provided a useful means to focus the physiological bases of psychological processes in humans and achieved considerable success in detailing mechanisms of attention and learning (e.g. Obrist 1981; Sokolov 1963). The determination of the functional significance of the reticular formation, i.e. its role in attention, motivation and learning was a major advance in neurophysiology, one that dominated the interest of physiologists and directed the thoughts and actions of physiological psychologists.

2. Personality and Arousal

During the period 1955–1970, there was considerable progress in the development of electrophysiological recording and measurement procedures and in mapping response patterns under a wide variety of conditions. With respect to personality, Duffy (1966) claimed "the degree of activation (that she demonstrated in various publications, i.e. Duffy 1962) appears to affect both sensory sensitivity and motor response, and is involved in those consistencies of behavior that we call personality characteristics." There was considerable interest in applying psychophysiological recording techniques to the study of anxiety, an individual difference trait that was widely supposed to be characterized by high activation patterns (e.g. Duffy 1970). As indicated in several comprehensive reviews, however, the outcome of this work was equivocal. For example, Duffy (1962: 273) concluded that "Any survey of physiological studies of personality must recognize the surprising fact that relatively few investigators have reported relationships of any magnitude between physiological measures and measures of behavior within the normal population. Since it is inconceivable that few relationships of consequence exist between differences in behavior and differences in so basic an aspect of response as that of activation, we are led to seek an explanation of the essentially negative findings of perhaps the majority of investigators." In her analysis, she pointed out that personality researchers mistakenly assessed the relation between physiological measures of activation and measures of directional aspects of behavior such as attitudes, values, aggressiveness and timidity. This approach ignored the fact that the direction taken by behavior and the intensity or energy mobilization with which the behavior occurs are relatively independent aspects of response. She also cited inadequacies in both the physiological and psychometric measures employed in this literature, and notably, "uncritical use of descriptive categories (trait names) which are 'impure' in the sense that they incorporate under one heading more than one dimension of behavior, and often dimensions which vary independently" (Duffy 1962: 278).

3. Eysenck and the Arousal Theory of Extraversion

The determination of extraversion and neuroticism as higher-order independent psychometric factors was an important feature of the personality typology advocated by Hans Eysenck (1959). The typology addressed an important limitation that was noted by Duffy. Because extraversion and neuroticism were both correlates of anxiety, as defined by most anxiety questionnaires that were employed in the early research on personality and activation, an unambiguous interpretation of effects was handicapped. In the schema that Eysenck proposed in the *The biological bases of personality* (1967: 230), the intensity modulating construct of arousal, as conceived by Duffy, was aligned with the introversion-extraversion dimension. Specifically, differences in behavior related to the extraversion dimension were identified with "differential thresholds in the various parts of the ascending reticular activating system."

The publication of *The biological bases of personality* was also a major advance in the attempt to explain individual differences in extraversion and neuroticism. In this text, contemporary developments in research on the physiological determinants of learning, attention and motivation were now drawn into the theoretical framework outlining the arousal theory of extraversion and neuroticism, specifically, cortico-reticular arousal for the former and limbic arousal for the latter. This work provided a neurophysiological basis for the hypothetical constructs presented in the preceding excitation-inhibition theory (Eysenck 1957). Although the central hypothesis was rather vaguely defined, proposing that introverts were characterized by higher levels of activity or lower levels of excitation in the cortico-reticular loop, the context of the theory was sufficiently seductive to inspire hundreds of experiments.

The arousal theory of extraversion outlined by Eysenck in 1967 continues to generate research initiatives. This interest is sustained in spite of important modifications to the theory put forth by Gray (1972) and by Brebner and Cooper (1974) and by the virtual demise of arousal theory in the physiological literature. This raises important questions of the success and validity of the arousal theory of extraversion. Have the causal bases of extraversion been revealed? What, if anything, has been achieved in this massive research endeavour? Overall, Duffy's view, cited above, that arousal affects both sensory sensitivity and motor response, and is involved in the expression of personality characteristics appears prescient, at least, with respect to extraversion.

Both the excitation-inhibition and arousal theories of extraversion enjoyed enormous heuristic success. The quantity of citations attests to that success. The effects that were reported and that have accumulated now offer a substantial corpus that allows some induction of the causal bases of extraversion to be made, in particular from those effects that have been replicated several times and from studies employing different methodologies and paradigms that converge on common processes. Three points can be briefly stated here.

First, from reviews of the psychophysiological literature, introverts and extraverts do not differ in tonic or basal levels of physiological activity. This conclusion is drawn from the absence of differences when skin conductance measures of arousal are obtained prior to stimulation and in conditions that have low arousal potential. Moreover, differences are seldom reported with EEG measures in low arousing conditions or during sleep. Thus, Eysenck's hypothesis of differences in base level of arousal receives little support from studies using psychophysiological methods (Matthews & Gilliland 1999; Stelmack 1990).

Second, there is a substantial body of evidence in research on the extraversion trait that converges on one general effect, namely the greater sensitivity (or reactivity) of introverts than extraverts to punctate, physical stimulation (Stelmack 1981; Stelmack & Geen 1992; Stelmack & Houlihan 1995). This effect can reasonably account for some social behavior exhibited by introverts, such as their preference for quieter environments and solitude, i.e. learning to avoid noisy environments and intense stimulation (Campbell & Hawley 1982; Geen 1984). The greater reactivity to physical stimulation for introverts than extraverts was observed with a wide range of methods and conditions that demonstrated the following: (1) lower absolute sensory sensitivity (e.g. Stelmack & Campbell 1974); (2) lower pain thresholds (e.g. Barnes 1975; Schalling 1971); (3) lower noise thresholds (e.g. Dornic & Ekehammar 1990); (4) larger skin conductance responses to brief, moderate intensity tones for introverts (e.g. Smith 1983; Stelmack 1979); (5) larger auditory event-related potential amplitudes to simple physical stimulation (e.g. Stelmack *et al.* 1977; Stelmack & Michaud-

Achorn 1985; Stenberg *et al.* 1990); (6) faster startle reflex response latencies for introverts than extraverts to moderate intensity noise bursts noise bursts (Britt & Blumenthal 1992); and (7) faster brainstem auditory evoked potentials (Bullock & Gilliland 1993; Stelmack & Wilson 1982; Swickert & Gilliland 1998).

Third, introverts and extraverts differ in their expression of motor behavior. In my view, these effects appear to be due to the faster initiation of movement for extraverts than introverts. This effect can reasonably account for the spontaneity, both active and social, that distinguishes extraverts from introverts (Barratt & Patton 1983). Extraverts are more talkative and initiate conversation more frequently than introverts during interview situations (Campbell & Rushton 1978) and are more restless (fidgety) in restricted environments (Gale 1969). Extraverts are also more disposed to physical activity and sports than introverts. (Eysenck *et al.* 1982; Kirkcaldy 1982). There is also a good deal of evidence that implicates basic differences between introverts in the performance of motor tasks. The effects demonstrating differences in the expression of motor behavior between introverts and extraverts include the following: (1) faster reaction time for extraverts than introverts (Barratt 1959; Robinson & Zahn 1988); (2) greater reminiscence effects on pursuit rotor tracking tasks for extraverts than introverts (Eysenck & Frith 1977); (3) more false positive errors for extraverts than introverts in reaction time tasks with speed instructions (Brebner & Flavell 1978); (4) faster movement time for extraverts than introverts on reaction time tasks (Doucet & Stelmack 1997, 2000; Stelmack *et al.* 1993); (5) larger amplitude Contingent Negative Variation (an event-related potential measure of response preparation) for extraverts than introverts (e.g. O'Connor 1982); and (6) slower motor reflex recovery for extraverts than introverts (Pivik *et al.* 1988; Stelmack & Pivik 1996).

Any theory of extraversion must accommodate the sensory and motor effects that have been consistently demonstrated. Given these data, there remains the task of identifying the neural circuits and neurochemical properties that serve these effects and functions that differentiate introverts and extraverts. Some of the psychophysiological research does, in fact, give quite specific information on this. Moreover, there have been several experiments suggesting that dopamine, a neurotransmitter that is thought to modulate the probability and strength of behavioral responses to sensory input (Le Moal & Simon 1991) may be implicated in variation in extraversion (Rammsayer *et al.* 1993; see Rammsayer in this book).

It is noteworthy that psychophysiological methods are largely unsuccessful in differentiating individuals along the neuroticism dimension, at least, in paradigms where physical stimulation is featured, as in the research on extraversion (Fahrenberg 1987; Matthews & Gilliland 1999). Event-related potentials, skin conductance responses and heart rate change are measures that are exquisitely sensitive to changes in stimulus intensity. The application of these recording procedures under conditions of simple physical stimulation, i.e. brief tones or light flashes, reveal that the sensory systems of introverts are more reactive or sensitive than extraverts. The same procedures, however, do not differentiate individuals along the neuroticism dimension, indicating that sensory sensitivity is not a factor underlying this construct. The failure to find consistent differences in sensory sensitivity for individuals who differ in neuroticism using psychophysical methods, i.e. sensory thresholds, pain thresholds, or psychological reports also endorses this view.

4. Sensation Seeking and the Optimal Level of Arousal

Arousal was the salient explanatory construct in Eysenck's (1967) theory of Extraversion and in Zuckerman's (1969a) theory of sensation seeking. Although there was some commonality in the conceptions, there are important differences in both the origins and the emphasis of the theories.

For Eysenck, the arousal construct was incorporated into the conditioning theory that formed the foundation of the extraversion theory. He stated: "Human beings differ with respect to the speed with which excitation and inhibition are produced, the strength of the excitation and inhibition produced, and the speed with which inhibition is dissipated. These differences are properties of the physical structures involved in making stimulus-response connections . . . . Individuals in whom excitatory potential is generated quickly and in whom excitatory potentials so generated are strong, are thereby predisposed to develop introverted patterns of behaviour and to develop dysthymic disorders in cases of neurotic breakdown" (Eysenck 1957: 114). In the 1967 version of Eysenck's theory of extraversion, the focus was on the stimulus intensity mediating function of arousal. The construct provided a discrete physiological basis for individual differences in attention and learning that were proposed to distinguish introverts and extraverts.

For Zuckerman, the arousal construct in sensation seeking theory emerged from his early work on the effects of sensory deprivation on psychological and physiological processes (e.g. Zuckerman 1969b). During the 1960s, the initial research on sensory deprivation was motivated by concerns about brainwashing that were quite intense during the Korean war and the cold war with the USSR. The effects of sensory deprivation on a wide variety of arousal indices was thoroughly explored, generally revealing a decrease in measures of arousal early in the isolation session with increasing levels of arousal developing with prolonged deprivation, especially if movement was restricted (Zubek 1969). There was also compelling evidence that during the course of sensory deprivation there was an increasing need for varied stimulus experience. As the duration of isolation increased, the number of responses initiated to receive auditory and visual stimulation increased (e.g. Zuckerman & Haber 1965). This research "provided a link between arousal in sensory deprivation and stimulus need and suggested the possibility that the 'stimulus hunger' of subjects aroused by sensory deprivation conditions might be reflected in other kinds of behavior outside the specific experimental condition. Work had already begun on a 'sensation seeking scale'; and this study raised the intriguing idea that such a scale would be predictive of arousal, operant response for stimulation, and other reactions to sensory deprivation" (Zuckerman 1979: 85).

The first Sensation Seeking Scale (SSS; Zuckerman *et al.* 1964) was intended to provide "an operational measure of the optimum level of stimulation and optimum level of arousal" (Zuckerman 1979: 91), primarily for use in sensory deprivation research. The theoretical basis for this work rested on the proposal that "every individual has characteristic levels of stimulation (OLS) and arousal (OLA) for cognitive activity, motor activity and positive affective tone" (Zuckerman 1969a: 429). An individual differences postulate was also put forward in which "a high-sensation seeker was conceived as someone who was happiest and functioned best at a high tonic level of arousal and therefore behaved in a way that would maintain such a high level" (Zuckerman 1979: 315). In effect, high-sensation seekers would seek stimulation in order to elevate arousal level to their optimum level.

Between 1969, the year that the theoretical bases of sensation seeking were formulated (Zuckerman 1969a) and 1979, the year that *The psychobiology of personality* was published (Zuckerman 1979), there was considerable research on sensation seeking and the optimum level of arousal hypothesis. The outcome of this work can be briefly summarized as follows:

First, from reviews of the psychophysiological literature, there is little evidence of individual differences in base level of arousal between high and low scorers in sensation seeking using measures of skin conductance level, EEG desynchronization, or resting heart rate. Thus, the notion that individuals with high scores on the sensation scale are characterized by low tonic levels of arousal is not supported.

Second, there is good evidence of differences in arousal responses to stimulation, with high-sensation seekers exhibiting larger (or stronger) responses than low-sensation seekers under some conditions. Specifically, high-sensation seekers exhibit larger skin conductance responses to novel stimulation than low-sensation seekers, notably to stimulus items that are relevant to the SSS, i.e. pictures of hang-gliding, marijuana smoking, mountain climbing, etc. (e.g. Smith *et al.* 1986). In general, these effects provide good support for the construct validity of the SSS.

Third, the most compelling evidence of arousal differences and sensation seeking is an augmenting-reducing effect observed with visual event-related potential changes to increases in the intensity of light flashes. Specifically, individuals with high scores on the Disinhibition subscale of the SSS exhibit an increase in amplitude of an ERP wave (P1N1) that develops at about 100 ms when recorded from a central vertex electrode. Those low in sensation seeking tend to exhibit a decrease in amplitude with an increase in intensity of the light flashes (Buchsbaum 1971; Lukas 1987). This effect can be understood in terms of the optimal level of arousal hypothesis, i.e. high-sensation seekers amplify stimulation or experience simple physical stimulation more intensely than low-sensation seekers. Alternatively, it can be argued that augmenting-reducing is an intensity effect in which high-sensation seekers are less sensitive to stimulation than low-sensation seekers, i.e. the low-sensation seekers initiate inhibitory, protective mechanisms in response to high intensity stimulation resulting in smaller responses. This view is endorsed by studies showing that high-sensation seeking is associated with greater pain tolerance, greater extraversion, less hypochondriasis, and higher absolute sensory thresholds (Goldman *et al.* 1983; Kohn *et al.* 1982). This indicates that high-sensation seekers engage in intense stimulating activities, not to achieve an optimum level of arousal, but simply because they can endure strong stimulation.

5. Conclusion: Beyond the Optimal Level of Arousal

In his Presidential Address to the American Psychological Association, D. O. Hebb (1974: 74) stated: "A science imposes limits on itself and makes its progress by attacking only those problems that it is fitted to attack by existing knowledge and methods. Psychology has made much progress in this century, and the rate of progress is accelerating, but it is limited and must be limited if it is to continue its progress — limited in the questions it asks, but sure in its results." As a scientist, it is helpful to be humble. Progress is often painstakingly slow, and the outcomes frequently contradict expectations. In this context, the period when the arousal construct was the main engine for research on the biological bases of personality did evince progress. Research did sharpen our understanding of both extraversion and sensation seeking and provided important clues to the nature of those personality traits. For Zuckerman (1979), the body of knowledge on sensation seeking that developed from work on the optimum level of arousal led to a major revision of sensation seeking theory, beyond the optimum level of arousal, that continues to influence our attempts to understand fundamental personality traits.

References

Barnes, G. (1975). Extraversion and pain. *British Journal of Social and Clinical Psychology, 14*, 303–308.

Barratt, E. (1959). Anxiety and impulsiveness related to psychomotor efficiency. *Perceptual and Motor Skills, 9*, 191–198.

Barratt, E. S., & Patton, J. (1983). Impulsivity: Cognitive, behavioral, and psychophysiological correlates. In: M. Zuckerman (Ed.), *Biological bases of sensation seeking, impulsivity and anxiety* (pp. 77–116). Hillsdale, NJ: Erlbaum.

Brebner, J., & Cooper, C. (1974). The effect of a low rate of regular signals upon the reaction times of introverts and extraverts. *Journal of Research in Personality, 8*, 263–276.

Brebner, J., & Flavell, R. (1978). The effect of catch-trials on speed and accuracy among introverts and extraverts in a simple RT task. *British Journal of Psychology, 69*, 9–15.

Britt, T. W., & Blumenthal, T. D. (1992). The effects of anxiety on motoric expression of the startle response. *Personality and Individual Differences, 13*, 91–98.

Buchsbaum, M. (1971). Neural events and the psychophysical law. *Science, 172*, 502.

Bullock, W. A., & Gilliland, K. (1993). Eysenck's arousal theory of introversion-extraversion: A converging measures investigation. *Journal of Personality and Social Psychology, 64*, 113–123.

Campbell, A., & Rushton, J. P. (1978). Bodily communication and personality. *British Journal of Social and Clinical Psychology, 17*, 31–36.

Cannon, W. B. (1915). *Bodily changes in pain, fear, hunger, and rage*. New York: Appleton-Century-Crofts.

Dornic, S., & Ekehammar, B. (1990). Extraversion, neuroticism, and noise sensitivity. *Personality and Individual Differences, 11*, 989–992.

Doucet, C., & Stelmack, R. M. (1997). Movement time differentiates extraverts from introverts. *Personality and Individual Differences, 23*, 775–786.

Doucet, C., & Stelmack, R. M. (2000). An event-related potential analysis of extraversion and individual differences in cognitive processing speed and response execution. *Journal of Personality and Social Psychology, 78*, 956–964.

Duffy, E. (1962). *Activation and behavior*. New York: Wiley.

Duffy, E. (1966). The nature and development of the concept of activation. In: R. N. Haber (Ed.), *Current research in motivation* (pp. 278–281). New York: Holt, Rinehart and Winston.

Duffy, E. (1972). Activation. In: N. S. Greenfield, & R. A. Sternbach (Eds), *Handbook of psychophysiology* (pp. 577–622). New York: Holt, Rinehart and Winston.

Elliot, R. (1964). Physiological activity and performance: A comparison of kindergarten children with young adults. *Psychological monographs, 78*, (10, No. 587).

Eysenck, H. J. (1957). *The dynamics of anxiety and hysteria*. London: Routledge & Kegan Paul.

Eysenck, H. J. (1959). *Manual for the Maudsley Personality Inventory*. San Diego: Educational & Industrial Testing Service.

Eysenck, H. J. (1967). *The biological basis of personality*. Springfield, IL: Thomas.

Eysenck, H. J., & Frith, C. D. (1977). *Reminiscence, motivation and personality*. New York: Plenum Press.

Eysenck, H. J., Nias, D. K. B., & Cox, D. N. (1982). Sport and personality. *Advances in Behavior Research and Therapy*, *4*, 1–56.

Fahrenberg, J., (1987). Concepts of activation and arousal in the theory of emotionality (neuroticism). In: J. Strelau, & H. J. Eysenck (Eds), *Personality dimensions and arousal* (pp. 99–120). New York: Plenum Press.

Gale, A. (1969). "Stimulus hunger": Individual differences in operant strategy in a button-pressing task. *Behaviour Research and Therapy*, *7*, 263–274.

Geen, R. G. (1984). Preferred stimulation levels in introverts and extraverts: Effects on arousal and performance. *Journal of Personality and Social Psychology*, *46*, 1303–1312.

Goldman, D., Kohn, P. M., & Hunt, R. W. (1983). Sensation seeking, augmenting reducing, and absolute auditory threshold: A strength of the nervous system perspective. *Journal of Personality and Social Psychology*, *45*, 405–411.

Gray, J. A. (1972). The psychophysiological basis of introversion-extraversion: A modification of Eysenck's theory. In: V. D. Nebylitsyn, & J. A. Gray (Eds), *Biological basis of individual behaviour* (pp. 182–205). London: Academic Press.

Hebb, D. O. (1949). *Organization of behavior*. New York: Wiley.

Hebb, D. O. (1955). Drives and the C.N.S. (conceptual nervous system). *Psychological Review*, *62*, 243–254.

Hebb, D. O. (1974). What psychology is about. *American Psychologist*, *29*, 71–79.

Jasper, H. H. (1949). Diffuse projection system: The integrative action of the thalamic reticular system. *Electroencephalography and Clinical Neurophysiology*, *1*, 405–419.

Johnson, A. K., & Anderson, E. A. (1990). Stress and arousal. In: J. T. Cacioppo, & L. G. Tassinary (Eds), *Principles of psychophysiology: Physical, social and inferential elements* (pp. 216–252). New York: Cambridge University Press.

Kaplan, A. (1964). *The conduct of inquiry: Methodology for behavioural science*. Scranton, PA: Chandler.

Kirkcaldy, B. D. (1982). Personality profiles at various levels of athletic participation. *Personality and Individual Differences*, *3*, 321–326.

Kohn, P. M., Hunt, R. W., & Hoffman, F. M. (1982). Aspects of experience seeking. *Canadian Journal of Behavioral Science*, *14*, 13–23.

Lacey, J. I. (1967). Somatic response patterning and stress: Some revisions of activation theory. In: M. H. Appley, & R. Trumbull (Eds), *Psychological stress: Issues in research*. New York: Appleton-Century-Crofts.

Le Moal, M., & Simon, H. (1991). Mesocorticolimbic dopaminergic network: Functional and regulatory roles. *Physiological Reviews*, *71*, 155–234.

Lindsley, D. B. (1951). Emotion. In: S. S. Stevens (Ed.), *Handbook of experimental psychology*. New York: Wiley.

Lukas, J. H. (1987). Visual evoked potential augmenting-reducing and personality: The vertex augmenter is a sensation seeker. *Personality and Individual Differences*, *8*, 385–395.

Malmo, R. B. (1959). Activation: A neurophysiological dimension. *Psychological Review*, *66*, 367–386.

Matthews, G., & Gilliland, K. (1999). The personality theories of H. J. Eysenck and J. A. Gray: A comparative review. *Personality and Individual Differences*, *26*, 583–626.

Moruzzi, G., & Magoun, H. W. (1949). Brainstem reticular formation and activation of the EEG. *Electroencephalograpy and Clinical Neurophysiology*, *1*, 455–473.

Obrist, P. A. (1981). *Cardiovascular psychophysiology*. New York: Plenum Press.

O'Connor, K. (1982). Individual differences in the effect of smoking on frontal-central distribution of the CNV: Some observations on smokers' control of attentional behaviour. *Personality and Individual Differences*, *3*, 271–286.

Olds, J., & Milner, P. (1954). Positive reinforcement produced by electrical stimulation of septal area and other regions of rat brain. *Journal of Comparative and Physiological Psychology*, *47*, 419–427.

Pivik, R. T., Stelmack, R. M., & Bylsma, F. W. (1988). Personality and individual differences in spinal motoneuronal excitability. *Psychophysiology*, *25*, 16–24.

Rammsayer, T., Netter, P., & Vogel, W. H. (1993). A neurochemical model underlying differences in reaction times between introverts and extraverts. *Personality and Individual Differences*, *14*, 701–712.

Robinson, T. N., & Zahn, T. P. (1988). Preparatory interval effects on the reaction time performance of introverts and extraverts. *Personality and Individual Differences*, *9*, 749–761.

Schalling, D. (1971). Tolerance for experimentally induced pain as related to personality. *Scandinavian Journal of Psychology*, *12*, 271–281.

Sokolov, E. N. (1963). *Perception and the conditioned reflex*. New York: Macmillan.

Smith, B. D. (1983). Extraversion and electrodermal activity: Arousability and the inverted-U. *Personality and Individual Differences*, *4*, 411–419.

Smith, B. D., Perlstein, W. M., Davidson, R. A., & Michael, K. (1986). Sensation seeking: Differential effects of relevant, novel stimulation on electrodermal activity. *Personality and Individual Differences*, *7*, 445–452.

Stelmack, R. M. (1979). Extraversion orienting reaction habituation rate and sensitivity to stimulation. In: H. D. Kimmel, E. H. van Olst, & J. R. Orlebeke (Eds), *The orienting reflex in humans* (pp. 647–656). New York: Erlbaum.

Stelmack, R. M. (1981). The psychophysiology of extraversion and neuroticism. In: H. J. Eysenck (Ed.), *A model for personality* (pp. 38–64). Heidelberg: Springer-Verlag.

Stelmack, R. M. (1990). The biological basis of extraversion: Psychophysiological evidence. *Journal of Personality*, *58*, 293–311.

Stelmack, R. M., Achorn, E., & Michaud, A. (1977). Extraversion and individual differences in auditory evoked response. *Psychophysiology*, *14*, 368–374.

Stelmack, R. M., & Campbell, K. B. (1974). Extraversion and auditory sensitivity to high and low frequency. *Perceptual and Motor Skills*, *38*, 875–879.

Stelmack, R. M., & Geen, R. G. (1992). The psychophysiology of extraversion. In: A. Gale, & M. W. Eysenck (Eds), *Handbook of individual differences: Biological perspectives* (pp. 227–254). New York: Wiley.

Stelmack, R. M., Houlihan, M., & McGarry-Roberts, P. A. (1993). Personality, reaction time, and event-related potentials. *Journal of Personality and Social Psychology*, *65*, 399–409.

Stelmack, R. M., & Michaud-Achorn, A. (1985). Extraversion, attention, and habituation of the auditory evoked response. *Journal of Research in Personality*, *19*, 416–428.

Stelmack, R. M., & Pivik, R. T. (1996). Extraversion and the effects of exercise on spinal motoneuronal excitability. *Personality and Individual Differences*, *21*, 69–76.

Stelmack, R. M., & Wilson, K. G. (1982). Extraversion and the effects of frequency and intensity on the auditory brainstem evoked response. *Personality and Individual Differences*, *3*, 373–380.

Stenberg, G., Rosen, I., & Risberg, J. (1990). Attention and personality in augmenting/reducing of visual evoked potentials. *Personality and Individual Differences*, *11*, 1243–1254.

Swickert, R. J., & Gilliland, K. (1998). Relationship between the brainstem auditory evoked response and extraversion, impulsivity, and sociability. *Journal of Research in Personality*, *32*, 314–330.

Zubek, J. P. (Ed.) (1969). *Sensory deprivation: Fifteen years of research*. New York: Appleton-Century-Crofts.

Zuckerman, M. (1969a). Theoretical formulations: I. In: J. P. Zubek (Ed.), *Sensory deprivation: Fifteen years of research* (pp. 407–432). New York: Appleton-Century-Crofts.

Zuckerman, M. (1969b). Variables affecting deprivation results. In: J. P. Zubek (Ed.), *Sensory deprivation: Fifteen years of research* (pp. 47–84). New York: Appleton-Century-Crofts.

Zuckerman, M. (1979). *Sensation seeking: Beyond the optimum level of arousal*. Hillsdale, NJ: Erlbaum.

Zuckerman, M., & Haber, M. M. (1965). Need for stimulation as a source of stress response to perceptual isolation. *Journal of Abnormal Psychology*, *70*, 371–377.

Zuckerman, M., Kolin, E. A., Price, L., & Zoob, I. (1964). Development of a sensation seeking scale. *Journal of Consulting Psychology*, *28*, 477–482.

Chapter 3

Warsaw Studies on Sensation Seeking

J. Strelau and M. Kaczmarek

1. Introduction

Marvin Zuckerman is one of the few differential psychologists who has been able to develop a theory of a temperament dimension, one which skillfully combines the correlational with the experimental approach, studies on humans with research on animals, behavior characteristics with biochemical and psychophysiological measures. This multidirectional approach made it possible for him to develop a causal theory of individual differences in sensation seeking (SS). Zuckerman presented his SS theory in many of his publications, some of which contain a general and comprehensive review (Zuckerman 1979, 1984, 1994).

We are considering SS as a temperament dimension because temperament refers to personality dimensions that have a biological basis. Using Zuckerman's (1992) criteria, also applied in our studies on temperament (Strelau 1983, 1998), they are present not only in man but also in other animal species. For these traits (dimensions) neurophysiological mechanisms or correlates can be identified. In one of his publications, *The biological foundations of the sensation-seeking temperament*, Zuckerman (1985) recognized his SS construct as belonging to the temperament domain. The concentration on temperament in the context of SS is not marginal for this presentation because for several decades the studies conducted in Strelau's laboratory have centered on temperament phenomena leading to our interest in SS.

To relate the SS construct to the temperament traits as studied in our laboratory, the Sensation Seeking Scale-Form IV (SSS-IV) and the Sensation Seeking Scale-Form V (SSS-V) were adapted for the Polish population from details described by Zuckerman (1979). The adaptation of the SS scales to cultures other than North American, in our case to Poland, which was under the Soviet regime for many decades, caused some difficulties (see Oleszkiewicz 1982; Andresen 1986). Among the many personality and temperament questionnaires known to us, the SS scales are the most culturally biased. Many items refer to behaviors (e.g. I have tried marijuana), situations (e.g. "wild" uninhibited parties) attitudes (e.g. I dislike "swingers") and activities (e.g. parachute jumping) unknown or rarely met in

On the Psychobiology of Personality
Edited by R. M. Stelmack

ISBN: 0-08-044209-9

other cultures, and, even when known, were hardly ever experienced by the subjects under study.[1]

Both SSS-IV and the SSS-V are composed of four subscales measuring the four following components of the SS construct: Thrill and Adventure Seeking (TAS), Disinhibition (Dis), Experience seeking (ES), and Boredom susceptibility (BS). Both versions of the test were applied in our laboratory. The SSS-IV inventory was adapted for the Polish population by Dorota Żychowska (1984) and the SSS-V by Zofia Oleszkiewicz (1982).

2. Psychometric Studies on the Relation Between Zuckerman's Sensation Seeking Constructs and Temperamental Traits Postulated by Strelau

In some of our studies, questions were asked about the relation between SS and the temperament traits as postulated by our theory in which two stages may be distinguished. The first stage centered on the Pavlovian approach. It led to the development of an inventory known as the Strelau Temperament Inventory (STI). In the second stage, the Regulative Theory of Temperament (RTT) was developed. As a consequence, a new inventory was constructed, the Formal Characteristics of Behavior-Temperament Inventory (FCB-TI). Both of those temperament measures were related to SS and some of our results are presented in the subsequent sections.

2.1. Sensation Seeking and Pavlov's Nervous System Properties

SS and the temperament constructs developed by Pavlov (1927), which were the focus of our studies for many years, have common elements. Both refer to man as well as to other animal species and both postulate neurophysiological mechanisms that underlie temperamental traits. They also have common roots in the concept of arousal that Pavlov interpreted in terms of excitation. Because we were strongly influenced by the Pavlovian and neo-Pavlovian traditions, we developed a temperament inventory aimed at assessing the basic Pavlovian properties of the central nervous system (CNS), i.e. strength of excitation, strength of inhibition and mobility of nervous processes. It is obvious that one cannot measure properties of the CNS by means of a paper and pencil technique. This procedure does not allow any insight into the physiological mechanisms to which these properties pertain. The CNS properties have the status of explanatory concepts belonging to Pavlov's (1927) theory of higher nervous system activity. This means that our inventories intended to measure temperament traits that were to be interpreted in terms of behavior within the Pavlovian theory of CNS properties (Strelau 1983; Strelau *et al.* 1999).

---

[1] When adapting the SSS-V to the Polish population, high school students were among the participants. A report about our study was delivered to the Minister of Education stating that the SSS questionnaire contains items that are morally doubtful. Under pressure by the official authorities, we were forced to interrupt the research conducted on high school students.

When referring to behavior, strength of excitation, understood as the ability to endure intense or long-lasting stimulation, is expressed in such domains as readiness for action, carrying on activity in highly stimulation situations, lack of emotional disturbances under stress situations and lack of evident changes in efficiency under intense or long-lasting stimulation.

Strength of inhibition, regarded by Pavlov as the functional capacity of the CNS for conditioned inhibition, especially as the ability to endure long-lasting inhibition, refers to such behaviors as restraining from reactions, delay of action and ability to interrupt an action. Broadly speaking, strength of inhibition expresses itself in the control of behavior. Mobility of the nervous system, understood as the ability of the CNS processes to switch from excitation to inhibition and conversely, expresses itself mainly in the ability to react quickly to changes in surroundings according to external conditions.

For the purpose of measuring CNS properties, as briefly described above, the Strelau Temperament Inventory (STI; Strelau 1972, 1983) was constructed and applied for almost 20 years in our laboratory. The STI, composed of three scales applied to the three CNS properties, was also adapted in more than a dozen language versions. Critical comments on the psychometric properties of the STI (Carlier 1985; Daum & Schugens 1986; Stelmack *et al.* 1985) led to a thorough revision of this inventory that resulted in the construction of a new psychometric instrument, the Pavlovian Temperament Survey (PTS; Strelau *et al.* 1999). This inventory is also composed of three scales marking the three CNS properties.

As mentioned above the temperament constructs, SS and the Pavlovian CNS properties, may be regarded as arousal-oriented concepts. Thus, it was reasonable to study the relation between them. We expected that strength of excitation would correlate with all SS components and that strength of inhibition would be inversely related, especially to DIS. This scale, more than the remaining SS scales, makes reference to socially unacceptable behaviors.

The most representative data regarding the relation between the SS components and the CNS properties were collected using the SSS-V and the PTS inventories. Table 1 presents median scores from 7 samples (two Polish, three German and one American) comprising more than 2000 subjects (see Strelau *et al.* 1999 for a detailed description).

Table 1: Sensation seeking and the Pavlov's CNS properties.

Sensation Seeking	**CNS Properties**		
	SE	**SI**	**MO**
Thrill and adventure seeking	0.34	0.00	0.30
Disinhibition	0.23	−0.26	0.13
Experience seeking	0.27	−0.05	0.25
Boredom susceptibility	0.20	−0.12	0.20
Total score	0.37	−0.15	0.28

Note: SE = Strength of Excitation; SI = Strength of Inhibition; MO = Mobility of the CNS. Total score = an aggregate score of all SSS-V subscales.

As can be seen in Table 1, our hypotheses regarding the relation between SS and Pavlovian properties are verified. In addition, SS correlates with mobility of the CNS. This is a reasonable result considering that high scorers on the SS scales and on mobility of the nervous system scales both prefer changes in behavior.

2.2. *Sensation Seeking and Temperament Traits as Proposed by the Regulative Theory of Temperament*

Some 20 years ago, we began to develop a theory of temperament known as the Regulative Theory of Temperament (RTT) which has been described in many publications (see Strelau 1983, 1993, 1998). The roots of this theory are based on the Pavlovian tradition and they refer to theories of arousal (Duffy 1957; Eysenck 1967; Gray 1964; Hebb 1955), and to Tomaszewski's (1978) theory of action. The development of the RTT was also influenced by our own experience, beginning in the late 1950s, in our studies on temperament.

The theory postulates a structure of temperament composed of six traits to be measured by the FCB-TI (Strelau & Zawadzki 1993, 1995). It has been adapted to eight different countries, including an American version (Zawadzki 2002). The six traits are:

- Briskness: tendency to react quickly, to keep a high tempo in performing activities, and to shift easily in response to changes in the surroundings from one behavior (reaction) to another.
- Perseveration: tendency to continue and to repeat behavior and experience emotional states after cessation of stimuli (situations) evoking this behavior or states.
- Sensory Sensitivity: ability to react to sensory stimuli of low stimulative value.
- Emotional Reactivity: tendency to react intensively to emotion-generating stimuli, expressed in high emotional sensitivity and in low emotional endurance.
- Endurance: ability to react adequately in situations demanding long-lasting or high stimulative activity and under intensive external stimulation.
- Activity: tendency to undertake behaviors of high stimulative value or to supply by means of behavior strong stimulation from the surroundings.

When relating the SSS scales to the FCB-TI scales, we hypothesized that Activity, as defined above, would be strongly related to all scales of SS, whereas Briskness and Endurance would correlate with TAS and ES. It was also predicted that Emotional Reactivity, closely related to Neuroticism (see Strelau & Zawadzki 1995), would correlate negatively with SS. The most representative results collected in our laboratory illustrating the relations between traits of the SSS and RTT scales again refer to SS as measured by the SSS-V inventory. Data from two following samples were collected. The first sample comprised 317 subjects (155 females and 162 males) aged 5 to 23 ($M = 19.1$; $SD = 2.40$). They were all high school or university students. Sample two comprised 217 subjects (169 females and 48 males) from 15 to 69 years of age ($M = 22.9$; $SD = 9.83$), representing high school and university students and 14 different professions (for more details see Strelau & Zawadzki 1995). The data are presented in Table 2.

Table 2: Sensation Seeking and Temperament Traits as Postulated by the RTT.

SSS-V Scales	Sample	FCB-TI Scales					
		BR	PE	SS	ER	EN	AC
TAS	1	0.28*	−0.26*	0.00	−0.33*	0.33*	0.40*
	2			0.02	−0.22*	0.17*	0.43*
ES	1	0.09	−0.10	0.13	−0.15*	0.09	0.31*
	2			0.17*	−0.18*	0.13	0.39
Dis	1	0.11	−0.15*	−0.07	−0.11	0.09	0.35*
	2			−0.14	−0.21*	0.15	0.36*
BS	1	0.08	−0.21*	0.01	−0.18*	0.03	0.35*
	2			−0.05	−0.10	−0.01	0.35*
Total score	1	0.21*	−0.26*	0.01	−0.28*	0.21*	0.50*
				−0.01	−0.27*	0.17*	0.56*

Note: TAS = Thrill and Adventure Seeking; ES = Experience Seeking; DIS = Disinhibition; BS = Boredom Susceptibility; BR = Briskness, PE = Perseveration; SS = Sensory Sensitivity; ER = Emotional Reactivity; EN = Endurance; AC = Activity. In sample two, the BR and PE were not included.
$^{*}p < 0.01$ (one tailed).

Our prediction regarding the close link between SS and Activity has been consistently confirmed. This effect is especially evident when the total score is taken into account. Also, the negative relation between SS and Emotional Reactivity was shown. Whereas, Briskness correlates with TAS and ES as predicted, the correlation between Endurance and these SS scales is evident only for TAS. The data show that perseveration is negatively correlated with the SS scales (except for ES). This is reasonable if we consider that in all of our studies Perseveration and Emotional Reactivity are rather highly correlated with each other (Zawadzki & Strelau 1997).

3. Sensation Seeking Related to Behavior and Behavior Disorders

In our laboratory, several studies were conducted on the relation of SS to preferences in painting and in music and to behavior problems, such as alcoholism, criminal acts, and maladjustment to family and school environments. In all these studies, temperament traits were measured by means of the PTS or FCB-TI inventories in addition to the SS scales.Our studies on SS can be grouped into three following areas:

(1) Sensation seeking as a predictor of antisocial and harmful behavior.
(2) Sensation seeking as a predictor of socially neutral behavior.
(3) Social expectation regarding the intensity of sensation seeking tendency and its impact on the risk of maladjustment to school and family environments.

3.1. Sensation Seeking as a Predictor of Antisocial and Harmful Behavior

Two separate studies were conducted in which SS was treated as a predictor of harmful or antisocial behaviors. These studies concern alcohol habits and committing aggressive as well as non-aggressive crimes.

3.1.1. Sensation seeking and alcohol abuse The relation between SS traits and problems with alcohol is well documented in the literature, especially among adolescents and young adults (Andrew & Cronin 1997; von Knorring *et al.* 1987; Zuckerman 1987). There are several different factors that are involved in drinking alcohol behavior. In general, three determinants can be distinguished: biological factors (Andersson & Magnusson 1990; Crabbe *et al.* 1994; Polich *et al.* 1994; von Knorring *et al.* 1987), social factors (Glenn & Nixon 1996; Simon *et al.* 1994) and individual psychological traits (Colder & Chassin 1997; Wennberg & Bohman 2002; Zuckerman 1987). Among individual psychological characteristics, temperament traits, understood as basic factors of personality, are the most common predictors of susceptibility to abuse alcohol (Wennberg & Bohman 2002; Zuckerman 1987).

The addiction to drinking alcohol is regarded as a heterogeneous phenomenon. According to the temperament-personality model suggested by Cloninger (1987), there are two different types of alcoholism. Type I is described by symptoms of binge drinking, feeling guilty following drinking, and attempts to self-limit the amount of alcohol consumed. As the authors suggest, Type I is characterized by the onset of alcohol abuse in adulthood i.e. after the age of 25 or older. On the other hand, Type II alcoholism is described by early onset of abuse, i.e. before age 25, breaking the law, aggressive behavior after alcohol drinking and unwillingness to reduce or stop drinking alcohol (Glenn & Nixon 1996). In terms of Cloninger's (1987) theory, Type II is characterized by a high level of novelty seeking and by low levels of harm avoidance and reward dependence. Type I is described by low novelty seeking, high harm avoidance, and high reward dependence.

It is apparent that high-sensation seeking is characteristic of Type II alcoholism. It must be underlined that consuming alcohol frequently and in large quantities does not lead to addiction directly. Rather, consuming alcohol should be treated as a risk factor. Zuckerman (1987) suggested that personality traits may be different for individuals who drink alcohol and do not have any special problems resulting from this behavior and for individuals for whom alcohol is the main source of their troubles in family and professional life. He claimed that SS may be an important factor in the etiology of alcoholism. High SS should be a characteristic of young people who drink alcohol and, because of their age, more frequently represent Type II alcoholism. Because of their short history of drinking alcohol, they rarely show symptoms of addiction to alcohol and their negative consequences.

Aleksandra Furowicz (1996) conducted a study that investigated SS and alcohol drinking habits in students. The sample consisted of 139 students from the universities in Kraków and Katowice (96 females and 43 males). They were between 19 and 26 years of age ($M = 21.00$; $SD = 1.25$). Most of them lived in dormitories and were unmarried. SS seeking was measured by the SSS-IV inventory whereas temperament was measured by the FCB-TI. The amount and frequency of drinking alcohol were assessed by the Questionnaire "A" (Engs *et al.* 1991). Items on this questionnaire assessed frequency of drinking alcohol, favorite type of alcohol (e.g. beer, wine, vodka), amount of consumption, subjectively perceived effects of drinking, and knowledge of objective effects of alcohol and the customs connected with it.

Subjects who declared that they drink alcohol at least once a week and/or consume large quantities constituted the high risk of alcoholism group (40 persons). Subjects who claimed that they do not drink at all or drink only on special occasions a few times a year formed the low risk of alcoholism group (36 persons). To verify the hypothesis that SS differentiates between the high and low risk of alcoholism groups, the scores of SSS-IV were compared between groups. Our hypothesis was confirmed. The high risk of alcoholism group was characterized by higher SS total scores and by higher scores on each of the separate scales. The largest differences between the groups were observed on the total SS score, and the DIS and the BS scales. Coefficients of correlation indicated that all of the SS scales were positively related to the amount of alcohol consumption. The correlations ranged from 0.20 (ES) to 0.69 (DIS) and the scales were significant at least at the 0.05 level.

We also tested the hypothesis that temperament traits measured by the FCB-TI are related to the risk of alcoholism. Higher Briskness, lower Emotional Reactivity, and lower Sensory Sensitivity scores characterized the high risk of alcoholism group. It is worth adding that dimensions of family environment measured in this study by the Family Environment Scale (Moose & Moose 1994) were modestly or even unrelated to the risk of alcoholism. The Family Environment Scale consists of 10 scales that measure three dimensions of family functioning. There were significant differences between the high and low risk of alcoholism groups for only three of the scales. Subjects at high risk for alcoholism are more independent in their families; their families were less committed to religious and moral issues; and their families were less demanding in respect to home duties.

In conclusion, our results are very similar to the outcomes on this subject that were obtained in previous studies in other countries. As Zuckerman (1987) shows, the relation between SS and alcohol habits is age-specific and may be influenced by socio-cultural changes. In the future, it might be worth considering whether the Polish political, social and economic transition after the collapse of the Soviet regime has modified this relation. But these are not the only changes that took place during the last decade. The social norms, values and life style, including drinking alcohol habits and prevalence of using illegal drugs, have also changed considerably.

3.1.2. Sensation seeking, crime and aggressiveness As Simo and Perez (1991) claim, many forms of antisocial behavior, such as robberies, burglaries, fights, and forgeries that involve risky, novel, and complex situations, can easily satisfy the need for stimulation. When referring to the construct of arousal, the SS dimension might be considered as an expression of high need for stimulation. Thus, it should not be surprising that people who committed crimes or delinquencies are more likely to be sensation seekers than law-abiding citizens. Many studies confirmed this view (Arnett 1996; Horvath & Zuckerman 1992; Newcomb & McGee 1991; Perez & Torrubia 1985). Studies have also shown that the relation between antisocial behavior and SS may differ under temporal and cultural influences. In any case, being a sensation seeker does not determine that one comes into conflict with law (see Hansen & Breivik 2001; Simon *et al.* 1994). Similar to the relation between SS and drinking alcohol habits, SS should be treated as one of the risk factors of criminal behavior.

The relation between aggressiveness (and types of aggressiveness) and SS (Netter & Rammsayer 1991), or traits related to the SS tendency (Ruchin *et al.* 1998), was also investigated. In a study conducted by Joanna Korczyńska (1998), SS was measured in two groups of young prisoners who differed in how they committed crimes, i.e. with or without aggression. The group of prisoners who committed crimes in an aggressive way was composed of 102 males (mean age = 19.52; SD = 0.92). There were 91 males (mean age = 20.04; SD = 0.37) in the group who committed crime without aggression. Schoolboys who attended vocational schools served as a control group (100 males; mean age = 17.45; SD = 0.61). The SSS-V, the FCB-TI, the Buss-Durkee Hostility Inventory (Buss & Durkee 1957), the Raven's Progressive Matrices (Raven 1960) and the Rokeach Value Survey (Rokeach 1985) were administered to all subjects. Also, reports of alcohol consumption when performing a crime were taken into account. All subjects who committed crimes were in prison when the study was conducted. They were sentenced to imprisonment for robbery (in case of a crime with aggression) or for theft or burglary (in case of a crime without aggression).

Two main hypotheses were assessed. First, it was predicted that SS is higher in the prisoner groups as compared to the control group. Secondly, it was expected that SS is higher in the group of prisoners sentenced for robberies compared to the rest of subjects. Neither hypothesis was confirmed. The only significant result obtained in this study was the difference in SS between the group of prisoners who committed crimes without aggression and who were under the influence of alcohol when committing crimes as compared to the remaining subjects. A lower total score on SS, lower ES and lower TAS characterized these prisoners. The results are shown in Table 3. There were no significant differences between groups for the RTT temperament traits.

In summary, the hypotheses regarding the relation between SS and criminal behavior that occurred with or without aggression was not confirmed. The reason may lie in the criteria for selecting the groups being studied. Korczyńska divided prisoners into aggressive and non-aggressive groups on the basis of the official records that might not correspond with their real experiences. It is also possible that the prisoners underrated their SS need.

3.2. Sensation Seeking as a Predictor of Socially Neutral Behavior

The second area of our studies on SS was centered on the relation between SS and some positive or socially neutral behavior, a research topic that was previously addressed in the literature. For example, Gomà-i-Freixanet (1995) found that pro-social risk, e.g. being a fireman or bodyguard, is related to SS dimensions. Also, sensation seekers more frequently engage in risky but socially approved activities or sports (Hansen & Breivik 2001). Studies were also conducted on the relation between SS and such socially neutral topics as humor (Forabosco & Ruch 1994) or music preferences. Litle and Zuckerman (1986) and McNamara and Ballard (1999) found that people's music preferences differed depending on their SS scores. McNamara and Ballard reported that those who are high on SS prefer rock music and dislike bland, soundtrack music.

One of the most interesting studies done in our laboratory in this field of research was an experiment conducted by Danuta Gebhardt (1997) to determine whether SS is linked to

Table 3: Differences between mean scores on temperament dimensions as measured by SSS Form V and the PTS among groups of prisoners differing in the character of committed crime and in the influence of alcohol during the criminal act.

Temperament Dimensions	Sentenced for Aggressive Crime		Sentenced for Non-Aggressive Crime		*F*
	Alcohol *M* (S.D.)	No Alcohol *M* (S.D.)	Alcohol *M* (S.D.)	No Alcohol *M* (S.D.)	
TAS	6.84 (2.38)	7.38 (2.47)	5.88 (2.72)	7.25 (2.50)	2.61*
DIS	6.40 (2.32)	6.00 (2.19)	5.75 (2.51)	5.48 (2.65)	1.56
ES	4.78 (1.92)	5.06 (1.89)	3.84 (1.14)	5.12 (2.20)	3.45**
BS	3.03 (1.90)	3.27 (1.84)	2.35 (1.70)	3.17 (1.68)	1.15
Total score	21.09 (5.76)	21.91 (6.12)	18.00 (5.88)	21.07 (7.01)	2.56*
BR	14.36 (2.81)	15.45 (3.45)	13.45 (3.76)	16.46 (2.99)	7.55**
PS	12.14 (3.83)	10.73 (4.15)	12.20 (4.37)	11.57 (4.84)	0.95
SS	13.29 (3.31)	14.84 (3.05)	13.23 (3.26)	14.22 (3.21)	2.24
ER	10.08 (3.81)	7.33 (3.68)	11.21 (4.26)	8.65 (4.33)	5.99**
EN	10.52 (4.26)	11.23 (4.85)	9.48 (4.70)	11.13 (4.33)	1.06
AC	12.89 (3.59)	14.50 (3.42)	13.10 (3.35)	12.87 (4.18)	1.69

Note: TAS = Thrill and adventure seeking; ES = Experience Seeking; DIS = Disinhibition; BS = Boredom Susceptibility; BR = Briskness, PE = Perseveration; SS = Sensory Sensitivity; ER = Emotional Reactivity; EN = Endurance; AC = Activity.

*$p < 0.05$.

**$p < 0.01$.

preferences in painting and in music. As already mentioned, studies on the preference in the type of music judged in terms of the level of stimulation need were conducted previously. In Gebhardt's (1997) study, differences in music tempo were recorded while other music parameters, such as style, theme, and instrumentality were controlled. It was assumed that faster tempo music would satisfy the need for stimulation more than slower tempo music. Thus, it was expected that high-SS participants would select faster pieces of music more frequently than lower-SS participants.

Similar reasoning was applied regarding the relation of SS to the preference of paintings. Color may be a variable on which pictures differ in their stimulation value. Predominately red, orange and yellow colors are perceived as optimistic, energetic and even irritable. These colors are considered as warm. Cold colors such as green and blue can denote such feelings and emotions as calm, relaxed and even sadness and pessimism (Zeugner 1965). Gebhardt (1997) assumed that the emotional states evoked by the differences in color reflect the stimulation value of each color. Warm colors are more stimulating than cold colors. Thus, sensation seekers should prefer warm colors whereas sensation avoiders will show preferences for cold colors. As in the case of the music study, other factors, i.e. style, painter, topic, were controlled.

Table 4: Coefficients of correlation between the sensation seeking dimensions and temperament traits measured by PTS and choices of warm vs. cold colors and fast vs. slow music.

Temperament Dimensions	Warm Color Choices	Fast Music Choices
General scale	0.72**	0.72**
Thrill and adventure seeking scale	0.55**	0.34*
Experience seeking	0.62**	0.59**
Disinhibition	0.54**	0.63**
Boredom susceptibility	0.73**	0.67**
Briskness	0.63**	0.57**
Perseveration	−0.32*	−0.30
Sensory sensitivity	−0.02	−0.14
Emotional reactivity	−0.22	−0.43**
Endurance	0.34*	0.39*
Activity	0.53**	0.39*

*$p < 0.01$.
**$p < 0.001$.

In the experiment, 53 persons participated (31 females and 22 males; 20–45 years, mean age = 21.5; $SD = 4.62$). They represented a variety of education levels and occupations. None of the participants performed music or painted professionally. Prior to the experiment, SS was assessed with the SSS-IV and RTT temperament traits were measured with the FCB-TI. During the experiment, subjects were asked to choose between two pieces of music that were each presented for 30 seconds. There were 15 pairs of music pieces. Within each pair, the pieces represented the same composer and in the most of the cases the selections were fragments from the same work. The presentation of the paintings to the subjects was similar. Pairs of paintings were exposed simultaneously. The paintings differed in color. There were 15 pairs. Each painting was exposed for 10 seconds.

Both hypotheses linking SS to preference of warm vs. cold coloring and preference of fast vs. slow music were confirmed. The correlation analysis of this study is shown in Table 4.

High scores on all of the SS scales were highly related to the choice of warm pictures and fast music. This experiment might be treated as an example showing that SS may influence a wide range of activity, even if this activity does not involve risk. It is noteworthy that the correlations showing the relation between the temperament traits measured by the FCB-TI and preferences in painting and in music are consistent with our expectation and with the data cited previously (see Table 2).

3.3. Social Expectations Regarding the Intensity of Sensation Seeking Tendency and its Impact on the Risk of Maladjustment to School and Family Environments

Findings show that SS is not a necessary determinant of antisocial behavior. Other individual characteristics as well as opportunities offered by the environment may influence how the need for stimulation will be expressed. Hansen and Breivik (2001) underlined the crucial impact of the social environment on the relation between SS and negative risk behavior. The authors claim that especially poor social environments, that do not offer many opportunities to satisfy the need for stimulation, dispose SS to express negative, antisocial behavior. Moreover, they observed that there are environmental presumptions and expectations concerning the ideal level of the SS tendency. According to Rowland and Heatherton (1987), there are cultural and social norms for the social desirability of SS. The question arises as to how this social expectation may modify the links between SS and risk of maladjustment to this environment.

The aim of the study representing the third area of our SS research was to examine the relation between SS and symptoms of maladjustment to the social environment. This relation was studied from two different points of view: (1) expected SS of adolescents by parents and teachers; and (2) discrepancy between expected SS and self-reported SS. The latter was considered as an index of the real temperament characteristic.

In a study conducted by Aleksandra Miklewska (2000) two questions were posed. (1) How does the expected level of SS influence the risk of maladjustment to the social environment? (2) How does the discrepancy between expected and real level of SS tendency influence such a risk? Two different social environments were also taken into account, family and school. To address the question regarding the relation between the discrepancy of expected and real level of SS and maladjusted behavior, Miklewska referred to the theory of "goodness of fit" developed by Chess and Thomas (1991). SS was considered as a temperament risk factor that predisposes maladjusted behavior when in interaction with an unfavorable environment, i.e. the degree of discrepancy between expected and real SS (Strelau 1995).

Miklewska (2000) hypothesized that when sensation seekers are confronted with social expectations of low level of the SS need, they may experience misfit. Consequently, they may develop symptoms of maladjustment that are expressed in antisocial behavior. Conversely, low sensation seekers, under the pressure of expectation of high intensity of the SS tendency, may also develop symptoms of maladjustment. The assumption was made that expectations regarding the SS trait are different for teachers and parents (mothers as well as fathers). Ballantine and Klein (1990) showed that Japanese teachers prefer behavior characterized by low- or moderate-level of the SS tendency. Lerner and Lerner (1983) discussed the relation between the expectations of the parents for the temperament of their child and the risk of misfit to family life. Miklewska (2000) assumed that ES and DIS are the most crucial SS components regarding the risk of maladjustment.

Overall, 141 triads consisting of adolescent, teacher and parent (mother or father) took part in this study. Temperament traits of adolescents (97 females and 44 males; 15–18 years, mean age = 15.75) were measured by means of the SSS-V, and the PTS. These tests were also administered to the teacher and to the parent (either mother or father) but with different instructions. They were asked to describe the "perfect child" (parent) and "perfect pupil" (teacher). The level of maladjustment was measured by means of the Maladjustment Scale (Pytka 1984). The scale consists of 6 subscales assessing different areas of social maladjustment. Only two subscales were applied in this study, i.e. maladjustment in the school and maladjustment in the family. Ratings on the scales were made by persons who exercised a significant socializing influence on the child, i.e. a teacher in the school environment and the parent in the family environment. The level of maladjustment to each environment was recorded as a general score.

The correlation between SS and the level of maladjustment in the family and in the school shows that there is a modest but significant positive relation between maladjustment to the family environment and ES ($r = 0.17$) as well as DIS ($r = 0.15$). To our surprise, no correlation was observed between the general score of maladjustment to the school environment and SS. Only when the items measuring frequency of conflicts with teachers and peers were considered was a significant relation between maladjustment to school environment and SS (ES and DIS) observed. However, regression analysis shows that if the full temperament model was tested, with all the SS and PTS scales as predictors, the only temperament dimensions which predicted maladjustment to family environment was balance of nervous processes measured by the ratio between the SE and the SI scales.

The next step in the analysis of the data treated the relation between maladjustment to both social environments and the expected SS tendency. Correlation analysis shows that the parent's expectation of their children's SS is positively related to the risk of maladjustment to the family environment. This means that adolescents who do not cope well with family demands have parents who expect higher ES ($r = 0.42$) as well as higher DIS ($r = 0.37$) of their child. A relation was also observed for maladjustment to the school environment. Pupils who have difficulties coping with demands in their school environment have teachers who expect lower DIS ($r = -0.37$). These findings are illustrated in Figure 1. This figure also shows coefficients of correlation between the level of maladjustment and two of the three temperament traits measured by PTS, Strength of Excitation and Mobility of the CNS.

The regression analysis indicated the important role of the expected SS tendency in predicting risk of maladjustment to the social environment, especially for family life. Expectation on both dimensions of SS—ES and DIS, predicts 21% of the variance of maladjustment in this area.

Finally, the relation between discrepancy in expected and real SS tendency and maladjustment was analyzed. The correlation analysis shows that discrepancy in expected and real ES is related to maladjustment in social environments, family life ($r = -0.21$) and

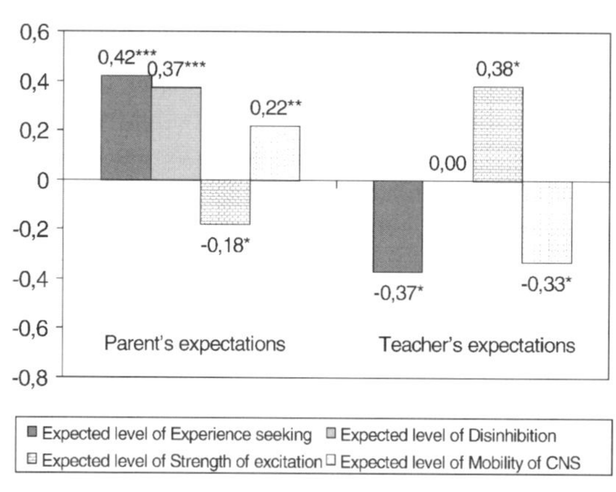

Figure 1: Correlation for parent and teacher expectation of the SS tendency in adolescents and temperament traits as measured by maladjustment to social environment and PTS. *Note:* $^{***}p < 0.001$; $^{**}p < 0.01$; $^{*}p < 0.05$.

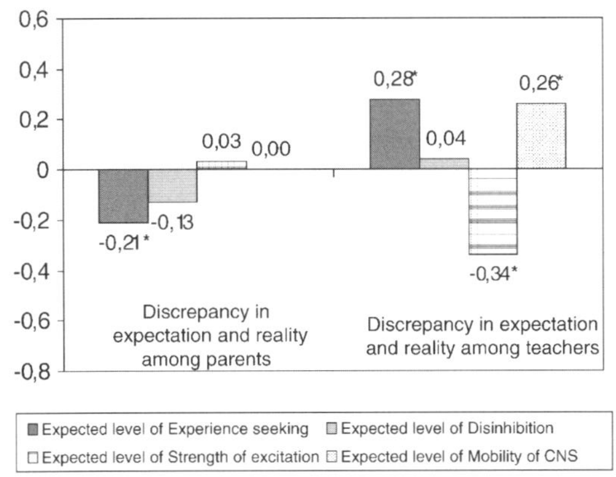

Figure 2: Correlation between maladjustment to the social environment and the discrepancy in expected and real sensation seeking tendency in adolescents as measured by the PTS temperament traits. *Note:* $^{***}p < 0.001$; $^{**}p < 0.01$; $^{*}p < 0.05$.

school ($r = 0.28$). The negative correlation between discrepancy in expected and real ES and the level of maladjustment in the family environment shows, as mentioned previously, that parent's higher expectation SS than real level of SS tendency is related to the more severe symptoms of maladjustment. It is notable that the discrepancy in respect to DIS is not related to maladjustment in both environments. Figure 2 illustrates these findings.

The results of this study demonstrate that environment is an important factor mediating SS and the risk of negative behavior. It suggests that there are social norms for the SS trait that can influence the risk of some behavior. It also shows that the expectations of the social environment (parent and teacher) are heterogeneous. The intensity of the SS need which may satisfy parent's expectation and develop a good fit to the family environment may be a source of difficulties in the school environment and vice versa.

4. Conclusions

The SS construct seems to be closely related to the Pavlovian CNS properties. All SS scales as well as the total SS score correlate positively, although rather moderately, with strength of excitation and mobility. When related to the RTT temperament traits, SS shows the highest correlation with activity and moderate but negative correlations with emotional reactivity and perseveration. In studies where SS was related to behavior and different types of behavior disorders it was found that:

- Individuals at high risk of alcohol addiction have higher SS scores on all SSS-IV scales compared to individuals who are at low risk of alcohol addiction.
- Juvenile prisoners who committed crime in which aggressive behavior was involved i.e. robberies, do not differ in the level of SS from prisoners who committed crime without aggressive behavior i.e. thefts or burglaries.

- High-sensation seekers prefer fast music tempo and warm color paintings, whereas sensation avoiders prefer slow music and cold color paintings.
- There are low positive correlations for the ES and DIS scales with level of maladjustment to school and family environments as measured in adolescents by means of self-report.
- The expectation of parents for ES and DIS of their children correlates positively with maladjustment. When the expectation of teachers of their pupils SS is taken into account, there is a negative correlation with maladjustment, but only for ES.
- The discrepancy between expected and real SS seems to be related to maladjustment in school and family environment. High discrepancy correlates negatively (but low) with ES when judged by parents and positively (also rather low) when judged by the teacher.

Data collected in our laboratory for over two decades indicate that SS as postulated by Marvin Zuckerman is an important personality/temperament dimension contributing substantially to the prediction of human behavior and behavior disorders. Our data also show that SS shares part of the variance with such traits as Strength of Excitation, Mobility of CNS processes, Activity and Briskness, temperament traits.

5. Summary

Several studies were presented in which SS, as postulated by Zuckerman and measured by SSS-IV and SSS-V, was related to two different domains of research. The first studies examined the relation between SS and temperament traits as measured by the Pavlovian Temperament Survey (PTS) and the Formal Characteristics of Behavior-Temperament Inventory (FCB-TI). The second domain dealt with studies in which SS was considered as a predictor of: (1) alcohol addiction and committing crime; (2) preference of kinds of paintings and music; and (3) risk of maladjustment to school and family environments. The results showed that SS: (a) shares some common variance with temperament as measured by PTS and FCB-TI; (b) plays a significant role as a predictor of behavior and behavior disorders.

References

Andresen, B. (1986). Reizsuche und Erlebnismotive 1: Eine psychometrische Reanalyse der SSS V Zuckermans im Kontext der MISAP Entwicklung [Sensation seeking and experience motives 1: A psychometric reanalysis of Zuckerman's SSS-V in the context of MISAP development]. *Zeitschrift für Differentiell and Diagnostische Psychologie*, *7*, 177–203.

Andersson, T., & Magnusson, D. (1990). Biological maturation in adolescence and the development of drinking habits and alcohol abuse among young males: A prospective study. *Journal of Youth and Adolescence*, *19*, 33–41.

Andrew, M., & Cronin, C. (1997). Two measures of sensation seeking as predictors of alcohol use among high school males. *Personality and Individual Differences*, *22*, 393–401.

Arnett, J. J. (1996). Sensation seeking, aggressiveness, and adolescent reckless behavior. *Personality and Individual Differences*, *20*, 693–702.

Ballantine, J. H., & Klein, H. A. (1990). The relationship of temperament and adjustment in Japanese schools. *The Journal of Psychology, 124*, 229–309.

Buss, A. H., & Durkee, A. (1957). An inventory for assessing different kinds of hostility. *Journal of Consulting Psychology, 4*, 343–349.

Carlier, M. (1985). Factor analysis of Strelau's Questionnaire and an attempt to validate some of the factors. In: J. Strelau, F. H. Farley, & A. Gale (Eds), *The biological bases of personality and behavior: Theories, measurement techniques, and development* (Vol. 1, pp. 145–160). Washington: Hemisphere.

Chess, S., & Thomas, A. (1991). Temperament and the concept of goodness of fit. In: J. Strelau, & A. Angleitner (Eds), *Exploration in temperament: International perspectives on theory and measurement* (pp. 15–28). New York: Plenum Press.

Cloninger, C. R. (1987). Neurogenetic adaptive mechanisms in alcoholism. *Science, 236*, 410–416.

Colder, C. R., & Chassin, L. (1997). Affectivity and impulsivity: Temperamental risk for adolescent alcohol involvement. *Psychology of Addictive Behaviors, 11*, 83–97.

Crabbe, J. C., Belknap, J. K., & Buck, K. J. (1994). Genetic animal models of alcohol and drug abuse. *Science, 264*, 1715–1723.

Daum, I., & Schugens, M. M. (1986). The Strelau Temperament Inventory (STI): Preliminary results in a West German sample. *Personality and Individual Differences, 7*, 509–517.

Duffy, E. (1957). The psychological significance of the concept of "arousal" or "activation." *The Psychological Review, 64*, 265–275.

Engs, R. C., Sławińska, J., & Hanson, D. (1991). The drinking patterns of American and Polish university studies: A cross national study. *Drug and Alcohol Dependence, 27*, 167–175.

Eysenck, H. J. (1967). *The biological basis of personality*. Springfield, IL: Thomas.

Forabosco, G., & Ruch, W. (1994). Sensation seeking, social attitudes and humor appreciation in Italy. *Personality and Individual Differences, 16*, 515–528.

Furowicz, A. (1996). Związek między zagrożeniem uzależnieniem alkoholowym a charakterystyką temperamntalną i środowiskową w populacji studentów [Relationship between temperament and environment and the risk of alcohol addiction among students]. Unpublished master thesis, Silesian University, Katowice, Poland.

Gebhardt, D. (1997). Preferencje kolorystyki malarskiej i tempa muzycznego w zależnośći od zapotrzebowania na stymulację [Preferences of coloring and music tempo depending on the intensity of stimulation need]. Unpublished master thesis, Silesian University, Katowice, Poland.

Glenn, S. W., & Nixon, S. J. (1996). Investigation of Cloninger's subtypes in a male alcoholic sample: Applications and implications. *Journal of Clinical Psychology, 52*, 219–230.

Gomà-i-Freixanet, M. (1995). Prosocial and antisocial aspects of personality. *Personality and Individual Differences, 19*, 125–134.

Gray, J. A. (1964). Strength of the nervous system and levels of arousal: A reinterpretation. In: J. A. Gray (Ed.), *Pavlov's typology* (pp. 289–364). Oxford: Pergamon Press.

Hansen, E. B., & Breivik, G. (2001). Sensation seeking as a predictor of positive and negative risk behaviour among adolescents. *Personality and Individual Differences, 30*, 627–640.

Hebb, D. O. (1955). Drives and the C.N.S. (conceptual nervous system). *Psychological Review, 62*, 243–254.

Horvath, P., & Zuckerman, M. (1992). Sensation seeking, risk appraisal, and risky behavior. *Personality and Individual Differences, 14*, 41–52.

von Knorring, L., Oreland, L., & von Knorring, A.-L. (1987). Personality traits and platelet MAO activity in alcohol and drug abusing teenage boys. *Acta Psychiatrica Scandinavica, 75*, 307–314.

Korczyńska, J. (1998). Temperamentalne uwarunkowania występowania agresji w dokonanym przestępstwie [Temperamental determinants of aggression in performing crime]. Unpublished master thesis, Silesian University, Katowice, Poland.

Lerner, J. V., & Lerner, R. M. (1983). Temperament and adaptation across life: Theoretical and empirical issues. *Life-span Development and Behavior*, *9*, 197–231.

Litle, P., & Zuckerman, M. (1986). Sensation seeking and music preferences. *Personality and Individual Differences*, *7*, 575–577.

McNamara, L., & Ballard, M. E. (1999). Resting arousal, sensation seeking and music preference. *Genetic, Social and General Psychology Monographs*, *125*, 229–250.

Miklewska, A. (2000). Charakterystyka temperamentalna uczniów i jej dopasowanie do oczekiwań rodziców i nauczycieli a przystosowanie spoeczne [Relationship between adolescents' temperament and temperamental fit to parents' and teachers' expectations and social adjustment]. Unpublished doctoral dissertation, Silesian University, Katowice, Poland.

Moose, R. H., & Moose, B. S. (1994). *Family Environment Scale Manual*. Paolo Alto, CA: Consulting Psychologist Press.

Netter, P., & Rammsayer, T. (1991). Reactivity to dopaminergenic drugs and aggression related to personality traits. *Personality and Individual Differences*, *12*, 1009–1017.

Newcomb, M. M., & McGee, L. (1991). Influences on sensation seeking on general deviance and specific problem behaviors from adolescence to young adulthood. *Journal of Personality and Social Psychology*, *61*, 614–628.

Oleszkiewicz, Z. (1982). Demand for stimulation and vocational preferences. *Polish Psychological Bulletin*, *13*, 185–195.

Pavlov, I. P. (1927). *Conditioned reflexes*. London: Oxford University Press.

Perez, J., & Torrubia, R. (1985). Sensation seeking and antisocial behaviour in a student sample. *Personality and Individual Differences*, *6*, 401–403.

Polich, J., Pollock, V. E., & Bloom, F. E. (1994). Meta-analysis of P300 amplitude from males at risk of alcoholism. *Psychological Bulletin*, *115*, 55–73.

Pytka, L. (1984). *Skala Nieprzystosowania Społecznego. Podręcznik* [Social Maladjustment Scale. Manual]. Warszawa: Centralny Ośrodek Metodyczny Poradnictwa Wychowawczo-Zawodowego.

Raven, J. C. (1960). Guide to the standard progressive matrices: Sets A, B, C, D, and E. London: H. K. Lewis.

Rokeach, M. (1985). *Value survey*. Sunnyvale, CA: Halgren Tests.

Rowland, G. L., & Heatherton, T. (1987). Social norms for the desirability of sensation seeking. *Personality and Individual Differences*, *8*, 753–755.

Ruchin, V. V., Eiseman, M., Hagglof, B., & Cloninger, C. R. (1998). Aggression in delinquent adolescents vs. controls in Northern Russia: Relations with hereditary and environmental factors. *Criminal Behaviour and Mental Health*, *8*, 115–126.

Simo, S., & Perez, J. (1991). Sensation seeking and antisocial behaviour in a junior student sample. *Personality and Individual Differences*, *9*, 965–966.

Simon, T. R., Stancy, A. W., Sussman, S., & Dent, C. W. (1994). Sensation seeking and drug use among high risk Latino and Anglo adolescents. *Personality and Individual Differences*, *17*, 665–672.

Stelmack, R. M., Kruidenier, B. G., & Anthony, S. B. (1985). A factor analysis of the Eysenck Personality Questionnaire and the Strelau Temperament Inventory. *Personality and Individual Differences*, *6*, 657–659.

Strelau, J. (1972). A diagnosis of temperament by nonexperimental techniques. *Polish Psychological Bulletin*, *3*, 97–105.

Strelau, J. (1983). *Temperament, personality, activity*. London: Academic Press.

Strelau, J. (1993). The location of the regulative theory of temperament (RTT) among other temperament theories. In: J. Hettema, & I. J. Deary (Eds), *Foundations of personality* (pp. 113–132). Dordrecht: Kluwer Academic Publishers.

Strelau, J. (1995) Temperament and stress: Temperament as a moderator of stressors, emotional states, coping, and costs. In: C. D. Spielberg, & I. G. Sarason (Eds), *Stress and emotion: Anxiety, anger, and curiosity* (Vol. 15, pp. 215–254). Washington: Hemisphere.

Strelau, J. (1998) *Temperament: A psychological perspective*. Plenum Press: New York.

Strelau, J., Angleitner, A., & Newberry, B. H. (1999). *Pavlovian Temperament Survey (PTS): An international handbook*. Göttingen: Hogrefe & Huber Publishers.

Strelau, J., & Zawadzki, B. (1993). The Formal Characteristics of Behaviour-Temperament Inventory (FCB-TI): Theoretical assumptions and scale construction. *European Journal of Personality*, *7*, 313–336.

Strelau, J., & Zawadzki, B. (1995). The Formal Characteristics of Behavior-Temperament Inventory (FCB-TI): Validity studies. *European Journal of Personality*, *9*, 207–229.

Tomaszewski, T. (1978). *Tätigkeit und Bewusstsein: Beiträge zur Einführung in die polnische Tätigkeitspsychologie* [Action and consciousness: Contribution to the introduction to Polish theory of action]. Weinheim and Basel: Beltz Verlag.

Wennberg, P., & Bohman, M. (2002). Childhood temperament and adult alcohol habits. A prospective longitudinal study from age 4 to age 36. *Addictive Behaviors*, *27*, 63–74.

Zawadzki, B. (2002). *Temperament — geny i środowisko. Porównania wewnątrz- i międzypopulacyjne* [Temperament-genes and environment: Intra- and interpopulation comparisons]. Gdańsk: Gdańskie Wydawnictwo Psychologiczne.

Zawadzki, B., & Strelau, J. (1997) *Formalna Charakterystyka Zachowania-Kwestionariusz Temperamentu (FCZ-KT): Podręcznik* [Formal Characteristics of Behaviour — Temperament Inventory (FCB-TI): Manual]. Warszawa: Pracowania Testów Psychologicznych PTP.

Zeugner, G. (1965). *Barwa i człowiek* [Humans and color]. Warsaw: Arkady.

Zuckerman, M. (1979). *Sensation seeking: Beyond the optimal level of arousal*. Hillsdale, NJ: Erlbaum.

Zuckerman, M. (1984). Sensation seeking: A comparative approach to a human trait. *Behavioral and Brain Sciences*, *7*, 413–471.

Zuckerman, M. (1985). Biological foundations of the sensation-seeking temperament. In: J. Strelau, F. H. Farley, & A. Gale (Eds), *The biological bases of personality and behavior: Theories, measurement techniques, and development* (Vol. 1, pp. 97–112). Washington: Hemisphere.

Zuckerman, M. (1987). Is sensation seeking a predisposing trait for alcoholism? In: E. Gottheil, K. A. Druley, S. Pashko, & S. P. Weinstein (Eds), *Stress and addiction* (pp. 283–301). New York: Brunner/Mazel.

Zuckerman, M. (1992). What is a basic factor and which factors are basic? Turtles all the way down. *Personality and Individual Differences*, *13*, 675–681.

Zuckerman, M. (1994). *Behavioral expressions and biosocial bases of sensation seeking*. New York: Cambridge University Press.

Żychowska, D. (1984). Reaktywność a postawy mężczyzn wobec seksu [Reactivity and the attitude of men towards sex]. Unpublished master thesis, University of Warsaw, Warsaw, Poland.

Part II

On the Identification and Structure of Personality Factors

Chapter 4

The Zuckerman-Kuhlman Personality Questionnaire: Origin, Development, and Validity of a Measure to Assess an Alternative Five-Factor Model of Personality

J. Joireman and D. M. Kuhlman

> A science of astronomy that made no distinctions among planets, stars, and galaxies, a geology that regarded every rock as a unique structure, or a biology that could only distinguish two-legged from four-legged creatures, would not progress very far in understanding or prediction (Zuckerman 1991: 1).

1. Introduction

At the most basic level, personality psychologists are interested in understanding the nature and causes of individual differences in response patterns across time and space, and using this knowledge to make predictions regarding future behavior. To accomplish these related goals, one must have both a theory and a measure of personality. Depending on the specific interests, goals, and philosophy of a researcher, this theory and assessment may be developed to understand more narrowly defined traits, such as sensation seeking, or broader dimensions of personality, such as introversion-extraversion. As readers familiar with his work will know, over the course of his prolific career, Marvin Zuckerman was interested in understanding personality at both ends of this spectrum.

In the early part of his career, Zuckerman introduced the soon to be widely studied trait of sensation seeking, to understand individual differences in reactions to sensory deprivation (for reviews, see Zuckerman 1979, 1994). In the latter part of his career, Zuckerman devoted increasing attention to understanding the nature and causes of basic dimensions of personality (Zuckerman 1991). In this research, Zuckerman began the development

On the Psychobiology of Personality
Edited by R. M. Stelmack

ISBN: 0-08-044209-9

of a biologically based model of fundamental dimensions that came to be known as the alternative Five-Factor Model (FFM), and he collaborated with Kuhlman in the development of an instrument to measure them, the Zuckerman-Kuhlman Personality Questionnaire (ZKPQ; Zuckerman *et al.* 1993). The alternative FFM is similar but not identical to the more traditional FFM, e.g. Costa and McRae (1992). In this chapter, we trace the origins, development and validity of the ZKPQ and suggest several directions for future research.

2. Development of the Alternative FFM and the ZKPQ-III

2.1. What is a Basic Dimension of Personality?

Behind any measure of personality, there are assumptions, implicit or explicit, that guide both development and interpretation. Of course, the nature of the assumptions determines the theoretical context that guides empirical research. In addition, the validity of the assumptions plays a major role in determining the utility of empirical outcomes for advancing our understanding of behavior and for the ability to predict, and perhaps modify, behavior. Given this, Zuckerman argued that researchers who are interested in identifying and assessing basic dimensions of personality must first address a fundamental question: what is a basic dimension of personality? It is principally the answer to this question that differentiates the Alternative FFM and ZKPQ-III from other the FFM models.

Zuckerman (1991, 1992) asserted that a basic dimension of personality should meet four criteria. First, it should be reliably identified across different methods, genders, ages, and cultures. Second, it should show moderate heritability. Advocates of the FFM model accepted and provided evidence for the first two criteria. There is less agreement on the next two criteria.

The third criterion put forth by Zuckerman is that a basic dimension should be identified in non-human species, especially species that are socially organized. On this point, Zuckerman (1992) notes that several of the FFM dimensions do not easily translate into behavioral patterns that are observed in non-human species. For example, Zuckerman points out that agreeableness and conscientiousness are more difficult to document in non-human species than are traits such as impulsivity and aggression.

The fourth criterion stated by Zuckerman is that significant biological markers are associated with a basic personality dimension. Advocates of the FFM model questioned the notion that a basic dimension should necessarily be associated with biological markers, suggesting "... it is poor science to explain the known on the basis of the unknown" (see Zuckerman 1991). Zuckerman (1992) countered by arguing that while much remains to be learned about the psychobiology of personality, evidence is beginning to accumulate that links biological mechanisms to various dimensions of personality.

Thus, with respect to the fundamental assumptions on the nature of basic personality dimensions, the alternative FFM and FFM are in partial agreement and partial conflict. As will be seen, the results of studies leading to the ZKPQ-III and the alternative FFM model constitute a similar pattern of overlap and uniqueness.

2.2. Development of the Alternative Five-Factor Model

Beginning in the late 1980s, Zuckerman and Kuhlman worked on a questionnaire to assess basic dimensions of personality. They followed a rational approach guided by the four criteria discussed above. They began by selecting scales already used as measures of temperament, e.g. Buss and Plomin's (1975) measures of emotionality, activity, sociability and impulsiveness. Measures that had high heritability or correlations with biochemical or psychophysiological measures were also selected, e.g. Eysenck's three superfactors of Extraversion (E), Neuroticism (N) and Psychoticism (P) and the Sensation Sensation Seeking Scales (Zuckerman 1994).

Zuckerman and Kuhlman anticipated that nine basic dimensions were possible: sociability, general emotionality, anxiety, hostility, socialization, sensation seeking, impulsivity, activity and social desirability. They selected 46 scales so that there would be at least three scale markers for each of the nine hypothesized factors.

For the initial study (Zuckerman *et al.* 1988), the 46 scales were completed by 271 students (178 females and 73 males). There was no clear support for a nine-factor solution in the initial analyses. Reported results were based on three separate factor analyses that varied from three to five to seven factors. To evaluate the cross-gender similarity of factors within each factor solution, male and female factor loadings were correlated. As an additional index of male/female factor similarity, the correlation between participants' factor scores based on their own, same-sex factor loadings and based on the factor scores from factor loadings of the opposite sex were computed. Results from both types of analyses revealed very good agreement on the factor solutions for men and women at the three-factor level, good agreement on four of the five factors at the five-factor level, and good agreement on six of the seven factors at the seven-factor solution.

The three-factor solution was very consistent with E, N, and P, from the Eysenck Personality Questionnaire (EPQ; Eysenck & Eysenck 1975). Scales with high loadings on the first factor, Extraversion-Sociability (E-Sy) included EPQ E, and scales measuring Sociability (Sy) and Activity (ACT). For the second factor, Neuroticism-Emotion (N-Emot), the scales with high-factor loadings were EPQ N, and scales measuring anxiety, anger, hostility, general emotionality lack of emotional control and work efficiency. For the third factor, Psychoticism-Impulsive Unsocialized Sensation Seeking (P-ImpUSS), the scales with high-factor loadings were EPQ P, independence, sensation seeking impulsiveness, socialization, planning, responsibility, restraint and social desirability.

Relations between the three- and five-factor models were examined and the correlations of factor scores computed for each model. E-Sy divided into two factors, Sy and ACT. The P-ImpUSS factor split into impulsive sensation seeking and aggressive sensation seeking. Correlations of factor scores for the five- and seven-factor solutions showed that N-Emot split into an Anger and an Anxiety factor.

This first study suggested the potential importance of distinguishing between anxiety and aggressiveness, which are combined in the EPQ N factor. In addition, they suggested that sociability and general energy/activity level, which are components of EPQ E, might be best viewed as separate basic dimensions of personality.

In their next study, 33 scales that proved to be the best markers for each of the seven factors in the study just described were selected from the original 46 scales (Zuckerman *et al.* 1991). This smaller number of scales, combined with a larger sample size ($n = 525$) improved the evaluation of the stability of the factors across genders. An examination of the scree plot for the 33 scales suggested either a three- or a five-factor solution. As in their previous work, a seven-factor solution was also examined. However, because one of the seven factors consisted of only one scale, only results for the other six factors were reported.

To evaluate the cross-gender similarity of the factor solutions, Tucker's congruency coefficients of factor loadings were calculated. For the three- and five-factor solutions, congruency was acceptably high, from 0.95 to 0.96, for corresponding factors and close to zero for diverging factors. The four-factor solution, congruency was not successful. In the six-factor solution, one factor found for males, labeled impulsiveness, could not be identified in females.

Further evaluation of similarity of males and females for the three and five factor solutions was performed using a technique developed by Kiers and ten Berge (1989) called simultaneous component analysis. In this analysis, a single principal component solution of specified dimensionality is determined that explains the maximum amount of variance for the groups that are compared. The variance explained by this single solution is compared to variance explained by solutions of the same dimensionality computed for each group separately. If there is little difference between the variances explained by separate and simultaneous solutions, this can be considered evidence for factor similarity (Caprara *et al.* 2000). A comparison of the results of the three-, four-, and five-factor analyses revealed that the simultaneous analyses explained virtually the same amount of variance as did separate factor analyses for men and women. This clearly indicates that the factor structures for men and women share a very high degree of overlap. These combined findings indicate that three- or five-factor solutions were quite robust for males and females.

As in our previous work, factor scores were correlated for factor solutions of varying dimensions. This analysis replicated their earlier findings. At the three-factor level, dimensions highly similar to EPQ E, N, and P were found. From the three- to five-factor solutions, E, labeled Sy, and P, labeled P-ImpUSS, remained virtually unchanged. However, N, labeled N-Emot, at the three-factor level split into three factors, Act, Neuroticism-Anxiety (N-Anx), and Aggression-Hostility (Agg-Host) at the five-factor level.

Zuckerman *et al.* (1991) argued that the three- and five-factor solutions can be seen as equally valid. Based on their meaningful hierarchical nature, they could be viewed as complementary rather than competing models. However, due to its greater specificity, researchers were encouraged to devote more attention to the development of the five-, rather than the three-factor model.

2.3. Measuring the Fundamental Dimensions of the Alternative FFM; Developing the ZKPQ

Zuckerman and Kuhlman next turned their attention to the development of an instrument to measure the five factors of the alternative FFM Model. The first version of the ZKPQ consisted of 100 items (20 items $\times$ 5 factors) from the 33 scales used in the Zuckerman *et al.* (1991) study. Items were selected that showed the highest correlation with the five-factor scores, weak correlations with the remaining factors, and weak correlations with the Crowne-Marlow social desirability scale. Items from published tests, and those that were unclear were re-written to form the ZKPQ-II.

The resulting 100-item scale was subsequently completed by a sample of 589 undergraduates. The scree plot for these 100 items provided strong evidence for the existence of five factors. Factor loadings from the five-factor solution showed that the majority of the items, i.e. 89, correlated 0.30 or higher on their respective factors with small loadings on the remaining four factors. These 89 items were retained to form the ZKPQ-III. Because the Sy factor was positively skewed, several new items were written for this scale. Most of these new items depicted introversion. Ten additional items were written to detect careless responding. The resulting 99 items make up the most recent version of the questionnaire known as the ZKPQ-III-R, which we will simply refer to as the ZKPQ.

2.4. The Present Version of the ZKPQ

The ZKPQ is a set of true/false statements that assess the basic dimensions of personality that constitute the alternative FFM. In alphabetical order they are:

(1) *Activity* (ACT). The 17 items in this scale reflect a preference for tasks that are both difficult and challenging, and a general preference for being on the go as opposed to being on the couch.
(2) *Aggression Hostility* (Agg-Host): The 17 items of this scale reflect rudeness, vengefulness and impatience with others, a "hot temper" and negatively reactive, confrontational non-verbal behavior.
(3) *Impulsive Sensation Seeking* (ImpSS). This 19-item scale reflects a need for change and novelty, a preference for uncertainty (risk) in social relationships and environments, and a tendency to forego planning coupled with acting on impulse with little concern for consequences.
(4) *Neuroticism-Anxiety* (N-Anx). This 19-item scale reflects a general lack of self-confidence and indecision, generalized negative emotionality (edginess, worry and fear), and a tendency to be sensitive to and easily hurt by criticism.
(5) *Sociability* (Sy): The 17 items of the Sy scale reflect aversion to social isolation, having many friends, a readiness to interact with strangers and a liking for large parties.

In addition to these 89 items, there is the 10-item Infrequency scale that can be used to detect careless responding. Zuckerman and Kuhlman hold the copyright to the ZKPQ but it is available to all interested researchers free of charge. The list of items and the scoring key for the ZKPQ is provided in Appendix. Since its initial development, a normative sample of 2377 University of Delaware undergraduates (904 males; 1473 females) has been generated. Interested researchers can obtain these data by contacting D. M. Kuhlman.

3. Research on the ZKPQ

3.1. Internal Consistency and Retest Reliability

Zuckerman (2002) reports acceptably high retest reliabilities for an American sample (n = 153). Over approximately one month, reliabilities were similar for males and females, specifically 0.8 for ImpSS, 0.84 for N-Anx, 0.78 for Agg-Host, 0.76 for Act and 0.83 for Sy. Zuckerman *et al.* (1993) reported internal reliabilities for the five ZKPQ scales that ranged from 0.70 to 0.86. There were sex differences for most scales. Men scored higher than women on ImpSS, Agg-Host, and Act. Women scored higher than men on N-Anx. Correlations among the factors ranged from −0.02 to 0.37, with the highest correlations emerging between ImpSS and Agg-Host and ImpSS and Sy.

3.2. Convergent and Discriminant Validity

To assess the convergent and discriminant validity of the ZKPQ sales, Zuckerman *et al.* (1993) included the following in a single factor analysis: (1) the five ZKPQ scales; (2) scales assessing E, N, and P from the EPQ; and (3) scales assessing E, N, Agreeableness, Conscientiousness and Openness to Experience from the NEO Personality Inventory-Revised (NEO PI-R; Costa & McCrae 1992). Four factors were found that accounted for 74% of the variance. The eigenvalue for the fifth factor was less than one and there was a negligible increase in variance explained by the five-factor solution. Thus, results from the four-factor solution were reported.

With respect to discriminant validity, all scales loaded at least twice as high on one factor than on the other three. The single exception was for ZKPQ ImpSS for which the highest loading was 0.74 and the second highest was 0.48. With respect to convergent validity, results demonstrated strong and meaningful overlap between the ZKPQ scales and those from both the EPQ and NEO-PI-R, as follows: (1) The ZKPQ Sy scale loaded on a factor with EPQ E and NEO E, as did ZKPQ ACT; (2) ZKPQ N-Anx loaded on a factor with EPQ N and NEO N; (3) ZKPQ ImpSS loaded with EPQ P and NEO Conscientiousness; and (4) ZKPQ Agg-Host loaded with NEO Agreeableness, as well as NEO Openness. That ZKPQ Act and NEO Openness failed to form their own factors was not surprising, given that each represented the only scale of its type within the factor analysis.

Other studies provide further support for the convergent validity of the ZKPQ by demonstrating that the five ZKPQ scales show meaningful relationships with relevant measures of temperament, sensation seeking, ego control and resiliency, reward and punishment expectancies, public and private self-consciousness, and social anxiety (cf. Joireman *et al.* 2003; Zuckerman *et al.* 1999).

The work summarized above suggests that the ZKPQ contains four scales that show high degree of internal and test retest reliability, as well as convergent validity with four fundamental dimensions of personality identified in Costa and McCrae's FFM: sociability, anxiety, impulsiveness and aggressiveness. To a great extent, the view of fundamental personality dimensions provided by FFM and alternative FFM appear quite similar. We consider this very good news because conceptual replication is compelling evidence for the general validity of any scientific enterprise, which in this case is the search for fundamental personality dimensions.

At the present time, the major difference between the alternative FFM and FFM appears to be the presence of a single factor on each test that has no conceptual equivalent on the other; Act for the ZKPQ and Conscientiousness for the NEO. Each of these unique factors is considered important. There is considerable evidence for their status as fundamental dimensions. Perhaps future work will lead to a "Hybrid-6" if researchers include scales to measure both activity and conscientiousness.

3.3. Translations of the ZKPQ

As noted previously, an important criterion for the alternative FFM model of basic personality dimensions is replication across different cultures. A number of recent studies report the results of analyses of ZKPQ translations into different languages, i.e. Chinese (Wu *et al.* 2000), Catalonian (Gomà-i-Freixanet *et al.*, in press), German (Ostendorf & Angleitner 1994), Japanese (Shiomi *et al.* 1995, 1996), and Spanish (Aluja *et al.* 2002, 2003; Gutiérrez-Zotes *et al.* 2001; Herrero *et al.* 2001; Peñate *et al.* 1999; Romero *et al.* 2002).

Research in China revealed that ImpSS and N-Anx demonstrate acceptable high levels of reliability, ranging from 0.68 to 0.81. Reliability for the remaining scales, ranging from 0.52 to 0.64, was somewhat lower than the traditionally accepted level of 0.70 (Wang *et al.* 2002a, 2004; Wu *et al.* 2000). Regarding concurrent validity, Wang *et al.* (2002b) also demonstrate that N-Anx and Agg-Host were positively correlated with depression as measured by the Plutchik and van Praag (1987) depression inventory. Wang *et al.* (2004) have shown meaningful links between the ZKPQ dimensions and scores on Livesley and Jackson's (in press) assessment of personality pathology.

From work in Barcelona by Gomà-i-Freixanet *et al.* (in press) on a Catalonian translation of the ZKPQ, reliabilities were reported that ranged between 0.73 and 0.83 for all scales except Agg-Host, for which alpha was 0.68. The congruence of factor loadings between the Catalonian speaking Spanish sample and the American (Delaware) comparison group is very high for all five factors.

In Germany, Ostendorf and Angleitner's (1994) translation of the ZKPQ has acceptably high reliabilities, ranging from 0.71 to 0.86 and, in support of its construct validity, meaningful relations with the big five dimensions assessed using the NEO-PI-R.

Research on a Japanese version of the ZKPQ (Shiomi *et al.* 1996) reports reliabilities on each scale ranging from 0.7 to 0.85 and evidence of acceptable congruence of factor loadings of the Japanese and American (Delaware) samples.

Several studies on a Spanish version of the ZKPQ revealed that its five factors demonstrate reasonably high levels of reliability, i.e. greater than 0.68 (Aluja *et al.* 2002, 2003; Gutiérrez-Zotes *et al.* 2001; Peñate *et al.* 1999), while one study (Romero *et al.* 2002) reported somewhat lower reliabilities on the dimensions of Sy (0.58) and Act (0.63). Aluja *et al.* (2003) also reported that a short 69-item form of a Spanish version of the ZKPQ tended to fit their data better than the original 89-item version. Thus, they suggested the adoption of this short form among Spanish-speaking respondents.

Two of the above Spanish studies also provided support for the construct validity of the ZKPQ. Similar to the findings of Zuckerman *et al.* (1993), Aluja *et al.* (2003) demonstrated that the ZKPQ scales were meaningfully linked to both the EPQ and FFM factors. Romero *et al.* (2002) provided further evidence for the construct validity of the ZKPQ by demonstrating that individuals scoring high on N-Anx, Agg-Host, and ImpSS reported higher levels of negative affect, whereas individuals scoring high on Act reported higher levels of positive affect, as assessed with the Positive and Negative Affect Scales (Watson *et al.* 1988).

In sum, these studies suggest that the five dimensions of personality assessed by translations of the ZKPQ are generally replicable in cross-cultural studies in Catalonia, Germany, Japan, Spain and also, to some degree, China. Research in each of these cultures also provided evidence for the construct validity of ZKPQ factors in relation to other measures of personality and adjustment. It is hoped that as future studies examine the reliability and validity of the ZKPQ factors across additional cultures and languages a more comprehensive picture of the cross-cultural generality of the alternative FFM will emerge.

3.4. Other Evidence for the Validity of the ZKPQ

A number of studies have compared average ZKPQ scores of at-risk groups, i.e. prostitutes and drug users with controls. ZKPQ scores were correlated with a several self-report measures of risk-taking behavior and psychological adjustment. The results of this work are evidence of the predictive and construct validity of the ZKPQ.

3.4.1. ZKPQ and self-reported risk-taking in college students In a recent study of college undergraduates, Zuckerman and Kuhlman (2000) found that high scores on the ImpSS scale predicted higher levels of self-reported drinking, smoking, drug use and sex in both men and women. Among men, higher scores on Agg-Host also predicted higher levels of drinking and risky driving, while Sy predicted higher levels of drinking, drug use, sex, and gambling. Among women, higher scores on Agg-Host predicted higher levels of drinking, smoking, and sex, while higher scores on Sy predicted higher levels of drinking and smoking.

3.4.2. ZKPQ correlates among drug users In one of the first ZKPQ studies in this area, Ball (1995) demonstrated that addiction severity and likelihood of continuing to use cocaine during treatment among cocaine-using men and women was positively correlated with scores on three of the ZKPQ scales, including ImpSS, N-Anx, and Agg-Host. Additional analyses revealed that individuals scoring higher on ImpSS and N-Anx reported a higher likelihood of experiencing a variety of psychiatric symptoms including depression, suicide attempts and/or ideation, attention problems, childhood abuse, and psychiatric treatment.

In a follow-up study involving pregnant and post-partum women classified as cocaine-abusing, Ball and Schottenfeld (1997) found that severity of drug abuse was, in a similar fashion, positively correlated with N-Anx, ImpSS, and Agg-Host, though the latter two relationships failed to reach the 0.05 level due to the small sample size. Drug abuse was negatively correlated with both Sy and ACT. High levels of N-Anx also predicted increased legal, family/social, and psychiatric problems, while higher levels of Agg-Host were associated with higher levels of legal and psychiatric problems, though again, neither of the latter relationships was significant due to a small sample size.

In the same study, higher levels of ImpSS also predicted higher levels of depression, violence and anxiety, and higher levels of risky sexual behavior such as having multiple partners, and having sex in exchange for drugs or money. Higher levels of N-Anx were associated with higher levels of depression, suicide attempts, anxiety, attention problems, and risky sexual behaviors (multiple partners, sex for money) and an increased likelihood of being tested for HIV. Finally, higher levels of Agg-Host were associated with higher levels of suicide attempts, violence, and attention problems, as well as all forms of risky sexual behaviors and an increased likelihood of being tested for HIV. In sum, Ball and colleagues have provided convincing evidence that the N-Anx, ImpSS, and Agg-Host scales of the ZKPQ predict theoretically meaningful and practically important outcomes among samples of drug-using individuals.

3.4.3. At-risk groups compared with controls Supporting the work of Ball, several studies that compared at-risk samples with controls also revealed meaningful relationships between several of the ZKPQ scales and risky and/or aggressive behavior. O'Sullivan *et al.* (1996) found that prostitutes scored significantly higher than controls on ImpSS, and marginally higher on Agg-Host. Within the prostitute group, average ImpSS was highest for cocaine users.

In another study, male adolescents serving time for crimes, ranging from assault and battery to murder, were compared to a control group of somewhat younger adolescent boys (Matykiewicz *et al.* 1997). The incarcerated group scored higher on the Agg-Host, but not the ImpSS scale of the ZKPQ. Incarcerated males also showed lower levels of CSF 5-hydroxyindoleacetic acid. In previous studies, 5-HIAA was linked to higher levels of violence (e.g. Castellanos *et al.* 1994). Correlations between 5-HIAA and Agg-Host were not reported.

3.4.4. Other groups compared with controls Complementing the work on at-risk groups, some research examined the relation between the ZKPQ dimensions and involvement in various sports, adjustment in response to spinal cord injury, and recollections of parenting styles.

In one study, male baseball and football athletes scored higher on ACT and lower on ImpSS and N-Anx than non-athlete controls. Female equestrian and field hockey/lacrosse athletes scored significantly higher on ACT and significantly lower on N-Anx compared to non-athlete controls (O'Sullivan *et al.* 1998).

Individuals who experienced spinal cord injuries about nine years previously were also studied (Thompson *et al.* 2003). Those individuals who had higher scores on ACT and Sy and lower scores on Agg-Host and N-Anx reported greater perceived meaning in life and better social adjustment. Purpose in life mediated the relation between adjustment and all personality dimensions except N-Anx.

In a retrospective study, individuals scoring high on N-Anx reported lower levels of father love and higher levels of father punishment (Kraft & Zuckerman 1999). For males from intact families, high scores on N-Anx were also associated with recollections of higher levels of control by both their mothers and fathers.

4. Conclusions and Future Directions

In this chapter, we traced the origin, development, and validity of the ZKPQ, an instrument designed to assess the alternative FFM model of personality that is grounded in the biological bases of personality. At this time, research in several cultures demonstrates the robustness of the alternative FFM model and the good internal reliability of the five ZKPQ scales. Work demonstrating the construct and predictive validity of the ZKPQ is also promising. For future research on the ZKPQ, there are some issues to resolve and strategies to follow.

4.1. Overlap and Differences Between the Alternative FFM and FFM Models

Again, these models are more similar than different. The overlap of models does endorse a schema of four basic dimensions. These four dimensions were identified by different research groups working from somewhat different theoretical perspectives and using different methods for scale construction.

With respect to the differences between models, we hope that future research will address two questions. First, what is gained by inclusion of the activity scale on the ZKPQ? Second, what might be lost by the absence of a ZKPQ scale to assess openness to experience?

4.2. Continued Cross-Cultural Development and Improvement of the ZKPQ

It is hoped that the number of ZKPQ translations will continue to increase, to focus on psychometric improvements of the ZKPQ, and to demonstrate the temporal stability of the scales. The work of Aluja and colleagues (2002, 2003) is a good example of such work.

4.3. More Validation Research

There are three paradigms for validation research but only two paradigms have received much attention. Work on correlations of the ZKPQ with other scales and comparisons of average scale scores between different groups have produced promising results. With regards to the latter paradigm, we suggest that researchers consider doing more than comparing scores on single scales. Although the ZKPQ scales appear to be rather independent in the general population, we feel that techniques such as cluster analysis may yield important information that is not provided by research that focuses on the dimensions separately. For example, the work of Ball and colleagues (Ball 1995; Ball & Schottenfeld 1997) suggests that high scores on three ZKPQ scales, N-Anx, ImpSS, and Agg-Host, may characterize certain categories of drug abusers. It is our hope that work following these first two validation paradigms will continue.

However, validation studies using the controlled laboratory paradigm are quite rare. We found a single published study by Breen and Zuckerman (1999) in which participants made bets in a controlled gambling task that was designed to provide a measure of "chasing," i.e. responding to losses by continuing to gamble until bankrupt. Chasers had higher scores than non-chasers on a subset of items from the ImpSS scale, specifically those relating to impulsiveness.

We hope to see an increase in the use of this laboratory paradigm for two reasons. First, laboratory tasks can be developed to confirm the construct validity of the scales. In the context of the current theory, specific behaviors that are relevant to the scales can be identified and manipulated. Second, research concerned with the cross-cultural generality of the ZKPQ can also benefit from this approach. Specifically, it would allow for the comparison of associations between the scales and behaviors across cultures. Such studies would increase knowledge beyond that provided by the demonstration of similarities of factor structures.

4.4. Use of the Internet

As stated above, the raw data (ZKPQ responses) for a large University of Delaware sample can be obtained by contacting M. Kuhlman. The Internet can be used to make such data more extensive and also accessible. We suggest the development of a multi-cultural raw data-base that is widely and easily available to all researchers, and hereby state our readiness to participate in its generation.

In addition to data sharing, the Internet can also be used for two types of data collection. Most obvious is the collection of responses to questionnaires. Widely available and user-friendly software for the development of interactive web pages greatly simplifies this task. Less obvious perhaps is the fact that controlled experiments can be run on the Internet as well. Here, a basic knowledge of computer programming allows for running experiments on the web. At the present time the only limitation is the collection of accurate reaction time data. In the future, we hope to see both types of Internet research on the ZKPQ.

4.5. Psychobiological Research

In light of the four criteria outlined by Zuckerman (1992) to establish a basic dimension of personality, future research should examine the biological correlates of, and genetic contributions to the five ZKPQ factors. The difficulties of such research notwithstanding, we anticipate that Marvin Zuckerman's important and extensive contributions to the psychobiology of personality will provide future researchers with inspiration to undertake it.

References

Aluja, A., García, Ó., & García, L. F. (2002). A comparative study of Zuckerman's three structural models for personality through the NEO-PI-R, ZKPQ-III-R, EPQ-RS, and Goldberg's 50-biploar adjectives. *Personality and Individual Differences*, *33*, 713–725.

Aluja, A., García, Ó., & García, L. F. (2003). Psychometric properties of the Zuckerman-Kuhlman personality questionnaire (ZKPQ-III-R): A study of a shortened form. *Personality and Individual Differences*, *34*, 1083–1097.

Ball, S. A. (1995). The validity of an alternative five-factor measure of personality in cocaine abusers. *Psychological Assessment*, *7*, 148–154.

Ball, S. A., & Schottenfeld, R. S. (1997). A five-factor model of personality and addiction, psychiatric, and AIDS risk severity in pregnant and postpartum cocaine misusers. *Substance Use and Misuse*, *32*, 25–41.

Breen, R. B., & Zuckerman, M. (1999). 'Chasing' in gambling behavior: Personality and cognitive determinants. *Personality and Individual Differences*, *27*, 1097–1111.

Buss, A. H., & Plomin, R. (1975). *A temperament theory of personality development*. New York: Wiley.

Caprara, G. V., Barbaranelli, C., Bermudez, J., Maslach, C., & Ruch, W. (2000). Multivariate methods for the comparison of factor structures in cross-cultural research — An illustration with the big five questionnaire. *Journal of Cross Cultural Psychology*, *31*, 437–464.

Castellanos, F., Elia, J., Kruesi, M., Gulotta, C., Mefford, L., Potter, W., Ritchie, G., & Rapport, J. (1994). Cerebrospinal fluid monoamine metabolites in boys with attention-deficit hyperactivity disorder. *Psychiatry Research*, *52*, 305–316.

Costa, P. T., Jr., & McCrae, R. R. (1992). Four ways five factors are basic. *Personality and Individual Differences*, *13*, 653–665.

Eysenck, S. B. G., & Eysenck, H. (1975). *Manual of the Eysenck Personality Questionnaire*. London: Hodder & Stoughton.

Gomà-i-Freixanet, M., Valero, S., Punti, J., & Zuckerman, M. (in press). Psychometric properties of the Zuckerman-Kuhlman Personality Questionnaire in a Spanish sample. *European Journal of Psychological Assessment*.

Gutiérrez-Zotes, J. A., Ramos-Brieva, J. A., & Ruiz, J. S. (2001). Desarrollo de la versión española del cuestionario de personalidad Zuckerman-Kuhlman (ZKPQ-III) y propiedades psicométricas [Development of the Spanish version of Zuckerman-Kuhlman personality questionnaire (ZKPQ-III) and psychometric properties]. *Psiquis*, *22*, 239–250.

Herrero, M., Vina, C., González, M., Ibáñez, I., & Peñate, W. (2001). El Cuestionario de Personalidad Zuckerman-Kuhlman-III (ZKPQ-III): Versión Española [The Zuckerman-Kuhlman (ZKPQ-III) Personality Questionnaire: Spanish version]. *Revista Latinoamericana de Psicología*, *33*, 269–287.

Joireman, J., Anderson, J., & Strathman, A. (2003). The aggression paradox: Understanding links among aggression, sensation seeking, and the consideration of future consequences. *Journal of Personality and Social Psychology*, *84*, 1287–1302.

Kiers, H. A. L., & ten Berge, J. M. F. (1989). Alternating least-squares algorithms for simultaneous component analysis with equal component weight matrices in 2 or more populations. *Psychometrika*, *54*, 467–473.

Kraft, M. R., & Zuckerman, M. (1999). Parental behavior and attitudes of their parents reported by young adults from intact and stepparent families and relationships between perceived parenting and personality. *Personality and Individual Differences*, *27*, 453–476.

Livesley, W. J., & Jackson, D. N. (in press). *Manual for the dimensional assessment of personality problems basic questionnaire*. London: Research Psychologists' Press.

Matykiewicz, L., La Grange, L., Vance, P., Wang, M., & Reyes, E. (1997). Adjudicated adolescent males: Measures of urinary 5-hydroxyindoleacetic acid and reactive hypoglycemia. *Personality and Individual Differences*, *22*, 327–332.

O'Sullivan, D. M., Zuckerman, M., & Kraft, M. (1996). The personality of prostitutes. *Personality and Individual Differences*, *21*, 445–448.

O'Sullivan, D. M., Zuckerman, M., & Kraft, M. (1998). Personality characteristics of male and female participants in team sports. *Personality and Individual Differences*, *25*, 119–128.

Ostendorf, F., & Angleitner, A. (1994). A comparison of different instruments proposed to measure the big five. *European Review of Applied Psychology*, *44*, 45–53.

Peñate, W., Ibáñez, I., & González, M. (1999). La cuatia y naturaleza de las dimensiones básicas de personalidad: Una approximación empírica [Amount and nature of basic personality dimensions: An empirical approximation]. *Analisis y Modificacion de Conducta*, *25*, 103–130.

Plutchik, R., & van Praag, H. M. (1987). Interconvertability of five self-reported measures of depression. *Psychiatry Research*, *22*, 243–256.

Romero, E., Leungo, M. ' A ., Gómez-Fraguela, J. A., & Sobral, J. (2002). La estructura de los rasgos de personalidad en adolescentes: El modelo de cinco factores y los cinco alternativos [The structure of personality traits in adolescents: The Five-Factor Model and the alternative Five]. *Psichothema*, *14*, 134–143.

Shiomi, K., Kuhlman, D. M., Zuckerman, M., Joireman, J. A., Sato, M., & Shinji, Y. (1996). Examining the validity and reliability of a Japanese version of the Zuckerman-Kuhlman Personality Questionnaire (in Japanese). *Hyogo University of Teacher Education Journal*, *28*, 1–13.

Shiomi, K., Shigemori, Y., Kuhlman, D. M., Joireman, J. A., & Sato, M. (1995). Constructing and evaluating a Japanese version of the Zuckerman-Kuhlman Personality Questionnaire (in Japanese). *Hyogo University of Teacher Education Journal*, *15*, 1–11.

Thompson, N. J., Coker, J., Krause, J. S., & Henry, E. (2003). Purpose in life as a mediator of adjustment after spinal cord injury. *Rehabilitation Psychology*, *48*, 100–108.

Wang, W., Cao, M., Zhu, S., Gu, J., Liu, J., & Wang, Y. (2002a). Zuckerman-Kuhlman's Personality Questionnaire in patients with major depression. *Social Behavior and Personality*, *30*, 757–764.

Wang, W., Du, W., Lieu, P., Lieu, J., & Wang, Y. (2002b). Five-factor measures in Chinese university students: Effects of one-child policy? *Psychiatry Research*, *109*, 37–44.

Wang, W., Du, W., Wang, Y., Livesley, W. J., & Jang, K. L. (2004). The relationship between the Zuckerman-Kuhlman Personality Questionnaire and traits delineating personality pathology. *Personality and Individual Difference*, *36*, 155–162.

Watson, D., Clark, L. A., & Tellegen, A. (1988). Development and validation of brief measures of positive and negative affect: The PANAS scales. *Journal of Personality and Social Psychology*, *54*, 1063–1070.

Wu, Y. X., Wang, W., Du, W. Y., Li, J., Jiang, X. F., & Wang, Y. H. (2000). Development of a Chinese version of the Zuckerman-Kuhlman personality questionnaire: Reliabilities and gender/age effects. *Social Behavior and Personality*, *28*, 241–249.

Zuckerman, M. (1979). *Sensation seeking: Beyond the optimal level of arousal*. Hillsdale, NJ: Lawrence Erlbaum.

Zuckerman, M. (1991). *Psychobiology of personality*. New York: Cambridge University Press.

Zuckerman, M. (1992). What is a basic factor and which factors are basic? Turtles all the way down. *Personality and Individual Differences*, *13*, 675–681.

Zuckerman, M. (1994). *Behavioral expressions and biosocial bases of sensation seeking*. New York, NY: Cambridge University Press.

Zuckerman, M. (2002). Zuckerman-Kuhlman Personality Questionnaire (ZKPQ): An alternative five-factorial model. In: B. De Raad, & M. Perugini (Eds), *Big five assessment*. Göttingen: Hogrefe & Huber.

Zuckerman, M., Joireman, J., Kraft, M., & Kuhlman, D. M. (1999). Where do motivational and emotional traits fit within three-factor models of personality? *Personality and Individual Differences*, *26*, 487–504.

Zuckerman, M., & Kuhlman, D. M. (2000). Personality and risk-taking: Common biosocial factors. *Journal of Personality*, *68*, 999–1029.

Zuckerman, M., Kuhlman, D. M., & Camac, C. (1988). What lies beyond E and N? Factor analyses of scales believed to measure basic dimensions of personality. *Journal of Personality and Social Psychology*, *54*, 96–107.

Zuckerman, M., Kuhlman, D. M., Joireman, J., Teta, P., & Kraft, M. (1993). A comparison of three structural models for personality: The big three, the big five, and the alternative five. *Journal of Personality and Social Psychology*, *65*, 757–768.

Zuckerman, M., Kuhlman, D. M., Thornquist, M., & Kiers, H. (1991). Five (or three) robust questionnaire scale factors of personality without culture. *Personality and Individual Differences*, *12*, 929–941.

Appendix A: The Scales of the ZKPQ-III-R

Note: The number in parentheses shows the position of the item in the ZKPQ.

Activity (ACT): A need for general activity and a preference for difficult non-trivial tasks
(5) T I do not like to waste time just sitting around and relaxing.
(13) T I lead a busier life than most people.
(18) T I like complicated jobs that require a lot of effort and concentration.
(23) F I do not have a great deal of energy for life's more demanding tasks.
(28) T I like a challenging task much more than a routine one.
(33) T I like to be doing things all of the time.
(38) F I can enjoy myself just lying around and not doing anything active.
(44) F I do not feel the need to be doing things all of the time.
(49) F I would like a job that provided a maximum of leisure time.
(54) T I usually seem to be in a hurry.
(59) T When on vacation I like to engage in active sports rather than just lie around.
(64) T I like to wear myself out with hard work or exercise.
(74) T I like to be active as soon as I wake up in the morning.
(83) T I like to keep busy all the time.
(88) T I can enjoy routine activities that do not require much concentration or effort.
(94) T When I do things, I do them with lots of energy.
(99) T Other people often urge me to "take it easy."

Aggression-Hostility (Agg-Host): A tendency towards rude or anti-social behavior; a readiness to be verbally aggressive.
(3) T I enjoy seeing someone I don't care for humiliated before other people.
(8) T When I get mad, I say ugly things.
(11) T It's natural for me to curse when I am mad.
(16) F I almost never litter the streets with wrappers.
(21) F I almost never feel like I would like to punch or slap someone.
(31) F If someone offends me, I just try not to think about it.
(36) T In many stores you just cannot get served unless you push yourself in front of other people.
(42) T If people annoy me I do not hesitate to tell them so.
(47) T When I am angry with people I do not try to hide it from them.
(57) F I generally do not use strong curse words even when I am angry.
(62) F I can easily forgive people who have insulted me or hurt my feelings.
(67) T When people disagree with me I cannot help getting into an argument with them.

(72) T I have a very strong temper.
(77) T I can't help being a little rude to people I do not like.
(86) F I am always patient with others even when they are irritating.
(91) T I often quarrel with others.
(97) T When people shout at me, I shout back.

Impulsive Sensation Seeking (ImpSS): A tendency to act quickly without planning and a general need for novelty, thrills and excitement.
(1) T I tend to begin a new job without much advance planning on how I will do it.
(6) F I usually think about what I am going to do before doing it.
(14) T I often do things on impulse.
(19) T I very seldom spend much time on the details of planning ahead.
(24) T I like to have new and exciting experiences and sensations even if they are a little frightening.
(29) F Before I begin a complicated job, I make careful plans.
(34) T I would like to take off on a trip with no preplanned or definite routes or timetables.
(39) T I enjoy getting into new situations where you can't predict how things will turn out.
(45) T I like doing things just for the thrill of it.
(50) T I tend to change interests frequently.
(55) T I sometimes like to do things that a little frightening.
(60) T I'll try anything once.
(65) T I would like the kind of life where one is on the move and travelling a lot, with lots of change and excitement.
(70) T I sometimes do "crazy" things just for fun.
(75) T I like to explore a strange city or section of town by myself, even if it means getting lost.
(79) T I prefer friends who are excitingly unpredictable.
(84) T I often get so carried away by new and exciting things and ideas that I never think of possible complications.
(89) T I am an impulsive person.
(95) T I like "wild" uninhibited parties.
Neuroticism-Anxiety (N-Anx): Worry and fearfulness, sensitivity to criticism and a lack of self-confidence.
(2) F I do not worry about unimportant things.
(7) T I am not very confident about myself or my abilities.
(15) T I often feel restless for no apparent reason.
(20) T I sometimes feel edgy and tense.
(25) T My body often feels all tightened up for no apparent reason.
(30) T I frequently get emotionally upset.
(35) T I tend to be oversensitive and easily hurt by thoughtless remarks and actions of others.
(41) T I am easily frightened.
(46) T I sometimes feel panicky.
(51) T I often think people I meet are better than I am.
(56) T Sometimes when emotionally upset, I suddenly feel as if my legs are unsteady.
(61) T I often feel unsure of myself.

(66) T I often worry about things that other people think are unimportant.
(71) T I often have trouble trying to make choices.
(76) T My muscles are so tense that I feel tired much of the time.
(80) T I often feel like crying sometimes without a reason.
(85) F I don't let a lot of trivial things irritate me.
(90) T I often feel uncomfortable and ill at ease for no real reason.
(96) T After buying something I often worry about having made the wrong choice.

Sociability (Sy): A general need for the company of others and an aversion to social isolation.
(9) T I tend to start conversations at parties.
(12) F I do not mind going out alone and usually prefer it to being out in a large group.
(17) F I would not mind being alone in a place for some days without any human contacts.
(22) T I spend as much time with my friends as I can.
(27) T I often find myself being "the life of the party."
(37) F I do not need a large number of casual friends.
(43) F I tend to be uncomfortable at big parties.
(48) T At parties, I enjoy mingling with many people whether I already know them or not.
(53) T I tend to start my social weekends on Thursday evenings.
(58) T I would rather "hang out" with friends than work on something by myself.
(63) F I would not mind being socially isolated in some place for some period of time.
(68) F Generally, I like to be alone so I can do things I want to do without social distractions.
(78) T I am a very sociable person.
(82) T I need to feel that I am a vital part of a group.
(87) F I usually prefer to do things alone.
(92) T I probably spend more time than I should socializing with friends.
(98) T I have more friends than most people do.

Infrequency Items: These can be used to detect careless responding
(4) T I never met a person that I didn't like.
(10) T I have always told the truth.
(26) T I always win at games.
(32) T I have never been bored.
(40) T I never get lost, even in unfamiliar places.
(52) T I never get annoyed when people cut ahead of me in line.
(69) T I never have any trouble understanding anything I read the first time I read it.
(73) T I have never lost anything.
(81) T No matter how hot or cold it gets, I am always quite comfortable.
(93) T It doesn't bother me if someone takes advantage of me.

Chapter 5

On the Alternative Five-Factor Model: Structure and Correlates

P. G. Schmitz

1. Zuckerman's Alternative Big Five Model of Personality

During the last two decades, Zuckerman has elaborated a model of personality that contains five basic dimensions. These dimensions are Impulsive Unsocialized Sensation Seeking (ImpSS), Neuroticism-Anxiety (N-Anx), Aggression-Hostility (Agg-Host), Sociability (Sy) and Activity (ACT). Zuckerman called his personality model the alternative Five-Factor Model (FFM) to distinguish it from the FFM of the Neuroticism, Extraversion, Openness to Experience Personality Inventory (NEO- PI; Costa & McCrae 1992a, b). The dimensions of the alternative FFM are assessed with the Zuckerman-Kuhlman Personality Questionnaire (ZKPQ).

The five dimensions are defined in the following way (cf. Zuckerman *et al.* 1993; Zuckerman 2002):

(1) *Impulsive Sensation Seeking* (ImpSS, 19 items) comprises two components, Impulsivity and Sensation Seeking. The impulsivity items refer to lack of planning and a tendency to act quickly on impulse without thinking. The sensation seeking items describe a general need for thrills or the willingness to take risks for the sake of excitement, a preference for unpredictable situations and friends, and the need for change and novelty.

(2) *Neuroticism-Anxiety* (N-Anx, 19 items) describes emotional upset, fearfulness, tension, worry, lack of self-confidence, sensitivity to criticism, and obsessive indecision.

(3) *Aggression-Hostility* (Agg-Host, 17 items) — about half of the items refer to the readiness to express verbal aggression while the other half refer to rude, thoughtless or antisocial behavior, vengefulness, spitefulness, a quick temper and impatience with others.

(4) *Sociability* (Sy, 17 items) contains two subcomponents, Parties and Friends and Isolation Intolerance. The first component describes liking big parties, interacting with many people, and having many friends. The second component refers to intolerance for social

On the Psychobiology of Personality
Edited by R. M. Stelmack

ISBN: 0-08-044209-9

isolation in highly sociable subjects, whereas unsociable persons like being alone and solitary activities. They show tolerance for isolation.

(5) *Activity* (ACT, 17 items) comprises also two components, Need for General Activity and Need for Work Activity. The first subdimension describes the need for general activity, impatience, and restlessness when there is nothing to do. The second subdimension refers to preference for challenging and hard work, an active busy life.

There is also a control scale, the *Infrequency* scale (10 items), that serves to eliminate persons with possibly invalid records.

The ZKPQ-II and later the revised version of the questionnaire, the ZKPQ-III, were made available by Zuckerman to the author to be used in several research projects at the University of Bonn. This contribution will refer to two of these research projects, namely to the Basic Dimensions Project and to the Inter-Cultural Competence Project.

1.1. Psychometric Properties of the Zuckerman-Kuhlman Personality Questionnaire

The ZKPQ II (Zuckerman *et al.* 1991) and the revised ZKPQ III (cf. Zuckerman *et al.* 1993) were applied in both research projects, the Basic Dimensions Project and the Inter-Cultural Competence Project.[1] To assess the correctness of the German translation of the ZKPQ, the technique of back-translation was used. There was a high degree of similarity between the English and German items. Table 1 shows the reliabilities (Cronbach's alphas) of the total score and the subscores of the German samples. The first two columns contain the Cronbach's alphas of the normative samples, 480 male and 710 female participants, collected between 1992 and 1999 within the Basic Dimensions Projects (Schmitz 1992, 1994a–c, 1999). They are equivalent to reliability coefficients reported by Zuckerman (2002). Retest reliabilities are also comparable to those reported by Zuckerman (2002). Factor analysis of items showed a five-factor solution. The factors found in that analysis could be identified as N-Anx, Sociability, ImpSS, ACT, and Agg-Host. Each item had a substantial loading on the factor to which it had been assigned (Schmitz 1999). When considering only loadings greater than 0.30, all 19 items of the N-Anx scale showed loadings above that criterion value, 14 of 17 items of the Sy scale, 18 of 19 items of the ImpSS scale, 16 of 17 items of the ACT scale, and 12 of 17 items of the Agg-Host scale. Various item and scale analyses illustrated that the German version of the ZKPQ shows satisfactory psychometric characteristics that are comparable to those reported in the ZKPQ literature (Schmitz 1992, 1994a–c).

In two earlier studies, Zuckerman and colleagues had shown that when factor analysing 46 questionnaire scales (Zuckerman *et al.* 1988) and 33 questionnaire scales (Zuckerman *et al.* 1991), Sy, ACT, N-ANX, Agg-Host, and ImpSS emerged at the five-factor level. At the three-factor level, the three superfactors of the Eysenck Personality Questionnaire (EPQ; Eysenck & Eysenck 1975) were clearly identified, i.e. Neuroticism (N), Extraversion (E),

[1] In these projects, a battery of instruments was employed. For reasons of similarity, participants were asked to use five-point-Likert-scales for all items in the present samples. This differs from Zuckerman's own procedure, where two-step-scales (i.e. "true" vs. "false") were used.

Table 1: Reliability (Cronbach Alpha) of the ZKPQ scales (Bonn version).

	Normative Sample		Range of Reliability (Studies: 1990–1999)	Retest-Reliability	
	Male (480)	**Female (710)**		**6 wks. (150)**	**7 mths. (75)**
Impulsive Sensation Seeking (ImpSS)	0.84	0.83	0.65–0.83	0.80	0.78
Sensation Seeking (SS)	0.83	0.81	0.73–0.88	0.83	0.78
Impulsivity (Imp)	0.76	0.69	0.65–0.83	0.76	0.75
Neuroticism-Anxiety (N-Anx)	0.91	0.86	0.83–0.91	0.84	0.80
Aggression Hostility (Agg-Host)	0.73	0.71	0.53–0.82	0.72	0.79
Activity (ACT)	0.87	0.80	0.78–0.91	0.79	0.78
Need for General Activity (GAC)	0.83	0.78	0.78–0.87	0.78	0.80
Need for work activity (WA)	0.63	0.58	0.56–0.68	0.65	0.73
Sociability (Sy)	0.87	0.86	0.84–0.88	0.84	0.82
Parties and Friends (PR)	0.83	0.78	0.75–0.86	0.85	0.83
Isolation Tolerance (IS)	0.85	0.86	0.78–0.88	0.82	0.79

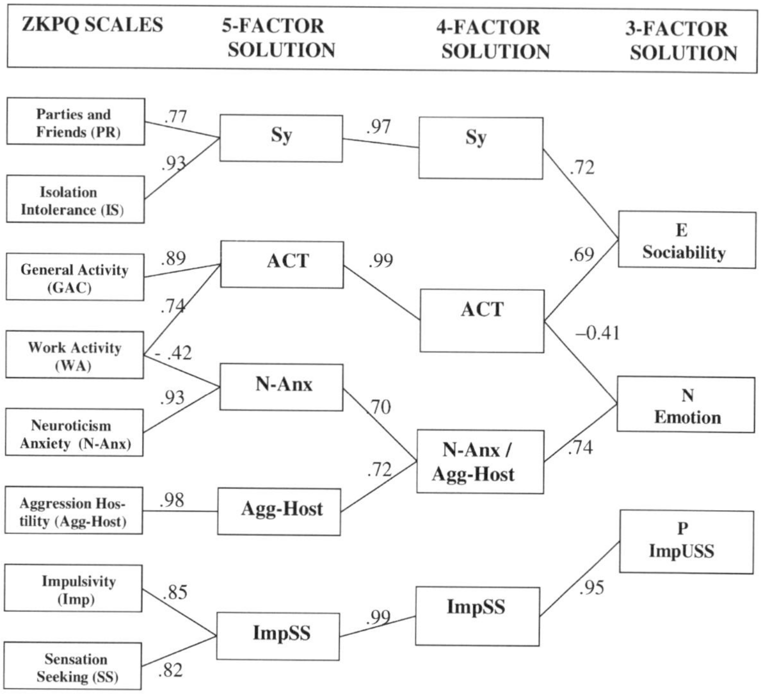

Figure 1: Five-, four-, and three-factor solutions for the ZKPQ dimensions and factor score correlations across levels when Eysenck Personality Questionnaire Scales are included in the analysis. E = Extraversion; N = Neuroticism; P-ImpUSS = Psychoticism-Unsocialized Sensation Seeking.

and Psychoticism (P). In a further study, comparable results were found (Zuckerman *et al.* 1993). The five dimensions emerged again at the five-factor level. EPQ E, N, and P could also be found at the three-factor level (Figure 1). In order to investigate the hierarchical structure at different factor levels, Schmitz (1999) factor-analysed the ZKPQ scale scores. But instead of using ZKPQ Sy total score, the Sy facets Parties and Friends and Isolation Intolerance were included. The subscale scores for Need for General Activity and Need for Work Activity entered the analysis instead of ACT. At the five-factor solution level, the ZKPQ FFM emerged. For the three-factor solution, EPQ N, E, and P were found. At the four-factor level, N-Anx and Agg-Host loaded on the same factor, illustrating that both could be considered as components of a general higher order factor, a factor identifiable as General Emotionality. Schmitz (1999) agreed with Zuckerman (2002) that the four-factor solution was not as reliable as the five- and three-factor solutions.

1.2. Structure of the Zuckerman-Kuhlman Personality Questionnaire

The follow-up studies within the Basic Dimensions Project aimed to test the alternative FFM by applying confirmatory factor analysis to investigate some structural models of the ZKPQ. The hypotheses tested were based on previous factor analysis findings in exploratory studies (cf. Schmitz 2003). Although five-factor solutions had been found when the analyses were conducted at the item level of the ZKPQ (Schmitz 1992), we had expected that at the scale level a four-factor solution would be found when using the facet scales proposed by Zuckerman (total of 8 scales). Two scales should show loadings on each of the four factors. The number of factors should be determined by the scree-test criterion and eigenvalues greater than 1.0. In fact, four factors emerged and were identified as ImpSS (markers were Impulsivity and Sensation Seeking), Sy (Isolation Intolerance, Parties and Friends), ACT (Need for General Activity and Need for Work Activity) and General (negative) Emotionality (markers: N-Anx, Agg-Host). Agg-Host emerged as a separate factor only in a five-factor solution, but no other variables loaded on this factor. In their 1993 study, Zuckerman *et al.* also found four factors when factor analysing the scale scores of the ZKPQ, NEO, and EPQ-R. The first two factors found were labelled N and E because they had loadings of the N and E scales of each questionnaire. The third factor had loadings from NEO Conscientiousness, ZKPQ ImpSS and EPQ P. The fourth factor was defined by NEO Aggreableness, ZKPQ Agg-Host and NEO Openness. In the Zuckerman *et al.* (1993) factor analysis, neither Openness nor ACT emerged as separate factors because each of these both potential factors was represented only by a single scale in the study.

Considering the findings of the exploratory factor analyses by Zuckerman *et al.* (1993), ZKPQ data were collected from a sample of 200 persons to assess the structural assumptions of the FFM in that analysis. LISREL was used to test whether a four- or a five-factor solution would fit the data collected. A FFM had to be rejected, but a four-factor solution adequately fit the data. The confirmatory factor analysis with five-factors matched the findings of the exploratory factor analyses to a high degree. Figure 2 presents the relevant model fit indices and shows the relations between variables and latent factors. According to Zuckerman's structural assumptions, the four latent factors were labelled ImpSS, N-Anx/Agg-Host, Sy and ACT. As expected, the facet scales of ImpSS, SY and ACT loaded on the corresponding latent factors even if the loadings vary considerably.

The best predictor of ImpSS is Sensation Seeking. Impulsivity shows a lower loading. A secondary loading is also allowed for the Parties and Friends scale, a facet ascribed by Zuckerman to Sy. Zuckerman *et al.* (1993) also found that the ImpSS scale score loads on both E/Sy and EPQ P/NEO Conscientiousness in their three- and four-factor solutions. Further, ImpSS and NEO Excitement Seeking scales showed marked loadings on E, Agreeableness and Conscientiousness in the five-factor solution for the EPQ, ZKPQ, and NEO facets analysis. Zuckerman *et al.* (1993) and Eysenck (1992a, b) considered the Agreeableness and Conscientiousness factors as components of P.

The second factor N-Anx/Agg-Host can possibly be interpreted as General Emotionality. In addition to Anxiety, the factor contains the component (defensive) Aggression or Anger (cf. Zuckerman 2002: 378). The latent factor in our model is best predicted by N-Anx. Secondary loadings are from Agg-Host, Parties and Friends (negatively) and Need for Work Activities (negatively). The high measurement error found for the Agg-host variable ($\delta = 0.92$) indicates that this variable is not explained well by the four factors of this confirmatory factor analysis. Consistent with the alternative FFM, Agg-Host has to be considered as a relatively independent dimension. However, with only one observable indicator in our study, an additional latent factor was not supported.

The third latent factor can be clearly interpreted as Sy. As predicted, it is related to both facet scales of Sy, i.e. Parties and Friends and Isolation Intolerance. There was a secondary

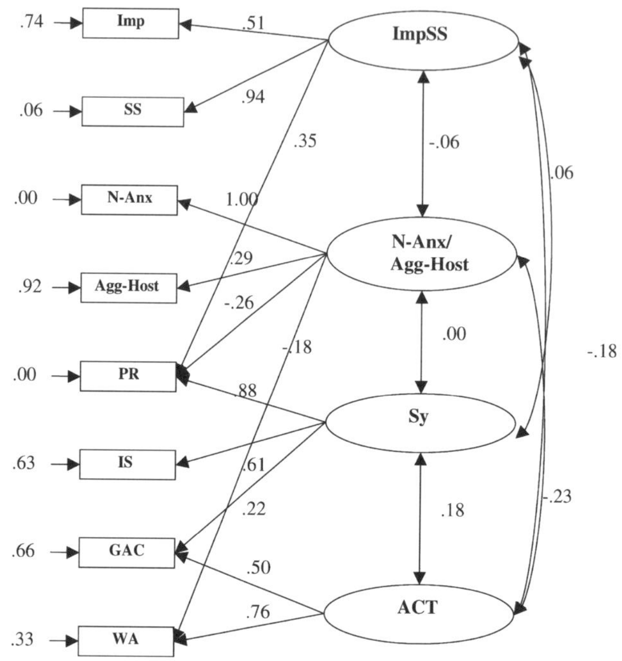

Figure 2: Confirmatory factor analysis of the four-factor solution of the ZKPQ dimensions and facet scales. N-Anx = Neuroticism-Anxiety; ImpSS = Impulsive Sensation Seeking; Sy = Sociability; Agg-Host = Aggression-Hostility; ACT = Activity; SS = Sensation Seeking; PR = Parties and Friends; WA = Work Activity; IS = Isolation intolerance; GAC = General Activity ($n = 200$; $\chi^2 = 5.78$, df = 11; GFI = 0.99; AGFI = 0.97, RMSEA = 0.000).

loading from the Sy factor on General Activity. According to Eysenck (1967, 1992a, b) and Costa and McCrae (1992a, b), ACT is considered as a component of E. In the Zuckerman *et al.* (1993) data, ACT also loads on E. The fourth factor is determined by both facet scales predicted to measure ACT in the alternative FFM.

The four-factor model does not contradict the alternative FFM because the number of latent factors accepted depends on the number of observable variables entered in the analysis. This time, eight scale scores were entered as observable variables and each of the four factors is primarily based on two observed variables. Three of them, i.e. ImpSS, Sy, and ACT, relate to their hypothetically predicted facets, whereas the N-Anx/Agg-Host factor loads on both, the N-Anx scale and Agg-Host scale. In the alternative FFM, there are no facets specified for the latter two dimensions. Therefore, it was decided to enter two additional scales in the next analyses to support the hypothetically derived independence of the N-Anx and Agg-Host dimensions. Two scales that appeared to closely resemble the concepts of the two ZKPQ dimensions were selected from the Guilford-Zimmerman Temperament Survey (GZTS), i.e. Emotionality and Friendliness for ZKPQ N-Anx and Agg-Host, respectively (Guilford & Zimmerman 1956; Guilford *et al.* 1976). Further, the General Activity scale was also included because in some studies the ACT factor did not appear very clear-cut (cf. Zuckerman *et al.* 1993). The postulated relations were also based on the results of previous studies (Schmitz 1999).

In different samples, Emotionality correlated highly with N-Anx, Friendliness with Agg-Host, and General Activity with ZKPQ ACT. A five-factor confirmatory factor analysis specifying alternative FFM dimensions was tested in a sample of 150 subjects. The best fitting solution, after carrying out some modifications of secondary loadings, is presented in Figure 3. As expected, the alternative FFM model could be accepted now. The ZKPQ

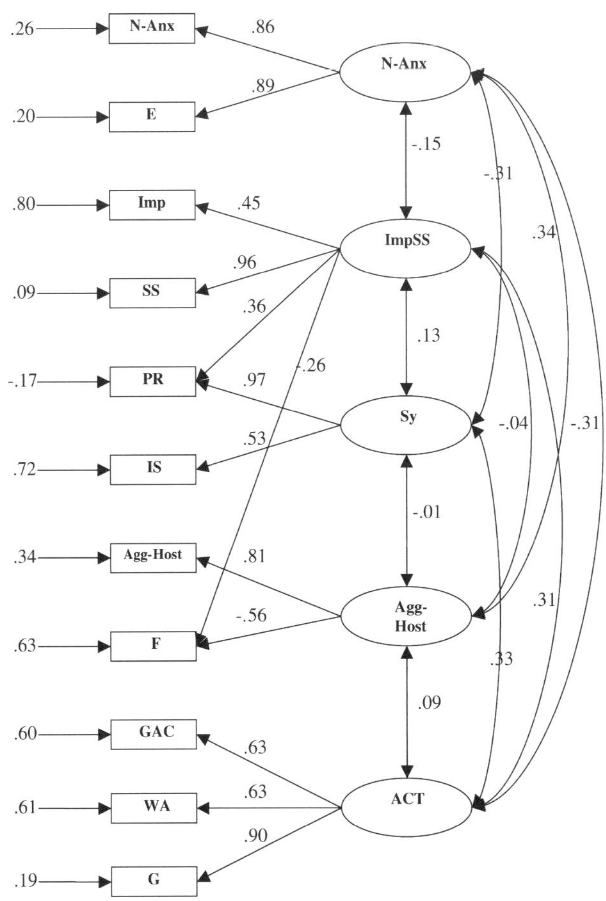

Figure 3: Confirmatory factor analysis of the five-factor solution of the ZKPQ dimensions and facet scales when the Guilford-Zimmerman Temperament Scales (GZTS) are included in the analysis. For the ZKPQ, N-Anx = Neuroticism-Anxiety; ImpSS = Impulsive Sensation Seeking; Sy = Sociability; Agg-Host = Aggression-Hostility; ACT = Activity; SS = Sensation Seeking; PR = Parties and Friends; WA = Work Activity; IS = Isolation intolerance; GAC = General Activity. For the GZTS, E = Emotionality; F = Friendliness; G = General activity ($n = 150$; $\chi^2 = 55.84$, df = 32; GFI = 0.93; AGFI = 0.85; RMSEA = 0.076).

facets and the GZTS variables showed loadings as they were hypothetically assigned to the alternative FFM. As in the previous study, ImpSS was more closely related to SS than to IMP, and again, the facet Parties and Friends was more strongly related to Sy than ImpSS. Further, it is of interest to see that the latent factor Agg-Host showed a stronger relation with the variable Agg-Host (0.81) than with GZTS Friendliness (−0.56). But Friendliness also showed a weak negative relation to ImpSS. That is not surprising. GZTS Friendliness and Personal Relations load on a second-order factor which Guilford (1975, 1977) called Paranoid Disposition that is somewhat similar to EPQ P.

Specific intercorrelations between latent factors hint at possible common higher order factors. For example, the correlation of N-Anx and Agg-Host could indicate a higher order factor of (negative) General Emotionality. Also, correlations of the ACT with Sy and N-Anx (negative) seem to point to a higher order factor.

1.3. The Relation Between the FFM and Alternative FFM

To distinguish his model from the established FFM (Costa & McCrae 1992a), Zuckerman *et al.* (1993) referred to his model as the alternative FFM. It seems important to ask how the models are related to each other and in what ways they are similar and different. The findings of joint factor analyses of ZKPQ and NEO scales suggest a large degree of convergence of both FFMs (cf. Costa & McCrae 1992b; Zuckerman *et al.* 1993). Two factors are considered as highly convergent, i.e. ZKPQ N-Anx/NEO N, and ZKPQ Sy/NEO E. Affinities are seen for ZKPQ ImpSS and NEO Conscientiousness and for ZKPQ Agg-Host and NEO Agreeableness. Zuckerman *et al.* (1993) predicted that these four major factors would emerge in a joint factor analysis of ZKPQ, NEO, and EPQ scales. The authors did expect that neither ZKPQ ACT nor NEO Openness would emerge as separate factors because each of them was only presented by a single scale within one of the three personality models. In fact, as predicted, four major factors emerged and were identified as E, N, Conscientiousness and Agreeableness. ACT loaded on E, as predicted by Eysenck and Eysenck (1975) and by Costa and McCrae (1992a, b). Openness showed a major loading on Agreeableness and a smaller loading on E (Zuckerman *et al.* 1993). Openness appeared as a fifth factor only when the NEO facet scales were factor analysed instead of the NEO major scales (Zuckerman *et al.* 1993). In the analysis on the facet scale level of the NEO, ZKPQ ACT showed a major loading on E and a smaller loading on Conscientiousness.

As has been shown, the alternative FFM (cf. Figure 3) could be verified when three scales from the GZTS were added to the ZKPQ facet scales, so that each hypothesized factor was indicated by at least two observable variables in the confirmatory factor analysis. In the following study, it was hypothesized that the alternative FFM would be supported by a confirmatory factor analysis over the joint ZKPQ and NEO scales together with the three GZTS scales Emotionality, Friendliness, and General Activity (that were also used in the above-mentioned study). Figure 4 shows the graph of the LISREL model that provided the best fit. The findings are similar to those found in earlier exploratory factor analyses (Schmitz 1999).

The latent factor N-Anx is clearly composed of the three N scales, NEO N, ZKPQ N-Anx, and EPQ N. The second latent factor, Sy, consists of high loadings of NEO E and ZKPQ Sy,

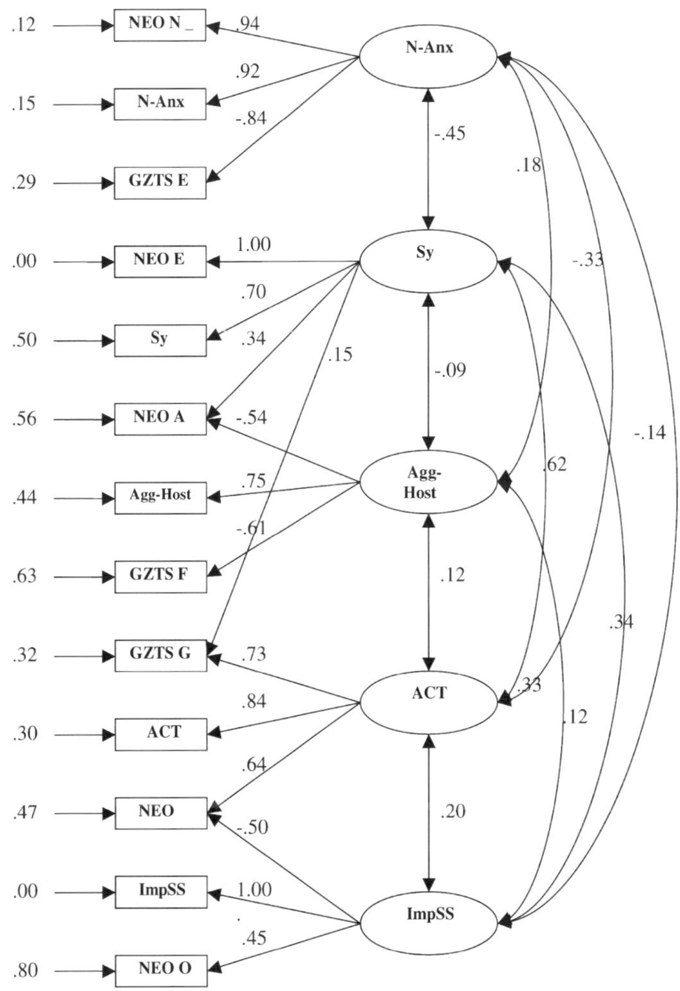

Figure 4: Confirmatory factor analysis of a Five-Factor Model including ZKPQ, NEO, and GZTS scales. N = Neuroticism; N-Anx = Neuroticism-Anxiety; E = Extraversion; Sy = Sociability; A = Agreeableness; Agg-Host = Aggression-Hostility; F = Friendliness; G = General activity; ACT = Activity; C = Conscientiousness; ImpSS = Impulsive Sensation Seeking; O = Openness (n = 174; χ^2 = 136.64, df = 53; GFI = 0.89; AGFI = 0.81; RMSEA = 0.096).

a minor loading of NEO Agreeableness and a small loading of GZTS General Activity. A secondary loading of the NEO Agreeableness scale on the Sy factor was accepted. It should be mentioned that in most analyses Agreeableness is more closely related to ImpSS than to EPQ P. But it is also obvious that in our model the two latent factors Sy and ACT are particularly highly intercorrelated. This might indicate the existence of a common higher order factor. Additionally, ACT shows a weaker negative correlation with N-Anx. Similar relations were also found in earlier studies (Schmitz 1999).

Further, there is a correlation between ImpSS and Sy that is difficult to interpret. This relation could be influenced by the Impulsivity scale, which is mainly an indicator of ImpSS, but also correlates weakly with Sy. In contrast to Zuckerman *et al.* (1993), Eysenck (1992a, b) considers Impulsivity as an indicator of E. Our data may indicate that Impulsivity is mostly a component of ZKPQ ImpSS, but it seems that Impulsivity also relates to E/Sy. As expected, the latent factor Agg-Host was shown to account for variance in the three components: ZKPQ Agg-Host, GZTS Friendliness (negative loading) and NEO Agreeableness (negatively). The latent factor ACT is related to ZKPQ ACT, GZTS General Activity and NEO Conscientiousness. As already mentioned, in the factor analysis of the NEO facet scales by Zuckerman *et al.* (1993), the Conscientiousness factor showed a secondary loading on ZKPQ ACT. This is consistent with an interpretation of the Conscientiousness dimension as related to achievement values or work-ethic beliefs frequently found in Westernized societies and to achievement-related behaviour patterns. One component of ZKPQ ACT, Need for Work Activity, also relates to achievement. The latent factor ImpSS is based on ZKPQ ImpSS and it is related negatively to Conscientiousness and positively to Openness. Openness seems to be connected with ImpSS probably due to the ImpSS component Sensation Seeking. The NEO facet Excitement Seeking also showed a secondary loading on the Openness to Experience factor in the analysis of the joint NEO facet and ZKPQ scales (Zuckerman *et al.* 1993). The findings of the analysis suggest that there is a great deal of convergence of these FFMs.

1.4. The Relation Between the Zuckerman-Kuhlman Personality Questionnaire and the Eysenck Personality Questionnaire

According to Zuckerman *et al.* (1993), the scales from the ZKPQ and the EPQ should load on E, N, and P as markers. This should be tested by means of a confirmatory factor analysis. To get at least three observable variables for each latent factor, it was decided to use ZKPQ facet scales. It was assumed, that the P factor should consist of the following observable variables: EPQ P, ZKPQ IMP and ZKPQ SS scales. N should include EPQ N and both ZKPQ factor scales relating to General Emotionality, i.e. N-Anx and Agg-Host. The E superfactor should show loadings of EPQ E and ZKPQ Need for Work Activity and components of the ZKPQ Sy, i.e. Intolerance for Social Isolation and Liking for Parties and Friends. According to EPQ model (Eysenck & Eysenck 1975), it was hypothesized that Sensation Seeking should also show a substantial loading on the E superfactor. Agg-Host should also load on P and ACT. Need for Work Activity loads on N. These minor secondary loadings, Sensation Seeking on E and Agg-Host on P, were also found in factor analyses of ZKPQ, NEO and EPQ scales (Zuckerman *et al.* 1993).

ACT did not load on N when analyses were conducted on the dimensional levels of the questionnaires applied in Zuckerman's study, but activity loaded weekly on N (negatively) when the analyses was computed on the facet level of the NEO. In the factor analyses of various questionnaire scales conducted in preceding studies ACT loaded negatively on N on a higher order factor level (Zuckerman *et al.* 1988, 1993).

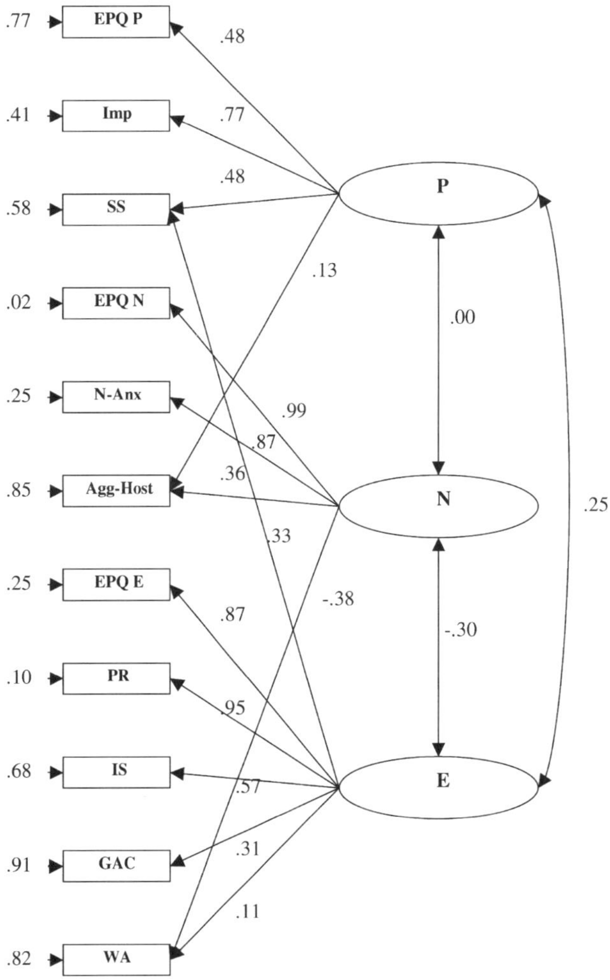

Figure 5: Confirmatory factor analysis of a Three-Factor Model including ZKPQ and Eysenck Personality Questionnaire (EPQ). P = Psychoticism; Imp = Impulsiveness; SS = Sensation Seeking; N = Neuroticism; N-Anx = Neuroticism-Anxiety; Agg-Host = Aggression-Hostility; E = Extraversion; PR = Parties and Friends; IS = Isolation intolerance; GAC = General Activity; WA = Work Activity (n = 120; $\chi^2 = 126.20$, df = 38; GFI = 0.88; AGFI = 0.80, RMSEA = 0.116).

As hypothesized the observed variables from both questionnaires, namely ZKPQ and EPQ, could be explained by the latent factors labelled P, E, and N as the graph of the model illustrates (cf. Figure 5). The first latent Factor P is composed by both sub-factors of ImpSS, Impulsivity and Sensation Seeking. But as predicted, the factor Agg-Host also shows a small loading on P ($\lambda = 0.13$). The latent factor N includes the variables EPQ N and ZKPQ N-Anx. Agg-Host also shows a smaller loading on N ($\lambda = 0.36$) than expected,

72% of the variance of this observed variable could not be explained by the latent factors N and P. Referring to research findings (Gray 1982; Valzelli 1981), Zuckerman suggests that Eysenck's N might be considered as a general Emotionality factor that splits into two relatively independent factors, namely N-Anx and Agg-Host, because both components of general Emotionality "have distinctive psychobiological bases" (Zuckerman *et al.* 1993: 763). In the three-factor model, Agg-Host shows a loading on each of the three superfactors. The highest loading was found for P ($a = 0.63$), with smaller loadings on N ($a = 0.32$) and E ($a = 0.27$). In our research, an alternative model tested, i.e. that the variable Agg-Host relates to each of the three latent factors, was not confirmed. The data from the German sample illustrates that Agg-Host relates to P and N, but not to E.

Concerning the facets of the ImpSS scale, Impulsivity loads clearly and only on the P factor, whereas Sensation Seeking has loadings on the P and E factors. In the present study, the latent N and E factors were slightly negatively correlated, which might be explained in part by the loadings of the variable Need-for-Work-Activity on both N (negatively) and E (positively). Usually, in factor analyses of EPQ, ZKPQ and NEO scales, N and E are slightly negatively correlated, normally somewhat less in the ZKPQ and in the EPQ than in the NEO (cf. Costa & McCrae 1992a; Eysenck & Eysenck 1975; Zuckerman 2002; Zuckerman *et al.* 1993). According to the last model, the latent variable P is best predicted in this study by ZKPQ Impulsivity and less by EPQP. This was also observed in the data presented by Zuckerman *et al.* (1993). As in Zuckerman *et al.* (1993), the best marker of N is EPQ N. N-Anx also a good predictor. Regarding E, the highest marker is the Sy component Parties and Friends that suggest that E could better be labelled sociability.

2. Validity Studies of the German Version of the ZKPQ

In the following, some correlates of the alternative FFM will be presented to show that the dimensions of the model help to understand individual differences in social behavior. The findings from the fields of acculturation and love-style research may serve to validate alternative FFM model in an additional and culturally different setting.

2.1. ZKPQ Personality Dimensions and Acculturation Styles

Migration can be considered as a central socio-political issue in societies at present. Persons deciding to migrate or being forced to migrate are often confronted with the challenge to adapt to a more or less different culture. Migration groups as well as individual migrants differ in how they adapt to a new culture they are confronted with.

2.1.1. Differences in acculturation strategies An acculturation model developed by Berry (1997) and applied by many researchers has been useful in scientific research to investigate differences in acculturation strategies (Berry *et al.* 1977). The acculturation model refers to two dimensions that relate to different forms of cognition, communication, and interaction that migrants have with the society and culture of the immigration country or host society as well as with their own cultural group. Dimension I can be described as

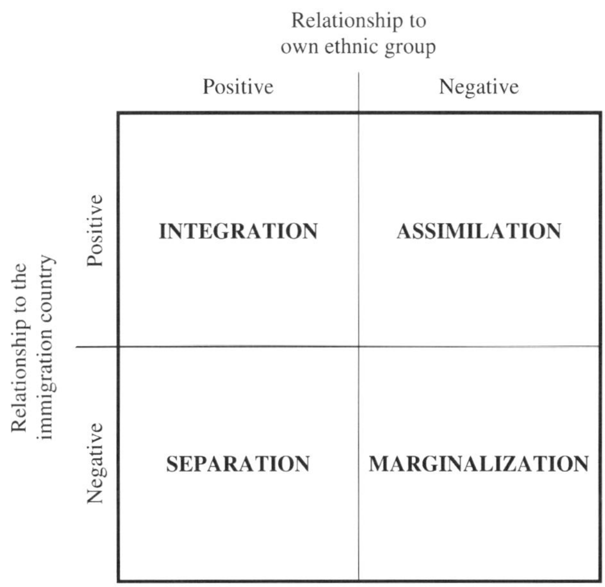

Figure 6: Acculturation styles, Integration, Assimilation, Separation, Marginalization, defined by the quality of the relationship to their the own ethnic group and the majority in the immigration country.

"contact and interaction with the host society" and dimension II as "maintenance of the culture of origin." The former relates to the question "Are the own cultural identity and customs of value to be maintained?" and the latter to the question "Are positive relations with the host society or other socio-cultural groups considered to be of value, and are they to be maintained?" Both dimensions are considered continua and individual differences of acculturative behavior are normal-distributed on each dimension (Schmitz 2003). When we artificially dichotomize each dimension to simplify matters for methodological reasons and combine both dichotomized dimensions then we will obtain a four-field table and each cell refers to a different prototype of acculturation strategy: integration, assimilation, separation, and marginalization (see Figure 6).

If we restrict the answers to our questions to "yes" or "no" we can define the four acculturation strategies as follows: answering "yes" to both questions we call integration. *Integration* can be defined as maintenance of the own cultural identity to a great extent and an effort towards becoming an integral part of the larger societal framework. Culture and customs of the host society are positively evaluated and parts of it are taken over and integrated in the own behavior and value system.

Assimilation means the abandonment of the own culture of origin and the maintenance of positive relations with the host society, with cultural values and behavior patterns being adopted. The aim is often to become a person whose behavior patterns and life style cannot be distinguished from that of a "real" member of the host society.

Separation is defined as maintenance of the own cultural identity and showing little interest in building up positive relations with other cultural groups and in taking over customs or accepting the host society's values. Interactions are restricted to a minimum of communication and social contacts.

Marginalization can be described as a type of reaction that develops when migrants give up their own cultural identity while at the same time they are not interested in maintaining close contact with either the host society or other socio-cultural groups living in the host country.

2.1.2. The influence of personality variables on acculturation Personality variables can be considered as central moderating factors during acculturation processes (Schmitz 2003). However, the number of personality variables that could be of interest in explaining the variety of individual differences in acculturative behavior can be considered relatively large. Therefore it could be of interest to refer to a limited number of factors accounting for a broad span of individual differences, such as basic personality dimensions derived from established models of personality, i.e. EPQ, NEO-PI, or ZKPQ.

Schmitz (1994a, b, 1995/1996, 2003) summarized research findings from different migrant groups collected before 1994, regarding the relations between acculturation styles preferred by migrants (assessed by questionnaires and ratings) and basic personality variables (e.g. EPQ-R, ZKPQ, Rokeach (1960) D-Scale).

Persons preferring Integration are emotionally more stable, less anxious and aggressive. They are more sociable and agreeable, and show more open-mindedness and activity. Obviously, they feel safer and they are more interested in exploring new situations. The contact with new cultures serves as an appropriate field of experience and they are able to break up their own value and belief system to take on new elements and integrate them into their own belief and behavior systems. They are flexible enough to modify easily strategies if it becomes obvious that certain strategies are not going to lead to success.

Assimilators show a higher degree of neuroticism and anxiety, but they are agreeable, friendly, and less aggressive. The high degree of activity helps them make an effort to assimilate to the new culture they are confronted with. Their sociable and friendly attitudes facilitate coming into contact with members of the host society, communicating with them, and joining their activities. It may be due to their elevated extent of neurotic tendencies and anxiety that they try to assimilate to a new social group quickly to avoid socio-cultural conflicts arising from perceived discrepancies between members of different social groups. Their acquired social competence helps assimilators to apply the Assimilation style as a suitable coping strategy.

Among migrants choosing Separation as an acculturative strategy, we also find a higher degree of neuroticism and its defining components such as emotionality, anxiety, and lack of self-assurance and feelings of self-esteem. Sometimes these traits are more marked among persons preferring Separation than with assimilators. Migrants belonging to this group have to cope with stressful acculturative situations trying to do this in accordance with the opportunities offered by the social situation they are in and according to their own psychological resources. As they are less active and frequently less agreeable, they often find it difficult to deal effectively with people of the host society as well as with other socio-cultural groups. This may lead to frustrations and to the experience of isolation and discrimination by the majority society. A high degree of closed-mindedness, the contrast pole of the openness dimension, makes it more difficult for them do modify their belief and behavior systems (cf. Rokeach 1960).

Migrants adopting the Separation strategy tend to show little interpersonal trust, in particular towards people they do not know very well. Their tendencies to react very emotionally in stressful situations lead to aggressiveness towards the host society and to withdrawal from contacts with members of the majority culture. This behavior becomes a vicious circle as the host society may react by showing increasing rejection and discrimination, which may reinforce the separating tendency for the migrants. To cope with these frustrating situations migrants may segregate and look for social contact within their traditional cultural group. But, we must understand that the preference for segregation does not always mean that migrants withdraw exclusively because of deficiencies in social behavior and negative emotionality. As we have already seen, auto-separation may be caused by a reappraisal of their own ethnic culture and be motivated by social and material opportunities given by their own ethnic group, advantages not always found in the host society. But it can be observed that in the latter case separation is not so extremely manifested and defensive aggressiveness towards the majority is not so marked.

Concerning the personality pattern of people showing Marginalization, there is some resemblance to that of migrants choosing Segregation. We also find neuroticism, aggressiveness, and a lack of interpersonal trust. But some differences become obvious. The quality of aggressiveness can be interpreted as less defensive and more antisocial — at least as manifest at the phenotype level.

With regard to our previous discussion, the following may be a plausible interpretation. Particularly during phases of high acculturative stress and when migrants do not receive adequate social support, marginalization can be considered a type of coping strategy to deal with social isolation and alienation. This may be because they are not willing to search for support due to their basic personality structure or they are not able to find support within their group of ethnic origin because the group does not exist or is not able to function as a basis for social support. Forms of distraction and pleasure seeking may be sought by consumption of alcohol and drugs — abuse and addiction can be the consequences. So it is not surprising to find that marginalization shows a close relationship with psychoticism, and its components impulsivity (i.e. lack of control) and psychopathy.

Finally, the dimension of sensation seeking, in particular the sub-dimension thrill and adventure seeking, is closely related to the motivation to leave one's own culture, to travel, and if possible, to live and work in other countries. If both sensation seeking and open-mindedness are central personality characteristics of individual migrants, and if they show a high degree of sociability and agreeableness that facilitates the acquisition of social skills, those migrants have an optimal opportunity to adjust to a new culture and to enjoy their new life in another country.

The findings mentioned earlier regarding the relation of acculturation styles and personality variables were further investigated in two cross-cultural research projects, where personality traits were assessed in addition to socio-cultural variables: International Comparative Studies of Ethnocultural Youth and Inter-Cultural Competence Project. The data were collected with different immigrant groups living in European Union countries, i.e. exchange students, seasonal workers, guest-workers, refugee-groups. The migrant groups

Table 2: Average correlation between ZKPQ dimensions and acculturation styles (range of correlation in brackets).

	Integration	Assimilation	Separation	Marginalization
Impulsivity	**−0.25**	−0.05	0.15	**0.40**
	(−0.09–0.30)	(−0.18–0.00)	(0.02–0.19)	(0.21–0.56)
Sensation	**0.23**	0.10	**−0.21**	**0.35**
seeking	(0.03–0.49)	(−0.02–0.62)	(−0.15–0.33)	(0.07–0.47)
Impulsive sens.	0.02	0.05	−0.05	**0.37**
seeking	(−0.05–0.09)	(−0.02–0.22)	(−0.08–0.02)	(0.13–0.52)
Sociability	**0.31**	0.14	**−0.33**	−0.17
	(0.29–0.36)	(−0.16–0.48)	(−0.17–0.43)	(−0.05–0.34)
Neuroticism-	−0.10	**0.28**	**0.20**	**0.30**
Anxiety	(−0.32–0.08)	(0.14–0.52)	(−0.09–0.34)	(0.15–0.59)
Aggression-	**−0.26**	−0.13	0.18	**0.37**
Hostility	(−0.16–0.43)	(−0.27–0.15)	(−0.15–0.25)	(0.14–0.66)
Activity	**0.22**	**0.26**	−0.04	**−0.23**
	(−0.06–0.32)	(−0.14–0.50)	(−0.14–0.28)	(−0.58–0.28)

Note: Correlations > 0.20 are in bold.

came from different cultures, i.e. Eastern European, Mediterranian, Asian, African, and Latin American. As in the preliminary studies the ZKPQ dimensions showed consistent correlational patterns for each acculturation style. Table 2 gives an overview of the findings. The table contains the average correlations between acculturation and the ZKPQ personality dimensions and the range of the correlations obtained from 26 samples.

Although the size of the correlations varies among the samples, the direction of the correlations shows a high degree of consistency. The average correlations between acculturation styles and personality dimensions correspond quite well to earlier findings, thus confirming the postulated hypotheses of previous research. Each acculturation strategy shows a different correlation pattern with the ZKPQ dimensions. Integration correlates positively with Sy and ACT and negatively with Agg-Host. This makes sense in so far as Integration depends on positive and friendly relationships with both the mainstream society and one's own cultural group. ACT is also a prerequisite that facilitates building social contacts and maintaining them over time. ZKPQ ImpSS is not correlated with Integration, but it is of interest to see that both components of this dimension show correlations that are in opposite directions. Impulsivity correlates negatively, whereas Sensation Seeking correlates positively with ImpSS. Impulsivity shows some affinity with unsocialized behavior, so it is not surprising to find it related with Marginalization. In contrast Sensation Seeking, often considered similar to Novelty Seeking, could be interpreted as an indispensable requirement to come in contact with a new culture and to be open to adapt new behavior patterns. Sy, ACT and Sensation Seeking are components of EPQ E (cf. Eysenck & Eysenck 1985), and as research findings illustrate, E has also been positively correlated with Integration (Schmitz 1994a, b, 1995/1996).

Assimilation and Separation show positive correlations with ZKPQ N-Anx. Behind both acculturation strategies, a tendency can be seen to deal with situations of uncertainty and ambiguity as it is frequently found among migrants. Persons with high scores on ZKPQ N-Anx are less emotionally stable and feel more insecure in situations of cultural conflicts. Assimilators solve this type of conflict by rejecting the traditional culture and by adopting the culture of the mainstream society, a way to be accepted more easily by members of the host society. Migrants choosing Separation feel also insecure, but they solve their problem by looking for social support within their own ethnic group, contact with the majority culture will be reduced or sometimes avoided. As a result, it is not surprising to see that Sensation Seeking is negatively related to Separation. In contrast to Assimilation, that shows a smaller negative correlation with Agg-Host, Separation is positively correlated with this dimension. As interview data from migrant samples show, a Separation strategy is frequently connected with negative feelings, or sometimes with hostile attitudes, and the mainstream society is considered as an out-group.

The highest average correlations are found for Marginalization. This acculturation style — a rather sporadic phenomenon — is considered a somewhat psychopathological behavior by most researchers (Berry 1997; Schmitz 2003). However, it occurs rarely in Western societies. High scores on the Marginalization scales are found in only about 1–3% of all cases. Persons having a middle range on the Marginalization scale are frequently very individualistic, are outsiders and often members of subculture-groups or gangs. Alcohol abuse and drug-addiction are more frequently found in this group. It is not surprising to see that Marginalization correlates positively with ImpSS, N-Anx and Agg-Host. These findings fit well with those discovered in earlier research where EPQ P and N correlated positively with Marginalization (Schmitz 1994a, b, 1995/1996).

Summarizing the main results regarding personality and acculturation, it can be assumed that individual differences in acculturation styles may be explained in part by personality factors, and further, that the alternative FFM model could help to understand why migrants prefer specific acculturative strategies.

2.2. *The Alternative FFM and Love Styles*

Love is one of the most central topics in everyday life, movies, art and literature. In social psychology a series of theories of love are presented. The most comprehensive theories of love are presented by Lee (1973, 1977), Hendrick and Hendrick (1986, 1987a–c), and by Sternberg (1986, 1988).

Lee's (1973, 1988) classification of love styles is based mostly on interview data. The classification system contains nine different types of love: three primary types Eros, Ludus, and Storge, and six secondary styles Mania, Pragma, Agape, Ludic Erotic, Storgic Erotic, and Storgic Ludus. The first three types can be represented as endpoints of a triangle and the rest are combinations of them. So Mania is a combination of Eros and Ludus, Pragma a combination of Ludus and Storge, and Agape a combination of Storge and Eros. Lee believes that love is an ideology and that these different types are influenced by culture and personal experience. Hendrick and Hendrick (1986) developed and validated a Love Attitude Scale (LAS) which is based on Lee's constructs. This scale measures six of Lee's components: Eros, Ludus, Storge, Mania, Pragma, and Agape. These six components are considered by Hendrick and Hendrick (1987b) as continuous variables, relatively stable over time and presenting independent dimensions. Individual patterns of love styles can be found.

Individuals high on Eros are described "to be intense and passionate, rather idealistic about sexuality, and to be disclosing to a love partner" (Hendrick *et al.* 1988: 980). The erotic lover possesses a clearly defined ideal of a person he loves, is highly attracted to a person he considers as ideal, and is highly motivated to become physically close to that person, expresses his feelings to the beloved person, and is interested to build up stable relationships. In contrast to erotic lovers, persons with high scores on Ludus do not have an ideal. They look for many interesting relationships. They like diversity in partnerships and they are not interested in lifelong relationships. Their orientation to love is "casual, permissive, and sometimes manipulative" (Hendrick *et al.* 1988: 980). Eros and Ludus display a relatively high degree of emotional arousal. Mania is similar to Eros and Ludus regarding the relationship to emotionality. Like the love style Eros, Mania includes idealism and disclosure, but not self-esteem. Agape refers to altruism, idealisism, and giving rather than taking in a person-to-person relationship. This style is committed to the partner, opposed to the permissiveness we find among persons high on Ludus. Storge is a slowly developing positive feeling to the partner, often starting with friendship. There is little passion, but when both partners are high on Storge they may share mutual interests. Love and sex are not primary goals, but accepted. Pragma is positioned between Ludus and Storge, and opposite to Eros. Emotions and passion are absent. A partner is chosen with regard to similarities in attitudes, beliefs, and interests. The choice is rational and pragmatic.

Research shows that individuals differ markedly with regard to love style patterns and these patterns are relatively stable over time. These differences in love attitudes and behavior are usually explained by the individual life experience and socio-cultural factors (cf. Baron & Byrne 2000; Goodwin & Findlay 1997; Lee 1973; Wan *et al.* 2000). But research has also related love styles to personality dimensions measured by the EPQ, ZKPQ, and NEO-PI (Davies 1996; Engel *et al.* 2002; Hendrick & Hendrick 1987b; Lester & Philbrick 1988; Mallandain & Davies 1994; Richardson *et al.* 1988; Wan *et al.* 2000; Woll 1989).

Lester and Philbrick (1988) correlated love styles with the Eysenck Personality Inventory scales (EPI; Eysenck & Eysenck 1964). Mania was significantly correlated with N. Eros and Ludus were associated with E. Woll (1989) used the EPI and the Love Attitude Questionnaire (Lasswell & Lasswell 1976) measuring Lee's six dimensions. Mania correlated with N and E; Eros, Ludus and Agape were associated with E and Storge with N. P was not assessed in the Woll and Lester and Philbrick studies because the EPI only measured E and N.

Davies (1996) applied the EPQ to measure Eysenck's N, E and P and the LAS which he considered as more reliable and valid than the Lasswell measures of love styles. He found E correlated positively with Eros and Ludus and N positively correlated with Mania, but negatively with Pragma. These correlations fit the findings reported by Woll (1989) and by Lester and Philbrick (1988). P was positively associated with Ludus and negatively with Storge and Agape. The last findings are not surprising as Storge was positively correlated with Sternberg's dimension Intimacy and Agape positively with Commitment, whereas Ludus related negatively to Sternberg's dimensions of Intimacy and Commitment (Aron & Westbay 1996; Hendrick & Hendrick 1989). P is characterized by adjectives such as cold, egocentric and impersonal (Eysenck & Eysenck 1985), i.e. the opposite of Sternberg's Companionate Love, which he defined as a combination of Intimacy and Commitment.

Recently, the relation between the NEO-PI dimensions and the LAS was investigated (Wan *et al.* 2000). They report higher correlations ($r > 0.20$) only for the dimension Mania. Mania correlates positively with N ($r = 0.47$), negatively with E ($r = -0.29$), and negatively with Conscientiousness ($r = -0.28$).

Engel *et al.* (2002) applied Sternberg's Triangular Love Scale which measures the degree of Intimacy, Passion and Commitment a person experiences toward a relationship partner. Conscientiousness and five of the six facets of Conscientiousness correlated positively with each of Sternberg's dimensions (higher correlations were found within the male sample). E correlates positively with Intimacy, and with regard to the facets of E, the highest positive correlation was found for Assertiveness. The findings of both studies, which applied five-factor measures, match those which had assessed personality with the EPQ scales.

Some research investigated the relation between Sensation Seeking Scales (SSS; Zuckerman 1994) and LAS. Hendrick and Hendrick (1987a) correlated the SSS with the LAS. They found that SSS total score, Disinhibition and Boredom Susceptibility were significantly correlated with Ludus.

Richardson *et al.* (1988) also employed the SSS and the LAS. They predicted that Ludus would relate more strongly to Sensation Seeking than other scales. As predicted, Ludus correlated with the SSS total score ($r = 0.35$). All sub-scores correlated significantly with Ludus with the largest correlation found for Disinhibition ($r = 0.39$) and Boredom Susceptability ($r = 0.30$). Pragma correlated negatively with the SSS total score ($r = -0.19$), Thrill and Adventure Seeking ($r = -0.16$), and Boredom Susceptability ($r = -0.18$). Similar findings were reported by Schmitz (2002) analysing data collected between 1990 and 1996. Ludus correlated also positively with the SSS Total ($r = 0.25$), Thrill and Adventure Seeking ($r = 0.15$), Experience Seeking ($r = 0.16$), Disinhibition ($r = 0.35$) and Boredom Susceptibility ($r = 0.30$); Pragma, Agape and Storge showed smaller negative correlations.

As research findings show, Sensation Seeking, as predicted by Zuckerman (1994), is clearly related to love styles, in particular to Ludus. Sensation Seeking is a subcomponent of ImpSS in the Alternative FFM. The question arises as to how the other personality dimensions are associated with the different love style components? With regard to the relation between love styles and personality dimensions that were assessed by the EPQ and NEO-PI, we hypothesized that ZKPQ N-Anx would be positively related to Mania and that Sy would be correlated with Eros. Data were collected with 255 persons (85 males, 170 females; age range: 20–46 years), the ZKPQ and the LAS were applied. Further, short interviews were conducted to get information about their behavior patterns in partner relationships.

Table 3 gives an overview of the correlations for the total sample. The general finding is that each dimension of the Alternative FFM shows a different love-style pattern. Further, it is of interest to split the ImpSS into the Impulsivity and Sensation Seeking components because both sub-factors showed specific correlation patterns with the love styles. As expected, Sensation Seeking correlates positively with Ludus and negatively with Pragma (cf. Richardson *et al.* 1988). Impulsivity also has a negative correlation with Pragma and a positive correlation with Agape, but Impulsivity does not correlate with Ludus at all.

Table 3: Correlation between ZKPQ dimensions and love styles.

	Eros	Ludus	Storge	Pragma	Mania	Agape
Impulsivity	−0.02	−0.03	−0.16	**−0.25**	−0.05	**0.31**
Sensation seeking	0.08	**0.33**	0.05	**−0.32**	−0.12	0.02
Impulsive sensation seeking	0.04	**0.20**	−0.05	**−0.36**	−0.11	**0.19**
Sociability	**0.37**	**−0.19**	0.07	−0.10	−0.05	0.15
Neuroticism/Anxiety	**−0.21**	0.15	**−0.19**	0.09	**0.17**	−0.12
Aggression/Hostility	−0.15	0.12	−0.15	0.02	**0.16**	**−0.23**
Activity	−0.01	**0.30**	0.03	**0.22**	**0.18**	−0.13

Note: Correlation coefficients in bold, $p < 0.01$.

The unexpected positive correlation of Impulsivity with Agape, found both for males ($r = 0.42$) and females ($r = 0.32$) can probably be explained by high agreement on items assessing Agape that reflect spontaneous and unreflected emotional reactions about the partner relationship. Further research has to investigate in which way Agape will become manifest in partnership behavior. In this context another finding is also interesting. Eros in the male sub-sample correlates positively with impulsivity ($r = 0.24$). Hendrick and Hendrick (1989) reported that both Eros and Agape are positively related to components of love intimacy, passion and commitment (Sternberg 1988). The three components are combined in a style labelled Consummate Love by Sternberg (1988). This style is considered as an ideal love relationship. But it has to be questioned which of Sternberg's components would explain the relation between impulsivity and Agape? It may be presumed that spontaneous and unreflected emotions are at least temporary components of passion, and that passion rather than intimacy and commitment is related to ZKPQ impulsivity sub-dimension.

Sy is positively correlated with Eros. This confirms Davies (1996) who reported a positive correlation with EPQ E. With regard to the Sternberg (1988) model, Eros can be interpreted as a combination of Passion and Intimacy that are frequently found with persons high on sociability (Hendrick & Hendrick 1989). Further, Eros is highly positively correlated with optimism and life satisfaction, which are characteristics found more frequently with persons with high scores on E or Sy. N-Anx and Agg-Host can be considered as factors inhibiting love relationships. Both dimensions relate to negative emotions. So it is not surprising to find them negatively correlated with Eros, but positively correlated with Mania in this study. Mania is an intense form of love or passion. Lovers are obsessed with their partner and experience an intense feeling of jealousy at the threat of loss. Persons high on Mania show a low degree of self-assurance. As interview data illustrate, two reaction patterns can appear, resignation, depression, helplessness on one hand and aggressive and hostile feelings on the other. These differences in behavior can be interpreted with regard to both of ZKPQ emotionality components, i.e. N-Anx and Agg-Host. But gender differences are also apparent: Agg-Host is more highly correlated with Mania for males ($r = 0.51$) than for females ($r = 0.15$). ZKPQ ACT also explains some differences in love styles. ACT is positively correlated with Ludus, Pragma and Mania. Sternberg's passion dimension can be interpreted as sexual urge or sexual drive or libido (cf. Eysenck 1976), which is marked in persons high on Eros, Mania and Ludus. Persons preferring Ludus as a favourite love style have to be active to realize this form of love. Observation of manic lovers shows that they are very active, but relatively unsuccessful in their relationship with partners. Interview data of subjects high on Pragma showed a high degree of commitment and engagement in different fields of their activities. Overall, the Alternative FFM provides an interesting point of departure to understand why persons differ in love behavior.

3. Conclusion

The alternative FFM does exhibit cultural universality, at least in the context of Western societies. As for contemporary personality models, the structure of the alternative FFM was replicated independently in German samples and the scales were validated with individual differences in social behavior. The findings we reported showed similar structural properties with those presented by Zuckerman *et al.* (1993). The data presented were collected in Germany with Germans and persons having immigrated to Germany from countries with different cultural backgrounds.

With regard to their origins, the EPQ superfactors and the alternative FFM emerged from psychobiological approaches to personality (Eysenck 1967; Eysenck & Eysenck 1985; Zuckerman 1983, 1991, 1993), whereas the NEO-PI (Costa & McCrae 1992b) developed from lexical analyses of trait terms in the language, i.e. a representation of personality in culture. Despite these differences in origin between the FFMs, a great deal of convergence was observed in the literature and in the present data. The results of the factor analyses support a hierarchical structure of personality dimensions, with the three EPQ superfactors, E, N, and P at the top, followed by a level of five factors for both the NEO-PI and ZKPQ. However, the results show too, that all scales and facets of the ZKPQ have specific variance. Further, correlates of the validation studies point out the usefulness of the individual facets as predictors for social behavior and the individual adaptation to the world.

References

Aron, A., & Westbay, L. (1996). Dimensions of the prototype of love. *Journal of Personality and Social Psychology*, *70*, 535–551.

Baron, R. A., & Byrne, D. (2000). *Social Psychology* (9th ed.). Boston: Allyn & Bacon.

Berry, J. W. (1997). Immigration, acculturation and adaptation. *Applied Psychology: An International Review*, *46*, 5–68.

Berry, J. W., Kalin, R., & Taylor, D. (1977). *Multiculturalism and ethnic attitudes in Canada*. Ottawa: Supply and Services.

Costa, P. T., Jr., & McCrae, R. R. (1992a). *Revised NEO personality inventory (NEO-PI-R)*. Odessa, FL: Psychological Assessment Resources.

Costa, P. T., Jr., & McCrae, R. R. (1992b). Four ways five factors are basic. *Personality and Individual Differences*, *13*, 653–665.

Davies, M. F. (1996). EPQ correlates of love styles. *Personality and Individual Differences*, *20*, 257–259.

Engel, G., Olson, K. R., & Patrick, C. (2002). The personality of love: Fundamental motives and traits related to components of love. *Personality and Individual Differences*, *32*, 839–853.

Eysenck, H. J. (1967). *The biological basis of personality*. Springfield, IL: Charles C. Thomas.

Eysenck, H. J. (1976). *Sex and personality*. London: Open Books.

Eysenck, H. J. (1992a). A reply to Costa and McCrae. P or A and C role of theory. *Personality and Individual Differences*, *13*, 867–868.

Eysenck, H. J. (1992b). Four ways five factors are not basic. *Personality and Individual Differences*, *13*, 667–673.

Eysenck, H. J., & Eysenck, M. W. (1985). *Personality and individual differences: A natural science approach*. New York: Plenum Press.

Eysenck, H. J., & Eysenck, S. B. G. (1964). *Manual of the Eysenck Personality Inventory*. London: University of London Press.

Eysenck, S. B. G., & Eysenck, H. J. (1975). *Manual of the Eysenck Personality Questionnaire*. San Diego, CA: Educational and Industrial Testing Service.

Goodwin, R., & Findlay, C. (1997). "We were just fated together" . . . Chinese love and the concept of yuan in England and Hong Kong. *Personal Relationships*, *4*, 85–92.

Gray, J. A. (1982). *The neuropsychology of anxiety: An enquiry into the septo-hippocampal system*. New York: Oxford University Press.

Guilford, J. P. (1975). Factors and factors of personality. *Psychological Bulletin*, *82*, 802–814.

Guilford, J. P. (1977). Will the real factor of extroversion-introversion please stand up! A reply to to Eysenck. *Psychological Bulletin*, *84*, 412–416.

Guilford, J. P., & Zimmerman, W. S. (1956). Fourteen dimensional temperament factors. *Psychological Monographs*, *70*, 1–26.

Guilford, J. S., Zimmerman, W. S., & Guilford, J. P. (1976). *The Guilford-Zimmerman temperament survey handbook*. San Diego: Edits.

Hendrick, C., & Hendrick, S. S. (1986). A theory and method of love. *Journal of Personality and Social Psychology*, *50*, 392–402.

Hendrick, C., & Hendrick, S. S. (1989). Research on love: Does it measure up? *Journal of Personality and Social Psychology*, *56*, 784–794.

Hendrick, S. S., & Hendrick, C. (1987a). Love and sex attitudes and religious beliefs. *Journal of Social and Clinical Psychology*, *5*, 391–398.

Hendrick, S. S., & Hendrick, C. (1987b). Love and sexual attitudes, self-disclosure and sensation seeking. *Journal of Social and Personal Relationships*, *4*, 281–297.

Hendrick, S. S., & Hendrick, C. (1987c). Multidimensionality of sexual attitudes. *Journal of Sex Research*, *23*, 502–526.

Hendrick, S. S., Hendrick, C., & Adler, N. L. (1988). Romantic relationships: Love, satisfaction, and staying together. *Journal of Personality and Social Psychology*, *54*, 980–988.

Lasswell, T. E., & Lasswell, M. E. (1976). I love you but I'm not in love with you. *Journal of Marriage and the Family*, *38*, 211–224.

Lee, J. A. (1973). *The colors of love: An exploration of the ways of loving*. Don Mills, Canada: New Press.

Lee, J. A. (1977). A typology of styles of loving. *Personality and Social Psychology Bulletin*, *3*, 173–182.

Lee, J. A. (1988). Love-styles. In: R. J. Sternberg, & M. L. Barnes (Eds), *The psychology of love* (pp. 38–67). New Haven, CT: Yale University Press.

Lester, D., & Philbrick, J. (1988). Correlates of styles of love. *Personality and Individual Differences*, *9*, 689–690.

Mallandain, I., & Davies, M. F. (1994). The colours of love: Personality correlates of love style. *Personality and Individual Differences*, *17*, 557–560.

Richardson, D. R., Medvin, N., & Hammock, G. (1988). Love styles, relationship experience, and sensation seeking: A test of validity. *Personality and Individual Differences, 9*, 645–651.

Rokeach, M. (1960). *The open and closed mind*. New York: Basic Books.

Schmitz, P. G. (1992). *Basic dimensions project report Number 1*. Bonn.

Schmitz, P. G. (1994a). Personnalité et acculturation [Personality and acculturation]. *Cahiers Internationaux de Psychologie Sociale, 24*, 33–53.

Schmitz, P. G. (1994b). Se puede generalizar el modelo de culturacion de John Berry [Can John Berry's model of acculturation be generalized?]. *Revista de Psicologia Social y Personalidad, 10*, 17–35.

Schmitz, P. G. (1994c). *Basic dimensions project report Number 2*. Bonn.

Schmitz, P. G. (1995/1996). Personalidade e processos de adaptação cultural [Personality and processes of cultural adaptation]. *Revista Portuguesa de Psicologia, 31*, 37–59.

Schmitz, P. G. (1999). *Basic dimensions project report Number 4*. Bonn.

Schmitz, P. G. (2002). Por qué son los estilos de amor tan diferentes? [Why are love styles so varying?]. Presentation at the IV Congreso Internacional de la Sociedad Espanola para el Estudio de la Ansiedad y el Estrés. Benidorm, September.

Schmitz, P. G. (2003). Psychosocial factors of immigration and emigration: An introduction. In: L. Loeb Adler, & U. P. Gielen (Eds), *Immigration and emigration in international perspective* (pp. 23–50). Westport, CT: Praeger.

Sternberg, R. J. (1986). A triangular theory of love. *Psychological Review, 93*, 119–135.

Sternberg, R. J. (1988). *The triangle of love*. New York: Basic Books.

Valzelli, L. (1981). *Psychobiology of aggression and violence*. New York: Raven Press.

Wan, W. W. N., Luk, C.-L., & Lai, J. C. L. (2000). Personality correlates of loving styles among Chinese students in Hong Kong. *Personality and Individual Differences, 29*, 169–175.

Woll, S. B. (1989). Personality and relationship correlates of loving styles. *Journal of Research in Personality, 23*, 480–505.

Zuckerman, M. (1983). *Biological bases of sensation seeking, impulsivity and anxiety*. Hillsdale, NJ: Erlbaum.

Zuckerman, M. (1991). *Psychobiology of personality*. New York: Cambridge University Press.

Zuckerman, M. (1993). Personality from top (traits) to bottom (genetics) with stops at each level between. In: J. Hettema, & I. J. Deary (Eds), *Foundations of personality* (pp. 73–100). Dordrecht, Netherlands: Kluwer.

Zuckerman, M. (1994). *Behavioral expressions and biosocial bases of sensation seeking*. Cambridge: Cambridge University Press.

Zuckerman, M. (2002). Zuckerman-Kuhlman Personality Questionnaire (ZKPQ): An alternative five-factorial model. In: B. De Raad, & M. Perugini (Eds), *Big five assessment* (pp. 377–396). Göttingen: Hogrefe & Huber.

Zuckerman, M., Kuhlman, D., Thornquist, M., & Kiers, H. (1991). Five (or three) robust questionnaire scale factors of personality without culture. *Personality and Individual Differences, 12*, 929–941.

Zuckerman, M., Kuhlman, D. M., & Camac, C. (1988). What lies beyond E and N? Factor analyses of scales believed to measure basic dimensions of personality. *Journal of Personality and Social Psychology, 54*, 96–107.

Zuckerman, M., Kuhlman, D. M., Joireman, J., Teta, P., & Kraft, M. (1993). A comparison of three structural the big five, and the alternative five. *Journal of Personality and Social Psychology, 65*, 757–768.

Chapter 6

Investigating the ZKPQ-III-R: Psychometric Properties, Relations to the Five-Factor Model, and Genetic and Environmental Influences on its Scales and Facets

A. Angleitner, R. Riemann and F. M. Spinath

1. Introduction

In this chapter, psychometric aspects of the Zuckerman-Kuhlman Personality Questionnaire (ZKPQ; Zuckerman *et al.* 1993) and the joint factor structure of the ZKPQ, the NEO-PI-R (Costa & McCrae 1992), and the Sensation Seeking Scales (SSS; Zuckerman 1979) are examined in two samples. In one sample, peer-report data was collected in addition to self-report data. Our analyses yield good reliability estimates for self- and peer-report versions of the ZKPQ and a high agreement between self and peer reports on the ZKPQ scales. Factor analyses show that all three instruments capture highly overlapping dimensions of individual differences. In a sample of 338 pairs of adult twins reared together, we analyse the genetic architecture of the ZKPQ scales. A simple additive genetic model best explains the individual differences in most ZKPQ scales. Between 51 and 43% of the total variance is attributable to genetic factors.

The development of the alternative Five-Factor Model (FFM) is only one of Marvin Zuckerman's many contributions to the study of individual differences. The alternative FFM is deeply rooted in a thorough analysis of factor analytic models of personality, temperament theories, and psychobiological research. It aims at a comprehensive description of personality and integrates several temperament traits, most notably sensation seeking and impulsivity, "in the broader family of traits" (Zuckerman 2002: 393). In contrast to the classic FFMs (e.g. Costa & McCrae 1992; Goldberg 1990), Zuckerman's approach closely links personality description and measurement to the question of the etiological homogeneity of broad personality dimensions. Thus, *alternative* does not primarily indicate that Zuckerman's model captures another personality sphere, but conveys the idea that the

On the Psychobiology of Personality
Edited by R. M. Stelmack

ISBN: 0-08-044209-9

basic dimensions should be etiologically homogenous. This approach can be developed by going beyond the analysis of phenotypic correlations. Studies of associations between personality traits and biological traits, as well as multivariate behavioral genetic analyses that identify traits with a common genetic basis, are important tools in pursuing this goal.

The first part of this chapter focuses on psychometric aspects of the ZKPQ, the standard instrument developed for the assessment of Zuckerman's alternative FFM. In a study using self- and peer-report data, the reliability and validity of the ZKPQ is examined. In addition, new factor analytic results clarifying the joint factor structure of the NEO-PI-R (Costa & McCrae 1992) and ZKPQ-scales are presented.

In the second part of this chapter, we provide the first quantitative genetic results from the Bielefeld Longitudinal Study of Adult Twins (BiLSAT; Spinath *et al.* 2002) that address the etiology of the measured constructs.

1.1. The Alternative Five-Factor Model

Zuckerman *et al.* (1988) and Zuckerman *et al.* (1991) aimed at integrating the SSS into a broader model of personality that they labeled the alternative FFM. On a rational basis, the authors selected scales from eight inventories including, for example, the Eysenck Personality Questionnaire (EPQ; Eysenck & Eysenck 1975); the Emotionality, Activity, Socability Inventory scales (Buss & Plomin 1984); and the Personality Research Form (Jackson 1974) representing nine domains they considered to be important and of relevance for temperament and personality. These domains were activity, sociability, impulsivity, socialization, sensation seeking, and emotionality (general, anxiety, hostility). Forty-six scales, including a scale to measure socially desirable responding, were selected and used in an exploratory factor analysis. Solutions with three factors, as well as five and seven factors, were inspected. Finally, the five-factor solution was considered to be the most robust and best interpretable solution. Four factors were labeled Activity (ACT), Neuroticism-Anxiety (N-Anx), Sociability (Sy), Impulsive Unsocialized Sensation Seeking (ImpUSS). A fifth factor was first termed Aggressive Sensation Seeking factor and later re-labeled to Aggression-Hostility (Agg-Host). In this five-factor solution, the four SSS scales showed loadings on the following factors: Experience Seeking (ES) and Thrill and Adventure Seeking (TAS) loaded on the ImpUSS factor, Disinhibition (DIS) and Boredom Susceptibility (BS) showed loadings on the Aggressive Sensation Seeking factor. Recently, this pattern was replicated in a German study aimed at testing the construct validity of the German SSS-V (Beauducel *et al.* 1999).

1.2. The Construction of the Zuckerman-Kuhlman Personality Questionnaire (ZKPQ)

Zuckerman *et al.* (1993) constructed ZKPQ as a measure for the alternative FFM. As an initial step for the item selection, factor scores were computed, using the data of the Zuckerman *et al.* (1991) study, and correlated with each item used in that study. With the exception of the EPQ items, all items were correlated with the factor scores in the total sample and the best 20 items were selected for each factor according to the following criteria: (1) the item correlated highest with the respective factor; (2) it showed only small correlations with other factors; and (3) it showed negligible correlations with Social Desirability as measured by the Crowne-Marlowe Social Desirability Scale (Crowne & Marlowe 1960). Next, many items were rewritten to complete the ZKPQ-II which consisted of a total of 100 items. Using another large sample of 589 subjects to test the factor structure of the inventory, a clear five-factor structure was found. Only 11 items failed to show clear loadings on the predicted factor. These items were eliminated which resulted in the ZKPQ-III containing 89 items. Because the existing Sy items deviated from normality, new Sy items were written and an additional ten items were constructed for measuring careless responding (Infrequency). The final questionnaire was re-labeled ZKPQ-III-R.

1.3. ZKPQ-III-R

The ZKPQ-III-R, with 99 items in its long form, shows satisfactory internal consistencies. Cronbach's Alpha for the five domain scales varied between 0.74 (ACT) and 0.82 (N-Anx) for males and between 0.76 (Agg-Host) and 0.84 (N-Anx) for females in the American sample. Similarly, N-Anx yielded the highest internal consistency in different language adaptations including the Spanish version (Gutiérrez-Zotes *et al.* 2001; Romero *et al.* 2002), the German adaptation (Ostendorf & Angleitner 1994), the Japanese (Shiomi *et al.* 1995) and the Chinese translations (Wu *et al.* 2000). Somewhat lower reliabilities were reported in the above mentioned studies for the domain scales Agg-Host and ACT.

In the following, we provide short descriptions of the ZKPQ-III-R scales and facets according to Zuckerman (2002: 382–383):

(1) Impulsive Sensation Seeking (ImpSS) is defined by two facets: (1) Impulsivity, denoting "a lack of planning and a tendency to act quickly on impulse without thinking;" and (2) Sensation Seeking, illustrating "a general need for thrills and excitement, a preference for unpredictable situations and friends, and the need for change and novelty."
(2) Neuroticism-Anxiety (N-Anx) describes "emotional upset, tension, worry, fearfulness, obsessive indecision, lack of self-confidence, and sensitivity to criticism."
(3) Aggression-Hostility (Agg-Host) depicts "readiness to express verbal aggression, rude, thoughtless or antisocial behavior, vengefulness, spitefulness, a quick temper and impatience with others."
(4) Activity (ACT) is differentiated into two aspects representing: (1) "the need for general activity and impatience and restlessness when there is nothing to do;" and (2) "need for work activity and a preference for challenging and hard work" and "a lot of energy for work and other tasks."
(5) Sociability (Sy) also consists of two facets: (1) Parties and Friends, "a liking of big parties, interacting with many people and having many friends;" and (2) intolerance for social isolation.
(6) The Infrequency scale described earlier is used to detect socially desirable responding. For convenience, we will use the shortened label ZKPQ to refer to the ZKPQ-III-R.

Studies investigating the convergent validity of the ZKPQ with other personality systems, such as the EPQ or the NEO-PI model (McCrae & Costa 1996), have documented the correspondence of the ZKPQ Sy and ZKPQ ACT with Extraversion (E). ZKPQ N-Anx correlates with Neuroticism (N), and the ZKPQ Agg-Host scale with Agreeableness (A) in McCrae and Costa's system. The ZKPQ ImpSS domain shows correspondence with EPQ Psychoticism (P) and negative associations with Conscientiousness (C) in the NEO-PI model (Zuckerman 2002). In a study in which different instruments proposed to measure the classic five factors, N, E, Openness to Experience (O), A and C were used, Ostendorf and Angleitner (1994) analyzed the joint structure of the NEO-PI-R (Costa & McCrae 1992), the PPQ (Kline & Lapham 1990), a set of 179 bipolar rating scales (Ostendorf 1990), and the ZKPQ (Zuckerman *et al.* 1993). A principal component analysis of the scales revealed that the ZKPQ does not cover the O domain and that the ZKPQ ACT scale relates more strongly to C in comparison to its proposed loading on E. This may mainly be due to the Need for Work Activity facet of the ACT scale. Furthermore, ImpSS loaded highest on the E factor and had a negative loading on C and a small to moderate loading on O.

1.4. Genetics of Sensation Seeking

To our knowledge, there are no published studies on the etiology of the ZKPQ scales. Because the ZKPQ is partly based on the SSS, we briefly review behavior genetic studies on the SSS here. Zuckerman (1979, 1994) suggests an innate biological basis for impulsivity and sensation seeking. Some earlier studies confirm that besides relations of sensation seeking with gonadal hormone levels (Daitzman *et al.* 1978) and levels of platelet monoamine oxydase (Schooler *et al.* 1978), sensation seeking may have a genetic basis. The total SSS as well as the four subscales TAS, DIS, ES and BS are moderately heritable (Fulker *et al.* 1980). In a study with adolescent twins, Koopmans *et al.* (1995) reported that the heritability of the subscales varied. The BS scale showed the lowest (48% for males, 54% for females) and the TAS scale the highest heritabilities (62% for males, 63% for females). Using a different study design, Hur and Bouchard (1997) replicated these moderate heritabilities by analyzing the SSS using small samples of monozygotic (MZ) and dizygotic (DZ) twins reared apart, thereby adding further support that there is some genetic basis of sensation seeking.

2. Aims of the Present Study

(1) There is ample evidence for the internal consistency of the SSS-V and the ZKPQ scales. However, as far as we know, no study has tested the self-peer agreement as a further aspect of evaluating the reliability and validity of the scales. We will present such data on self-peer convergence and the feasibility of the ZKPQ beyond the self-report domain.

(2) As shown in the study by Ostendorf and Angleitner (1994), there are some discrepancies in the loadings of the ZKPQ ImpSS and ACT scales. We will present new factor analytic studies that contribute to a clarification of the joint factor structure of the NEO-PI-R and ZKPQ scales.

(3) Zuckerman assumes a biological basis for the ZKPQ scales. Based on our Bielefeld Longitudinal Study of Adult Twins project, we will present first results concerning the etiology of the measured constructs and estimates for genetic and environmental influences.

3. Method

3.1. Participants

The data reported here are based on two samples. The first sample consists of $n = 141$ students of the Universities of Bielefeld and Jena (36 males, 105 females, age range: 18–59 years). The second sample is part of the BiLSAT project (see Spinath *et al.* 2002, for a more detailed description). In the third wave of the BiLSAT data collection (2000), 225 MZ twin pairs and 86 same-sex and 27 opposite-sex DZ twin pairs completed the ZKPQ-III-R. Zygosity was determined using a self-report questionnaire concerning physical similarity (Oniszczenko *et al.* 1993). The age of the twins in this sample varied between 21 and 75 years.

3.2. Measures

The Bielefeld-Jena sample was given the authorized German adaptations of the following instruments: ZKPQ (Zuckerman *et al.* 1993), NEO-PI-R (Costa & McCrae 1992; Ostendorf & Angleitner 2004) and the SSS-V (Zuckerman *et al.* 1978; German adaptation by Beauducel *et al.* 1999). Peer-report forms for these inventories were available and subjects were instructed to ask a good friend or relative to describe him or her on the peer-report forms of the tests. In the BiLSAT sample, the ZKPQ (self-report) and the NEO-PI-R (self- and peer-report forms) were included in the test battery that was mailed to the twins.

3.3. Behavior Genetic Analyses

It has been demonstrated that the effects of age and sex can bias heritability estimates (McGue & Bouchard 1984). Therefore, age- and sex-corrected scores were computed by regressing the personality scores of the twins on their age and sex. These standardized residuals were used in all correlation analyses as well as in the univariate structural equation analyses.

Genetic and environmental influences on phenotypic individual differences were estimated using maximum-likelihood model fitting. Goodness-of-fit indices and parameter estimates were obtained using the structural equation modeling software package Mx (Neale *et al.* 2002). Three sources of variance were considered in the analyses: (1) additive genetic effects at multiple loci (A); (2) environmental effects shared by twins (C); and (3) non-shared environmental influences and error variance (E). If twin similarities indicated the absence of shared environmental influences, an alternative ADE model was applied substituting the shared environmental parameter C with a parameter D modeling non-additive genetic dominance effects. Following the procedure described in detail by Neale and Cardon (1992), the following hypotheses were tested: (1) the data do not indicate any family resemblance (E model); (2) family resemblance is accounted for by additive genetic effects (AE model); (3) family resemblance is accounted for by environmental influences shared by twins (CE model); and (4) family resemblance is accounted for by additive genetic and shared environmental influences (ACE model). It was then tested whether the full ACE model fitted the data significantly better than the reduced model (AE or CE), using χ^2-difference likelihood-ratio tests. Among competing reduced models, we preferred the one with the lower Akaike Information Criterion value (AIC $= \chi^2 - 2$df; Akaike 1987). We followed the same rationale when D was tested instead of C.

4. Results

4.1. Psychometric properties of the ZKPQ and SSS-V scales

We will first report psychometric information on the ZKPQ and the SSS-V scales and the self-peer agreement based on the Bielefeld-Jena sample.

Table 1 documents, for the first time, that both the self- and the peer-report form of the ZKPQ showed satisfactory psychometric properties. Furthermore, there was a good correspondence between self-reports and acquaintance ratings. In both samples, the highest reliabilities were found for the scales N-Anx and ImpSS. The validity of the scales is good given that peer reports were available from a single peer. Self-peer agreement was highest for Sy ($r = 0.62$) and lowest for N-Anx ($r = 0.44$). The internal consistency estimates were replicable across different samples as indicated in Table 2. Table 3 gives comparable information for the SSS-V scales.

In the self-report form, internal consistency estimates of the SSS-V were somewhat lower than those for the ZKPQ scales. However, the peer-report form showed slightly better values. With the exception of the BS scale, high agreement between self and peer reports was also found for the SSS-V. The DIS and ES, as well as the total SSS score showed very high self-peer agreement.

4.2. The Factor Structure of the ZKPQ and the SSS-V Scales

In order to clarify some discrepancies in the loadings of the ZKPQ scales in the FFM, we used the following procedure. First, separate principal component analyses (PCA) were performed based on the 30 NEO-PI-R facet scales for self as well as for peer reports. The eigenvalues indicated a clear five-factor structure. The five factors were extracted, varimax rotated, and factor scores were derived. These NEO-PI-R factor scores were subsequently used for the factor analyses with the ZKPQ scales. Two analyses were run. For the Bielefeld-Jena sample, self and peer reports of the ZKPQ together with the NEO-PI-R self- and peer-report factor scores were factor analyzed. Several criteria for factor extraction converged

Table 1: Means, standard deviations, Cronbach's alphas, and self-peer agreement for ZKPQ domain and facet scales ($n = 141$, Bielefeld-Jena sample).

Scale	Self		Peer		Self Alpha	Peer Alpha	Self-Peer Agreement
	Mean	S.D.	Mean	S.D.			
Sociability	8.01	3.57	8.73	3.80	0.78	0.81	0.62**
Parties and Friends	3.06	2.15	3.54	2.16	0.73	0.71	0.63**
Isolation/Intolerance	4.96	2.25	5.21	2.33	0.74	0.78	0.54**
Impulsive Sensation Seeking	8.36	4.36	6.92	4.02	0.83	0.80	0.50**
Sensation Seeking	5.55	2.87	4.57	3.00	0.79	0.81	0.48**
Impulsivity	2.83	2.22	2.42	2.01	0.74	0.70	0.44**
Activity	8.33	3.43	8.96	3.69	0.74	0.78	0.56**
General Activity	3.21	2.31	3.48	2.61	0.71	0.78	0.55**
Work Effort	5.12	1.73	5.50	1.80	0.53	0.62	0.48**
Neuroticism-Anxiety	8.98	5.11	7.18	4.62	0.88	0.85	0.44**
Aggression-Hostility	7.51	3.24	6.84	3.54	0.72	0.77	0.57**
Infrequency	1.53	1.47	2.39	1.72	0.52	0.55	0.08

** $p < 0.01$ (two-tailed).

Table 2: Means, standard deviations, and Cronbach's alphas for ZKPQ domain and facet scales ($n = 844$; BiLSAT sample).

Scale	Self		Self Alpha
	Mean	S.D.	
Sociability	7.27	3.53	0.78
Parties and friends	2.61	2.02	0.71
Isolation/Intolerance	4.66	2.17	0.70
Impulsive sensation seeking	6.62	3.99	0.80
Sensation seeking	3.79	2.73	0.78
Impulsivity	2.83	2.03	0.68
Activity	9.20	3.76	0.78
General activity	3.98	2.63	0.78
Work effort	5.20	1.89	0.63
Neuroticism-anxiety	6.47	4.80	0.87
Aggression-hostility	6.58	3.26	0.75
Infrequency	1.78	1.56	0.53

on a clear five-factor solution. The varimax rotated factors explained 67.2% of the variance. The result of this analysis is given in Table 4. The ZKPQ scale N-Anx corresponds well with the Neuroticism domain of the NEO-PI-R. ZKPQ Sociability matches with NEO-PI-R E, Agg-Host corresponds with the negative pole of A in the FFM and ZKPQ ACT relates

Table 3: Means, standard deviations, and Cronbach's alphas in the self- and peer-report forms, and self-peer agreement for the SSS-V Scales ($n = 141$; Bielefeld-Jena sample).

Scale	Self		Peer		Self Alpha	Peer Alpha	Self-Peer Agreement
	Mean	S.D.	Mean	S.D.			
Thrill and Adventure Seeking (TAS)	5.42	2.62	4.47	3.10	0.73	0.83	0.58^{**}
Experience Seeking (ES)	6.37	1.85	5.45	2.00	0.53	0.57	0.67^{**}
Disinhibition (DIS)	4.30	2.47	3.67	2.65	0.71	0.78	0.69^{**}
Boredom Susceptibility (BS)	3.43	1.80	3.26	1.79	0.42	0.40	0.31^{**}
Total Sensation Seeking Score (SSS TOT)	19.56	6.05	16.61	6.63	0.79	0.83	0.68^{**}

$^{**}p < 0.01$ (two-tailed).

Table 4: Factor structure of the NEO-PI-R factor scores of the self- and peer-report forms and the ZKPQ domain scales (self and peer report) in the Bielefeld-Jena sample ($n = 141$).

NEO-PI-R Factor Scores	**N**	**E**	**O**	**A**	**C**	**h²**
S – N	**0.84**	−0.02	0.04	−0.07	−0.02	0.71
P – N	**0.85**	0.07	0.09	0.04	−0.02	0.73
S – E	0.07	**0.83**	0.02	0.11	0.02	0.70
P – E	−0.07	**0.85**	−0.03	−0.08	0.11	0.76
S – O	0.04	−0.07	**0.79**	0.16	0.13	0.67
P – O	0.11	0.00	**0.79**	0.09	0.02	0.65
S – A	0.10	−0.18	−0.08	**0.81**	−0.06	0.70
P – A	0.07	0.07	−0.08	**0.84**	−0.08	0.73
S – C	0.06	−0.12	−0.15	0.07	**0.77**	0.63
P – C	0.10	−0.14	−0.17	0.05	**0.81**	0.72
ZKPQ — Scales						
S – Sy	0.03	**0.81**	0.02	−0.15	0.05	0.68
P – Sy	0.00	**0.81**	0.11	−0.12	−0.06	0.68
S – ImpSS	−0.06	**0.50**	**0.60**	−0.19	−0.19	0.69
P – ImpSS	−0.20	**0.35**	**0.50**	−0.20	−0.30	0.55
S – ACT	−0.11	0.14	0.20	−0.03	**0.69**	0.55
P – ACT	−0.13	0.21	0.12	0.08	**0.68**	0.55
S – N-ANX	**0.84**	−0.08	0.09	0.10	−0.04	0.72
P – N-ANX	**0.80**	0.04	0.02	−0.16	0.01	0.66
S – AGG-HOST	0.18	0.12	−0.17	**−0.76**	−0.09	0.67
P – AGG-HOST	0.25	0.07	−0.15	**−0.77**	−0.10	0.68
Eigenvalues	3.15	3.81	2.41	2.37	1.69	

Note: All loadings >0.30 are listed in bold. 67.2% variance explained. S = Self-Report; P = Peer-Report. Scale abbreviations: N = Neuroticism; E = Extraversion; O = Openness to Experience; A = Agreeableness; C = Conscientiousness; Sy = Sociability; ImpSS = Impulsive Sensation Seeking; ACT = Activity; N-ANX=Neuroticism-Anxiety; AGG-HOST = Aggression-Hostility.

strongly to C. The ImpSS scale of the ZKPQ, however, is factorial complex and shows relations to the E and the O domains of comparable magnitude. This result is not in line with earlier studies (Aluja *et al.* 2002; Ostendorf & Angleitner 1994; Zuckerman 2002), in which ImpSS showed a higher negative association with the C domain.

To test the robustness of the factor structure, we performed a second PCA using the factor scores of the self- and peer-report forms of the NEO-PI-R and the scale values of the ZKPQ self reports from the BiLSAT sample. Members of twin pairs were entered as single subjects ($n = 839$). The varimax-rotated five-factor solution that explains 70.5% of the variance is presented in Table 5.

Table 5: Factor structure of the NEO-PI-R factor scores of the self- and peer-report forms and the ZKPQ domain scales (self report) in the BiLSAT sample ($n = 839$).

NEO-PI-R Factor Scores	N	E	O	A	C	h^2
S – N	**0.92**	−0.04	−0.04	−0.02	−0.05	0.86
P – N	**0.76**	−0.02	0.02	0.06	0.04	0.58
S – E	0.01	**0.89**	−0.04	−0.14	−0.05	0.82
P – E	0.02	**0.78**	0.02	0.10	0.04	0.63
S – O	0.01	0.02	**0.88**	−0.03	0.03	0.77
P – O	0.03	−0.06	**0.85**	0.07	−0.03	0.73
S – A	0.04	0.14	0.02	**0.87**	0.02	0.78
P – A	0.07	−0.05	−0.04	**0.77**	−0.10	0.62
S – C	0.05	0.02	−0.09	−0.06	**0.88**	0.78
P – C	0.01	−0.15	0.04	−0.05	**0.79**	0.66
ZKPQ – Scales						
Sociability	−0.04	**0.81**	−0.02	0.08	0.05	0.67
Impulsive SS	−0.10	**0.59**	**0.40**	**−0.33**	−0.22	0.67
Activity	−0.25	0.24	0.20	−0.08	**0.63**	0.56
Neuroticism-Anxiety	**0.89**	−0.01	0.01	−0.08	−0.10	0.80
Aggression-Hostility	**0.44**	0.19	−0.09	**−0.65**	0.01	0.67
Eigenvalues before rotation	2.60	2.69	1.61	1.91	1.78	

Note: All loadings >0.30 are listed in bold. 70.6% variance explained. S = Self-Report, P = Peer-Report. Scale abbreviations: N = Neuroticism; E = Extraversion; O = Openness to Experience; A = Agreeableness; C = Conscientiousness.

Again, ImpSS replicates its associations with the domains E and O. ACT also showed associations with C. Our analyses clearly document that the ZKPQ scales can be integrated in the FFM.

To clarify the position of the SSS-V scales in the factor space, we performed another PCA based on the NEO-PI-R self- and peer-factor scores, and self- and peer-scale values of the ZKPQ and SSS-V scales (Table 6).

A clear five-factor solution resulted which was varimax rotated. The five factors explained 60.5% of the variance. Surprisingly, three of the SSS-V scales, TAS, DIS, ES, showed their highest loadings on O. The BS scale exhibited strong relations to the negative pole of A.

4.3. Genetic Analyses of the ZKPQ Scales and Facets

We calculated twin similarities (intra-class correlations) first for MZ and separately for same- and opposite-sex DZ twins from the BiLSAT sample. Because similarity coefficients for the latter two groups did not differ significantly, we combined the data for subsequent analyses into a single DZ group.

Table 6: Factor structure of the NEO-PI-R factor scores of the self- and peer-report forms and the ZKPQ domain scales and SSS-V (self and peer report) in the Bielefeld-Jena sample (n = 141).

NEO-PI-R Factor Scores	**N**	**E**	**O**	**A-**	**C**	**h²**
S – N	**0.84**	−0.02	0.00	0.07	−0.02	0.70
P – N	**0.84**	0.10	−0.13	−0.02	−0.04	0.73
S – E	0.05	**0.81**	0.09	−0.13	0.03	0.69
P – E	−0.07	**0.86**	0.03	0.06	0.09	0.75
S – O	0.08	−0.12	**0.71**	−0.12	0.26	0.60
P – O	0.15	−0.04	**0.67**	−0.07	0.15	0.51
S – A	0.06	−0.18	−0.03	**−0.81**	−0.06	0.69
P – A	0.04	0.05	0.00	**−0.81**	−0.07	0.67
S – C	0.06	−0.09	−0.22	0.04	**0.70**	0.55
P – C	0.10	−0.14	−0.20	−0.05	**0.78**	0.68
ZKPQ — Scales						
S – Sy	0.04	**0.80**	0.05	0.15	0.08	0.68
P – Sy	0.01	**0.79**	0.16	0.13	−0.07	0.67
S – ImpSS	−0.04	**0.45**	**0.62**	0.24	−0.10	0.66
P – ImpSS	−0.18	0.34	**0.52**	0.25	−0.26	0.55
S – ACT	−0.11	0.15	0.10	0.05	**0.69**	0.52
P – ACT	−0.13	0.20	0.08	−0.05	**0.69**	0.54
S – N–ANX	**0.83**	−0.09	0.09	−0.08	−0.02	0.71
P – N–ANX	**0.80**	0.07	−0.03	0.10	−0.02	0.66
S – AGG – HOST	0.19	0.16	−0.23	**0.71**	−0.11	0.63
P – AGG – HOST	0.25	0.12	−0.24	**0.67**	−0.11	0.67
SSS — V scales						
S – TAS	**−0.36**	0.19	**0.51**	−0.02	−0.02	0.43
P – TAS	**−0.39**	**0.32**	**0.42**	−0.03	−0.12	0.45
S – DIS	−0.02	0.23	**0.58**	0.29	−0.29	0.55
P – DIS	−0.02	0.23	**0.48**	**0.32**	**−0.41**	0.55
S – ES	−0.14	0.08	**0.80**	0.00	−0.09	0.68
P – ES	−0.01	0.05	**0.77**	−0.08	−0.27	0.67
S – BS	−0.09	−0.01	0.21	**0.62**	0.09	0.44
P – BS	−0.01	−0.09	**0.31**	**0.50**	−0.17	0.38
Eigenvalues	2.61	3.62	5.73	2.90	2.08	

Note: All loadings >0.30 are listed in bold. 60.5% variance explained. S = Self-Report; P = Peer-Report. Scale abbreviations: N = Neuroticism; E = Extraversion; O = Openness to Experience; A = Agreeableness; C = Conscientiousness; Sy = Sociability; ImpSS = Impulsive Sensation Seeking; ACT = Activity; N-ANX = Neuroticism-Anxiety; AGG-HOST = Aggression-Hostility; TAS = Thrill and Adventure Seeking; DIS = Disinhibition; ES = Experience Seeking; BS = Boredom Susceptibility.

Table 7: Twin similarities (intra-class correlations) and confidence intervals for ZKPQ scales and facets in the BiLSAT sample.

Scales *n* (Pairs)	MZ (223–225)	DZ (113)
Sociability	0.51 (0.41–0.60)	0.27 (0.09–0.44)
Facet: Parties & Friends	0.47 (0.36–0.57)	0.23 (0.05–0.40)
Facet: Isolation Intolerance	0.50 (0.39–0.59)	0.27 (0.09–0.43)
Impulsive Sensation Seeking	0.42 (0.30–0.52)	0.30 (0.12–0.46)
Facet: Sensation Seeking	0.46 (0.35–0.55)	0.20 (0.02–0.37)
Facet: Impulsivity	0.23 (0.11–0.35)	0.34 (0.16–0.49)
Activity	0.48 (0.37–0.57)	0.29 (0.12–0.45)
Neuroticism-anxiety	0.42 (0.31–0.53)	0.09 (−0.10–0.27)
Aggression-hostility	0.46 (0.36–0.56)	0.22 (0.04–0.39)
Facet: General activity	0.45 (0.34–0.55)	0.24 (0.06–0.41)
Facet: Work effort	0.36 (0.24–0.47)	0.26 (0.08–0.42)
Infrequency	0.36 (0.24–0.47)	−0.01 (−0.19–0.17)

Note: Same- and opposite-sex DZ twins were combined prior to the analyses.

Table 7 shows that MZ twin similarity exceeded DZ twin similarity for all ZKPQ scales and facets except for the facet Impulsivity. The average MZ correlation across the five content scales reached 0.46 whereas the average DZ correlation was 0.23 indicating moderate to substantial genetic influences as well as substantial environmental influences of the non-shared variety. Even the Infrequency scale showed a pattern of higher MZ (0.36) compared to DZ (−0.01) correlations, although the absolute magnitude of similarity coefficients for this scale was lower than for most of the content scales.

Results from univariate genetic analyses reported in Table 8 include both fit indices and parameter estimates for the full ACE or ADE model as well as for the best fitting reduced model (typically, the AE model). Because the power of our sample was too low to obtain significantly better fit for the full model compared to the reduced models, we decided to present both results in order to provide the reader with the complete picture of findings.

The pattern of twin similarities reported earlier suggested additive genetic influences and non-shared environmental influences for most scales which is mirrored in the last four columns of Table 8. For 11 out of 13 content scales and facets, an AE reduced model provided the best fit with an average heritability of $a^2 = 0.46$ across scales, which means that almost half of the total variance was accounted for by additive genetic effects. The parameter estimates reported for the full model show that c^2 (shared environmental influences) and d^2 (genetic dominance) estimates were not only not statistically significant (their confidence intervals always included zero) but their absolute magnitude was small. The only exceptions to this rule were Impulsivity with regard to c^2,

Table 8: Univariate genetic analyses of ZKPQ scales and facets in the BiLSAT sample: Full and reduced model.

Scales	Model Fit		Parameter Estimates for Full Models				Model Comparison/Reduced Model Fit			Parameter Estimates for Reduced Models			
	Full Model	χ^2	a^2	c^2	d^2	e^2	Best Model	LRT	AIC	a^2	c^2	d^2	e^2
Sociability	ACE	2.01 ($p = 0.57$)	0.47 (0.12–0.59)	0.04 (0.00–0.35)	–	0.49 (0.41–0.59)	AE	0.06 (n.s.)	−1.94	0.51 (0.41–0.59)	–	–	0.49 (0.41–0.59)
Facet: Parties & Friends	ADE	6.29 ($p = 0.10$)	0.47 (0.00–0.56)	0.00 (0.00–0.54)	–	0.53 (0.44–0.63)	AE	0.00 (n.s.)	−2.00	0.47 (0.37–0.56)	–	–	0.53 (0.44–0.63)
Facet: Isolation Intolerance	ACE	0.36 ($p = 0.95$)	0.44 (0.08–0.58)	0.05 (0.00–0.36)	–	0.51 (0.42–0.62)	AE	0.10 (n.s.)	−1.90	0.49 (0.39–0.58)	–	–	0.51 (0.42–0.61)
Impulsive Sensation Seeking	ACE	2.09 ($p = 0.55$)	0.25 (0.00–0.52)	0.16 (0.00–0.43)	–	0.58 (0.48–0.69)	AE	0.89 (n.s.)	−1.11	0.43 (0.33–0.53)	–	–	0.57 (0.47–0.67)
Facet: Sensation Seeking	ADE	0.29 ($p = 0.96$)	0.35 (0.00–0.55)	–	0.10 (0.00–0.54)	0.54 (0.45–0.65)	AE	0.08 (n.s.)	−1.92	0.45 (0.35–055)	–	–	0.55 (0.45–0.65)
Facet: Impulsivity	ACE	4.02 ($p = 0.26$)	0.00 (0.00–0.29)	0.27 (0.01–0.37)	–	0.73 (0.63–0.83)	CE	0.00 (n.s.)	−2.00	–	0.27 (0.17–0.37)	–	0.73 (0.63–0.83)
Activity	ACE	1.56 ($p = 0.67$)	0.38 (0.04–0.57)	0.09 (0.00–0.39)	–	0.52 (0.43–0.63)	AE	0.32 (n.s.)	−1.68	0.49 (0.39–0.57)	–	–	0.51 (0.43–0.61)
Neuroticism-Anxiety	ADE	0.44 ($p = 0.93$)	0.00 (0.00–0.48)	–	0.43 (0.00–0.52)	0.57 (0.48–0.68)	DE	0.00 (n.s.)	−2.00	–	–	0.43 (0.32–0.52)	0.57 (0.48–0.68)
Aggression-Hostility	ADE	1.27 ($p = 0.74$)	0.45 (0.00–0.54)	–	0.00 (0.00–0.52)	0.55 (0.46–0.65)	AE	0.00 (n.s.)	−2.00	0.45 (0.35–0.54)	–	–	0.55 (0.46–0.65)
Facet: General Activity	ACE	2.75 ($p = 0.43$)	0.47 (0.14–0.56)	0.00 (0.00–0.29)	–	0.53 (0.44–0.64)	AE	0.00 (n.s.)	−2.00	0.47 (0.37–0.56)	–	–	0.53 (0.44–0.63)
Facet: Work Effort	ACE	0.43 ($p = 0.94$)	0.25 (0.00–0.48)	0.12 (0.00–0.39)	–	0.63 (0.52–0.75)	AE	0.50 (n.s.)	−1.50	0.38 (0.27–0.48)	–	–	0.62 (0.52–0.73)
Infrequency	ADE	1.59 ($p = 0.67$)	0.00 (0.00–0.37)	–	0.35 (0.00–0.45)	0.65 (0.55–0.77)	DE	0.00 (n.s.)	−2.00	–	–	0.35 (0.23–0.45)	0.65 (0.55–0.77)

Note: Same- and opposite-sex DZ twins were combined prior to the analyses. Average a^2 in reduced AE models: 0.46. a^2 = additive genetic variance; c^2 = shared environmental variance; d^2 = non-additive genetic variance; e^2 = nonshared environmental variance. LRT = likelihood ratio test. AIC = Akaike's information criterion.

and N-Anx and Infrequency with regard to d^2. Consequently, for these three scales the best fitting reduced model was either a CE (Impulsivity) or a DE model (N-Anx, Infrequency).

Taken together, our univariate analyses showed that with the sole exception of Impulsivity, the main source for familial resemblance on the ZKPQ scales and facets was genetic in origin. Environmental influences contributed mainly to differences between individuals.

5. Discussion

As expected, our study confirmed the good psychometric properties of the ZKPQ and the SSS in two independent German samples. The internal consistency estimates in our samples closely match those reported for the American normative sample (Zuckerman 2002). Only the facet scale Need for Work Activity consistently yielded notably lower reliability estimates in our samples (0.53 in the student sample and 0.63 in the twin sample). Although these estimates are still somewhat higher than those reported by Zuckerman for a Spanish sample (0.47 for males and 0.50 for females), they indicate that the homogeneity of this facet might be improved in the German version of the ZKPQ.

In our student sample, we collected peer-reports on the ZKPQ in addition to self- reports. The reliability of the peer-report scales is highly similar to the self-report scales. The agreement between self and peer reports is surprisingly high, especially for those scales that refer to easily observable behaviors. These results clearly demonstrate the convergent validity of the ZKPQ scales across different modes of data collection.

The joint factor analysis of NEO-PI-R factor scores and the ZKPQ using self- and peer-report data indicates that both inventories capture highly overlapping dimensions. The factor analysis of NEO-PI-R self and peer reports and ZKPQ self-report data from our twin sample confirms this result. The use of more reliable factor scores from the NEO-PI-R in both analyses, and the inclusion of two NEO-PI-R measures in the second analysis, results in factors clearly interpretable as the classic five factors. Despite this bias, the commonality estimates for the ZKPQ scales are only marginally smaller than those for the NEO-PI-R factor scores, which means that the variance of both the ZKPQ scales and the NEO-PI-R are almost equally well-explained by these factors.

Our results confirm earlier factor analytic studies with respect to the strong association between E and Sy as well as the association between N and N-Anx. However, our results are at odds with the previous research for the remaining ZKPQ scales. For ImpSS, we find high loadings on E and O in both of our samples and substantially smaller (negative) loadings on A and C. Ostendorf and Angleitner (1994) reported a high association of this scale to E and a negative loading on C. Whereas, in the study of Aluja *et al.* (2002), ImpSS showed the highest loading on C with secondary loadings on E and C. ZKPQ ACT loads high on C in our study and in the Ostendorf & Angleitner (1994) study, but shows the expected association with E in Aluja *et al.* (2002). Zuckerman (2002) reported moderate correlations of ACT with the NEO-PI-R scales E (0.36) and C (0.31). In both of our samples, we find the expected negative associations between Agg-Host and A. In our twin sample, there is a substantial secondary loading on N. Although the latter association was not found by Ostendorf and Angleitner (1994) and Aluja *et al.* (2002), it is consistent with the significant correlations of this scale with N and Emotionality reported by Zuckerman (2002).

Our factor analysis of NEO-PI-R factor scores, the ZKPQ scales and the SSS demonstrates one of the reasons why the different factor analytic studies fail to converge in detail. In this analysis, the O factor is located slightly closer to SS, resulting in marginally higher loadings of ImpSS on O and smaller loadings of this scale on E. All SSS scales, most notably E S, load on O, except BS. TAS and DIS show the expected secondary loadings on E and DIS loads on the negative pole of A. BS is associated with lack of A. These results corroborate the theorizing of Zuckerman (1994). Recently, Aluja *et al.* (2003) examined the relationship between E, O, and SS. They found very similar correlations between SS and E as well as O. Their results are in line with our study in that ES is strongly related to O and the correlations of BS with both E and O are low. The TAS and DIS scales correlate slightly higher with E than with O. These differences may be attributed to the use of factor scores based on all 30 NEO-PI-R facets in our study.

Our behavioral genetic analyses support the view that all dimensions measured by the ZKPQ have a biological basis. The heritability estimates vary in the narrow range from 0.51 to 0.43. Only for the facet scale Impulsivity did we not find evidence for any genetic influence (see twin correlations in Jang *et al.* 1998, for a small genetic effect on the NEO-PI-R facet scale Impulsivity). This is surprising as Impulsivity, for example, in Gray's theory (e.g. Pickering *et al.* 1999), is regarded as strongly associated to biological traits.

Even if we consider the parameter estimates for the full model, the environment shared by twins has only a negligible effect on the dimensions measured by the ZKPQ. Experiences not shared by twins explain about the same portion of variance as genetic effects. However, we have to take into account that in our univariate analyses effects of the non-shared environment are confounded with measurement error. Although the reliability of the ZKPQ scales is good, given the length of the scales, our reliability estimates as well as the retest reliabilities reported by Zuckerman (2002) suggest that 20% of the variance in ZKPQ scores must be attributed to measurement error. This means that estimates of the true effect of environmental influences not shared by twins vary between 0.29 and 0.37.

To conclude, we consider our combination of psychometric analyses, the factor analyses of phenotypic correlations, and behavioral genetic methods a step in the direction so strongly advocated by Marvin Zuckerman. We regard our factor analytic results as promising evidence for the convergence of the classic and alternative FFM. Divergence between different studies can plausibly be explained by the inclusion of different inventories and differences between samples, e.g. general population samples vs. student samples, which result in slightly different orientations of the axis in the five-dimensional space. Marginal differences between different language versions of the inventories, and true cultural differences may complicate comparisons between studies. The behavioral genetic analyses reported here, clearly show that the scales measured by the ZKPQ have a biological basis.

The lesson to be learned from Marvin Zuckerman's outstanding research is that no single approach can answer the basic questions of the study of individual differences alone. Experimental and quasi-experimental studies of single traits elucidate the biological basis of individual differences in sometimes very narrow behavioral domains. Factor analytic studies may help to understand how these traits relate to broader systems developed to describe individual differences that are important in a cultural context. Behavior genetic research

— both quantitative and molecular genetic analyses — are closely linked to experimental approaches and help to understand single traits as well as the structure of multiple-trait concepts.

References

Akaike, H. (1987). Factor analysis and AIC. *Psychometrika, 52*, 317–332.

Aluja, A., Garcia, O., & Garcia, L. F. (2002). A comparative study of Zuckerman's three structural models for personality through the NEO-PI-R, ZKPQ-III-R, EPQ-RS and Goldberg's 50-bipolar adjectives. *Personality and Individual Differences, 33*, 713–725.

Aluja, A., Garcia, O., & Garcia, L. F. (2003). Relationship among Extraversion, Openness to Experience, and Sensation seeking. *Personality and Individual Differences, 35*, 671–680.

Beauducel, A., Brocke, B., Strobel, A., & Strobel, A. (1999). Construct validity of Sensation Seeking: A psychometric investigation. *Zeitschrift für Differentielle und Diagnostische Psychologie, 20*, 155–171.

Buss, A. H., & Plomin, R. (1984). *Temperament: Early developing personality traits.* Hillsdale, NJ: Erlbaum.

Costa, P. T., Jr., & McCrae, R. R. (1992). *NEO-PI-R. Professional manual.* Odessa, FL: Psychological Assessment Resources.

Crowne, D. P., & Marlowe, D. (1960). A new scale of social desirability independent of psychopathology. *Journal of Consulting Psychology, 24*, 349–354.

Daitzman, R. J., Zuckerman, M., Sammelwitz, P. H., & Ganjam, V. (1978). Sensation seeking and gonodal hormones. *Journal of Biosocial Science, 10*, 401–408.

Eysenck, H. J., & Eysenck, S. B. G. (1975). *Manual of the Eysenck Personality Questionnaire (Junior and Adult).* London: Hodder & Stoughton.

Fulker, D. W., Eysenck, S. B. G., & Zuckerman, M. (1980). A genetic and environmental analysis of sensation seeking. *Journal of Personality Research, 14*, 261–281.

Goldberg, L. R. (1990). An alternative 'description of personality': The big five-factor structure. *Journal of Personality and Social Psychology, 59*, 1216–1229.

Gutiérrez-Zotes, J. A., Brieva, J. A. R., & Ruiz, J. S. (2001). Development of the Spanish version of the Zuckerman-Kuhlman Personality Questionnaire (ZKPQ-III) and psychometric properties [in Spanish]. *Psiquis, 22*, 19–30.

Hur, Y., & Bouchard, T. J., Jr. (1997). The genetic correlation between impulsivity and sensation seeking traits. *Behavior Genetics, 27*, 455–463.

Jackson, D. N. (1974). *Personality Research Form Manual.* Goshen, NY: Research Psychologists Press.

Jang, K. L., McCrae, R. R., Angleitner, A., Riemann, R., & Livesley, W. J. (1998). Heritability of facet-level traits in a cross-cultural twin sample: Support for a hierarchical model of personality. *Journal of Personality and Social Psychology, 64*, 1556–1565.

Kline, P., & Lapham, S. L. (1990). *The PPQ.* London: Pychometric Systems.

Koopmans, J. R., Boomsma, D. I., Heath, A. C., & van Doornen, L. J. P. (1995). A multivariate genetic analysis of sensation seeking. *Behavior Genetics, 25*, 349–356.

McCrae, R. R., & Costa, P. T., Jr. (1996). Toward a new generation of personality theories: Theoretical contexts for the Five-Factor Model. In: J. S. Wiggins (Ed.), *The Five-Factor Model of personality* (pp. 51–87). New York: Guilford Press.

McGue, M., & Bouchard, T. J. (1984). Adjustment of twin data for the effects of age and sex. *Behavior Genetics, 14*, 325–343.

Neale, M. C., Boker, S. M., Xie, G., & Maes, H. H. (2002). *Mx: Statistical modeling* (6th ed.). VCU Box 900126, Richmond, VA 23298: Department of Psychiatry.

Neale, M. C., & Cardon, L. R. (1992). *Methodology of genetic studies of twins and families*. Dordrecht, The Netherlands: Kluwer.

Oniszczenko, W., Angleitner, A., Strelau, J., & Angert, T. (1993). *The questionnaire of twins' physical resemblance*. Unpublished report. Department of Psychology, University of Warsaw, Poland.

Ostendorf, F. (1990). *Sprache und Persönlichkeitsstruktur. Zur Validität des Fünf-Faktoren-Modells der Persönlichkeit [Language and personality structure. On the structural validity of the Five-Factor Model of personality]*. Regensburg: Roderer.

Ostendorf, F., & Angleitner, A. (1994). A comparison of different instruments proposed to measure the Big Five. *European Review of Applied Psychology*, *44*, 45–53.

Ostendorf, F., & Angleitner, A. (2004). *NEO-Persönlichkeitsinventar (revidierte Form, NEO-PI-R) nach Costa und McCrae [NEO-Personality Inventory, revised form, NEO-PI-R according to Costa and McCrae]*. Göttingen: Hogrefe & Huber.

Pickering, A. D., Corr, P. J., & Gray, J. A. (1999). Interactions and reinforcement sensitivity theory: A theoretical analysis of Rusting and Larsen (1997). *Personality and Individual Differences*, *26*, 357–365.

Romero, E., Luengo, A., Gómez-Fraguela, J. A., & Sobral, J. (2002). The structure of personality traits in adolescence: The Five-Factor Model and the Alternative Five [in Spanish]. *Psicothema*, *14*, 134–143.

Schooler, C., Zahn, T. P., Murphy, D. L., & Buchsbaum, M. S. (1978). Psychological correlates of monoamine oxidase activity in normals. *Journal of Nervous and Mental Disease*, *166*, 177–186.

Shiomi, K., Shigemori, Y., Kuhlman, D. M., Joireman, J. A., & Sato, M. (1995). Constructing and evaluating a Japanese version of the Zuckerman-Kuhlman Personality Questionnaire. *Hyogo University of Teacher Education Journal*, *15*, 1–12.

Spinath, F. M., Angleitner, A., Borkenau, P., Riemann, R., & Wolf, H. (2002). German observational study of adult twins (GOSAT): A multimodal investigation of personality, temperament and cognitive ability. *Twin Research*, *5*, 372–375.

Wu, Y. X., Wang, W., Du, W. Y., Li, J., Jiang, X. F., & Wang, Y. H. (2000). Development of a Chinese version of the Zuckerman-Kuhlman Personality Questionnaire: Reliabilities and gender/age effects. *Social Behavior and Personality*, *28*, 241–250.

Zuckerman, M. (1979). *Sensation seeking: Beyond the optimal level of arousal*. Hillsdale, NJ: Erlbaum.

Zuckerman, M. (1994). *Behavioral expressions and biosocial bases of sensation seeking*. New York: Cambridge University Press.

Zuckerman, M. (2002). Zuckerman-Kuhlman Personality Questionnaire (ZKPQ): An alternative five-factorial model. In: B. DeRaad, & M. Perugini (Eds), *Big Five assessment* (pp. 377–396). Seattle: Hogrefe & Huber Publishers.

Zuckerman, M., Eysenck, S. B. G., & Eysenck, H. J. (1978). Sensation seeking in England and America: Cross-cultural, age, and sex comparisons. *Journal of Consulting and Clinical Psychology*, *46*, 139–149.

Zuckerman, M., Kuhlman, D. M., & Camac, C. (1988). What lies beyond E and N? Factor analyses of scales believed to measure basic dimensions of personality. *Journal of Personality and Social Psychology*, *54*, 96–107.

Zuckerman, M., Kuhlman, D. M., Joireman, J., Teta, P., & Kraft, M. (1993). A comparison of three structural models of personality: The Big Three, the Big Five, and the Alternative Five. *Journal of Personality and Social Psychology*, *65*, 757–768.

Zuckerman, M., Kuhlman, D., Thornquist, M., & Kiers, H. (1991). Five (or three) robust questionnaire scale factors of personality without culture. *Personality and Individual Differences*, *12*, 929–941.

Chapter 7

How the Impulsiveness and Venturesomeness Factors Evolved after the Measurement of Psychoticism

S. B. G. Eysenck

1. Introduction

When I first started out in psychology, H. J. Eysenck (who was to become my husband) had already published the Maudsley Personality Inventory (MPI; Eysenck 1959). My first task was to simplify the wording of some of the MPI items and thus the Eysenck Personality Inventory (EPI) was born (Eysenck & Eysenck 1964). The EPI purported to measure Extraversion (E), Neuroticism (N) and a Lie (L) score to detect dissimulation. Since E and N are incredibly robust dimensions, the standardization was relatively easy, although we were greatly concerned to include as many diverse subjects (age, sex, occupations, etc.) as possible to avoid the results that were obtained, often misleading, with just a student standardization population. N presented few problems of measurement but E items split into sociability, liveliness and impulsiveness (IMP) factors. For each study we embarked on, the loadings for E consistently produced high values for sociability and liveliness items (around 0.5–0.7) while the IMP items gave equally consistent but much more modest values (0.2–0.4).

While it was possible to use the EPI to measure sociability, liveliness and IMP, there was always the impression that the first two of these were a great deal more solid and reliable than the last. However, the content of the items that comprised the IMP factor was undoubtedly measuring impulsiveness, e.g. "Do you stop and think things over before doing anything?" and "Do you often do things on the spur of the moment?" Nevertheless, it seemed to us that while this was part of the story there clearly was a lot more to it. Before, however, pursuing the question of impulsiveness at this point, a different problem arose which occupied our thoughts and subsequent research.

The measurement of E and N was satisfactory to our minds, but something was lacking in the total description of personality. That something turned out undoubtedly to be

On the Psychobiology of Personality
Edited by R. M. Stelmack

ISBN: 0-08-044209-9

psychoticism (P) and it fell to me to try to adequately measure this in questionnaire form. Here was a problem indeed! It soon became obvious that one of the key features of P was uncooperativeness. How then, can you obtain replies from those subjects who would score highly on P when they are the very ones who would not co-operate and would likely decline to complete your questionnaire? Moreover, if they did complete the inventory their manipulativeness might tempt them to mislead.

2. Development of the Psychoticism Scale

From 1963, we produced one version of the P scale after another until the EPQ was standardised in 1975 (Eysenck & Eysenck 1968a, b, 1969, 1971, 1972, 1975, 1976). Even then, the fact that high P scorers tended to "bin" our questionnaire rather than help our research, meant that the scale constantly came out J shaped. In 1991, this problem was improved with the Eysenck Personality Scales (Eysenck & Eysenck 1991) in which the P scale was lengthened and some of its more aggravating statistical weaknesses were addressed (Eysenck *et al.* 1985a).

Meanwhile, the addition of the P scale clarified the position of impulsiveness. Factor analysis of P scale items plus the usual N and E items revealed that most, though not all, P items now switched from E to P. At last IMP items had consistently high loadings on this new scale, although there were still some loadings on E and some on N. Thorough research was needed and the conclusion that we came to at this point was that the EPQ could not deal adequately with the measurement of impulsiveness. Reluctantly, it was decided to construct an entirely new questionnaire for the measurement of impulsiveness.

3. Development of the Impulsiveness Questionnaire

3.1. Impulsiveness, Sensation Seeking and Venturesomeness

Again, we produced several preliminary versions of the impulsiveness questionnaire from 1977 to 1985 (Eysenck & Eysenck 1977, 1978, 1980) when the final version was published (Eysenck *et al.* 1985b). At first, factor analysis suggested that impulsiveness broke down into four factors, i.e. narrow IMP, Risk taking, Non-planning and Liveliness. These factors were positively correlated with each other and also with Sociability to varying degrees (Eysenck & Eysenck 1977).

The next question that arose was the relation of sensation seeking to impulsiveness. Where, we wondered, would this sensation seeking concept (Zuckerman 1979) fit into our personality system? Fortunately, Marvin Zuckerman visited our department at this crucial time and we were able to instigate a joint research to clarify the position of sensation seeking with respect to impulsiveness (Eysenck & Zuckerman 1978). Hence, we ran a factor analysis of both sets of items, the result of which gave us a surprisingly simple solution. There were two clearly distinct factors, one containing IMP items and the other composed of risk taking and sensation seeking items. We, therefore, called these factors IMP and Venturesomeness, respectively.

Because both of these factors were composed of seemingly similar items content-wise, it was deemed desirable to introduce a third factor whose questions would be regarded as buffer items. Rather than introducing haphazard items, we decided to use an empathy scale (Mehrabian & Epstein 1972) which subsequently proved to be a very useful adjunct to our questionnaire. By 1978, a 63-item impulsiveness questionnaire was constructed which now reduced the factors to three primary ones, namely IMP, Venturesomeness and Empathy (Eysenck & Eysenck 1978).

3.2. Impulsiveness and Venturesomeness in Children

In 1980, a 63-item questionnaire was devised for children, purporting to measure IMP, Venturesomeness and Empathy (Eysenck & Eysenck 1980). The questionnaire was completed by 299 boys and 204 girls and of these 251 boys and 143 girls also filled in the Junior EPQ (Eysenck & Eysenck 1975). IMP was correlated positively with P and N, negatively with L and slightly with E. Venturesomeness was correlated with E and rather less strongly with P and also negatively again with L. Empathy correlated negatively with P and slightly positively with N in these groups.

Also in 1980, this 63-item questionnaire was applied to 641 delinquent subjects at a detention centre, of whom 614 also completed the EPQ (Eysenck & McGurk 1980). Factor analysis confirmed that the structure was the same for delinquents as for a normal sample. As found in a normal group, only somewhat more clearly, the results showed that IMP aligned with P mainly and Venturesomeness was more correlated with E. Moreover, the positive correlation of Empathy with N and the negative correlation with P were again confirmed in this group of delinquents.

By 1983, 542 Canadian boys and 508 Canadian girls completed the Junior Impulsiveness Questionnaire (I_6; Saklofske & Eysenck 1983). Separate factor analyses for Canadian boys and girls yielded a similar structure to that obtained with British children. Sex differences showed that boys scored higher than girls on IMP and Venturesomeness but lower on Empathy.

It seemed of interest to include anti-social behavior in children into the equation (Eysenck 1981), and we consequently asked 118 boys and 309 girls to complete an Anti-social Behavior scale together with the I_6 impulsiveness scale and the Junior EPQ. This gave a fascinating matrix of correlations indicating a strong link between Anti-social Behavior in children and IMP and P and a weaker link with Venturesomeness, E and lack of Empathy. N was only slightly implicated for girls and hardly at all for boys.

To digress a little at this point, it may be of interest to note that a Criminality scale we devised at the same time as standardising the EPQ in 1975, produced the following item analysis results. On the adult scale, out of 34 items 14 were P, 18 were N and only 2 were E. The picture was somewhat different for children, where out of 40 items there were 13 P, 11 N and 16 E items. What was striking was the decrease in E items for adults thus suggesting that juveniles grow out of "high spirits" and mischievous misdemeanours, leaving the personality of adult criminals as more predominantly P and N, i.e. the pathological factors. In other words, naughty children may grow out of Anti-social Behavior as long as P and N are not overly involved; they presumably use their E characters to further social contacts, both personally and at work, rather than in an anti-social direction. Saklofske *et al.* (1978) subsequently confirmed these Criminality scale results.

We finally standardised both the Junior I_6 (Eysenck *et al.* 1984) and Adult I_7 (Eysenck *et al.* 1985a) impulsiveness questionnaires. A total of 1,505 children (633 boys and 872 girls) completed the Junior I_6 Inventory. This standardization study in 1984 quoted a table of reliabilities, intercorrelations of the factors and means and standard deviations for boys and girls for each age group from 8 to 15 years inclusive.

4. Development of the I_7 Adult Impulsiveness Questionnaire

In 1985, the I_7 Adult Impulsiveness Questionnaire was published (Eysenck *et al.* 1985b). It was completed by 1320 subjects (559 males and 761 females). Similar to the junior standardization, means and standard deviations were given in that article for eight age groups from 16 to 19 year olds to 50 to 89 year olds. A further sample of 383 males and 206 females completed the I_7 as well as the EPQ and the inter-correlations of all seven dimensions are given in that article. What this basically showed was that IMP correlated mainly with P (0.46) but also with E (0.39). Venturesomeness correlated mainly with E (0.37) and minimally with P (0.22) for males. The distinction was somewhat clearer for females, where IMP correlated with P (0.45) and (0.22) with E, while Venturesomeness correlated with E (0.44) but only (0.11) with P. This, then, was the development of our I_6 and I_7 impulsiveness scales.

5. Understanding Impulsiveness

There were, of course, many other impulsiveness scales available in addition to the I_6 and I_7 impulsiveness scales, notably those by Shalling (1970), Barratt and Patton (1983), Patton *et al.* (1995), Luengo *et al.* (1991). However, of particular note was a study by Dickman (1990) who found two IMP factors, which he called functional and dysfunctional respectively. He found that functional impulsiveness was related to E, while dysfunctional impulsiveness was related to P. This accords very well with our thinking, except that Dickman's functional impulsiveness is what we called Venturesomeness, whereas Dickman's dysfunctional impulsiveness, we called simply IMP. Remembering that Venturesomeness correlated mainly with E and IMP mainly with P, the functional and dysfunctional characteristics fit rather well. Dickman found, as we always did, that both kinds of impulsivity correlated with E and P to different degrees.

How then do we visualize these different forms of impulsiveness in behavioral terms? The analogy that comes to mind is that of the driver who overtakes on the brow of a hill with nil visibility as to oncoming traffic. The truly impulsive high P scoring type of driver simply never considers the possibility of oncoming traffic and certainly never envisages a crash ensuing from his action. He is minded to overtake, and impulsively does so, without thought of consequences. The venturesome high E scoring type of driver by contrast may also overtake in similar circumstances, but may be motivated by sensation seeking. He realises fully the danger that he is in and welcomes the adrenaline rush that this produces.

Clearly, there is some impulsiveness in both drivers' actions, but the mechanism seems different.

A complicating feature of the whole topic of impulsiveness is N. While P and E are involved, so is N up to a point. However, it seems as though the N component is restricted to IMP rather than Venturesomeness. Consequently, it has emerged that while venturesomeness is mainly an E feature, impulsiveness though mainly a P feature may share some N involvement. That, of course, implies that it is the pathological or dysfunctional side of impulsiveness.

While it is to be regretted that it was not feasible to measure impulsiveness adequately with the EPQ, it now appears to have been the right decision to create a whole new questionnaire to measure impulsiveness and venturesomeness, much more accurately than could have been achieved through the EPQ dimensions. Impulsiveness is a fascinating concept and once measured reliably can be of importance in the study of road safety, addiction and many other areas.

6. Summary

While attempting the measurement of impulsiveness with items from the EPQ E scale, it became obvious that there were additional aspects of impulsiveness that were not being tapped. When P was introduced, however, the place of impulsiveness became clearer. A new questionnaire separate from the EPQ, which, when factorially analyzed with the EPQ, revealed that impulsiveness items mainly belonged to P though partially still to E. This E component was called Venturesomeness, which unsurprisingly, also contained sensation seeking items. Importantly, it transpired that Dickman's (1990) functional and dysfunctional impulsiveness terms correlated with Venturesomeness and IMP, respectively.

References

Barratt, E. S., & Patton, J. H. (1983). Impulsivity: Cognitive behavioral and psychophysiological correlates. In: M. Zuckerman (Ed.), *Biological bases of sensation seeking, impulsivity and anxiety* (pp. 77–116). Hillsdale, NJ: Erlbaum.

Dickman, S. J. (1990). Functional and dysfunctional impulsivity: Personality and cognitive correlates. *Journal of Personality and Social Psychology*, *58*, 95–102.

Eysenck, H. J. (1959). *Manual of the Maudsley Personality Inventory*. London: University of London Press.

Eysenck, H. J., & Eysenck, S. B. G. (1964). *Manual of the Eysenck Personality Inventory*. London: University of London Press.

Eysenck, H. J., & Eysenck, S. B. G. (1968a). A factorial study of psychoticism as a dimension of personality. *Multivariate Behavioural Research*, 15–32.

Eysenck, H. J., & Eysenck, S. B. G. (1971). The orthogonality of psychoticism and neuroticism: A factorial study. *Perceptual and Motor Skills*, *33*, 461–462.

Eysenck, H. J., & Eysenck, S. B. G. (1975). *Manual of the Eysenck Personality Questionnaire*. London: Hodder and Stoughton.

Eysenck, H. J., & Eysenck, S. B. G. (1976). *Psychoticism as a dimension of personality*. London: Hodder and Stoughton.

Eysenck, H. J., & Eysenck, S. B. G. (1991). *Manual of the Eysenck Personality Scales*. London, UK: Hodder and Stoughton; San Diego, CA: Edits Publishers.

Eysenck, S. B. G. (1981). Impulsiveness and antisocial behaviour in children. *Current Psychological Research, 1*, 31–37.

Eysenck, S. B. G., Easting, G., & Pearson, P. R. (1984). Age norms for impulsiveness, venturesomeness and empathy in children. *Personality and Individual Differences, 5*, 315–321.

Eysenck, S. B. G., & Eysenck, H. J. (1968b). The measurement of psychoticism: A study of factor stability and reliability. *British Journal of Social and Clinical Psychology, 7*, 286–294.

Eysenck, S. B. G., & Eysenck, H. J. (1969). 'Psychoticism' in children: A new personality variable. *Research in Education, 1*, 21–37.

Eysenck, S. B. G., & Eysenck, H. J. (1972). The questionnaire measurement of psychoticism. *Psychological Medicine, 2*, 50–55.

Eysenck, S. B. G., & Eysenck, H. J. (1977). The place of impulsiveness in a dimensional system of personality description. *British Journal of Social and Clinical Psychology, 16*, 57–68.

Eysenck, S. B. G., & Eysenck, H. J. (1978). Impulsiveness and venturesomeness: Their position in a dimensional system of personality description. *Psychological Reports, 43*, 1247–1255.

Eysenck, S. B. G., & Eysenck, H. J. (1980). Impulsiveness and venturesomeness in children. *Personality and Individual Differences, 1*, 73–78.

Eysenck, S. B. G., Eysenck, H. J., & Barrett, P. T. (1985a). A revised version of the psychoticism scale. *Personality and Individual Differences, 6*, 21–29.

Eysenck, S. B. G., & McGurk, B. J. (1980). Impulsiveness and venturesomeness in a detention centre population. *Psychological Reports, 47*, 1299–1306.

Eysenck, S. B. G., Pearson, P. R., Easting, G., & Allsopp, J. P. (1985b). Age norms for impulsiveness, venturesomeness and empathy in adults. *Personality and Individual Differences, 6*, 613–619.

Eysenck, S. B. G., & Zuckerman, M. (1978). The relationship between Sensation Seeking and Eysenck's dimensions of personality. *British Journal of Psychology, 69*, 483–487.

Luengo, M. A., Carillo-de-la-Pena, M. T., & Otero, J. M. (1991). The components of impulsiveness: A comparison of the I7 Impulsiveness Questionnaire and the Barratt Impulsiveness Scale. *Personality and Individual Differences, 12*, 657–667.

Mehrabian, A., & Epstein, N. (1972). A measure of emotional empathy. *Journal of Personality, 40*, 525–543.

Patton, J. H., Stanford, M. S., & Barratt, E. S. (1995). Factor structure of the Barratt Impulsiveness Scale. *Journal of Clinical Psychology, 51*, 768–774.

Saklofske, D. H., & Eysenck, S. B. G. (1983). Impulsiveness and venturesomeness in Canadian children. *Psychological Reports, 52*, 147–152.

Saklofske, D. H., McKerracher, D. W., & Eysenck, S. B. G. (1978). Eysencks' theory of criminality: The C scale as a measure of antisocial behaviour. *Psychological Reports, 43*, 683–686.

Shalling, D. (1970). *Contributions to some personality concepts*. Doctoral dissertation, Department of Psychology, University of Stockholm.

Zuckerman, M. (1979). *Sensation seeking: Beyond the optimal level of arousal*. Hillsdale, NJ: Erlbaum.

Chapter 8

Stability of Personality Across the Life Span: A Meta-Analysis

P. G. Bazana and R. M. Stelmack

O God, give us serenity to accept what cannot be changed, courage to change what should be changed, and wisdom to distinguish the one from the other (Reinhold Niebuhr 1934).

1. Introduction

The desire to change or control personal tendencies is often a primary goal in our daily lives, in raising children, in counselling, and in the treatment of psychopathology and criminal behavior. A fundamental question that pertains to this goal is what is the extent to which personality is malleable and subject to the vagaries of everyday life experience? This question is also implicit in the issue concerning the degree to which innate dispositions or specific external circumstances influence individual differences in personality. To the extent that personality dispositions are relatively stable across the life span, the effect would endorse the view that personality is determined by inherited, physiological mechanisms. In this chapter, we present an analysis of evidence that addresses this issue of the stability of personality traits across the life span.

The notion of traits as descriptive constructs has a lengthy history in personality psychology. As early as 1937, Gordon Allport observed that without invoking the concept of traits, the stability of personal behavior over time could not be explained. The intervening years have seen a plethora of research, mostly factor analytic, into the nature of traits, with various competing models of personality descriptors proposed (e.g. Cattell *et al.* 1970; Costa & McCrae 1992a; Eysenck & Eysenck 1985; Guilford 1959; Norman 1963). In the past decade, consensus has emerged on the number of traits that are sufficient to describe personality, with a Five-Factor model (FFM) receiving widespread acceptance (Wiggins 1996). Moreover, many longitudinal studies have accrued, lending strong support to the trait perspective. Recently, attempts were made to organize these results in terms of the FFM (Costa & McCrae 1986; Soldz & Vaillant 1999).

On the Psychobiology of Personality
Edited by R. M. Stelmack

ISBN: 0-08-044209-9

Although there is a good deal of concordance across studies, samples, and psychometric instruments that describes and summarizes the results of longitudinal studies, a quantitative index of stability for each trait that takes such factors as age at study of inception and gender into account has not been established. In light of the compelling literature on the longitudinal stability of personality traits, the present study uses meta-analytic procedures to aggregate, summarize, and quantify the stability coefficients reported in extant longitudinal studies of traits.

2. The Five-Factor Model of Personality Traits

Traits are descriptive constructs, intervening variables inferred from behavior and invoked to account for the relations between observable variables. Guilford (1959) defined traits as "any distinguishable, relatively enduring way in which one individual varies from others" (p. 6). More specifically, traits are "the tendency for an individual to behave in a similar manner in diverse situations" (Brody 1988: 7). They are "dimensions of individual differences in tendencies to show consistent patterns of thoughts, feelings, and actions . . . over time as well as across situations" (McCrae & Costa 1990: 23–24).

Since the early 1960s, many factor analysts have determined that when comprehensive inventories of trait adjectives or behavioral descriptors are administered to individuals who then rate themselves on these characteristics, five robust, replicable factors emerge. This has also been demonstrated when individuals are rated by others (e.g. peers, parents, teachers). Though there have been minor differences in interpretation of the resulting factors, it is now widely agreed that neuroticism (N), extraversion (E), openness to experience (O), agreeableness (A), and conscientiousness (C) are fundamental dimensions describing human personality (Wiggins 1996).

The resulting FFM has been operationalized in an instrument termed the Neuroticism, Extraversion, Openness to Experience Personality Inventory (NEO-PI; Costa & McCrae 1985, 1989) and in a subsequent revised version (NEO-PI-R; Costa & McCrae 1992b) that incorporates scales for A and C. The model is depicted in Figure 1. Characteristics, or facets, associated with each of the traits are shown in the left column.

With the increasing adoption of the FFM, psychologists have reinterpreted past findings in light of current research. In a thoughtful history of the FFM, Digman (1996) pointed out that elements of the FFM were reported in the literature as early as 1915. Webb (1915) extracted a factor (C factor) defined by terms like conscientious and persevering. A reanalysis of the same data by Garnett (1919) also found evidence for an E factor. Later, Cattell (1933), using self-ratings of bipolar adjectives, uncovered C, E (which he termed surgency), a third factor defined by terms like good-natured and kind and thereby suggestive of A, and a fourth factor related to emotional instability and general maladjustment (N). This work was extended in the early work of Thurstone (1934) on self-ratings of trait adjectives and by Guilford (1936) and Guilford and Guilford (1939a, b).

In 1936, Allport and Odbert published their compendium of trait terms. This was the first attempt at a comprehensive cataloguing of personality trait descriptors used in common language. Though the availability of these descriptors might have had a facilitative effect in the field, the publication of Thurstone's seminal work *Multiple Factor Analysis* (1947) had

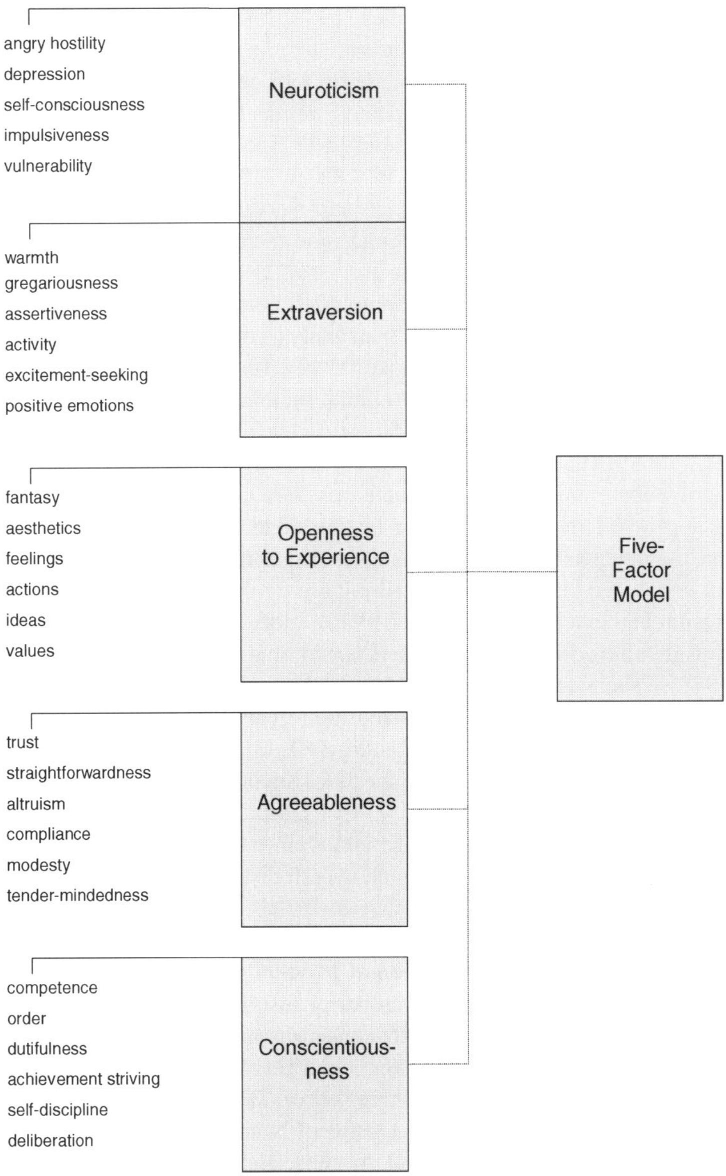

Figure 1: The Five-Factor model of personality traits.

a less positive influence. Although it was immediately accepted as the definitive text in the area, it contained one important short-coming. Thurstone advised that over extracting factors was better than under extracting factors from a matrix of correlations. The consequences of this suggestion became readily apparent in the subsequent work of many researchers and the development of trait measuring instruments, some of which are still widely used today.

Cattell, for example, in a series of studies (1944, 1947, 1948) found between nine and 16 factors. Interestingly, an analysis of Cattell's rating scales by Fiske (1949) yielded five factors that were stable for ratings made by self, peers and supervisors. Even Cattell admitted that only six factors were consistently replicated (Cattell 1950). Largely on the basis of these three studies, however, Cattell developed the Sixteen Personality Factors Questionnaire (16PF) an instrument still in widespread use (Cattell *et al.* 1970). The ten factors of the Guilford-Zimmerman Temperament Survey (Guilford *et al.* 1976) originated in a similar fashion. Thurstone (1951) found nine factors, laying the foundation for the Thurstone Temperament Schedule (1953).

By the 1960s, the availability of computers led some researchers to empirically test Thurstone's principle of over extraction. In an analysis of Cattell's scales and reanalysis of the data from Cattell (1947, 1948) and Fiske (1949), Tupes and Christal (1961) and Tupes and Kaplan (1961) uncovered only five reliable factors (cited in Digman 1996). Several other researchers also found five distinct factors in their respective studies (Borgatta 1964; Norman 1963; Smith 1967).

In spite of robust findings from numerous researchers, however, the widespread acceptance and belief in more than five factors continued. Notwithstanding his earlier assertion on the adequacy of five factors, Norman agreed that additional factors would probably be uncovered (1967). The overall picture by the end of the 1960s was a general lack of cohesion in the field (e.g. Cronbach 1970). Indeed, factor analytic research on traits met with considerable criticism by the late 1960s for this reason and for others. Specifically, Mischel (1973), a social learning theorist, argued that ratings of certain behaviors, regarded by most as evidence of traits, merely reflected stereotypes held by people about behavior in specific situations. Mischel and others (e.g. Argyle & Little 1972; Endler 1983; Hunt 1965) argued forcefully for this situationist perspective. Social psychologists coined the phrase "fundamental attribution error" (Ross *et al.* 1977), which asserts that people erroneously attribute causality to a trait rather than the situation, which is the real determinant. As a result of these arguments, combined with the overall disarray in the field, research on traits waned during the 1970s.

By the early 1980s, however, key developments led to a resurgence of factor analytic work on trait theory. Convincing refutation of Mischel's claims, centering largely around the methodology used in the studies, was partly responsible (Epstein 1983; Jackson & Paunonen 1985). More importantly, though, consensus was developing over the universality of N, E, and O (or a related variant) as fundamental personality descriptors. This was based on converging empirical evidence from three sources. First, Eysenck's voluminous factor analytic work led him to postulate the existence of N and E as universal trait descriptors. Cattell's development of the constructs of Anxiety, and Exvia, both higher-order factors derived from subscales of the 16PF, complemented Eysenck's work on N and E. Finally, Guilford too postulated (low) Emotional Health and Social Activity as measures of N and E, respectively.

These two factors emerged repeatedly in scores of factor analytic studies. Hence, by the early 1980s, it was difficult to dispute that at least two of the fundamental personality dimensions were N and E. To these, Eysenck added the Psychoticism dimension (Eysenck & Eysenck 1975). Costa and McCrae added Openness to Experience, and introduced the NEO-PI (1976); later, A and C were added (1985). Both the NEO-PI and its successor, the NEO-PI-R (Costa & McCrae 1992b), have been extensively validated. The FFM as operationalized in the NEO-PI and NEO-PI-R is robust across gender (Costa & McCrae 1988), age (Costa *et al.* 1980; Costa & McCrae 1988), method of assessment, i.e. self-ratings, ratings by others, computerized administration (Costa & McCrae 1988; Funder & Colvin 1991), and across various language, cultural, and racial groups (Church & Katibak 1989; Costa *et al.* 1991; McCrae & Costa 1997; Ostendorf 1990; Pulver *et al.* 1995).

Moreover, the five factors are structurally invariant across a wide variety of instruments (e.g. see Boyle 1989) and theoretical frameworks (e.g. Angleitner & Ostendorf 1994; Buss 1992; McCrae & Costa 1996). This is significant, because it allows psychologists to "group apparently dissimilar studies using scales with a variety of labels for the same underlying construct" (Costa & McCrae 1980: 73). This is a considerable understatement, because the impact of this change in methodological approach allowed for the consolidation of research spanning many decades.

Finally, longitudinal studies have demonstrated substantial temporal stability over a wide range of instruments and samples (e.g. Bromberger & Matthews 1996; Carmichael & McGue 1994; Costa & McCrae 1988; Dudek & Hall 1991; Gold & Henderson 1990; Helson & Pederson 1991; Wilhelm & Parker 1990; Wink 1992; Woodall & Matthews 1993).

3. Trait Stability

Reliability is a property of a psychometric instrument. Test-retest reliability indices are Pearson product-moment correlations between scores obtained at two different time periods for the same group of individuals. Psychometric instruments are reliable, to (sometimes widely) varying degrees.

Over longer time periods (one year or more), retest correlations will decrease, though they will almost invariantly remain positive. It is assumed that change in the trait is responsible for reductions in the test-retest coefficient. The retest correlation of the two sets of scores can be interpreted as a stability coefficient when the test-retest interval is substantial.

Differential or rank-order stability refers to invariance in the relative placement or rank-ordering of individuals' scores or ratings on a given trait within a particular cohort. Individuals within a group will obviously differ from one another on trait ratings. On the E dimension, for example, individuals can be rank-ordered by their scores. Studies on differential stability address the degree to which the relative placement of individuals remains the same over time; if the trait shows stability over time, then the person with the highest E score relative to the rest of the group should maintain his or her position in relation to that group.

Other forms of stability have also received attention. Ipsative stability refers to the relative salience and importance of a trait to a given individual over time (e.g. Block & Robins 1993). Mean-level stability refers to whether the average level of a trait shows normative increases or decreases over time (e.g. Costa & McCrae 1986), and is sometimes referred to as absolute stability (Gustavsson *et al.* 1997). Studies of ipsative and mean-level stability are rare when compared with studies of differential stability. The notion of relative ranking has been crucial to studies of temporal stability of traits. Only studies on differential stability or rank-order consistency will be considered in the present analysis. However, evidence of change in mean levels may, within certain contexts, provide some clues to why stability varies at certain ages or across gender.

4. Longitudinal Studies of Traits

Longitudinal research on the stability of traits spans more than six decades. The earliest reported study (for an interval greater than one year) was by Farnsworth (1938) who reported test-retest coefficients of 0.69 and 0.72 for N and E, respectively. The first large-scale study of the longitudinal consistency of personality in adulthood was conducted by Kelly (1955), who used data on 384 individuals collected over a 21-year span. His general conclusion was that a high degree of temporal stability was evident. Since then, many studies using various instruments, populations, and time-spans have been published. Overall, the evidence indicates that for normal populations ranging in age from early adolescence to late adulthood, the stability of personality traits is moderate to high.

Stability coefficients for N, for example, range from 0.17 over a 19-year period (Tuddenham 1959) to 0.86 over one year (Popham & Holden 1991). The approximate mean correlation for studies spanning one year is approximately 0.70, with a standard deviation (S.D.) of 0.15 (Baltes & Nesselroade 1972; Cattell & Cattell 1975; Eckert 1940; Gough 1975; Popham & Holden 1991; Taylor 1953). Note that periods less than one year are indicative of properties of the instrument rather than of trait stability. Mean correlations decrease in a step-wise fashion over longer intervals: the mean is 0.48 (S.D. = 0.14) over three years (Backteman & Magnusson 1981; Bates & Pandina 1989; Bromberger & Matthews 1996; Cook & Wolaver 1963; Farnsworth 1938; Hathaway & Monachesi 1963; Izard *et al.* 1993; Melamed *et al.* 1974; Wheeler & Schwartz 1989); 0.41 (S.D. = 0.12) for ten-year intervals (Caputo *et al.* 1966; Holmlund 1991; Wilhelm & Parker 1990); and 0.30 (S.D. = 0.12) for intervals of 18–20 years (Block 1971; Carmichael & McGue 1994; Conley 1985; Stevens & Truss 1985; Tuddenham 1959).

Similar results are reported for E. Coefficients range from 0.26 (Soldz & Vaillant 1999) over 45 years to a high of 0.80 over one to six years, i.e. Eckert (1940) and Costa and McCrae (1988) respectively. Overall, correlations for E are higher than for N (e.g. for data on three cohorts see Costa & McCrae 1977; for data on six cohorts see Viken *et al.* 1994).

The obvious limitation to describing results in this way, however, is that no attempt is made to account for sample size. For studies on N, E, O, A, and C sample size varies considerably, from a minimum of around 30 (Bolton 1979; Muntaner *et al.* 1988) to 1000 or more (Baltes & Nesselroade 1972; Plant & Telford 1966; Viken *et al.* 1994). In addition, this narrative approach is entirely descriptive. The reporting of means, standard deviations, and ranges, though by far the most widely used method of summarizing longitudinal data on traits, yields only general information that is often vague and imprecise.

Often results are based on a subjective determination of what studies should be included or on what results should be reported. To illustrate, in the above example, a mean correlation of 0.41 was reported for studies of N conducted over a ten-year period. Had the focus been on nine-year intervals, the mean correlation would have increased to 0.55, this result owing exclusively to a single study using three cohorts (Costa & McCrae 1977). Had results over a

12-year interval been selected, the correlation would rise to 0.61 (Costa *et al.* 1980; Stevens & Truss 1985).

4.1. Quantitative Reviews of Longitudinal Studies of Traits

In spite of obvious limitations to the traditional descriptive narrative review, only a handful of attempts at quantitatively summarizing longitudinal studies have been made. The first, by Crook in 1941, estimated the temporal stability of N and used visual as opposed to mathematical curve-fitting to generate a line of best fit to the plot of correlations (plotted against test interval). The curve showed a rapidly decelerating trend after about six months, and continuing negative acceleration over time. On the basis of the plots, stability coefficients can be estimated to be about 0.70, 0.64, 0.60, 0.57, 0.52, 0.49, and 0.46 over one to seven years, respectively. These are reasonable data and concordant with more recent studies. Data on E (Farnsworth 1938) also indicated a similar deceleration over time, with correlations of 0.74, 0.62, and 0.63 over periods of one, two, and 3.3 years.

The comprehensive *Stability and Change in Human Development* by Bloom (1966) was another important work. Though lacking a quantitative summary, Bloom concluded that trait change was evident well past 20 years of age and that the relation between trait stability and age could best be described as a positively sloped, negatively accelerated function. He also posited that stable characteristics are generally nonreversible: barring the effects of extreme environments or physical injury, extraverts are unlikely to become introverts, and highly anxious individuals will likely remain anxious over the life span.

Following Crook (1941), the next attempt at a quantitative summary of longitudinal studies was published 43 years later by Conley (1984). He used dimensions of the Eysenck Personality Questionnaire (EPQ; Eysenck & Eysenck 1975) to organize the results of 29 longitudinal studies. He applied a simple equation and visual curve-fitting to determine trait stability. His analysis was restricted to adolescents and adults from normal populations and he collapsed the data across gender, age, *and* trait. He reported that when corrected for attenuation (unreliability of the instrument) the longitudinally consistent correlations for traits, in general, were on the order of 0.98 for one year, 0.90 for five years, 0.82 for ten years, and 0.45 for 50-year intervals. These correlations represent the "true stability of the construct" (p. 11) but are only meaningful when applied to E because Conley only gave explicit data for E.

Schuerger *et al.* (1989) compiled a summary table of normative test-retest reliabilities for eight personality self-report inventories in a review that drew from 106 sources. Their conclusions were remarkably similar to those of Conley (1984). The test-retest interval was inversely related to the magnitude of the test-retest correlations of N and E over periods ranging from a few weeks to 15 years. Age at the beginning of study also varied inversely with retest correlations. In addition, they reported a significant association between internal consistency and magnitude of the retest correlation.

A recent study summarized this substantial body of literature using the FFM as an organizing framework (Roberts & Del Vecchio 2000). Although the primary purpose was to examine the relation between age at study inception and temporal stability, the authors also assessed the effects of interval and gender. Aggregated trait data was used instead of specific trait data for age and the authors reported that mean stability coefficients increased in a linear, stepwise manner over the life span. For participants in early adolescence, mean stability was 0.47; by old age, stability estimates were about 0.72. The test-retest interval was inversely related to overall trait stability, which decreased from a maximum of 0.55 at a one-year time span to 0.41 at 20 years, and 0.25 at 40 years. Gender had no effect on overall trait stability (0.49). The authors then examined the effect of type of trait on stability, treating specific traits as moderators. They reported mean stabilities of 0.50, 0.54, 0.51, 0.54, and 0.51 for N, E, O, A, and C, respectively.

Though these results are informative in a general way, the decision to conduct the analyses for interval, age, and gender without reference to specific traits is a shortcoming. Moreover, the method of aggregating results, specifically, the inclusion of individual cohorts over more than one interval (and in some cases several intervals) may have artificially inflated coefficients.

Overall, it can be concluded from the studies reviewed that several factors mediate the magnitude of test-retest correlations. Duration of the test interval exerts the largest influence, with smaller correlations found at longer intervals (Bloom 1966; Conley 1984, 1985; Costa & McCrae 1980; Crook 1941; Schuerger *et al.* 1989). Age at the inception of the study is a close second in terms of influence on test-retest correlations (Carmichael & McGue 1994; Costa & McCrae 1988; Finn 1986; Stevens & Truss 1985). Overall, the younger the individuals are at the beginning of the study, the smaller are the stability coefficients. The magnitude of the coefficient is also differentially influenced by gender for some traits (Barrett & Eysenck 1984; Feingold 1994; Lynn & Martin 1997). Psychometrically, test-retest reliability and internal consistency of the measures used also influence the magnitude of the correlations (Conley 1984; Schuerger *et al.* 1989). It is fairly well-established that self-ratings result in slightly larger correlations than ratings by others (e.g. Roberts & Del Vecchio 2000). Consequently, this issue will not be addressed in the present study.

5. Meta-Analysis of Longitudinal Studies of the Temporal Stability of Traits: Present Study

The term meta-analysis (MA) refers to methodologies for quantitatively summarizing an entire body of research in a given area (Hall & Rosenthal 1995; Johnson *et al.* 1995; Preiss & Allen 1995; Rosenthal 1995). The procedures involve gathering pertinent primary studies and converting the summary statistics from each into a standardized effect size. Population means can then be calculated. The MA is facilitated when the various studies use homogeneous methodologies. Because longitudinal studies of traits use Pearson correlation coefficients almost exclusively, such studies are well-suited to MA. Another advantage of MA is that variables that inflate or attenuate effect size in each study, termed moderators, can be analyzed across studies.

The use of MA in longitudinal research is relatively new. A PsychINFO search using meta-analysis and longitudinal as keywords revealed that no longitudinal MAs within psychology were conducted before 1983.

In the present study, FFM was used as a framework to organize and synthesize the data reported in primary studies. Relevant studies were located using ancestry methods and a computerized PsychINFO literature search. Papers cited in major reviews (e.g. Conley 1984, 1985; Costa & McCrae 1992b) were also retrieved. The PsychINFO search was conducted using the terms personality, trait, temperament, longitudinal, personality + longitudinal, trait + longitudinal, temperament + longitudinal, and others. The search identified 498 journal articles, books, book chapters, or dissertations, 96 of which were actual longitudinal studies that measured at least 1 trait variable over time.

5.1. Inclusion Criteria

Study selection proceeded in two stages. In the first stage, candidate studies were selected on the following criteria. Studies had to: (1) assess the stability of individual differences over time by means of test-retest correlations (in contrast to studies that assess change in mean levels of a trait within a cohort); (2) overtly use the trait concept and an instrument designed for measurement of traits, e.g. the Eysenck Personality Inventory (EPI; Eysenck & Eysenck 1964), NEO-PI or NEO-PI -R as measures of N and E; (3) employ constructs that have been demonstrated to be interpretable in terms of trait theory, e.g. some Myers-Briggs Type Indicator (MBTI; Meyers & McCaulley 1985) subscales are interpretable as measures of E, O, A, and C (McCrae & Costa 1989). Appropriate subscales of the GZTS may also be combined and interpreted as measures of N, E, O, A, and C (McCrae 1989); (4) report interval; (5) report age at study inception; (6) report sample size; (7) use normal populations; and (8) report the instrument used (note that projective tests were not used in the present analysis).

This selection procedure resulted in candidate studies that were then assessed using additional selection criteria: (1) age at inception of study had to be a minimum of ten years; (2) interval had to be a minimum of one year; (3) if the instrument used was ad hoc, as occurred in a small number of cases, it had to be derived from a major personality inventory; (4) when a study used the same sample over different intervals, only the longest period was used; and (5) a cohort was only used on one occasion.

Five variables shown to influence the temporal stability of traits were analyzed. First, the interval between study inception and termination was assessed. Analyses were conducted for each trait, and for all traits combined, i.e. aggregated sample. Secondly, the effect of gender on trait stability was evaluated. Thirdly, age at study inception was examined. The effect of age was analyzed in two ways. First, analyses were conducted for each trait, and for the aggregated sample (all traits combined). Secondly, data for the aggregated sample was sorted such that individuals in their teens were between 10.0 and 19.9 at both the beginning and end of any study. Thus, participants who were 10.0 at study inception would be between 11.0 and 19.9 at end of study; participants who were in their twenties at the beginning were no more than 29.9 at the end; and so on. For this age group analysis, data for individual traits were collapsed into an aggregated sample. Fourthly, year of publication of study was examined because MA studies on various constructs have shown that this may also mediate study outcome. Different historical periods may be more or less receptive to particular kinds of results or studies (Glass *et al.* 1981). For example, Mischel's challenge of the trait approach (1973) may have resulted in only studies with very robust findings being published during the 1970s. Even very recent studies have reported date-of-publication biases, e.g. Feist (1998).

Finally, the fifth variable analyzed was type of publication. It is possible that certain types of journals may favor particular types of studies and be more receptive to certain kinds of results. The editorial position of the journal *Personality and Individual Differences*, for example, states that "the traditional type of work on traits, abilities, attitudes, types and other latent structures underlying consistencies in behavior has in recent years been receiving rather short shrift in traditional journals of personality; *Personality and Individual Differences* aims to reinstate it to its proper place in psychology."

The potential moderating effect of subject attrition was not examined in the present study because it has been reported that the selective attrition of participants over time is not a significant determinant of trait stability (Finn 1986; Roberts & Del Vecchio 2000).

Fail-safe *N*, the number of additional studies required to nullify or reverse the conclusions drawn from the MA, was determined (Cooper 1979). This procedure addresses the file drawer problem (Rosenthal 1979, 1995), a form of publication bias. It is assumed that studies with significant results are more likely to be published, thereby biasing the results of the MA. Using the procedure developed by Orwin (1983) and a medium effect size of 0.50, at least 458 studies with non-significant results would be required to invalidate the results of the present study.

5.2. Coding of Moderators

Intervals were categorized into five classes: 1.0–2.9 years; 3.0–7.0 years; 8.0–14.0 years; 15.0–22.0 years; and 25.0 or more years. There were no intervals between 22.1 and 24.9 in the primary data. Males and females were classified. Age at study inception was also categorized into five classes, though in slightly different ways for the analyses of age and age groups. For the first age analysis, classes were 10.0–14.9 years; 15.0–19.9 years; 20.0–29.9 years; 30.0–49.9 years; and 50.0 or more years. For the analysis of age by group for the aggregated sample, classes were 10.0–19.9; 20.0–29.9; 30.0–39.9; 40.0–49.9; and 50.0 or more years.

Year of publication was classified as follows: studies from 1959 or earlier, 1960s, 1970s, 1980s, and 1990s. Finally, outlet was sorted into six categories: (1) psychometric test manuals; (2) journals of personality or genetics, e.g. *Personality and Individual Differences*, *Journal of Personality*, *Journal of Genetic Psychology*, *Genetic Psychology Monographs*; (3) developmental or gerontology journals, e.g. *Adolescence*, *Child Development*, *Developmental Review*, *Journal of Gerontology*, *Psychology and Aging*; (4) journals of general psychology, e.g. *American Psychologist*, *Annual Review of Psychology*, *Journal of General Psychology*, *Psychological Reports*, including journals of vocational and educational psychology; (5) *Journal of Personality and Social Psychology* and a very small number of closely related journals, e.g. *Journal of Social Behavior and Personality*, *Personality and Social Psychology Bulletin*; and (6) other publications including dissertations, conference presentations, and unpublished manuscripts. Book chapters were also sorted into appropriate categories. These classes are both meaningful theoretically and structured in such a way as to allow enough studies within each class, e.g. giving vocational and academic journals their own class would mean having only a few studies per class, thereby making analyses less sound. Data for year of publication and publication outlet were aggregated into a single sample.

5.3. Meta-Analyses

MAs were conducted in the following manner. Data for each trait were first analyzed in the absence of moderators. The MAs for each trait were conducted to examine whether effect sizes varied significantly with interval, gender, age at study inception, and age group. Data across traits were then aggregated for analysis without moderators, and for the effect of interval, gender, and age at study inception. MAs for year of publication and outlet were also conducted using only the aggregated sample.

An initial attempt to analyze age by interval using the five original categories for interval and the six original classes for age was not successful. There were not enough studies within each cell to generate meaningful results. Therefore, data was reclassified into three classes for age (10.0–19.9, 20.0–29.9, and $\geq$30.0) and four classes for interval ($\leq$3.0, 3.1–9.9, 10.0–19.9, $\geq$20.0). Overall, some aspects of the results remain difficult to interpret.

All MAs employed the Hedges and Olkin (1985) methods and used D-Stat, a statistical software package designed for meta-analytic research (Johnson 1995). The sample size and correlation for each study or independent cohort were used to determine weighted mean effect sizes and the associated 95% confidence interval. All correlations used in the analysis were uncorrected for attenuation. Hence, all were test-retest correlations and not stability coefficients. In a small number of cases, reported statistics were converted to correlations before being entered into the analysis. The resulting effect sizes are unbiased estimates of population values.

Homogeneity of effect sizes was determined for each analysis. The usual procedure in MA for dealing with non-homogeneous data is to systematically remove significant outliers until the Q-statistic is non-significant. This step-wise procedure begins with the largest outlier and removes it from the analysis; if the Q-statistic is still significant, then the next-largest outlier is removed, and so on. Within the context of the present study, however, the Q-statistic is expected, except in very rare circumstances, to be significant. This is because the simultaneous effects of interval and age at beginning of study will be confounded.

6. Outcome of Meta-Analysis of Longitudinal Studies of Personality

The primary studies used in the MA are marked with an asterisk in the reference section. A search of the published literature yielded 81 studies, employing 95 cohorts, that reported test-retest Pearson correlations between scores at the beginning and the end of the study and that used an established personality inventory. Each test-retest correlation used in the MA is based on data from an independent sample, which in most cases (75.9%) means that a specific study used a single cohort. In 24.1% of cases, however, a specific study used more than one cohort. For the purpose of describing and discussing MA results, the term, mean trait stability, refers to estimated mean population coefficients.

6.1. Mean trait Stability; No Moderators

Overall, mean trait stability for the aggregated sample and across the FFM traits, without reference to interval, age at study inception, or gender is 0.54. Mean stability for each of the five traits can be ranked as follows: E has the highest mean stability, $\rho = 0.59$. For N and O, the mean stability is $\rho = 0.52$. The mean stability is $\rho = 0.50$ for C and $\rho = 0.48$ for A.

6.2. Effect of Interval on Mean Trait Stability

Overall, mean trait stability is highest at shorter intervals and declines with increasing interval. The MA for the aggregated personality traits and for specific FFM traits is shown in Table 1. Figure 2 shows the plot of mean trait stability as a function of the mean of the interval class; this facilitates comparison across traits. Further, the curve for the aggregated data shows the expected decrease in magnitude with time, from a high of 0.59 at intervals less than three years to a low of 0.37 at intervals longer than 25 years. There is a plateau between intervals ranging from eight to 22 years.

For N and E, the plots are consistent with those of Conley (1984, Figure 3) and Schuerger *et al.* (1989, Figure 1). For both N and E, stability declines systematically from the shortest to the longest interval. The coefficient for N increases slightly (from 0.31 to 0.35) between the second longest and longest interval, but the increase is not significant. Mean stabilities for O, A, and C show the expected decrements over the first three intervals, but then stability increases sharply (and significantly) at the fourth. All three data points are based on data from the same four studies (Helson & Moane 1987; Kelly 1955; Stevens & Truss 1985; Tuddenham 1959). With the exception of mean stability for O, however, all coefficients reach their smallest magnitude by the longest interval.

6.3. Effect of Gender on Mean Trait Stability

When aggregated across all five traits, women and men have mean trait stabilities of the same magnitude ($\rho = 0.56$ and 0.55, respectively). On a trait-by-trait basis, women have more stable scores over time for both N ($\rho = 0.56$) and E ($\rho = 0.63$) than men ($\rho = 0.52$ and 0.60, for N and E respectively). These differences, though small, are significant for both traits. An opposite pattern is apparent with O ($\rho = 0.48$ and 0.55 for women and men, respectively) and A ($\rho = 0.51$ and 0.46 for women and men, respectively). Here men have more stable ratings over time, and the magnitude of the differences is larger; differences are significant for both traits. There is no gender-related difference in mean stability for C ($\rho = 0.50$).

6.4. Effect of Age at Study Inception on Mean Trait Stability

Figure 3 shows the plot of estimated mean stability coefficient against the mean for each age class for individual traits and for the aggregated sample. Generally, trends for all curves show similar patterns. For the aggregated sample and for individual traits, stability is lowest when participants at study initiation are youngest and highest when participants are

Table 1: Meta-analysis of retest interval for aggregated data and for traits.

Trait	Interval	ρ	95% CI	*N*	*k*	*Q*
AGG	<3	0.59	0.58–0.59	27404	82	2453.4^{**}
	3.0–7.0	0.56	0.55–0.56	66029	87	4074.2^{**}
	8.0–14.0	0.44	0.42–0.45	14814	61	1285.0^{**}
	15.0–22.0	0.43	0.41–0.44	7494	26	405.3^{**}
	≥25	0.37	0.35–0.40	3308	30	347.1^{**}
N	<3	0.58	0.56–0.59	6434	21	1222.9^{**}
	3.0–7.0	0.53	0.52–0.54	24515	25	1087.1^{**}
	8.0–14.0	0.44	0.42–0.46	4932	18	267.0^{**}
	15.0–22.0	0.31	0.26–0.35	963	6	28.9^{**}
	≥25	0.35	0.31–0.39	1081	9	46.9^{**}
E	<3	0.63	0.62–0.65	7553	19	634.5^{**}
	3.0–7.0	0.62	0.61–0.63	23947	23	1410.8^{**}
	8.0–14.0	0.51	0.48–0.53	3683	14	308.0^{**}
	15.0–22.0	0.42	0.40–0.44	4665	8	199.9^{**}
	≥25	0.36	0.32–0.41	909	7	104.2^{**}
O	<3	0.62	0.60–0.64	3392	12	55.7^{**}
	3.0–7.0	0.49	0.47–0.51	4998	13	359.0^{**}
	8.0–14.0	0.42	0.39–0.45	1786	9	144.4^{**}
	15.0–22.0	0.50	0.45–0.55	622	4	20.9^{**}
	≥25	0.47	0.42–0.53	564	6	63.6^{**}
A	<3	0.56	0.54–0.58	4762	14	198.2^{**}
	3.0–7.0	0.46	0.44–0.48	4840	14	88.5^{**}
	8.0–14.0	0.40	0.37–0.43	2372	11	161.2^{**}
	15.0–22.0	0.47	0.42–0.52	622	4	16.1^{**}
	≥25	0.36	0.30–0.43	455	5	70.7^{**}
C	<3	0.54	0.53–0.56	5263	16	143.0^{**}
	3.0–7.0	0.52	0.50–0.53	7729	12	183.0^{**}
	8.0–14.0	0.35	0.33–0.38	2041	9	285.8^{**}
	15.0–22.0	0.53	0.48–0.58	622	4	58.9^{**}
	≥25	0.31	0.23–0.39	299	3	38.7^{**}

$^{**}p < 0.01$.

oldest. Between these extremes, examination of individual traits reveals some interesting differences in the pattern of stability across age intervals.

For E, mean stability increases in a linear, stepwise fashion until about age 33, at which point it levels off at approximately $\rho = 0.69$. The pattern for N is similar, but there is a sharp

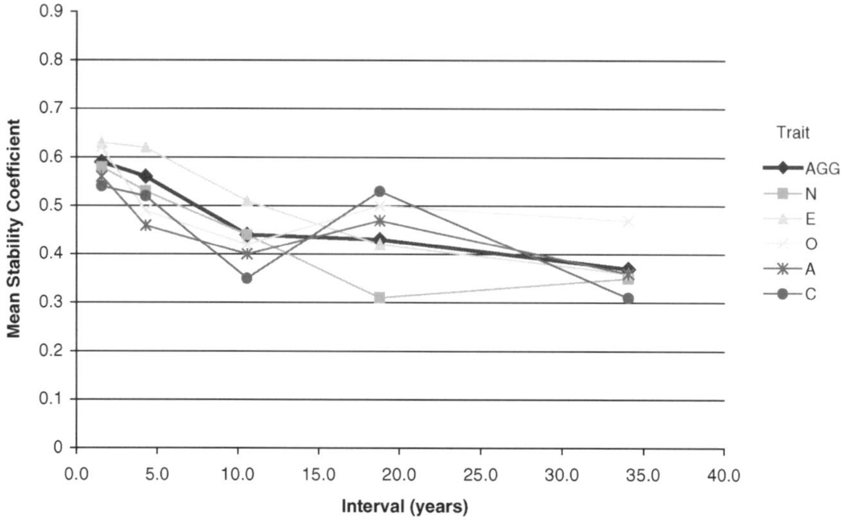

Figure 2: Estimated mean stability coefficients by interval.

decline, from $\rho = 0.45$ to 0.37, at about 17 years; stability also decreases significantly at about 45 years of age, after which it increases from $\rho = 0.56$ to 0.65. Overall, coefficients for N are lower than for E.

Mean stabilities for O, A, and C show abrupt and unexpected decrements at three locations. Coefficients for O and A both decrease at about 33 years of age (from $\rho = 0.57$ in

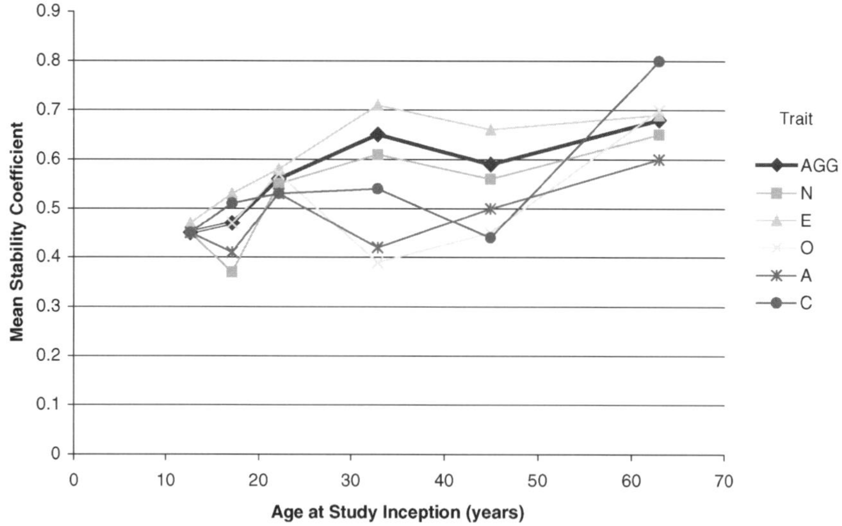

Figure 3: Estimated mean stability coefficient by age at study inception.

the preceding age class to 0.39 for O and from $\rho = 0.53$ in the preceding age class to 0.41 for A). Mean stability for A also decreases at 17 years, but the difference in magnitude, though significant, is negligible (from $\rho = 0.45$ to 0.41; confidence intervals overlap slightly). The mean stability coefficient for C decreases from 0.54 to 0.44 at 45 years of age. The magnitude of the difference is smaller than for O and A, and here the confidence intervals overlap considerably. It is important to note that three of these aberrant coefficients (for O and A at 33 years and for C at 45 years) are based on data from only three studies. With *k* this small, the vagaries of individual studies become more pronounced and the data generated are less reliable.

Mean stability for each of the five age groups increases in a stepwise fashion, from a low in the teenage years to a maximum for the oldest participants, with a slight but significant decrease for individuals in their forties. For participants in their teens at both beginning and end of study, mean stability is 0.48. For individuals in their twenties and thirties, $\rho = 0.59$ and 0.64, respectively. Mean stability decreases slightly to 0.60 for participants in their forties, then climbs again, to $\rho = 0.74$, for individuals fifty or older. This pattern is highly concordant with the aggregated data, which were not divided into age groups. Mean coefficients are 0.46, 0.56, 0.65, 0.59, and 0.68 for participants in their teens, twenties, thirties, forties, and for those over 50, respectively.

6.5. *Effect of Year of Publication on Mean Trait Stability*

Assessment of mean trait stability associated with year of publication for the aggregated sample shows that studies from the 1990s report the highest coefficients, $\rho = 0.57$. This value is significantly higher than coefficients from all other classes. Studies from the 1940s, 1950s, 1960s, and 1970s produced identical results, $\rho = 0.54$. Studies from the 1980s report significantly lower mean coefficients when compared with other classes, $\rho = 0.47$.

6.6. *Effect of Outlet on Mean Trait Stability*

Assessment of the moderating effect of publication outlet indicates that correlations reported in the *Journal of Personality and Social Psychology* were the highest overall, $\rho = 0.60$, followed by test manuals, $\rho = 0.58$; these values are not significantly different. The next largest correlations are found in general psychology journals, and in dissertations, conference presentations, and unpublished manuscripts, $\rho = 0.54$ for both outlets. Finally, the lowest correlations are from journals specializing in personality/genetics, $\rho = 0.50$, and journals focusing on developmental psychology and gerontology, $\rho = 0.48$. The correlations for these two outlets do not differ significantly. All mean trait stabilities for outlet are based on the aggregated sample.

7. Overview of Meta-Analysis of Personality Traits

Overall, the results are remarkably consistent with previous individual studies and narrative reviews that have addressed the same problems: how best to describe the effects of the passage of time, age at study inception, gender, and other variables on the stability of personality traits.

7.1. Trait Stability in the Absence of Moderators

Mean trait stability averaged across all traits, intervals, and ages at beginning of study was 0.54. This value is consistent with previous quantitative reviews (Conley 1984; Roberts & Del Vecchio 2000) and provides a ballpark figure of trait stability over the life span. Though substantial, this coefficient does not approach unity, evidence that some change occurs in the rank-ordering of individuals. The nature of that change can best be addressed on a trait-by-trait basis.

Assessment of the stability of individual traits indicates that E has the highest stability over time, 0.59. Most longitudinal studies (e.g. Bolton 1979; Conley 1985; Holmlund 1991; Muntaner *et al.* 1988; Pederson 1991) and many narrative reviews report test-retest correlations for E to be greater in magnitude than for any other trait (e.g. Costa & McCrae 1977, 1980). For the primary studies reported here, approximately 75% of studies that assessed both N and E reported larger test-retest correlations for E than for N.

N and O both have mean stabilities of 0.52, while values for C and A are 0.50 and 0.48, respectively. Costa and McCrae (1980) list three possible reasons why N might be less stable than E. First, high-N scorers may be more susceptible to stressors, thereby elevating scores on some occasions. The state-trait distinction may be at work here. Traits are considered to be highly stable, while states are changeable. Psychometric instruments, though ostensibly pure measures of traits, also measure an individual's state, though to a lesser degree (Usala & Hertzog 1991). N may be differentially sensitive to environmental stressors and so may be less stable overall, and certain periods in an individual's life might be more facilitative to the expression of N, e.g. the difficult transitional period of adolescence, or the so-called mid-life crisis. Ormel and Rijsdijk (2000) used structural equation modeling to determine the relative contributions of trait and state anxiety to scores. While trait anxiety accounted for about 38% of the variance in scores, state anxiety accounted for 34%, with error variance responsible for 23%. They attribute the low percentage for trait anxiety, however, to inadequate power (Ormel & Rijsdijk 2000). Secondly, the subjective distress associated with high-N scores may lead some individuals to attempt to change, either through their own efforts or through psychotherapy.

Thirdly, it may be easier to obtain valid and reliable indices of E than N. One possibility is that the sample of observations for E are more numerous than for N, and the other three other traits. There is concordance between the magnitude of the temporal stability of a variable and the number of observations used in its calculation (Epstein 1979; Schuerger *et al.* 1989). Specifically, aggregating over as many situations and occasions as possible increases both the magnitude of the test-retest correlations and, because error of measurement is reduced, the validity of the measure. Costa and McCrae (1995) note that when facet scores are aggregated, the domain scores have higher reliability and validity. Overall, including more valid measures of a construct increases test-retest reliability in a systematic fashion. In the present study, this relation is most apparent with number of items per scale and number of scales per instrument for each trait.

Among the instruments used in the primary studies, the California Personality Inventory (Gough 1975), the 16 PF, the GZTS, the EPQ, and the EPI have more items and scales measuring E or some facet of E than other traits. Together, the scales from these instruments account for about 30% of all correlations in the primary data. This is also found with observer or interviewer ratings of personality, e.g. in the studies of Bronson (1966), Mussen *et al.* (1980), and Tuddenham (1959).

If more scales are used in measuring a trait then it is likely that behavior over a greater number of different situations is being tapped. This will increase the magnitude of the test-retest correlations and hence the stability coefficient. In general, "broad, well-defined personality traits, particularly those that map onto common usage such as the Big 5 (Goldberg 1981), may show higher stabilities than traits that are more circumscribed or less familiar to the respondent" (West & Graziano 1989: 180). In contrast, scales measuring O, A, and C are somewhat under-represented in most instruments used in the MA debate.

The relatively small coefficient for A is contrary to the results of Roberts and Del Vecchio (2000) who report a stability coefficient of the same magnitude as E in their study. The most likely explanation is that Roberts and Del Vecchio (2000) include several studies not used in the present MA. These studies use peer-ratings of aggression as the sole marker for A (Bullock & Merrill 1980; Eron *et al.* 1972; Farrington 1978; Masten *et al.* 1985; Olweus 1977; Wiggins & Winder 1961). All of these studies report high retest correlations, e.g. 0.82 for Bullock and Merrill (1980), 0.72 for Olweus (1977). However, they are primarily based on short-term retest evaluations, mean interval = 3.8 years.

7.2. Interval and Trait Stability

For the aggregated sample, mean trait stability decreases in a linear, step-wise fashion over the five interval classes. This is a robust effect that is consistent with virtually all previous research on trait stability (e.g. Bloom 1966; Conley 1984; Costa & McCrae 1980; Stein *et al.* 1986; West & Graziano 1989). What is noteworthy is that even over intervals ranging from eight to 22 years, mean trait stability remains high at about 0.44.

The significant Q-values for all five traits indicate non-homogeneity, i.e. heterogeneity, of the effect sizes. This is expected because short-interval studies will have test-retest coefficients approaching the test-retest reliability of the instrument used; in other words, they will be quite large. Studies conducted over long intervals will have smaller test-retest coefficients. The disparity between the large and small coefficients will result in a significant Q-statistic.

The procedure for dealing with data like these is to determine the data point that contributes the most to the Q-statistic, and then to remove it from the analysis (Hedges & Olkin 1985). Presumably, this data point corresponds with the largest effect size and thereby accounts for the discrepant result. Within this type of analysis, and using this type of data, however, it is not possible to use outlier analysis and removal to yield homogeneous data. To illustrate, the three aberrant data points from Figure 2 will be examined. Mean stability coefficients for O, A, and C for the fourth interval, spanning 15.0–22.0 years with a mean of 18.8, are all significantly larger than coefficients for the preceding interval, which spans 8.0–14.0 years and has a mean of 10.6 years. For A and C, the coefficients for the fourth interval are also significantly larger than for the following interval, 25 or more years, mean interval equals 34.0 years. Examination of the homogeneity statistic for the four studies reveals that the study by Tuddenham (1959) contributes the most to non-homogeneity, −46.0, compared to −6.7 for the Helson and Moane study (1987), −22.5 for Kelly (1955), and −5.0 for the study by Stevens and Truss (1985).

Given the magnitude and significance of these differences, it is reasonable to assume that at least one of the studies reports anomalously large retest correlations. For each of these traits, the stability coefficients are based on the results from the same four studies. These are: Helson and Moane (1987), Kelly (1955), Stevens and Truss (cohort two; 1985), and Tuddenham (1959). Considering C, because the differences in magnitude of the correlations across the four studies is largest for this trait, the respective retest correlations are 0.65, 0.60, 0.42, and 0.10. Respective ages at study inception are 27, 20, 20, and 19, so it is unlikely that age is a confounding variable. Sample sizes are 81, 384, 85, and 72, also suggesting that sample size does not exert a confounding influence.

7.3. Gender and Trait Stability

Examination of gender as a potential moderator reveals that mean trait stability is equivalent for women and men, about 0.55, when data is collapsed across traits, intervals, and ages at beginning of study. Inspection of coefficients for individual traits, however, indicates that women generally, i.e. without reference to any other moderators, have more stable scores over time for N, 0.56 and 0.52 for women and men, respectively, and for E, 0.63 and 0.60 for women and men, respectively.

A four-year longitudinal study of normal adolescents (Ge *et al.* 1994) showed that women developed significantly higher mean levels of depressive symptoms than men. Though only measuring one facet of N, further analyses indicated that in adolescence, the propensity to maladaptation in the face of stressful life events was higher in women than in men. Woodall and Matthews (1993) also reported, in another four-year study, that female adolescents maintained higher stability values on indices of hostility, a facet of N, than men, with women showing lower mean levels of hostility at time one and time two than men. Overall, these findings have been confirmed in a number of studies (Brooks-Gunn 1991; Nolen-Hoeksema 1987), and extended to negative affect in others (Brooks-Gunn & Warren 1989; Swearington & Cohen 1985).

Simon and Thomas (1983) reported that women (mean age = 21 years) had significantly higher mean level scores for N and significantly lower mean level scores for E than men. In another study (Davis & Franzoi 1991), women had significantly higher mean levels of N, O, and C than men and also had larger test-retest correlations for all measures except empathic concern. On the E dimension, Baltes and Nesselroade (1972) found female adolescents to be more warm-hearted, while men were more dominant, assertive, aggressive, and excitement-seeking. Women were also more conscientious and persistent.

There is some conflicting evidence with respect to E, however. Although Costa and McCrae (1992) reported higher scores for women than men on all facets of N, women scored higher on all facets of E, with the sole exception of excitement-seeking, where men score higher. Muntaner *et al.* (1988) report significantly higher mean level scores for women on both N and E. Haan *et al.* (1986), in an assessment of traits spanning 50 years, reported that the period of greatest instability was the transition from late adolescence to early adulthood. Periods characterized by the greatest stability were early to middle adulthood, middle adulthood to late adulthood, and, most notably, childhood to early adolescence. These results are highly consistent with the present study, particularly with respect to N. Moreover, boys during the late adolescent- early adulthood transition had significantly lower test-retest correlations on measures of assertiveness and warmth, though stability was maintained for self-confidence. An opposite pattern was evident for girls, who had lower correlations for self-confidence but maintained consistent relative rankings on assertiveness and warmth. Over the duration of the life span, mean levels of self-confidence, outgoingness, and warmth showed strong linearly accelerated trends.

Ormel and Rijsdijk (2000), in a 16-year, five-wave study of N in adulthood, reported that mean levels for N were significantly higher at all time points for women. In contrast, Westenberg and Gjerde (1999) and Cohn (1991) report that women had significantly higher mean scores on ego development scales, which can be interpreted as crude measures of emotional health or maturity, which in turn are reflected in low scores on N. Westenberg and Gjerde (1999) also demonstrated that ego development for both women and men slows down and frequently stops after adolescence. They posit that adults may select their interpersonal environments to suit their level of ego development.

Stein *et al.* (1986) reported gender-related mean level differences in several traits. Specifically, women scored significantly higher than men on measures of generosity (A), law abidance (C), and orderliness (C), while men scored higher on indices of ambition (C), deliberateness (C), invulnerability (N), leadership (E), and self-acceptance. Moreover, scores for leadership and self-acceptance for women, low in early adolescence, increased substantially by late adolescence. For liberalism (O), scores obtained in early adolescence increased for boys and decreased for girls by late adolescence; by early adulthood, men and women were at about the same levels. In contrast, boys became less orderly between early and late adolescence, while the scores for girls increased over the period. There were no differences in E. Test-retest correlations for both genders were substantially larger for the period from late adolescence to early adulthood when compared with concordance between early and late adolescence. Correlations between scores obtained in early adolescence and early adulthood, were, of course, smallest in magnitude.

7.4. Age and Trait Stability

Trends for all curves depicted in Figure 2 show similar patterns. Stability is lowest when participants at the inception of the study are young and highest when participants are older. It has been demonstrated that age exerts a systematic influence on traits, raising the overall level of some and lowering the level of others (Costa & McCrae 1990). Studies by Costa *et al.* (Costa & McCrae 1989, 1992b; Costa *et al.* 1991) reported that adolescents and young adults were higher on N, E, and O scales, and lower on A and C scales than older individuals. The effect was replicated in a sample of young military recruits (Costa & McCrae 1994). Regardless of educational attainment, individuals in late adolescence were more intensely emotional, with higher scores on both negative affect (N) and positive affect (E), and were also less socialized, as evidenced by low scores on both A and C (Costa *et al.* 1991). The largest difference was on the excitement-seeking scale of E, with college students scoring much higher than adults. They also report that excitement seeking declines between adolescence and middle age (Zuckerman 1979). Many other studies have confirmed that stability is lower in adolescence (Carmichael & McGue 1994; Finn 1986; Haan *et al.* 1986; Helson & Moane 1987; Jessor 1983; Stein *et al.* 1986; Stevens & Truss 1985).

The position that a pervasive midlife crisis occurs with middle-aged men has not been vindicated (Costa & McCrae 1992b; Farrel & Rosenberg 1981; McCrae & Costa 1990). However, there is evidence that individuals who already have high scores on N show systematic increases in scores during this period (Cooper 1977; Costa & McCrea 1978, 1980; Farrell & Rosenberg 1981). Overall, the MA of age groups for the aggregated sample confirmed the finding that mean stability increases in a roughly linear fashion from the teen years till later life.

7.5. Effects of Year of Publication and Outlet on Traits Stability

Studies published in the 1990s report significantly higher retest correlations and studies from the 1980s report significantly lower correlations than studies from all other decades. What might account for these differences? It is unlikely that there is a systematic bias towards inflated test-retest correlations in studies from the 1990s. It is more reasonable to expect that, with the passage of time, "standards of research have become more rigorous, measures more critically scrutinized, replications demanded and provided" (Costa & McCrae 1990: 19; see also Eysenck & Eysenck 1985). If this is the case, then, overall, the 81 studies from the 1990s might better represent the true stability coefficient in the population rather than reflecting a systematic bias. Moreover, the coefficient approaches the upper bounds for the confidence intervals associated with coefficients from the 1940s, 1950s, 1960s, and 1970s. In other words, the magnitude of the difference, though significant, is not all that large.

The mean stability coefficient for studies from the 1980s poses a different problem, however. Here, the magnitude of the coefficient is considerably smaller than for the other time periods, and well outside of the boundaries for the corresponding confidence intervals. One hypothesis might be that journals were less receptive to studies reporting high retest correlations, possibly as a result of the challenge to trait theory throughout the 1970s. As many have noted, the renaissance in trait theory did not begin until early in the 1980s. To test this hypothesis, correlations from the periods 1970–1972, 1977–1979, 1980–1982, and 1987–1989 were examined with the expectation that coefficients would be highest for the first and fourth periods and lower for the periods between. This expectation was not met, with average correlations of 0.52, 0.55, 0.50, and 0.48 (uncorrected for sample size) reported for the four respective periods. Moreover, interval, age at study inception, and sample sizes were all similar for each period. Therefore, an explanation of why the mean stability coefficient for the 1980s is lower than for the other periods remains unresolved.

Mean stability coefficients for outlet can be grouped into three clusters. Studies published in the *Journal of Personality and Social Psychology*, and in test manuals report significantly higher test-retest correlations than studies from any other outlet, 0.60 and 0.58, respectively. In contrast, journals specializing in personality or genetics and in developmental psychology or gerontology reported significantly lower retest correlations overall, 0.50 and 0.49, respectively. Journals of general psychology as well as dissertations, conference presentations, and unpublished manuscripts report correlations that, when corrected for sample size, produce a stability coefficient of 0.54.

While it is possible that data reported in test manuals might be systematically inflated, it is highly unlikely that results from the *Journal of Personality and Social Psychology*, with its stringent requirements for publication, would be biased towards high retest correlations. As with studies from the 1990s, it is reasonable to assume that studies published in the *Journal of Personality and Social Psychology* probably better represent the true state of affairs. That the coefficient associated with journals of personality and genetics is among the lowest is somewhat surprising, if it is assumed that journals of this type would be more receptive to publishing data that is supportive of trait theory. One possibility is that some journals may have less stringent requirements for publication, and therefore publish studies with smaller sample sizes, leading to smaller effect sizes, and greater error variance.

Overall, it is reasonable to posit that higher estimates of trait stability are not the result of spuriously inflated test-retest correlations found in specific publication outlets within certain time periods. Recent studies published in the *Journal of Personality and Social Psychology* may provide data that more accurately reflects true trait stability in the population.

7.6. Factors Accounting for Trait Stability and Change

Although all of the mean stability coefficients are substantial, and comprise generally moderate to large effect sizes, they do not approach unity. Therefore, there is evidence in the present study for change as well as stability across the life span. Moreover, stability for some traits is mediated by gender, and age and gender interact. What factors might account for the observed stability and change in personality traits?

On the simplest level, two broad factors individually and interactively affect trait stability: these are genetics and biology, and the environment. The expression or development of some traits may be primarily determined by genetics while others are largely influenced by the environment. There can be differential influences of either genetics or environment at certain points in the individuals' life, and these may further by moderated by gender (Loehlin 1992; Viken *et al.* 1994).

Environment may be causally related to the stability of traits. Developmental studies suggest that a stable environment in childhood exerts a powerful influence on a wide variety of behaviors, many of which are maintained over the life span. Parental styles differentially reinforce social role models whereby children adopt gender-related characteristics (Feingold 1994). This interaction between the individual and the environment is further reinforced by expectancy effects, whereby gender stereotypes are socially and culturally reinforced. These factors may account for some of the variance observed in gender differences in such traits as aggression, compliance, dominance, and nurturance.

Genetic factors also play a causal role in trait consistency. Genetic or biological accounts of trait stability posit that traits are innate temperamental manifestations of underlying genotypes. The relative contributions of genes and environment are best assessed with twin studies. Tellegen *et al.* (1988) looked at personality similarity in twins reared together and apart. Heritabilities for traits ranged from 0.39 to 0.58, with an average of 0.48. Surprisingly, shared family environment was found to contribute negligibly to 12 of the 14 personality measures used in the study. McGue *et al.* (1993) performed behavior genetic analysis on a twin sample over an interval of ten years. The genetic influence on stability was greatest for the traits of negative emotionality (N) and positive emotionality (E). They report that, on average, "over 80% of the variance of the stable component of the Time 2 phenotype was associated with genetic factors" (p. 105), concluding that genetic factors are the prime determinant of stability in personality traits. Change in scores was attributed to the effects of unshared environment. These results were confirmed and extended in a developmental genetic analysis of N and E scores (Viken *et al.* 1994). Jang *et al.* (1996) assessed the genetic contribution to scores on the NEO-PI-R. The genetic contribution to trait scores was estimated to be: 41% for N; 53% for E; 61% for O; 41% for A; and 44% for C. The influence of shared environment was negligible for all traits, and unshared environment accounted for the remainder of the variance. These results concur with the more general analysis of Loehlin (1992).

On the basis of the available evidence, it is clear that genetics, shared and unshared environment, and interactions between these variables mediate the stability of personality traits. Stability is attributed to genetic influences and, to a lesser extent, shared environment; change is best accounted for by unshared environment (Jang *et al.* 1996; Loehlin 1992; McGue *et al.* 1993; Vernon *et al.* 1997; Viken *et al.* 1994).

Cognitive factors associated with biases in memory may also affect stability. One possibility is that individuals simply perceive themselves as having not changed over time, when in fact change has occurred. This memory effect might systematically inflate retest correlations. Several studies have addressed this issue.

In retrospective studies, participants are asked to recall how they responded in a previous test administration. Woodruff (1983) had participants complete a standard personality inventory under two conditions: (1) as they perceived themselves in the present (present condition); and (2) as they recalled answering at study inception 25 years earlier (retrospective condition). The recollections of the participants were of greater change than actually occurred. Although self-perceptions had changed, personality remained stable. An earlier study (Woodruff & Birren 1972) yielded similar results.

Another way of examining the role of memory is simply to have individuals indicate the degree of change experienced over the course of the study, then compare self-ratings with those of observers. Costa and McCrae (1988) asked participants to rate the degree to which they changed over a six-year period. Though some participants reported that they had changed a good deal, spouse ratings did not bear this out. They suggest that although self-concept may have changed for these individuals, personality traits did not.

Fleeson and Heckhausen (1997), in a study of perceived lifetime personality, had participants rate themselves on N, E, O, A, and C under three conditions: (1) as they were in the present; (2) as they recalled being in early adulthood; and (3) as they anticipated they would be in old age. Overall, results showed that many of the participants expected very substantial changes in almost all aspects of their personalities over the life span. These results address the problem of the so-called crystallized self-image, a type of memory effect hypothesized to account for trait stability (this problem is ameliorated by the use of observer reports). In short, the study suggests strongly that biases in favor of stability are not a confounding factor in studies of trait stability.

A mediating factor in longitudinal studies is that traits may not have equivalent meanings for people of different ages (Haan *et al.* 1986). For example, activity will clearly have quite different meanings for the 10-year old and the 65-year old. This refers to heterotypic continuity, which requires different operationalizations at different ages (Aspendorf & van Aken 1991: 122). Moss and Susman (1980) note that "differences in the definition of a personality variable tend to become progressively pronounced as the age interval between measurement increases" (p. 538). In contrast, homotypic continuity (Kagan 1971) means that the trait can be operationalized by the same measures at different ages (Aspendorf & van Aken 1991). A related methodological issue is that personality inventories are comprised of scales that are designed to assess stability, not change. The use of the same items at different ages may artificially inflate retest correlations.

The literal meaning of trait descriptors may be different for different researchers and across various instruments. Costa and McCrae (1990) note that correspondences between ostensibly identical constructs are "sometimes obscured by the labels psychologists have chosen for their scales. Two measures with the same label may measure different traits, and two measures of the same trait may have very different labels" (Costa & McCrae 1990: 28). An example of similarly labeled traits with quite different meanings is the distinction between impulsiveness as used by Costa and McCrae (1988), which is a facet of N, and impulsivity as used by Eysenck and Eysenck (1977) as a measure of Psychoticism. An example of different labels for measures of the same trait is tender-mindedness (Costa & McCrae 1988) and nurturance. Feingold (1994) reported although most assertiveness scales used in his MA differentiated between women and men, some did not.

8. Summary and Conclusions

A quantitative synthesis of longitudinal studies of personality traits was conducted using the FFM (Costa & McCrae 1992b) as an organizing framework. A search of the published literature yielded 81 studies, employing 95 cohorts, that reported test-retest Pearson correlations between scores at beginning and end of study and that used an established personality inventory. MA using the Hedges and Olkin (1985) algorithms was performed to determine the temporal stability of personality traits across the life span; estimates of the temporal stability of each trait were derived using the D-Stat (Johnson 1995) statistical package for MA. Only studies using intervals of one year or more were included. Studies of children less than ten years of age or of non-normal samples were not considered.

The temporal stability of Neuroticism (N), Extraversion (E), Openness to Experience (O), Agreeableness (A), and Conscientiousness (C) was assessed. Mean estimated stability coefficients were ranked as follows: E = 0.59; N = 0.52; O = 0.52; C = 0.50; and A = 0.48. The moderating effect of test-retest interval, gender, and age at study inception was examined. For all traits, mean stability was greatest at shorter intervals and declined systematically over time. Women had higher mean stability coefficients for N and E, but lower stability indices for O and C. An inverse relation was evident for mean trait stability and age at study inception, with substantial decrements in magnitude in late adolescence for N and A. Factors influencing stability and change in the temporal stability of traits are discussed.

The present study comprises the first meta-analytic summary of the moderating effects of interval, age, and gender on the temporal stability of traits on a trait-by-trait basis. Results from the 81 primary studies and 95 cohorts provide compelling evidence that personality traits show substantial stability over the life span. Moreover, there is strong support for the view that the FFM comprises a powerful tool to meaningfully synthesize studies using diverse instruments and trait concepts. Finally, the study contributes sound quantitative support to the conclusions of authors from scores of narrative reviews.

References

* References marked with an asterisk indicate studies used in the meta-analysis.

*Adams, S. H. (1994). Role of hostility in women's health during midlife: A longitudinal study. *Health Psychology*, *13*, 488–495.

Allport, G. W. (1937). *Personality: A psychological interpretation*. New York: Holt.

Allport, G. W., & Odbert, H. S. (1936). Trait names: A psycholexical study. *Psychological Monographs*, *47* (1, Whole No. 211).

Angleitner, A., & Ostendorf, F. (1994). Temperament and the big five factors of personality. In: C. F. Halverson, Jr., G. A. Kohnstamm, & R. P. Martin (Eds), *The developing structure of temperament and personality from infancy to adulthood* (pp. 69–90). Hilldale, NJ: Erlbaum.

Argyle, M., & Little, B. R. (1972). Do personality traits apply to social behavior? *Journal of Theory of Social Behavior*, *2*, 1–35.

*Aspendorf, J. B., & van Aken, M. A. G. (1991). Correlates of the temporal consistency of personality patterns in childhood. *Journal of Personality*, *59*, 721–730.

*Backteman, G., & Magnusson, D. (1981). Longitudinal stability of personality characteristics. *Journal of Personality*, *49*, 148–160.

*Baltes, P. B., & Nesselroade, J. R. (1972). Cultural change and adolescent personality development: An application of longitudinal sequences. *Developmental Psychology*, *7*, 244–256.

Barrett, P., & Eysenck, S. B. G. (1984). The assessment of personality factors across 25 countries. *Personality and Individual Differences*, *5*, 615–632.

*Bates, M. E., & Pandina, R. J. (1989). Individual differences in the stability of personality needs: Relations to stress and substance abuse during adolescence. *Personality and Individual Differences*, *10*, 1151–1157.

*Block, J. (1971). *Lives through time*. Berkeley, CA: Bancroft Books.

Block, J., & Robins, R. W. (1993). A longitudinal study of consistency and change in self-esteem from early adolescence to early adulthood. *Child Development*, *64*, 909–923.

Bloom, B. S. (1966). *Stability and change in human characteristics*. New York: Wiley.

*Bolton, B. (1979). Longitudinal stability of the primary and secondary dimensions of the 16PF-E. *Multivariate Experimental Clinical Research*, *4*, 67–71.

Borgatta, E. F. (1964). The structure of personality characteristics. *Behavioral Science*, *9*, 8–17.

Boyle, G. J. (1989). Re-examination of the major personality-type factors in the Cattell, Comrey, and Eysenck scales: Were the factor solutions by Noller et al. optimal? *Personality and Individual Differences*, *10*, 1289–1299.

Brody, N. (1988). *Personality: In search of individuality*. New York: Academic Press.

*Bromberger, J. T., & Matthews, K. A. (1996). A "feminine" model of vulnerability to depressive symptoms: A longitudinal investigation of middle-aged women. *Journal of Personality and Social Psychology*, *70*, 591–598.

*Bronson, W. C. (1966). Central organizations: A study of behavior organization from childhood to adolescence. *Child Development*, *37*, 125–155.

Brooks-Gunn, J. (1991). How stressful is the transition to adolescence for girls? In: M. E. Colten, & S. Gore (Eds), *Adolescent stress: Causes and consequences* (pp. 131–149). New York: Aldine de Gruyter.

Brooks-Gunn, J., & Warren, M. (1989). Biological and social contributions to negative affect in young adolescent girls. *Child Development*, *60*, 40–55.

Bullock, D., & Merrill, L. (1980). The impact of personal preference on consistency through time: The case of childhood aggression. *Child Development*, *51*, 808–814.

Buss, D. M. (1992). Manipulation in close relationships: Five personality factors in interactional context. *Journal of Personality*, *60*, 477–499.

*Cantoni, L. J. (1955). A study of emotional adjustment: The correlation of student and adult forms of the Bell Adjustment Inventory over a period of thirteen years. *Educational and Psychological Measurement*, *15*, 137–143.

*Caputo, D. V., Psathas, G., & Plapp, J. M. (1966). Test-retest reliability of the EPPS. *Educational and Psychological Measurement*, *26*, 883–886.

*Carmel, S., & Bernstein, J. (1989). Trait-anxiety and sense of coherence: A longitudinal study. *Psychological Reports*, *65*, 221–222.

*Carmichael, C. M., & McGue, M. (1994). A longitudinal study of personality change and stability. *Journal of Personality*, *62*, 1–20.

Cattell, R. B. (1933). Temperament tests: II: Tests. *British Journal of Psychology*, *23*, 308–329.

Cattell, R. B. (1944). Interpretation of the twelve primary personality factors. *Character and Personality*, *13*, 55–91.

Cattell, R. B. (1947). Confirmation and clarification of primary personality factors. *Psychometrika*, *12*, 197–220.

Cattell, R. B. (1948). The primary personality factors in women compared with those in men. *British Journal of Psychology*, *1*, 114–130.

Cattell, R. B. (1950). *Personality: A systematic theoretical and factual study*. New York: McGraw-Hill.

*Cattell, R. B., & Cattell, M. D. L. (1975). *Handbook for the Jr.-Sr. High School Personality Questionnaire*. Champaign, IL: Institute for Personality and Ability Testing.

Cattell, R. B., Eber, H. W., & Tatsuoka, M. M. (1970). *Handbook for the Sixteen Personality Factor Questionnaire (16PF)*. Champaign, IL: Institute for Personality and Ability Testing.

Church, A. T., & Katibak, M. S. (1989). Internal, external, and self-report structure of personality in a non-Western culture: An investigation of cross-language and cross-cultural generalizability. *Journal of Personality and Social Psychology*, *57*, 857–872.

Cohn, L. D. (1991). Sex differences in the course of personality development: A meta-analysis. *Psychological Bulletin*, *109*, 252–266.

*Conley, J. J. (1984). The hierarchy of consistency: A review and model of longitudinal findings on adult individual differences in intelligence, personality, and self-opinion. *Personality and Individual Differences*, *5*, 11–26.

*Conley, J. J. (1985). Longitudinal stability of personality traits: A multitrait-multimethod-multi-occasion analysis. *Journal of Personality and Social Psychology*, *49*, 1266–1282.

*Cook, D. L., & Wolaver, K. E. (1963). Teacher-pupil attitudes, personality, and teaching experience. Paper presented at the American Educational Research Association, Columbus, OH. Reported in: J. S. Guilford, W. S. Zimmerman, & J. P. Guilford (1976), *The Guilford-Zimmerman Temperament Survey handbook*. San Diego, CA: Edits Publishers.

Cooper, H. M. (1979). Statistically combining independent studies: A meta-analysis of sex differences in conformity research. *Journal of Personality and Social Psychology, 37*, 131–146.

Cooper, M. W. (1977). *An investigation of the male midlife period: A descriptive, cohort study.* Unpublished manuscript, University of Massachusetts at Boston.

*Costa, P. T., Jr., & McCrae, R. R. (1977–1978). Age differences in personality structure revisited: Studies in validity, stability, and change. *International Journal of Aging and Human Development, 8*, 261–275.

*Costa, P. T., Jr., & McCrae, R. R. (1980). Still stable after all these years: Personality as a key to some issues in adulthood and old age. In: P. B. Baltes, & O. G. Brim (Eds), *Life span development and behavior* (Vol. 3, pp. 65–102). New York: Academic Press.

Costa, P. T., Jr., & McCrae, R. R. (1985). *The NEO Personality Inventory manual.* Odessa, FL: Psychological Assessment Resources.

Costa, P. T., Jr., & McCrae, R. R. (1986). Personality stability and its implications for clinical psychology. *Clinical Psychology Review, 6*, 407–423.

*Costa, P. T., Jr., & McCrae, R. R. (1988). Personality in adulthood: A six-year longitudinal study of self-reports and spouse ratings on the NEO Personality Inventory. *Journal of Personality and Social Psychology, 54*, 858–863.

*Costa, P. T., Jr., & McCrae, R. R. (1989). *NEO-PI/NEO-FFI manual supplement.* Odessa, FL: Psychological Assessment Resources.

Costa, P. T., Jr., & McCrae, R. R. (1992a). Four ways five factors are basic. *Personality and Individual Differences, 13*, 653–665.

Costa, P. T., Jr., & McCrae, R. R. (1992b). *Revised NEO Personality Inventory and NEO Five-Factor Inventory.* Odessa, FL: Psychological Assessment Resources.

Costa, P. T., Jr., & McCrae, R. R. (1994). Set like plaster? Evidence for the stability of adult personality. In: T. F. Heatherton, & J. L. Weinberger (Eds), *Can personality change?* (pp. 21–40). Washington, DC: American Psychological Association.

Costa, P. T., Jr., & McCrae, R. R. (1995). Primary traits of Eysenck's P-E-N system: Three- and five-factor solutions. *Journal of Personality and Social Psychology, 69*, 308–317.

Costa, P. T., Jr., McCrae, R. R., & Arenberg, D. (1980). Enduring dispositions in adult males. *Journal of Personality and Social Psychology, 38*, 793–800.

Costa, P. T., Jr., McCrae, R. R., & Dye, D. A. (1991). Facet scales for agreeableness and conscientiousness: A revision of the NEO Personality Inventory. *Personality and Individual Differences, 12*, 887–898.

Cronbach, L. J. (1970). *Essentials of psychological testing* (3rd ed.). New York: Harper & Row.

*Crook, M. N. (1941). Retest correlations in neuroticism. *Journal of General Psychology, 24*, 74–101.

*Crook, M. N. (1943). A retest with the Thurstone Personality Schedule after six and one-half years. *Journal of General Psychology, 28*, 111–120.

*Davis, M. H., & Franzoi, S. L. (1991). Stability and change in adolescent self-consciousness and empathy. *Journal of Research in Personality, 25*, 70–87.

*Davis, T. N., & Satterly, D. J. (1969). Personality profiles of student teachers. *British Journal of Educational Psychology, 39*, 183–187.

Digman, J. M. (1996). The curious history of the Five-Factor Model. In: J. S. Wiggins (Ed.), *The Five-Factor Model of personality* (pp. 1–20). New York: Guilford Press.

*von Dras, D. D., & Siegler, I. C. (1997). Stability in extraversion and aspects of social support at midlife. *Journal of Personality and Social Psychology, 72*, 233–241.

*Dudek, S. Z., & Hall, W. B. (1991). Personality consistency: Eminent architects 25 years later. *Creativity Research Journal, 4*, 213–231.

*Dusek, J. B., & Flaherty, J. F. (1981). The development of the self-concept during adolescent years. *Monographs for the Society for Research in Child Development, 46* (4, Serial No. 191).

*Eckert, R. G. (1940). *A mental hygiene approach to speech instruction as a means to personal adjustment*. Unpublished doctoral dissertation, University of California. Reported in Bloom, B. S. (1964), *Stability and change in human characteristics*. New York: Wiley.

Endler, N. S. (1983). Interactionism: A personality model, but not yet a theory. *Nebraska symposium on motivation, 1982*. In: M. M. Page (Ed.), *Personality: Current theory and research* (pp. 155–200). Lincoln, NE: University of Nebraska Press.

Epstein, S. (1979). The stability of behavior: I: On predicting most of the people much of the time. *Journal of Personality and Social Psychology*, *37*, 1097–1126.

Epstein, S. (1983). Aggregation and beyond: Some basic issues on the prediction of behavior. *Journal of Personality*, *51*, 360–392.

Eron, L. D., Huesmann, L. R., Lefkowitz, M. M., & Walder, L. O. (1972). Does television cause aggression? *American Psychologist*, *27*, 253–263.

Eysenck, H. J., & Eysenck, M. W. (1985). *Personality and individual differences: A natural science approach*. New York: Plenum Press.

Eysenck, H. J., & Eysenck, S. B. G. (1964). *Manual of the Eysenck Personality Inventory*. San Diego, CA: Edits Publishers.

Eysenck, H. J., & Eysenck, S. B. G. (1975). *Manual of the Eysenck Personality Questionnaire*. San Diego, CA: Edits Publishers.

Eysenck, S. B. G., & Eysenck, H. J. (1977). The place of impulsiveness in a dimensional system of personality description. *British Journal of Social and Clinical Psychology*, *16*, 57–68.

*Farnsworth, P. R. (1938). A genetic study of the Bernreuter Personality Inventory. *Journal of Genetic Psychology*, *52*, 3–13.

Farrell, M. P., & Rosenberg, S. D. (1981). *Men at midlife*. Boston, MA: Auburn House.

Farrington, D. P. (1978). The family backgrounds of aggressive youth. In: L. A. Hersov, M. Berger, & D. Shaffer (Eds), *Aggression and anti-social behavior in childhood and adolescence* (pp. 73–94). Oxford, England: Pergamon Press.

Feingold, A. (1994). Gender differences in personality: A meta-analysis. *Psychological Bulletin*, *116*, 429–456.

Feist, G. J. (1998). A meta-analysis of personality in scientific and artistic creativity. *Personality and Social Psychology Review*, *2*, 290–309.

*Field, D., & Millsap, R. E. (1991). Personality in advanced old age: Continuity or change? *Journal of Gerontology: Psychological Sciences*, *46*, 299–308.

*Finn, S. E. (1986). Stability of personality self-ratings over 30 years: Evidence for age/cohort interaction. *Journal of Personality and Social Psychology*, *50*, 813–818.

Fiske, D. W. (1949). Consistency of the factorial structures of personality ratings from different sources. *Journal of Abnormal and Social Psychology*, *44*, 329–344.

Fleeson, W., & Heckhausen, J. (1997). More or less "me" in past, present, and future: Perceived lifetime personality during adulthood. *Psychology and Aging*, *12*, 125–136.

Funder, D. C., & Colvin, C. R. (1991). Explorations in behavioral consistency: Properties of persons, situations, and behaviors. *Journal of Personality and Social Psychology*, *60*, 773–794.

Ge, X., Lorenz, F. O., Conger, R. D., Elder, G. H., & Simons, R. L. (1994). Trajectories of stressful life events and depressive symptoms. *Developmental Psychology*, *30*, 467–483.

*Giuganino, B. M., & Hindley, C. B. (1982). Stability of individual differences in personality characteristics from 3 to 15 years. *Personality and Individual Differences*, *3*, 287–302.

Glass, G. V., McGaw, B., & Smith, M. L. (1981). *Meta-analysis in social research*. Beverly Hills, CA: Sage.

*Gold, S. R., & Henderson, B. B. (1990). Daydreaming and curiosity: Stability and change in gifted children and adolescents. *Adolescence*, *25*, 701–708.

Goldberg, L. R. (1981). Language and individual differences: The search for universals in personality lexicons. In: L. Wheeler (Ed.), *Review of personality and social psychology* (Vol. 2, pp. 141–165). Beverly Hills, CA: Sage.

*Gough, H. G. (1975). *Manual for the California Psychological Inventory*. Palo Alto, CA: Consulting Psychologists Press.

*Grigordias, S., & Fekken, G. C. (1992). Person reliability on the Minnesota Multiphasic Personality Inventory. *Personality and Individual Differences*, *13*, 491–500.

Guilford, J. P. (1936). Unitary traits of personality and factor theory. *American Journal of Psychology*, *48*, 673–680.

Guilford, J. P. (1959). *Personality*. New York: McGraw-Hill.

Guilford, J. P., & Guilford, R. B. (1939a). Personality factors D, R, T and A. *Journal of Abnormal and Social Psychology*, *34*, 230–238.

Guilford, J. P., & Guilford, R. B. (1939b). Personality factors N and GD. *Journal of Abnormal and Social Psychology*, *34*, 239–248.

Guilford, J. S., Zimmerman, W. S., & Guilford, J. P. (1976). *The Guilford-Zimmerman Temperament Survey handbook*. San Diego, CA: Edits Publishers.

*Gustavsson, J. P., Weinryb, R. M., Goransson, S., Pedersen, N. L., & Asberg, M. (1997). Stability and predictive validity of personality traits across 9 years. *Personality and Individual Differences*, *22*, 783–791.

Haan, N., Millsap, R., & Hartka, E. (1986). As time goes by: Change and stability in personality over fifty years. *Psychology and Aging*, *1*, 220–232.

Hall, J. A., & Rosenthal, R. (1995). Interpreting and evaluating meta-analysis. *Evaluation and the Health Professions*, *18*, 393–407.

*Harris, C. M. (1981). [Test-retest reliabilities of medical students at St. Mary's Hospital Medical School]. Unpublished raw data. Cited in: I. B. Meyers, & M. H. McCaulley (1985), *Manual: A guide to the development and of the Myers-Briggs type Indicator*. Palo Alto, CA: Consulting Psychologists Press.

*Harris, J. G., Jr. (1985). Congruence and temporal stability of multimethod profiles: A new pair of personality variables. *Journal of Personality*, *53*, 586–602.

*Hathaway, S. R., & Monachesi, E. D. (1963). *Adolescent personality and behavior: MMPI patterns of normal, delinquent, and dropout, other outcomes*. Minneapolis, MN: University of Minnesota Press.

Hedges, L. V., & Olkin, I. (1985). *Statistical methods for meta-analysis*. Stanford, CA: Stanford University Press.

*Helson, R., & Moane, G. (1987). Personality change in women from college to midlife. *Journal of Personality and Social Psychology*, *53*, 176–186.

*Helson, R., Roberts, B., & Agronick, G. (1995). Enduringness and change in creative personality and the prediction of occupational creativity. *Journal of Personality and Social Psychology*, *69*, 1173–1183.

*Helson, R., & Wink, P. (1992). Personality change in women from the early 40s to the early 50s. *Psychology and Aging*, *7*, 46–55.

*Holmlund, U. (1991). Change and stability of needs from middle adolescence to young adulthood in Swedish females. *European Journal of Personality*, *5*, 379–385.

Hunt, J. M. (1965). Validity in personality trait attribution. *American Scientist*, *53*, 80–96.

*Izard, C. E., Liberto, D. Z., Putnam, P., & Haynes, O. M. (1993). Stability of emotional experiences and their relations to traits of personality. *Journal of Personality and Social Psychology*, *64*, 847–860.

Jackson, D. N., & Paunonen, S. V. (1985). Construct validity and the predictability of behavior. *Journal of Personality and Social Psychology*, *49*, 554–570.

Jang, K. L., Livesly, W. J., & Vernon, P. A. (1996). Heritability of the Big Five personality dimensions and their facets: A twin study. *Journal of Personality*, *64*, 577–591.

*Jessor, R. (1983). The stability of change: Psychosocial development from adolescence to young adulthood. In: D. Magnusson, & V. L. Allen (Eds), *Human development: An interactional approach* (pp. 321–341). San Diego, CA: Academic Press.

*John, O. P., Cheek, J. M., & Klohnen, E. C. (1996). On the nature of self-monitoring: Construct explication with Q-sort ratings. *Journal of Personality and Social Psychology*, *71*, 763–776.

Johnson, B. T. (1995). *D-Stat: Software for the meta-analytic review of research literatures*. Hillsdale, NJ: Lawrence Erlbaum Associates.

Johnson, B. T., Mullen, B., & Salas, E. (1995). Comparison of three major meta-analytic approaches. *Journal of Applied Psychology*, *80*, 94–106.

Kagan, J. (1971). *Change and continuity in infancy*. New York: Wiley.

*Kelly, E. L. (1955). Consistency of the adult personality. *American Psychologist*, *10*, 659–681.

*Leon, G. R., Gillum, B., Gillum, R., & Gouze, M. (1979). Personality stability and change over a 30-year period – middle to old age. *Journal of Consulting and Clinical Psychology*, *47*, 517–524.

Loehlin, J. C. (1992). *Genes and environment in personality development*. Newbury Park, CA: Sage.

*Lovibond, P. F. (1998). Long-term stability of depression, anxiety, and stress syndromes. *Journal of Abnormal Psychology*, *107*, 520–526.

Lynn, R., & Martin, T. (1997). Gender differences in extraversion, neuroticism, and psychoticism in 37 nations. *The Journal of Social Psychology*, *137*, 369–373.

*Magnusson, D., & Backteman, G. (1978). Longitudinal stability of person characteristics: Intelligence and creativity. *Applied Psychological Measurement*, *2*, 481–490.

Masten, A. S., Morison, P., & Pellegrini, D. S. (1985). A revised class play method of peer assessment. *Developmental Psychology*, *21*, 523–533.

McCrae, R. R., & Costa, P. T., Jr. (1989). Reinterpreting the Myers-Briggs Type Indicator from the perspective of the five-factor model of personality. *Journal of Personality*, *57*, 17–40.

McCrae, R. R., & Costa, P. T., Jr. (1990). *Personality in adulthood*. New York: Guilford.

McCrae, R. R., & Costa, P. T., Jr. (1996). Toward a new generation of personality theories: Theoretical contexts for the five-factor model. In: J. S. Wiggins (Ed.), *The five-factor model of personality: Theoretical perspectives* (pp. 51–87). New York: Guilford.

McCrae, R. R., & Costa, P. T., Jr. (1997). Personality trait structure as a human universal. *American Psychologist*, *52*, 509–516.

*McGue, M., Bacon, S., & Lykken, D. T. (1993). Personality stability and change in early adulthood: A behavioral genetic analysis. *Developmental Psychology*, *29*, 96–109.

*Melamed, A. R., Silverman, M. S., & Lewis, G. J. (1974). Three-year follow-up of religious women on the 16 Personality Factor Questionnaire. *Review of Religious Research*, *15*, 64–70.

*Meyer, J. M., Heath, A. C., Eaves, L. J., Mosteller, M., & Schieken, R. M. (1988). The predictive power of Cattell's personality questionnaires: An eighteen-month prospective study. *Personality and Individual Differences*, *9*, 203–212.

Meyers, I. B., & McCaulley, M. H. (1985). *Manual: A guide to the development and use of the Myers-Briggs Type Indicator*. Palo Alto, CA: Consulting Psychologists Press.

*Mills, W. W. (1954). *MMPI profile pattern and scale stability throughout four years of college attendance*. Doctoral dissertation, University of Minnesota, Minneapolis, MN. Reported in: J. J. Conley (1984), The hierarchy of consistency: A review and model of longitudinal findings on adult individual differences in intelligence, personality, and self-opinion. *Personality and Individual Differences*, *5*, 11–26.

Mischel, W. (1973). Toward a cognitive social learning reconceptualization of personality. *Psychological Review*, *80*, 252–283.

Moss, H. A., & Susman, E. J. (1980). Longitudinal study of personality development. In: O. G. Brim, Jr., & J. Kagan (Eds), *Constancy and change in human development* (pp. 530–595). Cambridge, MA: Harvard University Press.

*Muntaner, C., Garcia-Sevilla, L., Fernandez, A., & Torrubia, R. (1988). Personality dimensions, schizotypal and borderline personality traits and psychosis proneness. *Personality and Individual Differences*, *9*, 257–268.

*Mussen, P., Eichorn, D. H., Honzick, M. P., Bieher, S. L., & Meredeth, W. (1980). Continuity and change in women's characteristics over four decades. *International Journal of Behavioral Development*, *3*, 333–347.

*Myers, I. B. (1973). *Retest reliability of the Type Indicator*. Unpublished manuscript. Reported in: I. B. Meyers, & M. H. McCaulley (1985). *Manual: A guide to the development and use of the Myers-Briggs Type Indicator*. Palo Alto, CA: Consulting Psychologists Press.

*Nichols, R. C. (1967). Personality change and the college. *American Education Research*, *4*, 173–190.

Nolen-Hoeksema, S. (1987). Sex differences in unipolar depression: Evidence and theory. *Psychological Bulletin*, *101*, 259–282.

Norman, W. T. (1963). Toward an adequate taxonomy of personality attributes: Replicated factor structure in peer nomination personality ratings. *Journal of Abnormal and Social Psychology*, *66*, 574–583.

Norman, W. T. (1967). *2800 personality trait descriptors: Normative operating characteristics for a university population*. Ann Arbor, MI: University of Michigan, Department of Psychology.

Olweus, D. (1977). Aggression and peer acceptance in adolescent boys: Two short-term longitudinal studies of ratings. *Child Development*, *48*, 1301–1313.

Ormel, J., & Rijsdijk, F. V. (2000). Continuing change in neuroticism during adulthood – structural modeling of a 16-year, 5-wave community study. *Personality and Individual Differences*, *28*, 461–478.

Orwin, R. G. (1983). A fail-safe N for effect size. *Journal of Educational Statistics*, *8*, 157–159.

Ostendorf, F. (1990). *Language and personality structure: Toward the validation of the Five-Factor Model of personality*. Regensburg, Germany: S. Roeder Verlag.

*Parnas, J., Teasdale, T. W., & Schulsinger, H. (1982). Continuity of character neurosis from childhood to adulthood. *Acta Psychiatrica Scandinavia*, *6*, 491–498.

Peabody, D. (1987). Selecting representative trait adjectives. *Journal of Personality and Social Psychology*, *52*, 59–71.

*Pederson, W. (1991). Mental health, sensation seeking and drug use patterns: A longitudinal study. *British Journal of Addiction*, *86*, 195–204.

*Plant, W. T. (1958). Changes in ethnocentrism associated with a two-year college experience. *Journal of Genetic Psychology*, *92*, 189–197.

*Plant, W. T., & Telford, C. W. (1966). Changes in personality for groups completing different amounts of college over two years. *Genetic Psychology Monographs*, *74*, 3–36.

*Popham, S. M., & Holden, R. R. (1991). Psychometric properties of MMPI factor scales. *Personality and Individual Differences*, *12*, 513–517.

Preiss, R. W., & Allen, M. (1995). Understanding and using meta-analysis. *Evaluation & the Health Professions*, *18*, 315–335.

Pulver, A., Allik, J., Pulkkinen, L., & Hamalainen, M. (1995). A Big-Five personality inventory in two non-Indo-European languages. *European Journal of Personality*, *9*, 109–124.

Roberts, B. W., & Del Vecchio, W. F. (2000). The rank-order consistency of personality traits from childhood to old age: A quantitative review of longitudinal studies. *Psychological Bulletin*, *126*, 3–25.

Rosenthal, R. (1979). The 'file drawer' problem and tolerance for null results. *Psychological Bulletin*, *86*, 638–641.

Rosenthal, R. (1995). Writing meta-analytic reviews. *Psychological Bulletin, 118*, 183–192.

Ross, L. D., Amabile, T. M., & Steinmetz, J. L. (1977). Social roles, social control, and biases in social-perception processes. *Journal of Personality of Personality & Social Psychology, 35*, 485–494.

*Schofield, W. (1953). A study of medical students with the MMPI: II: Group and individual changes after two years. *Journal of Psychology, 36*, 137–141.

Schuerger, J. M., Zarrella, K. L., & Hotz, A. S. (1989). Factors that influence the temporal stability of personality by questionnaire. *Journal of Personality and Social Psychology, 56*, 777–783.

*Simon, A., & Thomas, A. (1983). Means, standard deviations, and stability coefficients on the EPI for further education and college of education students. *Personality and Individual Differences, 4*, 95–96.

Smith, G. M. (1967). Usefulness of peer ratings of personality in educational research. *Educational and Psychological Measurement, 27*, 967–984.

*Soldz, S., & Vaillant, G. E. (1999). The Big Five personality traits and the life course: A 45-year longitudinal study. *Journal of Research in Personality, 33*, 208–232.

*Stacy, A. W., Newcomb, M. D., & Bentler, P. M. (1991). Social psychological influences on sensation seeking from adolescence to adulthood. *Personality and Social Psychology Bulletin, 17*, 701–708.

*Stein, J. A., Newcomb, M. D., & Bentler, P. M. (1986). Stability and change in personality: A longitudinal study from early adolescence to young adulthood. *Journal of Research in Personality, 20*, 276–291.

*Stevens, D. P., & Truss, C. V. (1985). Stability and change in adult personality over 12 and 20 years. *Developmental Psychology, 21*, 568–584.

*Stewart, L. H. (1964). Change in personality test scores during college. *Journal of Counseling Psychology, 11*, 211–220.

*Stricker, L. J., & Ross, J. (1964). An assessment of some structural properties of the Jungian personality typology. *Journal of Abnormal and Social Psychology, 68*, 62–71.

Swearington, E. M., & Cohen, L. H. (1985). Life events and psychological distress: A prospective study of young adolescents. *Developmental Psychology, 21*, 1045–1054.

*Taylor, J. A. A. (1953). A personality scale of manifest anxiety. *Journal of Abnormal and Social Psychology, 48*, 285–290.

Tellegen, A., Lykken, D. T., Bouchard, T. J., Wilcox, K. J., Segal, N. L., & Rich, S. (1988). Personality similarity in twins reared apart and together. *Journal of Personality and Social Psychology, 54*, 1031–1039.

Thurstone, L. L. (1934). The vectors of mind. *Psychological Review, 41*, 1–32.

Thurstone, L. L. (1947). *Multiple factor analysis*. Chicago, IL: University of Chicago Press.

Thurstone, L. L. (1951). The dimensions of temperament. *Psychometrika, 16*, 11–20.

Thurstone, L. L. (1953). *Thurstone Temperament Schedule*. Chicago, IL: Science Research Associates.

*Tuddenham, R. D. (1959). The consistency of personality ratings over two decades. *Genetic Psychology Monographs, 60*, 3–29.

Tupes, E. C., & Christal, R. E. (1961). *Recurrent personality factors based on trait ratings* (USAF ASD Tech. Rep. No. 61–97). Lackland Airforce Base, TX: U.S. AirForce.

Tupes, E. C., & Kaplan, M. N. (1961). *Similarity of factors underlying peer ratings of socially acceptable, socially unacceptable, and bipolar personality traits* (USAF ASD Tech. Rep. No. 61–48). Lackland Airforce Base, TX: U.S. Air Force.

*Usala, P. D., & Hertzog, C. (1991). Evidence of differential stability of state and trait anxiety in adults. *Journal of Personality and Social Psychology, 60*, 471–479.

Vernon, P. A., Jang, K. L., Aitken Harris, J., & McCarthy, J. M. (1997). Environmental predictors of personality differences: A twin and sibling study. *Journal of Personality and Social Psychology, 72*, 177–183.

*Viken, R. J., Rose, R. J., Kaprio, J., & Koskenvuo, M. (1994). A developmental genetic analysis of adult personality: Extraversion and neuroticism from 18 to 59 years of age. *Journal of Personality and Social Psychology*, *66*, 722–730.

*Watson, D., & McKee-Walker, L. (1996). The long-term stability and predictive validity of trait measures of affect. *Journal of Personality and Social Psychology*, *70*, 567–577.

Webb, E. (1915). Character and intelligence. *British Journal of Psychology Monographs*, *1*, 1–99.

*Weiss, J. (1980). [Longitudinal data of University of New Mexico Nursing Program]. Unpublished raw data. Reported in: I. B. Meyers, & M. H. McCaulley (1985), *Manual: A guide to the development and use of the Myers-Briggs Type Indicator*. Palo Alto, CA: Consulting Psychologists Press.

West, S. G., & Graziano, W. G. (1989). Long-term stability and change in personality: An introduction. *Journal of Personality*, *57*, 175–193.

Westenberg, P. M., & Gjerde, P. F. (1999). Ego development during the transition from adolescence to young adulthood: A 9-year longitudinal study. *Journal of Research in Personality*, *33*, 233–252.

*Wheeler, D. S., & Schwartz, J. C. (1989). Millon Clinical Multiaxial Inventory (MCMI) scores with a collegiate sample: Long-term stability and self-other agreement. *Journal of Psychopathology and Behavioural Assessment*, *11*, 339–352.

Wiggins, J. S. (1996). *The Five-Factor Model of personality: Theoretical perspectives*. New York: Guilford.

*Wilhelm, K., & Parker, G. (1990). Reliability of the Parental Bonding Instrument and Intimate Bond Measure scales. *Australian and New Zealand Journal of Psychiatry*, *24*, 199–202.

*Woodall, K. L., & Matthews, K. A. (1993). Changes in and stability of hostile characteristics: Results from a 4-year longitudinal study of children. *Journal of Personality and Social Psychology*, *64*, 491–499.

Woodruff, D. S. (1983). The role of memory in personality continuity: A 25 year followup. *Experimental Aging Research*, *9*, 31–34.

*Woodruff, D. S., & Birren, J. E. (1972). Age changes and cohort differences in personality. *Developmental Psychology*, *6*, 252–259.

*Yonge, G., & Regan, M. C. (1975). A longitudinal study of personality and choice of major. *Journal of Vocational Behavior*, *7*, 41–65.

Zuckerman, M. (1979). *Sensation seeking: Beyond the optimal level of arousal*. London: Wiley.

Chapter 9

The Genetic Basis of Substance Abuse: Mediating Effects of Sensation Seeking

A. M. Johnson and P. A. Vernon

1. Introduction

Most modern theories of personality are structured hierarchically, with broad higher-order dimensions predicting narrower trait-level variables. This approach is necessarily reductionist, proposing to summarize the majority of trait-specific variability with a smaller number of larger dimensions. Not surprisingly, therefore, significant research has been directed to determining what might be considered to be the most basic dimensions of personality — both with regards to the identification of how many factors are needed to describe personality, and what these factors might be called (Costa & McCrae 1992a; Eysenck 1947, 1967; Tupes & Christal 1992; Zuckerman 1992; Zuckerman *et al.* 1991, 1993). While these omnibus factors of personality have proven useful in the prediction of broadly defined behavioral criteria (Paunonen 2003), they raise the important question of "what makes a factor basic?" (Zuckerman 1992). Zuckerman (1992) suggested four characteristics that are critical to the identification of a "basic trait": (1) replication across methods, genders, ages, and cultures; (2) at least moderate heritability; (3) evidence of similar "personality" traits in non-human species; and (4) at least a partial foundation in biology.

The predominant method for identifying (and demonstrating) the factorial structure of personality is factor analysis — a statistical modeling procedure that aims to find latent constructs (variables that cannot be directly observed) that are responsible for the correlation between observed variables. A latent construct is represented by the shared variability of a number of observed variables, and these latent constructs are often called factors (Kim & Mueller 1978). The method relies on the assumption that each observed variable contains variance from two sources: variability that is shared with other variables, and variability that is unique to the variable. It is clear, therefore, that the nature of the factor structure in a set of data will be heavily determined by the variables included in the analysis (Zuckerman 1992, 1995; Zuckerman *et al.* 1993), and the practical implication of this statistical property of

On the Psychobiology of Personality
Edited by R. M. Stelmack

ISBN: 0-08-044209-9

factor analysis is that one is more likely to identify a stable factor if there is a preponderance of a particular construct (or constructs) within a particular data set. Similarly, if a latent construct is under-represented within the data set used for the factor analysis, it is unlikely to show up in the factor solution.

For this reason, it is important to have a systematic rationale for the selection of scales to be included in an analysis. The two basic rationales that have predominated within the literature are lexical models and biological models. Lexical models of personality rely on the assumption that language will evolve to produce the adjectives necessary to describe all aspects of personality. Accordingly, models of personality that are derived through a lexical approach tend to be derived from a distillation of large collections of adjectives that have been rationally and statistically sorted to produce basic personality traits — which are in turn sorted rationally and statistically into omnibus dimensions of personality (Goldberg 1990). Biological models of personality, on the other hand, are derived from a consideration of traits that are considered to be basic to human physiology or anatomy (Eysenck 1947, 1967; Zuckerman 1989; Zuckerman *et al.* 1991, 1993). In other words, these personality traits are traceable to physiological events, or physical differences among humans (Zuckerman 1995).

Arguably, the most widely cited personality model is Eysenck's (1947, 1967) "PEN" model, consisting of Psychoticism, Extraversion, and Neuroticism. Eysenck (1947, 1967) considered these three factors to be the most basic dimensions of human personality, with all dimensions beyond these factors attributable to some combination of the three. The PEN model was originally proposed as an analog to three basic adaptive behaviors observable among primates: sociability (extraversion), or the ability to interact cooperatively with peers to achieve complex goals; emotionality (neuroticism), or the ability to maintain appropriate levels of arousal in the face of a threat; and tough-mindedness (psychoticism), or the tendency to engage in aggressive behavior not linked to an obvious and proximal reward (Zuckerman 1989).

The Five-Factor Model (FFM; Costa & McCrae 1992b; Tupes & Christal 1992), on the other hand, is a widely cited model of personality derived from a lexical approach (Goldberg 1990). This is not to suggest, of course, that the FFM is not biologically relevant — all of the factors of the FFM have been demonstrated to be at least partially genetically determined (Jang *et al.* 1996; Johnson *et al.* 2004). Furthermore, the FFM shares two basic factors with Eysenck's (1947, 1967) PEN model, namely Extraversion, or Surgency and Neuroticism. Rather than a Psychoticism factor, however, the remaining dimensions of the FFM are described as Agreeableness, Conscientiousness or Dependability, and Openness to Experience or Culture (Costa & McCrae 1992b; Goldberg 1990; Tupes & Christal 1992).

Despite the success of the FFM, it is difficult to reconcile some robust and biologically relevant personality traits within its structure, such as masculinity/femininity (Paunonen & Jackson 2000) and sensation seeking (Ashton *et al.* 1998; Jackson *et al.* 1996; Paunonen & Jackson 1996). To this end, Zuckerman *et al.* (1991) proposed an alternative FFM, intended to represent the basic biological dimensions of personality. Like the PEN and FFM models, the Alternative FFM has an Extraversion factor termed Sociability, and a Neuroticism factor termed Anxiety. The remaining factors represent a rotation of the traditional FFM factor structure, and are termed Aggression-Hostility, Impulsive Unsocialized Sensation Seeking, and Activity (Zuckerman *et al.* 1991, 1993). Aggression-Hostility is similar to the negative pole of the FFM Agreeableness factor, and is typified by antisocial and verbally aggressive behavior. The Activity dimension is characterized by general restlessness and an inability to relax, and would be most similar to Extraversion in the FFM or the PEN model of personality. Finally, Impulsive Unsocialized Sensation Seeking is characterized by a lack of planning, and a tendency to act impulsively. While Impulsive Unsocialized Sensation Seeking is similar to Psychoticism (PEN), Neuroticism (FFM), or even Openness to Experience (FFM), it is more predictive of sensation seeking (the desire to seek out new experiences and sensations) than any of these traditional omnibus personality dimensions (Zuckerman *et al.* 1988). Impulsive Unsocialized Sensation Seeking might also be termed social deviance or nonconformity (Zuckerman *et al.* 1988).

Despite the utility of omnibus personality dimensions in the prediction of broad behavioral criteria (Paunonen 2003), very few genetic studies of addictive behaviors use these higher-order factor scores. When the goal is prediction of specific behaviors (such as alcohol and drug abuse), narrow traits (such as sensation seeking) may be more useful than broad traits (Zuckerman *et al.* 1988). Omnibus predictors of narrow behavioral traits usually result in less accuracy, and a poorer understanding of the theoretical underpinnings of a behavior (Ashton 1998; Ashton *et al.* 1995; Paunonen & Ashton 2001a, b).

2. Sensation Seeking

General sensation seeking, as measured by the Sensation Seeking Scale (SSS; Zuckerman *et al.* 1964), may be divided into sub-traits of: (1) Thrill and Adventure Seeking (TAS); (2) Experience Seeking (ES); (3) Disinhibition (DIS); and (4) Boredom Susceptibility (BS). TAS is typified by the desire to participate in potentially dangerous physical activities like skydiving that promise to produce elevated physical arousal. The high ES individual, on the other hand, is predisposed to seek out new experiences through the senses or the mind — either through exposure to a variety of external stimuli, by alteration of the mind (often with psychoactive drugs), or through nonconformist lifestyle choices. DIS is characterized by the pursuit of sensations through social-hedonistic activities, such as drinking and sex. Finally, BS refers to a distaste for routine activities and work, as well as boring people (Zuckerman 1971).

Sensation seeking was originally proposed to be a biologically relevant cluster of personality traits, related to an individual's sensitivity to environmental stimulation (Zuckerman & Link 1968; Zuckerman *et al.* 1972, 1974). To the extent that personality is a product of neurological processes, however, biology probably exerts its influence on personality through the action of neurotransmitters (Zuckerman 1995). It is, therefore, not surprising that neurotransmitters have been linked to sensation seeking behaviors in a variety of ways. Monoamine Oxidase (MAO) regulates levels of monoamines (such as dopamine and norepinephrine) by breaking them down — either after reuptake, or in the synaptic cleft (Nolte 1993). It was demonstrated that MAO is negatively correlated with sensation seeking (Zuckerman 1994), presumably due, at least in part, to the positive correlation between sensation seeking and dopamine (Netter & Rammsayer 1991). Interestingly, the relation between dopamine and sensation seeking does not appear to be symmetrical between high and low sensation seekers. Netter and Rammsayer (1991) administered haloperidol (a dopamine antagonist), and levodopa (the metabolic precursor to dopamine) to a group of healthy participants. Low sensation seekers became anxious, and began to process information more slowly when given the dopamine antagonist. Under similar conditions, however, high sensation seekers became more relaxed, but showed no performance decrement. This may suggest that while high sensation seekers are close to normal with regards to their dopaminergic system function, low sensation seekers have a significantly depressed system, i.e. with the administration of the dopamine antagonist, low sensation seekers resembled individuals with clinically significant dopamine deficiencies, such as Parkinson's disease (Netter & Rammsayer 1991).

Gonadal hormones also appear to be related to sensation seeking. Not only do men tend to demonstrate higher scores than women on all dimensions of sensation seeking (Zuckerman 1986b), but a positive correlation has been demonstrated between sensation seeking behaviors and testosterone (Daitzman & Zuckerman 1980). These effects may also be due to in utero exposure to gonadal hormones, as Resnick *et al.* (1993) have demonstrated that female co-twins in DZ opposite sex pairings tend to be masculinized by their male co-twin, as compared with female co-twins in DZ same sex pairings. The sub-facets of sensation seeking that seem to be most affected in this regard are DIS and ES, suggesting that these traits may be most susceptible to the effects of gonadal hormones.

3. Introduction to Behavior Genetics

A substantial amount of research has gone into the identification of neurotransmitter correlates of personality, and personality psychopathology. For example, low serotonin levels were related to depression (Delgado *et al.* 1990) and (as aforementioned), dopamine levels have been shown to be related to sensation seeking (Netter & Rammsayer 1991). It is, however, conceivable that the relationship between neurotransmitters and personality is reciprocal. In other words, it is equally plausible that serotonin levels are reduced by depressive affect, or that depressive affect is caused by reduced serotonin levels. Only through the use of behavior genetic methodology (and genetically informative data) is it possible to identify the causal direction of personality.

Figure 1a depicts a path diagram showing that the phenotypic correlation between twin-pairs (the curved lines at the top) can be accounted for by the additive genes that they share — 100% for MZ twins and 50% for DZ twins — and in terms of their common or shared environment, which by definition both types of twins share 100%. This figure also shows that any absence of correlation, or differences that may exist between the twins, is attributable to nonshared environmental factors (e), that one twin experiences and that his or her co-twin does not experience.

In standard univariate behavioral-genetic model fitting, estimates of these A, C, and E effects are used to recreate the MZ and DZ variance/covariance matrices of a particular variable and different models are compared in terms of the goodness-of-fit that they achieve to the observed variance/covariance matrices that are obtained from the twins' actual data. Typically, a full ACE model (Figure 1a) is applied first: this will always yield the best fit to the observed data. Reduced models can also be applied that systematically drop one or more of the parameters to identify more parsimonious models. Thus, an AE model can

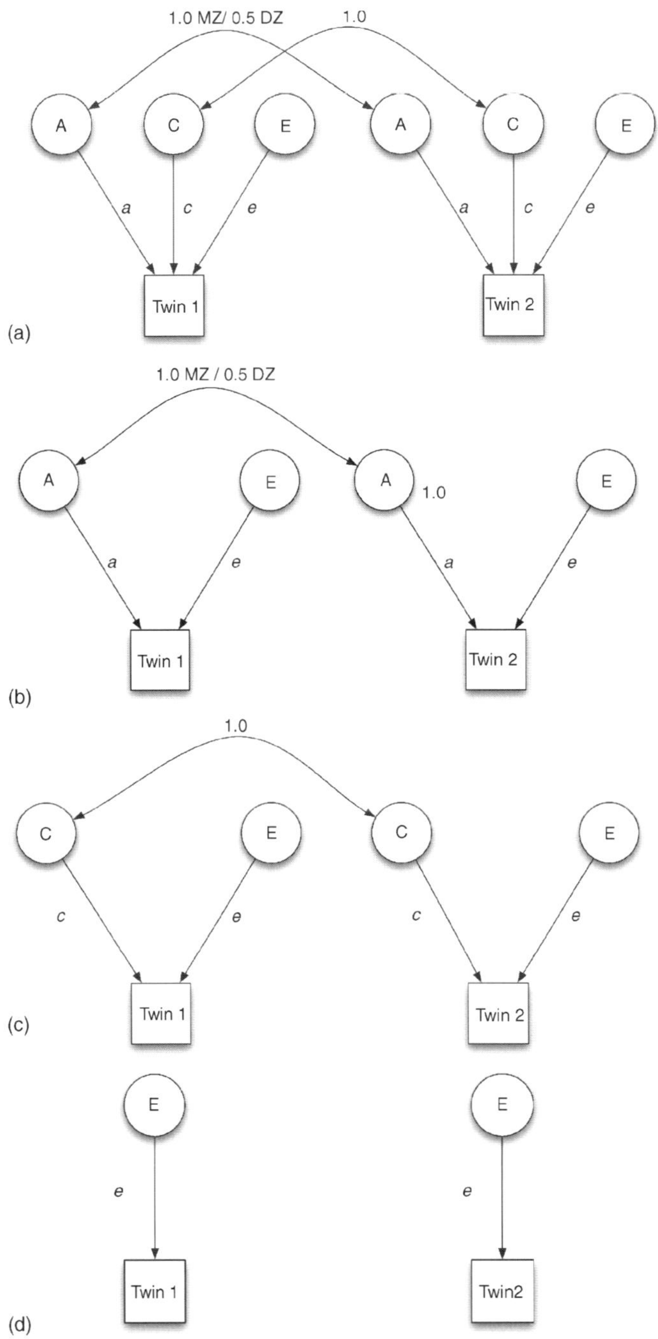

Figure 1: (a) ACE Path Diagram, (b) AE Path Diagram, (c) CE Path Diagram, (d) E Only Path Diagram, (e) ADE Path Diagram.

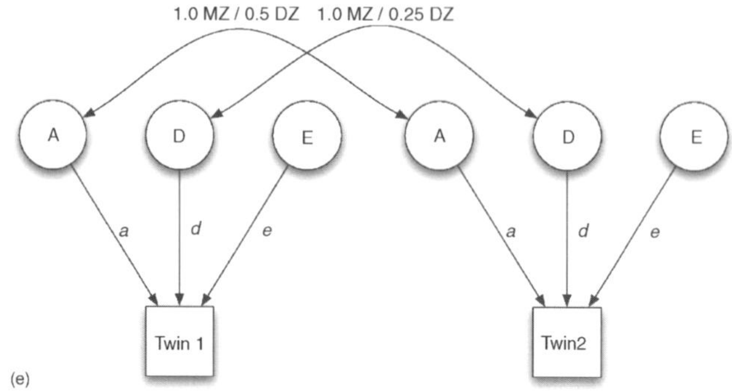

Figure 1: (*Continued*)

be fit (Figure 1b) to see whether shared environmental factors can be dropped without a significant worsening of fit. Fitting a CE model (Figure 1c) tests whether genetic effects can be dropped, and an E only model (Figure 1d) is also frequently tested, if only to confirm that it results in a significantly poorer model than other models. Note that the E only model could only work if in fact there was no correlation between the twins. Finally, the presence of dominance genetic effects can also be investigated (although data from MZ and DZ twins raised together cannot simultaneously test for A, D, C, and E effects) by fitting an ADE model, Figure 1e (Neale & Maes 1998). Once a model has been selected, its effects are used to estimate the heritability (and/or environmentality) of the variable.

If a researcher is interested in understanding what the correlations between two or more variables are attributable to, a multivariate model such as appears in Figure 2 can be examined. Models such as this compute twin cross-correlations: the extent to which one twin's score on a variable correlates with his or her co-twin's score on another variable. Multivariate models also provide estimates of genetic and environmental correlations between variables: that is, the extent to which those genes or environmental factors that contribute to one of the variables also contribute to the other variable. Perhaps the biggest advantage that multivariate behavior genetic analyses can give is that genetic and environmental correlations can exist even when there is no phenotypic correlation between two variables (Carey 1988). Thus, a phenotypic correlation of zero between two variables may mean that the variables have no shared etiology. It is also possible, however, that the variables in fact have sizeable genetic and environmental correlations, albeit of different signs and hence canceling each other out at the phenotypic level, and thus have shared etiologies of considerable interest; but this could only be revealed in a multivariate behavior genetic study.

The multivariate model shown in Figure 2 is referred to as a common pathway model (Neale & Maes 1998). This model is looking at three correlated domains relevant to this review — alcohol abuse, drug abuse, and tobacco abuse — and shows that the correlations between these variables can be attributed to the fact that common genetic and environmental factors (Ac, Cc, and Ec) impact on all three of them through a phenotypic latent variable (labeled "Sensation Seeking" in this example). To the extent that the variables correlate less than perfectly, this is attributed to specific genetic and environmental factors (As, Cs,

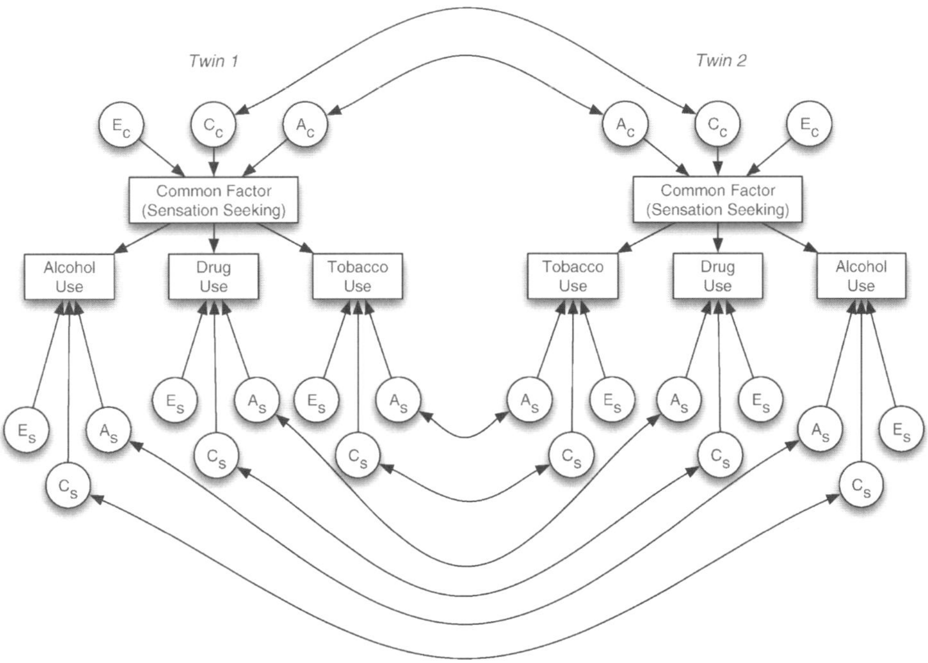

Figure 2: Common pathway model.

and Es) that underlie each of them. As was the case with univariate model fitting, a full multivariate ACE model can be examined first and then compared to reduced models that drop one or more of these effects.

Genetically informative data, and behavior genetic techniques, are thus quite useful in the identification of the structure of a disorder, and the development of a robust model of personality. Behavior genetic analyses cannot, however, generate information about specific genes (or allelic polymorphisms) that produce individual differences in personality, nor should a genetic correlation be interpreted as referring directly to molecular genetic information, e.g. the proportion of loci common between two variables (Carey 1988).

4. The Genetic Basis of Sensation Seeking

Fulker *et al.* (1980) reported the first behavior genetic analysis of sensation seeking, presenting data on the full SSS collected in a sample of 422 MZ and DZ twin-pairs. Results suggested a heritability of 0.58 for the total score, with the data demonstrating a significant interaction between genes and sex (30% of the genetic variability was found to be sex-specific). Eysenck (1983) presented individual scale score heritabilities in the same data set, and these data are summarized in Table 1.

These analyses were replicated by Koopmans *et al.* (1995) in a new data set based on the SSS. Unlike Eysenck (1983), however, these data showed no significant effects of sex, nor

Table 1: Univariate heritability estimates for sensation seeking scales.

	Eysenck (1983)				**Koopmans *et al.* (1995)**			
	Men		**Women**		**Men**		**Women**	
	A^2	E^2	A^2	E^2	A^2	E^2	A^2	E^2
TAS	0.45	0.55	0.44	0.56	0.62	0.38	0.63	0.37
ES	0.58	0.42	0.57	0.43	0.56	0.44	0.58	0.42
DIS	0.51	0.49	0.41	0.59	0.62	0.38	0.60	0.40
BS	0.41	0.59	0.34	0.66	0.48	0.52	0.54	0.46

Notes: TAS = Thrill and Adventure Seeking; ES = Experience Seeking; DIS = Disinhibition; BS = Boredom Susceptibility.

did they show a significant common factor underlying the four sensation seeking facets. Neither Eysenck (1983) nor Koopmans *et al.* (1995) found a significant effect from the shared environment, a result that agrees with the general findings of Plomin and Daniels (1987).

Further evidence of a genetic basis for sensation seeking was provided by Miles *et al.* (2001), i.e. evidence of a genetic basis to self-reported behavioral dimensions of sensation seeking. General risk taking attitudes showed a small degree of heritability and an even smaller (though non-zero) effect from the shared environment ($A^2 = 0.28$, $C^2 = 0.10$, $E^2 = 0.61$). More specific behavioral indicators such as riding motorcycles ($A^2 = 0.55$, $C^2 = 0.22$, $E^2 = 0.22$) and taking dangerous dares ($A^2 = 0.47$, $C^2 = 0.17$, $E^2 = 0.35$) demonstrated substantially more heritability, and all behaviors showed some effect of the shared environment.

While the results of behavior genetic investigations are indicative of heritability in a broad sense, they are not generally capable of isolating the specific gene (or genes) that are responsible for a given personality dimension (Carey 1988). Sensation seeking has the distinction of being the first personality dimension linked to a specific gene polymorphism (Benjamin *et al.* 1996; Ebstein *et al.* 1996). Given the demonstrated relationship between dopamine levels and sensation seeking at a phenotypic level (Netter & Rammsayer 1991), it is not surprising that the first candidate gene to be considered for linkage with sensation seeking was a dopamine receptor gene. Dopamine receptor D4 (DRD4) has a polymorphism caused by an amino acid segment that may be repeated between two and ten times among humans. The number of repeats present in the DRD4 polymorphism produces changes in the length, structure, and perhaps the function of the receptor site (van Tol *et al.* 1992). Ebstein *et al.* (1996) presented data on two groups of healthy participants that differed in the length of their DRD4 alleles. Individuals with long DRD4 alleles had significantly higher Novelty Seeking (NS) scores on the Tridimensional Personality Questionnaire (TPQ; Cloninger *et al.* 1994) than individuals with short DRD4 alleles. Benjamin *et al.* (1996) released simultaneous confirmation of this finding (in the same issue of *Nature Genetics*), demonstrating a similar relation between long and short DRD4 alleles on a NS dimension derived from the NEO-Personality Inventory (NEO-PI-R; Costa & McCrae 1992b).

Although several studies have corroborated these findings, using the TPQ in a similarly aged population (Benjamin *et al.* 2000; Ebstein *et al.* 1997; Noble *et al.* 1998; Ono *et al.* 1997; Ronai *et al.* 2001; Strobel *et al.* 1999), several studies have reported a failure to replicate the initial findings of Ebstein *et al.* (1996) and Benjamin *et al.* (1996). Malhotra *et al.* (1996) found no significant differences on the TPQ NS scale in a sample of men from a similar age range to Ebstein *et al.* (1996). Jonsson *et al.* (1997, 2002) also failed to replicate (in two independent studies), but used a different personality measure, the Karolinska Scales of Personality (Schalling *et al.* 1987). This suggests a possible instrumentation bias. Vandenbergh *et al.* (1997) failed to replicate the findings of Benjamin *et al.* (1996), using the same personality measure. This latter replication failure might have been due to the use of a significantly older sample. Gelernter *et al.* (1997) also failed to replicate these findings, using the TPQ in a variety of different populations (substance-dependent, personality-disordered, and healthy). Finally, Sander *et al.* (1997) failed to replicate these findings, possibly due to the fact that their sample was moderately older than the sample used by Ebstein *et al.* (1996). Even more damaging to the credibility of an association between DRD4 and novelty seeking is a recent meta-analysis of 20 DRD4 studies ($n = 3907$) that suggested that there is no significant association between DRD4 and novelty seeking.

5. The Genetic Basis of Alcohol Abuse

Alcohol abuse causes serious physical, social, and economic problems in three out of ten American families (Walters 2002). It is not surprising, therefore, that individuals are quite willing to accept genetic determinants in the etiology of alcoholism. Indeed, alcohol consumption is considered by many researchers to be at least partially determined by genetic factors (Han *et al.* 1999; Heath 1995; Heath *et al.* 1997; McGue 1993, 1994), with a particularly strong genetic determination among men (Grant *et al.* 1999). Walters (2002) reports results from a meta-analysis of 50 family, twin, and adoption studies, in which genetic factors account for 20–26% of the variability in alcohol misuse.

Genetic contributions to the etiology of alcoholism are not, however, best conceived as a simple univariate heritability estimate. Genetic factors may account for as much as 70% of the association between anti-social personality and alcohol dependence (Grove *et al.* 1990; Jang *et al.* 2000; Slutske *et al.* 1998), and the genetic correlation between alcohol consumption and stimulus-seeking behaviors is between 0.33 and 0.45 (Jang *et al.* 2000; Mustanski *et al.* 2003). Furthermore, there is a strong genetic correlation between alcohol consumption and alcohol problems (Mustanski *et al.* 2003), suggesting that there is a substantial overlap between the biological factors that predispose an individual to initiate drinking and the factors that predispose an individual to transition into alcohol abuse.

Finn *et al.* (2000) propose two pathways leading to alcohol abuse. In the first (and most direct) path, an individual is predisposed to social deviance, and this predisposition is expressed as alcoholism. This pathway does not propose any mediating effects of personality. The indirect pathway, however, suggests that an individual inherits an excitement-seeking temperament that (when coupled with positive alcohol expectancies) leads him/her to a regular consumption of alcohol. This regular consumption leads to alcohol dependency. This model is supported by findings suggesting that those who expect positive effects from alcohol consumption tend to drink more (Brown *et al.* 1985), as well as the finding that alcohol expectancy is moderately heritable (Gabrielli & Plomin 1985; Vernon *et al.* 1996).

Alcohol consumption has also been proposed to have a significant genotype by environment interaction. The heritability of alcohol consumption increases with age (Viken *et al.* 1999), suggesting that reasons for alcohol consumption early in life may be more related to environmental determinants, or even simple opportunity. Alcohol initiation has also been suggested to demonstrate a significant interaction with religiosity in women (Koopmans *et al.* 1999a). Koopmans *et al.* (1999a) demonstrated that 40% of the variation in alcohol initiation is attributable to genetics in non-religious women, while 0% of the variation is attributable to genetics among non-religious women. Men, on the other hand, show no significant interaction with religiosity, and demonstrate a 30% genetic and 60% shared environmental contribution for alcohol initiation.

Early studies of genes demonstrated to affect dopamine receptors at the D2 receptor sites (Blum *et al.* 1990) and D4 receptor sites (George *et al.* 1993; Muramatsu *et al.* 1996) have suggested direct genetic links to alcoholism. More recent studies, however, have found no significant relationship between alcoholism and either allele (Adamson *et al.* 1995; Chang *et al.* 1997; Geijer *et al.* 1997; Ishiguro *et al.* 2000; Parsian *et al.* 1997; Sander *et al.* 1997).

6. The Genetic Basis of Drug Abuse

Both sensation seeking traits (Zuckerman 1986a) and behavioral risk-taking evaluations (Adlaf & Smart 1983) have been demonstrated to be significant correlates of drug use, although they tend to predict illicit drug use better than alcohol consumption (Zuckerman 1987), a finding possibly related to the suggestion that high sensation seekers tend to prefer stimulants to depressants (Carrol & Zuckerman 1977). Sensation seeking has been suggested to explain approximately 29% of the variability in drug use (Pedersen *et al.* 1989) and between 12 and 17% of cannabis use (Teichman *et al.* 1989), with particularly strong relationships suggested for DIS, TAS, and ES (Zuckerman *et al.* 1984).

Like alcohol abuse, cannabis use is suggested to be the result of both genetic and environmental factors (van den Bree *et al.* 1998a, b; Cadoret 1992; Kendler *et al.* 2000, 2003; Miles *et al.* 2001; Tsuang *et al.* 1996, 1999). Miles *et al.* (2001) suggested a moderate heritability of cannabis use ($A^2 = 0.31$) and a more substantial effect of the shared environment ($C^2 = 0.47$). These findings add support to earlier findings that suggested an approximately equal distribution of variance estimates between genetic determinants, the shared environment, and unique environmental events (Tsuang *et al.* 1996). To understand the nature of the interplay between these genetic and environmental effects, however, it is helpful to consider drug abuse within a model of stage transitions, as proposed by Tsuang *et al.* (1999). This model suggests that there is a hierarchical progression towards drug abuse (and addiction): exposure; initiation of use; continuation of use, defined as using the substance more than five times in total; regularity of use, defined as using the substance at least once per week; and substance abuse, as defined by the DSM-IV.

Obviously, an individual must have physical access to a substance in order to initiate use. The transition from exposure to initiation of use may be mediated by sensation seeking (Zuckerman 1987) or antisocial personality disorder (Cadoret *et al.* 1995). Additionally, this behavior transition may also be influenced by peer groups (Cadoret 1992), and low levels of environmental risk, i.e. absence of corrupting influences may buffer against high familial risk (Legrand *et al.* 1999). The transition from first use to ongoing usage of the substance is likely mediated by a combination of genetic and environmental factors. The transition to regular use may be due to the positive affective state produced by the drug (Tsuang *et al.* 1999), but the transition from regular use to heavy use (and abuse) has been demonstrated to be strongly genetic (Cadoret 1992), with heritabilities ranging from 60 to 80% (Kendler *et al.* 2000).

Both DRD2 and DRD4 have been related to substance abuse. Significant associations have been reported between DRD2 and cocaine dependence (Noble *et al.* 1993), and polysubstance abuse (Comings *et al.* 1994; O'Hara *et al.* 1993). Significant associations have also been reported between DRD4 and heroin abuse (Kotler *et al.* 1997; Li *et al.* 1997), although some recent studies have failed to replicate these findings (Franke *et al.* 2000; Gelernter *et al.* 1997).

7. The Genetic Basis of Nicotine Dependence

Worldwide, tobacco use has been implicated in more than 3 million deaths per annum (Peto *et al.* 1996). Given that this is an eminently modifiable risk factor, it is not surprising that factors underlying tobacco use are frequent topics for study (Batra *et al.* 2003). Although environmental factors, such as peer pressure and religiosity, are frequently cited as having causal links to tobacco use, there is increasing evidence of the importance of genetic factors. Fisher (1958) presented the earliest evidence for a genetic determination of tobacco use, demonstrating a higher concordance rate among MZ twins than DZ twins.

While initial studies of tobacco use focused on the dichotomy of smokers and non-smokers, more recent studies have suggested that tobacco use may be subdivided into at least two general behavioral categories: smoking initiation, and smoking persistence (Han *et al.* 1999; Heath *et al.* 1991a, b; Koopmans *et al.* 1999b). Heath *et al.* (1991a) describe three potential models for the relationship between smoking initiation and smoking persistence (or smoking quantity as it is sometimes assessed). In the first model, a common liability model, smoking initiation and smoking quantity are co-determined by the same factor. In the second model, an independent liability model, factors leading to smoking initiation and smoking quantity arc uncorrelated. Finally, in the third model, a combined model, initiation and quantity are separate factors, but show significant interdependence. The model that best fits the data appears to be determined, at least in part, by an individual's age. The independent liability model has been suggested as the most appropriate model for individuals 12–24 years of age (Koopmans *et al.* 1999b) as well as 31 years of age and older (Heath *et al.* 1991a). For participants aged 18–30, Heath and Martin (1993) suggest that a combined model is the most parsimonious model of this relationship.

In addition to the impact of age on heritability of tobacco use, there is some evidence that suggests a different mechanism for heritability of tobacco use for men and women, with smoking initiation and persistence demonstrating substantially greater genetic determinance among men than women (Han *et al.* 1999; Madden *et al.* 1999). In a recent meta-analysis, however, Li *et al.* (2003) suggest that these sex effects are significantly different, depending on how tobacco use is defined. Smoking initiation demonstrated a significantly higher genetic determinance among women (55%) than among men (37%), while smoking persistence demonstrates a non-significantly higher genetic determinance among men (57%) than among women (46%).

As has been reported for alcohol and drug use, tobacco use has also been linked to dopamine receptor polymorphisms. As nicotine (the principal stimulant in tobacco) acts through the dopamine reward pathway (Nolte 1993), individuals with reduced dopamine receptor density may show deficits in this reward system. These deficits may translate into an increased liability to the development of nicotine dependence (Noble *et al.* 1994), presumably owing to an experience of increased reward when exposed to dopaminergic agents, such as nicotine. While the DRD1 gene has been linked to smoking initiation (Comings *et al.* 1997), the majority of evidence focuses on the importance of the DRD2 gene in the prediction of individuals most at risk for smoking initiation (Bierut *et al.* 2000; Comings *et al.* 1996; Wu *et al.* 2000; Yoshida *et al.* 2001).

8. Summary

Until very recently, the etiology of substance abuse has primarily been identified to be the result of psychological determinants, despite the classification of these tendencies as medical disorders, i.e. in the DSM-IV. Research on candidate genes that may impact on the development of substance abuse problems has, however, underscored the possibility that substance abuse may show a substantial genetic determination. The true determination of substance abuse may depend upon the interplay between these broad domains.

Swan *et al.* (1997) investigated the relation between alcohol, tobacco, and caffeine consumption, and found that the data were best described with a common pathway model, suggesting that a single variable might be responsible for the heritability of these potentially addictive behaviors. Koopmans *et al.* (1997) found similar evidence for a single latent variable mediating the relationship between alcohol and tobacco use, suggesting that this variable was largely determined by shared environment in 12–16 year olds, and predominantly determined by genetic factors among 17–25 year olds. Finally, Han *et al.* (1999) demonstrated that the initiation of alcohol, tobacco, and drug consumption was determined by a single latent phenotype.

What remains to be done, of course, is to identify this latent trait underlying the expression of substance abuse. As was previously mentioned, biology probably exerts its influence on personality through the action of neurotransmitters (Zuckerman 1995; Zuckerman *et al.* 1972, 1974), making it likely that the trigger for substance abuse lies somewhere among the myriad neurotransmitters that have been associated with the expression of these pathological tendencies. The demonstrated genetic and physiological determination of a sensation seeking personality, however, makes it equally likely that the latent trait purported to underlie alcohol, tobacco, and drug abuse is a sensation seeking dimension similar to that originally conceptualized by Zuckerman and Link (1968).

From a public health perspective, the identification of this latent trait is of immediate and practical import. While it is not, at the time of this writing, possible to engineer genotypes to reducc the likelihood of expressing addictive behaviors, the identification of the psychological variable associated with this latent phenotype may aid in the development of targeted interventions that address root causes of substance abuse — perhaps through the substitution of more socially (and physically) appropriate thrill-seeking sensations for an individual at-risk to pursue.

References

Adamson, M. D., Kennedy, J., Petronis, A., Dean, M., Virkkunen, M., Linnoila, M., & Goldman, D. (1995). DRD4 dopamine receptor genotype and CSF monoamine metabolites in Finnish alcoholics and controls. *American Journal of Medical Genetics*, *60*, 199–205.

Adlaf, E. M., & Smart, R. G. (1983). Risk-taking and drug-use behavior: An examination. *Drug and Alcohol Dependence*, *11*, 287–296.

Ashton, M. C. (1998). Personality and job performance: The importance of narrow traits. *Journal of Organizational Behavior*, *19*, 289–303.

Ashton, M. C., Jackson, D. N., Helmes, E., & Paunonen, S. V. (1998). Joint factor analysis of the Personality Research Form and the Jackson Personality Inventory: Comparisons with the Big Five. *Journal of Research in Personality*, *32*, 243–250.

Ashton, M. C., Jackson, D. N., Paunonen, S. V., Helmes, E., & Rothstein, M. G. (1995). The criterion validity of broad factor scales vs. specific factor scales. *Journal of Research in Personality*, *29*, 432–442.

Batra, V., Patkar, A. A., Berrettini, W. H., Weinstein, S. P., & Leone, F. T. (2003). The genetic determinants of smoking. *Chest*, *123*, 1730–1739.

Benjamin, J., Li, L., Patterson, C., Greenberg, B. D., Murphy, D. L., & Hamer, D. H. (1996). Population and familial association between the D4 dopamine receptor gene and measures of Novelty Seeking. *Nature Genetics*, *12*, 81–84.

Benjamin, J., Osher, Y., Kotler, M., Gritsenko, I., Nemanov, L., Belmaker, R. H., & Ebstein, R. P. (2000). Association between Tridimensional Personality Questionnaire (TPQ) traits and three functional polymorphisms: Dopamine receptor D4 (DRD4), serotonin transporter promoter region (5-HTTLPR) and catechol O-methyltransferase (COMT). *Molecular Psychiatry*, *5*, 96–100.

Bierut, L. J., Rice, J. P., Edenberg, H. J., Goate, A., Foroud, T., Cloninger, C. R., Begleiter, H., Conneally, P. M., Crowe, R. R., Hesselbrock, V., Li, T. K., Nurnberger, J. I., Jr., Porjesz, B., Schuckit, M. A., & Reich, T. (2000). Family-based study of the association of the dopamine D2 receptor gene (DRD2) with habitual smoking. *American Journal of Medical Genetics*, *90*, 299–302.

Blum, K., Noble, E. P., Shcridan, P. J., Montgomery, A., Ritchie, T., Jagadeeswaran, P., Nogami, H., Briggs, A. H., & Cohn, J. B. (1990). Allelic association of human dopamine D2 receptor gene in alcoholism. *Journal of the American Medical Association*, *263*, 2055–2060.

van den Bree, M. B., Johnson, E. O., Neale, M. C., & Pickens, R. W. (1998a). Genetic and environmental influences on drug use and abuse/dependence in male and female twins. *Drug and Alcohol Dependence*, *52*, 231–241.

van den Bree, M. B., Svikis, D. S., & Pickens, R. W. (1998b). Genetic influences in antisocial personality and drug use disorders. *Drug and Alcohol Dependence*, *49*, 177–187.

Brown, S. A., Goldman, M. S., & Christiansen, B. A. (1985). Do alcohol expectancies mediate drinking patterns of adults? *Journal of Consulting and Clinical Psychology*, *53*, 512–519.

Cadoret, R. J. (1992). Genetic and environmental factors in initiation of drug use and the transition to abuse. In: M. Glantz, & R. Pickens (Eds), *Vulnerability to drug abuse* (pp. 99–114). Washington, DC: American Psychological Association.

Cadoret, R. J., Yates, W. R., Troughton, E., Woodworth, G., & Steward, M. A. (1995). Adoption study demonstrating two genetic pathways to drug abuse. *Archives of General Psychiatry, 52*, 42–52.

Carey, G. (1988). Inference about genetic correlations. *Behavior Genetics, 18*, 329–338.

Carrol, E. N., & Zuckerman, M. (1977). Psychopathology and sensation seeking in "downers," "speeders," and "trippers": A study of the relationship between personality and drug choice. *The International Journal of the Addictions, 12*, 591–601.

Chang, F. M., Ko, H. C., Lu, R. B., Pakstis, A. J., & Kidd, K. K. (1997). The dopamine D4 receptor gene (DRD4) is not associated with alcoholism in three Taiwanese populations: Six polymorphisms tested separately and as haplotypes. *Biological Psychiatry, 41*, 394–405.

Cloninger, C. R., Przybeck, T., Svrakic, D. M., & Wetzel, R. (1994). *The temperament and character inventory (TCI): A guide to its development and use*. St. Louis: Center for Psychobiology of Personality.

Comings, D. E., Ferry, L., Bradshaw-Robinson, S., Burchette, R., Chiu, C., & Muhleman, D. (1996). The dopamine D2 receptor (DRD2) gene: A genetic risk factor in smoking. *Pharmacogenetics, 6*, 73–79.

Comings, D. E., Gade, R., Wu, S., Chiu, C., Dietz, G., Muhleman, D., Saucier, G., Ferry, L., Rosenthal, R. J., Lesieur, H. R., Rugle, L. J., & MacMurray, P. (1997). Studies of the potential role of the dopamine D1 receptor gene in addictive behaviors. *Molecular Psychiatry, 2*, 44–56.

Comings, D. E., Muhleman, D., Ahn, C., Gysin, R., & Flanagan, S. D. (1994). The dopamine D2 receptor gene: A genetic risk factor in substance abuse. *Drug and Alcohol Dependence, 34*, 175–180.

Costa, P. T., Jr., & McCrae, R. R. (1992a). Four ways five factors are basic. *Personality and Individual Differences, 13*, 653–665.

Costa, P. T., & McCrae, R. R. (1992b). *Revised NEO Personality Inventory (NEO-PI-R) and NEO Five-Factor Inventory (NEO-FFI) professional manual*. Odessa, FL: Psychological Assessment Resources.

Daitzman, R. J., & Zuckerman, M. (1980). Disinhibitory sensation seeking, personality, and gonadal hormones. *Personality and Individual Differences, 1*, 103–110.

Delgado, P. L., Charney, D. S., Price, L. H., Aghajanian, G. K., Landis, H., & Heninger, G. R. (1990). Serotonin function and mechanism of antidepressant action: Reversal of antidepressant-induced remission by rapid depletion of plasma atryptophan. *Archives of General Psychiatry, 47*, 411–418.

Ebstein, R. P., Nemanov, L., Klotz, I., Gritsenko, I., & Belmaker, R. H. (1997). Additional evidence for an association between the dopamine D4 receptor (D4DR) exon III repeat polymorphism and the human personality trait of Novelty Seeking. *Molecular Psychiatry, 2*, 472–477.

Ebstein, R. P., Novick, O., Umansky, R., Priel, B., Osher, Y., Blaine, D., Bennett, E. R., Nemanov, L., Katz, M., & Belmaker, R. H. (1996). Dopamine D4 receptor (D4DR) exon III polymorphism associated with the human personality trait of Novelty Seeking. *Nature Genetics, 12*, 78–80.

Eysenck, H. J. (1947). *Dimensions of personality*. New York, NY: Praeger.

Eysenck, H. J. (1967). *The biological basis of personality*. Springfield, IL: Charles C. Thomas.

Eysenck, H. J. (1983). A biometrical-genetical analysis of impulsive and sensation seeking behavior. In: M. Zuckerman (Ed.), *Biological bases of sensation seeking, impulsivity and anxiety* (pp. 1–36). Hillsdale, NJ: Lawrence Erlbaum.

Finn, P. R., Sharkansky, E. J., Brandt, K. M., & Turcotte, N. (2000). The effects of familial risk, personality, and expectancies on alcohol use and abuse. *Journal of Abnormal Psychology, 109*, 122–133.

Fisher, R. A. (1958). Lung cancer and cigarettes. *Nature, 182*, 108.

Franke, P., Nothen, M. M., Wang, T., Knapp, M., Lichtermann, D., Neidt, H., Sander, T., Propping, P., & Maier, W. (2000). DRD4 exon III VNTR polymorphism-susceptibility factor for heroin dependence? Results of a case-control and a family-based association approach. *Molecular Psychiatry*, *5*, 101–104.

Fulker, D. W., Eysenck, S. B. G., & Zuckerman, M. (1980). A genetic and environmental analysis of sensation seeking. *Journal of Research in Personality*, *14*, 261–281.

Gabrielli, W. F., Jr., & Plomin, R. (1985). Individual differences in anticipation of alcohol sensitivity. *Journal of Nervous and Mental Disease*, *173*, 111–114.

Geijer, T., Jonsson, E., Neiman, J., Persson, M. L., Brene, S., Gyllander, A., Sedvall, G., Rydberg, U., Wasserman, D., & Terenius, L. (1997). Tyrosine hydroxylase and dopamine D4 receptor allelic distribution in Scandinavian chronic alcoholics. *Alcoholism, Clinical and Experimental Research*, *21*, 35–39.

Gelernter, J., Kranzler, H., Coccaro, E., Siever, L., New, A., & Mulgrew, C. L. (1997). D4 dopamine-receptor (DRD4) alleles and novelty seeking in substance-dependent, personality-disorder, and control subjects. *American Journal of Human Genetics*, *61*, 1144–1152.

George, S. R., Cheng, R., Nguyen, T., Israel, Y., & O'Dowd, B. F. (1993). Polymorphisms of the D4 dopamine receptor alleles in chronic alcoholism. *Biochemical and Biophysical Research Communications*, *196*, 107–114.

Goldberg, L. R. (1990). An alternative "description of personality": The Big-Five factor structure. *Journal of Personality and Social Psychology*, *59*, 1216–1229.

Grant, J. D., Heath, A. C., Madden, P. A. F., Bucholz, K. K., Whitfield, J. B., & Martin, N. G. (1999). An assessment of the genetic relationship between alcohol metabolism and alcoholism risk in Australian twins of European ancestry. *Behavior Genetics*, *29*, 463–472.

Grove, W. M., Eckert, E. D., Heston, L., Bouchard, T. J., Jr., Segal, N., & Lykken, D. T. (1990). Heritability of substance abuse and antisocial behavior: A study of monozygotic twins reared apart. *Biological Psychiatry*, *27*, 1293–1304.

Han, C., McGue, M. K., & Iacono, W. G. (1999). Lifetime tobacco, alcohol and other substance use in adolescent Minnesota twins: Univariate and multivariate behavioral genetic analyses. *Addiction*, *94*, 981–993.

Heath, A. C. (1995). Genetic influences on alcoholism risk: A review of adoption and twin studies. *Alcohol Health and Research World*, *19*, 166–171.

Heath, A. C., Bucholz, K. K., Madden, P. A., Dinwiddie, S. H., Slutske, W. S., Bierut, L. J., Statham, D. J., Dunne, M. P., Whitfield, J. B., & Martin, N. G. (1997). Genetic and environmental contributions to alcohol dependence risk in a national twin sample: Consistency of findings in women and men. *Psychological Medicine*, *27*, 1381–1396.

Heath, A. C., & Martin, N. G. (1993). Genetic models for the natural history of smoking: Evidence for a genetic influence on smoking persistence. *Addictive Behavior*, *18*, 19–34.

Heath, A. C., Meyer, J., Eaves, L. J., & Martin, N. G. (1991a). The inheritance of alcohol consumption patterns in a general population twin sample: I. Multidimensional scaling of quantity/frequency data. *Journal of Studies on Alcohol*, *52*, 345–352.

Heath, A. C., Meyer, J., Jardine, R., & Martin, N. G. (1991b). The inheritance of alcohol consumption patterns in a general population twin sample: II. Determinants of consumption frequency and quantity consumed. *Journal of Studies on Alcohol*, *52*, 425–433.

Ishiguro, H., Saito, T., Shibuya, H., & Arinami, T. (2000). Association study between genetic polymorphisms in the 14–3–3 eta chain and dopamine D4 receptor genes and alcoholism. *Alcoholism, Clinical and Experimental Research*, *24*, 343–347.

Jackson, D. N., Paunonen, S. V., Fraboni, M., & Goffin, R. G. (1996). A five-factor vs. a six-factor model of personality structure. *Personality and Individual Differences*, *20*, 33–45.

Jang, K. L., Livesley, W. J., & Vernon, P. A. (1996). Heritability of the big five personality dimensions and their facets: A twin study. *Journal of Personality*, *64*, 577–591.

Jang, K. L., Vernon, P. A., & Livesley, W. J. (2000). Personality disorder traits, family environment, and alcohol misuse: A multivariate behavioural genetic analysis. *Addiction*, *95*, 873–888.

Johnson, A. M., Vernon, P. A., Harris, J. A., & Jang, K. L. (2004). A behavior genetic investigation of the relationship between leadership and personality. *Twin Research*, *7*, 27–32.

Jonsson, E. G., Ivo, R., Gustavsson, J. P., Geijer, T., Forslund, K., Mattila-Evenden, M., Rylander, G., Cichon, S., Propping, P., Bergman, H., sberg, M., & Nothen, M. M. (2002). No association between dopamine D4 receptor gene variants and novelty seeking. *Molecular Psychiatry*, *7*, 18–20.

Jonsson, E. G., Nothen, M. M., Gustavsson, J. P., Neidt, H., Brene, S., Tylec, A., Propping, P., & Sedvall, G. C. (1997). Lack of evidence for allelic association between personality traits and the dopamine D4 receptor gene polymorphisms. *American Journal of Psychiatry*, *154*, 697–699.

Kendler, K. S., Karkowski, L. M., Neale, M. C., & Prescott, C. A. (2000). Illicit psychoactive substance use, heavy use, abuse, and dependence in a U.S. population-based sample of male twins. *Archives of General Psychiatry*, *57*, 261–269.

Kendler, K. S., Prescott, C. A., Myers, J., & Neale, M. C. (2003). The structure of genetic and environmental risk factors for common psychiatric and substance use disorders in men and women. *Archives of General Psychiatry*, *60*, 929–937.

Kim, J., & Mueller, C. W. (1978). *Factor analysis: Statistical methods and practical issues*. Beverly Hills, CA: Sage.

Koopmans, J. R., Boomsma, D. I., Heath, A. C., & van Doornen, L. J. P. (1995). A multivariate genetic analysis of sensation seeking. *Behavior Genetics*, *25*, 349–356.

Koopmans, J. R., van Doornen, L. J., & Boomsma, D. I. (1997). Association between alcohol use and smoking in adolescent and young adult twins: A bivariate genetic analysis. *Alcoholism: Clinical and Experimental Research*, *21*, 537–546.

Koopmans, J. R., Slutske, W. S., van Baal, G. C. M., & Boomsma, D. I. (1999a). The influence of religion on alcohol use initiation: Evidence for genotype X environment interaction. *Behavior Genetics*, *29*, 445–453.

Koopmans, J. R., Slutske, W. S., Heath, A. C., Neale, M. C., & Boomsma, D. I. (1999b). The genetics of smoking initiation and quantity smoked in Dutch adolescent and young adult twins. *Behavior Genetics*, *29*, 383–393.

Kotler, M., Cohen, H., Segman, R., Gritsenko, I., Nemanov, L., Lerer, B., Kramer, I., Zer-Zion, M., Kletz, I., & Ebstein, R. P. (1997). Excess dopamine D4 receptor (D4DR) exon III seven repeat allele in opioid-dependent subjects. *Molecular Psychiatry*, *2*, 251–254.

Legrand, L. N., McGue, M., & Iacono, W. G. (1999). Searching for interactive effects in the etiology of early-onset substance use. *Behavior Genetics*, *29*, 433–443.

Li, M. D., Cheng, R., Ma, J. Z., & Swan, G. E. (2003). A meta-analysis of estimated genetic and environmental effects on smoking behavior in male and female adult twins. *Addiction*, *98*, 23–31.

Li, T., Xu, K., Deng, H., Cai, G., Liu, J., Liu, X., Wang, R., Xiang, X., Zhao, J., Murray, R. M., Sham, P. C., & Collier, D. A. (1997). Association analysis of the dopamine D4 gene exon III VNTR and heroin abuse in Chinese subjects. *Molecular Psychiatry*, *2*, 413–416.

Madden, P. A. F., Heath, A. C., Pedersen, N. L., Kaprio, J., Koskenvuo, M. J., & Martin, N. G. (1999). The genetics of smoking persistence in men and women: A multicultural study. *Behavior Genetics*, *29*, 423–431.

Malhotra, A. K., Virkkunen, M., Rooney, W., Eggert, M., Linnoila, M., & Goldman, D. (1996). The association between the dopamine D4 receptor (D4DR) 16 amino acid repeat polymorphism and novelty seeking. *Molecular Psychiatry*, *1*, 388–391.

McGue, M. (1993). From proteins to cognitions: The behavioral genetics of alcoholism. In: R. Plomin, & G. McClearn (Eds), *Nature, nurture, and psychology* (pp. 245–268). Washington, DC: American Psychological Association.

McGue, M. (1994). Genes, environment, and the etiology of alcoholism. In: R. Zucker, G. Boyd, & J. Howard (Eds), *The development of alcohol problems: Exploring the biopsychosocial matrix of risk* (pp. 1–40). Rockville, MD: U.S. Department of Health and Human Services.

Miles, D. R., van den Bree, M. B., Gupman, A. E., Newlin, D. B., Glantz, M. D., & Pickens, R. W. (2001). A twin study on sensation seeking, risk taking behavior and marijuana use. *Drug and Alcohol Dependence*, *62*, 57–68.

Muramatsu, T., Higuchi, S., Murayama, M., Matsushita, S., & Hayashida, M. (1996). Association between alcoholism and the dopamine D4 receptor gene. *Journal of Medical Genetics*, *33*, 113–115.

Mustanski, B. S., Viken, R. J., Kaprio, J., & Rose, R. J. (2003). Genetic influences on the association between personality risk factors and alcohol use and abuse. *Journal of Abnormal Psychology*, *112*, 282–289.

Neale, M. C., & Maes, H. M. (1998). *Methodology for Genetic studies of twins and families*. Dordrecht: Kluwer.

Netter, P., & Rammsayer, T. (1991). Reactivity to dopaminergic drugs and aggression related personality traits. *Personality and Individual Differences*, *12*, 1009–1017.

Noble, E. P., Blum, K., Khalsa, M. E., Ritchie, T., Montgomery, A., Wood, R. C., Fitch, R. J., Ozkaragoz, T., Sheridan, P. J., Anglin, M.D., *et al.* (1993). Allelic association of the D2 dopamine receptor gene with cocaine dependence. *Drug and Alcohol Dependence*, *33*, 271–285.

Noble, E. P., Ozkaragoz, T. Z., Ritchie, T. L., Zhang, X., Belin, T. R., & Sparkes, R. S. (1998). D2 and D4 dopamine receptor polymorphisms and personality. *American Journal of Medical Genetics*, *81*, 257–267.

Noble, E. P., St. Jeor, S. T., Ritchie, T., Syndulko, K., St. Jeor, S. C., Fitch, R. J., Brunner, R. L., & Sparkes, R. S. (1994). D2 dopamine receptor gene and cigarette smoking: A reward gene? *Medical Hypotheses*, *42*, 257–260.

Nolte, J. (1993). *The Human Brain: An Introduction to its Functional Anatomy* (3rd ed.). St. Louis, MO: Mosby Year Books.

O'Hara, B. F., Smith, S. S., Bird, G., Persico, A. M., Suarez, B. K., Cutting, G. R., & Uhl, G. R. (1993). Dopamine D2 receptor RFLPs, haplotypes and their association with substance use in Black and Caucasian research volunteers. *Human Heredity*, *43*, 209–218.

Ono, Y., Manki, H., Yoshimura, K., Muramatsu, T., Mizushima, H., Higuchi, S., Yagi, G., Kanba, S., & Asai, M. (1997). Association between dopamine D4 receptor (D4DR) exon III polymorphism and novelty seeking in Japanese subjects. *American Journal of Medical Genetics*, *74*, 501–503.

Parsian, A., Chakraverty, S., Fisher, L., & Cloninger, C. R. (1997). No association between polymorphisms in the human dopamine D3 and D4 receptors genes and alcoholism. *American Journal of Medical Genetics*, *74*, 281–285.

Paunonen, S. V. (2003). Big Five factors of personality and replicated predictions of behavior. *Journal of Personality and Social Psychology*, *84*, 411–424.

Paunonen, S. V., & Ashton, M. C. (2001a). Big Five factors and facets and the prediction of behavior. *Journal of Personality and Social Psychology*, *81*, 524–539.

Paunonen, S. V., & Ashton, M. C. (2001b). Big Five predictors of academic achievement. *Journal of Research in Personality*, *35*, 78–90.

Paunonen, S. V., & Jackson, D. N. (1996). The Jackson personality inventory and the five-factor model of personality. *Journal of Research in Personality*, *30*, 42–59.

Paunonen, S. V., & Jackson, D. N. (2000). What is beyond the big five? Plenty! *Journal of Personality*, *68*, 821–835.

Pedersen, W., Clausen, S. E., & Lavik, N. J. (1989). Patterns of drug use and sensation seeking among adolescents in Norway. *Acta Psychiatrica Scandinavica, 79*, 386–390.

Peto, R., Lopez, A. D., Boreham, J., Thun, M., Heath, C., Jr., & Doll, R. (1996). Mortality from smoking worldwide. *British Medical Bulletin, 52*, 12–21.

Plomin, R., & Daniels, D. (1987). Why are children in the same family so different from one another? *Behavioral and Brain Sciences, 10*, 1–60.

Resnick, S. M., Gottesman, I. I., & McGue, M. (1993). Sensation seeking in opposite-sex twins: An effect of prenatal hormones? *Behavior Genetics, 23*, 323–329.

Ronai, Z., Szekely, A., Nemoda, Z., Lakatos, K., Gervai, J., Staub, M., & Sasvari-Szekely, M. (2001). Association between Novelty Seeking and the –521 C/T polymorphism in the promoter region of the DRD4 gene. *Molecular Psychiatry, 6*, 35–38.

Sander, T., Harms, H., Dufeu, P., Kuhn, S., Rommelspacher, H., & Schmidt, L. G. (1997). Dopamine D4 receptor exon III alleles and variation of novelty seeking in alcoholics. *American Journal of Medical Genetics, 74*, 483–487.

Schalling, D., Åsberg, M., Edman, G., & Oreland, L. (1987). Markers for vulnerability to psychopathology: Temperament traits associated with platelet MAO activity. *Acta Psychiatrica Scandinavica, 76*, 172–182.

Slutske, W. S., Heath, A. C., Dinwiddie, S. H., Madden, P. A. F., Bucholz, K. K., Dunne, M. P., Statham, D. J., & Martin, N. G. (1998). Common genetic risk factors for conduct disorder and alcohol dependence. *Journal of Abnormal Psychology, 107*, 363–374.

Strobel, A., Wehr, A., Michel, A., & Brocke, B. (1999). Association between the dopamine D4 receptor (DRD4) exon III polymorphism and measures of Novelty Seeking in a German population. *Molecular Psychiatry, 4*, 378–384.

Swan, G. E., Carmelli, D., & Cardon, L. R. (1997). Heavy consumption of cigarettes, alcohol and coffee in male twins. *Journal of Studies on Alcohol, 58*, 182–190.

Teichman, M., Barnea, Z., & Ravav, G. (1989). Personality and substance use among adolescents: A longitudinal study. *British Journal of Addictions, 84*, 181–190.

van Tol, H. H., Wu, C. M., Guan, H. C., Ohara, K., Bunzow, J. R., Civelli, O., Kennedy, J., Seeman, P., Niznik, H. B., & Jovanovic, V. (1992). Multiple dopamine D4 receptor variants in the human population. *Nature, 358*, 149–152.

Tsuang, M. T., Lyons, M. J., Eisen, S., Goldberg, J., True, W. R., Lin, N., Meyer, J. M., Toomey, R., & Eaves, L. J. (1996). Genetic influences on abuse of illicit drugs: A study of 3,297 twin pairs. *American Journal of Medical Genetics, 67*, 473–477.

Tsuang, M. T., Lyons, M. J., Harley, R. M., Xian, H., Eisen, S., Goldberg, J., True, W. R., & Faraone, S. V. (1999). Genetic and environmental influences on transitions in drug use. *Behavior Genetics, 29*, 473–479.

Tupes, E. C., & Christal, R. E. (1992). Recurrent personality factors based on trait ratings. *Journal of Personality, 60*, 225–251.

Vandenbergh, D. J., Zonderman, A. B., Wang, J., Uhl, G. R., & Costa, P. T., Jr. (1997). No association between novelty seeking and dopamine D4 receptor (D4DR) exon III seven repeat alleles in Baltimore Longitudinal Study of Aging participants. *Molecular Psychiatry, 2*, 417–419.

Vernon, P. A., Lee, D., Harris, J. A., & Jang, K. L. (1996). Genetic and environmental contributions to individual differences in alcohol expectancies. *Personality and Individual Differences, 21*, 183–187.

Viken, R. J., Kaprio, J., Koskenvuo, M., & Rose, R. J. (1999). Longitudinal analyses of the determinants of drinking and of drinking to intoxication in adolescent twins. *Behavior Genetics, 29*, 455–461.

Walters, G. D. (2002). The heritability of alcohol abuse and dependence: A meta-analysis of behavior genetic research. *American Journal of Drug & Alcohol Abuse, 28*, 557–584.

Wu, X., Hudmon, K. S., Detry, M. A., Chamberlain, R. M., & Spitz, M. R. (2000). D2 dopamine receptor gene polymorphisms among African-Americans and Mexican-Americans: A lung cancer case-control study. *Cancer Epidemiology Biomarkers and Prevention*, *9*, 1021–1026.

Yoshida, K., Hamajima, N., Kozaki, K., Saito, H., Maeno, K., Sugiura, T., Ookuma, K., & Takahashi, T. (2001). Association between the dopamine D2 receptor A2/A2 genotype and smoking behavior in the Japanese. *Cancer Epidemiology Biomarkers and Prevention*, *10*, 403–405.

Zuckerman, M. (1971). Dimensions of sensation seeking. *Journal of Consulting and Clinical Psychology*, *36*, 45–52.

Zuckerman, M. (1986a). Sensation seeking and the endogenous deficit theory of drug abuse. *NIDA Research Monograph*, *74*, 59–70.

Zuckerman, M. (1986b). Sensation seeking: A biosocial dimension of personality. In: A. Gale, & J. A. Edwards (Eds), *Physiological correlates of human behaviour, Vol. 3: Individual differences and psychopathology* (pp. 99–115). San Diego, CA: Academic Press.

Zuckerman, M. (1987). Is sensation seeking a predisposing trait for alcoholism? In: E. Gottheil, K. A. Druley, S. Pasko, & S. P. Weinstein (Eds), *Stress and addictions* (pp. 283–301). New York, NY: Brunner/Mazel.

Zuckerman, M. (1989). Personality in the third dimension: A psychobiological approach. *Personality and Individual Differences*, *10*, 391–418.

Zuckerman, M. (1992). What is a basic factor and which factors are basic? Turtles all the way down. *Personality and Individual Differences*, *13*, 675–681.

Zuckerman, M. (1994). *Behavioral expressions and biosocial bases of sensation seeking*. New York, NY: Cambridge University Press.

Zuckerman, M. (1995). Good and bad humors: Biochemical bases of personality and its disorders. *Psychological Science*, *6*, 325–332.

Zuckerman, M., Ballenger, J. C., & Post, R. M. (1984). The neurobiology of some dimensions of personality. *International Review of Neurobiology*, *25*, 391–436.

Zuckerman, M., Bone, R. N., Neary, R., Mangelsdorff, D., & Brustman, B. (1972). What is the sensation seeker? Personality trait and experience correlates of the Sensation Seeking Scales. *Journal of Consulting and Clinical Psychology*, *39*, 308–321.

Zuckerman, M., Kolin, E. A., Price, L., & Zoob, I. (1964). Development of a Sensation Seeking Scale. *Journal of Consulting Psychology*, *28*, 477–482.

Zuckerman, M., Kuhlman, D. M., & Camac, C. (1988). What lies beyond E and N? Factor analyses of scales believed to measure basic dimensions of personality. *Journal of Personality and Social Psychology*, *54*, 96–107.

Zuckerman, M., Kuhlman, D. M., Joireman, J., Teta, P., & Kraft, M. (1993). A comparison of three structural models for personality: The Big Three, the Big Five, and the Alternative Five. *Journal of Personality and Social Psychology*, *65*, 757–768.

Zuckerman, M., Kuhlman, D. M., Thornquist, M., & Kiers, H. (1991). Five (or three) robust questionnaire scale factors of personality without culture. *Personality and Individual Differences*, *12*, 929–941.

Zuckerman, M., & Link, K. (1968). Construct validity for the Sensation-Seeking Scale. *Journal of Consulting and Clinical Psychology*, *32*, 420–426.

Zuckerman, M., Murtaugh, T., & Siegel, J. (1974). Sensation Seeking and cortical augmenting-reducing. *Psychophysiology*, *11*, 535–542.

Part III

Personality and Social Behavior

Chapter 10

Personality and Leisure Activity: Sensation Seeking and Spare-Time Activities

A. Furnham

1. Introduction

The literature on the relation between personality and leisure is disappointing despite both its theoretical and practical implications (Argyle 1996; Melamed *et al.* 1995; Tinsley & Tinsley 1986). The reason lies primarily in the classification of leisure activities. The measurement of leisure activities is based on the amount of time people spend in a variety of activities; the amount of money spent on them; and the amount of interest expressed in them. As a result, there are many time or money budget studies, free-time activity surveys and diary studies, and questionnaires designed to examine the meaning of leisure and attitudes to leisure. Yet nearly all of these approaches run into the problems of what activities to include and exclude in a very long list of possible leisure pursuits that are to be both comprehensive and parsimonious, and how to categorize leisure activities.

This a typical list: watching television; visiting friends or relatives; working around the yard or in the garden; reading magazines; reading books; going pleasure-driving; listening to records; going to meetings or participating in other organization activities; special hobbies; going out to dinner; participating in sports; playing cards, checkers, etc.; none of those listed; spending time at the drugstore, etc.; singing or playing a musical instrument; going to see a sports event; going to watch movies at a cinema; going to drive-in movies; going to dances; going to a play, concert or opera; going to lectures or adult education classes. Note how many activities are missing (e.g. what to watch on television or what sort of friends to visit and what to do with them), and even more importantly how very different activities (i.e. participating in sports), come under the same general heading. Clearly the devil lies in the details and to understand how personality predicts leisure choice and satisfaction we need a finer grain psychological classification of leisure. As there is still no comprehensive yet parsimonious classification of leisure activities, good research is inhibited in this area.

On the Psychobiology of Personality
Edited by R. M. Stelmack

ISBN: 0-08-044209-9

Shivers (1981) has argued that leisure can be conceived of in seven distinct ways:

(1) leisure as recreation — a time set aside for creativity and learning; a symbol of cultural achievement and educational betterment;
(2) leisure as pleasure — a source of happiness and moderate hedonism; leisure is a time of opportunity to avoid ennui and maximize preferred enjoyment;
(3) leisure as rejuvenation — leisure provides the necessary physiological and psychological stimulation and variety to return to work, which must be the primary arena for self-realization;
(4) leisure as a state of being — leisure is a self-perceived state of freedom that can only be defined in its *own* terms and not be activities performed;
(5) leisure as function — leisure can be thought of in terms of the functions it fulfils, such as relaxation, diversion, experience-broadening; it is essentially freedom from a certain number and kind of obligation;
(6) leisure as social stratification — leisure is the unrestrained and conspicuous spending of time/money by one class in order to live up to the concepts of others; it is the unproductive use of time, and evidence of the pecuniary ability to afford a life of idleness; and
(7) leisure as time — it is the discretionary or free time of any individual; it is the time not required to maintain biological function, economic worth and socio-cultural obligations. Leisure is choice.

Different researchers from different disciplines have tended to favor one conception or another. Personality theorists have tended to a functional and rejuvenation perspective. However, one reason why this research remains something of a backwater is because of the poor conceptualization of leisure. Science begins with description, then taxonomy, then understanding. Because there is no periodic table for leisure, research has been piecemeal.

Further, by definition Sensation Seeking (SS) researchers have been particularly interested in examining the relationship between SS and dramatic activities like dangerous sports. Any reviewer of the area is struck by the wide variety of leisure activities examined almost randomly. Equally, reviewers may be impressed by how often experimental hypotheses are confirmed in that the SS scale and sub-scales are systematically related to a wide variety of leisure activities.

More importantly we cannot really understand the relation between personality and leisure without understanding the relation between work and leisure. This is a highly salient point for this chapter as it implies that one cannot fully understand preferences for, satisfaction in, and time spent at, leisure, unless one understands the nature of the person's job as well. SS needs may be so well satisfied in the one, i.e. work, that they do not spill over to the other, i.e. leisure.

Indeed, there are three models of the job-leisure interface:

(1) *Spill over*: This refers to the easy transfer of attitudes, feelings and behaviors from one domain (the work place) to the other (the home). The idea is that people choose their work and make their home in ways that are contingent with their skills, personality and attitudes. People who are neat at home are neat at work; people who like to

control at home like to control at work; people who are sick at home are sick at work. We choose, change and modify both our jobs and our family in line with our preferences and predictions. In a sense we create both in terms of our needs, hopes and wants.

In turn, we become deeply frustrated when each or both does not fit in with our desires. When you first go home with a colleague you may be amazed by the similarities in their work style and home style. Those with paintings at work have them at home, the untidy at work are untidy at home, and the gadget obsessed has as many in the board as the bedroom. Their lives spill over and, if they are lucky, either/both are within their control. There is no discontinuity between the two. It makes the change easy, though it can lead to inappropriate behavior, particularly in the workplace where prescribed and proscribed behaviour is much more constrained.

(2) *Compensation*: This represents efforts to offset dissatisfaction and frustration in one domain by seeking satisfaction in the other. It is usually achieved by decreasing commitment and involvement in the one domain while increasing it in the other. Where your treasure is; there your heart is also, often where you genuinely choose to spend more time.

Compensation leads to psychological absorption and diverted attention. The workaholic may find it better being at work than at home. For the person seeming reluctant to go home it may be quite simply that at work they are admired and supported, given private space and time, and the company of peers. At home, on the other hand, they have much less personal time, feel they need to be the supporter not the supported and miss the company of adults. Equally the home may be a warm caring comfortable environment, while the workplace is cold, competitive, and stressful. Often, but by no means exclusively, men compensate at work, women at home. The office is a refuge for the one, while for the other it is the kitchen.

(3) *Segmentation*: This refers to the separation of work and family such that experience in the two domains do not influence one another. This may be seen as a natural diversion or a futile attempt to erect an unnatural boundary.

Segmentation occurs when people are totally focussed on the place/domain they are currently in. Equally people may adopt different personas and coping styles in the different places. So people may have problem-focussed strategies at work but emotional coping strategies at home. They are different people; not necessarily opposites but different. Just as the actor in repertory can, and has to be quite different characters week after week, so the segmenter is a compartmentalizer. They rarely worry about balance as they see the two things as unrelated to one another.

The central point here is that one needs to take account of, or co-vary, out work-based activities when studying leisure. Work like leisure is constrained: by personal factors like physique and ability; by economic factors like the local economy. Thus, a high SS might end up in a dull repetitive job making their leisure all the more important for expressing his/her personality. On the other hand a high SS individual who is a fire fighter may be so surfeited by stimulation at the end of the working day that he/she is happy to simply watch television. There is, therefore, an important interaction between work and leisure that should not be ignored in experimental studies.

2. Personality Traits and Leisure

A quarter of a century ago, Iso-Ahola (1976) argued that the salient literature can be simply categorized into two quite different approaches, namely the *trait approach*, which insists that personality exists in the individual being observed and the *attribution approach*, which claims that personality is in the eye of the beholder. The latter approach includes the processes by which people attribute personality factors to others on the basis of their knowledge of their sport/leisure preferences, attribution errors in the perception of the amount of freedom people have to choose their leisure, and how participants explain the causes of success and failure in their own and others' leisure behavior. Thus, while the trait approach is predominantly biological in conception, the attribution approach is essentially cognitive. While there remains some interest in the attribution approach, most research has concentrated on trait correlates of leisure preference and success. Certainly, as we shall see, nearly all SS researchers take a robustly biological approach.

In reviewing the relation between personality and leisure, Nias (1985: 61) concluded: "Personality has been shown to be related to interest preferences, but at a rather low level. Perhaps because of the specific nature of interest factors, it is expecting too much for general personality dimensions to show anything other than tenuous relations to them. A more fruitful approach might be to relate specific personality traits to the interest factor." Indeed, this is precisely what the SS researchers have done.

Nias (1985) was clearly influenced by need theory. He was concerned with the motives people have for pursuing specific interests. He pointed out a genetic component of interest preference, as well as the notion of family influence on interest development. In a study examining the relation between leisure pursuits and personality among adults, he showed that the trait Extraversion (E) was associated with drinking, talking with friends, and watching adventure and crime films (social activities). Neuroticism (N) on the other hand was unrelated to recreational interests. This is consistent with other findings that individuals with a marked preference for leisure activities are inclined to be outgoing, self-assured, versatile, expressive, enthusiastic and energetic.

The classic (original) trait concepts of E and N seem to be particularly predictive of leisure pursuits. As Brandstätter (1994) found, using time-sampling diaries, during leisure (and work) extraverts preferred high-stimulation social situations. Egloff and Gruhn (1996) showed that E and N were linked to preference for, and success in, endurance sports. Tri-athletes and long-distance runners were more extraverted and reported fewer physical complaints. Extraverts trained more, tended to be more successful, and tended to set themselves clearer goals than introverts. Certainly their results suggest that personality may influence attitudes to training, managing negative affect and goal setting, which in turn influences success in a particular sport.

Kirkcaldy, in a critical evaluation of the contribution of traits to sports, reported that:

> despite some inconsistencies, a certain degree of generalisation can be tentatively proposed. For instance, extraversion-introversion emerges as a trait associated with an interest in sport participation . . . the implication of extraversion with sport fits in well with the demands of strenuous activity and exercise. They are impulsive and pursue varied interests as a means

> of satiating their stimulus hunger. They prefer being with others rather than alone, enjoying participation in parties and other social gatherings (Kirkcaldy 1985: 257).

Kirkcaldy and Furnham (1991) found that E appears to be more influential in differentiating recreational interest preferences than N. Extraverts were particularly drawn towards activities of a social, playful kind — consistent with their needs for social interaction — as well as to dynamic, competitive, combat-oriented sports, in contrast to introverts, who tended to avoid such activities. There was no indication that extraverts were more inclined to express an interest in traditional team sports, e.g. football, ice-hockey, basketball and handball, as opposed to single sports (Kirkcaldy 1985). Neurotics appear to be less interested in competitive sports, although the magnitude of the relation was not significant.

It is unclear what percentage of the variance in leisure interests is explained by personality traits. Inevitably this depends on the particular traits measured as well as the specific leisure activity considered. However, as already mentioned, the selection of leisure pursuits is further restricted by other factors such as age (veterans are unlikely to pursue certain sports), geography (individuals may live too far away from mountain ranges to take part in climbing or skiing), money (limited finances prevent involvement in golf, ballooning, etc.), gender, class, ethnicity and health (Furnham 1990).

In his state-of-the-art book, *Behavioral expressions and biosocial bases of sensation seeking* (1994), Zuckerman reviewed the relation between SS and specific behaviors from art appreciation to vocations. Three chapters are tangentially, and one very specifically, related to this chapter. In the chapter on risk taking, Zuckerman (1994) reviewed papers that showed SS was systematically related to driver behavior (speed, general habits) injury proneness, sexual behavior, gambling, financial risk taking, travel and migration, fear of physical harm and smoking. Most of the studies confirmed hypotheses derived from the theory: for instance high, compared to low, SS drive faster and more recklessly (without seat-belts, while intoxicated) and are therefore more likely to have accidents. Many of these areas relate to leisure preference and experience. Thus, it seems that high SS are more likely to own fast cars, enjoy fast car sports more as a participant than an observer, but have a history of more traffic violations. Similarly, the personal sexual life of high SS may be quite different from those of low SS people. Predictably, they have more partners, indulge in a great variety of sexual habits and take more interest in sex in general. Equally, attitudes to, habits of, and preference for, gambling are systematically related to SS. In this sense whether a person gambles, their preferred gambling activity and how they respond while gambling may each be systematically related to his or her actual SS score.

In another chapter, Zuckerman (1994) looked specifically at SS as it relates to social, sexual and marital relationships. High SS are, predictably, more sociably dominant, self-disclosing and sexually permissive. Interestingly, the degree of similarity in SS partners predicts relationship satisfaction, though high SS couples are more at risk for divorce than low SS couples. In this sense, SS is related to social vs. non-social leisure activities.

However, it is probably in the area of holiday choice and experience that SS is most closely related to leisure. Thus, preference for adventure, as well as highly sociable holidays with variety and novelty, would be associated with SS. Inevitably age, income and opportunity constrain choice but even within those limitations it may be expected that an individual's history of holiday taking (as well as their specific activities on that holiday) may be an excellent, unobtrusive measure of their level of SS.

In a chapter on sport and vocations, Zuckerman (1994) reviewed the then growing literature that tended to confirm the straight-forward hypothesis that particularly risky, competitive and often highly sociable sports fulfils the high SS need for stimulation. He also points to the interesting literature on vocational choice, interest and satisfaction. Again, the extant literature confirms the obvious hypotheses. High SS seek out risky vocations like air traffic controller, the military and paramilitary professions. High SS may also seek out highly stimulating but non-risky occupations like journalism, medicine and psychotherapy. However, vocational choice and satisfaction is clearly associated with leisure mainly, through the process of compensation. Zuckerman (1994) notes that among those whose jobs fully satisfy their SS needs there is less need for extracurricular SS through sport.

Zuckerman (1994) also reviewed the literature on the oral passions of smoking, drinking, eating and drug taking. Again the literature tended to support the hypotheses of various SS researchers. Compared to low SS, high SS people drink and smoke more, use illegal drugs earlier and more frequently. SS is also related to food preferences. "Sensation seekers tend to be gourmets with a special taste for spicy and ethnic varieties of food as opposed to bland customary foods but they are not gourmands" (p. 257). Thus, if eating and drinking are considered leisure pursuits it may be possible to predict from SS test scores on food and drink consumption, experiences and preferences.

However, in Chapter 8 entitled "Vicarious experiences: art, media, music, fantasy and humor," Zuckerman (1994) reviews many studies salient to the topic of the chapter. The central tenet of this work is that art, music, literature and the media have, in varying capacity, the ability to arouse a person: "The stimulus qualities influencing arousal potential are intensity, novelty, complexity, change and suddenness of change, surprisingness, incongruity, uncertainty, size, color, sensory modality, emotional significance of the content, and associations with basic rewards or punishments. Everyone has experienced pain and its anticipation. Therefore, watching the image of a knife approaching a victim elicits a conditioned empathic response. From the time we first experience sexual arousal, certain images, such as nude bodies, become associated with that arousal and capable of eliciting it when presented in visual, auditory, or textual form" (p. 200).

Seven studies reviewed SS related to art and design preference. About the same number considered how SS scores related to media choice, preferences and reactions. Four studies looked at music preference, four at daydreaming and fantasizing and a similar number at humor appreciation. Zuckerman (1994) concludes thus: "Complexity and ambiguity are two qualities of visual stimuli that produce arousal. Liking for designs, art and music shows the interest of high SS in complex and ambiguous (as in complex abstract art) and intense (as in rock music) stimuli, and preferences of low SS for calming, low-tension art and music. Real life experience is generally more arousing than vicarious experience. It is more exciting to play a game than to watch others playing it, to do something risky rather than see others doing it, and to have sexual experiences rather than watching them in films or reading about them. However, for many low on SS vicarious experience may provide just the level of arousal they desire. Actual experience would push them beyond their optimal levels of arousals into the range of unpleasantness. High SS prefer to listen to live music in exciting surroundings whereas lows prefer to see and listen to it on television. High SS will watch television for the news reports, or use it as background while they are doing other things, but their interest is only peripheral. Based on their own reports and observed in an experiment, the high SS like to switch channels a lot keeping track of two or more programmes simultaneously. Low SS become more absorbed in a single programme. On traditional drinking nights, only the low SS are found in front of the television set. In photographs, television, films and reading, the high SS show a greater interest than the lows in morbid and sexual themes, whereas low SS find these themes distasteful and avoid them. High SS are more likely to be found among those attending sexually explicit (X-rated) movies and horror films. There is some evidence that the high SS may habituate more rapidly than lows to scenes in horror films. An awareness of the different kinds of media preferences in high and low SS has proved valuable in the design of media messages designed to discourage drug abuse" (pp. 220–221).

Further, he noted that daydreaming and fantasy are not strongly related to SS. Humor preferences reflect the cognitive styles of SS. High SS like nonsense humor, with incongruity or absurdity, whereas lows like humor in which the punch line neatly ties things up. Low SS tend not to enjoy sexual and nonsense humor. The rejection of sexual humour is particularly strong in those who are low on the Disinhibition (DIS) subscale of the SSS.

The preferences of SS in art, media, and humor reflect a liking for stimuli that arouse strong emotions, demand a suspension or reality, an acceptance of ambiguity or absurdity, and/or that vicariously involve spectators in activities that they find particularly rewarding particularly sex.

The remainder of this chapter attempts a selective up-date of this 10-year-old review. However, it is possible to make two rather disappointing observations from the more recent literature on the relation between SS and leisure. First, the literature has slowed down in the sense that there has been no growth, perhaps even a decline in interest in the relation of SS to leisure. Second there has been little theoretical development with an inclination to replication rather than innovation. Nevertheless, it seems that SS remains a more robust and predictive trait measure when it comes to understanding certain leisure preferences and satisfaction.

3. Sensation Seeking and Leisure

The literature on SS and leisure remains highly diverse and scattered. Much research concerns the association between SS and risk taking and evaluation (Rosenbloom 2003). Researchers have clearly seen the relevance of SS in leisure choice and experience and have set out to investigate usually clear hypotheses. Consider the following topics and findings.

3.1. Humor Appreciation

In a study across four samples, Ruch (1988) showed a clear association between SS subscales and enjoyment of humor. Experience Seeking (ES) and Boredom Susceptibility (BS) predicted the structural component in humor while DIS predicted the content. He concluded that "humor can be regarded as another area in which SS can express their need for intense, varied, novel and complex stimulation" (p. 871). Forabocso and Ruch (1994) examined the relation between SS and appreciation for three types of jokes: incongruity-resolution, nonsense and sexual humor. Results showed all SS sub-factors related to incongruity resolution, while ES related to appreciation of nonsense and BS and DIS correlated with liking sexual humour.

Given these findings it makes sense that SS is related to people's preference for all sorts of entertainment that portrays humor. Thus, preference and appreciation for books (as well as comics and magazines), films and videos, as well as live theatre and cabaret should systematically be related to SS. It will also predict how, when and why people use such things as the television remote control device (Weaver *et al.* 1996). A more recent paper by Lourey and McLachlan (2003) shows a clear relation between SS and both the perceived funniness of social cues and the overt expression of humor. The authors believe that perceiving events as being funny offers SS a novel source of stimulation and expressing humor an additional mode of experiencing intense stimulation.

3.2. Holidays

Gilchrist *et al.* (1995) tested the reasonable hypotheses that SS should be related to a preference for adventure holidays. Predictably, the Thrill and Adventure (TAS) subscale of the SS was highly significantly related to a preference for adventure holidays. The authors concluded that the SS concept and test "has potential as a psychometric tool in tourism research" (p. 513). The fact that SS has been associated with adventure activities (sports such as sky diving, hang-gliding, scuba diving, kayaking, skiing and mountaineering) attests to its usefulness in predicting certain types of leisure activities.

3.3. Hobbies

Most studies on preferred hobbies/past times have examined the relation with active high-risk activities. However, against this trend Joireman *et al.* (2002) looked at the relation between SS and involvement in the board game of chess. They found, as predicted, total SS and the TAS and DIS subscale scores were related to chess experience.

For over 30 years, there have been many papers on SS and sport. The earliest paper was published in 1974 by Hymbaugh and Garrett. In his review paper more than 20 years ago, Zuckerman (1983), related SS to sports as varied as auto-racing and scuba salvage diving. In his 1979 review, he noted: "Sensation seeking has been described as a biosocial motive determined in part by genetically determined differences in the biochemistry of certain neurotransmitters of the limbic systems that regulate approach, exploration and general activity.

The finding of low monoamine oxidase levels in mountain climbers presents the first evidence of an involvement of the central monoamine systems in a specific type of sport. What may risky sports, stressful life experiences and cocaine have in common, other than the fact that high SS may be attracted to them? Although the evidence is lacking for risky sports, and we largely extrapolate from animal studies of stress, it might be that all of these have a common biological pathway in the release of catecholamines stored in the neurons of limbic systems. At moderate levels of turnover, without excessive appraisal of threat, such release may temporarily activate or sensitize the intrinsic reward centres of the brain.

This sensitivity may characterize many participants in risky sports. We do not have to postulate unconscious death wishes or masculine protests to explain their desire for adventure and excitement. These desires, more characteristic of some than others, are part of our biological heritage. They are part of the source of much of our exploratory and creative activity as well as destructive behaviors in crime and war. Risky sports, along with travel, art, music, sex and social stimulation, can meet SS needs even if work cannot. Unfortunately for civilisations that cannot provide adventure and stimulation for the young that is not antisocial, crime and drugs may meet their needs. Recognition of the basic need and its scientific study are a first step in dealing with the problems that it may create" (p. 291).

Since then there have been many papers on the relation between SS and a wide range of sports as diverse as aerobic exercise (Babbitt *et al.* 1990), canoe and kayak paddlers (Campbell *et al.* 1993), and hang-glider pilots and golfers (Wagner & Houlihan 1994). Various papers have also looked at SS and more general sports interests (Franken *et al.* 1994; Schroth 1995) but most have followed the high vs. low risk distinction (Jack & Ronan 1998).

If one believes in the concept of recreational drug use, it is possible to argue that preference for drugs should be related to SS. Indeed, various studies have demonstrated this to be the case. Thus, Ball (1995) demonstrated that impulsive SS was related to greater cocaine abuse as well as psychiatric severity and symptoms. More recently, SS was linked to marijuana use (Ames *et al.* 2002).

SS has been linked to the choice of leisure pursuits and how people indulge in the activity. Thus, using the choice of driving cars as an example, it seems reasonable to assume that SS would be related to preference for driving per se; type of vehicle, destination and route; as well as driving style. Certainly the latter has been investigated. Furnham and Saipe (1993) showed TAS and BS linked to driver style, accidents and convictions. Ames *et al.* (2002) also found impulsive SS linked to driving under the influence of drugs.

4. Art Appreciation

There is a small but interesting and important literature on SS and art appreciation dating back over 30 years (Zuckerman *et al.* 1970), which will be examined in detail to illustrate the predictive power of SS in an area of research much neglected by personality researchers. There are, in fact, two distinct literatures depending on whether one is interested in art preference, i.e. liking of pictures, or art ability. The latter literature is however much more limited though recent studies have shown, rather well, that personality variables seem to be predictably and systematically related to art preference and experience, i.e. art education and knowledge, while cognitive ability, i.e. intelligence is related to art judgement (Furnham & Chamorro-Premuzic 2004).

Associations between SS and preferences in art and other imagery have been found by several studies (Zuckerman *et al.* 1972; Zuckerman & Neeb 1980). Zuckerman *et al.* (1993) used the SSS-V to examine the relation between personality and preferences for styles of paintings. High general SS liked expressionist paintings more than low, and high Experience Seekers liked semi-abstract paintings more than lows. Thus, high SS seemed to prefer complex, asymmetrical designs, which were suggestive of movement, while low SS preferred simple, symmetrical designs (Zuckermann *et al.* 1970). In addition, SS was associated with positive ratings of abstract, futurist, cubist paintings by Boccioni and abstract impressionistic paintings by Pollock. A positive correlation was also found between SS and positive ratings of representational paintings depicting aggressive scenes.

Preferential differences relating to content, as well as style, have also been found for SS, although it appears that, on the whole, content is less influential than the style and complexity of the art. Zuckerman *et al.* (1993) carried out two studies concerning SS and attitudes towards a selection of 19th century nature paintings that varied in actual artist, style, complexity and tension. An interaction was found for SS and the tension component. High and low SS did not differ in preference for paintings of medium and high tension from the low SS. However, the most salient influence was the degree of abstractness or representation. Complexity was not found to be relevant in this experiment either. Zaleski (1984) asked participants to choose the pictures they liked most from 21 paintings depicting images that were either positively emotionally arousing (e.g. celebratory scenes), negatively emotionally arousing (e.g. scenes of death), or neutral. The results showed a significant difference in the distribution of the first-choice picture among the three picture categories for high compared with low SS. Since surreal images may be regarded as possessing any or all of these attributes, it was predicted that total SS scores would be related positively to liking for surreal art, and negatively to liking for the representational pictures — which could be seen by high SS as boring and unchallenging.

Furnham and Bunyan (1988) found a negative correlation between total SS scores (as assessed by SSS Form V) and liking for complex representational paintings and a positive correlation between total SS scores and liking for complex abstract pictures. The style of the pictures was more strongly related to SS scores than the complexity of the images. They concluded that SS appears to account for 10–15% of the variance when it comes to art preference. Ruch *et al.* (1996) replicated this effect.

Furnham and Avison (1997) found that total SS scores were positively related to positive ratings of ten surreal paintings, and negatively correlated with positive ratings of ten representational paintings. TAS scores were not significantly correlated with positive ratings of either art genre; however, DIS scores were significantly correlated with positive ratings of surreal art, but not necessarily with disliking of representational paintings. "The finding here that preference for surreal art — with its ambiguous, incongruous, unusual imagery, is related to an individual's level of SS provides further support for the association of this trait and preferences for various forms of non-representational art that has been revealed by previous studies. ES has also been found in previous studies to be the SS component most strongly related to aesthetic preference and its salience in this study is consistent with this — liking for surreal art appears to be particularly associated with a person's receptivity to complexity, ambiguity and novelty experienced through the mind and the senses. It is interesting that ES appeared to be especially relevant to attitudes towards the surreal/non-traditional paintings and BS to attitudes towards representational paintings, and that they were each only predictive of preference for one of the art types. High ES does not necessarily predict a disliking for representational art, and high BS does not necessarily predict a liking for surreal art. A notable point here is that this is a fairly important distinction which would not be apparent if one were to only consider the total SS score and not its components" (p. 933).

Rawlings *et al.* (2000) looked at SS and preferences for music and paintings in two national samples. They found the ES subscale most consistently and clearly related to preferences for "hard rock" music and "violent abstract" art. Furnham and Walker (2001a, b) looked at preference for low painting styles: abstract, pop art, representational and Japanese. They found many hypotheses with the SS variables confirmed though psychological conservatism accounted for more of the variance.

Furnham and Walker (2001a, b) predicted that because TAS had previously been less highly correlated with aesthetic preference, the correlations would be weaker than for the DIS subscale but still significant. Because it was believed that pop art was closer in overall style to abstract and surreal art than to traditional, representational art, it was suggested that SS scores would be negatively related to positive ratings of representational art as has been established in various other studies. As predicted, the strongest correlations between TAS and DIS were for abstract art and the smallest for representational art.

What these studies show is that SS is systematically and predictably linked to art preference and an engagement with art activities. It is possible to take other art forms like literature, the cinema, the theatre and music even poetry derive hypotheses in line with sensation seeking theory that explain preference for as well as indulge in quite specific art forms.

5. Personality, Recreation and Competition

In one of the few thorough and theoretical reviews, Eysenck *et al.* (1982) considered the relation between personality and sport. Inevitably, they reviewed the literature in terms of Eysenck's three-factor model. However it is possible given the overlap between SS and Eysenck's three variables to postulate the relation between those variable and SS:

- Sportsmen and sportswomen tend to be characterized by an extraverted temperament. This seems equally true of outstanding performers and average performers, physical education students, and others who are at a much lower level than Olympic participants or champions in various sports. It is probable that most talented competitive sportspeople have high average, but not overly high SS scores.
- There are many different arguments about the low levels of cortical arousal level experienced by extraverts leading to their superior sporting performance. Among these are: high pain thresholds, SS, assertiveness and competitiveness, and generally a lack of cortical control and inhibition of ongoing behavior and immediate reactions. This finding is perfectly in accord with Zuckerman's theory though he would probably identify different mechanisms.
- There is a tendency for athletes, particularly outstanding ones, to be low on neuroticism scales, and to suffer less from anxiety than do non-sportsmen and women. The findings do not support this conclusion universally, but the trend is definitely in this direction, particularly with outstanding sportsmen. To an outsider the sensation seeker

is often extremely courageous, if not foolhardy, and could not be accused of negative affectivity.

- The reasons for the negative relation between excellence in sport and anxiety-neuroticism probably lies in the drive stimulus qualities of anxiety, which distract the athlete from his appointed task. The situation is complicated because of the curvilinear relation between anxiety as a drive and performance; the Yerkes-Dodson law is often invoked in this connection.
- The effects of sporting activities on personality are not really known, although there are many theories in this connection. It is often suggested that sporting activities may have a beneficial effect on personality, particularly in reducing depression and anxiety, but the evidence does not support such a view. However, in terms of SS, sport has the very real and important function of providing ideal stimuli to combat boredom.
- Driving a car may be regarded as a sporting activity, and is quite definitely related to personality, in the sense that both E and N are positively related to accident proneness. The combination of high N and high E is uniquely favourable for the occurrence of driving accidents. As we have seen, driving behavior was consistently related to SS.
- Sexual activity too may be regarded as partaking of the characteristics of a sport, these activities being carried out in many cases for amusement, and being physical in nature. Here too E has been found to be the personality component most commonly correlated with different types of sexual activity, such as early sexual activity, activity involving many different partners, activity indulged in frequently, etc. N appears to have a negative influence on sexual activity, being associated with frigidity, impotence, lack of orgasmic capacity, and other disorders. Again there is a growing literature that relates SS to sexual interests, preferences and behaviors.
- Most investigations use groups that are too heterogeneous to give clear-cut results. It has been found that even in apparently homogeneous groups, such as shooters, different types of shooting are correlated with different personality traits, by depending on such things as time allowed for reaction to the stimulus, etc. Where little time is allowed, extraverts excel but where much time is allowed, introverts do quite well. Such finer distinctions should always be looked at in future research. This is a highly salient point for the topic of this chapter for two reasons. First it speaks to the importance of understanding that each sport may fulfil different roles: there is attack and defence as well as the possibility of playing alone or together with others. Thus, the bowler and batsman in cricket, goalkeeper and striker in football, singles vs. doubles players in tennis may be differentially related to SS. In every sport, there can be dramatic differences: deep-sea vs. lake fishing; fly-fishing for salmon as opposed to canal fishing for pike; competitive vs. solo fishing. That is, to really understand the nature of the relation between SS and leisure we need to carefully explain precisely what the leisure activity involves. Secondly, most studies have shown that a finer grain analysis at the primary factor level of the SS dimension itself is beneficial. Thus, thrill and adventure seeking (TAS) may logically relate to one leisure activity while BS does not.
- Genetic factors are known to determine to a large extent both personality and physique; it has been shown that competence in many different sporting activities has a strong genetic component, accounting for between 70 and 90% of the total variance. This finding does not suggest that training cannot help people to improve their performance, but it does

suggest that selection for sport in general, and for specific types of sport in particular, should take account of personality and physique.

- Behavior modification, i.e. the application of psychological principles to learning and improvement in sport, could be of considerable importance in leading to greater achievement in sport. The possibilities of these methods have not yet been explored sufficiently to make a more definite statement.
- The techniques of behavior therapy (desensitisation, flooding, modelling) could be of considerable use in reducing anxiety insofar as this interferes with optimum performance. Here the evidence for the general usefulness of these methods is much stronger than for the methods of behavior modification, but little has been written about their application to sportsmen and sportswomen in particular. This illustrates the relative isolation of psychology from sport, and suggests that we already have methods of training and treatment that could, with advantage, be applied in this field.

6. The Effects of Leisure on Personality

Whereas personality has usually been treated as the independent variable in sport psychology by examining personality differences in preference for or effectiveness in specific sports, some research has considered personality as the dependent variable. Depending on the personality theory or model invoked, it is possible that various physical and social consequences that occur in sport and leisure could change certain aspects of personality functioning. Dienstbier (1984) proposed four possible mechanisms for personality change as a function of sport exercise:

(1) *Physiological changes.* Sports exercise can affect many physiological systems, including hormonal, which is known to have influential effects on mood and emotions. "If we define temperament as a long-term tendency toward certain moods or emotional dispositions, it is apparent that we should expect to see some effect upon such a measure after extreme training. Thus there seems a strong probability that changes in depression, anxiety and positive moods and emotions should follow directly (with no additional mediators) from physiological changes induced through running" (p. 250).

(2) *Self-perception of changes.* There appear to be potential self-concept and self-esteem consequences of sport that reduce body fat, redistribute weight, increase energy levels and lead to a more youthful appearance. "The amazing distances a healthy individual may be able to run after only a few months of training therefore can lead to an increased sense of one's ability to master challenges and to attain goals that seemed remote only months earlier. One's entire belief system about the degree to which one's life is self-determined or internal (versus other or fate-determined, or external) may be influenced by such significant successes" (p. 257).

(3) *Socialising and life-style changes.* Dedication to a particular sport or leisure activity brings with it life-style changes in such things as eating, drinking, smoking, sleeping and resting; in short, life-style. "Life-style changes mean different interaction patterns with different individuals who may have a substantial effect on personality functioning" (p. 257).

(4) *Expectations.* "Expectations and values may change as a function of being exposed to peers and coaches who share a quite different pattern of expectation about health, diet, and exercise. Gradually these new values and expectations are associated so as to change personality functioning" (pp. 258–259).

Although all of the above effects are possible, they are difficult to demonstrate, and the research evidence is patchy and problematic. Dienstbier (1984) listed six control features required to demonstrate some causal relation between exercise sport (leisure pattern) and personality. Studies must be longitudinal to demonstrate cause and effect; non-sport control groups must be involved in the before-after design; the control group should be engaged in some systematic activity capable of giving some of the psychological benefits as the sport; the control groups needs to be involved in a socially engaging activity; changes in lifestyle need to be co-varied out in analysis to ensure that this is not the cause of change; and the control group needs to be given similar expectations of personality change. When these various criteria are met, Then it will be possible to demonstrate personality change as a function of leisure sport.

This means that the extant literature is difficult to evaluate (Dienstbier 1984). For instance, Folkins and Sime (1981) concluded that there are no global changes in personality test scores after fitness training, while others reported more favorable results. For example, Jasnoski and Holmes (1991) used the 16PF to demonstrate that subjects became more imaginative, less shy and more apprehensive after a 15-week aerobic training program. However, there appears to be almost no literature on whether, how, when or why leisure activities have a systematic and measurable effect on SS.

7. Conclusion

There are many settings in which to test sensation seeking theories in the laboratory and the work place and also in the leisure preferences of individuals. It is not uncommon in application forms and job interviews for individuals to be asked what they do in their spare time. Presumably interviewers believe that this is a fruitful question because it gets at the "real nature of the person." Indeed many people have expressed interest in, and surprise about, the leisure time activities of other people. What, they often wonder, drives people to become stamp or birds-egg collectors while others go bungee jumping or sky diving.

There are three important observations from this research area. The first is that the SS trait variable and its factor scores relate systematically to a very wide variety of chosen leisure activities. It is not as many have assumed limited to dangerous sports. Secondly, the size of the correlations indicates that, while relations are significant, they are modest, accounting for some 10% of the variance. This suggests that many other factors determine leisure choice and satisfaction. Thirdly, until there is an agreed upon and sensitive psychological taxonomy of leisure activities, research in this area will be piecemeal and sporadic.

Marvin Zuckerman's theory and measures have significantly added to our understandings of preferences for more active, risky, thrilling types of leisure. Through the concept of SS, he has made it possible to describe, predict and understand leisure preferences.

References

Ames, S., Zogg, J., & Stacy, A. (2002). Implicit cognition, sensation seeking, marijuana use and driving behavior among drug offenders. *Personality and Individual Differences*, *33*, 1055–1072.

Argyle, M. (1996). *The social psychology of leisure*. Harmondsworth: Penguin.

Babbitt, T., Rowland, G., & Franken, R. (1990). Sensation seeking and participation in aerobic exercise classes. *Personality and Individual Differences*, *11*, 181–183.

Ball, S. (1995). The validity of an alternative five-factor measure of personality in cocaine abusers. *Psychological Assessment*, *7*, 148–154.

Brandstätter, H. (1994). Pleasure of leisure-pleasure at work: Personality makes the differences. *Personality and Individual Differences*, *16*, 931–946.

Campbell, J., Tyrrell, D., & Zingaro, M. (1993). Sensation seeking among white water canoe and kayak paddlers. *Personality and Individual Differences*, *14*, 489–491.

Dienstbier, R. (1984). The effect of exercise on personality. In: M. Sacks, & G. Buffone (Eds), *Running as therapy* (pp. 248–263). London: University of Nebraska Press.

Egloff, B., & Gruhn, J. (1996). Personality and endurance sports. *Personality and Individual Differences*, *21*, 223–239.

Eysenck, J., Nias, D., & Cox, D. (1982). Sport and personality. *Advances in Behaviour Research and Therapy*, *4*, 1–56.

Folkins, C., & Sime, W. (1981). Physical fitness training and mental health. *American Psychologist*, *36*, 373–389.

Forabocso, G., & Ruch, W. (1994). Sensation seeking, social attitudes and humour appreciation in Italy. *Personality and Individual Differences*, *16*, 515–528.

Franken, R., Hill, R., & Kierstead, J. (1994). Sport interest as predicted by the personality measures of competitiveness, mastery, instrumentality, expressivity and sensation seeking. *Personality and Individual Differences*, *17*, 467–476.

Furnham, A. (1990). Personality and demographic determinants of leisure and sports preference and performance. *International Journal of Sport Psychology*, *21*, 218–236.

Furnham, A., & Avison, M. (1997). Personality and preference for surreal paintings. *Personality and Individual Differences*, *23*, 923–935.

Furnham, A., & Bunyan, M. (1988). Personality and art preferences. *European Journal of Personality*, *2*, 67–74.

Furnham, A., & Chamorro-Premuzic, T. (2004). Personality, intelligence and art. *Personality and Individual Differences*, *36*, 705–715.

Furnham, A., & Saipe, J. (1993). Personality correlates of convicted drivers. *Personality and Individual Differences*, *14*, 329–336.

Furnham, A., & Walker, J. (2001a). Personality and judgement of abstract, pop art, and representational paintings. *European Journal of Personality*, *15*, 57–72.

Furnham, A., & Walker, J. (2001b). The influence of personality traits, previous experience of art, and demographic variables on artistic preference. *Personality and Individual Differences*, *31*, 997–1017.

Gilchrist, H., Povey, R., Dickinson, A., & Povey, R. (1995). The sensation seeking scale: It's use in a study of the characteristics of people choosing "adventure holidays". *Personality and Individual Differences*, *19*, 513–516.

Hymbaugh, K., & Garrett, J. (1974). Sensation seeking among sky divers. *Perceptual and Motor Skills*, *38*, 118.

Iso-Ahola, S. (1976). On the theoretical link between personality and leisure. *Psychological Reports*, *39*, 3–16.

Jack, S., & Ronan, K. (1998). Sensation seeking among high- and low-risk sports participants. *Personality and Individual Differences, 25*, 1063–1083.

Jasnoski, M., & Holmes, E. (1991). Influences of initial aerobic fitness, aerobic training and changes in aerobic fitness on personality functioning. *Journal of Psychosomatic Research, 25*, 553–556.

Joireman, J., Fick, C., & Anderson, R. (2002). Sensation seeking and involvement in chess. *Personality and Individual Differences, 32*, 509–515.

Kirkcaldy, B. (1985). The value of traits in sport. In: B. Kirkcaldy (Ed.), *Individual differences in movement* (pp. 248–259). Boston, MA: MTP Press.

Kirkcaldy, B., & Furnham, A. (1991). Personality and sex differences in recreational choices. *Sportwissenschaft, 20*, 43–56.

Lourey, E., & McLachlan, A. (2003). Elements of sensation seeking and their relationship with two aspects of humour appreciation. *Personality and Individual Differences, 35*, 277–285.

Melamed, S., Meir, E., & Samson, A. (1995). The benefits of personality leisure congruence-evidence and implications. *Journal of Leisure Research, 27*, 25–40.

Nias, D. (1985). Personality and recreational behaviour. In: B. Kirkcaldy (Ed.), *Individual differences in movement* (pp. 48–68). Lancaster: MTP Press.

Rawlings, D., Vidal, B., & Furnham, A. (2000). Personality and aesthetic preference in Spain and England: Two studies relating sensation seeking and openness to experience to liking for paintings and music. *European Journal of Personality, 14*, 553–576.

Rosenbloom, T. (2003). Risk evaluation and risky behaviour of high and low sensation seekers. *Social Behaviour and Personality, 31*, 375–386.

Ruch, W. (1988). Sensation seeking and the enjoyment of structure and content of humour. *Personality and Individual Differences, 9*, 861–871.

Ruch, W., Busse, P., & Schreurs, C. (1996, July). Sensation seeking and aesthetic preference. Paper presented at the 8th European Conference on Personality, Ghent, Belgium.

Schroth, M. (1995). A comparison of sensation seeking among different groups of athletes and non-athletes. *Personality and Individual Differences, 18*, 219–228.

Shivers, J. (1981). *Leisure and recreation concepts*. Boston: Allyn and Bacon.

Tinsley, H., & Tinsley, D. (1986). A theory of the attributes, benefits and causes of leisure experience. *Leisure Sciences, 8*, 1–45.

Wagner, A., & Houlihan, D. (1994). Sensation seeking and trait anxiety in hang-glider pilots and golfers. *Personality and Individual Differences, 16*, 975–977.

Weaver, J., Walker, J., McCord, L., & Bellamy, R. (1996). Exploring the links between personality and television remote-control device use. *Personality and Individual Differences, 20*, 483–487.

Zaleski, Z. (1984). Sensation seeking and preferences for emotional stimuli. *Personality and Individual Differences, 5*, 609–611.

Zuckerman, M. (1979). *Sensation seeking: Beyond the optimal level of arousal*. Hillsdale, NJ: Erlbaum.

Zuckerman, M. (1983). Sensation seeking and sports. *Personality and Individual Differences, 4*, 285–293.

Zuckerman, M. (1994). *Behavioral expressions and biosocial bases of sensation seeking*. Cambridge: Cambridge University Press.

Zuckerman, M., Bone, R., Neary, R., Mangelsdorf, D., & Brustman, B. (1972). What is the sensation seeker? Personality trait and experience correlates of the Sensation Seeking Scales. *Journal of Consulting and Clinical Psychology, 39*, 308–321.

Zuckerman, M., Neary, R., & Brustman, B. (1970). Sensation-seeking scale correlates in experience (smoking, drugs, alcohol, 'hallucinations' and sex) and preference for complexity (designs).

Proceedings of the 78th Annual Convention of the American Psychological Association (pp. 317–318). Washington, DC: American Psychological Association.

Zuckerman, M., & Neeb, M. (1980). Demographic influences in sensation seeking and expressions of sensation seeking in religion, smoking, and driving habits. *Personality and Individual Differences*, *1*, 197–206.

Zuckerman, M., Ulrich, R., & McLaughlin, J. (1993). Sensation seeking and reactions to nature paintings. *Personality and Individual Differences*, *15*, 563–576.

Chapter 11

Sensation Seeking and Participation in Physical Risk Sports

M. Gomà-i-Freixanet

1. Introduction

Our ancestors, when they were organized in hunter-gatherer societies, explored new territories in the pursuit of food and water, to have better opportunities for mating behavior and for child rearing. For example, we know that hunters who can engage successfully in the risky activity of hunting large animals signal their superior fitness (Smith & Bird 2000), and have more and healthier offspring, reinforcing the notion that successful hunting increases sexual access (Kaplan & Hill 1985) and choice. This exploratory behavior entailed gains (new resources, increased survival of the group) as well as risks that were mainly physical (increased probability of being injured or even losing one's life). Presently, in modern societies, human beings no longer need to explore new territories in search of food and water, but they still engage in exploratory behavior that entails risks. With the complexity of our contemporary societies, these risks are not limited to physical risks, but also entail legal, economic, social and political risks.

Because the concept of risk is treated in several different areas of knowledge, the term risk does not have a unitary meaning and interpretation. For example, in the field of international relations and politics, prospect theory tries to give a new insight into risky decision-making (Levy 1992, 1997). The cornerstone of this theory is that decision makers accept risks to avoid losses, but refuse to take risks to make comparable gains. Specifically, most people are risk averse when facing an opportunity for a gain, but are risk acceptant when facing the prospect of a loss. This theory assumes that one's willingness to take risks depends on how problems are framed. Thus, the situation often shapes the decision. There are, however, a sizeable number of subjects in experimental research who do not exhibit the framing effect (Kahneman *et al.* 1991). This does pose a challenge to the framing concept. It is clear that other factors than framing effects are important in the decision to take risks. Not taking individual differences into account may not be problematic in a field such as economics that is more concerned with modal behavior, but in international politics, where the behavior of

On the Psychobiology of Personality
Edited by R. M. Stelmack

ISBN: 0-08-044209-9

a single leader often can have dramatic policy consequences, the introduction of individual differences in the equation is of high importance.

Another theory devoted to risk is that of Weinstein (1980). In his seminal paper, Weinstein drew attention to the popular belief that people tend to think they are invulnerable, i.e. the expectation that misfortunes happen to others and not ourselves. This optimistic bias holds for a wide range of health and other outcomes. He used the term unrealistic optimism to define it. This theory draws attention to risk perception and the ways in which it may be mediated by experience. A recent work on a national sample of motorcyclists (Rutter *et al.* 1998) showed that the perceptions of risk predicted subsequent behavior, though generally in the direction not of precaution adoption but of precaution abandonment: the greater the perceived risk at time one, the more frequent the risky behavior at time two (one year later).

Reversal theory is a general theory of motivation, originally developed by Smith and Apter (1975). It strives to provide a systematic structure to explain the connections between arousal level, the subjective perception of emotion, the influence of social context, and behavior. In this theory, the concept of paradoxical behavior is described. In the context of reversal theory, this concept refers to conduct that is not essential for human survival but is "voluntarily undertaken and yet that appears to militate against the health, well-being, and even survival of the individual concerned, exposing him or her to gratuitous risk" (Apter & Batler 1997: 119–120). Such conduct includes the performance of potentially harmful behaviors (to self and/or others), e.g. participation in dangerous sports. Regarding the application of reversal theory in the field of sports, Kerr in a series of studies (Kerr 1989, 1991; Kerr & Svebak 1989) found that individuals who perform risky sports on a regular basis are arousal seekers as measured by the Arousal Avoidance subscale of the Telic Dominance Scale (TDS; Murgatroyd *et al.* 1978). Thus, it seems that individuals engaged in high-risk sports enjoy high arousal and indeed actively seek out situations where they can induce these pleasant feelings.

The three theories described above are common in that they try to describe behavior related to risk taking. Prospect theory emphasizes the situation in which the decision has to be taken, the frame, as an important variable in risk taking; the concept of unrealistic optimism focuses the influence of experience in the perception of risk; and reversal theory emphasizes the meta-motivational states, i.e. the particular kinds of experiences that people seek will depend on which particular frame of mind they are in at any given point in time. Surprisingly, none of these theories take individual differences in personality into account.

One theory that does involve the study of individual differences in risk taking and follows the trait theory tradition is Zuckerman's theory of Sensation Seeking (SS). Work on the first sensation seeking scale (SSS; Zuckerman *et al.* 1964) began in the early 1960s. It was based on the idea that there were consistent individual differences in optimal levels of stimulation and arousal, and that these differences could be measured with a questionnaire. Zuckerman described sensation seeking as "a trait defined by the need for varied, novel, and complex sensations and experiences and the willingness to take physical and social risk for the sake of such experience" (Zuckerman 1979: 10). This definition was first derived from types of items constituting the early forms of the SSS (until form V), and later from the research that related SSS scores to actual behavior, reported behavior, expectations, anticipations, and risk appraisals.

Minor changes to this definition were implemented (in italic) to adapt to empirical data. The current definition of SS is as follows: "Sensation seeking is a trait defined by the *seeking* of varied, novel, complex, and *intense* sensations and experiences, and the willingness to take physical, social, *legal*, and *financial* risks for the sake of such experience" (Zuckerman 1994: 27). Note that the term need has been substituted by the term seeking, as the former implies the subjective quality of compulsion and this does not seem to characterize the behavior of sensation seekers. The addition of intensity has been suggested because it seems that the common denominator of the sensations attractive to sensation seekers is that they all produce transient spurts of physiological arousal. The legal and financial types of risks were added because results from factor analyses of risk appraisal categories (Horvath & Zuckerman 1993) indicated that sensation seekers have a general risk-taking tendency regardless of the specific risk.

The SSS has undergone several revisions (forms II to VI), but since its publication in 1978, SSS-V has become the most widely used form of the scale (see Zuckerman 1979). Several improvements from previous versions were introduced in SSS-V. First, a total score was developed based on the sum of the four ten-item subscales. This replaced the General scale in SSS II and IV which was not a satisfactory measure of overall sensation seeking as it lacked items from the Disinhibition subscale. Second, the correlations among scales were reduced to define unique factors that still maintained some correlation in order to justify a total score. Third, some items were discarded to ensure cross-cultural as well as cross-gender reliability. Finally, the total length of the scale was reduced to 40 items, 10 for each subscale, as shorter scales are more convenient for research projects. The four SS scales are defined as follows:

(1) *Thrill and Adventure Seeking* (TAS). These items express a desire to engage in sports or other physically risky activities that provide unusual sensations of speed or defiance of gravity, such as parachuting, scuba diving, or skiing. Because most of the activities are not common, the majority of the items are expressed as intentions ("I would like . . .") rather than reports of experience. An attitude item that summarizes the factor is: "I sometimes like to do things that are a little frightening."
(2) *Experience Seeking* (ES). This factor considers the seeking of novel sensations and experiences through the mind and senses, as in arousing music, art, and travel, and through social nonconformity, as in association with groups on the fringes of conventional society (e.g. artists, hippies).
(3) *Disinhibition* (DIS). The items in this factor describe seeking sensation through social activities like parties, social drinking, and sex. An item describing the factor is: "I like to have new and exciting experiences even if they are a little unconventional or illegal."
(4) *Boredom Susceptibility* (BS). This factor describes an intolerance for repetitive experiences of any kind, including routine work and boring people. An item expressing the attitude is: "The worst social sin is to be a bore."

The SSS-V has been used in a wide range of projects, including studies on the psychophysiological and psychopharmacological bases of SS, on individual differences in social behavior of SS, on the identification of the place of SS in the structure of personality, and on applied research that examined the expression of SS in common daily life.

2. Sensation Seeking and Sports

One implication of the SS construct in the context of sports is that the particular sport discipline one is more likely to participate in may be based on whether one is high or low on the SS trait. Of course, additional factors such as physical ability, economic status and age are important determinants as well. But in this chapter we will review the contribution of the SS trait to the specific area of sports, and discuss research that is relevant to this specific issue. A comprehensive summary of research conducted in the area of SS and sport participation is given in Tables 1–3. These tables are based on Zuckerman's paper (1983) where sports were classified into high, medium or low physical risk according to the associated risks involved. High physical risk sports are those with a high probability of serious injury or death as a consequence of practicing such a sport. Sports like climbing, parachuting, speleology or white water kayaking, where subjects have to struggle with the strong forces of nature fit into this classification. Medium physical risk sports are those with a higher probability of being injured than encountering death, the arena where the sport takes place is limited and the environment is static. Sports like boxing, karate, rugby or American football are good examples in this category. Low physical risk sports have a very low probability of a fatal injury occurrence. Sports such as running, gymnastics, bowling or golf fit into this classification.

Tables 1–3 summarize 40 empirical studies that have been conducted on SS and risky sports. Only two papers that did not use the SSS, those of Kerr (1991) and Cogan and Brown (1999), were included. These authors used the Arousal Avoidance scale that is relevant to SS. In general, the studies reviewed compare groups participating in various kinds of sports with participants in other kinds of sports with similar or different level of risk, or with control groups. All but the two of studies reviewed are devoted to SS and sports. These studies do differ in several ways, including the sex of athletes, the kind of sport, the level of competition and the criteria of classification of individuals. Some of the studies differentiate genders, while others do not take this variable into account. Some use team sports such as rugby, while others use individual sports such as parachuting. Some compare different levels of competition, although the criteria are not the same in all the studies. Some studies use objective criteria such as height; other studies employ expert nominations, or membership on a national team. Others use different criteria to assign individuals to a given level of risk (number of accidents, level of uncertainty, inconsistency of the specific sports situations, or international grading systems as in kayaking or climbing). The control groups are also defined by different criteria, i.e. sports students, college students, general population or subjects selected specifically for not being enrolled in any risky sport. To make a more thoughtful analysis of the information that is reviewed, the tables are first analyzed individually, and then cross-analyzed to find similarities across them.

2.1. High Physical Risk Sports

The studies in Table 1 are grouped into three categories: (1) studies that compare high-risk sports with sports of similar level of risk; (2) studies that compare high-risk sports with

Table 1: Studies relating Sensation Seeking to high-risk sports.

Sport	Author	Experimental (sex, *n*)	Control (sex, *n*)	Differences		Notes
Scuba salvage diving	Bacon (1974)	Volunteer salvage divers	College students (matched)	↑ TAS = ES ↑ DIS ↑ BS ↑ Total		SSS-IV
Parachuting	Hymbaugh and Garrett (1974)	Sky-divers M & F 21	Non-sky-divers M & F (matched)	= TAS = ES = DIS = BS ↑ Total		SSS-II
Parachuting Racing Snowmobilers Police Firemen	Kusyszyn, Steinberg and Elliot (1974)	Risk-takers M 85	Civil servants & college students M 70	↑ TAS = ES = DIS = BS ↑ Total		SSS-IV
Mountain climbing	Fowler, von Knorring and Oreland (1980)	Climbers M 11, F 7 & students interested in climbing 9	Dental students not interested in climbing 32	↑ TAS = ES = DIS = BS ↑ Total		SSS-IV Climbers and interested have lower platelet MAO
Scuba diving (novices)	Heyman and Rose (1980)	Novice divers M 29, F 16	Same-sex students	Subscales not analysed ↑ Total		SSS-V SS correlated + time length of 1st free dive, — with depth of dive
Skiing	Connolly (1981)	Skiers M 27, F 18	Non-skiers from health-spa (matched)	↑ TAS = ES = DIS = BS ↑ Total		Skiers who had accidents higher than others on TAS, DIS, Total
Hang-gliding auto-racing	Straub (1982)	Hang-gliders^{1} M 33 Auto-racers^{2} M 22	Bowlers^{0} M 25	TAS 1 > 0 ES 1 > 0 DIS = BS = Total 1 > 0	TAS =0 ES 2 > 0 DIS 2 > 0 BS 2 > 0 Total 2 > 0	SSS-V High vs. low risk: more number of injuries.
Mountain climbing Parachuting Hang-gliding Racing	Zaleski (1984)	Miscellaneous risky sports M 60	Controls matched by age M 60	↑ TAS = ES ↑ DIS = BS		↑ risk takers on the Choice Dilemma Questionnaire, ↑ TAS & Intellectual Adventure Seeking.
Rock climbing	Robinson (1985)	Elite climbers M 30	Normative data M 377	↑ TAS ↑ ES = DIS = BS ↑ Total	↓STAI-T	SSS-V
Rock climbing	Levenson (1990)	Rock climbers M 18	Norms from college students M 686	↑ TAS ↑ ES ↓ DIS = BS ↑ Total		SSS-IV No data about significance.

Table 1: (*Continued*)

Sport	Author	Experimental (sex, *n*)	Control (sex, *n*)	Differences		Notes
Mountain climbing	Cronin (1991)	Climbers M & F 20	Control M & F 21	↑ TAS ↑ ES = DIS = BS ↑ Total		SSS-V College students.
Himalayas expedition	Gomà-i-Freixanet (1991)	Expeditioners[1] M 27 Mountain climbers & skiers[2] M 72 Sportsmen not related with mountaneering[3] M 221	Controls not engaged in any risky sports[0] M 54	TAS 123 > 0 2 > 3 ES 123 > 0 2 > 3 DIS 2 > 0 BS = TAS-OUT 23 > 0 Total 123 > 0 2 > 3	E 123 > 0 N = P = L = Imp = So =	SSS-V Controlling for age.
Surfing Windsurfing	Kerr (1991)	Surfers M 32 Sailboarders M 31	Weight traineers M 39	↓ PO ↓ SM ↓ AA ↓ Total		↑ risk sports arousal seekers & paratelic dominant individuals.
Parachuting Motor-cycle racing		Parachutists M 18 Motor-cycle racers M 21	Marathon runners M 17	= PO = SM ↓ AA ↓ Total		
Hang-gliding		Gliders M 25	General public M 25	= PO = SM	↓ AA = Total	
Rodeo Hang-gliding	Rainey, Amunategui, Agocs and Larick (1992)	Rodeo athletes[1] M 19 Hang-gliders[2] M 28	Baseball[3] players M 39 Wrestlers[4] M 29	TAS = ES 2 > 134 DIS 1 > 34 BS 2 > 34 Total 1 > 3 2 > 134		SSS-V College students. Rodeo not particularly ↑ on SS.
White-water	Campbell, Tyrrell and Zingaro (1993)	Canoe & kayak paddlers M & F 54	Norms from general population	↑ TAS = ES = DIS = BS = Total		SSS-V Anxiety correlated with TAS −0.30 & with Total −0.04
Speleology Alpinism Ski jumping	Rossi and Cereatti (1993)	Speleologists[1] ? 20 Alpinists[2] ? 20 Ski-jumpers[3] ? 7	Controls[0] ? 20	TAS 123 > 0 ES 12 > 0 DIS 123 > 0 BS 123 > 0 Total 123 > 0 1 > 3		SSS-V Sex not stated. Did not control for age. Number of accidents correlates with Total & TAS.
Parasailing	Cantón and Mayor (1994)	Parasailers M & F 21	Tennis M & F 30	↑ TAS ↑ ES ↑ DIS = BS ↑ Total	= PO ↑ SM ↓ AA ↑ Total	SSS-V Total SS correlates −0.40 with AA

Table 1: (*Continued*)

Sport	Author	Experimental (sex, *n*)	Control (sex, *n*)	Differences		Notes
Hang-gliding	Wagner and Houlihan (1994)	Hang-gliders M & F 170	Golfers M & F 90	↑ TAS ↑ ES ↑ DIS ↑ BS ↑ Total	= STAI-T	SSS-V
High risk sports	Gomà-i-Freixanet (1995)	Miscellaneous risky sports M 332	Controls not engaged in any risky sports M 54	↑ TAS = ES = DIS = BS = TAS-OUT ↑ Total	↑ E = N = P = L = Imp = So	SSS-V Controlling for age.
Everest expedition	Breivik (1996)	Everest expeditioners M 7	Elite climbers M 38	= TAS = ES = DIS ↑ BS = Total		SSS-V Sports students: TAS correlated 0.51 with physical risk, ES 0.47 with economic & 0.42 with intellectual risk, Total correlated with economic & physical risk.
		Everest expeditioners M 7	Sports students M 43	↑ TAS ↑ ES = DIS	↑ BS ↑ Total	
Bungee jumping	Michel, Carton and Jouvent (1997)	Bungee jumpers M 51, F 29	General public M 50, F 45	↑ TAS = ES = DIS = BS		In F, ES & BS positively correlated with number of jumps.
Rock climbing Skiing Piloting White-water	Slanger and Rudestam (1997)	Extreme[1] M 20 High risk takers[2] M 20	Athletes[0] M 20	TAS 1 = 2 Total 1 = 2 TAS 1 + 2 > 0 Total 1 + 2 = 0		SSS-V Controlling for age.
Parachuting	Breivik, Roth and Jorgensen (1998)	Expert M 21 Novice parachutists M 14	Sports students M 43	↑ TAS ↑ ES ↑ DIS ↑ BS ↑ Total	↑ E ↓ N ↑ P	SSS-V
		Expert parachutists M 21	Novice parachutists M 14	= TAS ↑ ES = DIS = BS = Total	= E = N ↑ P = STAI-T	
High risk sports	Jack and Ronan (1998)	High risk sports M & F 93	Low risk sports M & F 73	↑ TAS ↑ ES ↑ DIS ↑ BS	↑ TAS-OUT ↑ Total = Imp	SSS-V Controlling for age.
High risk sports	Zarevski, Marusic, Zolotic, Bunjevac and Vukosav (1998)	High risk sports M 94	Low risk sports M 94	↑ TAS ↑ ES ↑ DIS ↑ BS		SSS-V Discriminant analysis: ES, TAS, BS Regression analysis: ES, TAS

Table 1: (*Continued*)

Sport	Author	Experimental (sex, *n*)	Control (sex, *n*)	Differences		Notes
Snow boarding	Cogan and Brown (1999)	Snowboarders M 36	Badminton players M 26	= PO ↓ SM ↓ AA ↓ Total		Risk vs. safe sports: 1. more number of injuries 1. more serious injuries
High risk sports	Gomà-i-Freixanet (2001)	Miscellaneous risky sports F 52	Controls not engaged in any risky sports F 58	↑ TAS ↑ ES ↑ DIS = BS ↑ TAS-OUT ↑ Total	= E = N = P = L = Imp = So	SSS-V Controlling for age.
Physical risky activities	Hansen and Breivik (2001)	School students M & F 360 12–16 yrs				Positive correlation between SS & physical risky activities, mainly with TAS 0.43
Alpinism	Sánchez and Cantón (2001)	Alpinists M & F?	Mountain climbers M & F?	= TAS = ES = DIS = BS = Total		SSS-V Number of subjects by group not stated. 38 subjects in total M 27, F 11

Note: SSS = Sensation Seeking Scale; E = Extraversion; N = Neuroticism; P = Psychoticism; L = Lie; Imp = Impulsiveness; So = Socialization; STAI-T = Trait Anxiety; PO = Planning Orientation; SM = Serious mindedness; AA = Arousal Avoidance. TAS = Thrill and Adventure Seeking; ES = Experience Seeking; DIS = Disinhibition; BS = Boredom Susceptibility.

low-risk sports; and (3) studies that compare high-risk sports with controls. When high-risk sports are compared to sports of similar level of risk, sportspersons do not differ from each other on the SSS, neither on the specific subscales nor on the total score. Studies such as those of Gomà-i-Freixanet (1991), Rossi and Cereatti (1993), Breivik (1996), Breivik *et al.* (1998) and Sánchez and Cantón (2001) illustrate these findings. Subjects did not differ on other scales that were administered like Extraversion and Neuroticism from the Eysenck Personality Questionnaire (EPQ; Eysenck & Eysenck 1975), Impulsiveness from the Impulsiveness-Venturesomeness-Empathy Questionnaire (IVE; Eysenck & Eysenck 1978), and the Socialization scale from the California Psychological Inventory (CPI; Gough 1957), and trait-anxiety from the State-Trait Anxiety Inventory (STAI; Speilberger *et al.* 1970). These are the results we expected when comparing subjects practicing sports with similar level of risk.

When high-risk sports are compared to low-risk sports, the subjects differ on all subscales of the SSS as well as on the total scale (Cantón & Mayor 1994; Jack & Ronan 1998; Rainey *et al.* 1992; Wagner & Houlihan 1994; Zarevski *et al.* 1998). Subjects also differed on the variable named TAS-OUT in the studies that included it. As some of the items from the Thrill and Adventure Seeking (TAS) subscale are concerned with sports and activities that the athletes can actually be participating in, the TAS-OUT, being the sum of the remaining three subscales, controls for the possibility of variance in total SS scores being unduly influenced by sports participation.

Table 2: Studies relating Sensation Seeking to medium-risk sports.

Sport	Author	Experimental (sex, *n*)	Control (sex, *n*)	Differences	Notes
Body-contact sports	Stirling (1977)	Body-contact sports[1] M 14	Non-contact sports M 11 Non-athletes[0] M 11	TAS 1 > 0 ES = DIS 1 > 0 BS = Total 1 > 0	SSS-IV
Football	Cellini (1982)	Criminal offenders on probation or parole M 65		Total, TAS, ES, correlated with participation in football. Little correlation with non-contact sports	SSS-V Violent impulsive criminals: ↑ TAS, ↑ ES, ↑ Total. Football related to violent premeditated crime.
Rugby	Potgieter and Bisschoff (1990)	Rugby players M 35	Marathon runners	↑ TAS = ES = DIS = BS ↑ Total	SSS-V
Free-climbing Sports students	Rossi and Cereatti (1993)	Free climbers[1] ? 20 Sport students[2] ? 20	Controls[0] ? 20	TAS 2 > 0 ES 1 > 2 0 DIS 1 2 > 0 BS = Total 1 2 > 0	SSS-V Sex not stated. Did not control for age.
Karate	Cantón and Mayor (1994)	Karate M & F 53	Tennis M & F 30	= TAS = PO = ES ↑ SM = DIS ↑ AA = BS ↑ Total = Total	Total SS correlates −0.40 with AA
Different levels of risky sports	Davis and Mogk (1994)	Elite[1], subelite[2] athletes, sports students[3] M & F 30 by group	Non-athlete controls[0] M & F 30	TAS 2 3 > 0 E 3 > 0 ES = N = DIS = P 3 > 0 1 2 BS = L = Total =	M vs. F: ↑ DIS ↑ P M: N ↓ as ↑ excellence in sports

Note: SSS = Sensation Seeking Scale; E = Extraversion; N = Neuroticism; P = Psychoticism; L = Lie; Imp = Impulsiveness; So = Socialization; STAI-T = Trait Anxiety; PO = Planning Orientation; SM = Serious mindedness; AA = Arousal Avoidance; TAS = Thrill and Adventure Seeking; ES = Experience Seeking; DIS = Disinhibition; BS = Boredom Susceptibility.

When individuals who participate in high-risk sports are compared with controls (either college students, sports students, the general population, or simply non-athletes), the general tendency is still maintained with high significant scores in TAS, Experience Seeking (ES) and total scale, and even TAS-OUT. This pattern is not so clear with the Disinhibition (DIS) subscale. But when we take a closer look at the studies, we can observe that high-risk sportspersons when compared to the general population, and controlling for age (Gomà-i-Freixanet 1991, 2001; Zaleski 1984) also score significantly high on DIS. This effect is less clear when using sports students as a control group and it disappears totally when the contrast group is college students. This is probably due to the fact that these studies did not control for age and, in general, college students are younger than professional sportsmen. It is known that all SS scale scores decline with age (Zuckerman *et al.* 1978). Therefore, the older professionals, in general being in the 30–39 age range, by not differing significantly from college students, score higher compared to their age group.

Table 3: Studies relating Sensation Seeking to low-risk sports.

Sport	Author	Experimental (sex, *n*)		Control (sex, *n*)		Notes
Running	McCutcheon (1980)	Runners M 42, F 20	Non-runners	Males = TAS = ES ↓ DIS = BS = Total	Females ↓ TAS = ES = DIS = BS ↓ Total	Matched controls. No correlation of SSS with order of finish in races.
Gymnastics	Straub (1982)	Gymnasts F 28	Bowlers F 31	= TAS = ES = DIS = BS = Total		SSS-V
Physical Education Majors	Wykoff (1982)	Physical Education M 52, F 60	SSS college normative groups	=TAS = ES = DIS = BS = Total		SSS-V
Athletes	Gundersheim (1987)	Athletes M 123, F 51	Non-athletes M 43, F 122	Males ↑ TAS = ES = DIS ↑ BS ↑ Total	Females Athletes vs. Non-athletes ↑ Total	SSS-IV College students. Contact male athletes ↑ SS than non-contact.
Athletes	Hartman and Rawson (1992)	Athletes M & F 56	Non-athletes M & F 103	= TAS ↑ DIS ↑ Total		SSS-VI College students.
Athletes	Schroth (1995)	Athletes M & F 152	Non-athletes M & F 146	↑ TAS = ES ↑ DIS ↑ BS ↑ Total		SSS-V College students. Contact male athletes ↑ SS than non-contact.

Note: SSS = Sensation Seeking Scale; E = Extraversion; N = Neuroticism; P = Psychoticism; L = Lie; Imp = Impulsiveness; So = Socialization; STAI-T = Trait Anxiety; PO = Planning Orientation; SM = Serious mindedness; AA = Arousal Avoidance. TAS = Thrill and Adventure Seeking; ES = Experience Seeking; DIS = Disinhibition; BS = Boredom Susceptibility.

Thus, what these data exactly mean is that professional sportspersons actually score high on DIS.

Overall, high-risk sportspersons either compared to athletes practicing sports with lower level of risk or to controls controlling for age (either general population or college students) show higher scores on the total SSS and on all its subscales, except Boredom Susceptibility (BS) when compared to controls.

Some of these studies (e.g. Gomà-i-Freixanet 1991, 1995, 2001) also administered other questionnaires along with the SSS. They found that high-risk sportspersons, compared either to low-risk sportspersons or the general population, scored lower on the Arousal Avoidance scale of the TDS, and that they did not differ on the Impulsiveness scale of the IVE questionnaire when compared to either high or low level of risk and even to the control group. Compared to high or low-risk sportspersons, they also did not differ on the Trait Anxiety scale of the STAI inventory. When compared to controls they did not differ on the

Socialization scale of the CPI. On the Extraversion dimension from the EPQ, they scored significantly higher than the controls but did not differ from the other high-risk groups. These results show that sportspersons that practice sports with a high level of risk like the seeking of thrill, adventure, and unusual experiences, and are somewhat disinhibited and susceptible to routine. They also like practicing activities that increase arousal, they are neither impulsive nor anxious, and are extraverted and well socialized.

Thus, sportspersons practicing high-risk activities, whether in an elite group or not, enjoy extreme environments with great opportunities for encountering stimulation through the mind and senses such as height, depth, speed, a great amount of light or darkness, and changes in climatic conditions (wind, temperature); they like new, exciting and unconventional but not necessarily illegal experiences, and they have an intolerance for repetitive and routine experiences. They do not feel high levels of anxiety that could interfere with the highly skilled performance required at these extreme conditions and they plan these actions very carefully. This is evident in the planning of expeditions that may last for years because the purchase of equipment is very expensive and obtaining permissions is a lengthy process. Finally, although they are unconventional, they follow the social rules and are well socialized. We must not forget that in general high-risk sports are practiced in small groups (alpinism, climbing, speleology, parachuting) where one's behavior can interfere with the group and sometimes one's life relies on the companionship and loyalty of the group.

2.2. Medium Physical Risk Sports

Table 2 summarizes the empirical studies that have compared medium-risk sports either to lower risk sports, sports students or controls. Although there are not as many studies in Table 2 as in Table 1, they are sufficient to make group comparisons.

When compared to athletes practicing low-risk sports, subjects engaged in medium-risk sports score significantly high on TAS and total score (Potgieter & Bisschoff 1990). This pattern was not replicated in the study of Cantón and Mayor (1994) probably because male and female subjects constituted the sample and this circumstance could mask the differences. It is known that female subjects score lower on the SS trait. In studies comparing athletes in medium-risk sports to sports students (Davis & Mogk 1994; Rossi & Cereatti 1993), only Rossi and Cereatti find a significant difference on the ES subscale. Finally in comparisons of medium-risk sports to controls, athletes score significantly higher on TAS, DIS, and total score (Rossi & Cereatti 1993; Stirling 1977).

The comparisons seem to indicate that when we compare those who participate in medium-risk sports with those who participate in lower-risk sports or with control subjects, the former score higher on TAS and total scale score. When participants in medium-risk sports are specifically compared with controls, the DIS subscale appears as significantly different as well. These results probably could be explained by the following reasoning: when we compare medium-risk to low-risk sports, we are still comparing scores between athletes, even though they are participating in different levels of risky sports. Thus, both groups of athletes do not necessarily differ on DIS. By participating in sports with a different risk level it can be expected they do differ on the TAS subscale as this specifically measures thrill seeking. As control subjects are not engaged in any sports, the results on the DIS subscale could probably be related to the fact that athletes generally have social habits that are more open than those of non-athletes. In summary, sportspersons practicing medium-risk sports compared to low-risk sports and controls are thrill and adventure seekers and, specifically, when compared to subjects not practicing any given sport they exhibit the general pattern of athletes as being unconventional and open minded.

2.3. Low Physical Risk Sports

In Table 3, the available empirical data about the relationship between SS and low-risk sports is summarized. As expected, no significant differences were found when comparing groups both practicing low-risk sports (Straub 1982) or when comparing physical education students interested in sports with college normative groups (Wykoff 1982). However, a different pattern appears when comparing athletes vs. non-athletes (Gundersheim 1987; Hartman & Rawson 1992; Schroth 1995). The results obtained from these three studies merit much credit as contrary to other studies they are highly homogeneous: the selected sports were teams sports, all the subjects were college students, the sample consisted of male and female subjects and the number of subjects was high. Those practicing a low-risk sport compared to those not practicing any sport score significantly high on total scale score, TAS and DIS. The results seem to indicate that when we compare athletes practicing low-risk sports with non-athletes, controlling for age, sex, type of sport (team sports in these studies), and years of education (college students), the former are sensation seekers, thrill and adventure seeking, and more disinhibited. In relation to the DIS scale, as we said before, probably the difference is caused because team sports are related to competitions, and competitions entail frequent travel, meeting new people and celebrating the winning matches, especially in college settings where parties are so popular and welcome.

From the summary of Table 3, we can conclude that, regardless of gender, college athletes are higher sensation seekers than college non-athletes, although the sports practiced entail low levels of risk. If we consult the results found in the three tables, we can make additional comparisons that can help us to have a better understanding of the relation between SS and different levels of risky sports.

2.4. Comparing Sports with Similar Level of Risk

The review of the literature shows that when we compare groups engaged in sports with similar levels of risk, they do not differ significantly on any of the subscales of the SSS or on the total scale score. This holds regardless of whether: (1) they belong to an elite or near elite group as in the work of Davis and Mogk (1994); (2) they have made summits at heights higher that 8000 meters compared to elite mountain climbers (Breivik 1996; Gomà-i-Freixanet 1991); or (3) they belong to extreme as compared to high-risk takers as shown by Slanger and Rudestam (1997). These results mean that when sportspeople are at the top or upper level, they do not differ on the SS trait, i.e. all of them are attracted by variation and complexity, intense sensations, risks and adventures. Perhaps the level of SS should not be used to explain the difference between membership in the elite or near elite groups. Rather, other factors, such as constitutional differences (e.g. muscle fiber type) would be more appropriate.

2.5. Comparing Sports with Different Level of Risk

By contrasting different levels of risk in sports, we can distinguish three different levels, although comparing both extremes of risk shows the most clear cut result. When comparing high-risk sports vs. low-risk sports, those participating in high-risk sports differ on all subscales as well as in the total score. This means that high-risk sportspersons are genuine sensation seekers. When comparing high-risk vs. medium-risk levels (Gomà-i-Freixanet 1991), they still differ on TAS, ES and total score. When comparing medium to low levels of risk, they only differ on TAS and total score. These results mean that high-risk takers as compared to medium or low-risk takers are sensation seekers that like the thrill and adventure; are somewhat unconventional; and like new experiences involved in the practice of high-risk sports such as parachuting, climbing or motor racing.

2.6. Comparing Sportspersons Practicing Sports with Different Level of Risk to Controls

When risky sportspersons, either practicing high-, medium- or low-risk sports, are compared to control groups, a general pattern appears despite the different criteria used to classify the control groups, i.e. college students, sports students, general population. Compared to controls, risky sportspersons score higher in TAS, DIS and total scale score in all three levels of sport risk.

These results seem to indicate that compared to controls, risky sportspersons, either men or women, are high on the SS trait, on TAS and on the DIS subscale, e.g. Gomà-i-Freixanet 1991, 1995, 2001. Thus athletes, as compared to controls, like sports that provide unusual experiences and sensations, the opportunity for frequent travel, meeting new people, and the social activity associated with the participating in sporting activities. In the same way, they would not like sports characterized by routines, waiting time, and slow pace.

3. Overview

Overall, some general findings regarding the SS Scale and its subscales in relation to sports can be drawn from this review:

(1) The TAS subscale measuring thrill and adventure seeking seems characteristic of sports with high and medium levels of risk, and even of low-risk sports although to a lesser extent.
(2) The ES subscale measuring experience seeking through the mind and senses (notably cognitive) seems characteristic only of sports with high levels of risk.
(3) The BS subscale measuring boredom susceptibility only differs when comparing extreme levels of risk, that is, high- vs. low-risk sports.

(4) The total scale score and the DIS subscale seem characteristic of athletes at any level of risk as compared to control groups, or high-risk sports as compared to low-risk sports. Thus, what the total scale score measures seems to apply to sportspersons practicing sports with a given level of risk. In relation to DIS, we suggest that it relates to the liking of social activities around the sport, meeting new people, celebrating the summit or the winning game, being nonconformist and unconventional. This is in contrast to the more asocial aspect of the DIS subscale, such as disregard for social rules and taking drugs and alcohol.

These results, in general, match those found in previous reviews, but they add a new finding in relation to the DIS subscale. Since the last revision by Zuckerman (1994), a great deal of empirical research has been published on sports, and especially on high-risk sports. Some of the caveats that limited previous research and findings have been improved since the 1990s. For example, the number of subjects has been increased as some of the selected sport activities samples had small (less than 15) numbers of participants. Second, since that decade most studies use Form-V of the SSS, which has been improved, and thus the use of the same version facilitates comparisons and generalization of results. Third, statistical procedures were also improved, e.g. using covariance analysis to statistically control for age differences between groups. Finally, the refinement of methodology and the increase in the number of subjects has allowed separate analyses for males and females.

All in all, the results obtained in the research conducted since the 1990s seem to be more accurate from the methodological point of view than the previous ones and seem to indicate that TAS is mostly characteristic of sports with high and medium levels of risk; ES is only characteristic of sports with high levels of risk; BS only differs when comparing high vs. low levels of risk, and total and DIS seem characteristic of athletes at any level of risk as compared to controls, or high-risk sports as compared to low-risk sports. Thus, the SS theory provides a good framework to interpret the individual differences in the field of sport.

4. Conclusion

In this chapter, we reviewed the contribution of the SS trait to the specific area of sports, and discussed research that is relevant to this specific issue. One implication of the SS construct is that the particular sports discipline one is more likely to participate in may be based on whether one is high or low on the trait. A comprehensive summary of research conducted in the area of SS and sport participation shows that the TAS subscale measuring thrill and adventure seeking seems characteristic of sports with high and medium levels of risk, and even of low-risk sports although to a lesser extent. The ES subscale measuring experience seeking through the mind and senses seems characteristic only of sports with high levels of risk. The BS subscale measuring boredom susceptibility only differs when comparing extreme levels of risk, that is, high- vs. low-risk sports. The total scale score and the DIS subscale measuring disinhibition seem characteristic of athletes at any level of risk as compared to control groups, or high-risk sports as compared to low-risk sports. Thus, what the total SSS measures seems to apply to sportspersons practicing sports with a given level of risk. In relation to DIS, we believe it relates to the liking of social activities associated with the sport (like meeting new people, celebrating the summit, or the winning game), being nonconformist and unconventional. This is in contrast to the more asocial aspect of DIS like disregarding social rules and taking drugs and alcohol.

References

Apter, M. J., & Batler, R. (1997). Gratuitous risk: A study of parachuting. In: S. Svebak, & M. J. Apter (Eds), *Stress and health: A reversal theory perspective* (pp. 119–129). Washington, DC: Taylor & Francis.

Bacon, J. (1974). *Sensation seeking levels for members of high-risk organizations*. Unpublished manuscript. Described in: Zuckerman (1979, pp. 207–208).

Breivik, G. (1996). Personality, sensation seeking and risk taking among Everest climbers. *International Journal of Sport Psychology*, *27*, 308–320.

Breivik, G., Roth, W. T., & Jorgensen, P. E. (1998). Personality, psychological states and heart rate in novice and expert parachutists. *Personality and Individual Differences*, *25*, 365–380.

Campbell, J. B., Tyrrell, D. J., & Zingaro, M. (1993). Sensation seeking among whitewater canoe and kayak paddlers. *Personality and Individual Differences*, *14*, 489–491.

Cantón, E., & Mayor, L. (1994). The sensation of risk and motivational tendencies in sports: An empirical study. *Personality and Individual Differences*, *16*, 777–786.

Cellini, H. R. (1982). *Cognitive and personality trait differences of youthful offenders by property, violent impulsive, and violent premeditated offense groupings*. Unpublished doctoral dissertation, Southern Illinois University, Carbondale, IL.

Cogan, N., & Brown, R. I. F. (1999). Metamotivational dominance, states and injuries in risk and safe sports. *Personality and Individual Differences*, *27*, 503–518.

Connolly, P. M. (1981). *An exploratory study of adults engaging in the high-risk sport of skiing*. Unpublished masters thesis, Rutgers University.

Cronin, C. (1991). Sensation seeking among mountain climbers. *Personality and Individual Differences*, *12*, 653–654.

Davis, C., & Mogk, J. P. (1994). Some personality correlates of interest and excellence in sport. *International Journal of Sport Psychology*, *25*, 131–143.

Eysenck, H. J., & Eysenck, S. B. G. (1975). *Manual of the Eysenck Personality Questionnaire*. London: Hodder and Stoughton.

Eysenck, S. B. G., & Eysenck, H. J. (1978). Impulsiveness and venturesomeness: Their position in a dimensional system of personality description. *Psychological Reports*, *43*, 1247–1255.

Fowler, C. J., von Knorring, L., & Oreland, L. (1980). Platelet monoamine oxidase activity in sensation seekers. *Psychiatric Research*, *3*, 272–279.

Gomà-i-Freixanet, M. (1991). Personality profile of subjects engaged in high physical risk sports. *Personality and Individual Differences*, *12*, 1087–1093.

Gomà-i-Freixanet, M. (1995). Prosocial and antisocial aspects of personality. *Personality and Individual Differences*, *19*, 125–134.

Gomà-i-Freixanet, M. (2001). Prosocial and antisocial aspects of personality in women: A replication study. *Personality and Individual Differences*, *30*, 1401–1411.

Gough, H. G. (1957). *Manual for the California Psychological Inventory*. Palo Alto, CA: Consulting Psychologists Press.

Gundersheim, J. (1987). Sensation seeking in male and female athletes and nonathletes. *International Journal of Sport Psychology*, *18*, 87–99.

Hansen, E. B., & Breivik, G. (2001). Sensation seeking as a predictor of positive and negative risk behaviour among adolescents. *Personality and Individual Differences*, *30*, 627–640.

Hartman, M., & Rawson, H. E. (1992). Differences in and correlates of sensation seeking in male and female athletes and nonathletes. *Personality and Individual Differences*, *13*, 805–812.

Heyman, S. R., & Rose, K. G. (1980). Psychological variables affecting scuba performance. In: C. H. Nadeau, W. R. Holliwell, K. M. Newell, & G. C. Roberts (Eds), *Psychology of motor behaviour and sport*. Champaign, IL: Human Kinetics Press.

Horvath, P., & Zuckerman, M. (1993). Sensation seeking, risk appraisal, and risky behaviour. *Personality and Individual Differences*, *14*, 41–52.

Hymbaugh, K., & Garrett, J. (1974). Sensation seeking among skydivers. *Perceptual and Motor Skills*, *38*, 118.

Jack, S. J., & Ronan, K. R. (1998). Sensation seeking among high- and low-risk sports participants. *Personality and Individual Differences*, *25*, 1063–1083.

Kahneman, D., Knetsch, J. L., & Thaler, R. H. (1991). The endowment effect, loss aversion, and status quo bias. *Journal of Economic Perspectives*, *5*, 193–206.

Kaplan, H., & Hill, K. (1985). Hunting ability and reproductive success among male Ache foragers: Preliminary results. *Current Anthropology*, *26*, 131–133.

Kerr, J. H. (1989). Anxiety, arousal, and sport performance: An application of reversal theory. In: D. Hackfort, & C. D. Spielberger (Eds), *Anxiety in sports: An international perspective*. New York: Hemisphere.

Kerr, J. H. (1991). Arousal-seeking in risk sport participants. *Personality and Individual Differences*, *12*, 613–616.

Kerr, J. H., & Svebak, S. (1989). Motivational aspects of preference for and participation in risk and safe sports. *Personality and Individual Differences*, *10*, 797–800.

Kusyszyn, I., Steinberg, P., & Elliot, B. (1974, July). Arousal seeking, physical risk taking and personality. Paper read at the 18th International Conference of Applied Psychology, Montreal, Canada.

Levenson, M. R. (1990). Risk taking and personality. *Journal of Personality and Social Psychology*, *58*, 1073–1080.

Levy, J. S. (1992). Prospect theory and international relations: Theoretical applications and analytical problems. *Political Psychology*, *13*, 283–310.

Levy, J. S. (1997). Prospect theory, rational choice and international relations. *International Studies Quarterly*, *41*, 87–112.

McCutcheon, L. (1980). Running and sensation seeking. *Northern Virginia Community College Journal*, *Fall Issue*, 11.

Michel, G., Carton, S., & Jouvent, R. (1997). Recherche de sensations et anhédonie dans les conduites de prise de risque. Etude d'une population de sauteurs à l'élastique [Sensation seeking and anhedonia in risk taking behaviours: Study in bungee jumpers]. *L'Encéphale*, *23*, 403–411.

Murgatroyd, S., Rushton, C., Apter, M. J., & Ray, C. (1978). The development of the Telic Dominance Scale. *Journal of Personality Assessment*, *42*, 519–528.

Potgieter, J., & Bisschoff, F. (1990). Sensation seeking among medium- and low-risk sports participants. *Perceptual and Motor Skills*, *71*, 1203–1206.

Rainey, D. W., Amunategui, F., Agocs, H., & Larick, J. (1992). Sensation seeking and competitive trait anxiety among college rodeo athletes. *Journal of Sport Behavior*, *15*, 307–317.

Robinson, D. W. (1985). Stress seeking: Selected behavioural characteristics of elite rock climbers. *Journal of Sport Psychology*, *7*, 400–404.

Rossi, B., & Cereatti, L. (1993). The sensation seeking in mountain athletes as assessed by Zuckerman's Sensation Seeking Scale. *International Journal of Sport Psychology*, *24*, 417–431.

Rutter, D. R., Quine, L., & Albery, I. P. (1998). Perceptions of risk in motorcyclists: Unrealistic optimism, relative realism and predictions of behaviour. *British Journal of Psychology*, *89*, 681–696.

Sánchez, M. C., & Cantón, E. (2001). La práctica de actividad físico-deportiva de riesgo como herramienta preventiva de conductas desajustadas psicosocialmente [The practice of physical risky sports as a preventive tool for socially maladjusted behaviors]. *Revista de Psicología del Deporte*, *10*, 225–236.

Schroth, M. L. (1995). A comparison of sensation seeking among different groups of athletes and nonathletes. *Personality and Individual Differences*, *18*, 219–222.

Slanger, E., & Rudestam, K. E. (1997). Motivation and disinhibition in high risk sports: Sensation seeking and self-efficacy. *Journal of Research in Personality*, *31*, 355–374.

Smith, E. A., & Bird, R. L. (2000). Turtle hunting and tombstone opening: Public generosity as costly signalling. *Evolution and Human Behaviour*, *21*, 245–261.

Smith, K. C. P., & Apter, M. J. (1975). *A theory of psychological reversals*. Wilts, UK: Picton Publishing.

Speilberger, C., Gorsuch, R., & Lushene, R. (1970). *Manual for the State-Trait Anxiety Inventory*. Palo Alto, CA: Consulting Psychologists Press.

Stirling, J. (1977). *Strength of the nervous system, extraversion-introversion and kinaesthetic and cortical augmenting and reducing*. Unpublished doctoral dissertation, University of York, UK.

Straub, W. F. (1982). Sensation seeking among high and low risk male athletes. *Journal of Sport Psychology*, *4*, 246–253.

Wagner, A. M., & Houlihan, D. D. (1994). Sensation seeking and trait anxiety in hang-glider pilots and golfers. *Personality and Individual Differences*, *16*, 975–977.

Weinstein, N. D. (1980). Unrealistic optimism about future life events. *Journal of Personality and Social Psychology*, *39*, 806–820.

Wykoff, W. L. (1982). *Are physical education majors sensation seekers*? Unpublished manuscript. Cited in: Zuckerman (1983, p. 290).

Zaleski, Z. (1984). Sensation seeking and risk taking behaviour. *Personality and Individual Differences*, *5*, 607–608.

Zarevski, P., Marusic, I., Zolotic, S., Bunjevac, T., & Vukosav, Z. (1998). Contribution of Arnett's inventory of sensation seeking and Zuckerman's sensation seeking scale to the differentiation of athletes engaged in high risk and low risk sports. *Personality and Individual Differences*, *25*, 763–768.

Zuckerman, M. (1979). *Sensation seeking: Beyond the optimal level of arousal*. Hillsdale, NJ: Erlbaum.

Zuckerman, M. (1983). Sensation seeking and sports. *Personality and Individual Differences*, *4*, 285–293.

Zuckerman, M. (1994). *Behavioural expressions and biosocial bases of sensation seeking*. New York: Cambridge University Press.

Zuckerman, M., Eysenck, S. B. G., & Eysenck, H. J. (1978). Sensation seeking in England and America: Cross-cultural, age and sex comparisons. *Journal of Consulting and Clinical Psychology*, *46*, 139–149.

Zuckerman, M., Kolin, E. A., Price, L., & Zoob, I. (1964). Development of a sensation seeking scale. *Journal of Consulting Psychology*, *28*, 477–482.

Chapter 12

Personality Traits, Disorders, and Substance Abuse

S. A. Ball

1. Background: The Substance Abuse, Personality Trait and Disorder Connection

Through the efforts of many investigators over the past two decades, personality trait dimensions and personality disorder categories regained their status as important constructs in the addiction field. Perhaps more than any other personality trait researcher, Marvin Zuckerman embodied innovation and courage in his theories and investigations into the relation of personality and substance use. He attempted to connect the behavioral expressions of sensation seeking (SS) and drug use to underlying psychobiological systems and pursued this work at a time when the scientific zeitgeist not only devalued the concept of an addictive personality, but also questioned the very existence of personality traits.

Zuckerman's early conceptualization of drug use described sensation seeking (SS) as a behavioral attempt to maintain an optimal level of arousal (Carrol *et al.* 1982; Zuckerman 1979). From this seminal work, research evolved from searching for an additive personality type to a greater appreciation for the variability of personality functioning among individuals who use drugs and alcohol (Sutker & Allain 1988). Although there appears to be no consistent evidence for a singular addictive personality construct per se, there is evidence that certain personality traits play critical roles as risk factors, mediators, moderators, or consequences of the development, progression, and outcome of both substance abuse and personality disorders (see Barnes 1983; Cox 1985; Sher & Trull 1994; Sutker & Allain 1988). Overly simplistic or unidirectional cause-effect concepts have been replaced with developmentally complex models in which temperament, personality, parental behavior, peer and cultural influences, and deviant behavior interact to create greater susceptibility to substance abuse and personality disorders (Sutker & Allain 1988; Tarter 1988). Summaries of cross-sectional and longitudinal rescarch (Barnes 1983; Cox 1987) indicate that individuals later diagnosed with alcoholism had earlier exhibited higher impulsivity, hostility, and hyperactivity, and lower self-esteem and social conformity. Individuals already

On the Psychobiology of Personality
Edited by R. M. Stelmack

ISBN: 0-08-044209-9

diagnosed with alcoholism exhibited many of these traits as well as higher neuroticism (N), anxiety, introversion, depression, and antisocial behavior. Biologically influenced temperament traits (e.g. heightened activity, impulsivity, aggression, negative affect) appear to precede the development of early behavior problems (e.g. attention, conduct, risk taking, substance use and other deviant behaviors) which predict the later development of antisocial personality and substance use disorders (see reviews by Sher & Trull 1994; Sutker & Allain 1988; Tarter 1988). Behavioral disinhibition appears to increase the risk for problematic interactions with parents, teachers, and peers which increases risk for deficient socialization and early identification with a deviance-prone peer group, in which use of substances and antisocial behaviors are common (Tarter 1988).

Stimulated principally by the theories and findings of Zuckerman (1979), Cloninger (1987a), and others on the biological bases of personality, personality disorder, and substance abuse, investigators in the past 20 years created a body of work on the relation between personality and psychopathology in substance abusers that exceeds in quantity and quality the work for any other DSM Axis I disorder. As a broad diagnostic group, the Axis II Personality Disorders are the most common co-occurring disorders in treated substance abusers. Median prevalence rates of Axis II are especially high among treated opiate (79%) and cocaine (70%) dependent patients and somewhat lower in alcohol dependent samples (44%) (Verheul *et al.* 1998). Although studies that evaluate all Axis II disorders indicate that cluster B disorders are the most prevalent (antisocial, borderline, and less often narcissistic and histrionic), both cluster C (avoidant and dependent and less often obsessive-compulsive) and cluster A (paranoid and less often schizoid and schizotypal) disorders also seem to be highly prevalent among substance abusers. Co-occurrence of substance abuse and personality disorders is associated with greater substance abuse and psychiatric symptom severity (Brooner *et al.* 1997; Rounsaville *et al.* 1986; Rutherford *et al.* 1994) and greater susceptibility to relapse in the presence of craving, negative physical and emotional states, and interpersonal conflict (Kruedelbach *et al.* 1993; Nace *et al.* 1991). Several studies found that personality disorders are usually associated with worse outcomes when provided routine or less intensive addiction treatment (DeJong *et al.* 1993; Griggs & Tyrer 1981; Kofoed *et al.* 1986; Kosten *et al.* 1989; Nace & Davis 1993; Rounsaville *et al.* 1986). However, substance abusers with antisocial or borderline personality disorders improve as much as non-personality disordered patients when provided more intensive inpatient, psychosocial, psychotherapeutic, or behavioral interventions (Ball 2003; Verheul *et al.* 1998).

I am proud to count myself as one of Marvin Zuckerman's former graduate students and to be continuing some of his work in this area. In this chapter, I will summarize several studies I have conducted since leaving the University of Delaware and joining the Division of Substance Abuse faculty at Yale University School of Medicine's Department of Psychiatry. This research focused on SS, three different multi-trait measures, and one multidimensional typology model of personality and addiction. In addition to reviewing some of the broader issues and findings of other researchers, I will summarize my attempts to map the relation between substance abuse, personality disorders, and personality traits from the models of: (1) Zuckerman, as assessed by the Sensation Seeking Scale (SSS; Zuckerman *et al.* 1979) or the Zuckerman-Kuhlman Personality Questionnaire (ZKPQ; Zuckerman *et al.* 1993); (2) Cloninger, as assessed by the Temperament and Character Inventory (TCI; Cloninger *et al.* 1994); and (3) Costa and McCrae, as assessed by the NEO Personality Inventory (NEO-PI;

Costa & McCrae 1992a). Finally, I will review some evidence supporting the validity of a multidimensional addiction typology as a useful heuristic framework for conceptualizing the interconnections between personality and substance abuse.

2. Sensation Seeking and Substance Abuse

The relation between the SS trait and substance abuse in adolescents and adults is very well documented (see Zuckerman 1987, 1994). SS is associated with chronic substance dependence, vulnerability to drug use, age of onset, co-occurring psychiatric disorders (Kaestner *et al.* 1977; Montag & Birenbaum 1986; Sutker *et al.* 1978, 1979), and SS is an important family history dimension (Kosten *et al.* 1994; Luthar *et al.* 1992). SS has been shown to be a more powerful predictor of initial drug use and abuse across drug categories than other measures of personality or psychopathology (Andrucci *et al.* 1989; Jaffe & Archer 1987; Schwarz *et al.* 1978; Segal *et al.* 1980) and SS may be a particularly salient trait in the developmental trajectory of regular substance use during adolescence (Crawford *et al.* 2003). Longitudinal studies link SS and behavioral disinhibition with adolescent deviance and follow-up licit and illicit drug use in young adulthood (Block *et al.* 1988; Brook *et al.* 1986; Labouvie & McGee 1986; Newcomb & McGee 1991; White *et al.* 1985).

We first evaluated the familial associations of SS by comparing 201 opiate-addicted patients with their 133 siblings (Kosten *et al.* 1994). Patients and siblings who were substance abusers had higher scores than siblings who were not drug abusers on the SSS and all four subscales (Thrill and Adventure Seeking, Experience Seeking, Disinhibition, Boredom Susceptibility), even when controlling for gender, race, and age. The level of SS was also correlated among the drug-abusing siblings as well as with the age of first drug use, particularly for opiates, marijuana, and sedatives. Stepwise regression models indicated that a substance abuse diagnosis was the single best predictor of high SS on most subscales. We suggested that SS may mediate drug abuse in high-risk families, and that SS may be related to other risk factors associated with a more severe form of substance abuse (Kosten *et al.* 1993).

We pursued these initial findings in somewhat greater detail by conducting a comprehensive evaluation of SS, substance abuse severity, and psychiatric disorders in a clinical and community sample of 335 cocaine abusers (Ball *et al.* 1994). SS was negatively correlated with age of first use and onset of abuse/dependence for cocaine and alcohol. SS was also consistently related to self-reported lifetime use of other drugs with poly-drug users scoring higher than those who had not used these other drugs. As an additional comparison of diagnostic severity, the individual DSM III-R items for cocaine, alcohol, and marijuana dependence were summed, and all were positively correlated with SS. Cocaine abusers who met DSM III-R criteria for lifetime alcohol abuse or dependence scored higher on SS than did those who did not meet criteria.

Cocaine abusers diagnosed with antisocial personality disorder scored higher on SS, as did subjects with a lifetime history of conduct disorder or attention-deficit disorder. Subjects with a lifetime history of depression (major, minor, and depressive personality) and suicide attempts scored higher on SS. A family history of drug or alcohol abuse or affective disorders in first-degree relatives did not differentiate high and low SS probands (see also Kosten *et al.* 1993). However, subjects with a family history of antisocial personality, conduct, or attention-deficit disorder had higher SS scores than those without these disorders in their first-degree relatives. Finally, the relation between SS and several outcome measures was analyzed. SS did correlate positively with 12-month follow-up cocaine and alcohol dependence symptom severity, but generally accounted for the least variance among the various indicators of follow-up addiction severity. In addition, SS was weakly related to other outcomes.

3. Zuckerman's Alternative Five-Factor Model and Substance Abuse

As described more fully elsewhere in this volume, the ZKPQ-III is an alternative five-factor measure of biologically informed personality traits (Zuckerman *et al.* 1991). ZKPQ-III Neuroticism-Anxiety (N-Anx) is strongly related to what the other personality models call N or Negative Emotionality (e.g. Tellegen 1985; Watson *et al.* 1994), and ZKPQ-III Sociability (Sy) is similar to what other models call Extraversion. There is disagreement between the competing personality trait models about the remaining broad dimensions that centers mostly on whether a particular dimension is a higher level, primary trait or a narrower facet or component. Specifically, Zuckerman *et al.* (1993) view Impulsive-Sensation Seeking (ImpSS) and Aggression-Hostility (Agg-Host) as primary traits that are negatively related to Conscientiousness and Agreeableness, respectively, in the NEO five-factor model (Zuckerman 2003). However, Costa and McCrae (1992a) view Impulsiveness and Agg-Host as narrower facets of their N domain, and SS as a facet within the broader domains of Extraversion (excitement seeking facet) and Openness to Experience (particularly openness to actions, ideas, and aesthetics facets). Activity (ACT) is viewed as a facet of Extraversion (Costa & McCrae 1992a) rather than a primary temperament as in the ZKPQ-III or other models such as Buss and Plomin's (1975). The ZKPQ scales also overlap with the Cloninger's TCI dimensions, specifically ZKPQ Impulsive-Sensation Seeking (ImpSS) correlates highly with TCI Novelty Seeking, ZKPQ N-Anx correlates with TCI Harm Avoidance, ZKPQ Agg-Host correlates negatively with TCI Cooperativeness, and ZKPQ ACT correlates with TCI Persistence (Zuckerman & Cloninger 1996).

I have completed two studies validating the ZKPQ in outpatient cocaine abusers. In the first study (Ball 1995), 450 patients seeking outpatient treatment for cocaine abuse were evaluated with the ZKPQ, the Addiction Severity Index (ASI; McLellan *et al.* 1992), and clinical chart reviews, which yielded information about treatment response and outcome. ImpSS, N-Anx, and Agg-Host were significantly correlated with ASI impairment in the areas of substance abuse and psychiatric functioning. Outpatients reporting more recent use of cocaine scored higher on ImpSS and N-Anx. Patients scoring higher on ImpSS, Agg-Host, and ACT reported earlier first use of cocaine. Patients scoring higher on N-Anx reported more past treatment episodes and a stronger family history for alcohol and drug abuse. ImpSS and N-Anx were also the two scales more strongly related to psychiatric variables. Patients who scored higher on these two scales reported more childhood abuse, attention-concentration problems, lifetime depression and suicide attempts or serious ideation, and past psychiatric treatment. Patients scoring lower on Soc more often reported a history of attention and concentration problems and psychiatric treatment. Cocaine abusers with a history of violence and suicidal tendencies scored higher on Agg-Host.

ImpSS, N-Anx, and Agg-Host were related to abstinence and treatment response at discharge. Analyses of variance indicated that cocaine abusers who continued using throughout treatment scored higher on ImpSS and N-Anx than those who abstained or used cocaine infrequently. Cocaine abusers scoring higher on ImpSS kept fewer treatment appointments, were less successful at remaining for at least one month or completing treatment, and were also more often in need of immediate referral for inpatient treatment. Cocaine abusers immediately referred for inpatient treatment also scored higher on N-Anx and Agg-Host than patients who completed treatment. Early dropouts (less than 1 month) also scored higher on Agg-Host than those who completed treatment.

In order to identify a smaller number of personality subtypes, the five ZKPQ scales were cluster analyzed using a k-means approach. Subtype 2 ($n = 210$) cocaine abusers scored higher than Subtype 1 ($n = 240$) patients on N-Anx, ImpSS, and Agg-Host, but lower on Soc. There was no difference between the subtypes on the Act trait. As expected from the above findings, Subtype 2 cocaine abusers began using cocaine earlier and scored higher than Subtype 1 on ASI drug abuse, family, and psychiatric severity. At discharge, patients who were able to abstain or substantially reduce cocaine use and successfully complete treatment were more often Subtype 1 than Subtype 2. The less-severe Subtype 1 were more commonly men, stipulated by criminal justice, not abused as children, and relatively free of psychiatric symptoms. Subtype 2 were more commonly women, abused as children, non-stipulated, and recent users of cocaine who reported several lifetime psychiatric symptoms. These traits combined with hyperactivity, psychopathy, and substance abuse have been found to characterize a disinhibitory psychopathology syndrome (see Sher & Trull 1994).

In the second study, Ball and Schottenfeld (1997) evaluated the relation between addiction severity, psychiatric symptoms, AIDS-risk behaviors, and the ZKPQ-III in 92 pregnant and post-partum cocaine-abusing women in a comprehensive day treatment program. N-Anx was positively associated with ASI drug, legal, family, and psychiatric severity. The correlations between Agg-Host and drug, legal and psychiatric severity, and ImpSS with drug severity were marginally significant. Women reporting past addiction treatment scored higher on N-Anx than those with no prior treatment. ImpSS, N-Anx, and Agg-Host were all correlated with scores on the Beck Depression Inventory (Beck 1993). Patients reporting a history of depression, anxiety, suicidal tendencies, and attention difficulties scored higher on N-Anx. A history of suicidal tendencies, violence, criminal arrests, and attention difficulties also was associated with higher Agg-Host. ImpSS was related to a history of anxiety, depression, and violence, including arrests. Women reporting past psychiatric treatment scored higher on ImpSS and N-Anx.

Women who reported having sex with multiple partners scored higher on ImpSS, N-Anx, and Agg-Host than those reporting sex with few or no men. Women who reported engaging in sex to obtain drugs and sex to obtain money also scored higher on these traits than those who reported never having engaged in these high-risk behaviors. Women who reported being tested multiple times for human immunodeficiency virus (HIV) scored higher on N-Anx and Agg-Host. None of the personality traits were correlated with the percent of urines positive for cocaine, the total number of clinical contacts, or the number of weeks in which at least some services were received.

There have been several other studies using the ZKPQ in samples with documented or presumed substance abuse. Thornquist and Zuckerman (1995) evaluated psychopathic prisoners and found that psychopathy correlated with ImpSS, but only for Caucasian subjects. ImpSS also correlated with errors on an experimental task involving passive avoidance learning, suggesting a relative insensitivity to signals of punishment. Black (1993) found some association between ZKPQ traits and primary substances of choice in outpatients. Alcohol abusers scored higher than cocaine abusers on Soc and this was associated with higher rates of program completion. Cocaine abusers scored higher than alcohol abusers on N-Anx and Agg-Host and this was associated with higher rates of probation violation. At least half of the very high-risk prostitutes that were studied by O'Sullivan *et al.* (1996) were cocaine abusers. These subjects scored higher than controls on ImpSS with a trend toward higher Agg-Host. ImpSS was also related to substance abuse severity. In a study of college students, Zuckerman and Kuhlman (2000) found that ImpSS, Agg-Host, and Soc were all related to alcohol use and other risk taking behaviors, but only ImpSS was specifically associated with illicit drug and tobacco use.

4. Cloninger's Psychobiological Model Substance Abuse, and Personality Disorders

In addition to Zuckerman's work on the biological bases of personality and substance abuse, theoretical and empirical work by Cloninger (1987a, b) and colleagues on the genetics of alcoholism helped to re-position personality as an important construct in addiction research. In the original biosocial personality model, as assessed by the Tridimensional Personality Questionnaire (TPQ; Cloninger 1987a), deviations in Novelty Seeking, Harm Avoidance, and Reward Dependence were tied to specific neurotransmitter and behavioral systems and provided an underlying susceptibility for substance abuse and a range of personality disorders. Cloninger's (1987b) work was also important for advocating the concept that different personality dimensions and disorders were associated with different subtypes of alcoholism. Type 1 alcoholism was defined as a later onset, environmentally influenced, less severe disorder characterized by higher Harm Avoidance, and Type 2 was an earlier onset, genetically influenced, more chronic disorder characterized by higher Novelty Seeking. In all of these areas, the traits of impulsivity, novelty seeking, SS, or behavioral disinhibition had central roles.

We evaluated the relation between Cloninger's revised seven-factor model, as measured by the TCI and substance use indicators (see Ball 2002) in 370 inpatients and outpatients with alcohol and drug use disorders. The number of DSM-III-R substance dependence criteria met for a participant's substance of choice and the number of lifetime drugs used regularly were associated with higher TCI Novelty Seeking and Harm Avoidance, and lower Persistence, Self-Directedness, and Cooperativeness. An analysis of the frequency of recent drinking, i.e. past 30 days, indicated a positive association with Harm Avoidance and negative association with Reward Dependence and Self-Directedness. Higher Novelty Seeking and Harm Avoidance and lower Self-Directedness and Cooperativeness were associated with more poly-drug use. Higher Harm Avoidance and lower Reward Dependence and Self-Directedness were associated with greater ASI severity of alcohol-related problems, and lower Self-Directedness and Cooperativeness were associated with greater severity of ASI drug-abuse problems. Higher Novelty Seeking also was associated with an earlier age of onset of drug use problems, but was not associated with family history of substance abuse. Lower Cooperativeness was associated with an earlier age of onset for both drug and alcohol problems. A parental history of drug or alcohol abuse was associated with higher Harm Avoidance and lower Reward Dependence, Self-Directedness, and Cooperativeness.

Higher Novelty Seeking, Harm Avoidance, Self-Transcendence and lower Self-Directedness and Cooperativeness were associated with higher global psychiatric severity. Harm Avoidance and Self-Directedness also were associated with addiction-related psychiatric impairment on the ASI. Higher Novelty Seeking and lower Reward Dependence, Self-Directedness, and Cooperativeness also were associated with more childhood behavior symptoms. Higher Harm Avoidance was related to having at least one current and lifetime depressive diagnosis as well as a current and lifetime anxiety diagnosis. Similarly, lower Self-Directedness was found in participants meeting criteria for current and lifetime depressive disorders and current and lifetime anxiety disorders.

With regard to personality disorders, Cloninger (1987a) first proposed that deviations in Novelty Seeking, Harm Avoidance, and Reward Dependence form higher-order personality traits that, in their extreme expression, become personality disorders. For example, high Novelty Seeking and low Harm Avoidance dimensions as assessed by the TPQ defined a broader impulsive trait that, combined with other traits, characterize antisocial personality disorder. Novelty Seeking, Harm Avoidance, impulsiveness, and antisocial personality disorder are all strongly associated with substance use and abuse (Cloninger *et al.* 1993; Howard *et al.* 1997; Sher *et al.* 1995; Yoshino *et al.* 1994). In Cloninger *et al.*'s (1993) revised model and TCI measure, low Self-Directedness and Cooperativeness are conceptualized as critical dimensions for all personality disorders. The temperaments provide a specific risk for each Axis II personality disorder cluster: (A) Reward Dependence; (B) Novelty Seeking; (C) Harm Avoidance (Svrakic *et al.* 1993).

We evaluated the prevalence, reliability, and validity of DSM-III-R and DSM-IV personality disorders and the major dimensions of personality (NEO; TCI) in a sample of 370 opiate, cocaine, and alcohol-dependent outpatients and inpatients and 187 community controls. The majority of substance abusers (70%) met criteria for one or more personality disorders. Cluster B disorders were the most prevalent (61%), followed by Cluster C (34%), and Cluster A (22%). Antisocial (46%), borderline (30%), and avoidant (20%) were the most common specific personality disorders. We did not find strong support for predictions and preliminary findings that TCI Self-Directedness and Cooperativeness were critical for understanding or predicting all personality disorders (Ball *et al.* 1997a). Higher Harm Avoidance was associated with higher paranoid personality disorder severity, and lower Reward Dependence was associated with higher schizoid severity. Antisocial personality severity was correlated with higher Novelty Seeking and lower Self-Directedness. Borderline severity was associated with higher Harm Avoidance and lower Persistence, Self-Directedness, and Cooperativeness. Narcissistic severity was associated with lower Cooperativeness and Self-Directedness. Avoidant severity was correlated with higher Harm Avoidance and obsessive-compulsive personality disorder severity was associated with high Persistence. The number of personality disorder diagnoses received also showed a significant association with higher Harm Avoidance and lower Self-Directedness. Although

Self-Directedness did not appear to be critical for predicting all personality disorders, it was consistently associated with general psychopathology indicators, including mood, anxiety, and psychiatric symptoms (Ball *et al.* 1997b).

Because the TCI did not differentiate personality disorders as predicted from previous research, we undertook a more comprehensive analysis of the replicability and validity of the then relatively untested TCI dimensions (Ball *et al.* 1999). We did not replicate Cloninger's seven-dimension matrix, but instead found support for four factors that were replicated in both our substance-dependent clinical sample and community non-substance abusing sample using Procrustes rotations and which we labeled Harm Avoidance (low vigor), Sociability, Constraint, and Self-Transcendence. The four-factor structure was validated on other measures of personality, psychopathology, and substance abuse severity (see Ball *et al.* 1999).

5. The Costa and McCrae Five-Factor Model, Substance Abuse, and Personality Disorders

In comparison to the wealth of studies on Zuckerman's and Cloninger's psychobiological personality models in substance abusers, there have been relatively few studies examining substance dependence and the Costa and McCrae (1992a) five-factor model as assessed by the NEO PI-R. Of particular relevance to this chapter, Trull and Sher (1994) conducted a canonical correlation analysis that suggested two variables relevant to substance abuse in college students: (1) an indicator of general psychopathology (equal weighting of depression, anxiety, and substance abuse) characterized higher N and Openness and lower Conscientiousness; (2) a psychopathic personality indicator (positive weighting of substance abuse and negative weighting of depression) characterized by lower N, Agreeableness, and Conscientiousness and higher Extraversion. Likewise, Quirk and McCormick (1998) cluster analyzed the NEO-FFI in a sample of 3,256 male veteran substance abusers and found three subtypes appeared to vary along a continuum of severity defined by N (increasing), Agreeableness and Conscientiousness (both decreasing). The more extreme scoring subtype on these dimensions reported higher levels of depressive symptoms, hostile cognitions, impulsiveness, and polysubstance use (see also Piedmont & Ciarrocchi 1999).

As reported in Ball (2002), I found that NEO-FFI N was related to many substance use and Axis I psychiatric indicators, specifically substance dependence diagnostic severity, polydrug use, past 30-day drinking frequency, and greater ASI alcohol, drug, family, and psychiatric severity. N also was associated with a higher percentage of family members with alcohol problems and a parental history of substance abuse and was strongly associated with psychiatric symptom severity and diagnoses, especially current and lifetime anxiety and depressive disorders. Lower Extraversion was associated with a longer duration (years) of heavy substance use, more frequent alcohol use in the past 30 days, and higher ASI alcohol and psychiatric severity. Lower Extraversion was also associated with higher psychiatric symptom severity, current and lifetime anxiety and depressive diagnoses. Higher Openness was associated with past 30 day and lifetime use of cannabis and greater ASI family and psychiatric severity. It was associated with depressive, but not anxiety disorder, diagnoses. Lower Agreeableness was related to an earlier age of onset for alcohol and drug abuse, polydrug use, substance dependence severity, duration of lifetime opiate use, and psychiatric symptom severity. Lower Conscientiousness was associated with substance dependence severity, polydrug use, ASI psychiatric severity, psychiatric symptoms and a current diagnosis of depression.

In contrast to the few substance abuse studies, multiple studies have found that Costa and McCrae's (1992b) five broad domains account for significant variation in personality disorder dimensions in both normal (Costa & Widiger 2001; Schroeder *et al.* 1992; Watson *et al.* 1994; Wiggins & Pincus 1989) and clinical samples of non-substance abusers (Soldz *et al.* 1993; Trull 1992). As previously reported in the Ball *et al.* (1997b) study of inpatient and outpatient substance abusers, *t*-tests for those meeting vs. not meeting categorical DSM-IV personality disorder diagnoses indicated that individuals diagnosed with at least one personality disorder scored higher on NEO-FFI N and lower on Agreeableness and Conscientiousness. Individuals meeting diagnostic criteria for any Cluster A disorder scored higher on N and lower on Agreeableness. Individuals diagnosed with any Cluster B diagnosis scored higher on N and lower on Agreeableness and Conscientiousness. Individuals with any Cluster C diagnosis scored higher on N and lower on Extraversion. Pearson correlations for the association of the NEO-FFI domains with SCID-II personality disorder symptom counts were highly consistent with those found by Trull (1992) in a non-substance abuse sample. Regarding Cluster A, higher N and lower Agreeableness were associated with higher paranoid and schizotypal personality severity. Schizoid personality was associated with lower Extraversion. Regarding Cluster B, antisocial personality severity was correlated with lower Agreeableness and Conscientiousness. Borderline personality also was associated with lower Agreeableness and Conscientiousness, and higher N. Histrionic severity was associated with higher N and Extraversion, and narcissistic personality was associated with higher N and lower Agreeableness. Regarding Cluster C, avoidant personality severity was correlated with higher N and lower Extraversion and Conscientiousness. Dependent personality was associated with higher N and lower Agreeableness and Conscientiousness. Obsessive-Compulsive personality was associated with higher N.

Ben-Porath and Waller (1992) have suggested that an important test of clinical utility for personality measures is whether they provide incremental knowledge above and beyond other measures of psychopathology. Cloninger *et al.* (1993) and Svrakic *et al.* (1993) suggested that the new TCI provided a more complete characterization of personality and better differential diagnosis of personality disorders than the previous TPQ or other measures of personality (NEO) or psychopathology (DSM). Specifically, low Self-Directedness and Cooperativeness were hypothesized to be core dimensions of all personality disorders and the three temperaments differentiated the DSM clusters. In contrast, the NEO model hypothesizes that high N is a common substrate for many personality disorders and the other four domains (and more specific facets) differentiate each of the Axis II disorder (see Costa & Widiger 2001).

In Ball *et al.* (1997b), we compared the strength of associations between the NEO and the TCI and personality disorder severity. Using *t*-tests for dependent sample (*r* to *z*) correlations for the NEO vs. the TCI, we found that the NEO dimensions were more strongly associated than the TCI dimensions with personality disorder severity. As a more stringent test of the NEO-FFI and TCI scales' contribution to personality disorder prediction above and beyond symptoms of depression and substance abuse (see related analyses by

Svrakic *et al.* 1993; Trull & Sher 1994), we conducted hierarchical multiple regression analyses in which substance dependence and depression symptoms were entered into the model first, followed by the two personality trait models. The proportion of variance accounted for in all personality disorders was higher for the NEO than the TCI scales. NEO N, Extraversion, and Agreeableness were consistently stronger predictors across all disorders than the TCI dimensions that were significant predictors only for borderline and avoidant personality severity. With the exception of N (which was rendered non-significant by the earlier entry of the depression measure into the prediction model), the NEO-FFI traits remained significant predictors of personality disorders even when Axis I symptoms were taken into account. In particular, entering the substance dependence severity measure first had very little effect on the contribution of the NEO-FFI to personality disorder severity.

6. Multidimensional Addiction Typology, Personality Traits and Disorders

Some of the limitations in studies of personality and addiction over the past century include under- emphasizing the heterogeneity of addicted persons and evaluating personality constructs in isolation from other variables that mediate or moderate risk for addiction. As a greater appreciation for the heterogeneity of addicted persons has developed, personality factors may be viewed as etiologically or prognostically linked to some, but not necessarily all, subtypes of substance abusers. Although a trait-dimension model for describing personality pathology appears superior to the DSM categorical system, a broader theoretical framework for understanding the relation between personality, substance abuse, and personality disorders may be found through a typological (i.e. alternative categorical) system which organizes these diverse dimensions into broader subtyping constructs which are associated with different etiologies, patterns, and courses of the disorder. Although it is conceptually more parsimonious and practically easier to categorize subtypes by one dimension (e.g. personality traits, age of onset, family history), most of these dimensions are highly related with each other and no single dimension does as well as all of the dimensions considered together in predicting the course or outcome of substance abuse (Babor *et al.* 1992, 1988).

Several theorists (Babor *et al.* 1992; Cloninger 1987a, b; Morey & Skinner 1986) related personality traits to alcoholism in the context of such typological frameworks. A broad range of empirical research has supported the construct, discriminative, and predictive validity of two subtypes that differ on premorbid risk factors (including personality), severity of symptoms and consequences, and psychopathology (Babor *et al.* 1992; Ball 1996; Ball *et al.* 1995, 1997a; Schuckit *et al.* 1995). Both Babor *et al.*'s (1992) Type A and Cloninger's (1987b) Type 1 alcoholism represent a less severe subtype characterized by a later age of onset, lower heritability, fewer childhood risk factors, and less severe substance dependence and psychosocial impairment. Type B or 2 is more severe with an earlier onset, higher heritability, childhood behavior problems, novelty seeking, SS, and impulsive/antisocial behavior.

This Type A/B distinction has been validated across race, gender, substances of abuse, and treatment settings (Ball 1996; Ball *et al.* 1994, 1995, 1997a, 2000; Feingold *et al.* 1996).

Based on dimensions similar to those used in the Babor *et al.* (1992) alcoholism typology study, the Ball *et al.* (1995) cluster analysis of 399 cocaine abusers indicated that individuals were categorized best as being one of two types. Type B cocaine abusers (33%) exhibited greater evidence than Type A (67%) of premorbid risk factors, more severe drug and alcohol abuse, addiction-related psychosocial impairment, antisocial personality, and co-existing psychiatric problems. Further analyses indicated that Type B also had a greater history of aggression, criminality, violence, depression, suicide attempts, and substance abuse and psychiatric treatment episodes. They exhibited greater quantity, frequency, duration, severity, and adverse effects of cocaine abuse and had an earlier age of onset for alcohol abuse and antisocial personality disorder than did Type A. Type B scored higher than Type A on all Sensation Seeking subscales, aggression, criminality, violence, and social adjustment impairment. Thus, SS seemed to fit into this Type B (or II) schema in its association with earlier age of onset, male gender, childhood psychopathology, co-morbid (and family history of) antisocial behavior, greater symptom severity, polysubstance abuse, and impairment. These findings were consistent with Gurrera's (1990) description of two personality prototypes, one of which is characterized by high SS, Extraversion, Novelty Seeking, low Harm Avoidance and greater susceptibility to alcoholism, drug abuse, and Cluster B personality disorders (antisocial, histrionic, narcissistic, borderline).

We also extended this typology to other heterogeneous substance abuse samples (Feingold *et al.* 1996) and DWI offenders (Ball *et al.* 2000). In all of these studies, SS or impulsivity is a key typology variable. For example, in the DWI study, Type B drinkers appeared to encompass what other DWI subtyping systems have described as an aggressive SS, negative affect/nonassertive type (Donovan *et al.* 1983). These severe subtypes share in common heavier drinking patterns, higher accident risks, and worse follow-up outcomes, including risk for re-arrest and severe alcohol impairment (see Donovan & Marlatt 1982). We found that Type B DWI offenders had higher baseline and post-treatment indicators of symptom severity, psychosocial impairment, psychopathology, and worse coping confidence than Type As.

We also have extended the Type A/B model by mapping its relation to personality dimensions and disorders. Ball *et al.* (1997a) evaluated substance abuse subtype differences in DSM-IV personality disorders and normal personality dimensions in a diverse sample of inpatient and outpatient alcohol, cocaine, and opiate abusers. K-means clustering again suggested that a two-cluster solution was optimal for defining clearly separated subtypes of substance abusers. In the sample, 59% was grouped into one cluster (Type A), and 41% were Type B substance abusers. Proportionately more Type B substance abusers were diagnosed with a personality disorder (70% yes; 30% no) than were Type As (47% yes; 53% no). Higher rates of personality disorder diagnoses among Type B were found across the three DSM-IV clusters, although this difference was more pronounced for the DSM-IV Cluster B personality disorders. In addition, Type B substance abusers were diagnosed with more Axis II disorders than were Type As. Type B substance abusers scored higher than Type As on symptom counts for all of the DSM-IV personality disorders except schizoid personality disorder.

Regarding normal personality dimensions, Type B substance abusers scored higher on NEO-FFI N, and lower on Agreeableness and Conscientiousness than Type A. With regard to the TCI, Type B substance abusers scored higher on Novelty Seeking and Harm

Avoidance and lower on Cooperativeness and Self-Directedness than Type A. In summary, the above typology studies suggest that the traits of impulsivity, novelty seeking, SS, N or Harm Avoidance, and antisocial personality disorder (aggressiveness, disagreeableness, low conscientiousness and socialization) appear to be core dimensions of the more severe Type B. Type B substance abuse appears to have some similarity to a construct of secondary psychopathy in which N, anxiety, and depression may develop as potential consequences of a co-existing substance use disorder (see Sher & Trull 1994; Verheul *et al.* 1998). Our findings suggest that most Type Bs are not primary psychopaths, but rather experience significant emotional distress related to their addiction and psychiatric conditions.

Several studies have attempted to identify a smaller set of dimensions to predict typology membership and different studies have found different subsets of dimensions. For example, Ball *et al.* (1995) found that across the three sub-samples, antisocial personality and alcohol dependence severity were the best stand-alone dimensions predicting cocaine subtypes. Other dimensions found to be important in more than one other study include current and lifetime dependence severity, childhood behavior problems, substance use to reduce withdrawal symptoms, and medical problems (see summary by Ball 1996). As can be seen in this list, personality dimensions generally do not emerge as good stand-alone proxy measures of the A/B typology. In addition, given this level of variability in findings, it seems premature to eliminate any of the sub-typing dimensions from the model. A broad bio-psychosocial conceptual net seems most appropriate for guiding theory, research, predictions about the course of symptoms, and treatment decisions for a complex disorder like substance abuse. Single dimensions ultimately may be better for a specific purpose or for subgroups of patients. As Sher (1991) suggested, temperament or personality should be viewed as a critically important variable, but should not exist in isolation from broader etiological models of alcohol and drug use.

7. Conclusion

The NEO, ZKPQ, and TCI all measure constructs which are related to substance abuse and other psychiatric problems. Although these personality scales have some overlap, there are also substantial differences between the models. This frames my closing discussion regarding which measure or scales might best guide research into the role of personality in the etiology, course, and outcome of substance abuse. NEO N, ZKPQ N-Anx, and TCI Harm Avoidance are related constructs that appear to be important measures for a broad range of individuals who abuse substances (see review by Wills & Hirky 1996) and for psychiatric disorders in general. Higher NEO N was a defining feature of Trull and Sher's (1994) first canonical variable and appeared to be an indicator of general psychopathology. Research suggests that impulsivity/disinhibition predates the development of both substance abuse and antisocial personality (disinhibitory psychopathology) whereas N/emotionality develops more as a consequence of both disorders (see Sher & Trull 1994). Thus, N appears to be a general risk factor for psychopathology (or perhaps treatment seeking) and not specifically related to substance abuse or personality disorder.

NEO-FFI Extraversion, ZKPQ-III Soc, and TCI Reward Dependence have conceptual overlap, but have fewer relations to substance abuse and psychopathology in our studies, and inconsistencies in the literature seem in part related to when individuals are assessed in the development of their substance use problems. Lower NEO-FFI Agreeableness and TCI Cooperativeness and higher ZKPQ-III Agg-Host also overlap and have more consistent associations with both personality disorder and substance dependence severity. Lower NEO Extraversion, Agreeableness and Conscientiousness; higher ZKPQ ImpSS and Agg-Host; higher TCI Novelty Seeking and lower Self-Directedness and Cooperativeness all appear to be critical dimensions for the subtyping of substance abusers into more severely disordered and problematic (e.g. personality disordered) groups.

However, the four-trait inventories reviewed in this chapter (SSS, ZKPQ, TCI, NEO) differ markedly in their conceptualization of the one personality dimension that appears to be most relevant in cross-sectional, longitudinal studies of substance abuse. Although there is no single addictive personality trait or type, there is little dispute in the field regarding the importance of impulsivity, SS, or disinhibition in substance abusers. Research suggests that impulsivity/disinhibition predates the development of both substance abuse and antisocial personality whereas N/emotionality develops more as a consequence of both disorders (see Sher & Trull 1994).

On the surface, the NEO-PI-R appears to measure impulsivity directly as a facet of N. However, Costa & McCrae (1992a) define this facet more narrowly as an inability to control or resist craving and urges (e.g. for food, items, substances) while SS appears to be separated across two domains as facets of Extraversion and Openness to Experience. This definition of impulsiveness as craving is controversial and disputed in the personality field (see Tellegen 1985) and, more specific to this discussion, may contribute little information for understanding individual differences in clinical samples of addicted individuals. In fact, Costa and McCrae's (1992b) conceptualization of impulsivity is considerably broader and more complex, and includes the concepts of self-control, deliberation, planning, carelessness, self-discipline, and morality embedded within the NEO Conscientiousness domain. The five-factor model as assessed by the NEO has become the dominant personality model over the past two decades, and this popularity seems justified given its substantial empirical support in diverse national and cross-cultural community and clinical samples. Nonetheless, one specific limitation may be that the model fails to provide a widely accepted measure of a personality dimension that appears to be most relevant in cross-sectional and longitudinal studies of substance abuse.

Although widely used in substance abuse research, neither of Cloninger's instruments (TPQ or TCI) directly measures impulsivity. Rather, Cloninger conceptualizes narrower impulsive behaviors as subscales of Novelty Seeking and broader impulsivity as a combination of high Novelty Seeking and low Harm Avoidance. However, our research (Ball *et al.* 1999) suggested that impulsivity, i.e. lower Constraint, might be better characterized by high Novelty Seeking and low Self-Directedness. In contrast, the ZKPQ provides more specific coverage of impulsivity, SS, Aggression and Hostility traits. The SSS (Zuckerman 1979) provides even more detailed coverage of trait subscales that are highly relevant for substance abuse, including Thrill and Adventure Seeking (desire to take physical risks); Experience Seeking (seeking new experiences through unconventional behavior); Disinhibition (interest in going against conventional, social norms); Boredom Susceptibility (dislike for repetition and the need to seek change or novelty).

The ZKPQ remains in a much earlier stage of reliability and validity testing than either the TPQ/TCI or the NEO. It does not have narrower subscales for a more detailed description of the complexity of personality. Currently, the ZKPQ does not have an investigative team championing its use. The validity of the ZKPQ for personality disorders and other psychopathological conditions is untested, and it is not ready for use for clinical assessment purposes. The advantages of the TCI and the NEO over the ZKPQ include the breadth of these models and their inclusion of narrower facets or subscales that may be useful for subtyping or treatment planning purposes. The advantage of NEO over the TCI is its replicability and validity across cross-cultural clinical and community samples, its consistent association with personality disorders, and its growing connection to other dimensional models of abnormal personality such as those developed by Clark (1993) and Livesley *et al.* (1992) that together are pushing for changes to the DSM Axis II system.

To help bring some closure to this essay, I will briefly summarize three explanatory meta-models (for more complete discussion see Verheul *et al.* 1998) for the relation between personality and substance use and the high co-morbidity of personality disorder and addiction. The primary personality disorder model hypothesizes that personality traits contribute to the development of substance abuse, the secondary personality disorder model hypothesizes that substance abuse contributes to the development of personality disorders, and the common factors model hypothesizes that the two disorders share a common vulnerability that is presumably biological, but could be social-developmental. There is little research to support the secondary model and work on the common factors model is still very early in its development.

The current data most strongly support the primary personality model, and Verheul *et al.* (1998) described two alternatives for this model. First, personality may heighten risk for substance use due to relatively fixed, presumably brain-based, sensitivities to the positive (pleasurable arousal or social facilitation) and negative (e.g. stress reduction, negative affect regulation) reinforcement properties of psychoactive substances. In this model, for example, high SS or perhaps this trait combined with high levels of impulsivity and aggression (or other genetic risk factors such as family history) would be a direct risk factor for a substance use disorder. The evidence for a fixed or unidirectional model is quite mixed, especially when substance use is hypothesized to be driven by a need to self-medicate affects or maintain an optimal level of arousal or neuroadrenergic state. More complex developmental models place personality within the context of a challenging or changing environment in which other risk factors must be present for a substance use disorder to develop (see also Crawford *et al.* 2003). For example, heritable variations in SS would be seen as shaping reciprocal interactions with the environment and the gravitation toward particular (i.e. risky or deviant) peer groups or activities. In the absence of these social risk factors or easy availability of drugs and alcohol, substance use disorders would not develop, although conceivably other forms of risk taking, disinhibition, or deviance might.

Finally, we have argued that the role of personality dimensions and disorders in substance abuse may be best conceptualized within broader multidimensional addiction subtypes, such as Type A and B. The assessment of a personality trait like SS may be especially useful since it is one sub-typing dimension that can be measured easily, especially with recent short forms (Stephenson *et al.* 2003), before problems develop to identify types of individuals at risk for drug experimentation and pathological use toward whom prevention efforts can be targeted. For example, children and siblings of substance abusers may be a target group whose personality traits are especially important to assess (Luthar *et al.* 1992). Prevention and treatment could focus on teaching high SS individuals new activities which satisfy their motivational needs for novelty, risk, excitement, and avoiding boredom in ways that are less damaging to self or others (Sutker *et al.* 1978). As I have argued elsewhere (Ball 1998, 2003; Ball & Cecero 2001) an assessment of personality traits and disorders is critically important to the process of treatment development and efficacy testing. I have conceptualized a psychotherapeutic focus on personality trait dimensions (temperament and coping) that has informed a developing treatment model (Ball 1998; Ball & Young 2000). The reliable and valid assessment of personality traits and disorders in active substance abusers is very complicated due to the effects of intoxication, acute or protracted withdrawal symptoms, and other Axis I symptomatology (Ball *et al.* 2001; Verheul *et al.* 1998), and so we (Rounsaville *et al.* 1998) have established guidelines for distinguishing between personality disorder symptoms that are related to substance abuse vs. independent from substance abuse.

In conclusion, biologically informed personality traits such as Zuckerman's SS and alternative five, Cloninger's seven dimensions of temperament and character, and Costa and McCrae's five-factor model are all important constructs for understanding personality disorders and addictive behavior. Research has attempted to map the relations between personality and substance abuse and these complex associations are probably best conceptualized within a multidimensional model of risk factors.

Normal personality dimensions have an important role in facilitating an understanding of the complex etiology and interrelated course of psychiatric disorders, such as substance abuse and personality disorders (Sher & Trull 1994). Together with other genetic and environmental factors, personality traits such as those assessed in this chapter and other studies may be direct risk factors for substance use (e.g. Impulsivity, Novelty seeking, or SS), or be risk factors for personality disorders (e.g. low Agreeableness, high Agg-Host) which have substance abuse as an important behavioral expression, or they may be mediators or consequences of the severity of both disorders (e.g. N, Harm Avoidance). The measurement of normal temperament or personality dimensions may also facilitate the identification of types of individuals at increased risk for substance abuse and personality disorders toward whom prevention efforts can be targeted as well as understanding the relapse vulnerabilities of already addicted individuals.

Acknowledgments

Portions of this chapter are reprinted with the copyright permission of the American Psychological Association (Ball 1995, 2002; Ball *et al.* 1994, 1995, 1997a, b, 1999) and Guilford Press (Ball *et al.* 1998). The series of studies reviewed in this chapter have been funded through various grants from the National Institute on Drug Abuse, including R01 DA04029, R01 DA05592, R18 DA06915, R18 DA06963, R01 DA10012, and R01 DA14967. Correspondence concerning this chapter should be addressed to Samuel A. Ball, Ph. D., Yale University School of Medicine, VA CT (151D), 950 Campbell Avenue, West Haven, CT 06516 or through email to samuel.ball@yale.edu.

References

Andrucci, G. L., Archer, R. P., Pancoast, D. L., & Gordon, R. A. (1989). The relationship of MMPI and sensation seeking scales to adolescent drug use. *Journal of Personality Assessment*, *53*, 253–266.

Babor, T. F., Dolinsky, Z., Rounsaville, B. J., & Jaffe, J. (1988). Unitary vs. multidimensional models of alcoholism treatment outcome: An empirical study. *Journal of Studies on Alcohol*, *49*, 167–177.

Babor, T. F., Hofmann, M., DelBoca, F. K., Hesselbrock, V., Meyer, R. E., Dolinsky, Z. S., & Rounsaville, B. (1992). Types of alcoholics, I: Evidence for an empirically derived typology based on indicators of vulnerability and severity. *Archives of General Psychiatry*, *49*, 599–608.

Ball, S. A. (1995). The validity of an alternative five factor measure of personality in cocaine abusers. *Psychological Assessment*, *7*, 148–154.

Ball, S. A. (1996). Type A and B alcoholism: Applicability across subpopulations and treatment settings. *Alcohol Health & Research World*, *20*, 30–35.

Ball, S. A. (1998). Manualized treatment for substance abusers with personality disorders: Dual focus schema therapy. *Addictive Behaviors*, *23*, 883–891.

Ball, S. A. (2002). Big five, alternative five, and seven personality dimensions: Validity in substance dependent patients. In: P. T. Costa, Jr., & T. A. Widiger (Eds), *Personality disorders and the Five-Factor Model of personality* (2nd ed.). Washington, DC: American Psychological Association.

Ball, S. A. (2003). Treatment of personality disorders with co-occurring substance dependence: Dual focus schema therapy. In: J. J. Magnavita (Ed.), *Treating personality disorder*. New York: Wiley.

Ball, S. A., Carroll, K. M., Babor, T. F., & Rounsaville, B. J. (1995). Subtypes of cocaine abusers: Support for a Type A-Type B distinction. *Journal of Consulting and Clinical Psychology*, *63*, 115–124.

Ball, S. A., Carroll, K. M., & Rounsaville, B. J. (1994). Sensation seeking, substance abuse, and psychopathology in treatment seeking and community cocaine abusers. *Journal of Consulting and Clinical Psychology*, *62*, 1053–1057.

Ball, S. A., & Cecero, J. J. (2001). Addicted patients with personality disorders: Traits, schemas, and presenting problems. *Journal of Personality Disorders*, *15*, 72–83.

Ball, S. A., Jaffe, A. J., Crouse-Artus, M. S., Rounsaville, B. J., & O'Malley, S. S. (2000). Multidimensional subtypes, treatment outcome and matching in first time DWI offenders. *Addictive Behaviors*, *25*, 167–181.

Ball, S. A., Kranzler, H. R., Tennen, H., Poling, J. C., & Rounsaville, B. J. (1997a). Personality disorder and dimension differences between Type A and Type B substance abusers. *Journal of Personality Disorders*, *12*, 1–12.

Ball, S. A., Rounsaville, B. J., Tennen, H., & Kranzler, H. R. (2001). Reliability of personality disorder symptoms and personality traits in substance dependent inpatients. *Journal of Abnormal Psychology*, *110*, 341–352.

Ball, S. A., & Schottenfeld, R. S. (1997). A five-factor model of personality and addiction, psychiatric, and AIDS risk severity in pregnant and postpartum cocaine misusers. *Substance Use & Misuse*, *32*, 25–41.

Ball, S. A., Tennen, H., & Kranzler, H. R. (1999). Factor replicability and validity of the Temperament and Character Inventory in substance dependent patients. *Psychological Assessment*, *11*, 514–524.

Ball, S. A., Tennen, H., Poling, J. C., Kranzler, H. R., & Rounsaville, B. J. (1997b). Personality, temperament, and character dimension and the DSM-IV personality disorders in substance abusers. *Journal of Abnormal Psychology*, *106*, 545–553.

Ball, S. A., & Young, J. E. (2000). Dual focus schema therapy for personality disorders and substance dependence: Case study results. *Cognitive and Behavioral Practice*, *7*, 270–281.

Barnes, G. E. (1983). Clinical and prealcoholic personality characteristics. In: B. Kissin, & H. Begleiter (Eds), *The pathogenesis of alcoholism: Psychosocial factors* (Vol. 6, pp. 113–196). NY: Plenum Press.

Beck, A. (1993). *Beck depression inventory/Aaron T. Beck, Robert A. Starr*. San Antonio, TX.

Ben-Porath, Y. S., & Waller, N. (1992). "Normal" personality inventories in clinical assessment: General requirements and the potential for using the NEO Personality Inventory. *Psychological Assessment*, *4*, 14–19.

Black, J. J. (1993). *Predictors of outcome at an outpatient substance abuse center*. Unpublished doctoral dissertation. Newark, DE: University of Delaware.

Block, J., Block, J. H., & Keyes, S. (1988). Longitudinally foretelling drug usage in adolescence: Early childhood personality and environmental precursors. *Child Development*, *59*, 336–355.

Brook, J. S., Whiteman, M., Gordon, A. S., & Cohen, P. (1986). Dynamics of childhood and adolescent personality traits and adolescent drug use. *Developmental Psychology*, *25*, 394–402.

Brooner, R. K., King, V. L., Kidorf, M., Schmidt, C. W., & Bigelow, G. E. (1997). Psychiatric and substance use comorbidity among treatment-seeking opioid abusers. *Archives of General Psychiatry*, *54*, 71–80.

Buss, A., & Plomin, R. (1975). *A temperament theory of personality*. Hillside, NJ: Lawrence Erlbaum.

Carrol, E. N., Zuckerman, M., & Vogel, W. H. (1982). A test of the optimal level of arousal theory of sensation seeking. *Journal of Personality and Social Psychology*, *42*, 572–575.

Clark, L. A. (1993). *Manual for the schedule of nonadaptive and adaptive personality*. Minneapolis, MN: University of Minnesota Press.

Cloninger, C. R. (1987a). A systematic method for clinical description and classification of personality variants. *Archives of General Psychiatry*, *44*, 573–585.

Cloninger, C. R. (1987b). Neurogenetic adaptive mechanisms in alcoholism. *Science*, *236*, 410–416.

Cloninger, C. R., Przybeck, T., Svrakic, D. M., & Wetzel, R. (1994). *The temperament and character inventory (TCI): A guide to its development and use*. St. Louis: Center for Psychobiology of Personality.

Cloninger, C. R., Svrakic, D. M., & Przybeck, T. R. (1993). A psychobiological model of temperament and character. *Archives of General Psychiatry*, *50*, 975–990.

Costa, P. T., Jr., & McCrae, R. R. (1992a). *Revised NEO Personality Inventory and NEO Five-Factor Inventory*. Odessa, FL: Psychological Assessment Resources.

Costa, P. T., Jr., & McCrae, R. R. (1992b). Normal personality assessment in clinical practice: The NEO Personality Inventory. *Psychological Assessment*, *4*, 5–13.

Costa, P. T., Jr., & Widiger, T. A. (Eds) (2001). *Personality disorders and the Five-Factor Model of personality* (2nd ed.). Washington, DC: American Psychological Association Press.

Cox, W. M. (1987). Personality theory and research. In: H. T. Blane, & K. E. Leonard (Eds), *Psychological theories of drinking and alcoholism* (pp. 55–89). NY: Guilford Press.

Crawford, A. M., Pentz, M. A., Chou, C.-P., Li, C., & Dwyer, J. H. (2003). Parallel developmental trajectories of sensation seeking and regular substance use in adolescents. *Psychology of Addictive Behaviors*, *17*, 179–192.

DeJong, C., van den Brink, W., Harteveld, F. M., & van der Wielen, G. M. (1993). Personality disorders in alcoholics and drug addicts. *Comprehensive Psychiatry*, *34*, 87–94.

Donovan, D. M., & Marlatt, G. A. (1982). Personality subtypes among driving-while-intoxicated offenders: Relationship to drinking behavior and driving risk. *Journal of Consulting and Clinical Psychology*, *50*, 241–249.

Donovan, D. M., Marlatt, G. A., & Slazberg, P. M. (1983). Drinking behavior, personality factors and high-risk driving: A review and theoretical formulation. *Journal of Studies on Alcohol*, *44*, 395–428.

Feingold, A., Ball, S. A., Kranzler, H. R., & Rounsaville, B. J. (1996). Generalizability of the Type A/Type B distinction across different psychoactive substances. *American Journal of Drug and Alcohol Abuse*, *22*, 449–462.

Griggs, S. M., & Tyrer, P. J. (1981). Personality disorder, social adjustment and treatment outcome in alcoholics. *Journal of Studies on Alcohol*, *42*, 802–805.

Gurrera, R. J. (1990). Some biological and behavioral features associated with clinical personality types. *Journal of Nervous and Mental Disease*, *178*, 556–566.

Howard, M. O., Kivlahan, D., & Walker, R. D. (1997). Cloninger's tridimensional theory of personality and psychopathology: Applications to substance use disorders. *Journal of Studies on Alcohol*, *58*, 48–66.

Jaffe, L. T., & Archer, R. P. (1987). The prediction of drug use among college students from MMPI, MCMI, and sensation seeking scales. *Journal of Personality Assessment*, *51*, 243–253.

Kaestner, E., Rosen, L., & Appel, P. (1977). Patterns of drug abuse: Relationships with ethnicity, sensation seeking, and anxiety. *Journal of Consulting and Clinical Psychology*, *45*, 462–468.

Kofoed, L., Kania, J., Walsh, T., & Atkinson, R. (1986). Outpatient treatment of patients with substance abuse and co-existing psychiatric disorders. *American Journal of Psychiatry*, *143*, 867–872.

Kosten, T. A., Ball, S. A., & Rounsaville, B. J. (1994). A sibling study of sensation-seeking and opiate addiction. *The Journal of Nervous and Mental Disease*, *182*, 284–289.

Kosten, T. A., Kosten, T. R., & Rounsaville, B. J. (1989). Personality disorders in opiate addicts show prognostic specificity. *Journal of Substance Abuse Treatment*, *6*, 163–168.

Kruedelbach, N., McCormick, R. A., Schulz, S. C., & Grueneich, R. (1993). Impulsivity, coping styles, and triggers for craving in substance abusers with borderline personality disorder. *Journal of Personality Disorders*, *7*, 214–222.

Labouvie, E. W., & McGee, C. R. (1986). Relation of personality to alcohol and drug use in adolescence. *Journal of Consulting and Clinical Psychology*, *54*, 289–293.

Livesley, W. J., Jackson, D. N., & Schroeder, M. L. (1992). Factorial structure of traits delineating personality disorders in clinical and general population samples. *Journal of Abnormal Personality*, *101*, 432–440.

Luthar, S. S., Anton, S. F., Merikangas, K. R., & Rounsaville, B. J. (1992). Vulnerability to drug abuse among opioid addicts' siblings: Individual, familial, and peer influences. *Comprehensive Psychiatry*, *33*, 1–8.

McLellan, A. T., Kucher, H., Metzger, D., Peters, R., Smith, I., Grisson, G., Pettinati, H., & Argerious, M. (1992). The fifth edition of the Addiction Severity Index. *Journal of Substance Abuse Treatment*, *9*, 199–213.

Montag, I., & Birenbaum, M. (1986). Psychopathological factors and sensation seeking. *Journal of Research in Personality*, *20*, 338–348.

Morey, L. C., & Skinner, H. A. (1986). Empirically derived classifications of alcohol-related problems. In: M. Galanter (Ed.), *Recent developments in alcoholism* (Vol. 4, pp. 144–168). New York: Plenum Press.

Nace, E. P., & Davis, C. W. (1993). Treatment outcome in substance abusing patients with a personality disorder. *American Journal of Addictions*, *2*, 26–33.

Nace, E. P., Davis, C. W., & Gaspari, J. P. (1991). Axis II comorbidity in substance abusers. *American Journal of Psychiatry*, *148*, 118–120.

Newcomb, M. D., & McGee, L. (1991). Influence of sensation seeking on general deviance and specific problem behaviors from adolescence to young adulthood. *Journal of Personality and Social Psychology*, *61*, 614–628.

O'Sullivan, D. M., Zuckerman, M., & Kraft, M. (1996). The personality of prostitutes. *Personality and Individual Differences*, *21*, 445–448.

Piedmont, R. L., & Ciarrocchi, J. W. (1999). The utility of the Revised NEO Personality Inventory in an outpatient, drug rehabilitation context. *Psychology of Addictive Behaviors*, *13*, 213–226.

Quirk, S. W., & McCormick, R. A. (1998). Personality subtypes, coping styles, symptom correlates, and substances of choice among a cohort of substance abusers. *Assessment*, *5*, 157–170.

Rounsaville, B. J., Kosten, T. R., Weissman, M. M., & Kleber, H. D. (1986). Prognostic significance of psychopathology in treated opiate addicts. *Archives of General Psychiatry*, *43*, 739–745.

Rounsaville, B. J., Kranzler, H. R., Ball, S., Tennen, H., Poling, J., & Triffleman, E. (1998). Personality disorders in substance abusers: Relation to substance use. *Journal of Nervous and Mental Disease*, *186*, 87–95.

Rutherford, M. J., Cacciola, J. S., & Alterman, A. I. (1994). Relationship of personality disorders with problem severity in methadone patients. *Drug and Alcohol Dependence*, *35*, 69–76.

Schroeder, M. L., Wormsworth, J. A., & Livesley, W. J. (1992). Dimensions of personality disorder and their relationships to the big five dimensions of personality. *Psychological Assessment*, *4*, 47–53.

Schuckit, M. A., Tipp, J., Smith, T. L., Shapiro, E., Hesselbrock, V. M., Bucholz, K. K., Reich, T., & Nurnberger, J. I. (1995). An evaluation of Type A and B alcoholics. *Addiction*, *90*, 1189–1203.

Schwarz, R. M., Burkhart, B. R., & Green, S. B. (1978). Turning on or turning off: Sensation seeking or tension reduction as motivational determinants of alcohol use. *Journal of Consulting and Clinical Psychology*, *46*, 1144–1145.

Segal, B. S., Huba, G. J., & Singer, J. F. (1980). *Drugs, daydreaming, and personality: A study of college youth*. Hillsdale, NJ: Lawrence Erlbaum.

Sher, K. J. (1991). *Children of alcoholics: A critical appraisal of theory and research*. Chicago: University of Chicago Press.

Sher, K. J., & Trull, T. J. (1994). Personality and disinhibitory psychopathology: Alcoholism and antisocial personality disorder. *Journal of Abnormal Psychology*, *103*, 92–102.

Sher, K. J., Wood, M. D., Crews, T. M., & Vandiver, P. A. (1995). The Tridimensional Personality Questionnaire: Reliability and validity studies and derivation of a short form. *Psychological Assessment*, *7*, 195–208.

Soldz, S., Budman, S., Demby, A., & Merry, J. (1993). Representation of personality disorders in circumplex and five-factor space: Explorations with a clinical sample. *Psychological Assessment*, *5*, 41–52.

Stephenson, M. T., Hoyle, R. H., Palmgreen, P., & Slater, M. D. (2003). Brief measures of sensation seeking for screening and large-scale surveys. *Drug and Alcohol Dependence*, *72*, 279–286.

Sutker, P. B., & Allain, A. N. (1988). Issues in personality conceptualizations of addictive behaviors. *Journal of Consulting and Clinical Psychology*, *56*, 172–182.

Sutker, P. B., Archer, R. P., Brantley, P. J., & Kilpatrick, D. G. (1979). Alcoholics and opium addicts: A comparison of personality characteristics. *Journal of Consulting and Clinical Psychology*, *40*, 635–644.

Sutker, P. B., Archer, R. P., & Allain, A. N. (1978). Drug abuse patterns, personality characteristics, and relationships with sex, race, and sensation seeking. *Journal of Consulting and Clinical Psychology*, *46*, 1374–1378.

Svrakic, D. M., Whitehead, C., Przybeck, T. R., & Cloninger, C. R. (1993). Differential diagnosis of personality disorders by the seven factor model of temperament and character. *Archives of General Psychiatry*, *50*, 991–999.

Tarter, R. E. (1988). Are there inherited behavioral traits that predispose to substance abuse? *Journal of Consulting and Clinical Psychology*, *56*, 189–196.

Tellegen, A. (1985) Structures of mood and personality and their relevance to assessing anxiety, with an emphasis on self-report. In: A. H. Tuma, & J. D. Maser (Eds), *Anxiety and anxiety disorders* (pp. 681–706). Hillsdale, NJ: Lawrence Erlbaum.

Thornquist, M. H., & Zuckerman, M. (1995). Psychopathy, passive avoidance learning and basic dimensions of personality. *Personality and Individual Differences*, *19*, 525–534.

Trull, T. J. (1992). DSM-III-R personality disorders and the Five-Factor Model of personality: An empirical comparison. *Journal of Abnormal Psychology*, *101*, 553–560.

Trull, T. J., & Sher, K. J. (1994). Relationship between the Five-Factor Model of personality and axis I disorders in a non-clinical sample. *Journal of Abnormal Psychology*, *103*, 350–360.

Verheul, R., Ball, S., & van den Brink, W. (1998). Substance abuse and personality disorders. In: H. R. Kranzler, & B. J. Rounsaville (Eds), *Dual diagnosis and treatment: Substance abuse and comorbid medical and psychiatric disorders* (pp. 317–363). New York, NY: Marcel Dekker.

Watson, D., Clark, L. A., & Harkness, A. R. (1994). Structures of personality and their relevance to psychopathology. *Journal of Abnormal Psychology*, *103*, 18–31.

White, H. R., Labouvie, E. W., & Bates, M. E. (1985). The relationship between sensation seeking and delinquency: A longitudinal analysis. *Journal of Research in Crime and Delinquency*, *22*, 197–211.

Wiggins, J. S., & Pincus, A. C. (1989). Conceptions of personality disorders and dimensions of personality. *Psychological Assessment*, *1*, 305–316.

Wills, T. A., & Hirky, E. (1996). Coping and substance abuse: A theoretical model and review of the evidence. In: M. Ziedner, & N. S. Endler (Eds), *Handbook of coping: Theory, research, applications* (pp. 279–302). New York: Wiley.

Yoshino, A., Kato, M., Takeuchi, M., Ono, Y., & Kitamura, T. (1994). Examination of the tridimensional personality questionnaire hypothesis of alcoholism using empirically multivariate typology. *Alcoholism: Clinical and Experimental Research*, *18*, 1121–1124.

Zuckerman, M. (1979). *Beyond the optimal level of arousal*. Hillsdale, NJ: Lawrence Erlbaum.

Zuckerman, M. (1987). Biological connection between sensation seeking and drug abuse. In: J. Engel, & L. Oreland (Eds), *Brain reward systems and abuse* (pp. 165–173). New York: Raven Press.

Zuckerman, M. (1994). *Behavioral expressions and biosocial bases of sensation seeking*. New York, NY: Cambridge University Press.

Zuckerman, M. (2003). Zuckerman-Kuhlman Personality Questionnaire (ZKPQ): An alternative five-factorial model. In: B. DeRaad, & M. Perugini (Eds), *Big five assessment*. Seattle: Hogrefe & Huber Publishers.

Zuckerman, M., & Cloninger, C. R. (1996). Relationships between Cloninger's, Zuckerman's, and Eysenck's dimensions of personality. *Personality and Individual Differences*, *21*, 283–285.

Zuckerman, M., Kolin, E. A., Price, L., & Zoob, I. (1979). Development of a sensation seeking scale. *Journal of Consulting Psychology*, *28*, 477–482.

Zuckerman, M., & Kuhlman, D. M. (2000). Personality and risk taking: Common biosocial factors. *Journal of Personality*, *68*, 999–1029.

Zuckerman, M., Kuhlman, D. M., Joireman, J., Teta, P., & Kraft, M. (1993). A comparison of three structural models for personality: The big three, the big five and the alternative five. *Journal of Personality and Social Psychology*, *65*, 757–768.

Zuckerman, M., Kuhlman, D. M., Thornquist, M., & Kiers, H. (1991). Five (or three) robust questionnaire scale factors of personality without culture. *Personality and Individual Differences*, *23*, 929–941.

Chapter 13

Personality and Risky Behavior: Communication and Prevention

L. Donohew, M. T. Bardo and R. S. Zimmerman

1. Introduction

It has long been established that individuals who are high sensation seekers (SS) and impulsive decision makers are more likely to engage in drug use, risky sex, and other behaviors which can endanger their health (e.g. Carrol & Zuckerman 1977; Donohew *et al.* 1990; Segal 1976). Such persons have provided a challenge for those conducting campaigns intended to reduce these behaviors and may account for the high failure rate of prevention efforts (Flay & Sobel 1983; Rogers & Storey 1987). However, in recent years, compelling evidence has been offered that persuasive messages with novel components can attract and hold the attention of this prime target audience and bring about significant behavior change (Bardo *et al.* 1996; Donohew *et al.* 1994; Palmgreen *et al.* 2001; Zimmerman, Donohew *et al.* 2003).

Bardo and associates (e.g. Bardo & Hammer 1991; Bardo *et al.* 1993, 2001) and Zuckerman (1979, 1983, 1994) have cited neurobiological support for this approach. They proposed that exposure to novelty activates, at least in part, the same neural substrate that mediates the rewarding effects of drugs of abuse and argue that individual differences in response to novelty and drugs may relate to individual differences in the mesolimbic dopamine (DA) system of the brain.

In this chapter, we will describe some of the research mentioned above and focus the implications of this work for communication and prevention, including genetic and neurobiological foundations, models of information exposure and impulsive decision-making, and prevention studies drawing on the models. Most of the research reported here was conducted within an applied framework of prevention, funded by agencies of the National Institutes of Health (see Acknowledgments).

On the Psychobiology of Personality
Edited by R. M. Stelmack

ISBN: 0-08-044209-9

2. Genetic Connection Between SS and Drug Abuse Vulnerability

A host of genetic studies in humans indicate that vulnerability to drug abuse is heritable. Most work in this area is based on data collected from alcoholics (Cloninger & Begleiter 1990). In general, the strongest evidence for a genetic influence on alcoholism is obtained from the most severe alcoholic subtype (Johnson *et al.* 1996). With various drugs of abuse, including alcohol, considerable attention focused on genes encoding membrane proteins involved in dopamine (DA) neurotransmission. This research indicates that gene markers for DA D2 receptors are present more often in drug abusers than in control populations (Uhl *et al.* 1993).

The association between different gene markers and vulnerability to drug abuse may also be mediated, at least in part, by heritable personality traits. Among the most extensively studied personality traits in this area is sensation seeking or novelty seeking. In particular, recent work shows that genetic encoding for DA D4 receptors, which have considerable homology with the D2 subtype, may be associated with high novelty seeking in humans (Benjamin *et al.* 1996; Ebstein *et al.* 1996; Katz & Belmaker 1996). While this genetic link has not always been replicated across various sample populations, sensation seeking and novelty seeking have been positively correlated with use and abuse of drugs in different populations (Donohew *et al.* 1991; Wills *et al.* 1998; Zuckerman 1994). One interpretation of this relation is that high SS may be genetically predisposed to show enhanced sensitivity to drugs of abuse that activate DA pathways in the brain. Alternatively, high SS may simply be inclined to join social groups that engage in risky behaviors, such as drug use, and thus drug availability and peer pressure may play an important role in mediating the relation between sensation seeking and drug use.

Given the relation between sensation seeking and drug use among adolescents, it would be valuable to understand the basic neurogenetic mechanisms that may underlie this relation. One simple hypothesis that can be offered is that high SS differ from low SS in their response to drugs due to differences in the biological mechanisms involved in drug reward. Moreover, since the mesolimbic DA reward pathway plays a key role in drug reward (Wise 1998), it can be hypothesized further that the mesolimbic DA system may be more sensitive to drugs in high SS than in low SS. Some early work revealed that high SS have reduced monoamine oxidase (MAO) activity in blood platelets (Murphy *et al.* 1977). Since MAO is the major enzyme that metabolizes monoamine neurotransmitters such as DA, these results suggested that the activity of monoamine brain systems, and DA in particular, might differ between high and low SS. However, this conclusion is speculative presently, since platelet MAO activity is not a reliable index of MAO activity in the brain (Young *et al.* 1986). Additional work is needed to determine to what extent inherent differences in brain DA systems contribute, if at all, to the relation between sensation seeking and drug abuse vulnerability.

2.1. Using Animal Models to Investigate the Relation Between Sensation Seeking and Drug Abuse Vulnerability

In order to gain a more comprehensive understanding of the biological connection between SS and drug abuse vulnerability, models using laboratory animals can offer some useful information. Of course at this biological level of analysis we cannot measure personality traits, but we can operationally define species-specific behaviors that presumably represent an evolutionary precursor for the biological component of SS in humans. One important reason for developing animal models of SS is that modern neuroscientific and genetic techniques may be used to provide important clues about the role of specific neural systems in SS and how these systems are controlled by genetic and environmental factors. The use of recombinant inbred analyses, selective breeding, and genetic knockout techniques in mice may be particularly useful in this regard.

A second important reason to develop animal models of SS is that drug abuse vulnerability among high SS is difficult to study in adolescent humans. If high SS are biologically predisposed to abuse drugs, then presumably this predisposition exists prior to the first drug experience. Ideally, one would like to be able to study how high and low SS differ in their initial response to drug abuse, especially since there is some evidence that the subjective feeling of the first drug experience may predict later abuse in the general population (Haertzen *et al.* 1986). However, it is clearly unethical to expose adolescents to drugs for the first time. Thus, one can only rely on retrospective and subjective reports of the first drug experience, which provides only limited information about the individual differences in drug abuse vulnerability.

At the present time, there is little information about SS using nonhuman primates. Since SS in humans is based on a self-rated personality inventory, extrapolation of personality traits from nonhuman primates to humans must be done cautiously. Nonetheless, experimenter-ratings of nonhuman primate behavior can be used to categorize animals on the basis of various traits, including aggressiveness, curiosity, apprehensiveness, fearfulness and submissiveness. These traits are thought to be under both genetic and environmental control, and some effort has been made to explore the neurological basis for variations in these traits.

Recent work that examined trait variations among nonhuman primates identified at least two biological markers that may play a role, namely serotonin and plasma cortisol. Similar to humans, rhesus monkeys show a length variation in the genetic expression of the serotonin transporter protein, and this variation is under the control of early life experiences (Bennett *et al.* 2002). Early life experience has also been shown to play a prominent role in the behavioral and biological adaptation to stressful events during later adulthood, as expressed by the level of plasma cortisol. Fahlke *et al.* (2000) found that rhesus monkeys reared in the presence of peers, rather than in the presence of their mother, showed an exaggerated cortisol response to social separation during adulthood. When allowed to consume alcohol during young adulthood, these peer-raised monkeys also consumed more alcohol than mother-reared monkeys. These latter results are especially interesting when viewed in the context of evidence indicating that high SS humans have elevated plasma cortisol levels (Netter *et al.* 1996; Rosenblitt *et al.* 2001).

Laboratory rats and mice have been used extensively to investigate the potential biological connection between SS and drug abuse vulnerability. One animal model that has received considerable attention is the novelty "responder" test (Piazza *et al.* 1989). With this model, a random population of rats is placed individually into an inescapable novel chamber and the amount of locomotor activity is recorded. Based on the amount of activity displayed, each animal is categorized as either a high responder or a low responder, depending on whether they fall above or below the median of the group.

An alternative animal model, which is more analogous to the construct of SS in humans, is to allow rats to approach novel stimuli in a free-choice situation. For example, rats can be habituated to one set of contextual stimuli (visual, olfactory, tactile) and then be allowed to choose between the familiar context and a novel context (Klebaur *et al.* 2001). A variation of this model is to present rats with an array of different objects and then, after they have been familiarized with the objects, to embed a novel object into the array (Nicholls *et al.* 1992). Rats typically show a preference for the novel context or novel object. In addition, rats can be categorized as either high or low in novelty seeking based on the duration of free-choice exploration of the novelty. One advantage of this model, in contrast to the model in which rats are exposed to inescapable novelty, is that it seems to parallel the type of novelty preference observed in prelingual human infants (Fagan *et al.* 1986). In that latter work, infants are first familiarized with a distinctive visual pattern and then are shown a novel visual pattern along with the familiar pattern. Infants show an increase in preference for the novel pattern as measured by the duration of eye contact with the pattern. However, it is currently unknown if this early nonverbal test is related to scores on the SS personality inventory or to later vulnerability to drug abuse disorders.

A study by Piazza *et al.* (1989) illustrates how research with laboratory animals can be used to investigate the biological connection between SS and drug abuse vulnerability. In that study, a sample of randomly bred rats were categorized as high or low responders based on their individual activity levels in an inescapable novel compartment. When subsequently tested for their response to amphetamine, it was observed that high responders were more sensitive than low responders to locomotor stimulant effect of amphetamine. These animals were also assessed for their propensity to self-administer intravenous amphetamine in an operant conditioning chamber. High responders learned to make an operant response for amphetamine, whereas low responders did not. These results suggest that individual differences in response to novelty may predict the ability of amphetamine to serve as a reinforcer. Extrapolating this evidence to humans, it may be that high SS use drugs more frequently than low SS because they find the drug to be more reinforcing or pleasurable. Consistent with this view, preliminary evidence from a controlled human laboratory study has shown that high SS young adults are more sensitive to the subjective and physiological effects of both amphetamine and diazepam compared to low SS (Kelly *et al.* 1999). In essence, because high SSs have a high need for novelty, they may find that the drug experience is able to fulfill this need.

Other work has compared the ability of different animal models of SS to predict the abuse liability of amphetamine (Klebaur *et al.* 2001). In this study, rats were first assessed for their level of activity in an inescapable novel environment and for their novelty preference in a free-choice test. Similar to Piazza *et al.* (1989), using the inescapable novelty test, high responders self-administered more amphetamine than low responders. These individual differences were most robust when animals were allowed to self-administer low doses of intravenous amphetamine rather than high doses, and the effect was evident with both males and females. In contrast, individual differences in preference for a novel object or a novel chamber did not predict the rate of amphetamine self-administration. Interestingly, however, a related study found that individual differences in novelty preference did predict amphetamine conditioned place preference (Klebaur & Bardo 1999), which is an animal model of conditioned drug reward. Taken together, these results indicate that responses to inescapable novelty and to free choice novelty predict different components of drug reward.

Evidence indicates that exposure to novelty, whether in inescapable or free-choice tests, activates the mesolimbic DA system. Similar to the effects of amphetamine, rats exposed to novel environmental stimuli display an increase in locomotor activity (Bardo *et al.* 1990). Rats also show a conditioned place preference when novel objects are paired with one compartment of a place preference apparatus (Bevins 2001). When entering a novel compartment from a familiar compartment, there is a transient and rapid surge in DA relcase in the nucleus accumbens (Rebec *et al.* 1997), a limbic terminal region thought to be critical in drug reward. In addition, microinjection of the neurotoxin 6-hydroxydopamine into the mesolimbic DA system disrupts the increase in locomotion and rearing normally elicited by novel stimuli (Mogenson & Nielsen 1984). Novelty-induced place preference is also blocked by DA antagonist drugs (Misslin *et al.* 1984) and by destruction of the nucleus accumbens (Pierce *et al.* 1990).

There is not only evidence that novel stimulation and drugs of abuse activate a common DA reward pathway, but there is also research with laboratory animals indicating that individual differences in this biological system may mediate the relation between SS and drug abuse. Most of this work has been accomplished using the high and low responder rats assessed using inescapable novelty. High responders exhibit increased activity of the mesolimbic DA reward system following exposure to either novel stimulation or stimulant drugs (Hooks *et al.* 1992; Saigusa *et al.* 1999). As a result of the greater release of DA in the brain in high responders, there is also a compensatory increase in the reuptake of DA into the pre-synaptic neuron, as well as a down-regulation of DA D2 receptors in the brain (Hooks *et al.* 1994). Further, high responders have increased activity of the DA synthetic enzyme tyrosine hydroxylase, as well as an increased number of DA D1 receptor proteins (Saigusa *et al.* 1999). All of this neurochemical evidence points to an enhanced functioning of the mesolimbic DA reward pathway in the brain of high novelty responders.

Another biological marker that has been identified as a possible mediator of the relation between SS and drug abuse vulnerability is activity within the hypothalamic-pituitary-adrenal stress axis. High novelty responder rats have elevated levels of the stress hormone corticosterone (Piazza *et al.* 1991). Since corticosterone is known to potentiate the psychostimulant effects of amphetamine (Cador *et al.* 1993; Piazza & Le Moal 1998), this suggests that high responder rats may be more sensitive to the reinforcing effect of drugs. These results are consistent with the work cited earlier that high SS humans have elevated plasma cortisol levels (Netter *et al.* 1996; Rosenblitt *et al.* 2001) and are more sensitive to the reinforcing effect of amphetamine as measured by self-reports (Kelly *et al.* 1999).

Consistent with the evidence from humans, there is also considerable evidence from laboratory animals that SS or novelty seeking is a heritable trait. The heritability of this trait is illustrated clearly by the development of different lines of high and low novelty responder rats using selective breeding techniques (Cools & Gingras 1998). In addition, different inbred strains of mice are known to display a different level of locomotor activity in a novel apparatus (Crusio *et al.* 1989), as well as a different rate of contact with novel objects (Peeler & Nowakowski 1987). These inbred mouse strains display a wide variance in their responsiveness to the behavioral effects of various drugs of abuse (Crabbe *et al.* 1999). Along with these behavioral differences, strain differences have been observed in a number of neurochemical markers, including the markers directly related to the functioning of brain DA systems (Severson *et al.* 1981; Vadasz *et al.* 1992). Another report found strain differences in DA metabolism in the nucleus accumbens following exposure to an inescapable novel environment (Cabib *et al.* 1990).

While an individual's response to novelty is under some genetic control, it is also influenced by environmental factors. One important environmental factor that alters response to novelty is the amount of novel sensory stimulation that an individual encounters during development. A host of studies have shown that animals raised in an enriched stimulus environment display a wide range of neurobehavioral changes relative to animals raised in an impoverished stimulus environment (Renner & Rosenzweig 1987). In general, enriched rats find novelty to be less stressful than impoverished rats and they will approach novel stimuli more readily than impoverished rats. Compared to impoverished rats, enriched rats display less activity in an inescapable novel environment and they enter a novel compartment and manipulate novel objects more in a free-choice test (Renner & Rosenzweig 1987). Enriched rats also habituate to novel stimuli more rapidly than impoverished rats (Zimmermann *et al.* 2001).

Concomitant with these differences in response to novelty, enriched rats self-administer less amphetamine than impoverished rats (Bardo *et al.* 2001). Although the exact neural mechanism responsible for the enrichment-induced decrease in amphetamine self-administration remains to be elucidated, these findings suggest that stimulus enrichment may serve as a protective factor in stimulant abuse. This protection may be most apparent among high SS, as these individuals seem to require a greater optimal level of stimulus arousal than low SS. In any case, these results illustrate the potential utility of using information derived from controlled studies in laboratory animals to understand the biological linkage between SS and drug abuse vulnerability in humans.

2.2. *Non-Drug Alternative Reinforcers for High Sensation Seekers*

There is little doubt that the mesolimbic DA reward pathway has evolved in mammals as a critical neural substrate underlying the motivation to seek out and consume primary reinforcers, such as food, water and sexual encounters. In addition, the mesolimbic DA system seems to play a vital role in SS or novelty seeking behavior (Bardo *et al.* 1996). To the extent that both novelty and drugs of abuse activate the same mesolimbic DA system, this would suggest that stimuli that are high in sensation value would be most effective in substituting for drug reward. Moreover, since high SS have the greatest need for novelty and are willing to take the most risk to obtain novelty, perhaps the high sensation stimuli would be more effective in reducing drug use among high SS than low SS. This notion has led some investigators to develop more effective drug abuse prevention messages that specifically target high-risk SS (Donohew *et al.* 1991; Palmgreen *et al.* 2001). In addition, formative research using factor analysis and discriminant function analysis is beginning to provide comprehensive information on the kinds of activities high SS participate in (D'Silva *et al.* 2001). This latter work has shown that high SS can be discriminated from low SS on the basis of two factors, active-adventure and conflict-combat. This information may be especially useful for improving the effectiveness of drug abuse prevention interventions.

Pre-clinical evidence from laboratory animals has corroborated the basic idea that natural reinforcers and high sensation stimulus materials may be effective interventions for reducing drug self-administration, at least temporarily. For example, Nader and Woolverton (1991) demonstrated that when rhesus monkeys were given a choice between intravenous cocaine vs. food pellets (4 pellets), the frequency of cocaine choice was nearly 100%. When the number of food pellets was increased, frequency of cocaine choice decreased to below 50%. This decrease in cocaine choice could be partially overcome by increasing the dose of cocaine; however, when the number of food pellets was high (16 pellets), high doses of cocaine did not increase drug choice above 50%.

Other research has shown that the availability of a sweet drinking solution is effective in reducing drug intake in laboratory animals. For example, when given sucrose in addition to their daily ration of food, rats consumed less of an oral morphine solution than when given food alone (Kanarek & Marks-Kaufman 1988). This effect of sucrose was consistent across time. Rats given alternate weeks of exposure to sucrose consistently decreased consumption of the morphine solution when sucrose was available and increased consumption when the sucrose was removed. In addition, a sweet solution has been shown to decrease acquisition of intravenous cocaine self-administration in rats (Carroll & Lac 1993) and oral phencyclidine self-administration in rhesus monkeys (Campbell & Carroll 2000).

Much like the effect of food or a sweet solution in laboratory animals, alternative non-drug reinforcers also can reduce drug self-administration in humans. For example, studies indicate that abstinent alcoholics (Yamamoto *et al.* 1991) and opiate addicts (Morabia *et al.* 1989) crave and consume large amounts of sweet foods and beverages. In addition to non-drug reinforcers such as food, drug self-administration can also be reduced by money. Both heroin and cocaine self-administration have been altered as a function of the amount of money concurrently available (Comer *et al.* 1998; Hart *et al.* 2000). To date, however, there has not been a systematic investigation into the possibility that these non-drug reinforcers would differ in their efficacy to decrease drug self-administration between high and low SS.

3. Individual Differences and Prevention

The work in neurogenetics and neurobiology by Bardo and others offers support and even suggests avenues for studies of human communication and health behavior change. Also pointing toward approaches to prevention is the work of Caspi and colleagues (Caspi *et al.* 1997), who have identified what they call "risky personality types." They followed a cohort in New Zealand from age three ($n = 1{,}037$) to age 21 ($n = 961$). By age 21, they were measured on four health-risk behaviors: alcohol dependence, violent crime, risky sexual behavior, and dangerous driving habits. Persons displaying each of these characteristics had lower scores on scales indicating a need for safety and higher scores on those indicating a need for novelty. Individuals having a "risky personality" configuration at age 18 had displayed similar temperaments at age 3.

On the basis of data collected throughout the study, Caspi and associates (1997) suggest that "the origins of a personality type at risk for health behaviors may be found early in life and . . . the type stabilizes during adolescence" (p. 1061). They emphasized the importance of designing programs specifically to reach individuals on the basis of their different needs. This was the same conclusion arrived at independently by communication researchers concentrating on prevention of risky health behaviors (Reviewed in Donohew *et al.* 2003).

Hoyle *et al.* (2002) have also found positive correlations between measures of SS and every risk factor measured (such as deviance, perceived peer use of marijuana, and perceived family use of marijuana) and negative correlations with all protective factors measured (such as absence of depression, quality of home life, religiosity, and perceived sanctions against marijuana use).

3.1. Individual Differences Model of Information Exposure

It has been proposed that the search for novelty (e.g. Cloninger *et al.* 1996; Zuckerman 1979, 1994) is a fundamental survival behavior, in which detection of novel stimuli leads to alerting the system for fight or flight. Thus, as noted by Zuckerman (1979), novel stimuli can be either sources of reward or threats to survival.

A number of years ago, Donohew and associates began to examine the proposition that if novel stimuli bring about alerting responses, similar effects should occur when such stimuli are in the form of messages delivered either through the media or interpersonally, such as in a classroom (Bardo *et al.* 1996; Donohew *et al.* 1980, 1994; Zimmerman, Donohew *et al.* 2003).

Given that individuals who are higher SS are more likely to engage in drug use, risky sex, and other behaviors which can endanger their health, design of persuasive messages with novel components might be expected to attract and hold the attention of this prime target audience for prevention campaigns and might result in greater behavior change than had previously been accomplished (Donohew *et al.* 1991). Thus, sensation seeking has implications both on the preliminary alerting stage at which attention is attracted to a message, and on behavioral responses to the message itself. Donohew and colleagues contend that message choices frequently are made without awareness on the part of the individual, with novelty, movement, or other features of the messages triggering primary mechanisms, such as the reticular activating system (Donohew 1998; Donohew *et al.* 1980). Investigation of this hypothesis led to a series of laboratory and field experiments that began in 1985 and that continue today.

Much of the extensive series of experiments and field studies on improving the effectiveness of public health campaigns has been guided by an activation model of information exposure (for a review, see Donohew *et al.* 1998) in which the level of need for novelty and sensation is a fundamental component in the process of attending, affecting the likelihood that a stimulus in the form of a message will attract and hold the attention of any given individual. The model draws on Zuckerman's brain reward model of SS and treats messages as sources of stimulation that compete for attention with other stimuli in an individual's environment. It posits that messages with high sensation value are required in order to attract and hold the attention of individuals who are high SS. The model offers propositions about information choice behaviors, based on cognitive and activation needs. The central assumption of the theory is that human beings have individual levels of need for stimulation at which they are most comfortable, and that attention is a function primarily of an individual's level of need for stimulation and the level of stimulation provided by a stimulus source. From this, it is deduced that if individuals do not achieve or maintain this state upon exposure to a message, it is very likely that they will turn away and seek another source of stimulation that helps them achieve the desired state. If activation remains within some acceptable range, however, individuals are most likely to continue exposure to the information.

Palmgreen and Donohew (in press) define the sensation value of a message as the ability to elicit sensory, affective, and arousal responses. Messages high in sensation value should be more attractive to high SS, whereas low SS should prefer low sensation value messages. More recent versions of the model employ Zuckerman's Sensation Seeking Scale as a measure of need for stimulation and Everett and Palmgreen's (1995) Sensation Value Scale to measure the sensation dose of a message.

Early in the prevention studies, Bardo joined the project. His animal research involving novelty seeking and exploration of its neurobiological foundations (described earlier in this chapter) provided neurochemical validation not available in the human behavior studies. Bardo and Mueller (1991) noted that the re-conceptualization of SS as a brain reward model is important because the newer formulations place less emphasis on the differences between substances of abuse (e.g. stimulants and depressants) and instead focus on their common reward value. In recent years, Zimmerman also joined the project. He has extended the research to include impulsive decision-making as described below.

3.2. Impulsive Decision-Making

Impulsivity — an impulsive decision-making style — and SS are considered related personality traits (Buss & Plomin 1975; Eysenck & Eysenck 1977, 1978; Zuckerman *et al.* 1993). Zuckerman (1994) suggests that "while [impulsivity is] not an equivalent or supra-ordinate of sensation seeking, [it] is a highly related trait, particularly in its non-planning and risk-taking aspects." One of the five factors on the Zuckerman-Kuhlman Personality Questionnaire is labeled impulsive SS and is made up of impulsivity and SS items. However, Zimmerman and Donohew (1996) observe that impulsivity and SS are only moderately correlated[1] and view impulsive decision-making as one end of a continuum of decision-making styles. The styles vary from a consistently very rational decision-making style to one that is consistently impulsive. Zimmerman proposes that while rational decision-makers use beliefs about consequences of their actions, impulsive decision-makers use non-cognitive cues, including affective and physiological cues (as opposed to merely ignoring consequences), to make decisions.

Impulsive decision-making has been a component of the classroom interventions, but until a study currently underway, not of the media interventions. The information exposure

[1] Zimmerman's 11-item decision-making style scale has been shown to be moderately correlated with Eysenck's (1977) impulsivity scale (correlations of 0.31–0.65 in three samples of 100–650 high school students) and is more strongly related to risky sexual behavior (unpublished data). Internal consistency is generally in the 0.7–0.8 range and is comparable to that of the Eysenck scale, with a similar one-year test-retest correlation in high school students of approximately 0.5.

and impulsive decision-making models have guided numerous prevention interventions, many of which are described in more detail below.

3.3. Preliminary Studies

Characteristics of adolescents and young adults more likely to become drug users were identified in a study of students in grade seven through 12 (Donohew *et al.* 1990). Among students in the study, SS median scores rose sharply with the onset of puberty in the middle school years, then they leveled off near the end of high school. High SS were twice as likely as low SS to report that they drank beer and liquor during the past 30 days, three times as likely to have used marijuana, and seven times as likely to have used cocaine. SS were more likely in a laboratory experiment to attend to messages presented in a more novel (narrative) format than those presented in other formats.

3.4. Laboratory Experiments

3.4.1. Message sensation value and sensation seeking In other early studies in their program of research, Donohew *et al.* (1991) tested the proposition that messages designed to appeal to the needs for novelty and sensation of high SS would be more effective in reaching and influencing this high-risk group. They conducted a series of laboratory experiments in which both high SS and low SS subjects were exposed to anti-drug public service announcements (PSAs) either high in sensation value or low in sensation value. Sensation value was defined as the degree to which formal audiovisual features (such as more unusual format, greater frequency of editing techniques, faster and more frequent movement, and more intense music) and content of a televised message elicited sensory, affective, and arousal responses. Two PSAs were designed for a target audience 18–22 years of age, one aimed at high SS and the other at low SS. During formative research in preparation for designing the PSAs, a large number of commercials and PSAs were reviewed. From these, nine commercials and three PSAs were selected for testing. The PSAs ranged in adjudged sensation value from a peaceful, slow-paced ad for spaghetti sauce to an intense music video format automobile ad.

Individuals chosen from a randomly generated list of registered voters and from communication classes were administered Form V of the SSS and divided into high SS and low SS groups who were shown the commercials and PSAs and participated in two-hour focus group interviews on what they liked and disliked about the ads. The formative research revealed characteristics of televised messages having differential appeal for high SS and low SS young adults (aged 18–22). High SS reacted more positively to more novel and intense messages, preferring more novel formats and unusual use of formal features (such as extreme close-ups and heavy use of sound effects), high levels of suspense, tension, drama, and emotional impact and more intense, hard-edged music than low SS. The low SS preferred more closure at the end of a story, whereas high SS preferred drawing their own conclusions.

On the basis of the extensive formative research, characteristics of messages having differential appeal to high SS and low SS young adults were identified. These characteristics are: (1) novel, creative, unusual; (2) complex; (3) intense (auditory and visual); (4) physically arousing (exciting, stimulating); (5) emotionally strong; (6) graphic; (7) ambiguous; (8) unconventional; (9) fast-paced; and (10) suspenseful (Donohew *et al.* 1991; Palmgreen *et al.* 1991).

Thus, the degree to which formal and content features of a message elicit sensory, affective, and arousal responses was expected to substantially determine the likelihood that a message would be attended long enough for the persuasive content of a message to be understood. Two 30-second anti-drug PSAs were prepared, each involving the same concept, but one designed to appeal to high SS and the other to appeal to low SS.

Laboratory tests of the effects of the two versions on 18–22 year-old high SS and low SS were conducted on 207 young Caucasian and African-American adults. Participants in the study were divided into high SS and low SS groups on the basis of a median split on the sum of 37 non-drug-related items on the SSS, Form V. Within each group, participants were randomly assigned to a low sensation value (LSV), a high sensation value (HSV), or a control condition and shown televised messages. The experimental programming began with four minutes of a story from CBS Sunday Morning, followed by two 30-second commercials, then the HSV or LSV prevention PSA, three more 30-second ads, and the PSA again. Measures were taken on behavioral intention to call a hotline, attitude toward drugs, and drug use scales. All procedures were the same for the control condition except that the PSAs were not included in the content that was viewed.

The principal finding was an interaction effect between message sensation value and SS on the primary dependent measure, intent to call a hotline. The HSV message was more effective in getting high SS to call a hotline and the LSV message was more effective with low SS subjects. The strongest impact on behavioral intention was on high SS users of illicit drugs in the previous 30 days. Overall, viewers of the HSV messages reported more negative attitudes toward drugs than those viewing the LSV messages compared to their control groups.

The experiments, although providing evidence that message sensation value could be employed to reach high SS, involved forced-choice situations, in which viewers were instructed to attend messages. Would the same hold true in situations in which attending to other stimuli instead of watching television was an option?

3.4.2. Living room study The next study (Lorch *et al.* 1994) examined effects of message and program sensation value, SS, and drug use on visual attention to televised anti-drug public service announcements (PSAs) among 318 young adults given the opportunity one at a time to read from print media selections or to watch a half-hour television program including two presentations of the test PSAs, or both in a simulated living room. High and low SS were randomly presented television programs high or low in sensation value. High SS paid significantly greater attention to HSV programming and to PSAs embedded in such programming. Low SS, although paying greater attention to PSAs embedded in LSV programs, also watched a considerable portion of HSV programming.

A major implication of the study was that campaigns designed to reach high SS, the primary target audience, also would reach low SS, but programs not high in sensation value would not reach the prime target audience, high SS. The authors concluded that program sensation value and SS are important factors to be considered in the placement of televised drug abuse prevention messages.

3.4.3. Hotline study From a prevention perspective, the question now became the following: In a free-choice situation, i.e. an actual television campaign, could members of the primary target audience (high SS) be sufficiently motivated to call a hotline for further information? The field study (Palmgreen *et al.* 1995) involved designing five different televised drug abuse prevention messages (PSAs) intended to appeal to high SS, conducting surveys to determine programs primarily watched by high SS, purchasing time for the PSAs in the programs most frequently chosen, and producing a guidebook, "A Thrillseeker's Guide to the Bluegrass," which explained the concept of SS and offered a guide to activities available that might appeal to them. An effort was made to include all dimensions of the SS.

The campaign included 615 purchased television spots and 887 donated television spots. Data from pre- and post-campaign surveys, within-campaign surveys, and surveys of hotline callers all indicated that the campaign was successful in reaching high SS. In the hotline surveys, 73% of those calling were above the median on SS, 32% reported they had used illicit drugs in the past 30 days compared to 23% of the general population, and recall of message content was highest among high SS.

3.4.4. Peers, Sensation Seeking, and drug and alcohol use We have also investigated the prospective influence of individual adolescents' SS tendency and the SS tendency of named peers on the use of alcohol and marijuana, controlling for a variety of interpersonal and attitudinal risk and protective factors (Donohew *et al.* 1999). Data were collected from a cohort of adolescents ($n = 428$; 60% female) at three points in time, starting in eighth grade. Respondents provided information about SS, the positive character of family relations, attitudes toward alcohol and drug use, perceptions of the use of alcohol and marijuana by their friends, perceptions of influence by their friends to use alcohol and marijuana, and their own use of alcohol and marijuana. In addition, they named up to three peers, whose SS and alcohol and drug-use data were integrated with data from the respondents to allow for tests of hypotheses about peer clustering and substance use. Structural equation modeling analyses revealed direct effects of the SS of the peers on use of both marijuana and alcohol by the adolescent respondents own SS 2 years later. An unexpected finding was that the individual's own SS had indirect (not direct) effects on drug use two years later. These findings indicate the potential importance of SS as a characteristic on which adolescent peers cluster. Furthermore, the findings indicate that, beyond the influence of a variety of other risk factors, peer SS contributes to adolescents' substance use.

3.4.5. Two-cities study Recently completed studies have offered the most substantial evidence to date of our ability to bring about behavior change through media interventions. One was a study involving a controlled interrupted time-series design evaluating the effectiveness of televised anti-marijuana PSA campaigns targeted at high SS adolescents in Lexington, Kentucky, and Knoxville, Tennessee (Palmgreen *et al.* 2001). Specifically, television anti-marijuana HSV PSAs, designed and developed through formative research, were shown from January through April 1997, in Lexington. Similar campaigns were conducted from January through April 1998 in both Lexington and Knoxville. Beginning eight months prior to the first Lexington campaign and ending eight months after the 1998 campaigns, personal interviews (self-administered on laptop computers) were conducted with 100 randomly selected students in each county during each month (total $n = 6{,}400$). The population cohort followed was initially in the 7th through 10th grades and in the 10th grade through 7 months after high school graduation at completion of the study. Full sample medians were used to separate the Knox and Fayette monthly samples into groups of high and low SS. Time series regression analyses indicated that all three campaigns not only arrested, but actually reversed, upward developmental trends in past 30-day marijuana use among high SS adolescents. For example, 30-day use among Knoxville high SS rose in linear fashion from 16.6% initially to 33.0% over the 20-month pre-campaign period, then fell nearly 9% from the start of the campaign to the completion of data gathering 12 months later. The drop in the proportion of high SS using marijuana was 26.7%. The Lexington results were similar. The first campaign also reversed a strong upward trend in 30-day use among high SS. Time series regression models indicated that all changes in slopes were statistically significant ($p < 0.003$). It also should be noted that in both cities, low SS marijuana use was at the bottom of the charts, and did not show developmental increases over time.

3.5. Human Immunodeficiency Virus (HIV) Studies

Over the last nine years, Zimmerman, Donohew, and colleagues have been conducting studies in HIV prevention that focus on SS and impulsive decision-making. Findings will be presented here in four sections: correlation studies in the U.S., international correlation studies, mediation analyses, and intervention results.

3.5.1. Correlation studies in the U.S. In several studies conducted in U.S. populations over the past eight years, we assessed the relation between SS and impulsive decision-making on the one hand and sexual risk-taking on the other. In a sample of 2,949 ninth-grade students in 17 high schools in two mid-western U.S. cities, surveys were administered measuring SS and impulsive decision-making and their separate and combined relations to a number of indicators of sexual risk-taking. Measures of sexual risk-taking included intentions to have sex, ever had sex, number of lifetime sexual partners, been pregnant or caused a pregnancy, used a condom, had unwanted sex when drunk, had unwanted sex under pressure, used alcohol by self or partner before sex. Strong associations were found among sexually active students high on both SS and impulsive decision-making and weakest associations among students low on both measures (Donohew *et al.* 2000).

In 30 rural Kentucky high schools, 2,845 students completed surveys concerning demographic information, connection to family and school, attitudes, norms, and self-efficacy related to sex, communication with parents, religiosity, as well as sexual behavior. All putative risk and protective factors, including impulsive decision-making (odds ratio = 3.026) and SS (odds ratio = 2.697) were related to ever having had sexual intercourse. In a multivariate logistic regression analysis, however, results indicated that neither impulsive decision-making nor SS were significant predictors of having had sex; significant predictors were older age, being male, early puberty or physical development, attitudes about teens having sex, problem drinking, number of boyfriends or girlfriends, and perceived peer sexual activity. Among those sexually active, SS and impulsive decision-making were related to lifetime number of sexual partners ($r = 0.37$ and 0.22, respectively; Zimmerman, Hansen *et al.* 2003).

Three additional studies have assessed the relation of SS and impulsive decision-making in high-risk populations of U.S. adolescents: adolescent males in juvenile detention, adolescent females living in inner city housing developments, and young men who have sex with men. Results indicate relations of either or both variables to sexual risk taking in all three samples. Both were related to number of lifetime partners and unprotected anal intercourse, and impulsive decision-making was related in a multiple regression analysis to unprotected anal intercourse. Both young men who have sex with men variables were related to ever having had sex for the adolescent females living in inner city housing developments, and both were related to number of lifetime partners in this group. For the adolescent males in detention facilities, SS and impulsive decision-making were both related to age at first sexual experience, with higher SS and impulsive decision-makers having sex at an earlier age. Also in this group, high SS used condoms less frequently with both their girlfriends and other partners (Zimmerman, Cupp, Atwood *et al.* 2003).

3.5.2. International correlation studies Recently, Zimmerman and associates conducted research with 1,401 Ethiopian high school students to assess the impact of social clubs against acquired immunodeficiency syndrome (AIDS) on HIV-related knowledge, attitudes, self-efficacy, intentions, and behavior. SS and impulsive decision-making were also measured similarly as in U.S. surveys. Results indicated that while only 10.8% of the students had had sex, those who were impulsive decision-makers or high sensation-seekers were more than twice as likely to have done so, and in a multiple logistic regression equation, both variables were significant, with odds ratios of nearly 2 and significance levels of < 0.001.

Zimmerman and colleagues conducted a pilot study in Harare, Zimbabwe, with 141 students to assess some of the same variables and relations (Zimmerman, Cupp, Hansen *et al.* 2003). Most (61%) of the students were in Form 1 (equivalent to 8th grade), the rest in Form 2 (equivalent to 9th grade). Most students (57%) were female, all were Black, and their ages ranged from 12 to 16 (with a median of 13.75). Most (79%) reported having had no boyfriends or girlfriends, and 12% reported having had sexual intercourse. At the bivariate level, gender (females were more likely to have had sex, 21.4% vs. 3.8%) and high SS (odds ratio = 1.97) were related to having initiated sexual intercourse, and in a multiple logistic regression model, only gender was statistically significant (odds ratio = 5.85) while SS was not significant but had a meaningfully large odds ratio (1.85).

Results in South Africa only partially confirmed the U.S., Zimbabwe, and Ethiopia findings. Neither SS nor impulsive decision-making was related to ever having had sex in a sample of 646 9th and 10th grade South African students, 34.5% of whom had had sex. There was a significant relation, however, between SS and number of lifetime partners for those who were sexually active, with a correlation of 0.19, $p = 0.002$ (Karnell *et al.* 2003).

3.5.3. Mediation analyses Zimmerman and colleagues are currently involved in developing a model (which includes the individual difference variables of SS and impulsive decision-making) to help understand and explain sexual risk-taking. Two manuscripts recently submitted for publication assess the direct and indirect effects of these two variables on initiation of sexual activity and condom use, in relevant sub-samples over a 12–18 month time period of the adolescent sample in 17 urban high schools described earlier. The model proposes that social structural variables lead to environmental and individual difference variables; these in turn, lead to attitudes, perceived norms, and self-efficacy. In the final steps of the model, these social psychological variables, lead to intention; intention, along with situational variables and preparatory behaviors, leads to behavior.

Analyses involving the relation of SS and impulsive decision-making to initiation of sexual intercourse suggest several indirect, but no direct relations of the two individual difference variables to the outcome. SS was related to initiation of sexual activity through two of the social psychological variables, perceived norms and attitude about early sexual activity. High SS perceived that more of their friends were sexually active and had more positive attitudes about early sexual activity, than low SS. Both of these variables were, in turn related to intentions to have sex, and subsequently, initiation of sexual activity. Impulsive decision-making was related to initiation of sexual activity through two of the social psychological variables as well, attitudes about early sexual activity and refusal self-efficacy. Impulsive decision-makers had more positive attitudes about early sexual activity and lower refusal self-efficacy, both of which were related to intentions and behavior.

Analyses involving the relation of SS and impulsive decision-making to condom use revealed largely similar findings. Once again, effects of both individual difference variables were indirect rather than direct. SS was related to perceived friends' condom use and impulsive decision-making was related to attitudes about condoms and condom self-efficacy. High SS perceived that fewer sexually active friends used condoms; impulsive decision-makers had more negative attitudes about condoms and lower condom self-efficacy. These were all, in turn, related to condom use intentions and/or condom preparatory behaviors, and, ultimately to condom use.

3.5.4. Intervention results To date, four studies used SS and impulsive decision-making in the development of interventions to reduce risky sexual behavior. The first study, involving the 17 urban high schools discussed earlier (Zimmerman, Donohew *et al.* 2003) assigned schools to one of three conditions in a quasi-experimental design: (1) those receiving a 16-unit skills-based intervention, *Reducing the Risk*; (2) those receiving a curriculum adapted from it to include features designed to appeal to high SS and impulsive decision-makers, *Modified Reducing the Risk*; and (3) the schools' standard non-skills-based curricula as a comparison condition. The modified curriculum included more audio-visual materials, including short trigger films with teen-oriented music, involving peer facilitators in some of the lessons, introducing students to a young person living with HIV as a presenter for two of the lessons, using input from teens in creating more realistic, high risk-taking role plays for the classes to provide both greater involvement and rehearsal of responses, introducing more games and prizes into classroom exercises, and affording students a novel approach to the creation and observation of role-playing activities by incorporating video cameras into the classroom. Both of the skills-based curricula had significant, short-term impact on knowledge and response to sexual pressure. Those enrolled in the skills-based curricula also showed significant differences from the comparison group at the end of a year in initiation of sexual activity, but those adapted for higher SS did not show significant differences from the standard curriculum. It was speculated that failure of the *Modified Reducing the Risk* group to show differences from the other experimental group might have been a function of teacher, training, and population differences across schools. In designing for a follow-up study, a number of modifications were made to eliminate these possible differences.

There are preliminary results from a follow-up study involving nearly 3000 students in rural Kentucky high schools. A similar design was employed, in which schools were assigned to *Reducing the Risk, Modified Reducing the Risk*, and a comparison condition employing the schools' standard, non-skills-based curriculum. Follow-up data were collected at four to six months post-intervention and then again at 12–18 months post-intervention. Results indicate that both skills-based interventions had significant impact on attitudes toward waiting to have sex, knowledge, intention to have sex, initiation of sex, and refusal self-efficacy at either or both follow-up times. Additional analyses by individual scores on SS and impulsive decision-making are still in progress (Zimmerman, Clay *et al.* 2003).

Our research group's knowledge about high sensation seekers and impulsive decision-makers was drawn upon in conducting a pilot test of an alcohol and HIV prevention curriculum adapted from an American model and delivered to 9th grade students in five South African township schools (Karnell *et al.* 2003). The intervention was based on the "Project Northland" alcohol prevention curriculum developed at the University of Minnesota that was revised for use in South Africa. This randomized controlled trial of a 10-unit HIV and alcohol prevention curriculum (involving a total of 725 students in an intervention and control group) adapted from an American model demonstrated significant changes in HIV-related knowledge, HIV-related attitudes and intentions, and HIV and alcohol-related behavior among the 9th grade South African students. We found significant differences between students in the intervention and comparison groups in changes on several indicators, including intention to use a condom during the next three months, incidence of drinking during last sex, and self-efficacy of sex refusal.

In sum, the findings of the HIV study suggest that risk behavior interventions developed and tested in the West, after appropriate adaptation to the local cultural context, may bring about positive changes in risky behavior, attitudes, and intentions among school-going youth in other cultural settings. The strongest effects of the intervention tested in this study were found in HIV-related attitudes and intentions and HIV-related behaviors. All but one of the seven indicators in these areas, i.e. self-efficacy of condom use, changed in a desirable direction among intervention group students from pretest to posttest.

One additional intervention study, involving adolescent females in inner city housing developments, has taken an existing intervention (Sikkema *et al.* 2000) and modified it in ways expected to be more successful with impulsive decision-makers and high sensation seekers. Preliminary results indicate that, at six and/or twelve month follow-up, the psychosocial workshops and peer-led community activities led to increased knowledge about HIV/AIDS, increased condom self-efficacy, and lower intentions to have sex than those in the alternative (career intervention) group (Feist-Price *et al.* 2003).

4. Conclusion

Research described in this chapter differs significantly from other widely used approaches in studies of prevention of potentially harmful health behaviors in its fundamental assumptions about rational and non-rational approaches to behavior change. With support from animal studies involving the neurobiological bases of SS (and novelty) and impulsive decision-making, it is apparent that SS and impulsive decision-making play crucial roles in attention and persuasion. Thus, we have taken the position that they are complementary components of a decision-making process in humans that may or may not be rational. Generally weak results in earlier prevention studies which subscribe to rational models of decision-making may be attributed at least in part to the assumption in those studies that individuals carefully weigh possible choices and outcomes and rationally choose behaviors. It also has been at least implicitly assumed that messages are attended according to a similar heuristic. Yet, in the studies reported here, it seems apparent that the level of search for novelty in animals and for novelty and sensation in humans strongly influences what stimuli they attend, even when — in the case of humans — those stimuli are messages in the mass media or in the form of instruction in the classroom.

Thus, it can be argued that beyond the rational models of human behavior, the more primal forces reviewed here — novelty seeking, SS, and impulsive decision-making — should be considered both in the selection of primary audiences for prevention interventions and in the design of messages and other stimuli to reach them and bring about desired health behaviors. Further research is needed to better understand how to design messages for, impulsive decision-making and to better understand the direct and indirect effects of these forces on risky behaviors.

Acknowledgments

Research reported in this chapter was supported by Grant DA05312 from the National Institute on Drug Abuse (Michael Bardo, PI), Grant DA12964 from the National Institute on Drug Abuse (Michael Bardo, PI), Grant DA03462 from the National Institute on Drug Abuse (Lewis Donohew, PI), Grant 05312 from the National Institute on Drug Abuse (Lewis Donohew, PI; Philip Palmgreen and Elizabeth Lorch, Co-PIs, Grant DA06892 from the National Institute on Drug Abuse (Lewis Donohew, PI, Philip Palmgreen, Elizabeth Lorch, and William Skinner, Co-PIs), Grant AA10747 from the National Institute on Alcohol Abuse and Alcoholism (Lewis Donohew; PI, Rick Zimmerman, Co-PI), Grant DA04887 from the National Institute on Drug Abuse (Lewis Donohew, PI; Richard Clayton, Co-PI), Grant DA06892–08 from the National Institute on Drug Abuse (Lewis Donohew, PI; Philip Palmgreen, Elizabeth Lorch, and Rick Hoyle, Co-PIs), Grant R01-DA-12490 from the National Institute on Drug Abuse (Lewis Donohew, PI; Nancy Harrington, Rick Zimmerman, and Derek Lane, Co-Is); Grant R01-AA-10747 from the National Institute on Alcohol Abuse and Alcoholism (Rick Zimmerman, PI, Lewis Donohew, Co-PI), Grant R01-AA-013927 from the National Institute on Alcohol Abuse and Alcoholism (Rick Zimmerman, PI), Grant R01-MH-061187 from the National Institute on Mental Health (Rick Zimmerman, PI), Grant R01-MH-063705 from the National

Institute on Mental Health (Rick Zimmerman, PI, Phil Palmgreen Co-PI), and Grant R01-NR-008379 from the National Institute of Nursing Research (Rick Zimmerman, PI, Eric Anderman, Co-PI).

References

Bardo, M. T., Bowling, S. L., & Pierce, R. C. (1990). Changes in locomotion and dopamine neurotransmission following amphetamine, haloperidol, and exposure to novel environmental stimuli. *Psychopharmacology*, *101*, 338–343.

Bardo, M. T., Bowling, S. L., Robinet, P. M., Rowlett, J. K., Lacy, J. K., & Mattingly, M. (1993). Role of dopamine D1 and D2 receptors in novelty-maintained place preference. *Experimental and Clinical Psychopharmacology*, *1*, 101–109.

Bardo, M. T., Donohew, R. L., & Harrington, N. G. (1996). Psychobiology of novelty seeking and drug seeking behavior. *Behavioural Brain Research*, *77*, 23–43.

Bardo, M. T., & Hammer, R. P., Jr. (1991). Autoradiographic localization of dopamine D1 and D2 receptors in rat nucleus accumbens: Resistence to differential rearing conditions. *Neuroscience*, *45*, 281–290.

Bardo, M. T., Klebaur, J. E., Valone, J. M., & Deaton, C. (2001). Environmental enrichment decreases intravenous self-administration of amphetamine in female and male rats. *Psychopharmacology*, *155*, 278–284.

Bardo, M. T., & Mueller, C. W. (1991). Sensation seeking and drug abuse prevention from a biological perspective. In: L. Donohew, H. E. Sypher, & W. J. Bukoski (Eds), *Persuasive communication and drug abuse prevention* (pp. 209–226). Hillsdale, NJ: Lawrence Erlbaum.

Benjamin, J., Li, L., Patterson, C., Greenberg, B. D., Murphy, D. L., & Hamer, D. H. (1996). Population and familial association between the D4 dopamine receptor gene and measures of novelty seeking. *Nature Genetics*, *12*, 81–84.

Bennett, A. J., Lesch, K. P., Heils, A., Long, J. C., Lorenz, J. G., Shoaf, S. E., Champoux, M., Suomi, S. J., Linnoila, M. V., & Higley, J. D. (2002). Early experience and serotonin transporter gene variation interact to influence primate CNS function. *Molecular Psychiatry*, *7*, 118–122.

Bevins, R. A. (2001). Novelty seeking and reward: Implications for the study of high-risk behaviors. *Current Directions in Psychological Science*, *10*, 189–193.

Buss, A. H., & Plomin, R. (1975). *A temperament theory of personality development*. New York: Wiley.

Cabib, S., Algeri, S., Perego, C., & Puglisi-Allegra, S. (1990). Behavioral and biochemical changes monitored in two inbred strains of mice during exploration of an unfamiliar environment. *Physiology and Behavior*, *47*, 749–753.

Cador, M., Dulluc, J., & Mormede, P. (1993). Modulation of the locomotor response to amphetamine by corticosterone. *Neuroscience*, *56*, 981–988.

Campbell, U. C., & Carroll, M. E. (2000). Reduction of drug self-administration by an alternative non-drug reinforcer in rhesus monkeys: Magnitude and temporal effects. *Psychopharmacology*, *147*, 418–425.

Carrol, E. N., & Zuckerman, M. (1977). Psychopathology and sensation seeking in "downers," "speeders," and "trippers": A study of the relation between personality and drug choice. *The International Journal of the Addictions*, *12*, 591–601.

Carroll, M. E., & Lac, S. T. (1993). Autoshaping i.v. cocaine self-administration in rats: Effects of nondrug alternative reinforcers on acquisition. *Psychopharmacology*, *110*, 5–12.

Caspi, A., Harrington, H., Moffitt, T. E., Begg, D., Dickson, N., Langley, J., & Silva, P. A. (1997). Personality differences predict health-risk behaviors in young adulthood: Evidence from a longitudinal study. *Journal of personality and Social Psychology*, *73*, 1052–1063.

Cloninger, C. R., Adolfson, R., & Svrakic, N. M. (1996). Mapping genes for human personality. *Nature Genetics*, *13*, 3–4.

Cloninger, C. R., & Begleiter, H. (1990). *Genetics and biology of addiction*. New York: Cold Spring Harbor Press.

Comer, S. D., Collins, E. D., Wilson, S. T., Donovan, M. R., Foltin, R. W., & Fischman, M. W. (1998). Effects of alternative reinforcers on intravenous heroin self-administration by humans. *European Journal of Pharmacology*, *345*, 13–26.

Cools, A. R., & Gingras, M. A. (1998). Nijmegen high and low responders to novelty: A new tool in the search after the neurobiology of drug abuse liability. *Pharmacology, Biochemistry and Behavior*, *60*, 151–159.

Crabbe, J. C., Phillips, T. J., Buck, K. J., Cunningham, C. L., & Belknap, J. K. (1999). Identifying genes for alcohol and drug sensitivity: Recent progress and future directions. *Trends in Neuroscience*, *22*, 173–179.

Crusio, W. E., Schwegler, H., & van Abeelen, J. H. F. (1989). Behavioral responses to novelty and structural variation of the hippocampus in mice: I. Quantitative-genetic analysis of behavior in the open-field. *Behavioural Brain Research*, *32*, 75–80.

Donohew, L. (1998). Awareness, attention, and the tug of our primal past: Rethinking our target audiences for design of health messages. In: J. Trent (Ed.), *Communication: Views from the helm for the Twenty-First Century* (pp. 212–217). Needham Heights, MA: Allyn & Bacon.

Donohew, L., Helm, D., Lawrence, P., & Shatzer, M. (1990). Sensation seeking, marijuana use, and responses to drug abuse prevention messages. In: R. Watson (Ed.), *Drug and alcohol abuse prevention* (pp. 73–93). Camden, NJ: Humana Press.

Donohew, L., Hoyle, R., Clayton, R., Skinner, W., Colon, S., & Rice, R. (1999). Sensation Seeking and drug use by adolescents and their friends: Models for marijuana and alcohol. *Journal of Studies on Alcohol*, *60*, 622–631.

Donohew, L., Lorch, E. P., & Palmgreen, P. (1991). Sensation seeking and targeting of televised anti-drug PSAs. In: L. Donohew, H. Sypher, & W. Bukoski (Eds), *Persuasive communication and drug abuse prevention* (pp. 209–226). Hillsdale, CA: Lawrence Erlbaum.

Donohew, L., Lorch, E. P., & Palmgreen, P. (1998). Applications of a theoretic model of information exposure to health interventions. *Human Communication Research*, *24*, 454–468.

Donohew, L., Palmgreen, P., & Duncan, J. (1980). An activation model of information exposure. *Communication Monographs*, *47*, 295–303.

Donohew, L., Palmgreen, P., & Lorch, E. P. (1994). Attention, sensation seeking, and health communication campaigns. *American Behavioral Scientist*, *38*, 310–332.

Donohew, L., Palmgreen, P., Zimmerman, R., Harrington, N., & Lane, D. (2003). Health risk takers and prevention (pp. 165–170). In: D. Romer (Ed.), *Reducing adolescent risk*. Thousand Oaks, CA: Sage.

Donohew, L., Zimmerman, R., Cupp, P., Novak, S., Colon, S., & Abell, R. (2000). Sensation seeking, impulsive decision-making, and risky sex: Implications for risk-taking and design of interventions. *Personality and Individual Differences*, *28*, 1079–1091.

D'Silva, M. U., Harrington, N. G., Palmgreen, P., Donohew, L., & Lorch, E. P. (2001). Drug use prevention for the high sensation seeker: The role of alternative activities. *Substance Use and Misuse*, *36*, 373–385.

Ebstein, R. P., Novick, O., Umansky, R., Priel, B., Osher, Y., Blaine, D., Bennett, E. R., Nemanov, L., Katz, M., & Belmaker, R. (1996). Dopamine DA receptor (D4DR) exon III polymorphism associated with the human personality trait of novelty seeking. *Nature Genetics*, *12*, 78–80.

Everett, M., & Palmgreen, P. (1995). Influence of sensation seeking, message sensation value, and program context on the effectiveness of anti-cocaine PSAs. *Health Communication, 7*, 225–248.

Eysenck, S. B. G., & Eysenck, H. J. (1977). The place of impulsiveness in a dimensional system of personality description. *British Journal of Social and Clinical Psychology, 16*, 57–68.

Eysenck, S. B. G., & Eysenck, H. J. (1978). Impulsiveness and venturesomeness: Their position in a dimensional system of personality description. *Psychological Reports, 43*, 1247–1255.

Fagan, J. F., Singer, L. T., Montie, J. E., & Shepherd, P. A. (1986). Selective screening device for the early detection of normal or delayed cognitive development in infants at risk for later mental retardation. *Pediatrics, 78*, 1021–1026.

Fahlke, C., Lorenz, J. G., Long, J., Champoux, M., Suomi, S. J., & Higley, J. D. (2000). Rearing experiences and stress-induced plasma cortisol as early risk factors for excessive alcohol consumption in nonhuman primates. *Alcoholism: Clinical and Experimental Research, 24*, 644–650.

Feist-Price, S., Zimmerman, R. S., Cupp, P. K., Abell, R., & Goldsmith, S. (2003). *Results of a peer-led HIV prevention intervention for African-American adolescents in inner city housing developments*. Unpublished manuscript, University of Kentucky.

Flay, B. R., & Sobel, J. L. (1983). The role of mass media in preventing adolescent substance abuse. In: T. J. Glynn, C. G. Leukefeld, & J. P. Lundford (Eds), *Preventing adolescent drug abuse: Intervention strategies*. NIDA Research Monographs Series (47).

Haertzen, C. A., Kocher, T. R., & Miyasato, K. (1986). Reinforcements from the first drug experience can predict later drug habits and/or addiction: Results with coffee, cigarettes, alcohol, barbiturates, minor and major tranquilizers, stimulants, marijuana, hallucinogens, heroin, opiates and cocaine. *Drug and Alcohol Dependence, 11*, 147–165.

Hart, C. L., Haney, M., Foltin, R. W., & Fischman, M. W. (2000). Alternative reinforcers differentially modify cocaine self-administration by humans. *Behavioral Pharmacology, 11*, 87–91.

Hooks, M. S., Colvin, A. C., Juncos, J. L., & Justice, J. B. (1992). Individual differences in basal and cocaine-stimulated extracellular dopamine in the nucleus accumbens using quantitative microdialysis. *Brain Research, 587*, 306–312.

Hooks, M. S., Juncos, J. L., Justice, J. B., Meiergerd, S. M., Poviock, S. L., Schenk, J. O., & Kalivas, P. W. (1994). Individual locomotor response to novelty predicts selective alterations in D1 and D2 receptors and mRNAs. *Journal of Neuroscience, 14*, 6144–6152.

Hoyle, R., Stephenson, M., Palmgreen, P., Lorch, E., & Donohew, L. (2002). Reliability and validity of a brief measure of sensation seeking. *Personality and Individual Differences, 32*, 401–414.

Johnson, E. O., van den Bree, M. B. M., & Pickens, R. W. (1996). Subtypes of alcohol-dependent men: A typology based on relative genetic and environmental loading. *Alcoholism: Clinical and Experimental Research, 20*, 1472–1480.

Kanarek, R. B., & Marks-Kaufman, R. (1988). Animal model of appetitive behavior: Interaction of nutritional factors on drug seeking behavior. In: M. Winick (Ed.), *Control of appetite* (pp. 1–26). New York: Wiley.

Karnell, A., Cupp, P. K., Zimmerman, R. S., Feist-Price, S., & Bennie, T. (2003). *Efficacy of an alcohol and HIV prevention curriculum adapted for use in South Africa: Results of a pilot study in five township schools*. Manuscript submitted for publication.

Katz, M., & Belmaker, R. H. (1996). Dopamine D4 receptor (D4DR) exon III polymorphism associated with the human personality trait of novelty seeking. *Nature Genetics, 12*, 78–80.

Kelly, T. H., Delzer, T., Martin, C. A., Hays, L. R., Harrington, N. G., & Bardo, M. T. (1999). Behavioral effects of amphetamine and diazepam in high and low SS. Paper presented at the FASEB Summer Research Conference, Copper Mountain, CO.

Klebaur, J. E., & Bardo, M. T. (1999). Individual differences in novelty seeking on the playground maze predict amphetamine conditioned place preference. *Pharmacology, Biochemistry and Behavior*, *63*, 131–136.

Klebaur, J. E., Bevins, R. A., Segar, T. M., & Bardo, M. T. (2001). Individual differences in behavioral responses to novelty and amphetamine self-administration in female and male rats. *Behavioural Pharmacology*, *12*, 267–275.

Lorch, E. P., Palmgreen, P., Donohew, L., Helm, D., Baer, S. A., & D'Silva, M. U. (1994). Program context, sensation seeking, and attention to televised anti-drug public service announcements. *Human Communication Research*, *20*, 390–412.

Misslin, R., Ropartz, P., & Jung, L. (1984). Impairment of responses to novelty by apomorphine and its antagonism by neuroleptics in mice. *Psychopharmacology*, *82*, 113–117.

Mogenson, G. J., & Nielsen, M. (1984). Neuropharmacological evidence to suggest that the nucleus accumbens and subpallidal region contribute to exploratory locomotion. *Behavioral and Neural Biology*, *42*, 52–60.

Morabia, A., Fabre, J., Chee, E., Zeger, S., Orsat, E., & Robert, A. (1989). Diet and opiate addiction: A quantitative assessment of the diet of non-institutionalized opiate addicts. *British Journal of Addiction*, *84*, 173–180.

Murphy, D. L., Belmaker, R. H., Buchsbaum, M. S., Martin, N. F., Ciaranello, R., & Wyatt, R. J. (1977). Biogenic amine related enzymes and personality variations in normals. *Psychological Medicine*, *7*, 149–157.

Nader, M. A., & Woolverton, W. L. (1991). Effects of increasing the magnitude of an alternative reinforcer on drug choice in a discrete-trials choice procedure. *Psychopharmacology*, *105*, 169–174.

Netter, P., Hennig, J., & Roed, I. S. (1996). Serotonin and dopamine as mediators of sensation seeking behavior. *Neuropsychobiology*, *34*, 155–165.

Nicholls, B., Springham, A., & Mellanby, J. (1992). The playground maze: A new method for measuring directed exploration in the rat. *Journal of Neuroscience Methods*, *43*, 171–180.

Palmgreen, P., & Donohew, L. (in press). Effective mass media strategies for drug abuse prevention campaigns. In: W. J. Bukoski, & Z. Sloboda (Eds), *Handbook of drug abuse theory, science and practice*. New York: Plenum.

Palmgreen, P., Donohew, L., Lorch, E., Rogus, M., Helm, D., & Grant, N. (1991). Sensation seeking, message sensation value, and drug use as mediators of PSA effectiveness. *Health Communication*, *3*, 217–234.

Palmgreen, P., Donohew, L., Lorch, E. P., Hoyle, R. H., & Stephenson, M. T. (2001). Television campaigns and adolescent marijuana use: Tests of sensation seeking targeting. *American Journal of Public Health*, *91*, 292–296.

Palmgreen, P., Lorch, E. P., Donohew, L., Harrington, N. G., D'Silva, M., & Helm, D. (1995). Reaching at-risk populations in a mass media drug abuse prevention campaign: Sensation seeking as a targeting variable. *Drugs and Society*, *8*, 29–45.

Peeler, D. F., & Nowakowski, R. S. (1987). Genetic factors and the measurement of exploratory activity. *Behavioural and Neural Biology*, *48*, 90–103.

Piazza, P. V., Deminiere, J., Le Moal, M., & Simon, H. (1989). Factors that predict individual vulnerability to amphetamine self-administration. *Science*, *245*, 1511–1513.

Piazza, P. V., Deminiere, J. M., Maccari, S., Le Moal, M., Mormede, P., & Simon, H. (1991). Individual vulnerability to drug self-administration: Action of corticosterone on dopaminergic systems as a possible pathophysiological mechanism. In: P. Willner, & J. Scheel-Kruger (Eds), *The mesolimbic dopamine system: From motivation to action* (pp. 473–495). New York: Wiley.

Piazza, P. V., & Le Moal, M. (1998). The role of stress in drug self-administration. *Trends in Pharmacological Science*, *19*, 67–74.

Pierce, R. C., Crawford, C. A., Nonneman, A. J., Mattingly, B. A., & Bardo, M. T. (1990). Effect of forebrain dopamine depletion on novelty-induced place preference behavior in rats. *Pharmacology, Biochemistry and Behavior*, *36*, 321–325.

Rebec, G. V., Grabner, C. P., Johnson, M., Pierce, R. C., & Bardo, M. T. (1997). Transient increases in catecholaminergic activity in medial prefrontal cortex and nucleus accumbens shell during novelty. *Neuroscience*, *76*, 707–714.

Renner, M. J., & Rosenzweig, M. R. (1987). *Enriched and impoverished environments: Effects on brain and behavior*. New York: Springer-Verlag.

Rogers, E. M., & Storey, J. D. (1987). Communication campaigns. In: C. R. Berger, & S. H. Chaffee (Eds), *Handbook of communication science* (pp. 817–846) Newbury Park, CA: Sage.

Rosenblitt, J. C., Soler, H., Johnson, S. E., & Quadagno, D. M. (2001). Sensation seeking and hormones in men and women: Exploring the link. *Hormones and Behavior*, *40*, 396–402.

Saigusa, T., Tuinstra, T., Koshikawa, N., & Cools, A. R. (1999). High and low responders to novelty: Effects of a catecholamine synthesis inhibitor on novelty-induced changes in behaviour and release of accumbal dopamine. *Neuroscience*, *88*, 1153–1163.

Segal, B. (1976). Personality factors related to drug and alcohol use. In: D. J. Lettieri (Ed.), *Predicting adolescent drug abuse: A review of issues, methods, and correlates* (Publication Ms. ADM 77–299) Washington, DC: Department of Health, Education, and Welfare.

Severson, J. A., Randall, P. K., & Finch, C. E. (1981). Genotypic influences on striatal dopaminergic regulation in mice. *Brain Research*, *210*, 201–215.

Sikkema, K. J., Kelly, J. A., Winett, R. A., Solomon, L. J., Cargill, V. A., Roffman, R. A., McAuliffe, T. L., Heckman, T. G., Anderson, E. A., Wagstaff, D. A., Norman, A. D., Perry, M. J., Crumble, D. A., & Mercer, M. B. (2000). Outcomes of a randomized community-level HIV prevention intervention for women living in 18 low-income housing developments. *American Journal of Public Health*, *90*, 57–63.

Uhl, G., Blum, K., Noble, E., & Smith, S. (1993). Substance abuse vulnerability and D2 receptor genes. *Trends in Neuroscience*, *16*, 83–88.

Vadasz, C., Laszlovszky, I., De Simone, P. A., & Fleischer, A. (1992). Genetic aspects of dopamine receptor binding in the mouse and rat brain: An overview. *Journal of Neurochemistry*, *59*, 793–808.

Wills, T. A., Windle, M., & Cleary, S. D. (1998). Temperament and novelty seeking in adolescent substance use: Convergence of dimensions of temperament with constructs from Cloninger's theory. *Journal of Personality and Social Psychology*, *74*, 387–406.

Wise, R. A. (1998). Drug-activation of brain reward pathways. *Drug and Alcohol Dependence*, *51*, 13–22.

Yamamoto, M. E., Block, G. D., & Ishii, E. (1991). Food patterns among adolescents: Influence of alcohol consumption. *Alcoholism: Clinical and Experimental Research*, *15*, 359.

Young, W., Laws, E., Sharbrough, F., & Weinshilboum, R. M. (1986). Human monoamine oxidase: Lack of brain and platelet correlation. *Archives of General Psychiatry*, *43*, 604–609.

Zimmerman, R., & Donohew, L. (1996). Sensation seeking, impulsive decision-making, and adolescent sexual behaviors. Paper presented at the American Public Health Association, New York.

Zimmerman, R., Donohew, L., Sionean, C., Cupp, P., Feist-Price, S., & Helme, D. (2003). *Effects of a school-based, theory-driven HIV and Pregnancy Prevention Curriculum.*

Zimmerman, R., Hansen, G., Cupp, P., Donohew, L., Roberto, A., Dekhtyar, & Abner, E. (2003). *Predictors of early sexual initiation among rural adolescents*. Manuscript submitted for publication.

Zimmerman, R. S., Clay, C., Dekhtyar, O., Dudley, M., Atwood, K., Feist-Price, S., Cupp, P. K., & Ryans, C. (2003). *Alcohol and risky sexual behavior in three high-risk groups*. Unpublished manuscript, University of Kentucky.

Zimmerman, R. S., Cupp, P. K., Atwood, K., Dekhtyar, O., Feist-Price, S., & Hansen, G. (2003). An empirical test of a proposed multi-domain model of health-related behavior: Application to initiation of adolescent sexual behavior. Manuscript submitted for publication.

Zimmerman, R. S., Cupp, P. K., Hansen, G. L., Donohew, R. L., Dekhtyar, O., Roberto, A. J., & Abner, E. (2003). *The effects of a school-based HIV and pregnancy prevention program in rural Kentucky*. Unpublished manuscript, University of Kentucky.

Zimmermann, A., Stauffacher, M., Langhans, W., & Würbel, H. (2001). Enrichment-dependent differences in novelty exploration in rats can be explained by habituation. *Behavioural Brain Research, 121*, 11–20.

Zuckerman, M. (1979). *Sensation seeking: Beyond the optimal level of arousal*. Hillsdale, NJ: Lawrence Erlbaum.

Zuckerman, M. (Ed.) (1983). *Biological bases of sensation seeking, impulsivity, and anxiety*. Hillsdale, NJ: Lawrence Erlbaum.

Zuckerman, M. (1994). *Behavioral expressions and biosocial bases of sensation seeking*. Cambridge, UK: Cambridge.

Zuckerman, M., Kuhlman, D. M., Joireman, J., Teta, P., & Draft, M. (1993). A comparison of three structural models for personality: The big three, the big five and the alternative five. *Journal of Personality and Social Psychology, 65*, 757–768.

Part IV

Biological Bases of Personality:

A. Psychophysiological Analyses

Chapter 14

Neuroticism from the Top Down: Psychophysiology and Negative Emotionality

G. Matthews

> We should start from the top and work down, using the well-established psychological factors and considering how various biological systems may be involved in one or more of them
>
> (Zuckerman 1991: 424).

1. Introduction

There is near-universal agreement that neuroticism (N) is one of the most important human personality traits. The high N person is prone to anxiety, depression and other negative emotions, together with worry, mood swings and stress vulnerability. Conversely, the low N, emotionally stable person is calm and unworried. Studies of the nature of N focus on several of the issues central to Marvin Zuckerman's personality research: the biological basis of traits, their influence on learning and behavior, and their links with psychopathology. N has a substantial inherited component. Zuckerman (1991) estimates the broad heritability of the trait at about 0.40–0.60. Thus, N must influence brain development, so that meaningful differences between high and low N individuals should be evident in psychophysiological paradigms. Previously, theory has linked N to arousability of a reticulo-limbic-cortical system controlling emotion (Eysenck 1967; Eysenck & Eysenck 1985), or to sensitivity of brain systems for punishment and reward (Gray 1991; Pickering *et al.* 1997). It is believed that the brain systems underpinning N have profound influences on behavior, controlling the individual's ability to learn through conditioning, to function effectively in society, and to manage stressful encounters. Much evidence also implicates N in vulnerability to various emotional disorders (Zuckerman 1999), such as clinical anxiety and depression, although the causal paths between N as a vulnerability trait and symptomatology may not be straightforward (Matthews *et al.* in press).

On the Psychobiology of Personality
Edited by R. M. Stelmack

ISBN: 0-08-044209-9

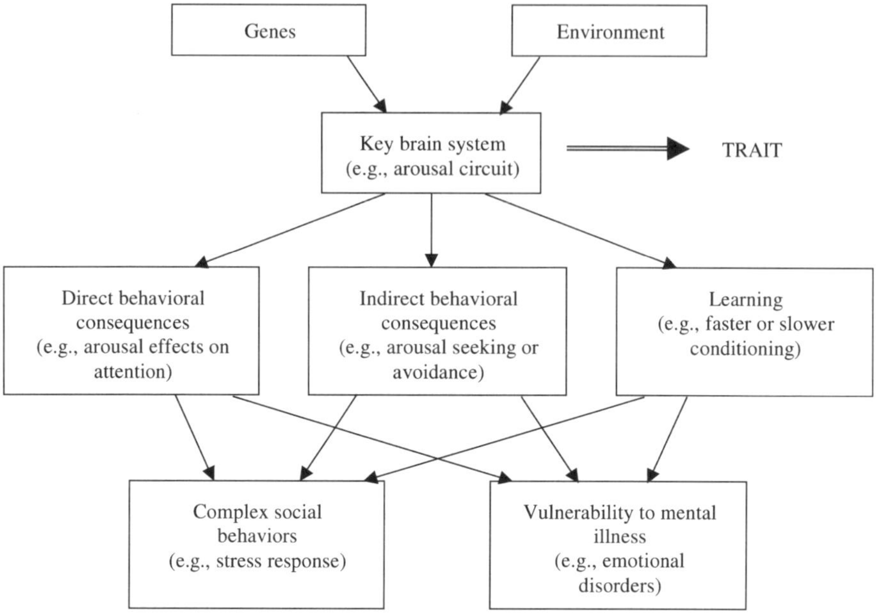

Figure 1: A bottom-up model for personality traits.

Traditional psychobiological theories of personality present a conceptually simple bottom-up model for understanding the emotional, behavioral and pathological consequences of neurotic personality (see Figure 1). Genes and environment interact to influence the structure and functioning of some key brain system that supports the trait. Individual differences in system function lead in turn to behavioral differences such as differential rates of learning. These behavioral attributes of personality generate individual differences in adaptation to life circumstances, that may be expressed either in variability in normal social behaviors, or in vulnerability to clinical disorder. For example, in Eysenck's (1967) theory, over-sensitivity of the emotional arousal circuit leads (among other consequences) to excessive emotionality that disrupts attention and performance, causing significant life difficulties for the high N person in stressful environments.

The attraction of the bottom-up approach is that it provides a single, unified theory of N that potentially explains a wide range of correlates of the trait, ranging from psychophysiological response to complex social behaviors. As Zuckerman (1991) discussed, the assumption is that N and other personality traits are *isomorphic* with brain systems. That is, each trait corresponds directly to a single brain system and, presumably, each discrete system supports a single trait. Thus, working upwards from a complete list of brain components would give a periodic table of traits that is essentially a brain map. Zuckerman (1991) argues cogently against the isomorphism assumption, as discussed further in the next section. Neuropsychological systems may participate in multiple behavioral functions that relate to different traits. Systems also frequently influence behavior interactively, rather than independently. In Zuckerman's analysis, there are no one-to-one mappings between traits and brain systems. Each trait is supported by multiple systems, and each system may contribute to multiple traits.

Zuckerman's psychometric studies (e.g. Zuckerman *et al.* 1993) recognize a hierarchical structure for traits that distinguishes relatively narrow, lower-level traits, such as impulsivity and sensation seeking, from the superfactors that constitute the basic dimensions of personality, such as N. Zuckerman's (1991) account of personality structure broadly favors the well-known Five-Factor Model with some differences in emphasis and detail, such as replacing (low) conscientiousness with a complex of psychoticism, impulsivity and unsocialized sensation seeking. Zuckerman (1991) suggests that narrow traits may often be closer to specific physiological systems than broad traits. As indicated by the opening quotation, he recommends that superfactors should be studied from the top-down. N probably relates to multiple systems that mediate different physiological and behavioral consequences of the trait.

The remainder of this chapter addresses the following issues. First, I will present a brief justification for Zuckerman's rejection of isomorphism, drawing on psychophysiological evidence, followed by a summary of Zuckerman's (1991) model for N. Next, I will argue that the non-isomorphism instantiated by the model may be extended by linking N to multiple cognitive processes as well as multiple neural systems. However, to do this forces recognition that different levels of explanation are required; I will introduce the tri-level explanatory framework of cognitive science to organize the many correlates of N. In the next section, I will outline my own cognitive-adaptive account of N. This theory accommodates several of Zuckerman's (1991) general principles, but with greater emphasis on cognitive processes and on the functional, adaptive significance of the behaviors typical of traits. I will conclude by summarizing Zuckerman's most distinctive contributions, and their relevance to the cognitive-adaptive theory of N.

2. The Failure of Isomorphism

2.1. Neuroticism from the Bottom Up

To appreciate Zuckerman's contribution, we must first appraise the leading bottom-up theories of N, those of Eysenck and Gray. Eysenck (1967), as we have seen, relates N to arousability of a system for emotion centered on the limbic system. The primary prediction is that, in stressful circumstances, N should be positively correlated with autonomic and cortical arousal. In fact (see Matthews & Gilliland 1999, 2001, for a full review), the evidence is only weakly supportive of this prediction. Although some authors (e.g. Gale *et al.* 2001) discern a trend towards higher cortical arousal in EEG data in high N persons, many well-designed studies fail to substantiate this result, or obtain complex interactions such that the effect of N depends on extraversion and situational factors. N fails to correlate with sensory evoked potential responses that might be expected to reflect arousal, although N is negatively correlated with latency of the P300 potential (Stelmack & Houlihan 1995). Similarly, studies using autonomic nervous system indicators such as electrodermal and electrocardiac response occasionally find stronger responses in higher N individuals, but there are numerous failures to confirm the prediction (e.g. Fahrenberg 1991). Indeed, there is a tendency for individuals high in N and trait anxiety to show reduced levels of electrodermal activity (Naveteur & Freixa i Baqué 1987; Wilken *et al.* 2000).

Gray's (e.g. 1991) theory starts from the assumption that trait anxiety, not N, is the causal influence on physiology and behavior, such that N is an amalgam of high anxiety and high impulsivity. However, in the more recent versions of the theory, N is aligned more closely with anxiety than with impulsivity, so that high N resembles trait anxiety, consistent with the high correlations observed between N and trait anxiety measures. In the best-known version of the theory, trait anxiety is governed by sensitivity of a behavioral inhibition system (BIS) that responds to threat signals by initiating behavioral freezing, orienting to the source of threat and increasing noradrenergic arousal. Thus, while the theory permits N to correlate with arousal response to threat, its main predictions concern the moderation of physiological and behavioral expressions of N by punishment signals. However, as with tests of the Eysenck theory, outcomes are mixed (Matthews & Gilliland 1999). For example, Stenberg (1992) found that trait anxiety (but not N) related to increased EEG beta activity in response to a negative emotional imagery condition, consistent with Gray's theory. Other studies have failed to confirm that N and/or trait anxiety moderate response to stimuli of negative valence (e.g. De Pascalis & Speranza 2000), or have found complex effects of personality that fail to conform to predictions from the Gray theory (e.g. Bartussek *et al.* 1996).

Thus, both the Eysenck and Gray theories fail to deal with what might be called the neurotic paradox. That is, the association between N and negative emotion is highly robust, and appropriately moderated by situational stress (Matthews *et al.* in press; Suls 2001). By contrast, although N relates to psychophysiological response on occasion, findings are weak and it is hard to isolate reliable moderator factors. It remains possible that an improved bottom-up theory might offer stronger support. Perhaps brain imaging techniques will isolate the key structures that control enhanced emotionality in high N persons. A small study reported by Canli *et al.* (2001), for example, found that N was positively correlated with brain activation to negative emotional stimuli in the middle frontal gyrus and middle temporal gyrus.

The latest version of Gray's theory (Corr 2002; Gray & McNaughton 2000) includes various substantial revisions. Trait anxiety (and hence N) is now linked to a fight-flight-freeze system (FFFS) as well as to the BIS, a system assigned a more constrained role than previously, in conflict resolution. Although states of fear (FFFS) and anxiety (BIS) are distinct, trait anxiety modulates both systems. Furthermore, the BIS may interact with the system for reward, the Behavioral Activation System (BAS), so that, contrary to Gray's earlier theory, trait anxiety and N may moderate response to reward signals (Corr 2002). The revised theory also places more emphasis on cognitive factors in response to threat. The BIS comprises various subsystems for evaluating and threat including some that are relatively primitive (amygdala), together with high-level, verbally mediated cognition. It is too early to say whether these modifications will improve the capacity of the theory to predict psychophysiological data (see Corr 2002, for an account of initial behavioral tests). However, the modifications are in line with Zuckerman's approach, in that they move away from a rigid isomorphism between brain systems and traits, they emphasize the interactive rather than independent influence of multiple systems, and they accommodate processes at different levels of abstraction from the neural substrate.

2.2. Turtles and Ladders: A Redescription of Neuroticism

Zuckerman's (1991) theory of neuroticism offers some reasons why N may not be straightforwardly correlated with autonomic arousal, even in stressful environments. In this section, I give a brief outline of the theory and its unique features. Zuckerman (1992) describes the oriental guru who portrays the world resting on a giant turtle. That turtle in turn stands on an even larger turtle, and from there on it is "turtles all the way down." The study of personality also requires turtles all the way down, in that multiple levels of understanding are needed. Zuckerman (1992) lists his seven turtles, from the top down, as traits, social behavior, conditioning, physiology, biochemistry, neurology and genetics. He states that "Each turtle is a distinct creature to be studied at its own level, but for a complete understanding of any turtle one cannot ignore the next turtle down who forms its foundation" (1992: 681).

In Zuckerman's (1991) psychophysiological theory, the somewhat different stack of turtles shown in Figure 2 supports N. The lowest level of genotype supports the next level of brain chemistry, feeding upward to influence successively, psychophysiology, emotion, cognition, trait emotionality and the supertrait of N. Two biochemical influences may be distinguished in the figure, relating to noradrenergic arousal and benzodiazepines (BZ), respectively. On the one hand, high levels of norephinephrine and epinephine produce autonomic arousal that may be a concomitant of anxiety along with other negative emotions such as anger. (These catecholamines may also influence the supertraits of Psychoticism-Impulsive Unsocialized Sensation Seeking (P-ImpUSS) and, via anger, Aggression-Hostility). The rather indirect role of noradrenergic arousal in anxiety may explain the weakness of the correlations between N and autonomic arousal. The other basis for N are the BZs that potentiate the effects of yet another neurotransmitter, γ-aminobutyric acid (GABA) that produces inhibition of brain nuclei implicated in anxiety, such as the locus coeruleus. More specifically, high N might be related to a decreased concentration of BZ receptors in areas such as amygdala, or to a high level of endogenous BZ inverse agonists, that may bias the identification of emotional arousal as anxiety.

At higher levels, there is integration of the multiple psychobiological systems. Zuckerman *et al.* (1999) suggest that N relates not just to negative effect, but also to congruent motivations and cognitions. Ball and Zuckerman (1990) developed the Generalized Reward and Punishment Expectancies Scale to assess these cognitive-motivational factors. These authors reported that N was significantly positively correlated with punishment expectancies ($r = 0.36$). The correlation between N and reward expectancies was smaller ($r = -0.26$), but also significant. A subsequent study (Zuckerman *et al.* 1999) confirmed and extended this result. Zuckerman (1999) elaborated the role of cognition in negative affective states in the context of anxiety and mood disorders. Distortions in self-beliefs, accompanied by biases in evaluation, selection attention and memory, appear to be an intrinsic part of disorders characterized by excessive negative affect. Similar but smaller magnitude cognitive distortions are also observed in normally functioning high N persons (Matthews *et al.* in press). However, as Zuckerman (1999) discusses, the causal role of cognitions in mood disorder is debatable, although diatheses may include aspects of cognition such as low self-esteem and attributional styles that promote self-blame and hopelessness.

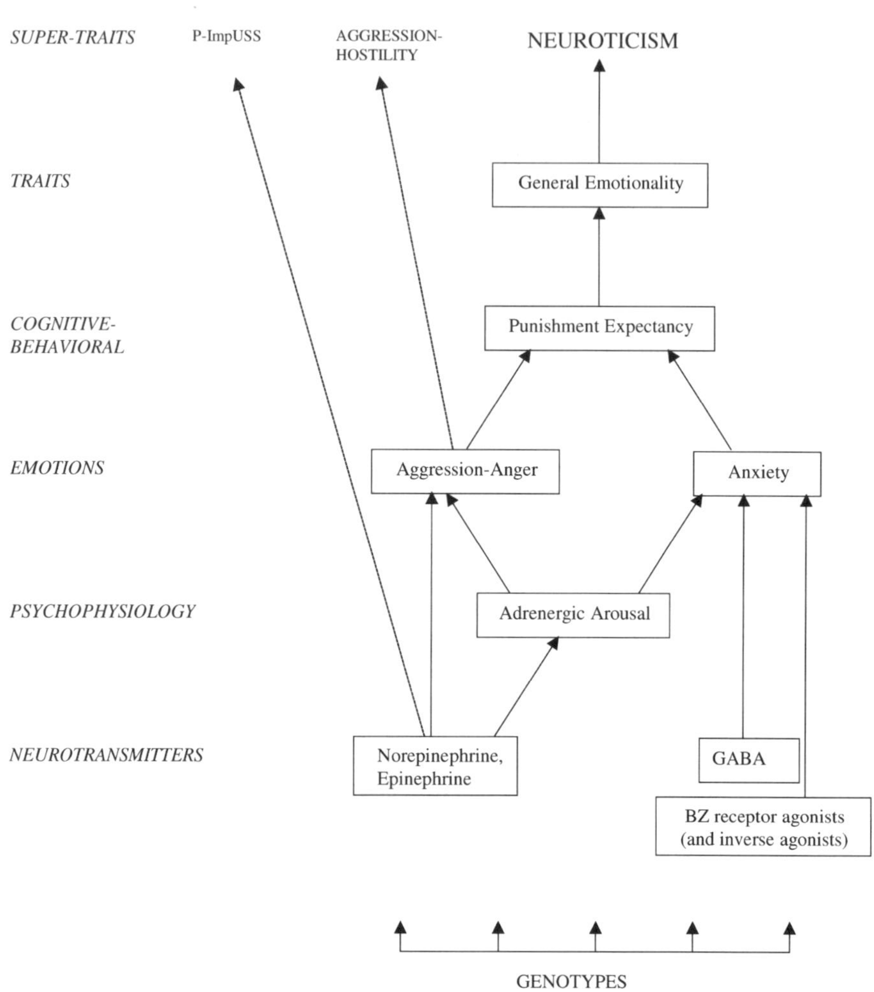

Figure 2: An outline of Zuckerman's (1991) psychobiological model for neuroticism.

Zuckerman (1991) also discusses the possible role of individual differences in emotion-regulation in N. There is an important theoretical issue here that is often neglected. Negative emotionality might simply reflect a gain parameter in some brain system such as, in Eysenck's formulation, the limbic system. That is, the higher N person outputs more negative emotion in response to some given threat or punishment stimulus. Alternatively, negative emotionality may relate to the extent of cortical regulation of lower-level systems for emotion, such as the amygdala. Regions of the frontal lobes may regulate the experience and behavioral expression of emotion generated subcortically. Zuckerman (1991) cites evidence that damage to orbitofrontal cortex and to the cingulate cortex reduces anxiety and N. These regions are critical to cortical modulation of limbic circuits, as evidenced by studies that link voluntary control of attention to threat stimuli to the anterior cingulate cortex

(Matthews *et al.* 2000a, b). N may relate not just to basic emotionality, but also to poor top-down regulation of subcortical systems, generating anxious impulsivity and lability of mood along with negative emotion. Consistent with the non-isomorphism principle, poor frontal control may also be linked to the P-ImpUSS trait.

Thus, Zuckerman (1991) presents a picture of the trait of neurotic emotionality emerging from several sources, including biochemical influences on emotion, subcortical structures such as the amygdala, cortical emotion-regulation systems such as orbitofrontal cortex, and various higher-order cognitive processes. This analysis successfully accommodates the manifold but elusive psychophysiological correlates of N, the neuropsychological evidence and the cognitive correlates of the trait. It is also consistent with emerging evidence from molecular genetics that suggests that associations between traits and specific polymorphisms are of small magnitude (Munafo *et al.* 2003). However, the analysis also sidesteps an important conceptual issue. How far can the personality model represented in Figure 2 be seen in reductionist terms, such that the operation of each level can be fully described in terms of constructs at the next level down, e.g. reducing expectancies to emotions, and emotions to neural processes? Alternatively, are the levels fully or partially autonomous, such that cognition, for example, is an emergent process that cannot be adequately described in terms of neural function? In the next section, I will describe a ladder of explanation taken from cognitive science that addresses this issue, softening some conceptual distinctions, e.g. between neurology and neurochemistry and sharpening others, e.g. between physical processes and information-processing.

3. A Cognitive Science Perspective on Neuroticism

3.1. Three Levels of Explanation

The classical theory of cognitive science (Pylyshyn 1999) distinguishes three levels of explanation for cognitive phenomena. The lowest level is the *biological* level, which provides a physical hardware account, in terms of neural function. The next level is the *symbol* or *syntactic* level, which specifies a virtual cognitive architecture supporting information-processing. The highest level is the *knowledge* or *semantic* level, which refers to the meaning of processing with respect to personal goals. This level requires an understanding in terms of intentionality and active adaptation to an external environment. Each level constitutes a viable explanatory framework: whether higher levels can be reduced to a biological account is left open. Matthews (2000) argues in favor of explanatory pluralism, i.e. limited but incomplete explanation of higher-level constructs in terms of lower-level constructs.

The tri-level framework provides alternate, complementary accounts of emotion (Matthews *et al.* 2000a, b). Emotion may be seen as an output of brain systems such as amygdala (biological explanation). Alternatively, emotion may be a product of symbolic computations such as appraising a stimulus as a threat (symbol-processing explanation). Thirdly, emotion may follow from assignation of personal meaning to an event, as described by Lazarus' (1999) transactional theory of emotion (knowledge-based explanation). Consequently, individual differences in emotionality may be variously explained in terms of neural function, computational accounts of cognition, or assignation of personal meaning.

3.2. Multiple Explanations for Correlates of Neuroticism

The tri-level cognitive science framework (Pylyshyn 1999) suggests a systematic approach to understanding the various empirical correlates of N and other traits (Matthews 1997, 2000). Different kinds of study are informative about different levels. Psychophysiological and neurochemical studies, exemplified by Zuckerman's work, delineate multiple attributes of neural functioning that contribute to the trait, but do not fully explain its behavioral expressions. Studies that relate N to specific information-processing operations allow specification of individual differences at the symbol-processing level. Traits may relate to parameters of the *functional architecture*: that is, properties of the memory stores, communication channels and other processing structures that support real-time computation (Matthews 2000). Studies of higher-level cognitions and thinking, such as those inspired by Lazarus' (1999) model of stress and emotion, link N to social-cognitive constructs, such as self-concept, personal goals and coping.

In previous reviews (e.g. Matthews 1999; Matthews & Dorn 1995; Matthews *et al.* 2000a, b; Zeidner & Matthews 2000) I have described some of the discrete cognitive correlates of N that may be allocated to symbol-processing or knowledge levels of explanation. One of the difficulties of human performance research is that the influence of external factors such as stressors and personality traits is often open to differing explanations. Some effects on performance are rightfully attributed to changes in basic information-processing functions, such as speed of execution of a particular computation, or changes in memory and attentional capacity. Other effects are strategic in nature, associated with changes in the person's understanding of the task, its personal relevance and the coping options the task situation affords. Thus, it is often unclear whether changes in selective attention, for example, reflect changes in functioning of the cognitive architecture, or changes in strategy and task goals. With this caution in mind, I next illustrate some cognitive correlates of N.

Much of the work that allows N to be related to basic information-processing comes from studies of trait anxiety, but, as Zuckerman (1999: 68) states, "The correlations of N with most trait anxiety tests are high enough to equate these two dimensions." A series of studies conducted by Derryberry and Reed (e.g. 1997, 2001) have identified various biases in attention associated with trait anxiety. Anxious individuals are slow to disengage attention from threatening stimuli, a process that may contribute to the well-known bias in selective attention exhibited by anxious individuals, although strategic processes may also influence this bias (Matthews & Wells 1999). In addition, anxiety relates to narrowing of attentional focus, evidenced by enhanced detection of local but not global targets, and to resistance to distraction. These multiple attentional mechanisms may be linked to attributes of the cognitive architecture because each can be linked to a specific neural system. These include attentional circuits in left posterior and left anterior cingulate, areas identified by Zuckerman (1991) as implicated in anxiety and N. Anxiety and N have also been linked to biases in implicit and explicit memory (e.g. Martin *et al.* 1983), but the data are less consistent than in the case of selective attention. Anxiety also relates to biases in thinking and verbal processing, such as interpreting ambiguous words and making predictive inferences, that serve to maintain awareness of threat (Calvo & Castillo 2001).

Other research links N and anxiety to self-regulative constructs at the knowledge level. Matthews *et al.* (2000a, b) identify low self-efficacy and self-esteem, pessimism in judgment and negative self-appraisals as constructs of this kind. In addition, neurotic individuals show preferences of coping strategies such as self-blame that are often ineffective, or even counterproductive. Furthermore, high N individuals display potentially dysfunctional styles of metacognition, that is, awareness and control of internal thoughts. N is linked to meta-worry (worry about worry), that promotes rumination and generalized anxiety, and to excessive monitoring of mood. Matthews and Wells (1999) argue that the deficits in attention and working memory typically associated with trait anxiety and N derive from these processes. High N individuals tend to cope with demanding tasks by allocating attention to self-referent executive processing which diverts attentional resources from the task at hand.

Thus, Zuckerman's (1991) analysis of N may be extended by seeing the trait as distributed both within and across levels of explanation. To fully capture the essence of neurotic personality, we need to relate N to multiple constructs at each level. Broadly, the trait encompasses sensitivity of physiological processes supporting negative emotion, bias in information-processing routines that assign codes for threat to stimulus representations, and personal meanings characterized by themes of personal inadequacy and insecurity. Zuckerman's (1991) major contribution is to show how N is distributed across multiple aspects of neural function. Additionally, N may be distributed across multiple information-processing components and higher-order cognitions.

4. From the Top Down: Adaptation and Neuroticism

The distributed account of neuroticism presented here may appear descriptively rich, but lacking the conceptual clarity of bottom-up theories. If N cannot be equated with any single brain system, how can we develop a coherent theory of the trait? In this section, I will outline an adaptive theory of N. The basic assumption is that the multifarious correlates of N gain coherence not from any common neurological foundation, but from common functional properties.

4.1. Individual Differences in Adaptation to Threat

The essence of the cognitive-adaptive theory proposed by Matthews (e.g. 1999) is that traits represent individual differences in styles of handling the key challenges of human life. People must make choices (consciously or not) about how much to compete or cooperate with others, how much effort to invest in activities geared towards short- and long-term gain, and so on. As Goldberg (1990) has suggested, the Big Five may represent the individual's orientation towards the areas of power, emotion, love, work and intellect. Each one of these major adaptive choices is too far-reaching to be supported by a single process alone. For example, to function successfully as an extravert requires biasing of multiple processes at all three of the cognitive science levels of description (Matthews 1999). Extraversion requires reward sensitivity and tolerance of high levels of stimulation (directly controlled by neural processes), attentional and linguistic capabilities for managing conversation (properties of the cognitive architecture) and personal confidence and proactive coping tendencies (knowledge level constructs).

Next, I will discuss how N may relate to individual differences in adaptation to threat.[1] The adaptive value of fear and anxiety as a motivator of self-protective behaviors such as escape has been widely discussed in the evolutionary psychological literature (e.g. Buss 1999; Marks & Nesse 1994). The organism that fails to respond quickly and effectively to stimuli such as dangerous animals and heights will not to survive to pass on its genes, so that fear responses to various threats constitute a set of inherited, species-typical mechanisms. However, individual differences in adaptation are not a simple matter of variation in the strengths or sensitivities of these mechanisms. As Zuckerman (1991) discusses, individual differences in human anxiety revolve primarily around social fears such as being criticized or rejected, rather than physical threats. Thus, picturesque anecdotes of people frightened by bears, snakes and even serpentine coils of rope are of dubious relevance to understanding personality.

Social threats are different in kind from the traditional physical threats in several key respects. First, social threats often develop over extended time periods, such as days or months, so there is less of an adaptive premium on rapid response; reflection on the threat may be advantageous. Second, social threats are often ambiguous: an apparently critical remark may be unintended to be so, or it may be an attempt at humor. Furthermore, malicious individuals may disguise their hostile intentions in order to perpetrate fraud or trickery. Thus, pattern-recognition mechanisms of the type that may drive response to spiders and snakes are ineffective, because there is no fixed template for the threat stimulus. Third, social threats often come from familiar people with whom the person threatened has a continuing relationship.[2] Over-sensitivity to physical threats carries few costs, but over-sensitivity to others is potentially damaging, in that the threat-sensitive person may be seen as paranoid, timid or hostile, depending on the exact response. Fourth, socially threatening situations often have an aspect of challenge to them, in that they offer potential benefits beyond negation of the threat. Evaluation during a formal test or examination is both threatening and potentially advantageous. Successful handling of personal criticism may lead to greater acceptance by others. Fifth, while a saber-toothed tiger may be assumed to be uniformly dangerous, social situations vary in the costs and gains they afford, and a strategy that works for one type of situation may be ineffective in another.

The complex nature of social threats implies that there may be a variety of viable strategies for adaptation. One strategy is avoidance of situations where one may be criticized or threatened, coupled with efforts to stay with secure places and people. Such a strategy entails a sensitive mental radar to detect the first signs of danger, including vigilant watchfulness and reflection on whether seemingly innocuous events are really as they seem, together

[1] Neuroticism, especially its depressive components, may also relate to orientation towards negative but non-threatening events such as those involving loss or harm. Susceptibility to frustration and anger is a further aspect of N. However, I focus on threat here as most of the experimental studies have used threat stimuli.

[2] Perceived threats of this kind may begin within infant-caregiver interactions, as explored by recent research relating attachment theory to personality (e.g. Stein *et al.* 2002).

with behavioral caution and readiness to engage in actions that may pre-empt or anticipate potential threats. A second strategy is to downgrade the significance of potential threats until the nature of the hazard is apparent, and then take appropriate action, which may involve direct confrontation of the threat, or even turning the situation to personal advantage. This strategy requires some "selective blindness" in avoiding distraction by ambiguous stimuli, coupled with skills for managing the threat at the point it becomes overt. Both strategies have advantages and disadvantages. The first, threat-avoidant strategy carries costs of wasting time and effort on managing threats that may never materialize, together with benefits related to avoiding danger or being prepared for it. The second strategy has the complementary costs of lack of readiness to react to an unexpected threat, and benefits of conserving resources for other activities and potentially gaining from meeting the threat head-on.

4.2. A Cognitive-Adaptive Theory of Neuroticism

Matthews (1999), Matthews *et al.* (in press) relates N to preferences for threat-management strategy. Rather than emphasize variation in overall threat sensitivity, it is supposed that handling threat is a major concern for all individuals. Where people differ is in the extent to which their first line of defense is to avoid threatening encounters, or to confront the threat directly. High N individuals may prefer avoidance and anticipation of threat, whereas low N persons are more disposed to accept direct exposure to threat. It is emphasized that these are preferences: the strategy chosen to handle a specific threat depends on a multitude of factors including previous learning, other concurrent motivations, mood state and various situational factors that influence the likely outcome of the strategy. Furthermore, neither strategy is seen as universally more adaptive than the other; how effective the strategy proves to be depends on the situation, and on the person's ability to "make it work for them" in the specific situation.

The adaptive hypothesis allows the common functional goal of threat handling to serve as the principle that unifies the various correlates of N. At the biological level of explanation, we have seen that, as described by Zuckerman (1991) and others, N correlates weakly with autonomic arousal, and with reactivity of structures such as amygdala that control negative emotionality and sensitivity to punishment stimuli. This low-level emotional reactivity is adaptive for an organism geared towards threat avoidance, in that even weak threat stimuli will activate the Behavioral Inhibition System described by Gray (1991), enhancing attention to potential threats that might otherwise be overlooked. By contrast, the low N organism that is prepared to wait until the threat becomes more salient gains through not having to divert attention and resources to dealing with weak threats that may not in fact materialize.

Those cognitive correlates of high N that reflect parameters of the cognitive architecture, i.e. basic processing components, may support the same adaptive strategies. We have seen that trait anxiety (and hence N) relate to several independent attentional processes such as slow disengagement from sources of threat and narrowed attentional focus in threatening conditions (Derryberry & Reed 1997, 2001; Matthews *et al.* 2000a, b). Although these processes are linked to specific brain areas, they must be understood at the symbol-processing level, as computations performed on abstracted representations (Matthews 2000).

Together, these attentional characteristics of negative emotionality may serve to maintain attention on potential threats, a strategy that is adaptive if the person aims to forestall dangerous encounters through anticipatory evasion. Conversely, the opposite set of biases may be potentially adaptive for the low N person following a direct-action strategy. As several studies show (e.g. Derryberry & Reed 2001; Fox *et al.* 2001), the low anxious person does not ignore threat, in that threat stimuli engage attention as quickly as they do in anxious individuals. However, less time is allocated to threat processing, given that attention disengages relatively quickly. Thus, the low N person may be more effective in maintaining ongoing activities and flexibility of attention in threatening environments, as for example, in continuing a conversation with a person of suspect motives.

At the knowledge level, the distinct styles of self-regulation of individuals high and low in N also support the mode of adaptation to threat. The high N person over-appraises threat, lacks self-confidence and is inclined to cope through emotion-focus and avoidance (e.g. Matthews *et al.* 2000a, b; Suls 2001). Thus, self-regulation is prone to be driven by the goal of maintaining personal security and the strategy of taking precautions to avoid the feared situation. By contrast, the more confident low N individual is likely to give relatively more priority to goals other than maintaining safety, and to engage in task-focused coping, in support of the more action-oriented adaptive style.

This analysis also offers a contrasting view to the hypothesis that negative emotion is a direct consequence of individual differences in neural functioning. Susceptibility to negative affect may be distributed across multiple levels of processing, including sensitivity of brain systems and neurochemistry, bias in the encoding of stimuli as threatening, and high-level social cognitions. Again, isomorphism breaks down both between and within levels of explanation. For example, evidence from experimental studies of stress demonstrates that changes in negative affect relate to multiple aspects of appraisal and coping (Matthews *et al.* 2002). Consistent with Lazarus' (1999) view that emotions signal the personal adaptive significance of interactions with the environment, the negative emotionality associated with N may represent an integration of multiple cognitive and neural biases.[3] Suls (2001) aptly refers to a neurotic cascade comprising multiple processes that link N to stress vulnerability.

4.3. *The Role of the Situation*

So far, I have described how the multiple attributes of individuals high and low in N may support different styles of adaptation to threat. However, in line with the interactionist approach to personality, the role of the situation is also important, for three reasons. The situation controls the efficacy of threat management strategies, calls for contextualized skills, and interacts dynamically with personal characteristics.

First, the adaptiveness of different strategies varies with the nature of the situation. The avoidant strategies of the high N person are likely to be most adaptive when the situation

[3] It is an open question whether or not negative emotionality has adaptive significance beyond signaling typical adaptive status. To the extent that negative emotion motivates attempts at mood-regulation, sensitivity to negative moods may support the adaptation of avoiding threatening situations that elicit anxiety and other stress responses.

is characterized by disguised, subtle or delayed threats, calling for vigilance and awareness of subtle cues. Conversely, the low N person is at an advantage in situations of clear and present danger, when hypervigilance for threat is redundant, and the emotion-focused coping strategies typical of the high N person divert attention from the immediate task, leading to performance deficits (Matthews & Wells 1999). Thus, personality relates to a preference for situations congruent with the preferred threat-management strategy, and high N individuals in fact tend to be under-represented in occupations characterized by stress and overt danger (Matthews 1999). In Zuckerman's words (1991: 402), "A neurotic searches for familiar and safe situations and people."

Second, successful adaptation often depends not on basic processing capabilities, but on learned cognitive and motor skills that are fine-tuned to the demands of particular environments. Thus, although the package of processing biases associated with N may sometimes have direct adaptive implications, processing biases often operate indirectly, through biasing skill acquisition (Matthews 1999). For example, social anxiety is characterized by coping behaviors (safety behaviors) specific to social interaction, such as gaze aversion and holding tight to objects to prevent shaking (Wells 2000). Matthews and Wells (1999) argue that bias in selective attention may not be solely a product of involuntary biases directly driven by parameters of the cognitive architecture, but also of learned skills for monitoring environments for specific threats.

Third, person-situation interaction is dynamic. The skills and processing biases that support the neurotic adaptation influence the person's situational exposure. Most simply, the neurotic person tends to avoid the feared situation, leading to loss of opportunity to develop direct threat-management skills. Behavioral avoidance also serves to maintain beliefs that the feared situation is threatening and beyond the individual's control (Wells 2000). Matthews (1999) suggests that the lower-level biases in neural function and information-processing operate as a platform for a more dynamic self-regulative system, as shown in Figure 3. In the high N individual, cognitive skills (e.g. maintaining awareness of danger), self-knowledge (e.g. lack of self-efficacy in confronting threat) and behavioral adaptations (avoidance of feared situations) tend to be mutually reinforcing, contributing to personality stability. As Zuckerman (1991: 124) states, "people who are prone to negative emotional states may elicit either avoidance or hostility in others, thereby confirming their views that people are basically unfriendly, or that they are worthless, or that the world is a threatening and frightening place." Dysfunctional cycles of person-situation interaction that lead to gross distortions of self-cognition may be especially important for the development and maintenance of anxiety and mood disorders (Matthews & Wells 1999). Although high N is not necessarily maladaptive in itself, it carries the risk of harmful and potentially pathological patterns of social interaction.

5. Conclusions

Zuckerman's (e.g. 1991) work on N has made a lasting contribution, especially to understanding the neurological bases of the trait. Much of this work fits comfortably into the mainstream of biological theories of personality, supporting the insights of Eysenck and Gray. However, I will conclude by highlighting three important principles

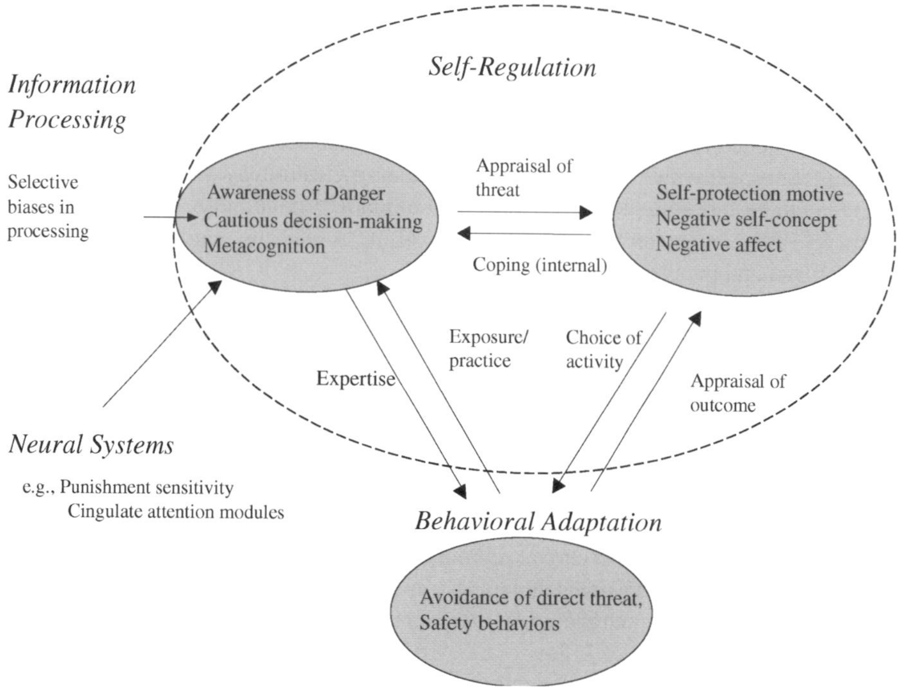

Figure 3: A dynamic cognitive-adaptive model for neuroticism.

that separate Zuckerman's stance from that of other biologically oriented theories, and provide a basis for integrating a psychophysiological perspective on N with cognitive perspectives.

The first principle is that brain systems and traits are non-isomorphic, so that the traditional bottom-up approach of placing a single trait on the foundation of a single brain system is over-simplified. Zuckerman's position that N is modestly linked to multiple brain systems helps to explain the weakness of the psychophysiological evidence for the Eysenck and Gray theories of N noted by Matthews and Gilliland (1999), while also encouraging researchers to pursue more subtle psychophysiological hypotheses. I have expanded the non-isomorphism principle here through application of the three levels of explanation of cognitive science. Just as N does not appear to correspond to any single brain process, so the trait also has multiple correlates at the symbol-processing and knowledge levels of explanation. Non-isomorphism applies in a different sense also: N is not isomorphic with any single level. Studies of neuroscience, of information-processing, and of high-level cognition and personal meaning all have an essential role in understanding the nature of neurotic personality.

Second, animal models are relevant only to the extent that functionally equivalent behaviors may be identified across different species. In the case of N, "One problem with animal models of fear is that the neurotic kind of fear in humans concerns social threat rather than threat of physical punishment (pain)" (Zuckerman 1991: 43). Thus, animal models are useful but incomplete. The cognitive-adaptive model I have presented here implies that the utility of animal models may be restricted to the lower levels of analysis of N. The expression of N as a self-regulative trait, characterized by distinct styles of appraisal and coping, may require a uniquely human-oriented perspective.

Third, like all biological psychologists, Zuckerman (1991) emphasizes genetic influences on traits, while also acknowledging the importance of gene-environment interaction. He also points out some limitations of evolutionary psychological approaches to personality. ". . . speculation about the adaptive values of these traits during the millions of years they have been evolving in our hominid ancestors is pointless unless we can understand the biological mechanisms that are *currently* mediating them" (Zuckerman 1991: 41). It is critical to distinguish adaptation in the sense of an inherited mechanism for handling a specific environmental challenge from adaptation more generally defined as a strategy for furthering attainment of a person's goals within a given environment (Matthews 1997). In this broader sense, adaptations may be learned rather than innate, and they may be directed towards socio-cultural goals rather than towards biological challenges. The cognitive-adaptive account of N (Matthews 1997) concerns this second sense of adaptation: understanding N requires attention to the costs and benefits of the styles of social behavior and information-processing associated with the trait. How inherited adaptations play into this wider adaptive process is an important question for future research.

Fourth, Zuckerman's perspective on person-situation interaction is subtler than the common stance of seeing situations simply as moderators of personality effects on behavior (see Endler & Parker's 1992, critique). In particular, personality traits relate to choices of situations and people, so that N relates to choosing the safe and familiar (Zuckerman 1991). Understanding such choices is critical to the cognitive-adaptive model, and the knowledge level of analysis in particular informs understanding of how safety goals may be especially powerful in guiding the behavior of high N persons. The interactionist perspective is also essential for understanding trait development. The high N or distress-prone child's preferences for clearly non-threatening situations may be critical in building skills for recognizing and finding safety, at the expense of acquiring skills for dealing directly with (predominantly social) threats.

In conclusion, Zuckerman's (1991) call to understand traits from the top down represents an important challenge to bottom-up theories that assume isomorphism between traits and brain systems. In this chapter, I have suggested that the cognitive-adaptive perspective on traits (Matthews 1999) extends Zuckerman's primarily biological analysis of N into the cognitive domain. It is proposed that N is not a direct expression of any brain system. Instead, the trait describes individual differences in strategies for adaptation to threat, with neurotics favoring strategies that avoid or pre-empt threat. Multiple processes to be understood in terms of the neural and cognitive architectures and higher-level social cognition support the individual's preferred strategy. The negative emotionality of the high N person is an emergent attribute of these multiple processes. The key task for future research is a functional analysis, to understand how individual differences in neurotic behavior relate to different adaptive outcomes across potentially threatening situations.

References

Ball, S. A., & Zuckerman, M. (1990). Sensation seeking, Eysenck's personality dimensions and reinforcement sensitivity in concept formation. *Personality and Individual Differences, 11*, 343–353.

Bartussek, D., Becker, G., Diedrich, O., Naumann, E., & Maier, S. (1996). Extraversion, neuroticism, and event-related potentials in response to emotional stimuli. *Personality and Individual Differences, 20*, 301–312.

Buss, D. M. (1999). *Evolutionary psychology: The new science of mind*. Boston: Allyn & Bacon.

Calvo, M. G., & Castillo, M. D. (2001). Bias in predictive inferences during reading. *Discourse Processes, 32*, 43–71.

Canli, T., Zhao, Z., Kang, E., & Gross, J. (2001). An fMRI study of personality influences on brain reactivity to emotional stimuli. *Behavioral Neuroscience, 115*, 33–42.

Corr, P. J. (2002). J. A. Gray's Reinforcement Sensitivity Theory: Tests of the joint subsystem hypothesis of anxiety and impulsivity. *Personality and Individual Differences, 33*, 511–532.

De Pascalis, V., & Speranza, O. (2000). Personality effects on attentional shifts to emotional charged cues: ERP, behavioural and HR data. *Personality and Individual Differences, 29*, 217–238.

Derryberry, D., & Reed, M. A. (1997). Motivational and attentional components of personality. In: G. Matthews (Ed.), *Cognitive science perspectives on personality and emotion* (pp. 443–473). Amsterdam: Elsevier.

Derryberry, D., & Reed, M. A. (2001). A multidisciplinary perspective on attentional control. In: C. L. Folk, & B. S. Gibson (Eds), *Attraction, distraction and action: Multiple perspectives on attentional capture* (pp. 325–347). New York: Elsevier.

Endler, N., & Parker, J. (1992). Interactionism revisited: Reflections on the continuing crisis in the personality area. *European Journal of Personality, 6*, 177–198.

Eysenck, H. J. (1967). *The biological basis of personality*. Springfield, IL: Thomas.

Eysenck, H. J., & Eysenck, M. W. (1985). *Personality and individual differences: A natural science approach*. New York: Plenum.

Fahrenberg, J. (1991). A differential psycho-physiology and the diagnosis of temperament. In: J. Strelau, & A. Angleitner (Eds), *Explorations in temperament* (pp. 317–333). New York: Plenum.

Fox, E., Russo, R., Bowles, R., & Dutton, K. (2001). Do threatening stimuli draw or hold visual attention in subclinical anxiety? *Journal of Experimental Psychology: General, 130*, 681–700.

Gale, A., Edwards, J., Morris, P., Moore, R., & Forrester, D. (2001). Extraversion-introversion, neuroticism-stability, and EEG indicators of positive and negative empathic mood. *Personality and Individual Differences, 30*, 449–461.

Goldberg, L. R. (1990). An alternative 'description of personality': The Big-Five factor structure. *Journal of Personality and Social Psychology, 59*, 1216–1229.

Gray, J. A. (1991). Neural systems, emotion and personality. In: J. Madden, IV (Ed.), *Neurobiology of learning, emotion and affect* (pp. 273–306). New York: Raven Press.

Gray, J. A., & McNaughton, N. (2000). *The neuropsychology of anxiety: An enquiry into the functions of the septo-hippocampal system* (2nd ed.). Oxford: Oxford University Press.

Lazarus, R. S. (1999). *Stress and emotion: A new synthesis*. New York: Springer.

Marks, I. M., & Nesse, R. M. (1994). Fear and fitness: An evolutionary analysis of anxiety disorders. *Ethology & Sociobiology, 15*, 247–261.

Martin, M., Ward, J. C., & Clark, D. M. (1983). Neuroticism and the recall of positive and negative personality information. *Behaviour Research and Therapy, 21*, 495–503.

Matthews, G. (1997). An introduction to the cognitive science of personality and emotion. In: G. Matthews (Ed.), *Cognitive science perspectives on personality and emotion* (pp. 3–30). Amsterdam: Elsevier.

Matthews, G. (1999). Personality and skill: A cognitive-adaptive framework. In: P. L. Ackerman, P. C. Kyllonen, & R. D. Roberts (Eds), *The future of learning and individual differences research: Processes, traits, and content* (pp. 251–270). Washington, DC: American Psychological Association.

Matthews, G. (2000). A cognitive science critique of biological theories of personality traits. *History and Philosophy of Psychology*, *2*, 1–17.

Matthews, G., Campbell, S. E., Falconer, S., Joyner, L., Huggins, J., Gilliland, K., Grier, R., & Warm, J. S. (2002). Fundamental dimensions of subjective state in performance settings: Task engagement, distress and worry. *Emotion*, *2*, 315–340.

Matthews, G., Deary, I. J., & Whiteman, M. C. (in press). *Personality traits* (2nd ed.). Cambridge: Cambridge University Press.

Matthews, G., Derryberry, D., & Siegle, G. J. (2000a). Personality and emotion: Cognitive science perspectives. In: S. E. Hampson (Ed.), *Advances in personality psychology* (Vol. 1, pp. 199–237). London: Routledge.

Matthews, G., & Dorn, L. (1995). Personality and intelligence: Cognitive and attentional processes. In: D. Saklofske & M. Zeidner (Eds), *International handbook of personality and intelligence* (pp. 367–396). New York: Plenum.

Matthews, G., & Gilliland, K. (1999). The personality theories of H. J. Eysenck and J. A. Gray: A comparative review. *Personality and Individual Differences*, *26*, 583–626.

Matthews, G., & Gilliland, K. (2001). Personality, biology and cognitive science: A reply to Corr (2000). *Personality and Individual Differences*, *30*, 353–362.

Matthews, G., Schwean, V. L., Campbell, S. E., Saklofske, D. H., & Mohamed, A. A. R. (2000b). Personality, self-regulation and adaptation: A cognitive-social framework. In: M. Boekarts, P. R. Pintrich, & M. Zeidner (Eds), *Handbook of self-regulation* (pp. 171–207). New York: Academic.

Matthews, G., & Wells, A. (1999). The cognitive science of attention and emotion. In: T. Dalgleish, & M. Power (Eds), *Handbook of cognition and emotion* (pp. 171–192). New York: Wiley.

Munafo, M. R., Clark, T. G., Moore, L. R., Payne, E., Walton, R., & Flint, J. (2003). Genetic polymorphisms and personality in healthy adults: A systematic review and meta-analysis. *Molecular Psychiatry*, *8*, 471–484.

Naveteur, J., & Freixa i Baqué, E. (1987). Individual differences in electrodermal activity as a function of subjects' anxiety. *Personality and Individual Differences*, *8*, 615–626.

Pickering, A. D., Corr, P. J., Powell, J. H., Kumari, V., Thornton, J. C., & Gray, J. A. (1997). Individual differences in reactions to reinforcing stimuli are neither black nor white: To what extent are they Gray? In: H. Nyborg (Ed.), *The scientific study of human nature: Tribute to Hans J. Eysenck at eighty* (pp. 36–67). London: Elsevier.

Pylyshyn, Z. W. (1999). What's in your mind? In: E. Lepore & Z. W. Pylyshyn (Eds), *What is cognitive science?* Malden, MA: Blackwell.

Stein, H., Koontz, A. D., Fonagy, P., Allen, J. G., Fultz, J. B., Brethour, J. R., Jr., Allen, D., & Evans, R. B. (2002). Adult attachment: What are the underlying dimensions? *Psychology and Psychotherapy: Theory, Research and Practice*, *75*, 77–91.

Stelmack, R. M., & Houlihan, M. (1995). Event-related potentials, personality and intelligence: concepts, issues and evidence. In: D. H. Saklofske, & M. Zeidner (Eds), *International handbook of personality and intelligence* (pp. 349–365). New York: Plenum.

Stenberg, G. (1992). Personality and the EEG: Arousal and emotional arousability. *Personality and Individual Differences*, *13*, 1097–1113.

Suls, J. (2001). Affect, stress, and personality. In: J. P. Forgas (Ed.), *Handbook of affect and social cognition* (pp. 392–409). Mahwah, NJ: Erlbaum.

Wells, A. (2000). *Emotional disorders and metacognition: Innovative cognitive therapy*. Chichester, UK: Wiley.

Wilken, J. A., Smith, B. D., Tola, K., & Mann, M. (2000). Trait anxiety and prior exposure to non-stressful stimuli: Effects on psychophysiological arousal and anxiety. *International Journal of Psychophysiology*, *37*, 233–242.

Zeidner, M., & Matthews, G. (2000). Personality and intelligence. In: R. J. Sternberg (Ed.), *Handbook of human intelligence* (2nd ed., pp. 581–610). Cambridge: Cambridge University Press.

Zuckerman, M. (1991). *Psychobiology of personality*. Cambridge: Cambridge University Press.

Zuckerman, M. (1992). What is a basic factor and which factors are basic? Turtles all the way down. *Personality and Individual Differences*, *13*, 675–681.

Zuckerman, M. (1999). *Vulnerability to psychopathology: A biosocial model*. Washington, DC: American Psychological Association.

Zuckerman, M., Joireman, J., Teta, P., Kraft, M., & Kuhlman, D. M. (1999). Where do motivational and emotional traits fit within three factor models of personality? *Personality and Individual Differences*, *26*, 487–504.

Zuckerman, M., Kuhlman, D. M., Joireman, J., Teta, P., & Kraft, M. (1993). A comparison of three structural models for personality: The big three, the big five, and the alternative five. *Journal of Personality and Social Psychology*, *65*, 757–768.

Chapter 15

The Multilevel Approach in Sensation Seeking: Potentials and Findings of a Four-Level Research Program

B. Brocke

1. Problems and Potentials of Correlational Personality Psychology

Personality theories based exclusively on correlational assumptions and questionnaire data are a basic prototype of mainstream personality psychology (Comrey 1995; Costa & McCrae 1992; Goldberg 1993). Theories of this type have at least two fundamental shortcomings, however. First, because they lack sufficiently specific descriptions of behavior and situations, they have no genuine potential for making scientific predictions. The item material used in the *adjective approach* of correlational trait theories is *trivially* maximally unspecific in this respect. Test takers, raters, and users are expected to evaluate, or specify for the application at hand, the tendency of individuals to engage in trait-specific behavior in imagined, arbitrary, especially typical (prototypical), modal, or all possible situations, though most instructions fail to even mention the situational context. This adjectival descriptor approach works with "virtual omnibus situations" (Brocke 2000). The *item approach*, on the other hand, is *notoriously* unspecific with respect to behavioral and situational variables, with some items being a little less unspecific than others.

Because predictions in these theories can, in the first instance, be based solely on the relations between trait scores and items, e.g. factor loadings or item total correlations, the disregard for behavioral and situational theory components takes full effect. The predictive potential of these theories — without utilizing criterion relations — cannot exceed the behavioral and situational content of the items on which they are based. Criterion relations, a second possible basis for predictions, are virtually all *ad hoc* in correlational theories of temperament and lack an explicit theoretical basis, i.e. are not genuine.

The second fundamental shortcoming of correlational theories of personality is at least as alarming: they are unsuitable for scientific explanations. This is not because they are based on traits and on correlational methods of analysis, but because they do not comprise

On the Psychobiology of Personality
Edited by R. M. Stelmack

ISBN: 0-08-044209-9

laws of causation or succession (If A then B). Without such laws, it is impossible to specify causes of the phenomena to be explained. In a similar context, Cronbach (1957) concluded that a correlational theory is merely a preliminary form of a substantial theory. He proposed that these kind of theories be evolved to scientific theories in the strict sense (i.e. theories permitting explanations) by complementing them with experimental (causal) components.

Which kinds of research approaches and strategies might help to overcome these two cardinal problems of mainstream research in the field of personality psychology?

2. Overcoming the Prediction and Explanation Dilemma: Multimodal Causal Theories of Personality

Relatively few strategies have been developed or applied in recent personality research to overcome the first cardinal problem, the prediction dilemma. Attention can be focused on four of these approaches: (1) In research programs seeking to develop methods to measure personality-related variables in the field (ambulatory diagnostics; e.g. Buse & Pawlik 1996; Fahrenberg & Myrtek 1996; Pawlik 1995; Pawlik & Buse 1996), behavioral and situational components are (of necessity) well elaborated and relatively specific; (2) Van Heck *et al.* (1994) have developed a version of the Five Factor Model (FFM) which specifies behavioral and situational factors within a paradigmatic research approach. Although this approach shows a great deal of potential, it has thus far been largely overlooked; (3) ten Berge and De Raad (2001) are developing a common taxonomy of situations and traits based on a variant of the FFM (AB5C); and (4) To complete purely correlational theories of personality with causal assumptions (postulates) (see below), it is necessary to specify treatment variables and dependent variables, i.e. at least one type of situation and behavior variables.

Causal research on individual differences is needed to overcome the second cardinal problem of purely correlational personality theories, the explanation dilemma. Pawlik, for example, maintains that "At present, the description of individual differences is much further advanced than their explanation" (Pawlik 1995, p. 34, own translation). "Causal research in differential psychology explores the reasons for individual differences" (p. 34). But precisely which form should this causal research take? Three strategies of causal personality research show particular potential: (1) multimodal causal personality research; (2) systematic multimodality; and (3) missing-link strategies.

(1) Multimodal causal personality theories, also known as causal multilevel theories, seem especially promising (cf. Brocke 2000; Eysenck 1981; Zuckerman, 1994). For the most part, these theories explain low-level correlations (Extraverts are sociable and outgoing) by reference to higher level causal assumptions (Extraverts are sociable and outgoing because they seek stimuli to compensate for cortical hypoarousal; theoretical explanation), which can be tested using quasi-experimental designs.
(2) In the case of systematic multimodality, the approach is not confined to one or two levels of causality or measurement, e.g. to psychophysiology and psychometric traits. Rather, a systematic multilevel approach aims to combine the respectively most revealing results

with regard to a specific research question, and irrespective of their level. In this way, the greatest possible depth of explanation may be obtained.

The key advantage of systematic multimodality consists in the synergy effects of the explanations. Findings on one level of explanation can throw light on problems/questions on another level which, given the current state of the art, would otherwise be difficult to solve.

(3) Missing-link strategy: Finally, in the domain of biopsychological theories of personality, multimodal causal trait theories based on traits which population genetic studies have shown to have high heritabilities and for which some molecular genetic localizations have already been ascertained seem particularly promising. High heritabilities and respective molecular genetic localizations seem to guarantee that a biopsychological basis for this trait exists and can be identified. In these cases, the biopsychological basis is a necessary connection — the missing link — between the molecular genetic information and the trait-specific behavior.

When, as in the present case, the multimodal causal theory is a theory of personality, it will necessarily incorporate a correlational or psychometric subtheory: the psychometric trait or psychometric trait system on which the multimodal causal assumptions are based and which constitutes the object of explanation. Such theories thus permit both the description and the explanation of individual differences, as was soon emphasized by H. J. Eysenck, and bridge the gap between correlational and causal (experimental) research, as advocated by Cronbach.

Biopsychological personality research has produced a number of such multimodal causal theories, particularly in recent years. These theories have paradigmatic character for the psychology of individual differences. In the following, the potential of multimodal causal personality research for overcoming the deficits of purely correlational personality research, particularly the prediction and explanation dilemma, will be illustrated by reference to Zuckerman's theory of sensation seeking. To begin, Zuckerman's approach will be briefly described as a multimodal causal theory and its explanatory potential will be outlined. The potential of multimodal causal personality research will then be demonstrated by a research program designed to systematically investigate aspects of sensation seeking across four different levels.

3. Multimodal Causal Research Strategies and Sensation Seeking: A Prototypical Theory

3.1. Levels of the Theory

Zuckerman (1992) postulates that traits should only be regarded as basic dimensions of personality if they have a biopsychological base. Furthermore, he states that the constitutional, biopsychological basic dimensions must have a hereditary-genetic base, and that behavioral genetic pathways transform the molecular genetic information to the level of overt behavior. On this basis, Zuckerman outlines a multilevel approach that provides a rough description of the structure of biopsychological personality theories.

Psychometric traits are located at the top (first level) of Zuckerman's hierarchy, resting on consistent social behavior patterns and habitual cognitive reactions to certain classes of situations (second level). Social behavior patterns and cognitive constructs are based on conditioning and learning (third level). Individual differences in conditioning processes or conditionability are based, among other things, on differences in cortical physiology (fourth level). Differences in psychophysiology, in turn, depend on particularities in biochemical systems (fifth level; e.g. neurotransmitters, enzymes, hormones), while neurotransmitter pathways mark out neurological systems and neural nuclei (sixth level). The seventh level consists of genetic information.

Hence, in this model, the domains of genetics, neurology, biochemistry, and physiology are seen as neurobiological bases for higher level psychological processes and systems such as conditionability, social behavior, and underlying traits (Zuckerman 1994a, b). With regard to these upper levels one point seems to be debatable, however. Behavioral dispositions (traits) can arguably be regarded as more basic than (trait-) specific behavior. Hence, it would seem to make more sense to invert the first and second levels of the model, so that socio-psychological behavior (overt and covert, including cognitive behavior and experience) is situated on the first level, traits on the second, and conditioning on the third.

In sensation seeking theory, the seven levels of the model and the connections between them have not yet been specified and elaborated completely and always systematically. Nevertheless, the assumptions of the theory and the findings available can be set in relation to the levels of this model. The neurological level (sixth level) is an exception here. Although assumptions on the neurochemical level are often relevant to the neurological domain, very few neuroanatomical findings in the strict sense referring directly to sensation seeking are currently available. An overview of the most important levels (excluding the sixth and third, for which also only few empirical findings are known) is provided in the following section.

3.2. The Psychometric Theory Component and Related Behavior

The genesis of this theory began with the development of the psychometric trait conception of sensation seeking, but the psychometric and biopsychological dimensions of sensation seeking evolved in parallel from the outset. It was not until a later phase of theory development that sensation seeking was placed within the broader field of personality and integrated into a more comprehensive model of personality traits, the Alternative Five Factor Model (AFFM; Zuckerman *et al.* 1988, 1991, 1993). In this model, sensation seeking is represented by the Impulsive Sensation Seeking (ImpSS) dimension, which is in turn embedded in the general factor Psychoticism-Impulsive Unsocialized Sensation Seeking (P-ImpUSS; Zuckerman 1993; Zuckerman *et al.* 1993).

The other four factors of the AFFM are Aggression-Hostility, Activity, Sociability, and Neuroticism-Anxiety. Simultaneous factor analyses with the Eysenck Personality Questionanaire-Revised (EPQ-R; Eysenck *et al.* 1985) and the NEO-Personality Inventory-Revised (NEO-PI-R; Costa & McCrae 1992) yielded a three- or four-factor solution (Zuckerman *et al.* 1993). Impulsive Sensation Seeking emerged to be part of a factor that was also defined by EPQ-R Psychoticism and NEO-PI Conscientiousness and Agreeableness. A further factor (the first) represents an Extraversion factor with Sociability and Activity.

A third factor describes the EPQ-R construct Neuroticism. Zuckerman postulates that Sensation Seeking has an internal structure consisting of four subscales. Based on the findings of Björk-Akesson (1990) and Horvath and Zuckerman (1993), he interprets these as primary factors and Sensation Seeking as a secondary factor (one-plus-four model).

Numerous studies have found evidence for relationships between sensation seeking and certain patterns of behavior and behavioral dispositions, e.g. vocational choices, preferences for certain kinds of sports, social behavior, aesthetic preferences, sexual experience, and alcohol and drug use. The theory components presented in the following form a basis for explaining these patterns of behavior and behavioral dispositions (primary and secondary factors).

3.3. The Biopsychological Theory Components

In line with Eysenck (1963, 1967), sensation seeking theory draws on the concept of the optimum level of arousal to explain the behavior characteristic of sensation seekers. High sensation seekers tend to be underaroused, i.e. below the optimum level of arousal of the Ascending Reticular Activation System (ARAS). They seek to attain this optimum arousal level by exposure to novel, intense, and complex stimuli or sensations. It was originally assumed that high sensation seekers have habitually lower baseline levels of tonic arousal, but this assumption was not confirmed by EEG indicators of activity (Golding & Richards 1985; Passini *et al.* 1977; Watson *et al.* 1979) or by peripheral indicators, although findings were not entirely consistent (Feij *et al.* 1985; Neary & Zuckerman 1976; Ridgeway & Hare 1981; Smith *et al.* 1989; Stern *et al.* 1981; Zuckerman *et al.* 1988). The assumption that high and low sensation seekers have different habitual baseline levels of arousal was thus substituted by the notion that the two groups have different degrees of arousability (Zuckerman 1997).

Behavioral particularities of sensation seekers that have been associated with individual differences in arousability are described and explained, above all, in the context of the orienting and the defensive reflex. Whereas high sensation seekers still show an orienting response (heart rate deceleration) to novel stimuli of moderate intensity, low sensation seekers already display a defensive reflex. Moreover, high sensation seekers show a stronger electrodermal orienting response to stimuli that are of personal interest to them. This relationship is attributed to the specific arousability of high sensation seekers. However, it only applies to novel stimuli of moderate intensity.

In terms of electrocortical activity, the assumed specific arousability of high sensation seekers is reflected in contexts such as the augmenting/reducing paradigm. This concept was originally introduced by Petrie (1967) to measure the degree to which subjects overestimate or underestimate the intensity of a stimulus following prolonged stimulus bombardement. The concept was assumed to reflect differences in the central nervous system. Buchsbaum and Silverman (1968) developed the now prevailing version of the augmenting/reducing paradigm using evoked potentials (EP). When the intensity of a stimulus increases, high sensation seekers respond with a significantly more pronounced increase in early negative (N1) and positive peaks (P1, P2) than low sensation seekers. Beginning with a study by Zuckerman *et al.* (1974) this finding has been replicated in numerous empirical studies.

A review of early augmenting/reducing studies including animal experiments (Lukas & Siegel 1977) is given in Zuckerman (1990). However, the findings of these studies are not entirely consistent, especially across the visual and auditory modality (cf. Carrillo-de-la-Peña 1992).

Later studies of the 1990s primarily showing improved methods in utilising the augmenting/reducing paradigm yielded further evidence supporting the augmenting disposition of high sensation seekers (Brocke *et al.* 1999, 2000; Hegerl *et al.* 1995; Zuckerman 1994a). However, some inconsistencies still require clarification (Carrillo-de-la-Peña 2001), and various suggestions for improving methods of specifying augmenting/reducing dispositions have recently been made (Beauducel *et al.* 2000).

Of particular significance for understanding the augmenting disposition of sensation seekers is the assumption that individual differences in augmenting/reducing are modulated primarily by serotonergenic activity, and that augmenting can be taken as an indicator of low central serotonergenic neurotransmission, particularly in the primary auditory cortex. Using dipole source analysis represents an important methodological advance in this context (Hegerl *et al.* 2001; Hegerl & Juckel 1993). Clinical studies (Gallinat *et al.* 2000; Tuchtenhagen *et al.* 2000) and animal experiments (Juckel *et al.* 1997, 1999) provide evidence to support the assumption of serotonergic modulation of augmenting/reducing.

On the neurochemical level of the model (Zuckerman 1994a, 1995), sensation seeking is seen in the context of the broader dimension Psychoticism-Impulsive Unsocialized Sensation Seeking (P-ImpUSS) and contrasted with the traits Extraversion-Sociability and Neuroticism-Anxiety (Zuckerman 1993, 1996). Individuals with high scores on the P-ImpUSS dimension show:

(1) Pronounced approach as an expression of increased dopaminergic activity and of the directly or indirectly modulating effects of the activity of sex hormones, particularly testosterone, and type B monoamine oxidase (MAO).
(2) Low inhibition as a result of low serotonergic activity.
(3) Low cortical and autonomic arousal in consequence of low noradrenergic activity, which is in turn affected by the activity of dopamine β-hydroxylase (DBH), endorphins, and gamma-aminobutyric acid (GABA).

Many of the assumptions postulated in this model as regards the approach, inhibition, and arousal systems, as well as the relative significance of monoaminergic neurotransmission for the functioning of these systems, are also advocated in other approaches, particularly by Gray (1991a, b), Cloninger (1987), and Depue (Depue & Collins 1999). The concept of activity of a neurotransmitter system shows some vagueness, however. Does high neurotransmitter activity imply a high rate of synthesis, low reuptake and storage of neurotransmitters, sensitivity or density of pre- or post-synaptic receptors? Zuckerman (1995) himself draws attention to these difficulties, without being able at present to make his model more specific in this respect.

On the genetic level, numerous findings support Zuckerman's assumption of a genetic basis of sensation seeking. An early population genetic study (Fulker *et al.* 1980) computed a heritability estimate (in the strict sense) of $h^2 = 58\%$ for the sensation seeking total score (SSS IV). More recent studies have not been able to confirm the assumption that all subscales share a common genetic factor. However, the heritability scores for the subscales were of approximately the same magnitude as in the first study (Hur & Bouchard 1997; Koopmans *et al.* 1995). Pogue-Geile *et al.* (1998) report much lower heritabilities.

In view of the substantive similarities between sensation seeking and novelty seeking, and the assumed dopaminergic modulation of sensation seeking, it seems primarily worth referring to findings on the relationship between novelty seeking and functional polymorphisms for dopaminergic activity. While many studies have found a relationship with the dopamine D4 receptor gene (DRD4), many other studies have failed to replicate this finding (Kluger *et al.* 2002). Furthermore, the neurochemical model indicates that functional polymorphisms for serotonergic and noradrenergic activity are of particular relevance. Meanwhile first attempts to identify moderator variables and interactions with such potentially relevant polymorphisms have been undertaken (see Benjamin *et al.* 2000; Strobel *et al.* 2003a).

Numerous studies have now also investigated the direct associations between sensation seeking and polymorphisms with dopaminergic relevance, with the *Bal I* polymorphism of the DRD3 gene, the *TaqI* A1 allele of the D2 receptor gene, the serotonin transporter polymorphism (5-HTTPR), and the DRD4 exon III polymorphism. However, only three studies have found evidence for a significant relationship between sensation seeking and polymorphisms (Duaux *et al.* 1998; Ratsma *et al.* 2001; Strobel *et al.* 1999). Various methodological reasons for these inconsistent results have been proposed and discussed (e.g. Brocke *et al.* 2003).

4. A Four-Level Research Program on Sensation Seeking

As mentioned above, the causal multilevel approach to sensation seeking theory not only allows individual differences to be described (and assessed), it also makes it possible to explain these differences on various levels. The research project described in the following demonstrates the advantages of causal multilevel theories of personality over purely correlational trait theories. The project was designed to systematically investigate explanatory assumptions of sensation seeking theory on four different levels. As is standard practice in experimental personality research, quasi-experimental designs and, to some extent, correlational analysis strategies were applied. In other words, the test sometimes is weaker than some of the theoretical assumptions under investigation.

The project focused on the impact of monoaminergic neurotransmitters on personality traits, especially sensation seeking, novelty seeking, and related concepts. In line with the multilevel approach, the project was not restricted to the neurochemical level. The research questions were also investigated on the molecular genetic, psychophysiological, and psychometric levels. For instance, findings on individual differences on augmenting/reducing were not only replicated on the psychophysiological level. Also neurochemical and molecular genetic factors which could help to explain these electrocortical differences, were analyzed in consecutive studies.

4.1. Overview

As described above, a positive correlation between sensation seeking and augmenting (i.e. a strong intensity dependence) can be regarded as a key characteristic of sensation seeking on the psychophysiological level. The assumed primarily serotonergenic modulation of augmenting/reducing is of particular interest in the present context. Individual particularities in serotonergic modulation might help to explain the strong intensity dependence of sensation seekers.

For some time now, certain personality traits and patterns of behavior (sensation seeking, novelty seeking, impulsivity, aggressiveness) have been associated with central serotonergic activity (e.g. Cloninger 1986, 1987; Hegerl *et al.* 1995; Zuckerman 1994a). It can also be assumed that some clinical disorders (affective disorders, addictive behavior, aggression, compulsion) are linked to dysregulation of the neurotransmitter serotonin. The efficacy of drugs affecting central serotonergic activity in the treatment of depressive disorders, for instance, supports this assumption (Hegerl & Juckel 1993).

These findings raise the question of whether the aspects of central serotonergic activity that are characteristic of sensation seeking/impulsivity and affective disorders respectively are related or correspond. Is this serotonergic characteristic a common diathesis variable or a common constitutional factor of sensation seeking and affective disorders? Are high sensation seekers particularly vulnerable to affective disorders?

Two key findings of Zuckerman, which show a significant correlation between sensation seeking and affective disorders on the psychometric level, indicate the possibility that the relationship between sensation seeking and affective disorders may be based on common constitutional factors (Cronin & Zuckerman 1992; Zuckerman & Neeb 1979). Using the SSS-V, Zuckerman and Neeb (1979) were able to differentiate between patients with a reported history of bipolar depression or bipolar affective disorders (BAD) and healthy controls. Cronin and Zuckerman (1992) showed that BAD patients have significantly higher Sensation Seeking scores (on the Disinhibition and Boredom Susceptibility subscales) than healthy respondents, even though half the patients were in a depressive episode (not manic) at the time of the study.

Population genetic studies indicate that sensation seeking, as well as unipolar and bipolar depression, display high heritabilities. If this is indeed the case, the question arises as to the molecular genetic bases of these findings. Are preliminary molecular genetic specifications of these findings now available? To what extent do functional polymorphisms with relevance for central serotonergenic neurotransmission play a role here?

In the studies described below, these questions, which span four levels of the sensation seeking approach, were investigated systematically.

4.2. Sensation Seeking and Intensity Dependence (Augmenting/Reducing) of the Acoustic Evoked Potential (AEP)

The experiments conducted in the first study (Brocke *et al.* 1999) were primarily based on a test of the key finding on the psychophysiological level that high sensation seekers are characterized by a strong intensity dependence or augmenting. Although this finding has been replicated in numerous studies (see Section 3.3), some inconsistencies do remain, making further investigation necessary.

The 32 participants in this study (18 female, 14 male; mean age 23.4) completed three personality inventories: the Sensation Seeking Scale, Form V (SSS-V) (Zuckerman 1994a),

Table 1: Correlations between traits and slopes of N1/P2-, N1- and P2 amplitudes.

Slope	SSS-V	TAS	ES	ZKPQ-IMPSS
N1/P2 (C3)		0.35*,a		
N1/P2-Median (C3)		0.36*,a		
N1/P2-Median (Cz)		0.32*,a		
N1 (C3)			0.56**	0.56**
N1 (Cz)			0.36*	0.45*
N1 (C4)			0.44*	0.48**
P2 (C3)	0.38*		0.54**	0.39*
P2 (Cz)	0.38*		0.52**	0.40*
P2 (C4)			0.52**	0.50**

Notes: SSS-V = sensation seeking total score; TAS = thrill and adventure seeking; ES = Experience Seeking; ZKPQ-IMPSS = ZKPQ-impulsive sensation seeking.
Source: From Brocke *et al.* (1999). Copyright 1999 by Pergamon. Reprinted by permission.
[a] One-tailed.
*$p < 0.05$.
**$p < 0.01$.

the Zuckerman Kuhlmann Personality Questionnaire (ZKPQ; Zuckerman *et al.* 1993), and the Impulsiveness Venturesomeness Empathy Questionnaire (IVE; Eysenck *et al.* 1990; Eysenck & Eysenck 1991). Within the augmenting/reducing paradigm, tones of different intensities were sounded at 1000 Hz. One hundred tones were presented for every intensity level; the intensity of the tones varied randomly. The individual N1/P2 components of the acoustic evoked potential for each level of intensity were ascertained and regression lines were calculated across the levels of intensity. The slopes of the individual regression lines were taken as an indicator of the intensity dependence. In addition, medians of the slopes between all possible combinations of two intensity levels were calculated.

As shown in Table 1, the slope of the N1/P2 amplitudes at electrode site C3 across the four levels of intensity up to 90 dB correlated significantly with the Thrill and Adventure Seeking (TAS) subscale of the SSS-V (see Brocke *et al.* 1999, for details). The median slopes (median of the slopes between all possible combinations of two intensity levels) also correlate significantly with TAS. Figure 1 shows the relationship between TAS and N1/P2 amplitudes. Furthermore, the Experience Seeking (ES) subscale and ZKPQ-IMPSS correlate strongly with the slopes calculated separately for N1 and P2.

The results of this study replicate findings, repeatedly demonstrated, of a correlation between sensation seeking and the augmenting disposition (i.e. between TAS and the N1/P2 amplitude). Because the slope was calculated on the basis of the N1/P2 amplitude, this replication is in line with the findings reported by Hegerl *et al.* (1988) and Hegerl and Juckel (1993), who also used the N1/P2 amplitudes.

Above and beyond this classic result (based on N1/P2 amplitudes), the additional finding of a high correlation of ES and ZKPQ-IMPSS with the intensity-dependent slopes for

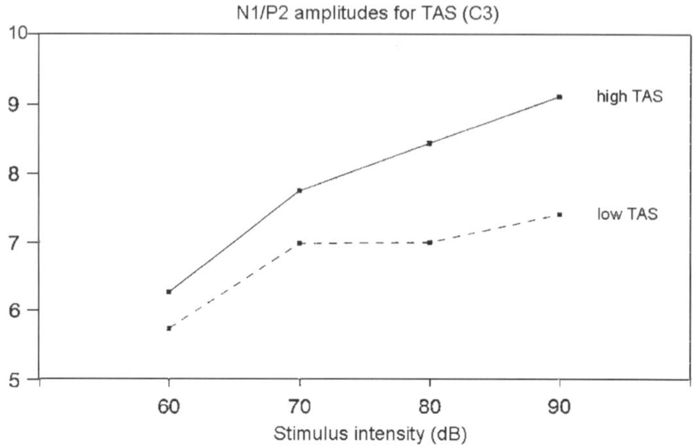

Figure 1: N1/P2 amplitudes at electrode site C3 in μV for SSS-V subscale TAS. *Source*: From Brocke *et al.* (1999). Copyright 1999 by Pergamon. Reprinted by permission.

N1 and P2, which were calculated separately, indicates that there may be several ways to compute parameters for augmenting/reducing (see Connolly & Gruzelier 1986). However, because N1 and P2 are not yet as well established as the other parameters (N1/P2 calculated differently; first Coursey *et al.* 1975; then Hegerl & Juckel 1993), the reliability and validity of the individual parameters are still in need of clarification. These questions were addressed systematically in a study by Beauducel *et al.* (2000), and the key results were integrated in the following replication studies exploring the relationship between sensation seeking and intensity dependence of the AEP.

4.3. Serotonergic Modulation of Intensity Dependence: Common Characteristics of Sensation Seeking and Bipolar Affective Disorders (BAD)

In the same vein, one objective of the second study (Brocke *et al.* 2000) was to replicate the correlation between sensation seeking and intensity dependence once more, taking account of the findings presented by Beauducel *et al.* (2000). In response to the recommendations of this study for improving and standardizing the augmenting/reducing paradigm, particular attention was paid to three points: (1) At least five or six intensity levels seem to be necessary for reliable measurements of intensity dependence; (2) The P2 and N1/P2 amplitudes of the AEP are the comparatively best (most reliable) indicators (although all indicators should always be reported as a matter of principle); and (3) To control the quality of the indicators of an individual study, their reliability should always be determined, if possible as a retest estimate.

The main focus of the study was first on the question of whether certain features of central serotonergic activity are common to sensation seekers and patients with affective disorders. A second main focus lay on the influence of serotonin agonists on the intensity dependence exhibited by individuals with bipolar and unipolar depression. Third, it examined whether correspondences for the expected psychophysiological communalities of sensation seekers and BAD patients could be found on the behavioral or psychometric level.

There are some indications that the particularities of the intensity dependence of the AEP observed in sensation seekers also occur in certain clinical disorders, e.g. affective disorders and alcoholism. Following the seminal work by Buchsbaum *et al.* (1971), several studies found that BAD patients, like sensation seekers, are characterized by a strong intensity dependence (i.e. a pronounced augmenting disposition). It has also emerged that clinical responders to antidepressant or prophylactic medication — i.e. patients whose symptoms improved under therapy — are augmenters, while nonresponders tend to be reducers (Hegerl & Herrmann 1990; Hegerl & Juckel 1993; Hegerl *et al.* 2001). In addition, Buchsbaum's results indicate that individuals with unipolar depression (UPD) exhibit a lower intensity dependence than healthy controls, meaning that they are reducers, a finding that seems difficult to explain, however (see below).

As yet, little is known about the effects of antidepressant and prophylactic medication with serotonergic relevance on the intensity dependence of BAD and UPD patients. Buchsbaum *et al.* (1971) observed a significant decrease in the intensity dependence of bipolar patients receiving lithium (flattening effect). Some studies found the same effect for other patient groups treated with tricyclic antidepressants and selective serotonin reuptake inhibitors (SSRI; von Knorring 1982; von Knorring *et al.* 1980; for a summary, see Hegerl & Juckel 1993). Overall, however, it has not yet been clarified whether this flattening effect is stable or merely a transient effect experienced during the first phase of medication, since pre/post studies with a medication-free baseline condition and sufficient intervals between the treatment and the retest are not yet available. The question thus arises of whether the stronger intensity dependence of BAD patients compared to healthy controls receiving antidepressant or prophylactic medication really does change (stably) in terms of a flattening effect, and whether the intensity dependence of the two groups is similar under these conditions.

The Buchsbaum *et al.* (1971) study does not allow firm conclusions to be drawn about the effects of lithium (prophylactic medication) on the intensity dependence of UPD patients. To date, studies on the effects of antidepressant or prophylactic medication on UPD patients have, for the most part, been confined to clinical responsiveness studies.

Because sensation seekers and BAD patients are assumed to share certain psychophysiological characteristics, the second study also investigated whether the two groups have communalities on the behavioral or psychometric level. The psychophysiological findings corroborate this assumption and are consistent with the psychometric findings on the relationship between sensation seeking and affective disorders mentioned above.

Of the 42 patients participating in this study, 21 were diagnosed with a bipolar affective disorder (BAD) and 21 with a major depression (unipolar group or UPD). A group of 24 healthy controls also participated. There were no significant differences in the age and gender distributions of the three groups.

As in the first study, the augmenting/reducing paradigm was implemented. To control the reliability of the measurements, the EEG was recorded in two sessions at an interval of about three weeks. Tones were presented at six levels of intensity (59, 71, 79, 88, 92, 96 dB SPL). The stimuli (1000 Hz, 30 ms presentation time) were sounded in random order.

Table 2: Retest reliabilities for ASF slopes (controls and patients).

Parameters	C3	Cz	C4
Controls ($n = 24$)			
P1/N1	0.19	0.30	0.31
N1/P2	**0.77**	**0.71**	**0.59**
P1	0.18	0.02	0.14
N1	0.38	0.07	0.06
P2	**0.61**	**0.77**	**0.67**
Patients ($n = 28$)			
P1/N1	0.22	0.34	0.17
N1/P2	0.17	0.38	0.18
P1	0.20	0.25	**0.43**
N1	**0.53**	**0.58**	0.21
P2	**0.41**	**0.61**	**0.47**

Note: Pearson correlation >0.40 are in bold.
Source: From Brocke *et al.* (2000). Copyright 2000 by Karger. Reprinted by permission.

Reliability of the AEP parameters (intensity dependence). The results indicate that, in line with the ideas reported in Beauducel *et al.* (2000), the retest reliabilities for the various AEP parameters differed considerably (Table 2). In the control group, the ASF slopes for the P2 and N1/P2 components showed satisfactory retest reliabilities at all electrode sites. The slopes of the regression lines for the P1, N1, and P1/N1 amplitudes were not reliable, however. The reliabilities of the median slopes did not differ systematically from those of the ASF slopes.

For patients, the pattern of reliabilities was less consistent than for healthy controls (Table 2). The N1/P2 slope was not reliable for patients, but acceptable values were obtained for the P2 slopes at all electrode sites, and for the N1 slopes at sites C3 and Cz.

Sensation seeking and intensity dependence (healthy controls). The expected positive correlation between sensation seeking and intensity dependence of the AEP was again confirmed for the healthy participants (control group) in this study (Table 3). At both recording sessions, the strongest relationships between sensation seeking (SSS-V total score) and intensity dependence were found for the P2 slopes, i.e. the parameter with the highest reliabilities. This finding remained stable when the measurements were aggregated across both sessions.

Although the P1 and N1 slopes, which were not reliable for the healthy controls, also correlated with sensation seeking (SSS-V total score) in some cases, the pattern of results was inconsistent. When aggregated across both recording sessions, the P1 and N1 slopes showed significant correlations with the SSS-V total score at C4. The same held for the N1 slopes at the first point of measurement. For the N1/P2 components, a correlation was found with the SSS-V TAS subscale at C3 at the second session ($r = 0.36, p > 0.05$, one-tailed). The findings of this replication study thus are particularly informative as they show how

Table 3: Pearson correlations of the ASF slopes with the SSS-V total score in controls ($n = 24$).

Parameters	First Recording Session			Second Recording Session			Aggregated Across Session		
	C3	Cz	C4	C3	Cz	C4	C3	Cz	C4
P1/N1	0.01	−0.01	−0.10	−0.04	0.08	−0.01	−0.02	0.04	−0.06
N1/P2	0.07	0.16	0.00	0.27	0.23	0.16	0.18	0.21	0.09
P1	0.34	0.27	0.29	0.11	0.15	0.26	0.29	0.30	0.37*
N1	0.30	0.30	0.37*	0.12	0.04	0.22	0.24	0.20	0.40*
P2	0.29	0.37*	0.35*	0.45*	0.34*	0.41*	0.41*	0.38*	0.42*

Source: From Brocke *et al.* (2000). Copyright 2000 by Karger. Reprinted by permission.
*$p < 0.05$, one-tailed.

the differing reliabilities of the parameters impact on the relationship between sensation seeking and intensity dependence, as previously demonstrated by Beauducel *et al.* (2000).

Clinical groups and intensity dependence. To examine the group differences in intensity dependence, data from the first recording session were submitted to a 2 × 3 repeated-measures ANOVA, including group and position (C3, Cz, C4). The group differences between UPD, BAD and controls were tested seperately. As expected, analyses revealed larger ASF slopes, i.e. a stronger intensity dependence, for BAD patients when controlled for medication by means of covariates, namely as a group main effect for the P1/N1 slopes [$F(1, 37) = 5.91$, $p < 0.05$]. When medication was not controlled, no effect for the slopes reached the level of significance. This finding is in line with the assumption that the medication administered to the BAD patients levels out the slopes (flattening effect), meaning that the differences between BAD patients and healthy controls disappear (Buchsbaum *et al.* 1971; Hegerl & Juckel 1993).

UPD patients were found to have a smaller P2 slope than healthy controls [$F(1, 43) = 5.91, p < 0.05$]. This effect disappeared when controlled for medication [$F(1, 38) = 1.34$, n.s.]. The same pattern emerged for the N1/P2 slopes. This implies that the medication administered to the UPD patients may account for their smaller ASF slopes. On the other hand, of course, it may be that UPD patients not receiving medication still exhibit smaller slopes, as reported by Buchsbaum *et al.* (1971), for example.

Irrespective of any differences in comparison with healthy controls, however, why do BAD and UPD patients differ in intensity dependence, which is presumably subject to serotonergic modulation? The difference in the serotonergically modulated intensity dependence of BAD and UPD patients could be attributable to a specific interaction effect in sensation seekers (and BAD patients), i.e. to the frequently postulated interaction of low central serotonergic and high central dopaminergic neurotransmission, as in sensation seekers (Zuckerman 1994). The results of the fourth study conducted in the present project support this assumption (see Section 4.5).

Overall, however, because it was only possible to control the effects of medication on intensity dependence (i.e. the augmenting/reducing disposition) by means of statistical analysis, these results should be seen with caution. Even if groups of sufficient size could be obtained for each condition, there will always be confounding effects (e.g. type of disorder and medication) that cannot be completely controlled. These limitations are typical of naturalistic settings, however, and are difficult to avoid, since it is neither possible nor advisable to leave patients unmedicated. Further studies, especially with more restrictive medication or pre/post designs, could help to further clarify the characteristic intensity dependence of BAD and UPD patients and the effects of antidepressant and prophylactic medication on these groups. However, studies of this type are not easily to realize.

Psychometric relations: Clinical groups and sensation seeking. On the psychometric level, these results confirm the assumption that BAD patients score significantly higher on sensation seeking than either UPD patients or healthy controls (Figure 2). As expected, BAD patients were found to have significantly higher SSS-V total scores than UPD patients [$t = -2.29$, $p < 0.05$, one-tailed]. This replicates the results of Zuckerman and Neeb (1979), Cronin and Zuckerman (1992), and Carton *et al.* (1992). Some of the results reported by Carton *et al.* (1992), however, could only be replicated with reservations, because the differences between UPD patients and healthy controls showed only as tendency. However, reanalyses showed that the sensation seeking personality trait did not modulate the group differences in the ASF slopes. The group-specific differences in sensation seeking did not account for any additional variance in the ASF slopes. This finding indicates that the group characteristics and sensation seeking are highly dependent and that they account for a large proportion of the common variance in the ASF slopes.

In sum, this second study highlights some of the psychophysiological and psychometric differences between BAD patients, UPD patients, and healthy controls. These results are consistent with the few existing findings on these relations when controlled for medication. Furthermore, when the effects of medication are not controlled, the findings are compatible

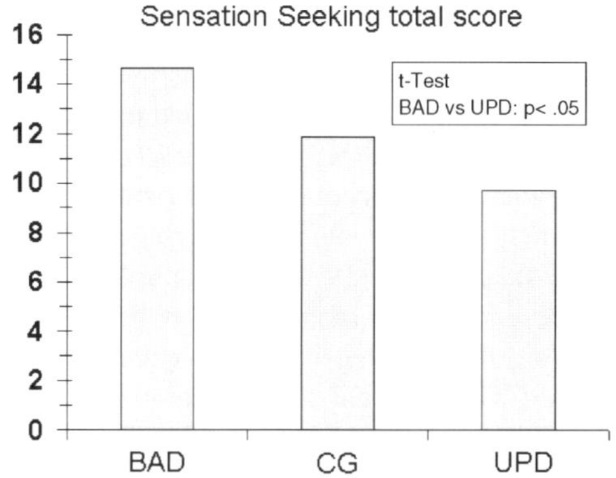

Figure 2: Scores on the SS total score for Bipolar Affective Disorder (BAD), Control Group (CG) and Unipolar Depression (UPD). *Source:* From Brocke *et al.* (2000). Copyright 2000 by Karger. Reprinted by permission.

with the previously reported characteristics of medicated BAD patients, i.e. the flattening effect of the slopes under antidepressant or prophylactic medication. In view of the naturalistic setting, however, these findings should be seen with caution and regarded as preliminary.

4.4. Does Experimental Manipulation of Serotonergic Neurotransmission Affect the Intensity Dependence of the AEP?

Our understanding of the existing findings on the relationship between sensation seeking, affective disorders, and intensity dependence would be much enhanced if it were possible to provide additional evidence for the relationship between central serotonergic activity and intensity dependence by direct experimental manipulation in humans. Although the relationship has been shown by direct manipulation in animal experiments, most previous human research in this area has taken an indirect approach. Further corroboration of this relationship by direct experimental manipulation in humans would have the additional benefit of underscoring the validity of a particularly useful indicator of central serotonergic activity.

Hegerl (e.g. Hegerl & Juckel 1993) was the first to present results supporting the assumption that the intensity dependence of the AEP serves as a biological marker for central serotonergic activity, especially of the primary auditory cortex (PAC). Sensory processing in the primary auditory cortex is modulated by serotonergic neurotransmission. High serotonergic neurotransmission in the PAC, e.g. on account of a high firing rate in the raphe nuclei, leads to lower intensity dependence.

The assumption that the AEP augmenting/reducing tendency can serve as an indicator for central serotonergic activity is supported by numerous findings without direct experimental manipulation, for instance the results of studies in personality psychology showing a positive correlation between certain personality characteristics with typically low serotonergic neurotransmission (e.g. sensation seeking, impulsivity) and augmenting (review of earlier studies in Zuckerman 1990; see also Carillo-de-la-Pena 1992). More recent studies have increasingly adopted suggestions for the methodological improvement and standardization of the augmenting/reducing paradigm (Brocke *et al.* 1999; Hegerl *et al.* 1992, 1995, 2000). Numerous studies have shown that the augmenting tendency serves as a predictor for clinical SSRI responsiveness in depression (for an overview, see Hegerl & Juckel 1993; Hegerl *et al.* 2001). In animal research, the changes prompted by microinjections of 5-HT1A agonists were in line with expectations: intensity dependence decreased on systemic application and increased when local injections were administered to the dorsal raphe nuclei. Corresponding effects, again in line with expectations, emerged when 5-HT2A (ketanserin) and 5-HT1A (spiperone) antagonists were administered (Juckel *et al.* 1997, 1999). Finally, more recent studies (Croft *et al.* 2001; Tuchtenhagen *et al.* 2000) have shown an increased augmenting tendency in subjects consuming ecstasy. This is associated with reduced central serotonergic neurotransmission resulting from impaired receptor function.

Only a few studies with healthy humans are direct tests of the hypothesis that the intensity dependence of the AEP serves as a biological marker for central serotonergic activity. Therefore our third study (Debener *et al.* 2002) was designed as a direct experimental manipulation of the relationship between intensity dependence and central serotonergic activity, involving what is known as a tryptophan depletion study. In the acute tryptophan depletion (ATD) paradigm, central serotonin availability is decreased by dietary means (see below for details). Findings from numerous experimental studies with humans and animals (Carpenter *et al.* 1998; Moore *et al.* 2000; Nishizawa *et al.* 1997) indicate that the ATD is an efficient means of manipulating central serotonergic activity. However, few ATD studies have as yet specifically tested the hypothesis that augmenting/reducing is an indicator for serotonergic function (e.g. Dierks *et al.* 1999).

The goal of this third study was thus to investigate whether ATD-induced changes in the central serotonergic availability impact on the intensity dependence of the AEP. Although the procedure involves direct manipulation of central serotonergic neurotransmission, the specific indicator hypothesis is tested only indirectly, because this global manipulation does not allow direct conclusions to be drawn about specific effects on the serotonergic activity of the primary auditory cortex.

It was originally assumed (Hegerl & Juckel 1993; Hegerl *et al.* 2001) that the ATD-induced decrease in the central serotonin level would be reflected by an increase in the ASF-slopes of the individual components (i.e. P1, N1, P2, P1/N1, N1/P2). However, recent studies, though confirming the basic assumptions on the intense 5-HT innervation of the primary auditory cortex and early cortical auditory processing (Kähkönen *et al.* 2002a), suggest a negative correlation of ATD and intensity dependence (Kähkönen *et al.* 2002b). The results presented by Dierks *et al.* (1999) also point in this direction.

Eighteen healthy female students at Dresden University of Technology participated in a within subject double-blind placebo-controlled cross over study with repeated measurements. Participants in the depletion condition were given a 50 g mixture of 15 amino acids without tryptophan; those in the placebo condition were given a mixture containing tryptophan. To determine the intensity dependence of the AEP, participants were exposed to the augmenting/reducing paradigm in the form used in the second study. Measurements were taken before the amino-acid mixture was ingested, and again five and six hours after ingestion. There were two sessions for either the treatment or placebo condition (counterbalanced) with a one week interval.

Figure 3 shows grand average AEP P1, N1, and P2 at electrode site Cz for six stimulus intensities and the three conditions. Mean N1 and P2 amplitudes enhanced with increasing stimulus intensity, as can be seen from Figure 3. Retest reliabilities (one week interval) of the N1/P2 ASF-slopes for the pre-ingestion baseline revealed moderate stabilities, between $r = 0.56$ and $r = 0.58$ depending on the electrode site.

A two-way repeated-measures ANOVA with factors treatment (depletion/placebo) and session (post 1, post 2) included as within factors, and positions collapsed across the central scalp sites, did not reveal a significant main effect for either treatment or session. The hypothesized treatment *x* session interaction was not significant either. Additional one-way ANOVAs, conducted separately for each condition (pre/baseline, post 1, post 2), did not reveal a significant effect for either depletion or placebo sessions. Because of the relatively small sample size, group differences, especially for high and low sensation seekers, were not investigated.

As such, this third study did not substantiate our original assumption that intensity dependence increases under acute tryptophan depletion. The insignificant findings may

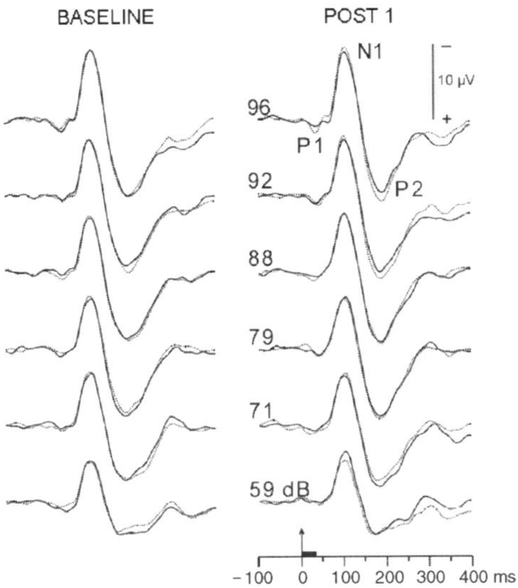

Figure 3: Grand averaged ($n = 18$) auditory evoked potentials P1, N1 and P2 at electrode site Cz, for six different stimulus intensities before (Baseline), five (Post 1) and six hours (Post 2) after ingestion of a 50 g amino-acid mixture. *Note:* Dotted lines indicate the placebo condition (mixture containing tryptophan), and solid lines indicate the depletion condition (mixture without tryptophan). *Source*: From Debener *et al.* (2002). Copyright 2002 by Elsevier Science. Reprinted by permission.

be attributed to some limitations in the study. Because the sample was relatively small and contained only women, it was not possible to consider groups with different serotonin-modulated reactivities (e.g. high vs. low sensation seekers) separately. The decision to administer a 50 g (as opposed to 100 g) dose of amino-acid mixture to avoid adverse side-effects could impact on results, as could the timing of the second point of measurement only six hours after ingestion. However, these limitations are not easy to overcome.

Summarizing the results of recent studies of this approach the finding of a negative correlation between ATD and intensity dependence seems to be surprising, and to contradict deductions based on Hegerl's assumptions (Hegerl & Juckel 1993). But the brain serotonin system is complex and recent studies suggest that other deductions can, in fact, be drawn from Hegerl's approach (see Kähkönen *et al.* 2002b; Priotti-Cecchini *et al.* 1997). Explanations have to take into account that multiple types and subtypes of receptors have different, excitatory or inhibitory, actions on different physiological processes. This situation is further complicated by the adaptive changes of receptors for instance after acute drug challenge (up-regulation). Yatham *et al.* (2001) showed that ATD decreased 5-HT2 receptor binding in various areas including temporal and frontal regions. Finally, ATD effects can impact differently on cerebral functions via presynaptic or postsynaptic receptors over time. As such, recent findings indicating a lower intensity dependence after ATD do seem to be compatible with the core assumptions of Hegerl's approach after all.

4.5. Molecular genetic variation of sensation seeking: Monoamine relevant polymorphisms and intensity dependence

Quantitative genetic studies have shown high heritabilities of sensation seeking (see Section 3.3) and BAD. This raises the question as to the molecular genetic bases of these findings. In view of the assumed monoaminergic modulation of sensation seeking, it seems worth considering the role of functional polymorphisms in monoaminergic neurotransmission.

Because individual differences in serotonergic neurotransmission are likely to be attributable, at least in part, to variation in serotonin-relevant genes, functional variants of these genes can be expected to account for some of the interindividual variance in a serotonergic modulated intensity dependence. A functional polymorphism of the serotonin transporter gene (5-HTTLPR) has been shown to be associated with transporter expression and function (Lesch *et al.* 1996). The presence of the short form (s) of this polymorphism impairs the gene transcription efficiency and reduces serotonin transporter levels and serotonin reuptake (as compared to the long form, l). 5-HTTLPR has been associated with several traits assumed to be modulated by serotonergic neurotransmission including anxiety-related traits (Lesch 2001).

The goal of the fourth study (Strobel *et al.* 2003b) was thus to investigate whether 5-HTTLPR is associated with the intensity dependence of the AEP. However, the data currently available did not allow us to make a directed prediction as to whether the short 5-HTTLPR allele leads to less or more serotonergic neurotransmission. Studies in humans have shown that the short allele is associated with higher scores in anxiety-related traits which presumably reflect higher serotonergic function (Lesch *et al.* 1996). However, animal studies with serotonin transporter gene knockout mice point in the opposite direction (reduced levels in various brain areas). Because of these difficulties, we hypothesized — without specifying a direction — that individuals with distinct 5-HTTLPR genotypes would differ with regard to the AEP intensity dependence (augmenting/reducing).

Furthermore, there are indications of dopaminergic influences on the intensity dependence of the AEP. Juckel *et al.* (1997) showed that application of the D1/D2 agonist apomorphine significantly reduced intensity dependence in cats. Other findings point in the same direction, e.g. Bruneau *et al.* 1986, found that high dopaminergic neurotransmission correlates with weak intensity dependence. At present, the empirical evidence indicates that the DRD4 exon III polymorphism is most likely to impact on the dopaminergic modulation of personality variables, particularly novelty seeking and sensation seeking (Ebstein *et al.* 1996; Strobel *et al.* 1999). Benjamin *et al.* (2000), Auerbach *et al.* (1999) and Strobel *et al.* (2003b) found interactive effects of 5-HTTLPR and DRD4 Exon III on individual differences in personality traits. The polymorphism consists of a 48 bp sequence with two to ten repetitions, the four and seven repeat being the most frequent alleles. A similar interaction effect may also be of importance in the modulation of the intensity dependence.The fourth study thus additionally investigated possible interaction effects of serotonergic and dopaminergic neurotransmission on the intensity dependence of the AEP.

Sixty individuals completed personality questionnaires before and after EEG recording within the augmenting/reducing paradigm (see above). Methods of EEG recording and AEP analysis followed our previous studies (Brocke *et al.* 1999, 2000).

Reliabilities of the linear N1/P2 slope at C3, Cz and C4, were notable, with the highest reliability observable for Cz ($r = 0.83$) and the lowest for C4 ($r = 0.70$). Reliabilities of the median slopes were comparably high (0.70–0.80). As expected the reliabilities of the N1/P2 slopes were higher than those for the N1, and P2 slopes, respectively.

To assess whether 5-HTTPLR influences the intensity dependence of the AEP an ANOVA was performed with repeated measures on electrode position (within-subjects factor) and 5-HTTLPR genotype (ll vs. ls vs. ss) as a group (between-subjects) factor. The results showed no position effect and no significant interaction of position and 5-HTTLPR genotype (group) on the intensity dependence of the AEP (N1/P2 median slopes). There was a significant between-subjects effect of the 5-HTTPLR polymorphism on the intensity dependence ($F_{2,57} = 5.03, p = 0.010$; s. Figure 4).

This effect accounted for 15% of the variance of the N1/P2 median slopes. Post hoc tests showed that individuals with the 5-HTTLPR ll polymorphism had higher slopes than individuals with the ls polymorphism. No differences in intensity dependence (N1/P2 median slopes) were observed for the two other comparisons (ll vs. ss and ls vs. ss).

Analyses of a potential interaction effect of 5-HTTLPR and DRD4 exon III on the intensity dependence could only be performed under restricted conditions. Because there were only two individuals with and five individuals without the DRD4 exon III 7 repeat allele in the 5-HTTLPR ss group, analyses could only be run for the 5-HTTLPR ll vs ls comparison. However, a two factors repeated measures ANOVA (electrode position × 5-HTTLPR) revealed that neglecting the ss group did not alter the effect of 5-HTTLPR on

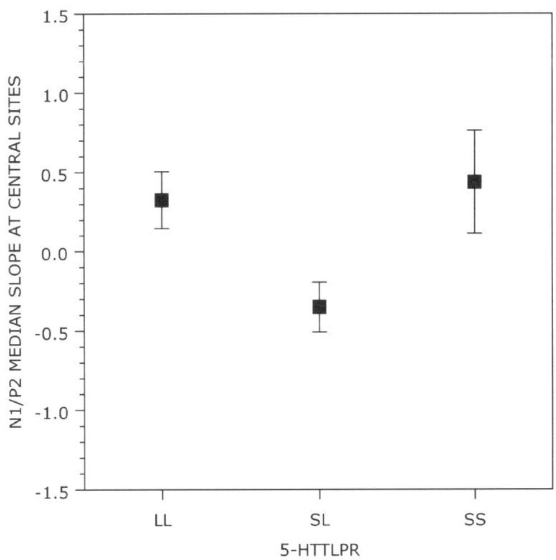

Figure 4: N1/P2 median slopes (collapsed across three central scalp sites C3, Cz, C4) of subgroups defined by 5-HTTLPR genotype (ll group: $N = 23$; ls group: $N = 30$; ss group: $N = 7$); 5-HTTLPR main effect, $p = 0.01$; post hoc comparisons: ll vs. ls, $p = 0.02$; other post hoc comparisons $p > 0.05$. *Source:* From Strobel *et al.* (2003b). Copyright 2003 by Wiley-Liss. Reprinted by permission.

the AEP intensity dependence ($\eta^2 = 0.13$). A subsequent three-factor repeated measures ANOVA with electrode position as within-subjects factor and 5-HTTLPR (ll vs. ls) and DRD4 exon III (absence vs. presence of the 7 repeat allele) as group factors again revealed a significant main effect of 5-HTTLPR on AEP intensity dependence but no DRD4 exon III main effect. There was no significant position effect, no interaction effect between position and DRD4 exon III and no three-way interaction between the polymorphisms and position. With respect to a potential between-subjects interaction effect of the polymorphisms, the analysis revealed that although there was no DRD4 exon III main effect and no interaction of the polymorphisms, the main effect of 5-HTTLPR on the AEP intensity dependence (N1/P2 median slopes) was even more pronounced ($\eta^2 = 0.18$). Figure 5 illustrates how the main effect of 5-HTTLPR on the intensity dependence is influenced by including DRD4 exon III as a second group factor in the ANOVA.

In summary, the fourth study supports the assumption of a relation between interindividual variation in serotonergic function and individual differences in the intensity dependence of the AEP. The results showed a significant effect of the serotonin transporter polymorphism 5-HTTLPR on the AEP intensity dependence. Individuals with the ll-allele (more efficient transporter) had steeper N1/P2 slopes than individuals with the ls allele. This relation is stronger when DRD4 exon III is additionally considered in the analyses. Further research is needed, however, to allow an interpretation of the results with regard to the assumption of lower serotonergic function in individuals with steeper ASF slopes.

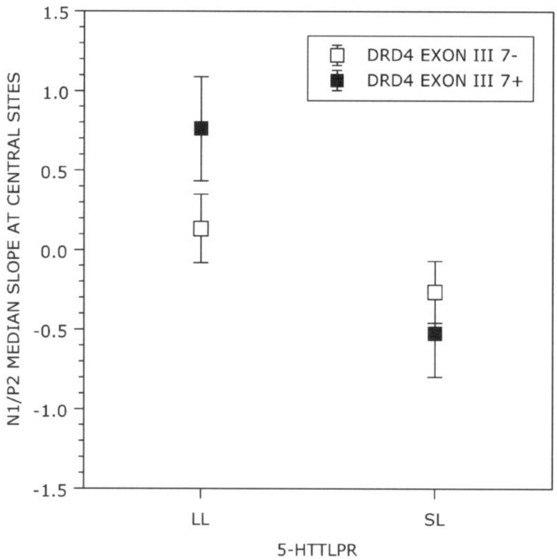

Figure 5: N1/P2 median slopes (collapsed across three central scalp sites C3, Cz, C4) of subgroups defined by 5-HTTLPR genotype and by the absence (7−) vs. presence (7+) of the DRD4 exon III 7 repeat allele (ll/7-group, $N = 16$; ll/7+, $N = 7$; ls/7−, $N = 20$; ls/7+, $N = 10$); 5-HTTLPR main effect, $p = 0.002$; DRD4 exon III main effect and 5-HTTLPR × DRD4 exon III interaction $p > 0.05$. *Source:* From Strobel *et al.* (2003b). Copyright 2003 by Wiley-Liss. Reprinted by permission.

5. Outlook

The results of the studies presented, systematically exploring aspects of sensation seeking on four different levels, can be summarized as follows. On the psychophysiological level, the key finding of a positive correlation between sensation seeking and the intensity dependence of the AEP was replicated once more in the studies. BAD patients seem to share a common characteristic with sensation seekers, they are both characterized by a strong intensity dependence of the AEP. The results with regard to UPD patients are less clear. It may be that the interactive influences of the serotonergic and dopaminergic polymorphisms have differential effects on the two groups. We did not succeed in our aim of manipulating serotonergic neurotransmission and serotonergic modulated AEP intensity dependence more directly in the present study. First results have been seen in more recent investigations, however, once again raising the question of the direction of the effects on the complex serotonergic system. Our results support the assumption that at least two functionally relevant polymorphisms influence the intensity dependence of the AEP. This seems to be reflected, in part at least, in the results on the psychometric level, which reveal BAD patients to exhibit higher sensation seeking scores than UPD patients.

To summarize, in contrast to the dominant correlational structural theories, the sensation seeking theory goes far beyond a descriptive approach (Brocke 2000). The research program presented, in which consecutive studies systematically investigate aspects of sensation seeking on four different levels, highlights the merits of Zuckerman's approach. As a multimodal causal theory of personality with explanatory potential, it has paradigmatic character as do some other biopsychological theories, primarily the influential PEN theory (Eysenck 1967; Eysenck & Eysenck 1985; cf. Brocke & Battmann 1992). To draw on Cronbach (1957), theories of this kind are not just preliminary forms of a substantial theory, but substantial scientific theories in their own right. Nevertheless, given the current state of research and the predominance of quasi-experimental designs, we should remain cautious about making causal interpretations.

Sensation seeking theory also has some weaknesses, however, and is in need of enhancement in several respects. These include some vague and unresolved aspects of its assumptions. We have already drawn attention to the ambiguity of assuming a transmitter to have high or low neurotransmission. Some assumptions still appear rather unspecific; e.g. that of a relationship between low serotonergic neurotransmission and low inhibition. Hypotheses such as these can only be regarded as the first rudimentary outlines of an explanation.

Zuckerman's theory has entailed very swift revisions of some of the original explanations. This particularity could also be of benefit, however, as it is compatible with the concept of a top-down theory (Brocke & Bartussek 1993; Zuckerman 1994b). Theories of this kind start by focusing on their psychometric subtheories, and only later attempt to find biopsychological explanations for them. The resulting biopsychological explanatory assumptions are thus often rather preliminary in nature and frequently have pilot character. However, this also means that the biopsychological base of such theories remains much more receptive to new forms of explanation as biopsychological basic research continues to develop. As such, these theories have great developmental potential.

The successive attempts to explain individual differences in the augmenting/reducing of acoustic evoked potentials described in the present paper highlight the particular receptiveness of sensation seeking theory to progress in neuroscience. Recent neurogenetic developments, which may help to account for individual differences in augmenting/reducing, seem particularly promising in this connection. The prospect of explaining aspects of affective disorders as extreme forms of sensation seeking also has great developmental potential (Brocke *et al.* 2000; Zuckerman 1999). Ultimately, the success of a biopsychological theory of sensation seeking may hinge on whether it is possible to integrate new findings from biopsychological basic research continuously, and to use these new insights to further develop the theory.

Acknowledgments

Parts of Paragraphs 3 and 5 are based on Brocke, Strobel and Müller (2003).

I would like to thank André Beauducel for his helpful comments.

References

Auerbach, J., Geller, V., Lazar, S., Shinwell, E., Belmaker, R. H., Levine, J., & Ebstein, R. (1999). Dopamine D4 receptor (D4DR) and serotonin transporter promoter (5-HTTLPR) polymorphisms in the determination of temperament in 2-month-old infants. *Molecular Psychiatry, 4*, 369–373.

Beauducel, A., Debener, S., Brocke, B., & Kayser, J. (2000). On the reliability of augmenting/reducing: Peak amplitudes and principal component analysis of auditory evoked potentials. *Journal of Psychophysiology, 14*, 226–240.

Benjamin, J., Osher, Y., Kotler, M., Gritsenko, I., Nemanov, L., Belmaker, R. H., & Ebstein, R. P. (2000). Association between tridimensional personality questionnaire (TPQ) traits and three functional polymorphisms: Dopamine receptor D4 (DRD 4), serotonin transporter promoter region (5-HTTLPR), and catechol O-methyltransferase (COMT). *Molecular Psychiatry, 5*, 96–100.

ten Berge, M., & De Raad, B. (2001). The construction of a joint taxonomy of traits and situations. *European Journal of Personality, 15*, 253–276.

Björk-Akesson, E. (1990). *Measuring sensation seeking*. Göteborg: Acta Universitatis Gothoburgensis.

Brocke, B. (2000). Das bemerkenswerte Comeback der Differentiellen Psychologie. Glückwünsche und Warnungen vor einem neuen Desaster [The remarkable comeback of personality psychology: Congratulations and warnings against a new disaster]. *Zeitschrift für Differentielle und Diagnostische Psychologie, 21*, 5–30.

Brocke, B., & Bartussek, D. (1993). Biopsychologische Persönlichkeitstheorien: Entwicklungsperspektiven und Ergebnisse [Biopsychological theories of personality: Developmental perspectives and findings]. In: L. Montada (Hrsg.), *Bericht über den 38. Kongress der Deutschen Gesellschaft für Psychologie in Trier 1992* (pp. 850–853). Göttingen: Hogrefe & Huber.

Brocke, B., & Battmann, W. (1992). The arousal-activation theory of extraversion and neuroticism: A systematic analysis and principal conclusion. *Advances in Behaviour, Research and Therapy, 14*, 211–246.

Brocke, B., Beauducel, A., John, R., Debener, S., & Heilemann, H. (2000). Sensation seeking and affective disorders: Characteristics in the intensity dependence of acoustic evoked potentials. *Neuropsychobiology, 41*, 24–30.

Brocke, B., Beauducel, A., & Tasche, K. (1999). Biopsychological bases and behavioral correlates of sensation seeking: Characteristics in the intensity dependence of auditory evoked potentials. *Personality and Individual Differences, 26*, 1103–1123.

Brocke, B., Strobel, A., & Müller, J. (2003). Sensation Seeking: Eine biopsychologische Mehr-Ebenen-Theorie [Sensation Seeking: A biopsychological multi-level theory]. In: M. Roth, & P. Hammelstein (Eds), *Sensation Seeking: Konzeption, diagnostik und anwendung* (pp. 29–51). Göttingen: Hogrefe & Huber.

Bruneau, N., Barthelemy, C., Jouve, J., & Lelord, G. (1986). Frontal auditory-evoked potential augmenting-reducing and urinary homovanillic acid. *Neuropsychobiology, 16*, 78–84.

Buchsbaum, M. S., Goodwin, F., Murphy, D., & Borge, G. (1971). AER in affective disorders. *American Journal of Psychiatry, 128*, 19–25.

Buchsbaum, M. S., & Silverman, J. (1968). Stimulus intensity control and the evoked cortical response. *Psychomatic Medicine, 30*, 12–22.

Buse, L., & Pawlik, K. (1996). Ambulatory behavioral assessment and in-field performance testing. In: J. Fahrenberg, & M. Myrtek (Eds), *Ambulatory assessment* (pp. 29–50). Göttingen: Hogrefe & Huber.

Carpenter, L. L., Anderson, G. M., Pelton, G. H., Gudin, J. A., Kirwin, P. D. S., Price, L. H., Heninger, G. R., & McDougle, C. J. (1998). Tryptophan depletion during continuous CSF sampling in healthy human subjects. *Neuropsychopharmacology, 19*, 26–35.

Carrillo-de-la-Peña, M. T. (1992). ERP augmenting/reducing and sensation seeking: A critical review. *International Journal of Psychophysiology, 12*, 211–220.

Carrillo-de-la-Peña, M. T. (2001). One-year test-retest reliability of auditory evoked potentials (AEPs) to tones of increasing intensity. *Psychophysiology, 38*, 417–424.

Carton, S., Jouvent, R., Bungener, C., & Widlöcher, D. (1992). Sensation seeking and depressive mood. *Personality and Individual Differences, 13*, 843–849.

Cloninger, C. R. (1986). A unified biosocial theory of personality and its role in the development of anxiety states. *Psychiatric Developments, 3*, 167–226.

Cloninger, C. R. (1987). A systematic method for clinical description and classification of personality variants. A proposal. *Archives of General Psychiatry, 44*, 573–588.

Comrey, A. L. (1995). *Manual and handbook of interpretations for the Comrey Personality Scales.* San Diego: EdITS Publishers.

Connolly, J. F., & Gruzelier, J. H. (1986). Persistent methodological problems with evoked potential augmenting-reducing. *International Journal of Psychophysiology, 3*, 299–306.

Coursey, R. D., Buchsbaum, M. S., & Frankel, B. L. (1975). Personality measures and evoked responses in chronic insoniacs. *Journal of Abnormal Psychology, 24*, 239–249.

Costa, P. T., Jr., & McCrae, R. R. (1992). *Revised NEO Personality Inventory (NEO-PI-R) and NEO Five-Factor Inventory (NEO-FFI) professional manual.* Odessa, FL: Psychological Assessment Resources.

Croft, R. J., Klugman, A., Baldeweg, T., & Gruzelier, J. H. (2001). Electrophysiological evidence of serotonergic impairment in long-term MDMA ("ecstasy") users. *American Journal of Psychiatry, 158*, 1687–1692.

Cronbach, L. J. (1957). The two disciplines of scientific psychology. *American Psychologist, 12*, 671–684.

Cronin, C., & Zuckerman, M. (1992). Sensation seeking and bipolar affective disorder. *Personality and Individual Differences, 13*, 385–387.

Debener, S., Strobel, A., Kirschner, K., Kranczioch, C., Hebenstreit, J., Maercker, A., Beauducel, A., & Brocke, B. (2002). Is auditory evoked potential augmenting/reducing affected by acute tryptophan depletion? *Biological Psychology, 59*, 121–133.

Depue, R., & Collins, P. (1999). Neurobiology of the structure of personality: Dopamine, facilitation of incentive motivation, and extraversion. *Behavioral and Brain Sciences*, *22*, 491–569.

Dierks, T., Barta, S., Demisch, L., Schmeck, K., Englert, E., Kewitz, A., Maurer, K., & Poustka, F. (1999). Intensity dependence of auditory evoked potentials (AEPs) as biological marker for cerebral serotonin levels: Effects of tryptophan depletion in healthy subjects. *Psychopharmacology*, *146*, 101–107.

Duaux, E., Gorwood, P., Griffon, N., Bourdel, M.-C., Sautel, F., Sokoloff, P., Schwartz, J. C., Ades, J., Loo, H., & Poirier, M. F. (1998). Homozygosity at the dopamine D3 receptor gene is associated with opiate dependence. *Molecular Psychiatry*, *3*, 33–336.

Ebstein, R. P., Novick, O., Umansky, R., Priel, B., Osher, Y., Blaine, D., Bennett, E. R., Nemanov, L., Katz, M., & Belmaker, R. H. (1996). Dopamine D4 receptor (D4DR) exon III polymorphism associated with the personality trait of Novelty Seeking. *Nature Genetics*, *12*, 78–80.

Eysenck, H. J. (1963). *Experiments with drugs*. New York: Pergamon.

Eysenck, H. J. (1967). *The biological bases of personality*. Springfield, IL: Charles C. Thomas.

Eysenck, H. J. (1981). *General features of the model*. Berlin: Springer.

Eysenck, H. J., & Eysenck, M. W. (1985). *Personality and individual differences: A natural science perspective*. New York: Plenum.

Eysenck, H. J., & Eysenck, S. B. G. (1991). *Manual of the Eysenck Personality Scale (EPS-Adult)*. London: Hodder and Stoughton.

Eysenck, S. B. G., Daum, I., Schugens, M. M., & Diehl, J. M. (1990). A cross-cultural study of impulsiveness, venture-sameness and empathy: Germany and England. *Zeitschrift für Differentielle und Diagnostische Psychologie*, *11*, 209–213.

Eysenck, S. B. G., Eysenck, H. J., & Barrett, P. (1985). A revised version of the psychoticism scale. *Personality and Individual Differences*, *6*, 21–29.

Fahrenberg, J., & Myrtek, M. (Eds) (1996). *Ambulatory assessment*. Göttingen: Hogrefe & Huber.

Feij, J. A., Orlebeke, J. F., Gazendam, A., & van Zuilen, R. (1985). *Sensation seeking: Measurement and psychophysiological correlates*. Washington, DC: Hemisphere.

Fulker, D. W., Eysenck, S. B. G., & Zuckerman, M. (1980). A genetic and environmental analysis of Sensation Seeking. *Journal of Research in Personality*, *14*, 261–281.

Gallinat, J., Bottlender, R., Juckel, G., Munke-Puchner, A., Stotz, G., Kuss, H. J., Mavrogiorgou, P., & Hegerl, U. (2000). The loudness dependency of auditory evoked N1/P2-component as a predictor of the acute SSRJ response in depression. *Psychopharmacology*, *148*, 404–411.

Goldberg, L. R. (1993). The structure of phenotypic personality traits. *Psychologist*, *48*, 26–34.

Golding, J. F., & Richards, M. (1985). EEG spectral analysis, visual evoked potential and photic driving correlates of personality and memory. *Personality and Individual Differences*, *6*, 67–76.

Gray, J. A. (1991a). *The neuropsychology of temperament*. New York: Plenum Press.

Gray, J. A. (1991b). *The psychology of fear and stress* (2. Aufl). Cambridge: Cambridge University Press.

van Heck, G. L., Perugini, M., Caprara, G. V., & Tröger, J. (1994). The Big Five as tendencies in situations. *Personality and Individual Differences*, *16*, 715–731.

Hegerl, U., Gallinat, J., & Juckel, G. (2001). Event-related potentials. Do they reflect serotonergic neurotransmission and do they predict clinical response to serotonin agonists? *Journal of Affective Disorders*, *62*, 93–100.

Hegerl, U., Gallinat, J., & Mrowinski, D. (1995). Sensory cortical processing and the biological basis of personality. *Biological Psychiatry*, *37*, 467–472.

Hegerl, U., & Herrmann, W. M. (1990). Event-related potentials and the prediction of differential drug response in psychiatry. *Neuropsychobiology*, *23*, 99–108.

Hegerl, U., & Juckel, G. (1993). Intensity dependence of auditory evoked potentials as an indicator of central serotonergic neurotransmission: A new hypothesis. *Biological Psychiatry*, *33*, 173–187.

Hegerl, U., Karnauchow, L., Herrmann, W. M., & Müller-Oerlinghausen, B. (1992). Intensity dependence of auditory evoked N1/P2 component and personality. *Neuropsychobiology*, *26*, 173–187.

Hegerl, U., Prochno, J., Ulrich, G., & Müller-Oerlinghausen, B. (1988). Are auditory evoked potentials suitable for predicting the response to lithium prohylaxis? A study on the effects of repeated measurement, age, gender and personality on the amplitude/stimulus intensity function in healthy volunteers. *Pharmacopsychiatry*, *21*, 336–337.

Horvath, P., & Zuckerman, M. (1993). Sensation seeking, risk appraisal, and risky behavior. *Personality and Individual Differences*, *14*, 41–52.

Hur, Y.-M., & Bouchard, T. J., Jr. (1997). The genetic correlation between impulsivity and sensation seeking traits. *Behavior Genetics*, *27*, 455–463.

Juckel, G., Hegerl, U., Molnár, M., Csepé, V., & Karmos, G. (1999). Auditory evoked potentials reflect serotonergic neuronal activity — a study in behaving cats administered drugs acting on 5-HT1A autoreceptors in the dorsal raphe nucleus. *Neuropsychopharmacology*, *21*, 710–716.

Juckel, G., Molnár, M., Hegerl, U., Csepé, V., & Karmos, G. (1997). Auditory-evoked potentials as indicator of brain serotonergic activity — first evidence in behaving cats. *Biological Psychiatry*, *41*, 1181–1195.

Kähkönen, S., Ahveninen, J., Pennanen, S., Liesivuori, J., Ilmoniemi, R. J., & Jääskiläinen, I. P. (2002a). Serotonin modulates early cortical processing in healthy subjects. Evidence from MEG study with trypophan depletion. *Neuropsychopharmcology*, *27*, 862–868.

Kähkönen, S., Jääskeläinen, I. P., Pennanen, S., Liesivuori, J., & Ahveninen, J. (2002b). Acute tryptophan depletion decreases intensity dependence of auditory evoked magnetic N1/P2 dipole source activity. *Psychopharmacology*, *164*, 221–227.

Kluger, A. N., Siegfried, Z., & Ebstein, R. P. (2002). A meta-analysis of the association between DRD4 polymorphism and novelty seeking. *Molecular Psychiatry*, *7*, 712–717.

von Knorring, L. (1982). Effect of impramine and zimelidine on the augmenting-reducing response of visual-evoked potentials in healthy volunteers. *Advanced Biological Psychiatry*, *9*, 81–86.

von Knorring, L., Johannson, F., & Almay, B. (1980). Augmenting/reducing response in visual evoked potentials in patients with chronic pain syndromes. *Advanced Biological Psychiatry*, *4*, 55–62.

Koopmans, J. R., Boomsma, D. I., Heath, A. C., & van Doornen, L. J. P. (1995). A multivariate genetic analysis of sensation seeking. *Behavior Genetics*, *25*, 349–356.

Lesch, K. P. (2001). Serotonin transporter: From genomics and knockouts to behavioral traits and psychiatric disorders. In: M. Briley, & F. Sulser (Eds), *Molecular genetics of mental disorders* (pp. 221–267). London: Martin Dunitz.

Lesch, K. P., Bengel, D., Heils, A., Sabol, S. Z., Greenberg, B. D., Petri, S., Benjamin, J., Muller, C. R., Hamer, D. H., & Murphy, D. L. (1996). Association of anxiety-related traits with a polymorphism in the serotonin transporter regulatory region. *Science*, *274*, 1527–1531.

Moore, P., Landolt, H. P., Seifritz, E., Clark, C., Bhatti, T., Kelsoe, J., Rapaport, M., & Gillin, J. C. (2000). Clinical and psychological consequences of rapid tryptophan depletion. *Neuropsychopharmacology*, *23*, 601–622.

Neary, R. S., & Zuckerman, M. (1976). Sensation seeking, trait and state anxiety, and the electrodermal orienting reflex. *Psychophysiology*, *13*, 205–211.

Nishizawa, S., Benkelfat, C., Young, S. N., Leyton, M., Mzengeza, S., DeMontigny, C., Blier, P., & Diksic, M. (1997). Differences between male and females in rates of serotonin synthesis in human brain. *Proceedings of the National Academy of Sciences of the USA*, *94*, 5308–5313.

Passini, F. T., Watson, C. G., Dehnel, L., Herder, J., & Watkins, B. (1977). Alpha wave feedback training therapy in alcoholics. *Journal of Clinical Psychology*, *33*, 292–299.

Pawlik, K. (1995). Persönlichkeit und Verhalten: Zur Standortbestimmung von differentieller Psychologie. In: K. Pawlik, H. Bock, S. Bodenburg, L. Buse, & G. Sammer (Eds), *Bericht über den*

39. Kongress der Deutschen Gesellschaft für Psychologie in Hamburg 1994 (pp. 31–49). Göttingen: Hogrefe & Huber.

Pawlik, K., & Buse, L. (1996). Verhaltensbeobachtung in Labor und Feld. In: K. Pawlik (Ed.), *Grundlagen und Methoden der Differentiellen Psychologie* (Enzyklopädie der Psychologie, Serie VIII, Bd. 1, pp. 359–394).

Petrie, A. (1967). *Individuality in pain and suffering*. Chicago: University of Chicago Press.

Pogue-Geile, M., Ferrell, R., Deka, R., Debski, T., & Manuck, S. (1998). Human Novelty-Seeking Personality Traits and Dopamine D4 receptor polymorphisms: A twin and genetic association study. *American Journal of Medical Genetics, 81*, 44–48.

Priotti-Cecchini, A., Afra, J., & Schoenen, J. (1997). Intensity dependence of the cortical auditory evoked potentials as a surrogate marker of central nervous system serotonin transmission in man: Demonstration of a central effect for the 5HT agonist zolmitriptan (311C90, Zolmig). *Cephalgia, 17*, 849–854.

Ratsma, J. E., van der Stelt, O., Schoffelmeer, A. N. M., Westerveld, A., & Gunning, W. B. (2001). P3 event-related potential dopamine d2 receptor al allele, and sensation seeking in adult children of alcoholics. *Alcoholism: Clinical and Experimental Research, 25*, 960–967.

Ridgeway, D., & Hare, R. D. (1981). Sensation seeking and psychophysiological responses to auditory stimulation. *Psychophysiology, 18*, 613–618.

Smith, B. D., Davidson, R. A., Smith, D. L., Goldstein, H., & Perlstein, W. (1989). Sensation seeking and arousal: Effects of strong stimulation on electrodermal activation and memory task performance. *Personality and Individual Differences, 10*, 671–679.

Stern, G. S., Cox, J., & Shahan, D. (1981). Feedback in pulse rate change and divergent affective reactions for high and low sensation seekers. *Biofeedback and Self Regulation, 6*, 315–326.

Strobel, A., Debener, S., Schmidt, D., Hünnerkopf, R., Lesch, K.-P., & Brocke, B. (2003a). Allelic variation in serotonin transporter function associated with the intensity dependence of the auditory evoked potential. *American Journal of Medical Genetics, 118B*, 41–47.

Strobel, A., Lesch, K. P., Jatzke, F., Petzold, F., & Brocke, B. (2003b). Further evidence for a modulation of novelty seeking by DRD4 exon III, 5-HTTLPR, and COMT val/met variants. *Molecular Psychiatry, 8*, 371–372.

Strobel, A., Wehr, A., Michel, A., & Brocke, B. (1999). Association between the dopamine D4 receptor (DRD4) exon III polymorphism and measures of Novelty Seeking in a German population. *Molecular Psychiatry, 4*, 378–384.

Tuchtenhagen, F., Daumann, J., Norra, C., Gobbele, R., Becker, S., Pelz, S., Sass, H., Buchner, H., & Gouzoulis-Mayfrank, E. (2000). High intensity dependence of auditory evoked dipole source activity indicates decreased serotonergic activity in abstinent ecstasy (MDMA) users. *Neuropsychopharmacology, 22*, 608–617.

Watson, C. G., Jacobs, C., & Herder, J. (1979). Correlates of alpha, beta and theta wave production. *Journal of Clinical Psychology, 35*, 364–369.

Yatham, I. N., Liddle, P. F., Shia, I. S., Lam, R. W., Adam, M. J., Athanasios, P., & Ruth, T. J. (2001). Effects of rapid tryptophan depletion on brain 5-HT2 receptor: A PET study. *British Journal of Psychiatry, 178*, 448–453.

Zuckerman, M. (1990). The psychophysiology of sensation seeking. *Journal of Personality, 58*, 313–345.

Zuckerman, M. (1992). What is a basic factor and which factors are basic? Turtles all the way down? *Personality and Individual Differences, 13*, 675–681.

Zuckerman, M. (1993). P-Impulsive sensation seeking and its behavioral, psychophysiological and biochemical correlates. *Neuropsychobiology, 28*, 30–36.

Zuckerman, M. (1994a). *Behavioral expressions and biosocial bases of sensation seeking*. New York: Cambridge University Press.

Zuckerman, M. (1994b). Impulsive unsocialized sensation seeking: The biological foundations of a basic dimension of personality. In: J. E. Bates, & T. D. Wachs (Eds), *Temperament and individual differences at the interface of biology and behavior* (pp. 219–255). Washington: APA.

Zuckerman, M. (1995). Good and bad humors: Biochemical bases of personality and its disorders. *Psychological Science*, *6*, 325–332.

Zuckerman, M. (1996). The psychobiological model for impulsive unsocialized sensation seeking: A comparative approach. *Neuropsychobiology*, *34*, 125–129.

Zuckerman, M. (1997). The psychobiological basis of human nature. In: H. Nyborg (Ed.), *Tribute to Hans J. Eysenck at eighty* (pp. 3–16). New York: Elsevier.

Zuckerman, M. (1999). *Vulnerability to psychopathology. A biological model.* Washington: APA.

Zuckerman, M., Kuhlmann, D. M., & Camac, C. (1988). What lies beyond E and N? Factor analyses of scales believed to measure basic dimensions of personality. *Journal of Personality and Social Psychology*, *54*, 96–107.

Zuckerman, M., Kuhlmann, D. M., Joireman, J., Teta, P., & Kraft, M. (1993). A comparison of three structural models for personality: The big five, and the alternative five. *Journal of Personality and Social Psychology*, *65*, 757–768.

Zuckerman, M., Kuhlmann, D. M., Thornquist, M., & Kiers, H. (1991). Five (or three) robust questionnaire scale factors of personality without culture. *Personalilty and Individual Differences*, *12*, 929–941.

Zuckerman, M., Murtaugh, T. T., & Siegel, J. (1974). Sensation seeking and cortical augmenting-reducing. *Psychophysiology*, *11*, 535–542.

Zuckerman, M., & Neeb, M. (1979). Sensation seeking and psychopathology. *Psychiatry Research*, *1*, 255–264.

Zuckerman, M., Simons, R. F., & Como, P. G. (1988). Sensation seeking and stimulus intensity as modulators of cortical, cardiovascular, and electrodermal response: A cross-modality study. *Personality and Individual Differences*, *9*, 361–372.

Chapter 16

On the Psychophysiology of Extraversion

V. De Pascalis

1. Introduction

Initial research on individual differences in personality centered on the development of questionnaires. These were the only available tools for the description and prediction of behavior. Later, trait models were developed that attempted to move from personality description to a multilevel causal form of explanation. As noted by Gale and Eysenck (1992), psychometric methods have achieved good levels of predictive validity for psychologically and socially important human behaviors. This success in describing personality bolstered attempts to identify the biological substrate of psychometric derived indices of individual variation.

Scores on psychometric instruments are examined using a variety of procedures that record bioelectrical signals. These include procedures to monitor autonomic nervous system activity, such as electrodermal and cardiac recordings, and cortical activity, with electroencephalographic and event-related potential procedures. Investigations of elementary physiological events in normal thinking, feeling, and interacting individuals are now feasible. The techniques provide windows through which psychological processes and neurological generators of bioelectric activity can be observed unobtrusively (see, e.g. the recent *Handbook of Psychophysiology* by Cacioppo *et al.* 2000). A number of different psychophysiological responses and methods are applied to verify hypotheses and for further exploration of the biological bases of temperament and personality dimensions, notably extraversion (E), neuroticism (N) and sensation seeking (SS). The research on biological and psychophysiological determinants of temperament and personality emerged from specific hypotheses proposed by Pavlov and Eysenck in their classic experimental research on personality (Eysenck 1963, 1967; Nebylitsyn & Gray 1972; Strelau 1983).

This chapter begins with a brief outline of the main hypotheses that were explored using psychophysiological methods to study individual differences in personality, with specific emphasis on the extraversion trait. Subsequently, the most consistent psychophysiological results will be described and discussed.

On the Psychobiology of Personality
Edited by R. M. Stelmack

ISBN: 0-08-044209-9

2. The Physiological Bases of Personality: Extraversion and the Inverted-U

Eysenck (1967) proposed that individual differences in E could be understood in terms of differences in optimal levels of arousal. This concept was previously elaborated by Hebb (1955) and linked to functions of the ascending reticular activating system (ARAS; Moruzzi & Magoun 1949). This system regulated the activation of the cortex. It was advanced that the set point of activation (threshold) of the ARAS of introverts was lower than for extraverts. Extraverts, on the other hand, who were characterized by higher thresholds of arousal in the ARAS, reach their optimal level of arousal at higher levels of stimulation. Although the physiological mechanisms of arousal and arousability were not explicitly defined, the hypothesis of optimal level of arousal proved to have strong heuristic value. The arousal hypothesis attracted a great number of studies on individual differences in E, N and SS using electrocortical and autonomic indices of activation of the ARAS.

Zuckerman's interest in the role of catecholamines in personality led him to the work of Stein (1978) and Gray (1982, 1987). They attributed a central role to dopamine in approach motivation and reward mechanisms of the mesolimbic system. An analysis of the literature on the monoamines led Zuckerman to reconsider the optimal level of arousal theory. Instead of the ARAS, he focused on the activity of the brain catecholamine systems, i.e. dopaminergic and noradrenergic systems (Zuckerman 1979, 1984). Positive mood, exploratory activity and sociability (extraversion) are expressions of optimal levels of catecholamine activity. Some years later, Zuckerman (1991, 1994) formulated a model in which monoamine neurotransmitters play a leading role in personality traits. He linked dopamine to approach motivation, serotonin to behavioral inhibition and norepinephrine (and GABA) to arousal mechanisms.

In his review of the biological bases of personality, Eysenck (1990) outlined the problems encountered by the researcher in attempting to link physiological functioning, behavior, and personality. One of the most relevant problems raised by Eysenck (1990) concerns the fact that a single physiological measure cannot be considered a representative index of general cortical arousal or excitation. It is known, in fact, from psychophysiological research (Lacey 1967; Lacey & Lacey 1958) that certain events, such as emotional stimuli, may act in different ways in different physiological systems, depending on individual differences, i.e. response specificity. One individual may be prone to react to a threatening stimulus through a rapid increase in skin conductance activity; another through an increase in heart rate; and a third through a more pronounced activation of the EEG, and so forth. Therefore, no single physiological measure is sufficient to describe the complexity of the response. One possible way to resolve this issue is to take measures that are representative of a large number of systems and to score physiological changes in the activity of the most relevant systems.

Eysenck's (1967) view of physiological arousal is multidimensional because he postulates two distinct systems: cortical and visceral arousal. Although it is clear that there are numerous dimensions of arousal (Vanderwolf & Robinson 1981), it is not clear how different psychophysiological indices are composed to evaluate the reactivity of different arousal systems. From this perspective, a failure to support Eysenck's theory may be due to inaccuracy of the measuring method, or to a wrong choice of the physiological variable.

Moreover, the fact that each individual may be more sensitive to certain stimuli and less sensitive to others, i.e. stimulus specificity, may also contribute to experimental error. Individual variability in floor and ceiling effects and the difficulty in defining resting levels of a given physiological measure also pose some difficulty for evaluating the association between personality and neurophysiological measures (Eysenck 1990).

The well-known Yerkes-Dodson law (Yerkes & Dodson 1908) and the Pavlovian law of transmarginal inhibition (Pavlov 1928) also present a challenge in linking personality, behavior and physiological response. Both laws describe a nonlinear relation between stimulus and response. With increasing intensities of stimulation, the strength of response at first increases and then declines, producing an inverted-U. This inverted-U relation appears to hold for the interactive effects of E and arousal manipulations on performance and neurophysiological functioning. Arousing or stressful conditions tend to improve (or have lesser effect on) the performance of extraverts, but impair that of introverts (Revelle *et al.* 1987). To explain findings of this kind, it is generally assumed that introverts are optimally aroused, but extraverts are normally under-aroused. Increasing the intensity of stimulation increases the arousal of extraverts to the optimal level, but leads to over-arousal for introverts. However, to make a precise prediction is difficult. It can be predicted that the high-arousal of introverts, as compared to the low-arousal of extraverts, will lead to a reversal of the stimulus-response relation at a lower point of stimulus intensity than would happen for extraverts, but it is difficult to know the precise switching point. Nevertheless, both the Yerkes-Dodson law and transmarginal inhibition effects have been demonstrated for a multiplicity of behavioral responses (Eysenck & Eysenck 1985). Direct physiological evidence in support of the relation between arousal measures and performance is limited. It was observed, however, that with direct stimulation of the medial reticular formation in chimpanzees the performance is optimal for specific ranges of excitation (Fuster & Uyeda 1962).

3. Extraversion and Skin Conductance Level

The base level of electrodermal activity, or skin conductance level (SCL), is an index of tonic arousal either in the baseline resting condition or in a brief period preceding stimulation during the experimental condition. Individual differences in tonic arousal between introverts and extraverts were usually assessed with SCL measurements during periods preceding stimulation or during conditions involving simple sensory stimulation. Differences in tonic levels of electrodermal activity between introverts and extraverts are seldom observed when simple sensory stimulation is used and when subjects are not challenged by task demands (see, e.g. Coles *et al.* 1971; Davis & Cowles 1988; Kishimoto 1977; Nielsen & Petersen 1976; Smith 1983). However, some consistent findings have emerged when subjects are challenged by task demands. In particular, Fowles *et al.* (1977) compared SCL for introverts and extraverts during a series of tones varying in both stimulus intensity and amount of stress preceding the tones. Results from this study indicated that SCL is higher for extraverts at higher levels of stress and SCL is higher in introverts for lower levels of stress. In the study by Smith *et al.* (1986), introverts had higher SCLs than extraverts while they were engaged in a task requiring sustained attention and introverts were less affected by a distraction condition than were extraverts.

Electrodermal lability, i.e. the rate of spontaneous fluctuations of skin conductance response (SCR) in the absence of specific stimulation, is also considered as an index of tonic arousal (e.g. Barland & Raskin 1973). In some studies, introverts were found to exhibit a higher rate of nonspecific SCR compared to extraverts (Coles *et al.* 1971; Gange *et al.* 1979; Mangan & O'Gorman 1969).

4. Extraversion and Skin Conductance Responses

Recording of SCRs was a common procedure for assessing the arousal hypothesis. Sokolov's (1963) model of attention and the orienting response (OR) often provided a context for this work. In terms of the OR model, Eysenck (1967) predicted that introverts would exhibit stronger OR, i.e. larger SCR amplitude, and slower habituation or more persistent SCRs, compared to extraverts. These predictions were widely tested and a number of reviews of this literature are available (Eysenck 1990; Eysenck & Eysenck 1985; Graham 1979; O'Gorman 1977; Smith 1983; Stelmack 1981, 1990; Stelmack & Geen 1992). In their review of the literature, Stelmack and Geen (1992) concluded that introverts consistently exhibit greater SCR amplitudes than extraverts to simple visual stimuli and auditory stimuli of moderate intensity (75–90 dB). This effect was mainly observed in the greater initial SCR amplitude, slower habituation rate, or greater SCR amplitude to habituated stimuli following a stimulus change (Crider & Lunn 1971; Fowles *et al.* 1977; Gange *et al.* 1979; Mangan & O'Gorman 1969; Nielsen & Petersen 1976; Smith *et al.* 1981; Stelmack *et al.* 1979, 1983; Wigglesworth & Smith 1976; Zahn *et al.* 1994). Studies using auditory stimulation of low-intensity (60 dB or lower intensity) fail to differentiate introverts and extraverts (Bartol & Martin 1974; Coles *et al.* 1971; Hastrup 1979; Koriat *et al.* 1973; Krupski *et al.* 1971; Mangan 1974; Mangan & O'Gorman 1969; Sadler *et al.* 1971; Siddle & Heron 1976).

Studies using high-intensity sounds (greater than 90 dB) found a reversed relation between E and SCR, i.e. SCR amplitude was smaller for introverts, compared to extraverts (Smith *et al.* 1981, 1983, 1984; Wigglesworth & Smith 1976). The reverse relation for moderate and high-intensity tones was clearly demonstrated by Wigglesworth and Smith (1976) using 80 and 100 dB tones. The effect was attributed to transmarginal inhibition, a mechanism thought to protect the individual from harmful effects of high-intensity stimulation. It was proposed that this inhibition is initiated at lower levels of stimulation for introverts (Eysenck 1981).

Similarly, Geen (1984) reported that introverts prefer stimuli of lower intensity compared to extraverts. When introverts received bursts of noise stimuli at the stimulus intensity preferred by extraverts, introverts exhibited a greater number of evoked SCRs indicating a higher level of activation for these subjects. Extraverts that received noise bursts at the intensity preferred by the introverts displayed the smallest number of SCRs. No differences between E groups were obtained when noise bursts were delivered at the intensity level preferred by each group. These results are in line with the generally accepted view that stimulation of moderate intensity evokes a positive affective response (positive hedonic tone) whereas high-intensity stimuli are regarded as sources of discomfort (negative hedonic tone).

Smith and colleagues implemented an interesting approach to understand the relation between E and arousal in examining the differential effects of systematic arousal manipulation on extraverts and introverts (Smith *et al.* 1981, 1983). Arousal level was manipulated by varying the amount of caffeine that was ingested. Introverts exhibited larger SCRs under placebo and low stimulant dosages, whereas extraverts were more responsive with higher dosages. This study was followed by another project where arousal level was varied by caffeine dosage, stimulus intensity, and the presence or absence of a preparatory stimulus (Smith *et al.* 1984). The preparatory signal reduces the response to the stimulus that follows it. Subjects were assigned low, medium or high doses of caffeine or a placebo that were previously placed in a randomly numbered vial. Subjects heard two sets of tones of 1500 Hz with one tone at each of six intensities, 60, 70, 80, 90, 100, and 110 dB. In one set of tones, a 4.5 sec preparatory light signal onset before each tone. The light signals reduced SCR amplitudes only at the highest level of stimulus intensity. Introverts had higher overall SCL and SCR magnitudes compared to extraverts. As is shown in Figure 1, introverts had larger SCRs at the lowest three stimulus intensities, whereas with increasing stimulus intensity the group differences were diminished. In fact, introverts produced slightly smaller responses than extraverts at the highest intensity.

Another interesting effect observed in this SCR study is illustrated in Figure 2. In the non-signal condition, response amplitudes decreased for introverts with increasing dosage level of caffeine, whereas the extraverts displayed an increase in response amplitude with increasing dosage. With the presentation of the preparatory signal, introverts showed a larger initial decrease in responsiveness from the placebo to the lowest caffeine level, followed by an increase in responsiveness for the condition in which the preparatory signal was delivered. For extraverts, in contrast, the presence of the signal did not

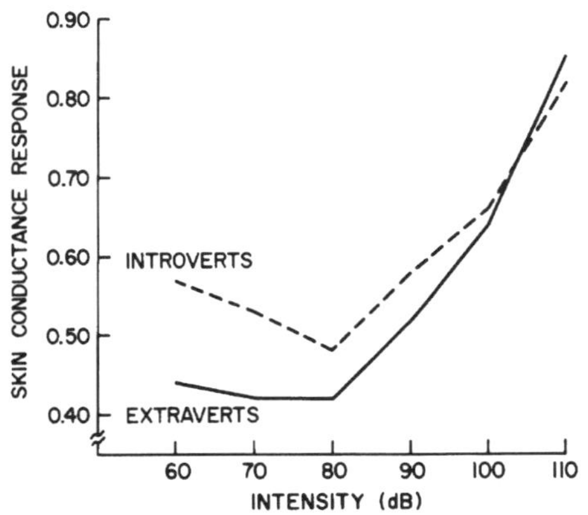

Figure 1: Skin conductance response (SCR) of introverts and extraverts as a function of stimulus intensity. *Source:* From "electrodermal activity and extraversion: Caffeine, preparatory signal and stimulus intensity effects," by B. D. Smith *et al.* (1984), *Personality and Individual Differences*, *5*, Figure 1, p. 62. Copyright by Elsevier Science Ltd. Reprinted by permission.

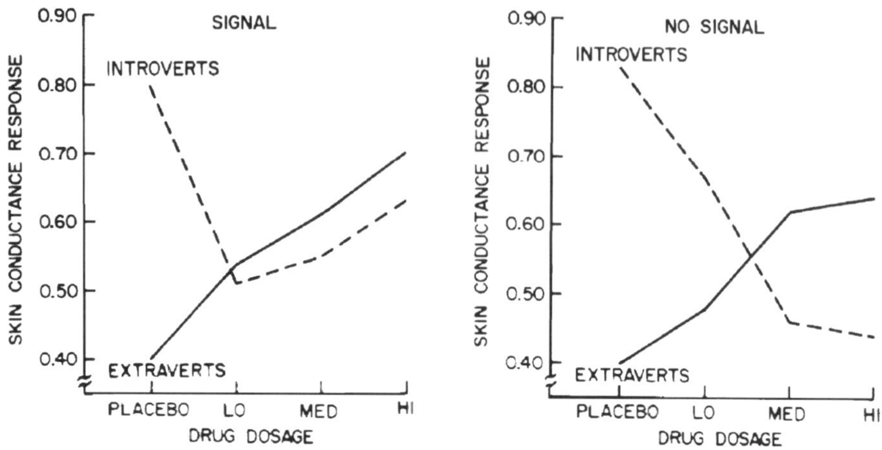

Figure 2: Interaction between personality groups (introverts vs. extraverts) and preparatory stimulus on skin conductance responses. *Source:* From "Electrodermal activity and extraversion: Caffeine, preparatory signal and stimulus intensity effects," by B. D. Smith *et al.* (1984), *Personality and Individual Differences*, *5*, Figure 3, p. 63. Copyright by Elsevier Science Ltd. Reprinted by permission.

appreciably change the response pattern as a function of caffeine dosage level. In terms of the tonic measure of SCL, an increase in SCL was observed with increasing levels of caffeine dosage and higher SCLs in introverts than in extraverts. Smith *et al.* (1984) discussed their findings in terms of the greater focus of attention induced by higher levels of arousal.

In a later study, Smith *et al.* (1986) controlled attention demands by randomly assigning half of extraverts and introverts to an attention condition and the other half to a distraction condition. Subjects received two blocks of 19 habituation trials each. One block included a test stimulus and the other included a dishabituation stimulus, i.e. a previously habituated stimulus that followed the novel test stimulus. In one of the two trial blocks an auditory, preparatory signal preceded each stimulus. Overall, introverts showed larger SCRs, and greater SCR to the dishabituation stimuli than extraverts. As expected, the preparatory signal reduced responding significantly more for introverts compared to extraverts. The distraction condition affected responses of extraverts more than it did for introverts.

The notion that introverts are morning types, i.e. have higher arousal levels and better performance in the morning than extraverts, was advanced by a number of authors (e.g. Revelle *et al.* 1987). Wilson (1990) assessed this hypothesis with a psychophysiological method by employing a self-monitoring electrodermal recording system that enabled participants to record their SCL throughout the day. Sixty-one men and 50 women measured their own SCL hourly throughout one working day, and recorded their activities and drug intake. Although it appeared that introverts were more highly aroused than extraverts in the morning, these effects were not statistically significant.

5. Extraversion, Heart Rate, and Cardiovascular Measures

A number of cardiovascular measures have been used to explore arousal differences between introverts and extraverts. In the majority of cases no differences between extraverts and introverts on baseline or tonic heart rate (HR) were reported (e.g. Myrtek 1984; Pearson & Freeman 1991). However, HR changes in response to stimuli or environmental changes yielded some more consistent findings. For example, Gange *et al.* (1979), in an experiment on vigilance, found no HR differences between introverts and extraverts during a baseline period. They did observe higher HR for introverts than for extraverts in all vigilance conditions, including a condition in which no task was performed.

Graham and Clifton (1966) suggested that phasic HR deceleration is the cardiac component of the orienting response and that phasic acceleration is the cardiac component of the defensive response. If we assume that, with increasing intensities of stimulation, introverts are more reactive than extraverts, it follows that introverts are more likely to display more pronounced HR accelerations to these stimuli than extraverts. Moreover, extraverts should display more pronounced HR decelerations to stimuli of low and moderate intensities. Results obtained in the study by Orlebeke and Feij (1979) indicate that introverts had a greater rate of HR acceleration to a tone of 60-dB intensity over the first five trials than did extraverts. However, this finding remains difficult to evaluate because only tones of a single level of intensity were used.

In a subsequent study, Hirschman and Favaro (1980) recorded HR activity during the presentation of highly aversive pictures known to elicit defensive reactions (e.g. photographs depicting mutilation). The average HR over the five beats preceding each stimulus onset and over 15 beats that followed it was analyzed for groups of introverts and extraverts. Extraverts did not show HR changes over the first eight post-stimulus beats and continuous deceleration thereafter. On the other hand, introverts initially showed a HR acceleration, but this response pattern was followed by a HR deceleration. These HR reactions to aversive stimuli can be considered in agreement with the hypotheses of Orlebeke and Feij (1979).

Geen (1984) measured pulse rates (PR) of introverts and extraverts during two paired associate learning experiments in which they either chose the level of intensity of noise to be heard or were assigned to one of four levels of noise stimulation, low, intermediate-low, intermediate-high, and high intensities. In both experiments, extraverts preferred higher intensity levels than introverts. There were no differences between groups when they were stimulated by the noise level that was preferred either by themselves or assigned to yoked members of the same personality classification. It was observed that preferred levels of stimulation in introverts and extraverts are related to arousal levels in the form of an inverted U, with introverts exhibiting higher PR than extraverts at intermediate levels of stimulation.

Pearson and Freeman (1991) engaged introverts and extraverts on an arithmetic task with various levels of difficulty. Although baseline levels were identical for the two groups, introverts showed larger HR reactivity to the task than extraverts. This difference was due to the fact that extraverts had no HR changes during the task, whereas introverts showed significantly higher HR during task performance. The easy condition produced the least difference while during moderate and difficult conditions there were equally large differences between groups.

In another study by Richards and Eves (1991), personality and temperament measures were compared between subjects who showed HR accelerative defensive responding (accelerators) and subjects whose HR remained relatively unchanged during the interval following high-intensity auditory stimulation. Introverts and subjects with low N scores, compared to extraverts and stable subjects, showed higher levels of HR throughout the experiment.

Kaiser *et al.* (1997) examined HR changes for individuals with high and low levels of N, E, and psychoticism (P). They were instructed to listen to the presentation of 10 auditory tones (60 dB, 1 kHz), i.e. an irrelevant condition, and then they were required to count the tones (relevant condition). High P subjects had smaller heart rate changes to the irrelevant stimuli and smaller differences between the relevant and irrelevant conditions than did low P subjects. High N subjects, compared to low N subjects, showed enhanced cardiac responding to relevant stimuli, but there were no effects of differences in E. The absence of differences between introverts and extraverts may be attributed to the easy task demands and low-intensity stimulation that were employed. As previously noted, differences between extraverts and introverts are consistently observed with stimulation of moderate intensity.

In Gray's (1970, 1973) modification of Eysenck's (1967) model of personality, anxiety, i.e. high N, low E, is characterized by sensitivity to signals of punishment. This disposition is mediated by a behavioral inhibition system (BIS). On the other hand, impulsiveness, i.e. low N, high E, is characterized by sensitivity to reward. This disposition is mediated by a behavioral activation system (BAS). Fowles (1980) argued that HR activity is a good index of the BAS. This, of course, leads to the prediction that higher levels of impulsivity are associated with higher levels of cardiovascular activity in response to reward stimuli. This hypothesis is somewhat at odds with the lower cardiac responses to physical stimulation of extraverts noted in this literature review.

This issue was examined by De Pascalis *et al.* (1996) who reported that high and low N subjects, as well as introverts and extraverts, were differentiated with the HR deceleration response. Extraverts were more sensitive to signals of reward, i.e. more pronounced HR deceleration to signals indicating the winning of a fixed amount of money, whereas introverts were more sensitive to signals of punishment, i.e. more pronounced HR decelerations for signals indicating a loss of a fixed amount of money. High N exhibited more pronounced anticipatory HR slowing than low N to signals of both reward and punishment. These results appear consistent with Gray's theory. However, as Matthews and Gilliland (1999) pointed out in their comparative review of the personality theories of Eysenck and Gray, it is curious that introverts, but not high N, should be especially sensitive to punishment signals.

6. Extraversion and the Electroencephalograph

Psychophysiological recording is a direct source of data for monitoring the ongoing electrical activity of the brain during perceptual and cognitive processes. High levels of arousal are indexed by low amplitude, high-frequency activity in the alpha range (8–13 Hz). The EEG, however, does have limitations as an indicator of the ongoing brain activity. First, because the EEG is recorded using electrodes placed on the scalp, activity of the cortex is not assessed directly. Second, because of volume conductivity of the electrical field in the brain, the EEG is composed of a mixture of electrical activities generated from different parts of the cortex. This may produce erroneous impressions of the source of activity from any specific area of the cortex. In spite of these limitations, EEG measures not only provided reliable indices of brain damage, but they proved to be a good way to study physiological processes underlying arousal, attention, memory, vigilance, emotion, and cognitive activities. This was apparent from the first EEG recording of alpha rhythm by Berger (1929). From this initial demonstration, there were great expectations that this technique could be employed to study the basic brain functions that mediate mental activity. Some years after Berger's discovery, Lemere (1936) suggested that the electrical activity of the brain is related in some way to personality style. The optimism for this new method was encouraged by the discovery of the function of ascending reticular). activating system (ARAS) as an arousal system of the brain (Magoun 1963; Moruzzi & Magoun 1949). Later, numerous studies investigated the relation between personality and the properties of the bioelectrical activity of the brain. A prominent area has been the association of EEG-alpha activity, recorded from the posterior regions of the skull, and individual differences in arousal between introverts and extraverts. The desynchronization of the EEG, i.e. the transition from high-amplitude, low-frequency (alpha activity) to low amplitude, high-frequency (beta activity), was linked to the increased activity of the ARAS when attention is directed to incoming stimulation or to response generation (Table 1).

After the discovery of the ARAS, some valuable insights were gained concerning the neurological generators of EEG activity (Cooper *et al.* 1965). In 1967, H. J. Eysenck incorporated those advances in understanding of the arousal system in a reformulation of his theory of personality. Eysenck proposed that individual differences in E and N are determined by differences in cortical arousal that can be indexed by EEG measures

Table 1: Mean spectral peak amplitudes of alpha (8–13 Hz) activity for introverts and extraverts over the left frontal region (FP1, F3, and F7), over the right frontal region (FP2, F4, and F8), and the central regions (Fz, Cz) where extraverts were found to have significantly higher levels of alpha activity.

	Mean (μV)	**S.D.**	**Minimum (μV)**	**Maximum (μV)**
Introversion	4.5	1.57	2.0	8.2
Extraversion	6.8	3.17	0.7	15.8
Low anxiety	5.6	2.98	2.0	15.8
High anxiety	5.9	2.64	0.7	11.6
Tender minded	5.4	3.15	0.7	15.8
Tough poise	6.1	2.44	2.0	11.6
Subduedness	6.2	3.26	2.3	15.8
Independent	5.4	2.41	0.7	11.6

($^{*}p < 0.05$; $^{**}p < 0.01$). From "Extraversion-introversion and 8–13 Hz waves in frontal cortical regions," by Y. Tran *et al.* (2001), *Personality and Individual Differences*, *30*, Table 2, p. 210. Copyright by Elsevier Science Ltd. Reprinted by permission.

(Eysenck 1967). There was considerable research interest in this arousal hypothesis. However, the enthusiasm for exploring individual differences in arousal and psychological processes with EEG measures diminished considerably because of difficulties in obtaining response-specific measures. Moreover, the evidence for linking EEG measures and personality differences has been judged inconsistent. Investigation of the relation between individual differences in personality and EEG measures of arousal has not yielded any reliable findings (Gale 1983; Stelmack 1990; Stelmack & Geen 1992).

The extensive literature that examined the relation between EEG and personality was reviewed first by Gale (1981, 1983). During the past three decades, some studies have found a positive relation between EEG alpha activity and extraversion, i.e. greater EEG alpha activity for extraverts (Gale *et al.* 1969; Marton & Urban 1966; O'Gorman & Mallise 1984; Savage 1964; Zuckerman 1991). Others reported a negative relation between EEG alpha activity and E, i.e. greater EEG alpha activity in introverts, an effect that contradicts the arousal hypothesis (Broadhurst & Glass 1969; Young *et al.* 1971) or no differences between introverts and extraverts (Fenton & Scotton 1967; Gale *et al.* 1971). Gale (1981) suggested that these inconsistent results reflect a pervasive weakness in the research methods and designs that characterize this work.

According to Gale (1981, 1983), one potential confounding factor is the arousal level elicited in the studies reviewed. Gale rated experimental conditions that require solving problems or time-controlled tasks as high-arousal experiments. Conditions in which participants are asked to do nothing, but to keep their eyes closed and not fall asleep are rated as low-arousal experiments. Gale (1981, 1983) concluded that high and low arousal conditions were not appropriate for studying relations between personality and EEG since differences between the two introverts and extraverts are masked at the extreme poles of arousal conditions. Conditions of very low arousal would produce strong feelings of boredom in extraverts and thus they are likely to attempt to increase their arousal levels. In contrast, with high levels of stimulation introverts produce the paradoxical reaction of reduced indices of arousal as postulated by the Pavlovian law of transmarginal inhibition. For the evaluation of the relation between E and EEG, Gale (1983) suggests conditions that elicit intermediate levels of arousal. This is where subjects are allowed some mild interaction with the experimenter, such us receiving instructions to open and close their eyes.

Cortical levels of activation or arousal have been associated to amplitude and frequency of the alpha rhythm (Gale 1983; Golan & Neufield 1996). High amplitudes and low frequency of the alpha rhythm are associated with a low level of arousal, while low amplitudes and a high frequency are associated with a high level of arousal. In the cases in which subjects are instructed to open and close their eyes, which require alertness without concentration, it is hypothesized that extraverts will display higher amplitudes and faster alpha waves than introverts. Gale's hypothesis was tested in three experiments using testing with eyes open and eyes closed as the two conditions. O'Gorman and Mallise (1984) carried out the first experiment in which subjects were engaged in a number of arousal conditions. E was measured using the EPQ and a measure of amplitude EEG-alpha activity was obtained. Contrary to Gale's hypothesis, extraverts were found to have more pre-stimulus alpha activity than introverts under all conditions except opening and closing eyes on instruction where the reverse was observed.

In a subsequent study in which subjects were required to open and close their eyes on instructions, O'Gorman and Lloyd (1987) reported that subjects with high scores on narrow impulsiveness showed less alpha spectral power than subjects with low scores. This study also failed to confirm Gale's hypothesis, since no differences in alpha activity were found between extraverts and introverts. In the third more recent study by Tran *et al.* (2001), four factors were controlled as possible sources of equivocal results in previous research in this field. These factors were: (1) the cortical site where the alpha wave is measured; (2) the method used for EEG analysis; (3) the questionnaire used; and (4) the age of the subjects engaged. Fast Fourier Transform was used in this study to analyze the EEG and spectral peak amplitude in the alpha band (8–13 Hz) was measured. EEG was recorded from frontal, central, and posterior scalp sites while subjects opened and closed their eyes on instructions. To reduce possible bias, a diverse sample of participants with a broad age range (22–60 yrs) was tested. Subjects completed Cattell's 16 Personality Factor questionnaire and from those results E and other dimensions were derived as second-order personality traits. Frontal EEG alpha activity was found to be associated with E, with extraverts showing larger spectral peak amplitudes in the alpha band than introverts but only at frontal recording sites. In contrast, at posterior sites of the scalp, no significant associations were found.

The findings by Tran *et al.* (2001) do support Gale's hypothesis and Eysenck's (1967) theory of E. Furthermore, they indicate the importance of the frontal regions of the brain in the development of personality. This also supports Gray's (1970) suggestion that the physiological basis of arousal levels in extraverts and introverts should involve the frontal lobes as a component of a negative feedback loop including the orbital frontal cortex, the medial septal area and the hippocampus.

Venturini *et al.* (1981) measured spectral characteristics of spontaneous EEG and characteristics of the alpha attenuation responses (AAR) to acoustic stimulation (90 dB) for introverts and extraverts. The AAR characteristics consisted of AAR latency from stimulus onset, duration of the AAR, AAR instability, and duration of transitory resynchronization. Although no significant differences were found in basic alpha rhythm, significant differences between extraverts and introverts were found in the AAR characteristics. Extraverts habituated to the auditory stimulus while introverts were more responsive to auditory stimulation. It is advantageous to include these measures of AAR in future studies on individual differences because they provide specific indices of the physical characteristics of the alpha generating system.

7. Extraversion and Event-Related Potentials

Event-related potentials (ERPs), formerly termed evoked potentials, are event-related voltage changes in the ongoing EEG activity that are time-locked to sensory, motor, and cognitive events. ERPs can be used to identify and classify perceptual, memory and linguistic operations. These potentials arise from the synchronous activities of neuronal populations engaged in information processing. The ERPs are usually obtained by signal averaging, i.e. by summation of the time-locked electrocortical responses that occur on each repetition of the event. The averaging procedure assumes that the ERP and the background EEG summate independently. As averaging proceeds, the ERP waveform summates, while the random background EEG (noise) decreases in amplitude as the sum proceeds. This method extracts the event-related activity that is often difficult to distinguish in the ongoing EEG activity.

One of the useful applications of ERP measurement is to demarcate the timing and classification of specific stages of information processing. Under specific conditions, ERPs can be recorded for each sensory modality. A characteristic waveform corresponds to each modality. The components (or peaks) of the ERP waveform are usually labeled positive or negative according to their latency and polarity. The latency of a component is usually given in milliseconds. The earlier a peak or component emerges, the more likely that the peak is determined by physical characteristics of the stimulus (exogenous component). Time periods as short as 10 ms are associated with the auditory brainstem response. The majority of ERP studies investigated responses that occur in the first 100–500 ms following a stimulus. Early components (N100, P200) relate to sensory properties of stimuli and to selective attention. Later ERP waves are used to index endogenous cognitive activity.

The positive going ERP component at 300 ms (P300) is related to processes that involve classifying or updating memory representations of stimuli. The amplitude of the P300 increases as the demand for cognitive resources increases and as the significance of the event and its relevance to the subject increases. The latency of the P300 measure appears to be independent of the time needed for response-related processes. It is a good index of the time needed to categorize and evaluate the stimulus. The endogenous generated components of P300 or later components, e.g. N400 or P650, are sensitive indices of selective attention and decision-making activity (Hillyard & Picton 1987; Rugg & Coles 1995). A number of ERP paradigms were used to evaluate differences in cortical arousal between introverts and extraverts.

8. Extraversion and Event-Related Potentials to Auditory Stimulation

Stelmack *et al.* (1977) reported the first ERP results consistent with the arousal hypothesis by showing that introverts are more sensitive to auditory stimulation than extraverts. They recorded ERPs to low- (0.5 Hz) and high- (8.0 Hz) frequency tones at three levels of intensity (40, 55, and 80 dB) in two experiments with a total of 60 subjects differing in degree of E. Subjects were required to count a series of alternating high- and low-frequency tones to increase the level of attention. Introverts exhibited greater amplitude of the N1-P2 peak than extraverts with the low-frequency tones of 55 and 80 dB. No differences between extraversion groups were observed with high-frequency tones. The authors suggested that employing low-frequency auditory stimulation facilitated the observation of differences between introverts and extraverts because the individual variability of ERPs to low-frequency tones is greater than for high-frequency tones (Rothman 1970). The larger amplitude of ERP response (N1-P2) of introverts to low-frequency moderate intensity tones is illustrated in Figure 3. A subsequent study by Bruneau *et al.* (1984) reported that when tones are presented by alternating high and low frequencies or by varying the intensity of the tones in a series, differences between introverts and extraverts are more likely than when tones are presented in a repetitive fashion.

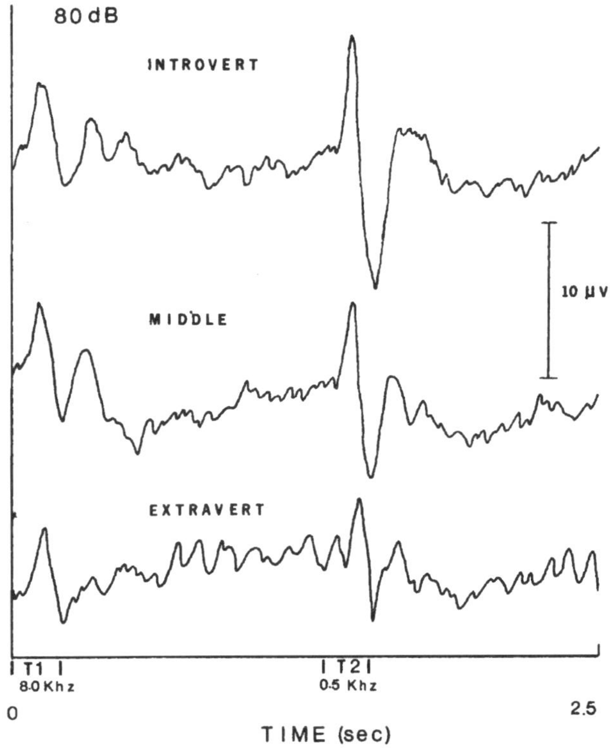

Figure 3: N1-P2 peak amplitude of the auditory evoked response to high (8.0 kHz) and low (0.5 kHz) frequency tones delivered at 80 dB for introverts, middle and extraverts. *Source:* From "Extraversion and individual differences in auditory evoked response," by R. M. Stelmack *et al.* (1977), *Psychophysiology*, *14*, Figure 2, p. 371. Copyright by Blackwell Publishing Ltd. Reprinted by permission.

Stelmack and Michaud-Achorn (1985) demonstrated that in a repetitive series of stimuli with short inter-stimulus intervals, the enhanced N1-P2 peak amplitude for introverts, notably at the central recording site Cz, is only observed for the first stimulus in the series. This is because response amplitude is greatly reduced after the first stimulus, an effect suggesting that the recovery cycle of the response is not completed.

De Pascalis and Montirosso (1988) used a tone-probe paradigm to elicit ERPs while participants identified target words in meaningful and meaningless speech passages. For extraverts, N2 peak amplitude was larger in the meaningful than in the meaningless condition, whereas the reverse was observed for introverts. For extraverts, this finding was paralleled by higher ratings of subjective engagement in the meaningful than in the meaningless condition, whereas the reverse trend was observed for introverts. The authors interpreted these findings as indicative of differences in sensory discrimination between introverts and extraverts. Moreover, extraverts displayed smaller P2 amplitude in the left hemisphere than introverts. No differences between groups were found in the right hemisphere. This finding is consistent with the larger N1-P2 amplitude for introverts reported by Stelmack *et al.* (1977).

This review of auditory ERP studies indicated that the larger N1 and P2 amplitudes for introverts than extraverts is consistent with the arousal hypothesis, i.e. greater arousability for introverts than extraverts. It is also clear, however, that N1 and P2 components are influenced by exogenous, physical properties of the stimuli and thus, reflect differences in sensory reactivity between groups. When the task is complex and late components of the ERPs are involved, i.e. N2 or P3, the differences in E would be understood in terms of processing capacity.

9. Extraversion, Attention, Cognition, and Event-Related Potentials

There were numerous attempts to link attention and cognitive components of the ERPs to E. Reviews of ERP and E indicate similar problems as those reported in the EEG studies (Eysenck 1990, 1994; Stelmack & Geen 1992; Zuckerman 1991) with a considerable degree of variation in testing conditions, stimulus characteristics, and subject selection. The P300 ERP component appears to be a promising measure to differentiate introverts from extraverts. It is known that the P300 component reflects cognitive and attention processes. As Eysenck (1994) pointed out, habituation, orienting responses, and stimulus classification are processes that are associated with both P300 and the concept of cortical arousal and that P300 could be used with advantage in testing the E-arousal hypothesis.

Daruna *et al.* (1985) were the first to report a significant link between the P300 amplitude and extraversion. They compared introverts and extraverts using a selective attention paradigm. Subjects were instructed to predict the occurrence of high- or low-frequency tones. Introverts displayed larger P300 amplitude over frontal, central and parietal sites than extraverts (see Figure 4). Task performance failed to discriminate the groups. The authors interpreted this finding as indicating that introverts allocated more attention resources to the task than extraverts (Kramer *et al.* 1987; Polich 1987). O'Connor (1983) also reported larger P300 amplitude for introverts than for extraverts using a varied reaction time (RT) paradigm.

Subsequently, Pritchard (1989) examined the relation between P300 amplitude and E using an auditory oddball paradigm in which P300 as elicited by infrequently occurring target tones in a series of standard tones. He failed to find an inverse relation between P300 amplitude and E. Differences in the selection of subjects and in the stimulus conditions used make it difficult to compare the results among these studies. Moreover, the larger P300 amplitude seen in introverts may not be evident in initial trials or in sessions using a small number of trials. This is because it has been shown that this difference may be due to the greater habituation in extraverts and thus more likely to occur only after subjects had spent sufficient time on the task to produce habituation. Ditraglia and Polich (1991) observed this habituation effect. They elicited ERPs using a simple two-tone auditory discrimination task with a two-trial block replication procedure. P300 amplitude to the target stimuli declined significantly between the two blocks for extraverts, but did not change across trial blocks for the introverted group (see Figure 5). These results were consistent with Eysenck's suggestion that habituation is faster in extraverts. This finding is also in agreement with the greater

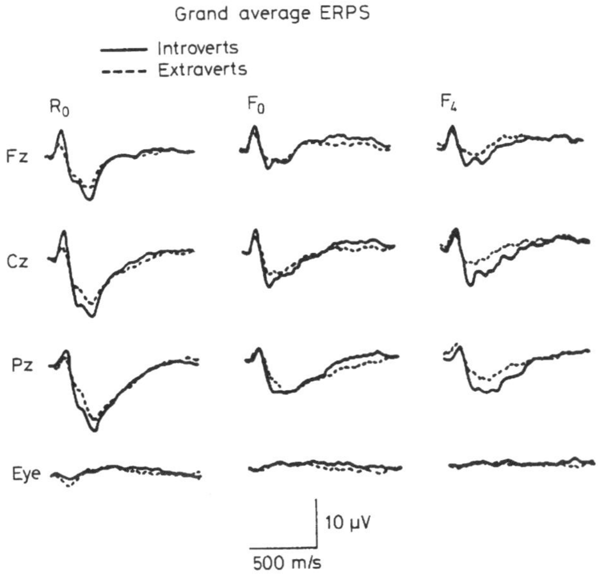

Figure 4: Grand average of the auditory evoked response for introverts ($n = 12$) and extraverts ($n = 12$). Evoked responses are shown as a function of rare (R0) low-frequency tones (0.6 kHz; 6.5 dB), frequent (F0) high frequency tones (2.4 kHz, 65 dB) occurring immediately before a rare tone. *Source:* From "Introversion, attention and the late positive component of event-related potentials," by J. H. Daruna *et al.* (1985), *Biological Psychology, 20*, Figure 1, p. 254. Copyright by Elsevier Science Ltd. Reprinted by permission.

vigilance usually exhibited by introverts (Eysenck & Eysenck 1985) and with EEG-alpha attenuation response findings previously obtained in our laboratory (Venturini *et al.* 1981). In this case, extraverts habituated to auditory clicks, while introverts did not. Subsequently, Cahill and Polich (1992) manipulated the target stimulus probability while setting time-on-task to a minimum to avoid habituation effects. Under these conditions, extraverts produced larger P300 peaks than introverts. Extraverts also displayed a significant stimulus probability effect by producing a steeper increase of peak amplitude with diminishing target stimulus probability.

In a later study by Polich and Martin (1992), male and female subjects were engaged in three target tone detection tasks that varied the probability of target stimulus occurrence. The P300 elicited by target tones provided some results that supported previous findings. In male subjects, introverts showed greater P300 amplitude than extraverts, while female subjects did not show such trends. These results appear in the same direction as the P300 findings from previous studies (Daruna *et al.* 1985; Ditraglia & Polich 1991), but not from others (Cahill & Polich 1992; Pritchard 1989). The reason for this discrepancy is not clear. It is possible that Polich and Martin have used a more complex task than simple target tone detection or it may be related to the influence of the habituation rate of the P300 for different personality types (Ditraglia & Polich 1991; O'Gorman 1977).

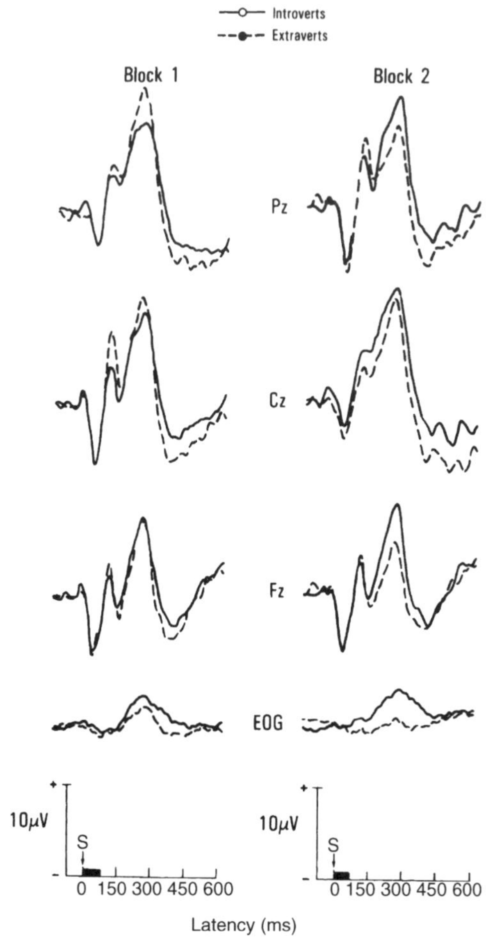

Figure 5: Event-related potentials and electro-ocular activity (EOG) for introverts ($n = 16$) and extraverts ($n = 16$) recorded over central regions (Fz, Cz, Pz) across trial blocks 1 and 2, each composed by 20 target trials. *Source:* From "P300 and intraverted/extraverted personality types," by G. M. Ditraglia and J. Polich (1991), *Psychophysiology*, *28*, Figure 1, p. 180. Copyright by Blackwell Publishing Ltd. Reprinted by permission.

Similar to other electrocortical measures, the relation between the P300 component and the E dimension is not simple. However, this does not imply that the P300 is not a valuable tool for testing personality theory. Ortiz and Maojo (1993) recorded ERPs from extreme scorers on E while introverts and extraverts were engaged in an auditory oddball task. Latency and amplitude of P300 component were measured. Introverts had greater P300 amplitude than extraverts over Fz, Cz, and Pz. There were no significant differences between groups for P300 latency. The P300 amplitude for introverts was more than three times that of extraverts. These findings are contrary to findings reported by Pritchard (1989), but confirm earlier work of O'Connor (1983) and Daruna *et al.* (1985).

Stenberg's (1994) review of these effects suggests that P300 is larger in extraverts when the task is cognitively demanding. Brocke *et al.* (1996) reported two studies, one using an auditory vigilance task and the other using a visual vigilance task with a high level of task difficulty. They maintained that differences between introverts and extraverts might be better evidenced by situations requiring an effortful response. In both studies, larger P300 amplitude, mainly across frontal electrode sites was observed for introverts than extraverts under vigilance conditions with a high level of task difficulty. No group differences were observed when task difficulty was very low.

Subsequently, Brocke *et al.* (1997) engaged introverts and extraverts in a 32-minute visual vigilance task under three different experimental conditions: (1) without acoustic stimulation; (2) with 40 dB SPL; and (3) with 60 dB SPL white noise. Introverts showed larger P300 amplitudes in the baseline and 40 dB white noise conditions, whereas extraverts had a larger P300 amplitude in the 60 dB condition. These results were explained by authors in terms of the control theory of arousal. That is, in monotonous situations extraverts increase their effort as reflected in a steady decrease in the P300 amplitude. For these subjects the constant decline in stress due to additional stimulation (60 dB white noise) was reflected in a steady increase in the P300 amplitude. In contrast, situations with low degree of stimulation are more suitable for introverts and demand a low degree of compensatory effort (increase in P300 amplitude). An alternative explanation of these results is that, in general, introverts are more sensitive to stimulation than extraverts and that the higher intensity stimulation competes for attention resources with the visual stimuli during the vigilance task.

A significant relation between E and ERP responses across low- and high-effort demanding tasks was also observed in a study of our own (De Pascalis 1993). Subjects were engaged in two visual and auditory stimulus-recognition tasks of low and high difficulty. A significant positive relation between E and ERP responses to targets was found for difficult recognition tasks across both visual and auditory stimuli. Easy recognition tasks failed to evidence a significant relation between E and ERP responses.

During a difficult stimulus recognition task, a positive relation was observed between E, frontal 40-Hz ERP response, an index of focused arousal. This effect was observed in the left hemisphere for both visual and auditory modalities. A similar positive relation between E and frontal N2 peak amplitudes was obtained for auditory stimuli. These effects contrast with results of a later study (De Pascalis 1994) using a visual stimulus recognition task under stress and no-stress conditions. A significant negative relation was obtained between E and frontal P2 and N2 peak amplitudes both for the no stress and stress conditions. These results also suggested that the frontal cortex plays a leading role in differentiating extraverts from introverts with ERP components that index attention and discrimination during the stimulus recognition process (i.e. the P2 and N2 ERP components).

In a recent study on E by Gurrera *et al.* (2001), the P300 wave was elicited by novel auditory stimuli during an auditory discrimination paradigm. Three types of stimuli were used: frequent (70%) nontarget tones, infrequent (15%) target tones, and infrequent (15%) non-target novel sounds. Frequent tones (1 kHz) and target tones (1.5 kHz) were 97 dB short duration (50 msec) tone pips. Novel sounds were 50–150 msec in duration and had a more complex spectrum than the sinusoidal tone pips, but were of comparable average intensity. A positive relation between E and frontal P300 amplitude was observed to these high-intensity novel tones.

With respect to P300 latency, there is little experimental evidence for any consistent differences between introverts and extraverts.

10. Extraversion and Auditory Brainstem Responses

Auditory brainstem responses (ABRs) are short-latency evoked potentials that emanate from the auditory pathways and nuclei of the brain stem. ABRs develop within the first 10 ms of stimulation. The neural generators are better understood than the later ERP components that develop between 100 and 800 ms. The ABR waves I-VII are thought to emanate from the synchronous action potentials of successively higher levels of the ascending auditory pathway. ABR waves labeled I and II reflect activity of the distal and proximal portions of the auditory nerve, respectively, and waves III, IV and V reflect activity in the cochlear superior olive, and lateral lemniscus, and inferior culliculus, respectively. The generator of waves VI and VII are at present less defined (see Hughes *et al.* 1988; Møller 1994), but wave VII seems to relate to initial cortical projection activity. The ABR is reliably sensitive to stimulus intensity (Hecox & Galambos 1974). The amplitudes of the ABR waves increase exponentially with increasing stimulus intensity (Wilson & Stelmack 1982). Latency increases as stimulus intensity is reduced, an effect that is observed in all sensory modalities, and is attributed to a diminished rate of neural firing (Picton *et al.* 1977).

Compared to other ERPs, the ABR is notably resistant to fatigue or habituation. The ABR does not change in amplitude or latency after 20 minutes of continuous stimulation (Salamy 1984) or during different stages of sleep and arousal, including metabolic coma. The seven waves of the ABR are indexed by absolute latency from stimulus presentation and by their inter-peak latencies (i.e. the conduction times from one peak to another peak). Faster peak latencies or conduction times are thought to reflect higher levels of neural activity. ABR peak amplitude measures are less reliable than ABR latency (see Chiappa 1997; Hall 1992). In a recent article, the reliability for peak latency was greater than for peak-to-trough amplitude and much greater than for baseline-to-peak amplitude measures (Stelmack *et al.* 2003). The ABR is manifestly insensitive to sleep, attention or arousal conditions, i.e. there is little or no effect of these conditions on ABR latency and amplitude.

There is a general consensus that the stability of ABRs across arousal states either assessed through subjective measures or environmental manipulations means that the ABR indexes peripheral rather than central nervous system (Chiappa 1997; Stelmack 1990). There is, however, some evidence that the ABR may be sensitive to changes in attention (e.g. Lukas 1980) and to drug-induced modulations of central nervous system arousal centers (e.g. Church & Shucard 1987). This suggests that the ABR may also reflect the influence of ARAS levels. The ABR, however, is less sensitive to arousal states than other measures of central nervous system activity.

A number of ABR reports indicate that introverts exhibit faster wave V latency and faster wave I-V conduction times than extraverts. Stelmack and Wilson (1982) compared the ABR of introverts and extraverts that were elicited by brief clicks varying in intensity from 55–90 dB. They found positive correlations between E and latency the ABR for wave I and wave V at 75, 80 and 85 dB. This finding led the authors to state that differences between introverts and extraverts are evident in peripheral nervous system processes and the effects could not be predicted from the activity of the ARAS. It is known that the inhibitory influence of the olivo-cochlear bundle on the auditory nerve (wave I), the cochlear nucleus (wave II) and the inferior colliculus (wave V) is reduced or absent for intensities above 75 dB and, in any event, the inhibitory effects are independent of the ARAS (Desmedt 1975). And again, the ABR is manifestly insensitive to sleep, attention or arousal conditions.

The faster ABR latency for introverts than extraverts was also reported in several other studies (e.g. Andress & Church 1981; Bullock & Gilliland 1993; Cox *et al.* 2001; Swickert & Gilliland 1998). On the other hand, Gilliland and colleagues (Bullock & Gilliland 1993; Matthews & Gilliland 1999; Swickert & Gilliland 1998) argue that faster brainstem transmission in introverts is a result of increased arousal of the brainstem reticular formation because the auditory pathway (as many other brainstem pathways) receives collaterals from and projects collaterals to the reticular formation (Guyton 1981; Klepper & Herbert 1991; Scheibel 1980). This view is compatible with Eysenck's (1967) arousal theory in that individual differences in the ABR reflect the influence of differential arousal of the ARAS.

In a recent study, Bar-Haim (2002) assessed the response characteristics of the acoustic reflex arc of introverts and extraverts. Because of the anatomical overlap between the neural pathway of the acoustic reflex arc and the generators of the earlier ABR waves (waves I, II and III), it was assumed that increased abnormalities in ABR functioning among introverts would confirm that initial peripheral action of the auditory system is responsible for individual differences between introverts and extraverts as indicated by ABR measures. Introverts displayed a greater incidence of abnormal middle ear acoustic reflexes and lower acoustic reflex amplitudes than extraverts. Unexpectedly, these differences were more pronounced for stimuli presented at a frequency of 2 kHz compared to lower-frequency stimuli presented at 0.5 and 1 kHz. Stelmack and Wilson (1982) also reported a similar interaction of stimulus frequency and extraversion for ABR wave V latency, i.e. introverts showed shorter wave V latencies than extraverts for 2 kHz tones, but not for 0.5 kHz stimuli. The reason why 2 kHz is more effective than 0.5 kHz may lay in the fact that ABRs are reliably elicited by the onset of abrupt click stimuli that excite mainly high-frequency nerve fibres. Low-frequency tones that are characterized by relatively slow rise times are less effective in eliciting discernible ABRs (see Stelmack & Wilson 1982). Results from this study support the position that faster ABR latencies in introverts, compared to extraverts, are the product of differential sensitivity and functioning of peripheral nervous system mechanisms rather than central arousal processes.

11. Extraversion and Contingent Negative Variation

In a reaction time task where a warning signal is presented prior to an imperative signal to respond, a negative brain potential, termed the contingent negative variation (CNV), is generated prior to the imperative stimulus (Walter *et al.* 1964). This ERP wave is considered as an index of preparation for a motor response. This response is localized primarily over the fronto-central region of the brain. In typical CNV paradigms, the interval between the warning stimulus and the imperative stimulus that requires a motor response varies between 1 and 4 sec. The CNV wave is composed of early and late components (Rohrbaugh & Gaillard 1983). The early component is considered to be a general response to salient or novel stimuli. The late component is related to the readiness potential, i.e. the slow negative brain potential shift preceding a motor response (Kornhuber & Deecke 1965). It is generally accepted that larger late CNVs are associated with shorter reaction times.

Significant differences between introverts and extraverts were reported in a number of CNV studies. In several reports, the CNV was larger for extraverts than for introverts in neutral or control conditions (Lolas & de Andraca 1977; Plooij-van Gorsel & Janssen 1978; Werre *et al.* 1973). Werre (1983) reported that distraction smoothed the differences in CNV response between extraverts and introverts. Later, Dincheva *et al.* (1984) observed that extraverts displayed larger CNV amplitude than introverts during a control condition. They also observed that extraverts were more susceptible to distraction than introverts as evidenced by a greater reduction in CNV amplitude when novel tones were presented unexpectedly. Subsequently, Piperova-Dalbokova *et al.* (1984) confirmed the larger CNV amplitude of extraverts than introverts.

In a CNV study by Werre (1986), a significant correlation between CNV amplitude and extraversion was found. The most salient effect was evident when motivated young adult students performed a novel reaction time task. A significant positive correlation between CNV amplitude and E was found. In contrast, there were no significant effects when they repeated a standard task or performed a dual task, i.e. a second task in addition to the standard task. In a more recent study, Werre *et al.* (2001) observed that caffeine increased early CNV amplitude (between 600 and 1600 ms after S1) for extraverts and decreased CNV amplitude for introverts. Chlordiazepoxide, regarded as an inhibitory drug, had the opposite effect. Early CNV was not correlated with reaction time and decreased in amplitude across consecutive sessions. In contrast, there were no significant drug effects on late CNV or on RT, either with or without an interaction with extraversion. Late CNV showed also a strong negative correlation with reaction time, but early CNV had a positive effect on this relation. E was negatively correlated with reaction time.

12. Extraversion and Motor Control

There is a general consensus that E is characterized by individual differences in the expression of motor behavior (Brebner & Cooper 1974; Eysenck 1957; O'Connor 1989; Stelmack 1985). Extraverts have been found to be more active and restless in restricted environments (Gale 1969) and to be more active and involved in athletic activities than introverts (Eysenck *et al.* 1982). Extraverts tend to speak more often in interview situations (Campbell & Rushton 1978) and to have a greater preference for physical activity (Furnham 1981). However, in the pursuit-rotor tracking task, which requires refined motor control, introverts tend to perform more effectively than extraverts (Frith 1971; Horn 1975). Introverts also tend to emit less frequent responses than extraverts (Brebner & Cooper 1974) and they exhibit fewer false positive errors in a reaction time task that favored response sets (Brebner & Flavell 1978).

With respect to reaction time tasks, faster reaction times for extraverts than introverts were observed in several studies (Barratt 1967; Buckalew 1973; Keuss & Orlebeke 1977;

Robinson & Zahn 1988). However, null effects were reported in several other studies (Casal *et al.* 1990; Gupta & Nicholson 1985; Hummel & Lester 1977).

While it is generally accepted that there are individual differences in the expression of motor behavior between extraverts and introverts, the physiological bases of these differences remain largely unexplored. Pivik *et al.* (1988) examined individual differences in motoneuronal excitability by recording the spinal monosynaptic H-reflex for subjects who varied in E. It was recorded as the action potential of the evoked reflex from the calf muscle of the leg. Pairs of electrical pulses were presented at varying interstimulus intervals (50 msec–2 sec). Reflex recovery was calculated as a ratio of the reflex amplitude of the second stimulus (H2) in the pair to the first stimulus in the pair (H1). With increasing interpulse intervals, the reflex response amplitude of the second pulse increases, or recovers, relative to the first pulse. Using this method, the authors observed that extraverts displayed reduced motoneural excitability as determined by analysis of recovery functions. These differences are shown in Figure 6.

Extraverts did not differ from introverts in the intensity of the stimulation required to elicit muscle action potentials or the conduction velocity of the nerve of those potentials. The authors concluded that the observed effects were not attributable to differences in initial levels of excitability, but rather to the reduced motor excitability in the central nervous system.

Britt and Blumenthal (1991) examined differences in motoneuronal sensitivity between introverts and extraverts by recording startle reflexes. Brief bursts of white noise stimuli were presented at 85 and 60 dB intensity with and without a prepulse tone. For introverts, the latency of the startle response was shorter at 85 dB intensity than at 60 dB, whereas for extraverts, there was no difference in response latency for the two intensity levels of stimuli. The authors argued that extraverts might have a less sensitive motoneuronal system. The corollary of this interpretation is that this is an intensity effect reflecting the greater sensitivity of introverts to sensory stimulation.

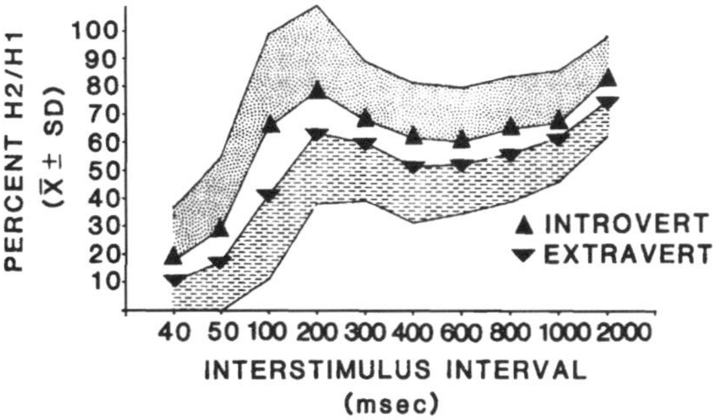

Figure 6: Percent motoneural reflex recovery functions for introverts ($n = 23$) and extraverts ($n = 36$) at increasing inter-stimulus intervals. *Source:* From "Personality and individual differences in spinal motoneuronal excitability," by R. T. Pivik *et al.* (1988), *Psychophysiology*, *25*, Figure 3, p. 20. Copyright by Blackwell Publishing Ltd. Reprinted by permission.

Moderate exercise also appears to have differential effects on mood or perceived arousal. Extraverts report that they are more energetic after a brisk 10-min walk, whereas introverts describe themselves as less tense (Thayer *et al.* 1987). Stelmack and Pivik (1996) also observed this effect. They reported that a brisk 10-min exercise increased General Activation scores, as measured by Activation-Deactivation Adjective Check List (Thayer 1978). Extraverts reported greater increases in energetic arousal than introverts. In this study, the effect of exercise on motoneuronal excitability, as measured by H-reflex recovery functions, was also investigated. Significant personality group differences in H-reflex recovery function were limited to the longer inter-pulse intervals. Introverts displayed greater motoneuronal recovery than extraverts during the pre-exercise period, an effect that replicated previous findings (Pivik *et al.* 1988). Exercise reduced these individual differences by increasing excitability for extraverts.

It has been reported that levels of dopamine-beta-hydroxylase (DBH) are increased following exercise, an effect that may be indicative of reduced dopaminergic activity (Bove *et al.* 1984; Calhoon 1988). Furthermore, levels of DBH are negatively correlated with extraversion (Calhoon 1988). The consistency of these effects is influenced by the strenuousness of the exercise and the level of fitness of participants (Calhoon 1991). Stelmack and Pivik (1996) speculate that moderate exercise may have the effect of reducing dopaminergic activity and that this may have increased spinal motoneuronal excitability (as measured by H-reflex recovery functions) especially for extraverts.

Another line of research examined individual differences in E by means of independent measures of decision time (DT) and movement time (MT). In this research, response time measures are obtained by means of a response panel to make use of a home button. The DT is scored as the time from stimulus onset to the release of the home button, and the MT as the time from this release to the subsequent press of a target button. Thus, the DT reflects central processes such as speed of stimulus recognition, stimulus evaluation and response organization (Sanders 1998; Sternberg 1985). MT is largely independent of cognitive requirements in the task and is a good measure of speed of response execution (Doucet & Stelmack 1997, 2000; Jensen & Munro 1979; Theios 1975).

There are some studies on extraversion that measured both DT and MT (Doucet & Stelmack 1997, 2000; Muniz-Fernandez & Paz-Caballero 1984; Rammsayer 1995, 1998; Rammsayer *et al.* 1993; Stelmack *et al.* 1993). No DT differences between extraverts and introverts are reported in all of these studies, whereas there is some evidence that extraverts have faster MTs than introverts (Doucet & Stelmack 1997; Rammsayer 1995; Stelmack *et al.* 1993). This finding also endorses the view that individual differences in extraversion are related to peripheral levels of the central nervous system (Stelmack & Pivik 1996).

To account for individual differences in speed of responding and motor control between extraverts and introverts, Brebner and Cooper (1974) advanced the idea that central mechanisms of stimulus analysis or response organization can be in one of two states, excitation or inhibition. In tasks demanding stimulus analysis, introverts are characterized by greater stimulus excitation and lower stimulus inhibition, whereas extraverts are characterized by the opposite pattern. In tasks demanding response organization, introverts are characterized by greater response inhibition and lower response excitation, whereas extraverts are characterized by the opposite pattern. According to Brebner's model (Brebner 1985, 1990), introverts are more disposed to analysis of sensory information than extraverts, whereas extraverts are disposed to faster motor response preparation. Rammsayer and Stahl (2002) used recordings of lateralized readiness potentials (LRPs) to test Brebner's hypothesis that the latency of central response organization is shorter for extraverts than for introverts.

The LRP has emerged as an important tool in mental-chronometry approach since it provides a discrete index that traces the time course of stimulus processing from stimulus onset to response execution (e.g. Gratton *et al.* 1988; Kutas & Donchin 1980; Smid *et al.* 1987). The LRP is derived from the readiness potential (Kornhuber & Deecke 1965) that appears several hundred milliseconds prior to voluntary hand movements and reflects the asymmetrical cortical activation ipsi- and contra-lateral to the responding hand (Gratton *et al.* 1988; Rugg & Coles 1995). Processing time associated with stimulus analysis is indexed by stimulus-locked LRP latency, i.e. the time interval between stimulus onset and LRP onset. Response-locked LRP latency, i.e. the time interval between the onset of the LRP and completion of the motor response, indexes speed of response organization. Thus, using a LRP recording method may help in highlighting differences between introverts and extraverts in both stimulus analysis and response organization.

Rammsayer and Stahl (2002) engaged two groups of extraverted and introverted women in a two-choice go/no-go reaction-time task while LRP recordings were obtained from left- and right-central scalp sites overlying the primary motor cortex. Reaction times were significantly longer for introverts than for extraverts. This behavioral difference in performance was partially paralleled by the LRP data. There were no significant differences in stimulus-locked LRP latencies. However, response-locked LRP latencies were substantially shorter for extraverts compared to introverts. The authors concluded that the observed differences in response-locked LRP latencies between introverts and extraverts indicate that individual differences in E are referred to differences in fundamental motor processes (Doucet & Stelmack 1997, 2000; Stelmack & Pivik 1996). This study is one of the first to provide electrophysiological evidence of faster central response organization in extraverts compared to introverts, a result supporting Brebner's (1983, 1985) model of extraversion.

Concurrent with the study of Rammsayer and Stahl (2002), Houlihan *et al.* (2002) also conducted an LRP experiment. Subjects were engaged in an easy two-stimulus task in which the predictability about the imperative stimulus was varied. ERPs were derived to examine P300 amplitude and latency to the imperative stimulus as well as LRP from electrodes over the motor cortex. LRP onset was earlier in extraverts than introverts in all conditions, while no significant differences were obtained for the P300 component. Again, these findings provide evidence for faster central motor processes in extraverts and suggest that LRP is a valid and sensitive approach to study individual differences in extraversion in terms of both sensory and motor components of information processing.

13. Conclusions

There is a substantial body of evidence, at different levels of brain processes, linking extraversion to individual differences in stimulus processing and motor behavior. Introverts, compared to extraverts, are characterized by greater electrodermal and electrocortical reactivity to sensory stimulation. There is little evidence that introverts and extraverts differ in tonic or basal levels of electrocortical and autonomic activity. This conclusion is derived from the fact that there are no E-related differences in skin conductance levels for conditions inducing low levels of arousal and in skin conductance levels preceding stimulation. Similarly, E-related differences are rarely observed with EEG measures obtained during low-arousal conditions or sleepiness. When physiological arousal is manipulated by administering central nervous system stimulants (e.g. caffeine, nicotine) or depressants (e.g. Chlordiazepoxide), systematic effects that are consistent with arousal theory predictions (Eysenck 1967) are observed with electrodermal response and event-related potential measures. These effects support the view that introverts are more arousable than extraverts, i.e. they are characterized by enhanced reactivity to stimulation. They do not support the notion that individual differences in extraversion are characterized by individual differences in tonic arousal. However, it is not clear whether the enhanced sensitivity to stimulation of introverts reflects differences in central or peripheral nervous system processes or both.

The E-related effects on ABRs indicated that the greater sensitivity of introverts may be referred to differences in axonal or synaptic transmission at the level of auditory nerve. The experimental evidence supports the view that the arousal construct itself cannot be generalized. A main reason lays in the fact that extraversion-related differences are linked to arousability rather than to base levels of tonic arousal. Furthermore, ERP differences in E are not evident across the full continuum of intensity levels, but mainly for stimulation of moderate intensity. Another limiting aspect of the arousal hypothesis lies in the fact that psychophysiological response measures of arousal are not similarly effective in detecting individual differences in E. Significant effects also depend on specific task requirements. The arousal hypothesis has received considerable support using SCR and ERP to auditory stimulation and to a lesser extent ERPs to visual stimulation. HR measures, on the other hand, yielded mixed results.

The experimental evidence of individual differences in motoneurnoal excitability introduced a new line of research on the biological concomitants of extraversion. On a variety of tasks requiring a motor response, there is good evidence that extraverts differ from introverts in their expression of motor behavior. Recent research has demonstrated that this difference is in both peripheral response execution processes and on central stimulus analysis and response selection processes. Recent research has demonstrated faster movement times and earlier onset of LRPs in extraverts than introverts.

References

Andress, D. L., & Church, M. W. (1981). Differences in brainstem auditory evoked responses between introverts and extraverts as a function of stimulus intensity. *Psychophysiology*, *18*, 156.

Bar-Haim, Y. (2002). Introversion and individual differences in middle ear acoustic reflex function. *International Journal of Psychophysiology*, *46*, 1–11.

Barland, G. H., & Raskin, D. C. (1973). Detection of deception. In: W. F. Prokasy, & D. C. Raskin (Eds), *Electrodermal activity in psychological research* (pp. 417–477). New York: Academic Press.

Barratt, E. S. (1967). Perceptual-motor performance related to impulsiveness and anxiety. *Perceptual and Motor Skill*, *25*, 485–492.

Bartol, C. R., & Martin, R. B. (1974). Preference for complexity as a function of neuroticism, extraversion and amplitude of orienting response. *Perceptual and Motor Skills, 38*, 1155–1160.

Berger, H. (1929). Über das electrenkephalogramm des Menschen. *Archives für Psychiatie und Nervenkrankheiten, 87*, 527–570. Translated and reprinted in: P. Gloor (1969), [Hans Berger on the electroencephalogram of man.] *Electroencephalography and Clinical Neurophysiology* (Suppl. 28).

Bove, A. A., Dewey, J. D., & Tyce, G. M. (1984). Increased conjugated dopamine in plasma after exercise training. *Journal of Laboratory and Clinical Medicine, 104*, 77–85.

Brebner, J. (1983). A model of extraversion. *Australian Journal of Psychology, 35*, 349–359.

Brebner, J. (1985). Personality theory and movement. In: B. Kirkcaldy (Ed.), *Individual differences in movement* (pp. 27–42). Lancaster: MTP Press.

Brebner, J. (1990). Psychological and neurophysiological factors in stimulus-response compatibility. In: R. W. Proctor, & T. G. Reeve (Eds), *Stimulus-response compatibility: An integrated perspective* (pp. 241–260). Amsterdam: Elsevier.

Brebner, J., & Cooper, C. (1974). The effect of a low rate of regular signals upon the reaction times of intrverts and extraverts. *Journal of Research in Personality, 8*, 263–276.

Brebner, J., & Flavell, R. (1978). The effect of catch-trials on speed and accuracy among introverts and extraverts in a simple RT task. *British Journal of Psychology, 69*, 9–15.

Britt, T. W., & Blumenthal, T. D. (1991). Motoneuronal insensitivity in extraverts as revealed by the startle response paradigm. *Personality and Individual Differences, 12*, 387–393.

Broadhurst, A., & Glass, A. (1969). Relationship of personality measures to the alpha rhythm of the electroencephalogram. *British Journal of Psychiatry, 115*, 199–204.

Brocke, B., Tasche, K. G., & Beauducel, A. (1996). Biopsychological foundations of extraversion: Differential effort reactivity and the differential P300 effect. *Personality and Individual Differences, 21*, 727–738.

Brocke, B., Tasche, K. G., & Beauducel, A. (1997). Biopsychological foundations of extraversion: Differential effort reactivity and state control. *Personality and Individual Differences, 22*, 447–458.

Bruneau, W., Roux, S., Perse, J., & Lelord, G. (1984). Frontal evoked responses, stimulus intensity control, and the extraversion dimension. *Annals of the New York Academy of Sciences, 425*, 546–550.

Buckalew, L. W. (1973). Relationship between a physiological and personality index of excitability. *Physiological Psychology, 1*, 158–160.

Bullock, W. A., & Gilliland, K. (1993). Eysenck's arousal theory of introversion-extraversion: A converging measures investigation. *Journal of Personality and Social Psychology, 64*, 113–123.

Cacioppo, J. T., Tassinary, L. G., & Berntson, G. G. (2000). Psychophysiological science. In: J. T. Cacioppo, L. G. Tassinary, & G. G. Berntson (Eds), *Handbook of psychophysiology* (2nd ed., pp. 3–23). Cambridge: Cambridge University Press.

Cahill, J. M., & Polich, J. (1992). P300, probability and introverted/extroverted personality types. *Biological Psychology, 33*, 23–35.

Calhoon, L. L. (1988). Explorations into the biochemistry of sensation-seeking. *Personality and Individual Differences, 9*, 941–949.

Calhoon, L. L. (1991). Sensation seeking, exercise, and dopamine-beta-hydroxylase. *Personality and Individual Differences, 12*, 903–907.

Campbell, A., & Rushton, J. P. (1978). Bodily communication and personality. *British Journal of Social and Clinical Psychology, 17*, 31–36.

Casal, G. B., Caballo, V. E., Cueto, E. G., & Cubos, P. F. (1990). Attention and reaction time differences in introversion-extraversion. *Personality and Individual Differences, 11*, 195–197.

Chiappa, K. H. (1997). *Evoked potentials in clinical medicine*. Philadelphia: Lippincot-Raven.

Church, M. W., & Shucard, D. W. (1987). Theophylline-induced changes in the mouse brainstem auditory evoked potential. *Neurotoxicology and Teratology*, *9*, 59–66.

Coles, M. G. H., Gale, A., & Kline, P. (1971). Personality and habituation of the orienting reaction: Tonic and response measures of electrodermal activity. *Psychophysiology*, *8*, 54–63.

Cooper, R., White, A. L., Crow, H. J., & Walter, H. G. (1965). Comparison of sub-cortical, cortical, and scalp activity using chronically indwelling electrodes in men. *Electroencephalography and clinical Neurophysiology*, *18*, 217–228.

Cox, F., Luz, E., Gilliland, K., & Swickert, R. J. (2001). Congruency of the relationship between extraversion and the brainstem auditory evoked response based on the EPI vs. the EPQ. *Journal of Research on Personality*, *35*, 117–126.

Crider, A., & Lunn, R. (1971). Electrodermal lability as a personality dimension. *Journal of Experimental Research in Personality*, *5*, 145–150.

Daruna, J. H., Karrer, R., & Rosen, A. J. (1985). Introversion, attention and the late positive component of event-related potentials. *Biological Psychology*, *20*, 249–259.

Davis, C., & Cowles, M. (1988). A laboratory study of temperament and arousal: a test of Gale's hypothesis. *Journal of Research in Personality*, *22*, 101–116.

De Pascalis, V. (1993). Hemispheric asymmetry, personality and temperament. *Personality and Individual Differences*, *14*, 825–834.

De Pascalis, V. (1994). Personality and temperament in the event-related potentials during stimulus recognition tasks. *Personality and Individual Differences*, *16*, 877–889.

De Pascalis, V., Destro Fiore, A., & Sparita, A. (1996). Personality, event-related potential (ERP) and heart rate (HR): An investigation of Gray's theory. *Personality and Individual Differences*, *20*, 733–746.

De Pascalis, V., & Montirosso, R. (1988). Extraversion, neuroticism and individual differences in event-related potentials. *Personality and Individual Differences*, *9*, 353–360.

Desmedt, J. E. (1975). Physiological studies of the efferent recurrent auditory system. In: W. D. Keidel, & W. D. Neff (Eds), *Handbook of sensory physiology* (Vol. 5). Berlin: Springer.

Dincheva, E., Piperova-Dalbokova, D., & Kolev, P. (1984). Contingent negative variation (CNV) and the distraction effects in extraverts and introverts. *Personality and Individual Differences*, *5*, 757–761.

Ditraglia, G. M., & Polich, J. (1991). P300 and introverted/extraverted personality types. *Psychophysiology*, *28*, 177–184.

Doucet, C., & Stelmack, R. M. (1997). Movement time differentiates extraverts from introverts. *Personality and Individual Differences*, *23*, 775–786.

Doucet, C., & Stelmack, R. M. (2000). An event-related potential analysis of extraversion and individual differences in cognitive processing speed and response execution. *Personality and Individual Differences*, *78*, 956–964.

Eysenck, H. J. (1957). Drugs and personality: I. Theory and methodology. *Journal of Mental Science*, *103*, 119–131.

Eysenck, H. J. (1963). *Experiments with drugs*. Oxford: Pergamon Press.

Eysenck, H. J. (1967). *The biological basis of personality*. Springfield: Thomas.

Eysenck, H. J. (1981). General features of the model. In: H. J. Eysenck (Ed.), *A model for personality* (pp. 1–37). Berlin: Springer-Verlag.

Eysenck, H. J. (1990). Genetic and environmental contributions to individual differences: Three major dimensions of personality. *Journal of Personality*, *58*, 245–261.

Eysenck, H. J. (1994). Personality: Biological foundations. In: P. A. Vernon (Ed.), *The neuropsychology of individual differences* (pp. 151–207). London: Academic Press.

Eysenck, H. J., & Eysenck, M. W. (1985). *Personality and individual differences: A natural science approach*. New York: Plenum.

Eysenck, H. J., Nias, D. K. B., & Cox, D. N. (1982). Sports and personality. *Advances in Behavior Research and Therapy, 4*, 1–56.

Fenton, G. W., & Scotton, L. (1967). Personality and the alpha rhythm. *British Journal of Psychiatry, 113*, 1283–1289.

Fowles, D. C. (1980). The three arousal model: Implications of Gray's two-factor learning theory for heart rate, electrodermal activity and psychopathy. *Psychophysiology, 17*, 87–104.

Fowles, D. C., Roberts, R., & Nagel, K. (1977). The influence of introversion-extraversion on the skin conductance response of stress and stimulus intensity. *Journal of Research in Personality, 11*, 129–146.

Frith, C. D. (1971). Strategies in rotary pursuit tracking. *British Journal of Psychology, 62*, 187–197.

Furnham, A. (1981). Personality and activity preference. *British Journal of Social Psychology, 20*, 57–68.

Fuster, J. M., & Uyeda, A. A. (1962). Facilitation of tachistoscopic performance by stimulation of midbrain tegmental points in the monkey. *Experimental Neurology, 6*, 384–406.

Gale, A. (1969). "Stimulus hunger": Individual differences in operant strategy in a button-pressing task. *Behaviour Research and Therapy, 7*, 263–274.

Gale, A. (1981). EEG studies of extraversion-introversion: what's the next step? In: R. Lynn (Ed.), *Dimensions of personality: Papers in honour of H. J. Eysenck* (pp. 181–207). Oxford: Pergamon.

Gale, A. (1983). Electroencephalographic studies of extraversion-introversion: A case study in the psychophysiology of individual differences. *Personality and Individual Differences, 4*, 371–380.

Gale, A., Coles, M. G. H., & Blaydon, J. (1969). Extraversion-introversion and the EEG. *British Journal of Psychology, 60*, 209–223.

Gale, A., Coles, M. G. H., Kline, P., & Penfold, V. (1971). Extraversion-introversion, neuroticism and the EEG: Basal and response measures during habituation of the orienting response. *British Journal of Psychology, 62*, 533–543.

Gale, A., & Eysenck, M. W. (Eds) (1992). *Handbook of individual differences: Biological perspectives*. New York: Wiley.

Gange, J. J., Geen, R. G., & Harkins, S. G. (1979). Autonomic differences between extraverts and introverts during vigilance. *Psychophysiology, 16*, 392–397.

Geen, R. G. (1984). Preferred stimulation levels in introverts and extraverts: Effects on arousal and performance. *Journal of Personality and Social Psychology, 46*, 1303–1312.

Golan, Z., & Neufield, M. Y. (1996). Individual differences in alpha rhythm as characterizing temperament related to cognitive performances. *Personality and Individual Differences, 21*, 775–784.

Graham, F. K. (1979). Distinguishing among orienting, defensive, and startle reflexes. In: H. D. Kimmel, E. H. van Olst, & J. F. Orlebeke (Eds), *The orienting reflex in humans* (pp. 137–167). Hillsdale, NJ: Lawrence Erlbaum.

Graham, F. K., & Clifton, R. K. (1966). Heart rate change as a component of the orienting response. *Psychological Bulletin, 65*, 305–320.

Gratton, G., Coles, M. G. H., Siveraag, E. J., Eriksen, C. W., & Donchin, E. (1988). Pre- and post-stimulus activation of response channels: A psychological analysis. *Journal of Experimental Psychology: Human Perception and Performance, 17*, 246–266.

Gray, J. A. (1970). The psychophysiological basis of introversion-extraversion. *Behaviour Research and Therapy, 8*, 249–266.

Gray, J. A. (1973). Causal theories and how to test them. In: J. R. Royce (Ed.), *Multivariate analysis and psychological theory* (pp. 409–463). New York: Academic Press.

Gray, J. A. (1982). *The neuropsychology of anxiety: An enquiry into the functions of the septo-hippocampal system*. Oxford: Oxford University Press.

Gray, J. A. (1987). The neuropsychology of emotion and personality. In: S. M. Stahl, S. D. Iverson, & E. C. Goodman (Eds), *Cognitive neurochemistry* (pp. 171–190). Oxford: Oxford University Press.

Gupta, A., & Nicholson, J. (1985). Simple visual reaction time, personality and strength of the nervous system: A signal-detection theory approach. *Personality and Individual Differences*, *6*, 461–469.

Gurrera, R. J., O'Donnell, B. F., Nestor, P. G., Gainski, J., & McCarley, R. W. (2001). The P3 auditory event-related brain potential indexes major personality traits. *Biological Psychiatry*, *49*, 922–929.

Guyton, A. C. (1981). *Textbook of medical physiology* (6th ed.). Philadelphia: Saunders

Hall, J. W. (1992). *Handbook of auditory evoked responses*. New York: Allyn & Bacon.

Hastrup, J. L. (1979). Effects of electrodermal lability and introversion on vigilance decrement. *Psychophysiology*, *16*, 302–310.

Hebb, D. O. (1955). Drives and the CNS (conceptual nervous system). *Psychological Review*, *62*, 243–254.

Hecox, K., & Galambos, R. (1974). Brainstem auditory evoked responses in human infants and adults. *Archives of Otolaryngology*, *99*, 30–33.

Hillyard, S. A., & Picton, T. W. (1987). Electrophysiology of cognition. In: V. B. Mountcastle, F. Plum, & S. R. Geiger (Eds), *Handbook of physiology. Section 1: The nervous system* (pp. 519–571). Bethesda, MD: American Physiological Society.

Hirschman, R., & Favaro, L. (1980). Individual differences in imagery vividness and voluntary heart rate control. *Personality and Individual Differences*, *1*, 129–133.

Horn, P. D. (1975). Evidence for the generality of reminiscence function of extraversion and neuroticism. *Journal of Psychology*, *90*, 41–44.

Houlihan, M. E., Pritchard, W. S., Guy, T. D., & Robinson, J. H. (2002). Smoking/nicotine affects the magnitude and onset of lateralized readiness potentials. *Journal of Psychophysiology*, *16*, 37–45.

Hughes, J. R., Helgason, C. M., & Wilbur, A. (1988). Neuroanatomic correlations with the late waves of the brain-stem auditory evoked potential. *Electroencephalography and Clinical Neurophysiology*, *71*, 367–374.

Hummel, H., & Lester, D. (1977). Extraversion and simple reaction time. *Perceptual and Motor Skills*, *45*, 1236.

Jensen, A. R., & Munro, E. (1979). Reaction time, movement time, and intelligence. *Intelligence*, *3*, 121–126.

Kaiser, J., Beauvale, A., & Bener, J. (1997). The evoked cardiac response as a function of cognitive load differs between subjects separated on the main personality dimensions. *Personality and Individual Differences*, *22*, 241–248.

Keuss, P. J. G., & Orlebeke, J. F. (1977). Transmarginal inhibition in a reaction time task as a function of extraversion and neuroticism. *Acta Psychologica*, *41*, 139–150.

Kishimoto, Y. (1977). Visual vigilance performance of extraverts and introverts under two conditions of signal frequency. *Japanese Journal of Psychology*, *48*, 53–57.

Klepper, A., & Herbert, A. (1991). Distribution and origin of noradrenergic and serotonergic fibers in the cochlear nucleus and inferior colliculus of the rat. *Brain Research*, *557*, 190–201.

Koriat, A., Averill, J. R., & Malmstrom, E. J. (1973). Individual differences in habituation: some methodological and conceptual issues. *Journal of Research in Personality*, *7*, 88–101.

Kornhuber, H. H., & Deecke, L. (1965). Hirnpotentialanderungen bei Willkurbewegungen und passiven Bewegungen des Menschen: Bereitschaftspotential und reafferente Potentiale. *Pfluegers Archives für die gesammte Physiologie*, *248*, 1–17.

Kramer, A. F., Siveraag, E. J., & Braune, R. (1987). A psychophysiological assessment of operator workload during simulated flight missions. *Human Factors*, *29*, 145–160.

Krupski, A., Raskin, D. C., & Bakan, P. (1971). Physiological and personality correlates of commission errors in an auditory vigilance task. *Psychophysiology*, *8*, 304–311.

Kutas, M., & Donchin, E. (1980). Preparation to respond as manifested by movement-related brain potentials. *Brain Research*, *202*, 95–115.

Lacey, J. I. (1967). Somatic response patterning and stress: Some revisions of activation theory. In: M. H. Appley, & R. Trumbull (Eds), *Psychological stress: Issues in research* (pp. 14–44). New York: Appleton-Century-Crofts.

Lacey, J. I., & Lacey, B. C. (1958). Verification and extension of the principle of autonomic response stereotyping. *American Journal of Psychology*, *71*, 50–73.

Lemere, F. (1936). The significance of individual differences in the Berger rhythm. *Brain*, *9*, 366–375.

Lolas, F., & de Andraca, I. (1977). Neuroticism, extraversion, and slow brain potentials. *Neuropsychobiology*, *3*, 12–22.

Lukas, J. H. (1980). Human auditory attention: The olivocochlear bundle may function as a peripheral filter. *Psychophysiology*, *17*, 444–452.

Magoun, H. W. (1963). *The waking brain* (2nd ed.). Springfield, IL: Thomas.

Mangan, G. L. (1974). Personality and conditioning: Some personality and cognitive psychophysiological parameters of classical appetitive (sexual) GSR conditioning. *Pavlovian Journal of Biological Psychology*, *9*, 125–135.

Mangan, G. L., & O'Gorman, J. G. (1969). Initial amplitude and rate of habituation of orienting reaction in relation to extraversion and neuroticism. *Journal of Experimental Research in Personality*, *3*, 275–282.

Marton, M., & Urban, I. (1966). An electroencephalographic investigation of individual differences in the process of conditioning. Proceedings of the 18th International Congress of Experimental Psychology, Symposium 9, Moscow, 106–109.

Matthews, G., & Gilliland, K. (1999). The personality theories of H. J. Eysenck and J. A. Gray: A comparative review. *Personality and Individual Differences*, *26*, 583–626.

Møller, A. R. (1994). Auditory neurophysiology. *Journal of Clinical Neurophysiology*, *11*, 284–308.

Moruzzi, G., & Magoun, H. W. (1949). Brain stem reticular formation and activation of the EEG. *EEG Clinical Neurophysiology*, *1*, 455–473.

Muniz-Fernandez, J., & Paz-Caballero, M. D. (1984). Tiempo de reaccion y personalidad. [Reaction time and personality]. *Informes de Psicologia*, *3*, 153–161.

Myrtek, M. (1984). *Constitutional psychophysiology*. London: Academic Press.

Nebylitsyn, V. D., & Gray, J. A. (1972). *Biological bases of individual behavior*. New York: Academic Press.

Nielsen, T. C., & Petersen, K. E. (1976). Electrodermal correlates of extraversion, trait anxiety, and schizophrenism. *Scandinavian Journal of Psychology*, *17*, 73–80.

O'Connor, K. (1983). Individual differences in components of slow cortical potentials: Implications for models of information processing. *Personality and Individual Differences*, *4*, 403–410.

O'Connor, K. (1989). A motor psychophysiological model of smoking and personality. *Personality and Individual Differences*, *10*, 889–901.

O'Gorman, J. G. (1977). Individual differences in habituation of human physiological responses: A review of theory, method and findings in the study of personality correlates in non-clinical populations. *Biological Psychology*, *5*, 257–318.

O'Gorman, J. G., & Lloyd, J. E. M. (1987). Extraversion, impulsiveness and EEG alpha activity. *Personality and Individual Differences*, *8*, 169–174.

O'Gorman, J. G., & Mallise, L. R. (1984). Extraversion and the EEG: II. A test of Gale's hypothesis. *Biological Psychology*, *19*, 113–127.

Orlebeke, J. F., & Feij, J. A. (1979). The orienting reflex as a personality correlate. In: H. D. Kimmel, E. H. Van Olst, & J. F. Orlebeke (Eds), *The orienting reflex in humans* (pp. 567–585). Hillsdale, NJ: Erlbaum.

Ortiz, T., & Maojo, V. (1993). Comparison of the P300 wave in introverts and extraverts. *Personality and Individual Differences*, *15*, 109–112.

Pavlov, I. P. (1928). *Lectures on conditioned reflexes*. New York: Liveright.

Pearson, G. L., & Freeman, F. G. (1991). Effects of extraversion and mental arithmetic on heart rate reactivity. *Perceptual and Motor Skills*, *72*, 1235–1244.

Picton, T. W., Woods, D., Baribeau-Brown, J., & Healey, T. (1977). Evoked potential audiometry. *Journal of Otolaryngology*, *6*, 90–119.

Piperova-Dalbokova, D., Dincheva, E., & Urgelles, L. (1984). Stability of contingent negative variation (CNV) and extraversion-introversion. *Personality and Individual Differences*, *5*, 763–766.

Pivik, R. T., Stelmack, R. M., & Bylsma, F. W. (1988). Personality and individual differences in spinal motoneuronal excitability. *Psychophysiology*, *25*, 16–24.

Plooij-van Gorsel, P. C., & Janssen, R. H. C. (1978). Contingent negative variation (CNV) and extraversion in a psychiatric population. In: C. Barber (Ed.), *Evoked potentials: Proceedings of an international evoked potentials symposium* (pp. 505–514). Lancaster: Medical and Technical Publications.

Polich, J. (1987). Task difficulty, probability and inter-stimulus interval as determinants of P300 from auditory stimuli. *Electroencephalography and Clinical Neurophysiology*, *68*, 311–320.

Polich, J., & Martin, S. (1992). P300, cognitive capability and personality: A correlational study of university undergraduates. *Personality and Individual Differences*, *13*, 533–543.

Pritchard, W. S. (1989). P300 and EPQ/STP personality traits. *Personality and Individual Differences*, *10*, 15–24.

Rammsayer, T. (1995). Extraversion and alcohol: Eysenck's drug postulate revisited. *Neuropsychobiology*, *32*, 197–207.

Rammsayer, T. (1998). Extraversion and dopamine. Individual differences in response to changes in dopaminergic activity as a possible biological basis of extraversion. *European Psychologist*, *3*, 37–50.

Rammsayer, T., Netter, P., & Vogel, W. H. (1993). A neurochemical model underlying differences in reaction times between introverts and extraverts. *Personality and Individual Differences*, *14*, 701–712.

Rammsayer, T., & Stahl, J. (2002). Extraversion-related differences in motor activation as revealed by lateralized readiness potentials. *International Journal of Psychophysiology*, *45*, 19 (Abstract).

Revelle, W., Anderson, K. J., & Humphreys, M. S. (1987). Empirical tests and theoretical extensions of arousal-based theories of personality. In: J. Strelau, & H. J. Eysenck (Eds), *Personality dimensions and arousal* (pp. 17–36). New York: Plenum.

Richards, M., & Eves, F. (1991). Personality, temperament and the cardiac defense response. *Personality and Individual Differences*, *12*, 999–1004.

Robinson, T. N., & Zahn, T. P. (1988). Preparatory interval effects on the reaction time performance of introverts and extraverts. *Personality and Individual Differences*, *9*, 749–761.

Rohrbaugh, J. W., & Gaillard, A. W. K. (1983). Sensory and motor aspects of the contingent negative variation. In: A. W. K. Gaillard, & W. Ritter (Eds), *Tutorials in ERP research: Endogenous components* (pp. 269–310). Amsterdam: North Holland.

Rothman, H. H. (1970). Effects of high frequencies and intersubject variability on the auditory evoked cortical response. *Journal of the Acoustical Society of America*, *47*, 569–573.

Rugg, M. D., & Coles, M. G. H. (1995). The ERP and cognitive psychology: Conceptual issues. In: M. D. Rugg, & M. G. H. Coles (Eds), *Electrophysiology of mind: Event-related brain potentials and cognition* (pp. 27–39). Oxford: Oxford University Press.

Sadler, T. G., Mefferd, R. B., & Houck, R. L. (1971). The interaction of extraversion and neuroticism in orienting response habituation. *Psychophysiology*, *8*, 312–318.

Salamy, A. (1984). Maturation of the auditory brainstem response from birth through early childhood. *Journal of Clinical Neurophysiology*, *1*, 239–329.

Sanders, A. F. (1998). *Elements of human performance: Reaction Processes and attention in human skills*. Mahwah, NJ: Lawrence Erlbaum.

Savage, R. D. (1964). Electrocerebral activity, extraversion and neuroticism. *British Journal of Psychiatry*, *110*, 89–100.

Scheibel, A. B. (1980). Anatomical and physiological substrates of arousal: A view from the bridge. In: J. A. Hobson, & M. A. B. Brazier (Eds), *The reticular formation revisited* (pp. 55–66). New York: Raven Press.

Siddle, D. A. T., & Heron, P. A. (1976). Effects of length of training and amount of tone frequency change on amplitude of autonomic components of the orienting response. *Psychophysiology*, *13*, 281–287.

Smid, H. G., Mulder, G., & Mulder, L. J. (1987). The continuous flow model revisited: Perceptual and central motor aspects. *Electroencephalography and Clinical Neurophysiology* (Suppl. 40), 270–278.

Smith, B. D. (1983). Extraversion and electrodermal activity: Arousability and the inverted-U. *Personality and Individual Differences*, *4*, 411–419.

Smith, B. D., Rockwell-Tischer, S., & Davidson, R. (1986). Extraversion and arousal: Effects of attentional conditions on electrodermal activity. *Personality and Individual Differences*, *7*, 293–303.

Smith, B. D., Rypma, C. B., & Wilson, R. J. (1981). Dishabituation and spontaneous recovery of the electrodermal orienting response: Effects of extraversion, impulsivity, sociability and caffeine. *Journal of Research in Personality*, *15*, 233–240.

Smith, B. D., Wilson, R. J., & Davidson, R. A. (1984). Electrodermal activity and extraversion: Caffeine, preparatory signal and stimulus intensity effects. *Personality and Individual Differences*, *5*, 59–65.

Smith, B. D., Wilson, R. J., & Jones, B. E. (1983). Extraversion and multiple levels of caffeine-induced arousal: Effects of overhabituation and dishabituation. *Psychophysiology*, *15*, 29–34.

Sokolov, E. N. (1963). *Perception and the conditioned reflex*. London: Pergamon Press.

Stein, L. (1978). Catecholamines and opioid peptides. In: M. A. Lipton, D. Mascio, & K. F. Killman (Eds), *Psychopharmacology: A generation of progress* (pp. 569–581). New York: Raven Press.

Stelmack, R. M. (1981). The psychophysiology of extraversion and neuroticism. In: H. J. Eysenck (Ed.), *A model for personality* (pp. 38–64). Berlin: Springer-Verlag.

Stelmack, R. M. (1985). Personality and motor activity: A psychological perspective. In: B. Kirkcaldy (Ed.), *Individual differences in movement* (pp. 153–213). Lancaster: Medical and Technical Publications.

Stelmack, R. M. (1990). Biological bases of extraversion: Psychophysiological evidence. *Journal of Personality*, *58*, 293–311.

Stelmack, R. M., Achorn, E., & Michaud, A. (1977). Extraversion and individual differences in auditory evoked response. *Psychophysiology*, *14*, 368–374.

Stelmack, R. M., Bourgeois, R. P., Chain, J., & Pickard, C. W. (1979). Extraversion and the orienting reaction habituation rate to visual stimuli. *Journal of Research in Personality*, *13*, 49–58.

Stelmack, R. M., & Geen, R. G. (1992). The psychophysiology of extraversion. In: A. Gale, & M. W. Eysenck (Eds), *Handbook of individual differences: Biological perspectives* (pp. 227–254). New York: Wiley.

Stelmack, R. M., Houlihan, M., & McGarry-Roberts, P. A. (1993). Personality, reaction time, and event-related potentials. *Journal of Personality and Social Psychology*, *65*, 399–409.

Stelmack, R. M., Knott, V., & Beauchamp, C. M. (2003). Intelligence and neural transmission time: A brain stem auditory evoked potential analysis. *Personality and Individual Differences*, *34*, 97–107.

Stelmack, R. M., & Michaud-Achorn, A. (1985). Extraversion, attention, and habituation of the auditory evoked response. *Journal of Research in Personality, 19*, 416–428.
Stelmack, R. M., & Pivik, R. T. (1996). Extraversion and the effects of exercise on spinal motoneuronal excitability. *Personality and Individual Differences, 21*, 69–76.
Stelmack, R. M., Plouffe, L., & Falkenberg, W. (1983). Extraversion, sensation seeking, and electrodermal response: probing a paradox. *Personality and Individual Differences, 4*, 607–614.
Stelmack, R. M., & Wilson, K. (1982). Extraversion and the effects of frequency and intensity on the auditory brainstem evoked response. *Personality and Individual Differences, 3*, 373–380.
Stenberg, G. (1994). Extraversion and the P300 in a visual classification task. *Personality and Individual Differences, 16*, 543–560.
Sternberg, R. J. (1985). *Beyond IQ: A triarchic theory of human intelligence*. Cambridge: Cambridge University Press.
Strelau, J. (1983). *Temperament personality activity*. London: Academic Press.
Swickert, R. J., & Gilliland, K. (1998). Relationship between the brainstem auditory evoked response and extraversion, impulsivity, and sociability. *Journal of Research on Personality, 32*, 314–330.
Thayer, R. E. (1978). Factor analytic and reliability studies on the Activation-Deactivation Adjective Check List. *Psychological Reports, 42*, 747–756.
Thayer, R. E., Cook, M. W., Hooe, E. S., & Lotts, D. J. (1987). Exercise-induced arousal change as a function of extraversion. Paper presented at the meeting of the International Society for the Study of Individual Differences, Toronto.
Theios, J. (1975). The components of response latency in simple human information processing tasks. In: P. M. A. Rabbitt, & S. Dornic (Eds), *Attention and performance V* (pp. 418–440). London: Academic Press.
Tran, Y., Craig, A., & McIsaac, P. (2001). Extraversion-introversion and 8–13 Hz waves in frontal cortical regions. *Personality and Individual Differences, 30*, 205–215.
Vanderwolf, C. H., & Robinson, T. E. (1981). Reticulo-cortical activity and behavior: A critique of the arousal theory and a new synthesis. *The Behavioral and Brain Sciences, 4*, 459–514.
Venturini, R., De Pascalis, V., Imperiali, M. G., & San Martini, P. (1981). EEG alpha reactivity and extraversion-introversion. *Personality and Individual Differences, 2*, 215–220.
Walter, W. G., Cooper, R., Aldridge, V. J., McCallum, W. C., & Winter, A. L. (1964). Contingent negative variation: An electric sign of sensorimotor association and expectancy in the human brain. *Nature, 203*, 380–384.
Werre, P. P. (1983). Contingent negative variation and interindividual differences. In: R. Sinz, & M. K. Rosenzweig (Eds), *Psychophysiology, memory, motivation and event-related potentials in mental operations* (pp. 337–342). Amsterdam: Elsevier.
Werre, P. F. (1986). Contingent negative variation: Relation to personality, and modification by stimulation and sedation. In: J. Strelau, F. H. Farley, & A. Gale (Eds), *The biological bases of personality and behavior, psychophysiology, performance and application* (Vol. 2, pp. 77–90). Washington: Hemisphere.
Werre, P. F., Favery, H. A., & Janssen, R. H. C. (1973). Contingent negative variation and personality. *Electroencephalography and Clinical Neurophysiology, 34*, 739.
Werre, P. F., Mattie, H., & Berretty, E. W. (2001). Contingent negative variation, extraversion, reaction time and drug effects. *Personality and Individual Differences, 30*, 1083–1094.
Wigglesworth, M. J., & Smith, B. D. (1976). Habituation and dishabituation of the electrodermal orienting reflex in relation to extraversion and neuroticism. *Journal of Research in Personality, 10*, 437–445.
Wilson, G. D. (1990). Personality, time of day and arousal. *Personality and Individual Differences, 11*, 153–168.

Wilson, K. G., & Stelmack, R. M. (1982). Power functions of loudness magnitude estimations and auditory brainstem evoked responses. *Perception and Psychophysics*, *31*, 561–564.

Yerkes, R. M., & Dodson, J. D. (1908). The relation of strength of stimulus to rapidity of habit-formation. *Journal of Comparative Neurology and Psychology*, *18*, 459–482.

Young, J. P. R., Lader, M. H., & Fenton, G. W. (1971). The relationship of extraversion and neuroticism to the EEG. *British Journal of Psychiatry*, *119*, 667–670.

Zahn, T. P., Kruesi, M. J. P., Leonard, H. L., & Rapaport, J. L. (1994). Autonomic activity and reaction time in relation to extraversion and behavioral impulsivity in children and adolescents. *Personality and Individual Differences*, *16*, 751–758.

Zuckerman, M. (1979). *Sensation seeking: Beyond the optimum level of arousal*. Hillsdale, NJ: Erlbaum.

Zuckerman, M. (1984). Sensation seeking: A comparative approach to a human trait. *Behavioral and Brain Sciences*, *7*, 413–471.

Zuckerman, M. (1991). *Psychobiology of personality*. Cambridge: Cambridge University Press.

Zuckerman, M. (1994). *Behavioral expressions and biosocial bases of sensation seeking*. New York: Cambridge University Press.

Chapter 17

Brain Imaging Studies of Personality: The Slow Revolution

R. J. Haier

> . . . a great personality may possibly make a great brain, but no brain can make a great personality (W. Hanna Thomson, *Brain and Personality*, 1911: 234).

> The ground of character [i.e. personality] is to be sought in the nervous organization which governs the inhibitions . . . we should still be on our search for the physical basis and location of the inhibition (A. A. Roback, *The Psychology of Character*, 1928: 541).

> Scarcely anyone has ever thought of questioning the existence of traits as the fundamental dispositions of personality (G. W. Allport, *Personality: A Psychological Interpretation*, 1949: 286). But the information is too meager to warrant at the present time a physiological account of the operation of traits. *Ibid*: 319.

> In psychology, as in other sciences, knowledge has been advanced by new techniques and new instruments, as well as by new modes of thought . . . (Aubrey Lewis, in the Forward to Hans Eysenck's, *The Scientific Study of Personality*, 1952: vii).

> The beauty of a psychobiological approach [to personality] is that progress in understanding biological structure and function is not only possible but is inevitable (M. Zuckerman, *Psychobiology of Personality*, 1991: 427).

On the Psychobiology of Personality
Edited by R. M. Stelmack

ISBN: 0-08-044209-9

1. Introduction

Once upon a time, not so long ago, many American psychologists believed that personality traits did not exist and that the idea of any neurobiological basis to personality was simply foolish reductionism. Marvin Zuckerman was a lonely exception. I first met Marvin in the late 1970s when, as a true pioneer, he prowled the corridors of the National Institute of Mental Health (NIMH) in Bethesda. He was working with collaborators measuring things like monoamine oxidase (MAO), evoked potentials, and brain chemistry metabolites in cerebral spinal fluid and correlating the various measures to scores on his sensation seeking trait scales (Ballenger *et al.* 1983; Zuckerman *et al.* 1980). Now, there is a resurgence of interest in individual differences in personality (and intelligence) and the revolution in neuroscience has energized the search for a biological basis of personality traits. We know there must be a biological basis simply because genetic studies confirm modest to high heritability for a number of personality traits (Bouchard & Loehlin 2001; Bouchard & McGue 1990; Bouchard *et al.* 1998) and genes work through biology. Modern personality researchers have caught up to Marvin's neurobiological approach (Zuckerman 1979, 1984, 1995) and other early attempts to define neurobiological models of personality (Eysenck 1967; Gray 1970).

Advances in brain imaging technology can be used to help identify the neurobiology and the neuroanatomy of personality traits just as this technology is helping understand learning (Haier 2001; Haier *et al.* 1992), memory (Alkire *et al.* 1996, 1998), intelligence (Haier *et al.* 1988, 2003), and even consciousness (Alkire *et al.* 2000; Alkire & Haier 2001). However, whereas brain imaging methods are now a staple of cognitive research, the transition from personality research based on psychometrics to research using brain imaging methods is still sporadic and at a very early stage. We will review how brain imaging has been used in personality research and highlight some issues that have impeded progress.

2. Review of Imaging Studies

2.1. The First Blood Flow Study of Personality

In a pioneering paper, Mathew *et al.* (1984) used the xenon inhalation technique to correlate regional blood flow with the Eysenck Personality Inventory (Eysenck & Eysenck 1964) scales in 51 normal female volunteers (mean age = 32, SD = 8.3). This technique traced radioactive gas that mixed with air as the subject breathed and the gas entered the blood stream. Detectors were placed over 16 scalp locations (8 in each hemisphere). Blood flow was assessed over a ten-minute period while the subject rested with eyes closed. Significant inverse correlations between blood flow at all 16 detectors and Extraversion were found with the correlations ranging from −0.24 to −0.41. There were no significant correlations with the Neuroticism scale. These results were cautiously interpreted as consistent with Eysenck's hypothesis of an inverse association between Extraversion and general cortical arousal. Like EEG measures of the day, the xenon gas technique was limited to surface detections and it was unable to provide detailed spatial resolution. Nonetheless, this study clearly pointed the way for future experiments. Two other subsequent reports used the xenon gas technique to study personality traits in smaller samples (Stenberg *et al.* 1990, 1993). However, the newer brain imaging technology of Positron Emission Tomography (PET) was becoming available with the capability of measuring function throughout the entire brain with much better spatial resolution.

2.2. *The First Positron Emission Tomography of Personality*

The first attempt at using PET to study personality was reported at the second meeting of the Hans Eysenck and Marvin Zuckerman (among others) inspired International Society for the Study of Individual Differences in 1985. It was subsequently published in a book chapter (Haier *et al.* 1987). PET was first used for clinical research about 1980. I had given personality tests to a number of subjects in PET studies being conducted at the University of California at Irvine 1984–1985. The intention was to see if personality traits correlated with regional brain function. The PET technique is based on injecting a special low-level radioactive sugar tracer, ^{18}F-flurodeoxyglucose (FDG), into a person while they are engaged in a mental task. The harder any part of the brain works to perform the task, the more FDG is taken up by that part of the brain and the more signal would be detected in that location during the scanning. Many early PET studies were done while subjects rested with their eyes closed instead of while engaged in a mental task. Since the choice of task (or no task) determined the regional pattern of brain activity, this was a critical element of PET research design. For studies of personality, no particular task was obviously relevant and even if one was, the expense of PET scans (about $2500 per person in 1985; about $1200 in 2003) precluded an exploratory, non-funded study or even pilot work to develop a proper task. This is a primary problem that has limited functional brain imaging research in personality to this day.

In 1985, the University of California at Irvine was conducting a PET study of generalized anxiety disorder. I asked the subjects, 18 outpatients with generalized anxiety disorder and 9 normal controls, to complete the Sensation Seeking Scale (Zuckerman 1971) and the Eysenck Personality Questionnaire (EPQ; Eysenck & Eysenck 1975) prior to their PET scans. The design included two baseline, pre-drug PET scans per person. During FDG uptake, one scan used the Continuous Performance Test (CPT) where the subject viewed random digits and pressed a button for each zero, i.e. an attention task condition. For the other scan, a control task of the same CPT stimuli was used but with instructions to view the stimuli passively, i.e. a no-task condition without instructions to press the button for any target. Brain function during each condition was quantified as glucose metabolic rate (GMR) and correlations with personality scores were computed for both quantified GMR and relative GMR, i.e. GMR within an area divided by whole brain GMR to correct for individual differences in whole brain GMR. Brain areas were defined, *a priori*, with a stereotactic brain atlas approach.

By current standards, everything about this design and analysis was rudimentary. The results, based on a small sample and limited accuracy of anatomical localization, were regarded as exploratory and interpreted with caution. Only two-tailed tests were used because there were few clear directional, *a priori*, hypotheses about brain areas and personality traits. Interpretation of increased or decreased GMR in an area was problematic because increased GMR could signify more inhibitory activity as well as more excitatory activity. We found a tentative pattern of positive correlations between GMR in frontal and temporal areas and the EPQ measure of Extraversion. Areas of the caudate and putamen (dopamine areas) were also correlated with Extraversion. Other areas showed negative correlations with EPQ Psychoticism. The cingulate, the thalamus, the hippocampus, and the parahippocampus also showed correlations with various scales, especially in right hemisphere. Correlations with the Zuckerman scales were plentiful throughout the brain, but a clear pattern was not apparent. At the time, it was clear that this data set was not adequate to address personality issues. Despite the many difficulties, this study did demonstrate the potential of brain imaging to identify the functional neuroanatomy of personality traits. We enthusiastically concluded our discussion by saying, "It is now possible to design new experiments to extend the scientific investigation of personality from the realms of behavior and psychometrics to the deep recesses of the brain itself" (Haier *et al.* 1987: 266).

Not much happened. Researchers interested in personality had very limited access to imaging technology, which required collaboration with other specialties not usually interested in personality research and high budgets virtually unknown in psychometric personality studies. Scanning large samples with tasks appropriate to personality issues would be required along with image analysis techniques that could address multiple problems of anatomical localization and statistical inference.

Four years later, an abstract of a PET study (Semple *et al.* 1991) reported a significant correlation between the EPQ Neuroticism Scale and GMR in areas of the frontal lobe in 27 normals, males and females combined (mean age = 29), but this was not replicated in another sample of 44 volunteers scanned with different parameters. Details were limited and a full report was never published so no conclusions can be reached about these findings.

2.3. The First Single Photon Emission Tomography Study of Personality

In 1994, Ebmeier *et al.* used a variation of the PET method, single photon emission tomography (SPECT), to measure regional blood flow in 51 normal, mostly elderly volunteers, who were selected as controls for other studies. The age and sex of the participants was not reported. The scans were obtained while most subjects rested, but subgroups performed various tasks. All subjects completed the EPQ separately from the imaging. Anatomical localization was based on a stereotactic atlas approach to define 15 regions of interest in each hemisphere using only two brain slices. Blood flow within regions of interest was determined and a principal components analysis was used to extract brain factors after controlling for age. Four brain factors were identified, fronto-temporal, cingulate, sub-cortical, fronto-parietal.

The three EPQ scales, Extraversion, Neuroticism, and Psychoticism, were correlated with each factor. Of the 12 possible correlations, only Extraversion and the cingulate factor were correlated ($r = 0.46$). Despite numerous difficulties in this study which were mostly derived from using subjects and task conditions that were selected for other projects, the statistical approach was a good attempt at addressing a fundamental problem in brain imaging, that of having many intercorrelated variables and small sample sizes. As computing technology improved and voxel-by-voxel analysis became possible, however, this problem grew even more complex and required a different statistical approach. The modern studies discussed below now use standard image analysis programs like Statistical Parametric Mapping (Friston *et al.* 1995).

2.4. The NEO Personality Inventory Scales in Imaging Studies

Fischer *et al.* (1997) used PET to measure regional blow flow by scanning the distribution of mildly radioactive water injected into the blood stream. This PET technique is an alternative to measuring glucose metabolic rate with FDG. Both techniques use the same hardware and regional blood flow and GMR are highly correlated. Thirty female volunteers (mean age 32, $SD = 6.1$) were scanned while viewing an emotionally neutral video for about four minutes as a control condition for an anxiety study. A Swedish version of the NEO Personality Inventory-Revised (NEO PI-R; Costa & McCrae 1992) was used to form groups by a median split on the Extraversion and Neuroticism scales. A number of specific regions-of-interest were defined *a priori* by a brain atlas approach. For extraverts, higher blood flow was observed in caudate and putamen (dopamine areas); no cortical areas differed in blood flow between extraverts and introverts. No differences were found between high and low Neuroticism groups. In a separate analysis, Type A subjects showed higher blood flow than Type B subjects in areas of the hypothalamus and the hippocampus (Fredrikson *et al.* 1999). Overall, this work had a number of methodological strengths and some of the same weaknesses of earlier studies. The strongest results highlighted the potential importance of a relation between dopamine and Extraversion, as had been only suggested in earlier work (Haier *et al.* 1987).

The next PET blood flow study used more sophisticated image analysis procedures that allowed better anatomical localization of findings (Johnson *et al.* 1999). This group scanned 18 normal volunteers, ten males and eight females with a mean age of 30 years ($SD = 8.5$). Blood flow in every image voxel throughout the entire brain was correlated to scores on only one NEO scale — Extraversion. Using a criterion of $r > 0.60$ ($p < 0.005$, one-tailed), 17 areas had significant correlations, uncorrected for multiple comparisons, with Extraversion. Most of these areas were identified in the earlier less sophisticated imaging studies, although some earlier studies were not cited. It is not clear why one-tailed tests were used instead of more conservative two-tailed tests, since there was no hypothesized *a priori* directional relation between most brain areas and personality. Moreover, none of the correlations were corrected for age, which ranged from 19 to 48 years. Age is a well-known influence on cerebral blood flow. This was a disappointing study because, although it used the most sophisticated analyses to date, the sample size was still too small to study individual differences and the subjects were scanned at rest, which is essentially an uncontrolled condition. The use of only one personality scale also makes interpretation difficult. For all these reasons, the results really provided no new insights as the 1990s "Decade of the Brain" neared its end.

2.5. The Temperament and Character Inventory Scales in Imaging Studies

In another SPECT study, Sugiura *et al.* (2000) correlated regional blood flow during rest with scores on the three scales of the Temperament and Character Inventory (TCI; Cloninger 1987), Novelty Seeking, Harm Avoidance, and Reward Dependence for 30 volunteers. There were 13 males and 17 females with an age range of 26 to 61 years. Voxel-by-voxel correlations were computed and some promising positive and negative correlations were reported, $p < 0.005$, one-tailed, uncorrected for multiple comparisons, for cingulate, insula, parahippocampus, pre- and post-central gyrus, and parts of the frontal lobe. However, the effects of age and sex on blood flow were not removed and, given there was no correction for multiple comparisons, these one-tailed tests at $p < 0.005$ must be interpreted with caution. Most of the areas showing significant correlations were also noted in previous studies. Because this study shared the limitations of previous studies, these results added little to our understanding of the issue.

A similar study (Youn *et al.* 2002) used PET and FDG instead of SPECT to find correlates of the same three TCI scales. Subjects were 19 normal volunteers (13 males, six females; mean age = 26, SD = 9.9), scanned during rest. Voxel-by-voxel analysis was done with Statistical Parametric Mapping (99) without removing age or sex effects. For statistical tests a criterion of $p < 0.005$, one-tailed, uncorrected for multiple comparisons, was employed. GMR results include negative correlations with novelty seeking for areas in precentral gyrus, parahippocampus, and middle temporal lobe and a positive correlation in middle frontal gyrus. Only negative correlations were found with harm avoidance in areas of temporal cortex and anterior cingulate. Only positive correlations were found with reward dependency in areas of temporal lobe and the orbital frontal gyrus. According to the authors, these areas were somewhat different than those reported by the similar Sugiura *et al.* (2000) SPECT study of the TCI. Like the earlier attempts with Extraversion and Neuroticism, both studies using the TCI scales failed to use a cognitive task instead of rest; both failed to correct for age and sex effects; and both used liberal statistical analyses uncorrected for multiple comparisons in small samples. It is no surprise to find inconsistent results.

A third SPECT study correlated blood flow with scores on seven TCI scales in 20 normal male subjects, 20–33 years of age (Turner *et al.* 2003). A novel aspect of this study was that the imaging occurred while each subject completed the TCI items. Whether this is a good control of mental state is arguable. Because their initial regression analyses did not show linear relations with personality scores, a quartile method was used that revealed many nonlinear relations (activations and deactivations) between the TCI scales and regional blood flow in a number of areas throughout the brain. So many relations were found that additional study is necessary with a larger sample and a more controllable task before these data can be assessed.

2.6. PET Receptor Studies of Personality

The PET technology can also be used to assess various neurotransmitter receptor systems. Glucose or blood flow PET studies are indexes of general activity, closely tied to neuronal function, and regional glucose and blood flow results are often used to infer the activity of neurotransmitter systems known to be involved with the areas identified. PET receptor studies assess specific neurotransmitter systems more directly. Typically, a radiotracer is attached to a drug that has an affinity to block certain receptors (at least more than it blocks other receptors). For example, Farde *et al.* (1997) assessed dopamine D2 receptor density using PET and the radioligand [^{11}C] raclopride. The data were correlated to 15 scales of the Karolinska Scales of Personality (Schalling *et al.* 1987). There were 24 normal participants, 14 men and ten women, who ranged in age from18 to 38 years. Results, uncorrected for age, showed a significant correlation between D2 receptor density in the putamen and scores on the detachment scale and on the irritability scale.

Subsequent attempts to replicate a relation between dopamine and similar scales with PET were mixed (Kestler *et al.* 2000; Laakso *et al.* 2000; Leyton *et al.* 2002; Suhara *et al.* 2001; Yasuno *et al.* 2001). PET studies examining the relation between serotonin receptor activity and personality are similarly inconsistent (Moresco *et al.* 2002; Rabiner *et al.* 2002). For the most part, the samples of participants in PET receptor studies consisted of both males and females with a wide range in age. The studies also employed a variety of personality scales. Nonetheless, in conjunction with other types of research, receptor-imaging studies have great potential to help identify the brain systems that are important to personality.

2.7. The First Uses of Functional Magnetic Resonance Imaging in Personality Studies

In 2001, Canli *et al.* reported a new, potentially exciting approach to research on personality and the brain using functional magnetic resonance imaging (fMRI). Building on imaging experiments of response to emotional stimuli, they scanned 14 female volunteers, with an age range of 19–42 years, while they passively viewed pictures with either a positive or a negative emotional content. Although this study was designed to compare brain activation patterns between positive and negative emotion, each subject also completed the NEO scales. Voxel-by-voxel correlations between positive and negative stimuli were determined for each scale at $p < 0.001$, uncorrected for multiple comparisons and without removing any age effects. Extraversion correlated positively with increased activation to positive stimuli in areas of the frontal lobes, temporal lobes, and parts of the caudate, putamen, and amygdala. Some of the same areas were correlated to Neuroticism (Extraversion and Neuroticism were correlated, $r = -0.42$, NS). Most of these significant areas were reported in previous studies. Although this study also had a small sample and used liberal statistical criteria, the design included a task during the scanning that was relevant to personality. This was a welcome first. The spatial resolution of fMRI is also better than other functional imaging. At the very least, this study demonstrated the important finding that some personality variables can influence emotional response in the brain and therefore, cognitive studies of emotion should take account of individual differences in personality scores among the subjects just as age and sex must be considered. Canli *et al.* (2002) made this point dramatically in another fMRI study of 15 volunteers by showing that Extraversion was correlated to the degree of activation in the amygdala during happy stimuli. Only the amygdala data were reported.

Gray and Braver (2002) conducted an fMRI study of working memory in 14 normal subjects, six males and eight females, with an age range of 19 to 27 years. They also collected data on two personality measures that were based on Jeffery Gray's theory (Gray 1970, 1982). Scores on the measures of behavioral approach sensitivity, an impulsivity dimension, and behavioral inhibition sensitivity, an anxiety dimension, were correlated to activity in regions of interest in parts of the anterior cingulate, the only area reported. The complex analyses involved collapsing two emotion-based stimulus conditions and applying multivariate statistical procedures. The analysis was limited by the small sample size and by combining males and females, uncorrected for age. Consequently, there is a need for replication, but this study follows the recent trend of including an experimental manipulation in an imaging study and investigating how personality variables influence results.

2.8. Structural Magnetic Resonance Imaging and Personality

Another approach with potential may be structural brain imaging. Size and volume of various brain structures can be determined from low cost MRI. For example, one important study (Pujol *et al.* 2002) measured the surface area of the anterior and posterior cingulate in 100 subjects, 50 males and 50 females. They found positive correlations between the TCI Harm Avoidance scale and activity in the right anterior cingulate. The left posterior cingulate was positively correlated with Novelty Seeking. The method used to determine size, however, has a number of limitations and cannot be applied to all brain areas.

Structural MRI can also measure gray and white matter concentrations throughout the entire brain using the recently developed voxel-based-morphometry approach (Ashburner & Friston 2000; Good *et al.* 2001). We are applying this approach to NEO PI-R personality data in 25 normal controls. Preliminary analyses, removing age and sex effects, show several significant correlations. For example, scores on the Neuroticism scale are positively correlated with gray matter concentrations in limbic areas including the amygdala, i.e. more gray matter in these areas for those high on the Neuroticism scale. The Extraversion scale is negatively correlated with the putamen, an important dopamine area (low Extraversion goes with greater gray matter). The Openness scale is positively correlated with gray matter in the left middle and inferior temporal lobe. Unlike functional images, structural images are completely independent of cognitive task, so these relationships between gray matter and personality may prove to be more replicable. A complete analysis and report are underway.

3. Conclusions

We are now at the 20th year anniversary of the Mathew *et al.* (1984) paper correlating cortical blood flow assessed with the xenon technique and Extraversion, and it is 18 years since the first PET study correlated GMR throughout the brain with several personality dimensions. What is the subsequent progress? The bad news is readily apparent. Every functional imaging study trying to identify brain areas correlated to personality traits have major limitations and flaws, as described in the preceding review. Functional brain imaging results are dependent on the cognitive state of the subject, so studies "at rest" are essentially uncontrolled, and in my view, not easily interpretable. Small samples, often confounding sex and age effects, have limited statistical power and similarly yield results difficult to interpret. At this point, inconsistencies abound and replications are few so that no strong specific or general findings about personality and regional brain function are apparent from the imaging studies. The most that can be said is tentative — there may a dopamine connection to Extraversion (via the caudate and putamen) and the amygdala may be involved in Extraversion and Neuroticism; frontal and temporal cortex may also be related to several personality dimensions.

The good news is that this field is wide open for discovery. Most of the shortcomings to date derive from adding the collection of personality data to small sample studies designed for other purposes. The mistakes of the past are easily addressed, given proper funding and studies designed specifically to address personality issues. For example, subjects could be selected for high or low scores on at least two personality traits (median splits are used when subjects have not been selected for high or low scores and medians are not the best way to divide people into personality groups). Then the subjects should be scanned at least twice, once engaged in a task to highlight areas thought to be involved in one personality measure and once engaged in a task to highlight the other personality measure. Although PET remains expensive, fMRI is considerably less so and, as demonstrated in recent studies, has great potential for personality research. Compared to the complexities and expense of obtaining brain imaging, testing subjects on multiple measures of personality is relatively easy and should be considered so that studies using the same measures can be compared.

Imaging studies shine light into the "black box" (as Behaviorists referred to the brain) and they are helping identify the brain areas and systems that underlie some important aspects of personality. Ultimately, this information, combined with other kinds of psychopharmacology and neurotransmitter studies and molecular genetics, will lead to a detailed understanding of the neurobiological basis of personality. Such an understanding is likely to rival the wildest expectations of earlier, modern personality researchers who studied psychophysiology (Gale 1973; Strelau 1983), perception (Witkin *et al.* 1954), and even brain lesions (Powell 1981). This has long been the vision of Marvin Zuckerman and other pioneers of personality research. As more and more psychologists use revolutionary brain imaging and neuroscience techniques, the realization of this vision may be near.

References

Alkire, M. T., & Haier, R. J. (2001). Correlating in vivo anaesthetic effects with ex vivo receptor density data supports a GABAergic mechanism of action for propofol, but not for isoflurane. *British Journal of Anaesthesiology*, *86*, 618–626.

Alkire, M. T., Haier, R. J., & Fallon, J. H. (2000). Toward a unified theory of narcosis: Brain imaging evidence for a thalamocortical switch as the neurophysiologic basis of anesthetic-induced unconsciousness. *Conscious Cognition*, *9*, 370–386.

Alkire, M. T., Haier, R. J., Fallon, J. H., & Barker, S. J. (1996). PET imaging of conscious and unconscious verbal memory. *Journal of Consciousness Studies*, *3*, 448–462.

Alkire, M. T., Haier, R. J., Fallon, J. H., & Cahill, L. (1998). Hippocampal, but not amygdala, activity at encoding correlates with long-term, free recall of nonemotional information. *Proceedings of the National Academy of Science*, *95*, 14506–14510.

Allport, G. W. (1949). *Personality: A psychological interpretation*. New York: Henry Holt and Company.

Ashburner, J., & Friston, K. J. (2000). Voxel-based morphometry — the methods. *Neuroimage, 11*, 805–821.

Ballenger, J. C., Post, R. M., Jimerson, D. C., Lake, C. R., Murphy, D., Zuckerman, M., & Cronin, C. (1983). Biochemical correlates of personality traits in normals: An exploratory study. *Personality and Individual Differences, 4*, 615–625.

Bouchard, T. J., & Loehlin, J. C. (2001). Genes, evolution, and personality. *Behavior Genetics, 31*, 243–273.

Bouchard, T. J., & McGue, M. (1990). Genetic and rearing environmental-influences on adult personality: An analysis of adopted twins reared apart. *Journal of Personality, 58*, 263–295.

Bouchard, T. J., McGue, M., Hur, M., & Horn, J. M. (1998). A genetic and environmental analysis of the California Psychological Inventory using adult twins reared apart and together. *European Journal of Personality, 12*, 307–320.

Canli, T., Sivers, H., Whitfield, S. L., Gotlib, I. H., & Gabrieli, J. D. E. (2002). Amygdala response to happy faces as a function of extraversion. *Science, 296*, 2191.

Canli, T., Zhao, Z., Desmond, J. E., Kang, E. J., Gross, J., & Gabrieli, J. D. E. (2001). An fMRI study of personality influences on brain reactivity to emotional stimuli. *Behavioral Neuroscience, 115*, 33–42.

Cloninger, C. R. (1987). A systematic method for clinical description and classification of personality variants: A proposal. *Archives of General Psychiatry, 44*, 573–588.

Costa, P. T., & McCrae, R. R. (1992). *Revised NEO Personality Inventory (NEO-PI-R) and NEO Five-Factor Inventory (NEO-FFI) professional manual*. Odessa, FL: Psychological Assessment Resources.

Ebmeier, K. P., Deary, I. J., Ocarroll, R. E., Prentice, N., Moffoot, A. P. R., & Goodwin, G. M. (1994). Personality associations with the uptake of the cerebral blood-flow marker (99m)Tc-Exametazime estimated with single-photon emission tomography. *Personality and Individual Differences, 17*, 587–595.

Eysenck, H. J. (1952). *The scientific study of personality*. New York: Macmillan Company.

Eysenck, H. J. (1967). *The biological basis of personality*. Springfield: Charles C. Thomas.

Eysenck, H. J., &. Eysenck, S. B. G. (1964). *Manual for the Eysenck Personality Inventory*. San Diego: Educational and Industrial Testing Service.

Eysenck, H. J., & Eysenck, S. B. G. (1975). *Manual of the Eysenck Personality Questionnaire*. San Diego: Hodder & Stoughton.

Farde, L., Gustavsson, J. P., & Jonsson, E. (1997). D2 dopamine receptors and personality traits. *Nature, 385*, 590.

Fischer, H., Wik, G., & Fredrikson, M. (1997). Extraversion, neuroticism and brain function: A PET study of personality. *Personality and Individual Differences, 23*, 345–352.

Fredrikson, M., Wik, G., & Fischer, H. (1999). Higher hypothalamic and hippocampal neural activity in type A than type B women. *Personality and Individual Differences, 26*, 265–270.

Friston, K. J., Holmes, A. P., Worsley, K. J., Poline, J. P., Firth, C. D., & Frackowiak, R. S. J. (1995). Statistical parametric maps in functional imaging: A general linear approach. *Human Brain mapping, 2*, 189–210.

Gale, A. (1973). The psychophysiology of individual differences: Studies of extraversion and the EEG. In: P. Kline (Ed.), *New approaches to psychological measurement* (pp. 211–256). New York: Wiley.

Good, C. D., Johnsrude, I. S., Ashburner, J., Henson, R. N., Friston, K. J., & Frackowiak, R. S. (2001). A voxel-based morphometric study of ageing in 465 normal adult human brains. *Neuroimage, 14*, 21–36.

Gray, J. A. (1970). Psychophysiological basis of introversion-extraversion. *Behaviour Research and Therapy*, *8*, 249–266.

Gray, J. A. (1982). *The neuropsychology of anxiety: An inquiry into the functions of the septo-hippocampal system.* Oxford: Oxford University Press.

Gray, J. R., & Braver, T. S. (2002). Personality predicts working-memory-related activation in the caudal anterior cingulate cortex. *Cognitive Affective and Behavioral Neuroscience*, *2*, 64–75.

Haier, R. J. (2001). PET studies of learning and individual differences. In: J. L. McClelland, & R. S. Siegler (Eds), *Mechanisms of cognitive development: behavioral and neural perspectives* (pp.123–145). Hillsdale, NJ: Lawrence-Erlbaum.

Haier, R. J., Siegel, B. V., MacLachlan, A., Soderling, E., Lottenberg, S., & Buchsbaum, M. S. (1992). Regional glucose metabolic changes after learning a complex visuospatial/motor task: A positron emission tomographic study. *Brain Research*, *570*, 134–143.

Haier, R. J., Siegel, B. V., Nuechterlein, K. H., Hazlett, E., Wu, J. C., Paek, J., Browning, H. L., & Buchsbaum, M. S. (1988). Cortical glucose metabolic rate correlates of abstract reasoning and attention studied with positron emission tomography. *Intelligence*, *12*, 199–217.

Haier, R. J., Sokolski, K., Katz, M., & Buchsbaum, M. S. (1987). The study of personality with positron emission tomography. In: J. Strelau, & H. J. Eysenck (Eds), *Personality dimensions and arousal* (pp. 251–267). New York: Plenum Press.

Haier, R. J., White, N. S., & Alkire, M. T. (2003). Individual differences in general intelligence correlate with brain function during nonreasoning tasks. *Intelligence*, *31*, 429–441.

Johnson, D. L., Wiebe, J. S., Gold, S. M., Andreasen, N. C., Hichwa, R. D., Watkins, G. L., & Ponto, L. L. B. (1999). Cerebral blood flow and personality: A positron emission tomography study. *American Journal of Psychiatry*, *156*, 252–257.

Kestler, L. P., Malhotra, A. K., Finch, C., Adler, C., & Breier, A. (2000). The relation between dopamine D2 receptor density and personality: Preliminary evidence from the NEO personality inventory-revised. *Neuropsychiatry Neuropsychololology and Behavioral Neurolology*, *13*, 48–52.

Laakso, A., Vilkman, H., Kajander, J., Bergman, J., Paranta, M., Solin, O., & Hietala, J. (2000). Prediction of detached personality in healthy subjects by low dopamine transporter binding. *American Journal of Psychiatry*, *157*, 290–292.

Leyton, M., Boileau, I., Benkelfat, C., Diksic, M., Baker, G., & Dagher, A. (2002). Amphetamine-induced increases in extracellular dopamine, drug wanting, and novelty seeking: A PET/[11C]raclopride study in healthy men. *Neuropsychopharmacology*, *27*, 1027–1035.

Mathew, R. J., Weinman, M. L., & Barr, D. L. (1984). Personality and regional cerebral blood-flow. *British Journal of Psychiatry*, *144*, 529–532.

Moresco, F. M., Dieci, M., Vita, A., Messa, C., Gobbo, C., Galli, L., Rizzo, G., Panzacchi, A., De Peri, L., Invernizzi, G., & Fazio, F. (2002). In vivo serotonin 5HT(2A) receptor binding and personality traits in healthy subjects: A positron emission tomography study. *Neuroimage*, *17*, 1470–1478.

Powell, G. E. (1981). A survey of the effects of brain lesions upon personality. In: H. J. Eysenck (Ed.), *A model for personality* (pp. 65–87). Berlin: Springer-Verlag.

Pujol, J., Lopez, A., Deus, J., Cardoner, N., Vallejo, J., Capdevila, A., & Paus, T. (2002). Anatomical variability of the anterior cingulate gyrus and basic dimensions of human personality. *Neuroimage*, *15*, 847–855.

Rabiner, E. A., Messa, C., Sargent, P. A., Husted-Kjaer, K., Montgomery, A., Lawrence, A. D., Bench, C. J., Gunn, R. N., Cowen, P., & Grasby, P. M. (2002). A database of [(11)C]WAY-100635 binding to 5-HT(1A) receptors in normal male volunteers: Normative data and relationship to methodological, demographic, physiological, and behavioral variables. *Neuroimage*, *15*, 620–632.

Roback, A. A. (1928). *The psychology of character.* New York: Harcourt Brace.

Schalling, D., Asberg, M., Edman, G., & Oreland, L. (1987). Markers for vulnerability to psychopathology: Temperament traits associated with platelet MAO activity. *Acta Psychiatrica Scandinavica*, *76*, 172–182.

Semple, W. E., Cohen, R. M., Foer, J., King, A. C., Nordahl, T., Zametkin, A., Kosmidis, M., Andreason, P. J., & Goyer, P. (1991). Orbital frontal cortex metabolism and personality in normals: Results from two PET studies. *Biological Psychiatry*, *29*, 174–185.

Stenberg, G., Risberg, J., Warkentin, S., & Rosen, I. (1990). Regional patterns of cortical blood-flow distinguish extraverts from introverts. *Personality and Individual Differences*, *11*, 663–673.

Stenberg, G., Wendt, P. E., & Risberg, J. (1993). Regional cerebral blood-flow and extraversion. *Personality and Individual Differences*, *15*, 547–554.

Strelau, J. (1983). *Temperament, personality, activity*. New York: Academic Press.

Sugiura, M., Kawashima, R., Nakagawa, M., Okada, K., Sato, T., Goto, R., Sato, K., Ono, S., Schormann, T., Zilles, K., & Fukuda, H. (2000). Correlation between human personality and neural activity in cerebral cortex. *Neuroimage*, *11*, 541–546.

Suhara, T., Yasuno, F., Sudo, Y., Yamamoto, M., Inoue, M., Okubo, Y., & Suzuki, K. (2001). Dopamine D2 receptors in the insular cortex and the personality trait of novelty seeking. *Neuroimage*, *13*, 891–895.

Thomson, W. H. (1911). *Brain and personality*. New York: Dodd, Mead & Company.

Turner, R. M., Hudson, I. L., Butler, P. H., & Joyce, P. R. (2003). Brain function and personality in normal males: A SPECT study using statistical parametric mapping. *Neuroimage*, *19*, 1145–1162.

Witkin, H. A., Lewis, H. B., Hertzman, M., Machover, K., Meissner, P. B., & Wapner, S. (1954). *Personality through perception*. New York: Harper & Brothers.

Yasuno, F., Suhara, T., Sudo, Y., Yamamoto, M., Inoue, M., Okubo, Y., & Suzuki, K. (2001). Relation among dopamine D2 receptor binding, obesity and personality in normal human subjects. *Neuroscience Letters*, *300*, 59–61.

Youn, T., Lyoo, I. K., Kim, J. J., Park, H. J., Ha, K. S., Lee, D. S., Abrams, K. Y., Lee, M. C., & Kwon, J. S. (2002). Relationship between personality trait and regional cerebral glucose metabolism assessed with positron emission tomography. *Biological Psychology*, *60*, 109–120.

Zuckerman, M. (1971). Dimensions of sensation seeking. *Journal of Consulting and Clinical Psychology*, *36*, 45–52.

Zuckerman, M. (1979). *Sensation seeking: Beyond the optimal level of arousal*. Hillsdale, NJ: Erlbaum.

Zuckerman, M. (1984). Sensation seeking: A comparative approach to a human trait. *Behavioral and Brain Sciences*, *7*, 413–434.

Zuckerman, M. (1991). *Psychobiology of personality*. New York: Cambridge University Press.

Zuckerman, M. (1995). Good and bad humors: Biochemical bases of personality and its disorders. *Psychological Science*, *6*, 325–332.

Zuckerman, M., Buchsbaum, M. S., & Murphy, D. L. (1980). Sensation seeking and its biological correlates. *Psychological Bulletin*, *88*, 187–214.

Chapter 18

Electrophysiological Correlates of Sensation Seeking Behavior in Rats, Cats, and Humans

J. Siegel

1. Introduction

This festschrift paper for Marvin Zuckerman describes my collaborative work with him that dates back to the early 1970s. Even then, Zuckerman was interested in the biological basis of sensation seeking (SS) and sought to collaborate with my laboratory — at the time I was working on the neural control of sleep and arousal. I summarize here our early collaborative study, using human subjects, and my subsequent cat and rat work that explored electrophysiological correlates (visual evoked potentials) of SS behavior. A final project described here are initial experiments that explore the brain biochemical mechanisms (neurotransmitters) that determine the evoked potential and behavioral differences that characterize low- and high-sensation seekers.

2. Sensation Seeking, Augmenting and Reducing in Humans

My augmenting/reducing and sensation seeking collaboration with Marvin Zuckerman started in the early 1970s when Monte Buchsbaum (1971) published a short note in Science that showed a relationship between SS, as measured by Zuckerman's (1971) Sensation Seeking Scale and visual evoked potential (VEP) augmenting and reducing. Marvin asked me to collaborate with him and a graduate student, Tom Murtaugh, on a project to follow up this lead. In my lab, at that time, we were doing cat experiments with implanted electrodes to record evoked potentials (EPs) to light flash and to acoustic stimuli. We were looking at the effects of arousal levels on visual and auditory EPs as recorded from the visual and auditory cortices and their associated thalamic nuclei. We moved some of my equipment to Marvin's lab and proceeded to record VEPs from scalp leads of human subjects (undergraduate students at the University of Delaware). A Grass photostimulator generated light flashes of five different intensities and a Grass polygraph was used to amplify the brain

On the Psychobiology of Personality
Edited by R. M. Stelmack

ISBN: 0-08-044209-9

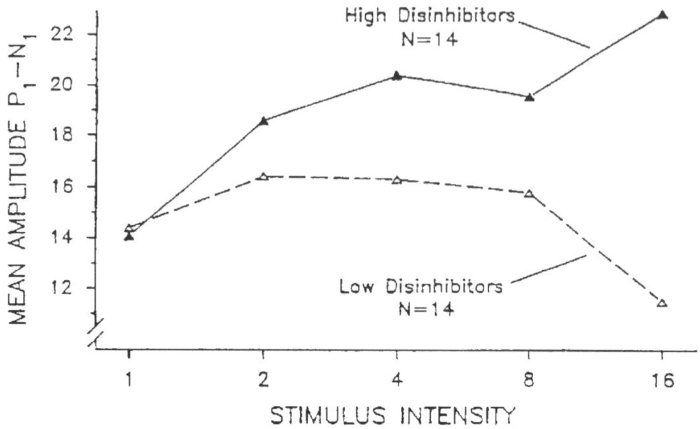

Figure 1: Mean VEP amplitudes for low and high disinhibition scorers at each level of stimulus intensity. *Source:* From Zuckerman, M., Murtaugh, T., and Siegel, J. (1974). Sensation seeking and cortical augmenting-reducing. *Psychophysiology. 11*, 535–542. Reprinted with permission from the author.

activity from the scalp leads. A large 7-channel Sanborn FM tape recorder stored the raw electroencephalogram (EEG) signals as they were generated. Off-line, the EEG voltages were fed into a Nuclear Chicago computer to digitize the EEG signal that was time-locked to the flash and then average those individual digitized VEPs over 120 sweeps. The resulting average was printed out on a Moseley X-Y plotter. This was in 1973. In preparing this manuscript I reminisced about the equipment we used at the time. In approximate figures, the 8-channel Grass polygraph cost $1,000/channel, the Sanborn tape recorder was $10,000, the Nuclear Chicago computer was $15,000, and the X-Y plotter was $2,000. That totaled $35,000. Today we can do all that, plus more, with a desktop PC and printer for about $3,000. The evolution of laboratory instrumentation in electrophysiology from the 1960s when I started, to now has been an interesting side aspect of my research over the years.

The main finding of that experiment is shown in Figure 1, taken from the paper we published in *Psychophysiology* (Zuckerman *et al.* 1974). Subjects who scored high on the Disinhibition subscale of the Sensation Seeking Scale showed augmenting of the first positive-negative amplitude VEP waves (P1-N1) at the highest flash intensity and low disinhibitors exhibited a dramatic reduction of that VEP amplitude at the highest flash intensity.

3. Sensation Seeking, Augmenting and Reducing in Cats

As an animal researcher, I thought it would be of interest and of value to explore the underlying neural mechanisms of the augmenting/reducing — SS relation. Invasive studies with animals would permit that. We were already doing VEP work with animals; what was needed was an animal model of SS behavior.

My students and I had been using cats in experiments for a number of years and had observed that cats show large individual differences along a number of behavioral dimensions. In some of our studies, cats were brought into the lab and permitted to roam around and get used to us and to the laboratory environment prior to being used in the experiment. We observed that some cats were highly exploratory. They would jump onto tables and generally interact with people in the lab. In contrast, others retreated to a quite corner, often under a table, and were quite passive.

Jeff Lukas, a graduate student in my lab at the time, formalized our observations by setting up a number of standard conditions. He rated the cats along seven dimensions of behavior. These were exploration, activity level, aggression, withdrawal, visual contact, emotionality, and responsiveness. The cats were then prepared for electrophysiological recordings and VEP data were recorded to light flashes of five different intensities. The same equipment used in the human research was used in the cat study (Lukas & Siegel 1977).

The same VEP component that showed augmenting or reducing in the human was evaluated in these cats. We found that the behaviorally responsive cats showed VEP augmenting and the least responsive animals were VEP reducers. Figure 2, taken from the paper we published in Science (Lukas & Siegel 1977), shows the cortical VEPs from the least behaviorally responsive animal in the experiment and from one of the most responsive cats. The highly responsive cat (who showed marked SS behavior), was clearly an augmenter (see the five traces in part C of Figure 2). The least responsive cat showed a progressive decrease in VEP amplitudes as flash intensities increased (traces A in Figure 2).

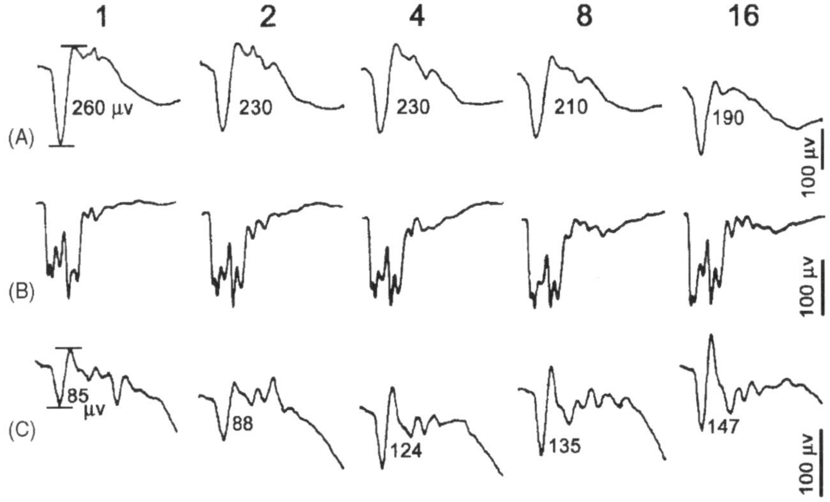

Figure 2: VEP averages recorded from the visual cortex (A) and thalamus (B) of a VEP reducer and cortical recordings (C) from an augmenter cat. *Source:* From Lukas, J. H., and Siegel, J. (1977). Cortical mechanisms that augment or reduce evoked potential in cats. *Science*, *198*, 73–75. Reprinted with permission from the American Association for the Advancement of Science.

In this animal study, electrodes were placed within the brain and we were not limited to scalp leads, as is the case in human work. We asked if VEP augmenting and reducing recorded at the cortex is merely a reflection of a difference that occurs deeper within the brain or is augmenting/reducing a cortical phenomenon. The cortical VEP, particularly the early component, is primarily a function of input from the lateral geniculate of the thalamus, which in turn receives directly from the retina. In this study we placed electrodes into the optic radiation fibers that carry the visual message from the lateral geniculate body to the visual cortex. We were looking at the neural signal before it reached the cortex. As seen in traces B of Figure 2, that message recorded simultaneously with the cortical potentials from the least responsive cat (the cortical reducer), showed no sign of reducing with increasing flash intensity. In fact, the early component of the thalamocortical signal (which is the basis of the cortical component that augments or reduces), showed an increase in amplitude with increasing flash intensity. So neural activity from the thalamus shows the expected psychophysical function, i.e. increasing neural response with increasing stimulus intensity. We concluded that there is something different occurring at the cortex of responsive vs. non-responsive (high- and low-sensation seeking) cats.

4. Sensation Seeking, Augmenting and Reducing in Rats

We now felt that we had an animal model for a relation between an important dimension of behavior (SS) and a specific brain event, i.e. VEP augmenting or reducing). The VEP response may be thought of as a biological marker for this complex and important behavioral trait. This is an interesting observation, but having a biological marker for a behavioral trait provides minimal understanding of the biological basis for the behavior. It is simply a correlation. What is required is the ability to do invasive studies to determine the biological mechanisms that cause the relationship between the SS behaviors and the VEP augmenting and reducing. Our animal model permits that. However, we felt that a laboratory rat model would be of greater value than a cat model for a number of reasons — namely the ability to explore and manipulate genetic factors, short generational times, and a large body of experimental techniques and behavioral data that are available for the rat. Another consideration is the principle of using animals as low on the phylogenetic scale consonant with the experimental question asked. So the question was: do rats show differences in SS-like behaviors?

At that point in time, I was on a sabbatical leave in Heidelberg, Germany, and was giving a talk in Magdeburg, then a part of East Germany, describing this research. After I had presented the cat work described above, someone in the audience commented that he was familiar with a researcher in Zurich, Switzerland who was breeding two strains of rats that have behavioral traits that are remarkably similar to the high and low SS cats I had been talking about. I contacted Peter Driscoll in Zurich and visited him there to learn about his two rat lines. Driscoll described work that he and others had done showing that Roman High Avoidance (RHA) rats, as they are called, exhibited greater locomotor behavior, exploratory behavior, alcohol consumption, and aggression and less inhibitory control of behavior than did the Roman Low Avoidance (RLA) rats. These are the same terms used to describe high and low SS humans. In addition, richer behavioral data existed for the rat than for the cat.

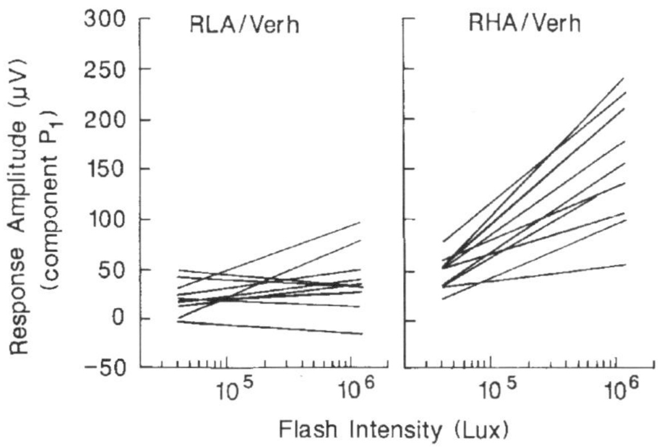

Figure 3: The least squares regression functions of VEP response amplitudes of component P1 against flash intensity for each of 10 RHA and 10 RLA rats. The abscissa represents the range of flash intensities. *Source:* From Siegel, J., Gayle, D., Sharma, A., and Driscoll, P. (1996), The locus of origin of augmenting and reducing of visual evoked potentials in rat brain, *Physiology and Behavior*, *54*, 287–291. Reprinted with permission from Elsevier.

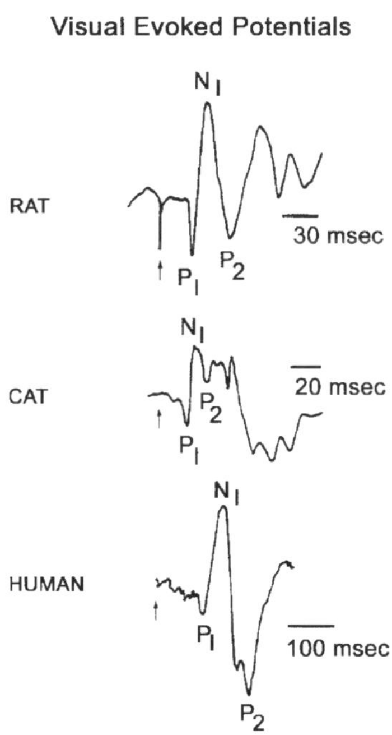

Figure 4: VEPs recorded from the cortex of a rat, cat, and human. The same components, P1–N1, augment or reduce in each species. The arrows indicate the time of flash occurrence. *Source:* From Siegel, J., and Sisson, D. (1993). Evoked field potentials — Beyond correlates of behavior. In: Haschke *et al.* (Eds), *Slow potential changes in the brain* (pp. 151–165). Birkhauser Boston. Reprinted with permission from Springer-Verlag.

Peter Driscoll and I arranged for his rats, bred in Zurich, to be shipped to Delaware after I returned from sabbatical. In Delaware, these rats were then submitted to electrophysiological testing.

The data we collected showed that RHA rats had significantly steeper slopes of components P1 and P1-N1 than did the RLA rats (Siegel *et al.* 1993). The two lines of rats were VEP augmenters and reducers, respectively. Figure 3 shows the least squares regression function of VEP response amplitude of component P1 against log flash intensity of 10 RLA (left panel) and 10 RHA rats (right panel). There is almost no overlap of the P1 slopes between the two lines of rats; 8 of 10 RHA rats had slopes greater than any of the RLA rats. Of great importance for the position that there is a common physiological basis for the SS behaviors in the three species thus far tested is the fact that VEPs recorded from the three species, as shown in Figure 4, have essentially the same waveform (initial positivity-negativity). More to the point, the same early components, P1 and P1-N1, augment or reduce in the human, cat, and rat.

5. Locus of Origin of Augmenting and Reducing in the Rat Brain

Prior to investigating the neural differences recorded at the cortex that underlie VEP augmenting/reducing in the two lines of rats, it was important to be sure that

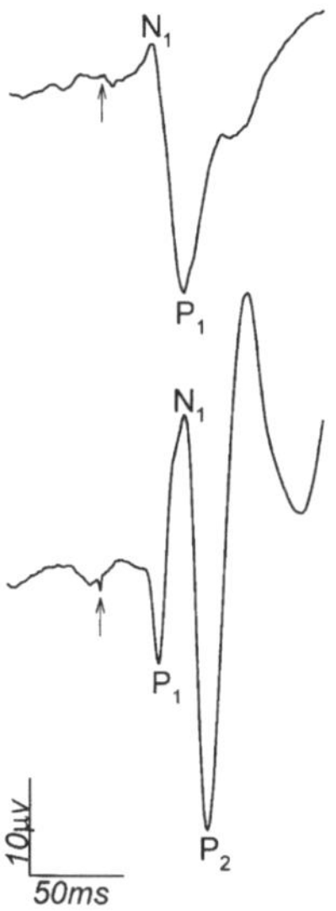

Figure 5: Averaged VEPs in response to a middle-intensity light flash recorded simultaneously from a rat lateral geniculate nucleus (top trace) and visual cortex (bottom trace). The arrows indicate the time of flash occurrence. *Source:* From Siegel, J., Gayle, D., Sharma, A., and Driscoll, P. (1996). The locus of origin of augmenting and reducing of visual evoked potentials in rat brain. *Physiology and Behavior*, *54*, 287–291. Reprinted with permission from Elsevier.

augmenting/reducing is a cortical phenomenon. We had evidence from our cat experiment with recordings from the subcortical thalamic radiations that this was the case, but we wanted to confirm this in the rat. To accomplish this, we again used RHA and RLA rats (using another infusion of rats from Zurich). In addition to recording VEPs from the visual cortex, as in the previous rat study, we inserted a fine electrode into the dorsal lateral geniculate nucleus of the thalamus. The electrode was lowered until it yielded a maximum amplitude response of an initial component that had a shorter latency than P1 recorded from the visual cortex. VEP responses recorded simultaneously from the lateral geniculate and the visual cortex are illustrated in Figure 5. The first geniculate component was a small negative deflection (N1) with a peak latency 3 ms shorter than the first cortical component, P1. There was no other geniculate component that preceded cortical P1; we therefore assume that the first geniculate component is the field potential correlate of the thalamocortical volley responsible for the first cortical component. Forty-two rats (22 RHA and 20 RLA) yielded VEP data from histologically verified electrode placements in the dorsal lateral geniculate (Siegel *et al.* 1996).

As in our previous study with these Roman rats, component P1 recorded from the cortex of RHA rats showed clear augmenting relative to the P1 amplitude of the RLA rats. This is shown in the right panel of Figure 6. The major new finding in this study was that the lateral geniculate component, N1, which provides the visual cortex with the volley responsible for the first cortical component, P1, showed no difference of augmenting and reducing between the two lines of Roman rats. This is seen in the left panel of Figure 6. This finding is consistent with our previous cat work in which we recorded from the thalamic radiations that innervate

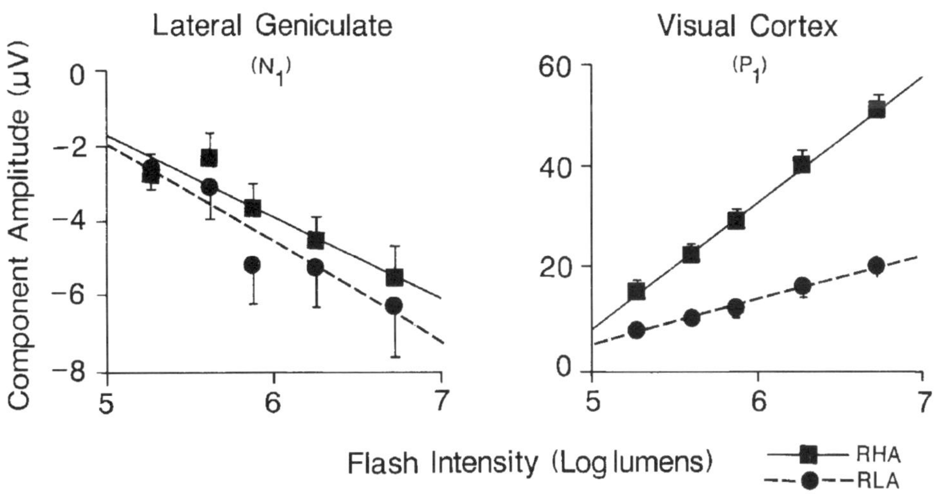

Figure 6: The least squares regression functions of VEP mean amplitudes recorded simultaneously from the lateral geniculate (left panel) and visual cortex (right panel) of 22 RHA and 20 RLA rats. Error bars refer to the SEM. For components recorded at the cortex, the error bars are so small that they are sometimes embedded in the symbols. *Source:* From Siegel, J., Sisson, D. F., and Driscoll, P. (1993). Augmenting and reducing of visual evoked potentials in Roman high- and low-avoidance rats. *Physiology and Behavior*, *54*, 707–711.

the visual cortex. However, recording from the lateral geniculate is direct evidence that the augmenting-reducing difference recorded at the cortex in the rat is not due to a difference occurring at the thalamus and is not, therefore, a reflection of events at the thalamus.

These data indicate that we can concentrate on the cortex as the brain area to investigate in order to determine the neurochemical differences between augmenting and reducing animals. Our long-term goal in this project was to understand the neural mechanisms basic to individual differences in SS and risk-taking behavior. There is no basis to expect a causal relationship between SS behavior on one hand and VEP augmenting/reducing on the other hand. The major factors that determine visual activity at the cortex are retinal and thalamic events. These visual processes should be independent of factors that determine behavioral or personality traits. The observed correlation between VEP augmenting-reducing and SS behavior requires a third factor that exerts a common influence on the other two. We speculate that this third factor is one or more of the subcortical, extra-thalamic systems that have, so called, non-specific or diffuse projections to the entire cortical mantle.

These structures, schematically illustrated in Figure 7, are transmitter-specific which make them well suited for pharmacological manipulation. They are the dopaminergic ventral tegmental area, serotonergic raphe nuclei, adrenergic nucleus locus coeruleus, and

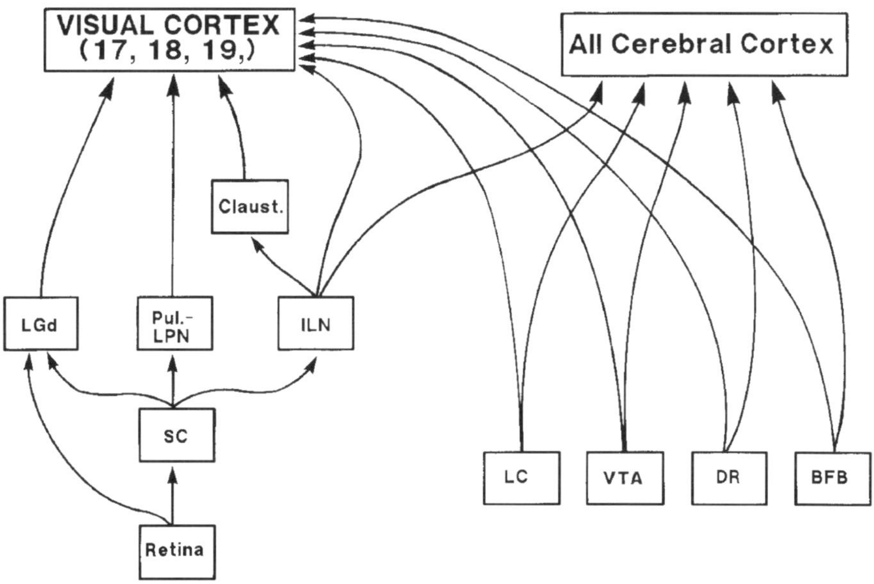

Figure 7: Lateral geniculate and extrageniculate projections to visual cortex. BFB = basal forebrain (nucleus basalis); Claust. = claustrum; DR = dorsal raphe nucleus; ILN = intralaminar nuclei of the thalamus; LC = locus ceoruleus; LGd = lateral geniculate nucleus, dorsal part; Pul LPN = pulvinar-lateral posterior nucleus complex of the thalamus; SC = superior colliculus; VTA = ventral tegmental area. *Source:* From Siegel, J., and Driscoll, P. (1996). Recent developments in an animal model of visual evoked potential augmenting/reducing and sensation seeking behavior. *Neuropsychobiology*, *34*, 130–135. Reprinted with permission from Karger.

the cholinergic basal forebrain. There is evidence from a number of labs that these nuclei are often not the prime influence, but exert modulatory effects upon target cells. Areas of cortex that receive modulatory influences include those that are involved with behavioral traits related to SS as well as sensory cortex from which VEPs are recorded. Under this common modulatory influence, the visual system would be biased to produce VEPs in the direction of augmenting or reducing and, similarly, regions of the brain that control SS behaviors such as risk taking and impulsivity would be biased to express more or less of these traits. We postulate that there are individual differences, genetically influenced, in the tonic and, perhaps, phasic activity of the subcortical modulating system(s) such that the different areas of the brain that control visual processing and behavioral traits are modulated similarly within individuals and differently between individuals.

6. Neurotransmitters, Augmenting and Reducing in Rats

Our first approach to this was to investigate the role of neurotransmitters that determine or influence the amplitude of cortical components P1 and N1, the components that augment or reduce. To do this we devised a perfusion chamber that was cemented to the skull above a hole over the exposed visual cortex. With the dura removed and the pia perforated, the cortex was superfused with artificial cerebrospinal fluid as VEPs were recorded from an electrode

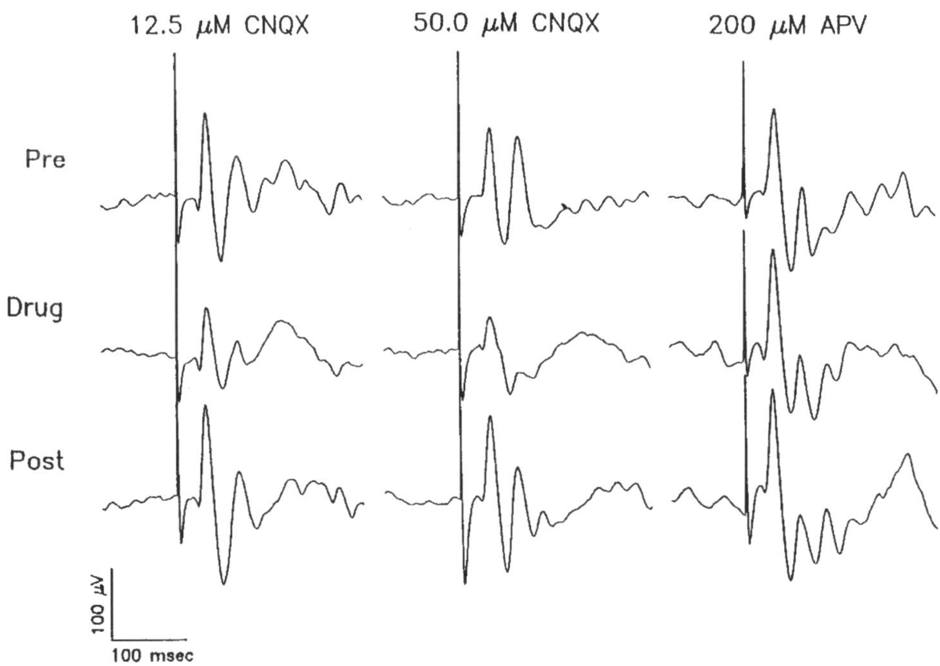

Figure 8: Visual event-related potentials (VEP) averages recorded before, during, and after superfusion of the visual cortex with two doses of 6-cyno-7-nitroquinoxaline-2,3-dione (CNQX) and one dose of AP5 (designated APV on the figure).

placed within the perfusion chamber on the cortical surface. The superfusion fluid contained, at different times, concentrations of neurotransmitter agonists and antagonists to determine the influence of these transmitters on VEPs recorded from that region of cortex. The intensity of the visual stimulus was selected to produce VEPs that were midway within the dynamic range of responses recorded from the cortex. This served to optimize the ability to detect a neurotransmitter influence that would result in an augmenting or a reducing of the VEP.

Our first study looked at the role of excitatory amino acid (EAA), known to be the primary neurotransmitter that mediates the geniculocortical response. Kynurenic acid (KYN), a non-selective EAA antagonist, superfused over the visual cortex had the effect of decreasing components N1 and N2 in a dose-dependant fashion. This indicates that an EAA transmitter (probably glutamate) mediates these cortical components. We next determined whether neural activity that produces these components is mediated by N-methyl-D-aspartate (NMDA) or non-NMDA glutamate receptors. Figure 8 shows the data for cortical superfusion with 6-cyno-7-nitroquinoxaline-2,3-dione (CNQX), a non-NMDA antagonist, and 2-amino-5-phosphonopentanoic acid (AP5), a selective NMDA antagonist. VEPs in the top and bottom rows were recorded during superfusion with artificial cerebrospinal fluid prior to and after perfusion with the drug treatment, shown in the middle row of traces. VEPs are averages from four rats at each drug treatment. CNQX, the non-NMDA antagonist, produced a dose-dependant decrease of N1 and N2, as did KYN. AP5, the selective NMDA antagonist, produced no effect on early VEP components. These data, together with the KYN findings, suggest that short latency neural activity generated by EAA transmitter in rat visual cortex is mediated by non-NMDA receptors. This makes sense. NMDA glutamate receptors are associated with synapses involved with plasticity, as seen in hippocampal circuits for memory. In the visual system, especially at synapses that provide short latency information about the visual signal, we do not want plasticity. At this early step of sensory processing, the cortex should be provided with veridical information about the sensory stimulus.

These findings were interesting, but this work was preparatory to investigating the role of dopamine, serotonin, and norepinephrine in the modulation of VEP components that augment or reduce. Those neurotransmitters are likely candidates for influences that modulate cortical processes in multiple areas of the cerebral cortex. These neurotransmitters (and their agonists and antagonists) would then be explored for influences on SS type behaviors. That work remains to be done.

References

Buchsbaum, M. (1971). Neural events and the psychophysical law. *Science*, *172*, 502.

Lukas, J. H., & Siegel, J. (1977). Cortical mechanisms that augment or reduce evoked potential in cats. *Science*, *198*, 73–75.

Siegel, J., Gayle, D., Sharma, A., & Driscoll, P. (1996). The locus of origin of augmenting and reducing of visual evoked potentials in rat brain. *Physiology and Behavior*, *60*, 287–291.

Siegel, J., Sisson, D. F., & Driscoll, P. (1993). Augmenting and reducing of visual evoked potentials in Roman high- and low-avoidance rats. *Physiology and Behavior*, *54*, 707–711.

Zuckerman, M. (1971). Dimensions of sensation seeking. *Journal of Personality*, *36*, 45–52.

Zuckerman, M., Murtaugh, T., & Siegel, J. (1974). Sensation seeking and cortical augmenting-reducing. *Psychophysiology*, *11*, 535–542.

B. Biochemical Analyses

Chapter 19

Personality and Hormones

P. Netter

1. Introduction

The study of the relations between hormones and personality is based on ancient ideas of the four humors or fluids of the body, melanchole (black bile), chole (yellow bile), sanguine (blood) and phlegm (mucus) as described by Hippocrates (460 BC 1978). A balance between these humors was thought to be essential for personal health and a "temperated soul," whereas an imbalance in the humors was expressed in various illnesses and moods (Galen 170 BC 1938). The Latin word *temperare*, meaning to blend in proper proportion, later gave rise to the term temperament as it is used in the description of character. The excess of one of these fluids was thought to cause typical character qualities, i.e. melancholic, choleric, sanguine and phlegmatic. This general concept that bodily fluids may be responsible for behavior, or even for differences in personality, experienced a renaissance when it became possible to measure hormones in urine and blood in the first half of the 20th century.

It is only recently, however, that scientific investigations began to explore the functions and mechanisms of hormones in the expression of personality differences. When relating basal levels as well as treatment-induced changes in hormones to personality, interest shifted to the questions of whether genetic and/or environmental influences were responsible underlying factors and of how central nervous mechanisms transform experiences into signals for transmitter release and subsequent changes in hormone levels. There are several hormones that attracted particular interest in personality psychology. These are the hormones that are associated with the hypothalamo-pituitary-adrenal (HPA) axis as well as those of the gonadal pituitary adrenal (HPG) axis, like testosterone and estrogen. It must be emphasized, however, that there is an interaction between the two and also with the adrenomedullary axis (represented by catecholamines from the adrenal medulla and sympathetic nerves) that must be kept in mind when presenting data for the hormone domains separately (see Figure 1).

With respect to personality, the hormones most widely studied are cortisol, the hormone representing the HPA axis, and testosterone representing the HPG axis. In addition, the association between peripheral catecholamines and personality was studied in early, but currently less popular, psychoendocrinological issues in research on personality and

On the Psychobiology of Personality
Edited by R. M. Stelmack

ISBN: 0-08-044209-9

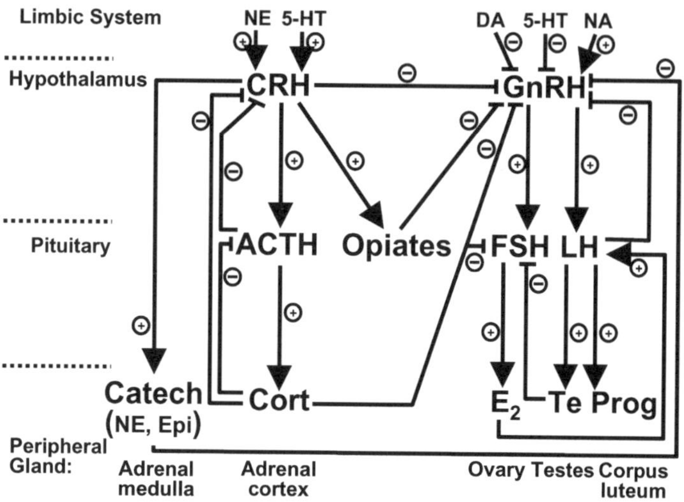

Figure 1: Interaction of the HPA (left) and GPA axis (right) and with catecholamines and opiates. *Note:* ⊥ = inhibition; ↑ = stimulation; NE = norepinephrine; 5-HT = serotonin; DA = dopamine; CRH = corticotropin releasing hormone; GnRH = gonadotropin releasing hormone; ACTH = adrenocorticotropic hormone; FSH = follicle stimulating hormone; LH = luteinizing hormone; Catech = catecholamines; NE = norepinephrine; epi = epinephrine; Cort = cortisol; E2 = estrogen; Te = testosterone; Prog = progesterone. − = leading to decrease, + = leading to increase.

hormones. Therefore, this contribution will mainly focus on cortisol and on testosterone in their relation to personality and on the association of personality with the adrenomedullary catecheolamines.

The female gonadal hormones, thyroid hormones, and the abundant source of various peptides will not be addressed in this chapter. It is, however, necessary to obtain a general overview of how hormones are related to each other by feedback mechanisms, and of why contradictory results may be reported depending on the stage of development of a hormonal imbalance in subjects scoring high and low on certain personality traits. Some introductory remarks are required in order to understand the interaction between hormones secreted from peripheral glands and their regulating peptides from the pituitary and the higher centers of the hypothalamus and the limbic system as well as the basic mechanisms and mediators of hormone action.

1.1. Regulating Feedback Systems, Mechanisms of Hormone Action, and Rhythmic Variations of Hormones

Most of the glandular hormones are regulated by hypothalamic and pituitary peptides (see Figure 1). When the hormone level in the periphery rises, the pituitary receives the signal to stop further peptide secretion for stimulating the particular hormone. There is another feedback loop from the pituitary to the hypothalamus, because the pituitary peptides are guided by releasing and inhibiting factors released from the hypothalamus, corticotropin releasing hormone (CRH) for the HPA axis and gonadotropin releasing hormone (GnRH) for the HPG axis. These are inhibited when pituitary hormones are increased, but as shown in Figure 1, GnRH, in particular, is inhibited by a number of additional mechanisms. A third loop relates neurotransmitters released from the limbic system to the hypothalamic peptides. These neurotransmitters, serotonin, noradrenalin, dopamine, are discussed in other chapters in this book. These influences explain the close relationship between hormone responses and neurotransmitter-related challenge tests. The regulation of hormonal systems has frequently been represented as a feedback system as described in technical devices that adjust the actual value to the norm value set by the system.

Furthermore, the regulatory principals of most hormones are governed by diurnal rhythms, some of which are linked to wake-sleep patterns, e.g. prolactin, growth hormone, or thyroid stimulating hormone; others, like adrenocorticotropic hormone (ACTH), are not linked to wake-sleep patterns, although they follow a clear pattern of diurnal variation. Cortisol exhibits the most pronounced variation with zenith developing in the morning between 6.00 and 9.00 a.m. and the nadir developing around midnight. Other hormones are governed by rhythms of longer periods, like the monthly rhythm of the female sex hormones estrogen and progesterone.

1.2. Mediators of Hormone Responses

It must be kept in mind that the mediators of differences in hormone responses or levels are due to:

(1) the sensitivity of central nervous system receptors that are influenced by releasing hormones and underlie the same mechanisms of stimulation and inhibition as the neurotransmitter receptors;
(2) the sensitivity and responsiveness of the autonomic nervous system influenced by the peripheral glands;
(3) differences in peripheral metabolism; and
(4) gender, age and personality associated differences in the distribution of fat and muscle tissue that may be responsible for differences in hormone levels and reactions, e.g. testosterone is metabolized into estrogen in the fatty tissue.

Mediators of hormone levels, however, may be different from those of hormone response values and will therefore be dealt with separately in the following sections.

2. The Relation of Cortisol to Personality Variables

It must be kept in mind when analyzing the relation of cortisol to personality that it is not just the stress hormone that is well known in psychology. Cortisol, which is produced from the zona fasciculata of the adrenal cortex, has many different functions. For example, cortisol has a role in carbohydrate metabolism by increasing blood glucose, metabolizing muscle proteins, increasing cholesterol, decreasing the development of connective tissue, decreasing immune reactions, increasing the production of hydrochloridic acid in the stomach and sensitizing the cardiovascular system for the action of catecholamines. In particular, it acts on central nervous system processes, such as memory, perhaps by increasing the transition time at the synapses. Personality correlates investigated in combination with this multi-functional hormone must consider that some of the relations to personality may be mediated by metabolic, autonomic nervous system or cardiovascular mechanisms that contribute indirect effects on the relations between hormones and personality.

Most of the research on cortisol came from stress research that was first conducted on animals and from clinical observations in depressed patients. From stress studies on animals, Selye (1936, 1946) developed the concept of a general adaptation syndrome. This was conceived as a universal response of the organism to any kind of a strong stressor. The general adaptation syndrome comprised phases of an alarm reaction in which resources are mobilized in order to increase sympathetic arousal. In the initial phase, cardiovascular and catecholamine responses provide energy for fight or flight. This is followed by a phase of resistance in which the organism tries to cope with the stressor. Finally, there is a phase of exhaustion in which the release of cortisol is increased. From this conception, many experimental studies with animals and humans were aimed at identifying experimental conditions that determine the size and course of cortisol responses. The number of psychological and physical stressors investigated is enormous. The overall conclusion, summarized by Munck *et al.* (1984), was that cortisol increase might be viewed as the attempt of the organism to counteract an overactivity of "detrimental defence mechanisms of the organism." It soon emerged from animal research (Henry & Stephens 1977) and from research in humans based on the model of learned helplessness (Seligman 1975), that the extent to which a stress event can be predicted and controlled is essential for the size and course of the hormone response.

In clinical research, it was observed that depressed patients had higher cortisol baseline values and signs of a disturbed feedback loop of the HPA axis as revealed by pathological outcomes of challenge tests. So traits associated with the state of stress induced anxiety, as well as those associated with depression and lack of controllability as exhibited in learned helplessness, and with coping strategies and defence mechanisms as in repression/sensitization were particularly relevant for research on cortisol responses. These traits may be grouped together as the major construct of neuroticism.

2.1. Cortisol and Depression/Anxiety/Neuroticism/Sensitization

Neuroticism, depression, anxiety, and sensitization from the repression-sensitization construct share a large amount of variance. Although their relevance may be derived from different perspectives, they will be discussed together with respect to cortisol.

The relations between cortisol baseline values and depression, neuroticism, anxiety are rather weak (Windle 1994). In several studies of healthy subjects with depression or neuroticism related personality traits, no relation between cortisol and depression was observed (Gerra *et al.* 1992, 1996); Harris *et al.* 1989; Ravindran *et al.* 1996). Weak effect sizes were observed in a large male sample (Dabbs & Hopper 1990) and in a sample with a large age range in which age was not statistically controlled (Chodzko-Zaijko & O'Connor 1986). It must be emphasized, that even in clinically depressed samples, there is only a certain percentage of cases where high baseline values are exhibited. The disturbance of the HPA axis takes time to develop. High levels of cortisol may be first induced by constant feelings of being stressed and then result in desensitization of receptors and lower production of cortisol. The same may be true to a lesser degree in non-clinical samples with subclinical dysphoria or depression in which some subjects may be responsible for elevated cortisol group means. For instance, a sample of bulimic women tested by Hemmeter *et al.* (1991) scored higher on depression than controls and they exhibited higher cortisol baseline levels.

It must be remembered, however, that high cortisol levels are sometimes indicative of a non-exhausted HPA-axis. Therefore, it is not surprising that some studies also report higher values in low depressives, e.g. Ballenger *et al.* (1983), Brandstaedter *et al.* (1991).

A similar controversial situation is found when measures related to trait anxiety are correlated to basal cortisol levels or when measures of neuroticism are investigated. Sometimes consideration of the time perspective is helpful in producing positive associations. For instance, taking measurements over a longer period of time produced results showing higher baseline values for high-anxiety subjects (Rose *et al.* 1968) or subjects exhibiting neurotic traits, like low autonomy, low self-esteem, or high somatic complaints (Lindfors & Lundberg 2002). Also, when restricting measurements to the early morning, higher neuroticism scores were associated with higher cortisol values 30 minutes after awakening, but not later in the morning (Wüst *et al.* 2000). Sometimes, the variability of baseline values is more informative than the baseline values themselves. Adler *et al.* (1997) reported that the variability of cortisol across five nights was associated with neuroticism, while the baseline levels were not.

The study of differences in cortisol responses may be more promising than the study of baseline levels. Cortisol responses can be studied in two ways: (1) by examining the effect of stressful stimulation; and (2) by the dexamethasone suppression test (DST). With DST, the CRH feedback mechanism is tested by administering a steroid compound that suppresses CRH in normal subjects and that consequently suppresses the cortisol response. Due to a failure in feedback mechanisms, so-called non-suppression is observed for depressed persons. This was tested in a study by McCleery and Goodwin (2001) with respect to neuroticism. They used a modified version of the DST, the DEX-CRH test. In addition to dexamethasone, CRH is administered in order to stimulate cortisol secretion by CRH when testing the feedback loop. Surprisingly, high neurotic subjects, expected to be vulnerable to depression, exhibited less pronounced cortisol responses. It may be that the blunted cortisol response of persons scoring high on neuroticism is consistent with the lower cortisol stress responses that were reported in several studies of depressed persons (Croes *et al.* 1993; Gotthardt *et al.* 1995; Hemmeter 2000; Netter *et al.* 1991; Trestman *et al.* 1991).

This reduced cortisol responsiveness may be due to desensitization of receptors. That this may also apply to trait anxiety is demonstrated in an experiment performed by Hubert and de Jong-Meyer (1992) with a sample of 64 males (Figure 2). They were exposed to an emotionally arousing film, *The Shining*, for two hours. High-anxiety subjects, defined by the State-Trait Anxiety Inventory (Spielberger *et al.* 1970) did not respond with an

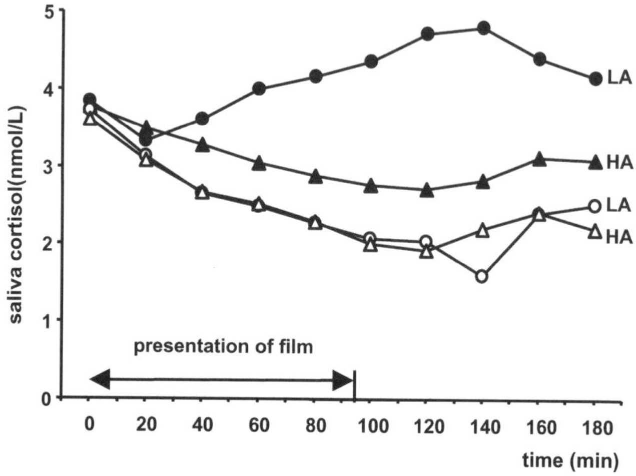

Figure 2: Cortisol responses of high (HA) and low anxiety (LA) males ($N = 64$) exposed to an emotionally arousing film (black font) and a neutral film (open font). Modified after Hubert and de Jong-Meyer (1992).

increase in cortisol to the arousing film. Low-anxious subjects exhibited the expected cortisol increase to the arousing film, but not to the neutral movie. There are, however, experimental conditions in which high-anxiety subjects exhibit larger cortisol increases. Specifically, cortisol increases were observed when children were exposed to a competitive game in which they were criticized by a confederate of the experimenter (van Goozen *et al.* 1998).

In addition to a blunted or an exaggerated response, lack of habituation and adaptation is a feature particularly prominent in high neuroticism and high-anxiety subjects. A lack of habituation has been shown by Gerra *et al.* (2001) and by Kirschbaum *et al.* (1995). They observed that the cortisol responses of those subjects having higher cortisol values at the beginning of the experiment did not habituate when they were exposed to the same stressor on consecutive days. Those subjects who did not habituate exhibited higher scores on neuroticism-related personality traits.

Similar observations hold with respect to adaptation. Low adaptability on the psychological level is a particular feature of subjects scoring high on neuroticism (Hennig *et al.* 1998; Netter *et al.* 1998a). This is reflected by their inability to adapt to sleeping, eating, and working requirements of the environment. This type of rigidity is also exhibited in their hormone responses. In a study on shift work with nurses, the neurotic and more stress responsive subjects were unable to shift their cortisol peak from morning to evening (the time of onset of work), whereas the more psychologically adapted subjects were able to adapt their hormone peaks to the time of waking and sleeping (Hennig *et al.* 1998). This shows that the adaptability of hormones is congruent with the adaptability of behavior to the requirements of the day (Netter *et al.* 1998a).

These examples show that the experimental setting, the type of stressor, the age of subjects, and the duration and time course of the stressful experience are important variables that are relevant to the amplitude, duration and time course of the cortisol response.

The construct of repression-sensitization is also associated with differences in hormone responses. Many studies reported that under stress conditions, not only are psychophysiological measures like heart rate and blood pressure higher in repressors than in sensitizers, but hormone responses are also higher. Concomitantly, repressors report a lower subjective experience of stress and anxiety than sensitizers.

In spite of the attempt to distinguish sensitization from trait anxiety and neuroticism (Krohne 1996; Weinberger *et al.* 1979), this has never been fully achieved. Therefore, it is not surprising that sensitizers, like subjects scoring high on anxiety and neuroticism, may have smaller cortisol responses to stress conditions. Repressors were observed to respond with larger cortisol increase than sensitizers (Rohrmann 1998). This would reflect a sort of healthy response to stressful events by repressors. The blunted response of sensitizers is comparable to that of high-anxiety subjects.

2.2. Cortisol and Extraversion/Achievement Motivation

Although cortisol has never been explicitly investigated with respect to differences between extraverts and introverts, there is indirect evidence from some studies suggesting that extraversion shows similar relations to cortisol as psychological stability (the opposite of neuroticism). For example, in two studies with children, Gunnar *et al.* (1997) observed that children whose cortisol values were high at school and low at home were rated as sociable, competent, and well-liked by their peers, whereas children who either had constantly high values when returning back to their families or exhibited an inverse pattern, i.e. high values at home and lower ones at school, were rated as unsociable and exhibiting negative affectivity. Here features of introversion mingle with neuroticism.

An experiment relating to achievement motivation illustrates that cortisol reactions may only be reliably associated with a personality dimension if the stressor is relevant for that particular trait. In an experiment performed by Müller and Netter (1992) on 64 healthy male students, subjects were classified on an achievement motivation questionnaire (Hermans *et al.* 1978) and then exposed to mental and physical stressors, i.e. a letter cancellation and electrical stimulation of the skin, respectively. One group of subjects was exposed to both stressors in balanced order in a controllable condition, i.e. given correct feedback for performance in the letter cancellation test and allowing subjects to control the amount of electrical stimulation that they received in the physical stress condition. The other group was exposed to an uncontrollable condition, i.e. false feedback was given and the experimenter determined the amount of electrical stimulation that was applied. The results for changes of saliva cortisol are presented in Figure 3.

It is evident that only those high on achievement motivation and who were exposed to the uncontrollable mental stressor exhibited a cortisol increase. This would confirm Henry's model (Henry & Stephens 1977) which predicts that uncontrollability leads to elevated cortisol levels as opposed to controllable conditions where testosterone increases and cortisol decreases. The results indicate that individual differences are not observed under all conditions. In the electrical pain condition, there were no differences in cortisol response between achievement motivation groups or between controllable and uncontrollable conditions.

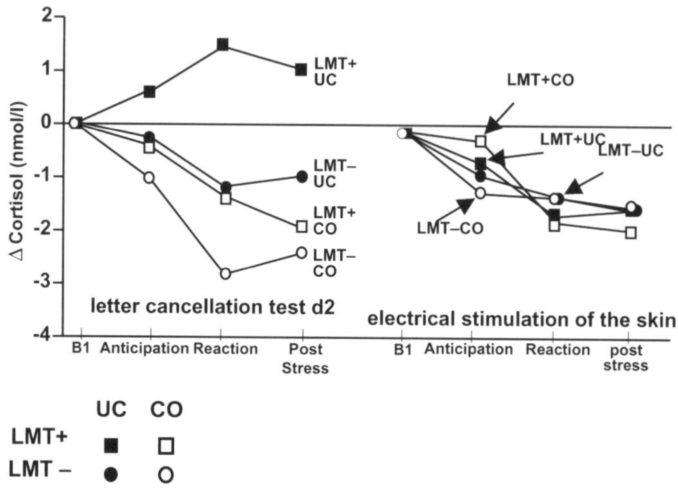

Figure 3: Cortisol responses in male subjects ($N = 64$) grouped/divided according to achievement motivation and subjected to a controllable (co) and uncontrollable (uc) mental (left panel) and physical stressor (right panel). Modified after Müller and Netter (1992). *Note:* LMT+ = high motivation; LMT− = low motivation.

2.3. Cortisol and Psychoticism-Related Traits: Aggression, Sensation Seeking, Impulsivity, Type-A Behavior

Although novelty seeking shares some common variance with extraversion, it is included in this group of psychoticism-associated traits, because the relation of novelty seeking to cortisol response resembles that of aggression, impulsivity, and psychoticism.

According to Mazur (1995), sensation seekers, representing the opposite of depressed and anxious subjects, should also show the opposite relation to cortisol. Indeed, some studies confirm the hypothesis that sensation seekers have low cortisol baseline values (Ballenger *et al.* 1983; Rosenblitt *et al.* 2001). This effect is evident for the Sensation Seeking Scales of Boredom Susceptibility, Disinhibition, and Experience Seeking, but not Thrill and Adventure Seeking, nor is this effect observed for women (Rosenblitt *et al.* 2001).

In a large study by Gerra *et al.* (1999), the relation between cortisol baseline levels and Sensation Seeking was not confirmed. There is some evidence for an increase of cortisol with age, although this effect is somewhat equivocal. In the Gerra study, the age range of participants was large, from 19 to 60 years. The inverse relation between cortisol and age might have confounded the relation between sensation seeking and cortisol, because sensation seeking decreases with age.

In general, when testing cortisol response values in relation to sensation seeking, no significant effects are observed. For example, in the study by Gerra *et al.* (1998a), the stressor of techno-music did not differentially affect the cortisol levels of high- and low-sensation seekers. Other biochemical measures, specifically betaendorphine and noradrenaline, did differentiate high and low sensation seekers.

Results relating aggression to cortisol yield are compelling. When basal values are related to the more pathological type of social deviance, most studies show negative correlations between cortisol values in urine, cerebrospinal fluid or blood, and the degree of aggressive behavior (Ballenger *et al.* 1983; Bergman & Brismar 1994; Scerbo & Kolko 1994; Virkkunen 1985).

Studies correlating questionnaire scores on aggression scales with cortisol in nonpathological groups observe positive correlations for subscales like irritability (Gerra *et al.* 1996), verbal aggression and low inhibition of aggression (Westrin *et al.* 1998). This suggests that neuroticism-related aggression may be positively related to high cortisol baseline values, paralleling the relation reported for high anxiety, whereas aggression associated with the Psychoticism dimension of the Eysenck Personality Scale (Eysenck & Eysenck 1975) is characterized by low baseline values.

When testing stress-induced cortisol responses in high and low aggressive persons and in conditions designed to induce aggression, high aggressive persons tend to respond with large increases in cortisol. This effect was observed in a study by Gerra *et al.* (1997) where cortisol reactions were measured after playing a competitive computer game (Cherek 1981). This game required the subject to gain as many points as possible while playing against a computer controlled "competitor." When the competitor begins to subtract points from the subject, the subject retaliates. The number of retaliation points is considered as a measure of provoked aggression. In this case, high aggressive persons responded with larger cortisol reactions.

As shown in Figure 4, the type of stressor may determine the time course of cortisol reactions. The data were obtained by Suarez *et al.* (1998) in a sample of young boys

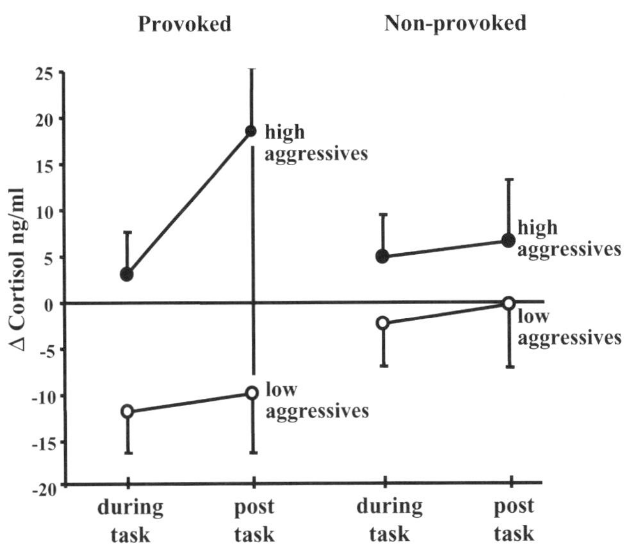

Figure 4: Baseline-corrected cortisol change values in high and low aggressives performing solvable tasks under conditions with (left) and without (right) provocation. Modified after Suarez *et al.* (1998).

who were divided into high and low aggressive groups according to the Cook and Medley Hostility Questionnaire (Cook & Medley 1954). They were then challenged by provocation, i.e. an offensive reproach expressed by the experimenter when the boys were performing a mental task. In the condition in which provocation took place, high aggressive subjects responded with an increase of cortisol only after the stressor was terminated. Evidently, the personal attack induced a delayed cortisol response. There were no differences between high and low aggressive groups in the condition without provocation. High aggressive subjects, however, did exhibit change values slightly, but not significantly above the low aggressive subjects in the condition without provocation.

Evaluation of cortisol values in children defined as type-A personality (impulsive, impatient, hostile, and with high need to control others) revealed that baseline values as well as responses may be moderated by specific additional characteristics of these subjects, notably whether they exhibit high or low academic performance. Spangler (1995) found that only those children defined as type-A, who also exhibited poor performance at school and low motivation for school work, had low cortisol values in the morning. Similarly, a stress response analysis of cortisol values was conducted on medical students defined as type-A or type-B and classified according to their performance on a medical examination. Type-A students who performed above the median on the examination had particularly high cortisol increases during the anticipation period of the examination, whereas type-B subjects performing well on the examination had particularly low levels of cortisol that did not increase during the anticipation period (Jones *et al.* 1986).

The personality and cortisol research may be summarized as follows:

(1) Personality differences in cortisol baseline and responses indicate that cortisol may sometimes serve as a protecting hormone "against hyperreactions of defence mechanisms of the organism," as Munck *et al.* (1984) claim. High cortisol levels and responses do not only indicate uncontrollability and despair, especially high in depressives, but sometimes also indicate a successful defence reaction. Low levels of cortisol may mean that subjects do not need to respond with stress reactions because the condition is not experienced as stressful. Or, low cortisol levels may mean that the organism may no longer be able to respond with a cortisol increase due to exhaustion of resources, i.e. following the exhaustion period in Selye's model of the general adaptation syndrome (Selye 1936).

(2) Depressive subjects do not share high baseline values with pathologically depressive patients, but they do sometimes exhibit the same blunted cortisol stress reactions indicating a disturbed feedback regulation of their HPA axis.

(3) Cortisol baseline and response values may differentiate antisocial from neurotic aggression, the former exhibiting low values and lower responses as opposed to the traits of irritability as a characteristic of neurotic subjects who exhibit high baseline and high response values.

(4) Sensation seekers seem to exhibit the pattern of low cortisol levels that are characteristic of antisocial aggression.

(5) Type-A subjects only exhibit larger cortisol responses if their achievement motivation and successful performance is taken into account.

3. The Relation of Testerone to Personality

Because testosterone is a hormone that is distributed differently in males and females, most investigations deal with those personality traits observed to be more pronounced in males, like aggression, dominance, sensation seeking and psychoticism. They also deal with type-A behavior and extraversion. So this complex will be dealt with in more detail. Testosterone only has a marginal role in depression, neuroticism and anxiety.

3.1. Testosterone and Aggression-Related Traits: Aggression, Dominance, Sensation Seeking, Impulsivity, Type-A Behavior

According to Mazur and Booth (1998) the causal relation between testosterone and aggression works both ways. Induction of aggression and aggressive behavior may produce increases in testosterone, and high testosterone levels may induce aggression. Research dealing with aggressiveness as a trait employed both aggression and testosterone as the independent variable.

It is widely accepted that most studies analyzing the relation of baseline levels of testosterone to aggression conclude that higher testosterone levels are associated with more aggressive behavior. A more detailed analysis, however, suggests that high testosterone baseline levels are apparent only in subgroups, i.e. very high aggressive subjects, those of low socioeconomic status, those who are younger and those with an onset of antisocial behavior at a young age. Similarly, the application of testosterone does not induce an aggressive state in all cases (for a review see Christiansen 1999).

A path analysis performed by Olweus *et al.* (1988) revealed that basal testosterone value was directly related to provoked aggression, but only indirectly via low frustration tolerance to spontaneous aggression. It has never been shown, however, that testosterone can differentiate between physical and verbal aggression.

Also when considering baseline testosterone values in relation to impulsivity, it emerges that higher values are associated with high impulsivity (O'Connor *et al.* 2002), probably because this trait has a large overlap with aggression. It is also possible, however, to separate impulsive aggression from pathological aggression by the evaluation of the responses to a serotonergic challenge test. The response to the serotonergic drug fenfluramine is typically blunted for impulsive aggressives, while only pathological aggressives often have merely high testosterone values (Dolan *et al.* 2001; Virkkunen *et al.* 1994). Similarly, type-A behavior, also characterized by high impulsivity, is usually associated with higher testosterone baseline levels (Zumoff *et al.* 1984).

Testosterone response values elicited by stress conditions are more interesting than basal levels. As shown in Figure 1, there is a reciprocal interaction between the HPA- and the HPG-axis. This interaction is responsible for the fact that severe stressors that elicit an increase in cortisol, such as operations, accidents, and physical exhaustion, lead to a decrease of testosterone or to no change at all (Christiansen 1999). When tested with stressors under laboratory conditions, changes in testosterone in high and low aggressive persons are fairly similar, although perhaps the response initiates from a different baseline level.

Because experiments on changes in testosterone in animals mainly involved observations of aggression and submission, experiments in humans were frequently disposed to use aggressive provocation to study changes in testosterone. Sometimes, subjects scoring high on scales of aggressiveness also produce higher testosterone increases upon provocation in experiments. Indeed, the animal model put forward by Henry and Stephens (1977) of testosterone increase in dominant animals and decrease in submissive animals, could be confirmed in humans who were either winners or losers in experimental games.

Usually the amount of aggressive behavior in experimental conditions is independent of the increase of testosterone of the subjects. However, some studies indicate that there is a reciprocal interaction between testosterone and aggressive behavior as put forward by Mazur and Booth (1998). This interaction was confirmed in an experiment where normal male students were exposed to frustration and provocation in a game designed according to the Master Mind model (Netter *et al.* 1998b). Two competitors in the game are required to guess the color combinations that each player must remember. In the version used in the experiment, the experimenter told the partner of the subject (who was a confederate of the experimenter placed in a different room) the color combination of the opponent. The communication took place by color displays and response buttons by which the two players could signal punishments or approval for wrong and correct guesses respectively. Subjects who showed the highest increase in testosterone also exhibited the most aggressive behavior as measured by rating their partner as aggressive in the game (see Figure 5B). Furthermore, if testosterone is used as the dependent variable, the subjects scoring high on self-ratings of overt aggression show increases of their testosterone levels when exposed to a condition of boredom for two hours in an experiment (see Figure 5A, Netter *et al.* 2001).

There is also the question of how testosterone relates to the trait of aggression in females. Testosterone is produced by females in the adrenal gland, but of course, to a much lesser degree than by males. Testosterone is also associated with personality traits for females. It

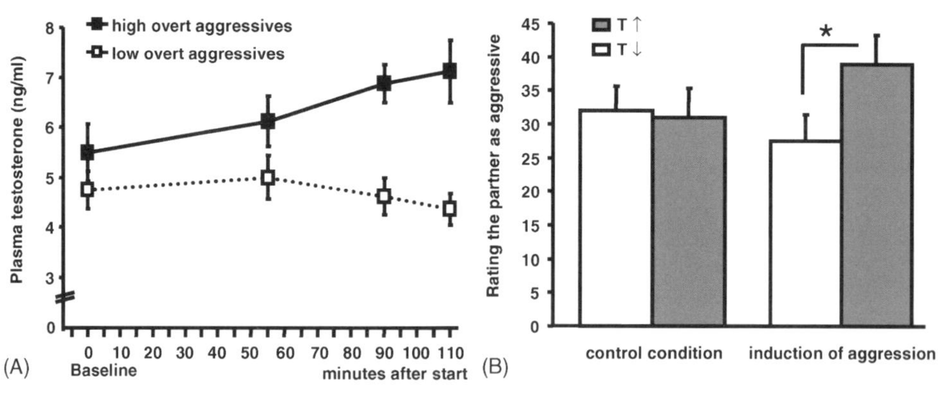

Figure 5: (A) Plasma testosterone in aggressive and non-aggressive subjects exposed to 2 hours of boredom. (B) The influence of induction of aggression in subjects with increase (↑) and decrease (↓) of plasma testosterone (T) on their ratings of their partners in a game with or without induction of aggression by losing and provocation.

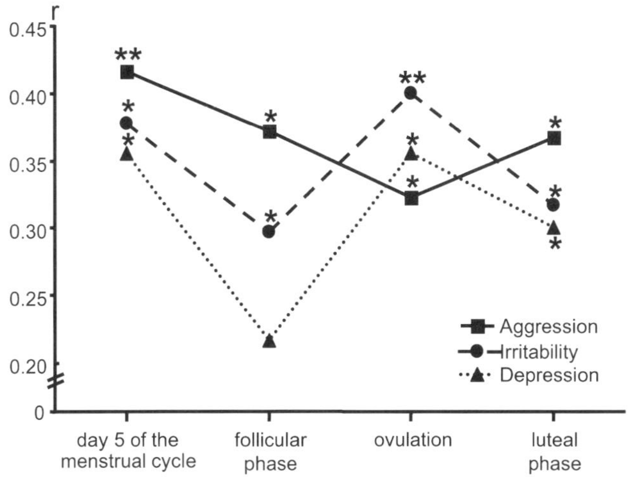

Figure 6: Correlations between plasma testosterone and mood ratings at different phases of the menstrual cycle. *Note:* * = $p < 0.05$; ** = $p < 0.01$. Modified after Netter *et al.* (1998a).

is usually assumed that females with high testosterone levels indulge in very aggressive and male-type activities, like motor bike riding, having tattoos or interest in racing. But, it has been shown, at least in students, that testosterone levels measured throughout a menstrual cycle correlate with states of depression, irritability, and aggressiveness in different phases of the menstrual cycle as indicated in Figure 6. At the time of ovulation, the depressive state outweighs aggressive feelings with respect to its correlation with the testosterone level. So it seems that testosterone has different correlates for females and males. This may only be valid in females of a higher academic level as observed in this study. In contrast, path analyses performed between different aspects of aggression and testosterone levels by Harris *et al.* (1996) yielded very similar path models for males and females. This may be due to the assessment of a more heterogeneous mixed population in their study.

3.2. *Testosterone and Dominance*

As revealed by factor analysis, dominance overlaps with aggression to a great extent and also with facets of extraversion, such as self-assertiveness, leadership, optimism, and competence. Dominance also shares the power motive and the joy of dominating others with aggressiveness. High positive correlations were frequently observed between testosterone and dominance, in particular when dominance was based on observer ratings (Schaal *et al.* 1996). The correlations are somewhat lower when dominance is assessed by self-ratings as in the early studies by Daitzman and Zuckerman (1980) and Udry and Talbert (1988).

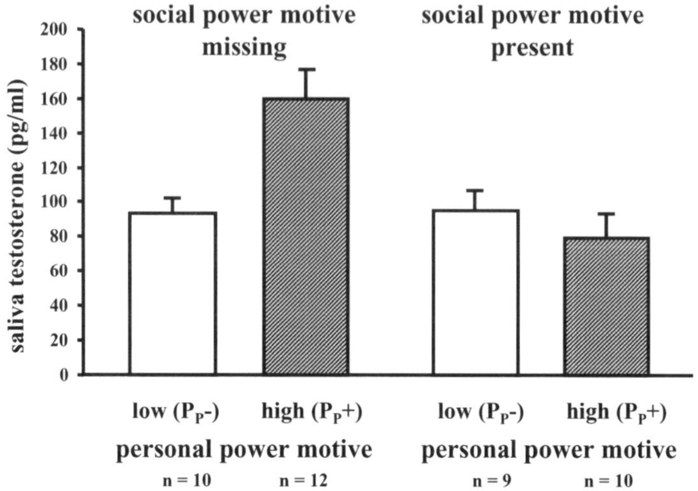

Figure 7: Baseline-corrected testosterone change values in subjects scoring high (Pp+) and low (Pp−) on personal power motive and on social power motive when listening to a story about an expected match reported from the view of a winner. Modified after Schultheiss *et al.* (1999).

It must be emphasized, however, that different aspects of dominance should be considered. Schultheiss *et al.* (1999) showed that testosterone increase was only observed in subjects who exhibited the power motive on a personal basis without a socially based power motive. This was demonstrated in an experiment in which subjects had to listen to a tape representing a winner in a competitive game and subsequently when performing a competitive game themselves (see Figure 7).

For females, testosterone baseline levels were also correlated with higher scores on scales of dominance. Of course, there are fewer studies investigating dominance in females. Evidently the stimulation of testosterone in situations of competition is not easily achieved in females (Mazur & Booth 1998).

3.3. Testosterone and Extraversion

Higher baseline values of testosterone were associated with initiative, sociability, and activity (Baucom *et al.* 1985; Udry & Talbert 1988). In an interesting experiment performed by Dabbs *et al.* (2001), subjects were asked to enter a room and to interact with another person, either by giving a talk or by engaging in a conversation. Ratings by uninformed observers identified subjects as being active, self-assertive, and goal-oriented or the opposite. Subsequently, it was determined that the active, self-assertive and goal-oriented group had the higher testosterone baseline levels. It was also observed that mothers who received testosterone-like substances, such as progestin, during pregnancy bore children who were more active, robust, happy, and more object-oriented, rather than emotionally reactive, when confronted with problems (Reinisch & Sanders 1987).

3.4. Testosterone and Sensation Seeking

Zuckerman (1983) claimed that one of the major biological features of high sensation seekers is their higher testosterone baseline level, an effect that is independent of age. Some studies found that high testosterone levels were limited to the Disinhibition scale (e.g. Daitzman *et al.* 1978). Several studies failed to observe a relation between sensation seeking and testosterone (Rosenblitt *et al.* 2001; Wang *et al.* 1997). There are few studies assessing the relation of testosterone response values to sensation seeking.

3.5. Testosterone and Depression/Anxiety/Neuroticism

With respect to the question of testosterone deficiency, depression is the most intensively investigated personality characteristic. The demonstration of testosterone deficiencies were primarily derived from the analysis of depressed males in clinical studies (e.g. Barrett-Connor *et al.* 1999). Anxiety and stress sensitivity also show a negative relation to testosterone levels (Francis 1981).

It should be noted that testosterone levels decrease and depression scores increase with age. Age can be a confounding variable in the relation of testosterone and depression. However, lower testosterone values for depressed males were observed in large samples even after controlling for the effect of age (e.g. Barrett-Connor *et al.* 1999).

It is also worthwhile to analyze the course of hormone values over time instead of using levels or response increases. For example, Adler *et al.* (1997) found that neuroticism was more highly associated with the variability of testosterone production across five nights than with the average level.

4. Catecholamines and Personality

In addition to their functional significance as central nervous system neurotransmitters, the relation of catecholamines, noradrenaline (NA), adrenaline, and dopamine, to individual differences in personality were also studied. In the early stages of stress research, the catecholamines were thought to relate to different emotions (Ax 1953; Funkenstein 1955). Although at that time it was not yet possible to measure the catecholamines from their differential effects on α- and β-adreno-receptors, it was concluded from patterns of psychophysiological responses that NA relates to activity and aggression, whereas adrenaline relates to anxiety and fear. It should also be noted that the mean anxiety scores are higher for females than males and that mean aggression scores are higher for males than females. Therefore, gender should be taken into account in the analysis of catecholamines and personality. There is a clear relation of higher catecholamine baseline and stress induced increases in catecholamines for males. Furthermore, it must be remembered that NA also increases with age. Thus, age may act as a confounding factor in its relation to aggression which decreases with age.

4.1. Catecholamines and Neuroticism/Anxiety

From stress research, it was concluded that catecholamines increase with the extent of induction of anxiety. Although higher baseline levels of both adrenaline and NA were observed in panic patients (Villacres *et al.* 1987), the relation of these catecholamines to trait anxiety in healthy subjects is marginal and inconsistent. Stress responses clearly reveal higher catecholamine increases in high-anxious subjects (Arnetz *et al.* 1985). However, as shown in Figure 8, this effect may depend on the type of stressor that is employed (Netter 1991).

Males and females scoring high and low on the STAI anxiety scale were exposed to a physical stressor, i.e. venipuncture, and to a mental stressor, i.e. word alliteration. As can be seen from Figure 8, high-anxious males responded in the most pronounced way to both catecholamines, whereas low anxious males and female subjects were not differentially affected. Of course, these two stressors may differ not only in the quality of stressor, physical or mental, but also in their intensity. In any case, these interactions between gender, anxiety, and the stressor suggest that catecholamine responses should be viewed as depending on several internal and external factors simultaneously. Moreover, it is important to note that anxious subjects are often characterized not only by high levels of catecholamines but also

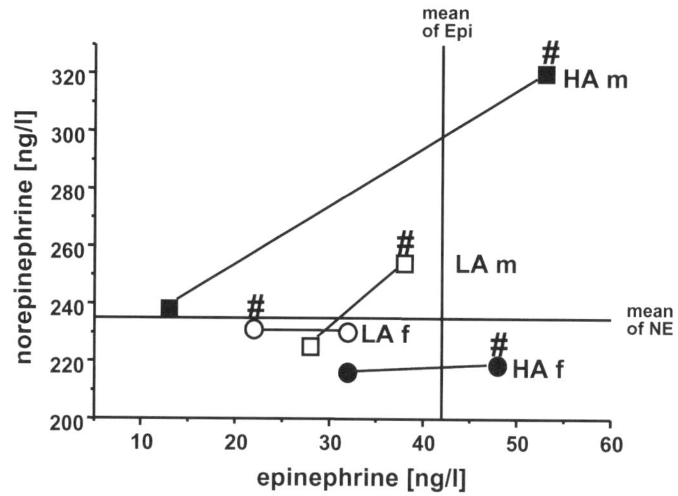

Figure 8: Relationship between norepinephrine (NE) and epinephrine (Epi) responses to venipuncture and word alliteration stress in a sample of male and female subjects divided according to trait anxiety scores. For norepinephrine, the interaction of Gender × Stressor × Anxiety is significant. *Note:* HA = high anxiety; LA = low anxiety; m = male; f = female; # = venipuncture; plain symbol = word alliteration stress. Modified after Netter (1991).

Table 1: Patterns of catecholamine baseline concentrations. Modified after Murphy and Redmond (1975).

Catecholamines	General Depression Type I	Agitated Anxious Depression
Epinephrine	–	↑
Norepinephrine	–/↓	↓
Dopamine	↓	↑

Note: ↓ = decreased, ↑ = increased, – = unchanged compared to controls.

by the slow return to baseline values (Netter & Vogel 1991; Vogel & Netter 1989). The pattern of relations between NA and A may also be very relevant for personality traits; high A and relatively lower NA is usually associated with higher trait anxiety (Netter 1991).

Based on the catecholamine hypothesis of depression, as put forward by Schildkraut (1965), the relation between depression and catecholamine levels was also investigated. As depicted in Table 1, it is worthwhile to show how differences between agitated depression and general depression are reflected in different levels of catecholamines. It is evident that general depression is characterized by low dopamine with no marked change of adrenaline and NA, whereas agitated depression shows increases in dopamine as well as in adrenaline, but lower levels of NA.

From the psychiatric literature, it is clear that small catecholamine responses are frequently observed in high depressives. This effect may also be observed in subjects scoring high on neuroticism. Those excreting high adrenaline levels during a performance challenge exhibit greater ego strength than those with lower levels (Johansson *et al.* 1973; Rauste-von-Wright *et al.* 1981). Neurotic subjects sometimes also show a delayed increase in catecholamine response under stress and a prolonged return to baseline values. It is not clear if this is because they cannot discriminate between a stressful and non-stressful condition or, rather, if this reflects a delayed response.

In summary, it appears that highly anxious subjects respond very sensitively with adrenaline and NA; depressive subjects exhibit a low baseline production and responsiveness; and neurotics seem to be characterized by inappropriate responses to stress.

4.2. Catecholamines and Extraversion/Activity

According to Eysenck's theory of cortical arousal, introverts should exhibit higher catecholamine levels in their brains, but brain and peripheral catecholamines are not highly correlated. However, in a study by Miller *et al.* (1999), baseline values of both NA and adrenaline were higher for introverts than for extraverts. Similarly, response values were also larger in introverts (Meyer-Bahlburg & Strobach 1971; Netter *et al.* 1994). Individual differences in catecholamines were more intensively investigated for activity and achievement than for introversion/extraversion. Higher values of both adrenaline and NA were observed in subjects with higher subjective feelings of activation (Netter 1983) and objective measures of performance (O'Hanlon & Beatty 1976; Rauste-von-Wright *et al.*

1981). As observed for psychologically stable subjects, extraverts also display response curves that usually show faster return to baseline values. When responding to consecutive stressors, active, extraverted, achievement-oriented subjects are characterized by values of adrenaline and NA that are above the median, whereas for less active subjects, the hypo-responsivity of both hormones is rather pronounced (Netter 1983).

4.3. Catecholamines and Aggression

Because aggression was linked to NA, there were attempts to observe the effect in normal subjects. Higher NA baseline values for high aggressive subjects were reported in some experiments (Castellanos *et al.* 1994; Fine & Sweeny 1968). It must be noted, however, that high NA values are often induced by greater muscle activity that may be more pronounced in aggressive subjects. Adrenaline is also higher in more aggressive subjects as demonstrated in large studies by Miller *et al.* (1999) and by Netter and Neuhäuser-Metternich (1991). In stress conditions, high aggressives sometimes exhibit greater increases in adrenaline, but occasionally there is also a delayed return of the NA response to baseline values, as observed in neurotic subjects (Netter & Neuhäuser-Metternich 1991). These findings seem to relate to neurotic aggression, whereas in a study by Hare (1972) psychopaths showed less responsive changes in skin conductance to adrenaline injections.

4.4. Catecholamines and Impulsivity/Type-A Behavior

Impulsivity is characterized by low adrenaline baseline values (Seeber *et al.* 1985). However, type-A personality, which shares a large part of variance with impulsivity, was associated with high adrenaline baseline values (Cameron 1994; Schneider 1994). Also, with respect to response values, type-A persons consistently show greater catecholamine increases when challenged by achievement and competition-related experimental conditions (Berman & Magnusson 1979; Rauste-von-Wright *et al.* 1981).

4.5. Catecholamines and Sensation Seeking

According to Zuckerman's theory, NA baseline values are low in sensation seekers. This view is based on the negative correlation between the NA metabolite MHPG and sensation seeking (Arqué *et al.* 1988; Ballenger *et al.* 1983), in particular, for the Experinence Seeking and Disinhibition scales of the Sensation Seeking Scale (Zuckerman *et al.* 1964). Surprisingly, Gerra *et al.* (1999) reported a positive correlation between NA baseline values in plasma and Novelty Seeking on the Temperament and Character Inventory (Cloninger *et al.* 1994). It may be that the MHPG values measured in the cerebrospinal fluid by Ballenger *et al.* reflect NA levels in the brain, whereas those measured by Gerra in plasma reflect sympathetic activity. Even if sensation seekers have higher baseline values, which again may be due to their greater motor activity, their response values in stress conditions are certainly smaller than those of low sensation seekers (Gerra *et al.* 1998a, b).

In summary, it may be concluded that the response curves of hormones after stressors, as well as the pattern of relations between levels or responses of adrenaline and NA may be more informative than just the size of the response. Dienstbier (1989) put forward a theory that summarizes individual differences in catecholamines. The theory explains the association between catecholamines and personality on the basis of animal studies and of developmental considerations. He assumes that a prenatal or early infancy exposure to strong stress conditions that elicited large increases of catecholamines renders the individual more stress resistant, but also more sensitive to stress-induced catecholamine increases. Individuals with this history have a robust resistance to stress. They have low catecholamine baseline values, a larger and faster increase and a rapid decline in response after the end of the stressor. They therefore have better adaptation to stress and challenging performance conditions. It may be added that they probably also have larger NA than adrenaline responses. These would be the psychologically stable, extravert, non-aggressive subjects with low anxiety. In contrast, psychopaths, and perhaps also sensation seekers of the high psychoticism type as defined on the Eysenck Personality Scale (Eysenck & Eysenck 1975) are characterized by low baseline levels as well as response levels of both adrenaline and NA.

Overall, these findings are consistent with the stress model put forward by Henry and Stephens (1977) and by Henry and Wang (1998). The model predicts that in situations that an individual rates as easy to manage, NA is released. With continuously reduced control, anxiety increases. Passive coping strategies are then mobilized that are accompanied by an increase in adrenaline, so that the ratio from NA to adrenaline is reduced. In the final phase, ACTH and cortisol are released when an inability to exercise control or to escape are signalled. So it may be concluded that the relation between catecholamines and the HPA activation is determined by the degree of uncertainty and uncontrollability of a condition. When this is translated into personality research, the uncontrollable stress condition in the Henry model can be referred to neurotics, depressives, and high-anxiety subjects, who experience many situations as conditions of helplessness and who do not often rely on their own resources (Biondi & Picardi 1999).

References

Adler, L., Wedekind, D., Pilz, J., Weniger, G., & Huether, G. (1997). Endocrine correlates of personality traits: A comparison between emotionally stable and emotionally labile healthy young men. *Neuropsychobiology, 35*, 205–210.

Arnetz, B. B., Edgren, B., Levi, L., & Otto, U. (1985). Behavioral and endocrine reactions in boys scoring high on Sennton neurotic scale viewing an exciting and partly violent movie and the importance of social support. *Social Science and Medicine, 20*, 731–736.

Arqué, J. M., Unzeta, M., & Torrubia, R. (1988). Neurotransmitter systems and personality measurements: A study in psychosomatic patients and healthy subjects. *Neuropsychobiology, 19*, 149–157.

Ax, A. F. (1953). The physiological differentiation between fear and anger in humans. *Psychosomatic Medicine, 15*, 433–442.

Ballenger, J. C., Post, R. M., Jimerson, D. C., Lake, C. R., Murphy, D. L., Zuckerman, M., & Cronin, C. (1983). Biochemical correlates of personality traits in normals: An exploratory study. *Personality and Individual Differences, 4*, 615–625.

Barrett-Connor, E., Von Muhlen, D. G., & Kritz-Silverstein, D. (1999). Bioavailable testosterone and depressed mood in older men: The Rancho Bernardo study. *Journal of Clinical Endocrinology and Metabolism, 84*, 573–577.

Baucom, D. H., Besch, P. K., & Callahan, S. (1985). Relation between testosterone concentration, sex role identity, and personality among females. *Journal of Personality and Social Psychology, 48*, 1218–1226.

Bergman, B., & Brismar, B. (1994). Hormone levels and personality traits in abusive and suicidal male alcoholics. *Alcoholism: Clinical and Experimental Research, 18*, 311–316.

Berman, L. R., & Magnusson, D. (1979). Overachievement and catecholamine excretion in an achievement-demanding situation. *Psychosomatic Medicine, 51*, 181–188.

Biondi, M., & Picardi, A. (1999). Psychological stress and neuroendocrine function in humans: The last two decades of research. *Psychotherapy and Psychosomatics, 68*, 114–150.

Brandstaedter, J., Baltes-Goetz, B., Kirschbaum, C., & Hellhammer, D. H. (1991). Developmental and personality correlates of adrenocortical activity as indexed by salivary cortisol: Observations in the age range of 35 to 65 years. *Journal of Psychosomatic Research, 35*, 173–185.

Cameron, O. G. (1994). *Adrenergic dysfunction and psychobiology*. Washington, DC: American Psychiatric Press.

Castellanos, F. X., Elia, J., Kruesi, M. J. P., & Gulotta, C. S. (1994). Cerebrospinal fluid monoamine metabolites in boys with attention-deficit hyperactivity disorder. *Psychiatry Research, 52*, 305–316.

Cherek, D. R. (1981). Effects of smoking different doses of nicotine on human aggressive behavior. *Psychopharmacology, 75*, 339–345.

Chodzko-Zaijko, W., & O'Connor, P. (1986). Plasma cortisol, the dexamethasone suppression test and depression in normal adult males. *Journal of Psychosomatic Research, 30*, 313–323.

Christiansen, K. (1999). Hypophysen-Gonaden-Achse: Mann [Pituitary-gonadal axis: Males]. In: C. Kirschbaum, & D. Hellhammer (Eds), *Psychoendokrinologie und Psychoimmunologie* [Psychoendocrinology and psychoimmunology] (pp. 141–222). Göttingen: Hogrefe & Huber.

Cloninger, C. R., Przybeck, T. R., Svrakic, D. M., & Wetzel, R. D. (1994). *The temperament and character inventory (TCI): A guide to its development and use*. St. Louis: Center for Psychobiology of Personality.

Cook, W. W., & Medley, D. M. (1954). Proposed hostility and pharisaic-virtue scales for the MMPI. *Journal of Applied Psychology, 238*, 414–418.

Croes, S., Merz, P., & Netter, P. (1993). Cortisol reaction in success and failure condition in endogenous depressed patients and controls. *Psychoneuroendocrinology, 18*, 23–35.

Dabbs, J. M., Bernieri, F. J., Strong, R. K., Campo, R., & Milun, R. (2001). Going on stage: Testosterone in greetings and meetings. *Journal of Research in Personality, 35*, 27–40.

Dabbs, J. M., & Hopper, C. H. (1990). Cortisol, arousal and personality in two groups of normal men. *Personality and Individual Differences, 11*, 931–935.

Daitzman, R., & Zuckerman, M. (1980). Disinhibitory sensation seeking and gonadal hormones. *Personality and Individual Differences, 1*, 103–110.

Daitzman, R. J., Zuckerman, M., Sammelwitz, P., & Ganjam, V. (1978). Sensation seeking and gonadal hormones. *Journal of Biosocial Science, 10*, 401–408.

Dienstbier, R. (1989). Arousal and physiological toughness: Implications for mental and physical health. *Psychological Review, 96*, 84–100.

Dolan, M., Anderson, I. M., & Deakin, J. F. (2001). Relationship between 5-HT function and impulsivity and aggression in male offenders with personality disorders. *British Journal of Psychiatry, 178*, 352–359.

Eysenck, S. B. G., & Eysenck, H. J. (1975). *Manual of the Eysenck personality questionnaire*. London: Hodder & Stoughton.

Fine, B. J., & Sweeny, D. R. (1968). Personality traits, situational factors, and catecholamine excretion. *Journal of Experimental Research in Personality*, *3*, 15–27.

Francis, K. T. (1981). The relationship between high and low trait psychological stress, serum testosterone, and serum cortisol. *Experientia*, *37*, 1296–1297.

Funkenstein, D. (1955). The psychology of fear and anger. *Scientific American*, *192*, 74–80.

Galen (1938). *Peri kraseon* [On temperaments] (K. Lamera Translated ancient to modern Greek). *Papyros library: The collected works of ancient Greek writers* (Vol. 24). Athens: Papyros (original work written ca. 170 AD).

Gerra, G., Avanzini, P., Zaimovic, A., Fertonani, G., Caccavari, R., Delsignore, R., Gardini, F., Talarico, E., Lecchini, R., Maestri, D., & Brambilla, F. (1996). Neurotransmitter and endocrine modulation of aggressive behavior and its components in normal humans. *Behavioral Brain Research*, *81*, 19–24.

Gerra, G., Avanzini, P., Zaimovic, A., Sartori, R., Bocchi, C., Timpano, M., Zambelli, U., Delsignore, R., Gardini, F., Talarico, E., & Brambilla, F. (1999). Neurotransmitters, neuroendocrine correlates of sensation-seeking temperament in normal humans. *Neuropsychobiology*, *39*, 207–213.

Gerra, G., Volpi, R., Delsignore, R., Caccavari, R., Gaggiotti, M. T., & Montani, G. (1992). ACTH and beta-endorphin responses to physical exercise in adolescent women tested for anxiety and frustration. *Psychiatry Research*, *41*, 179–186.

Gerra, G., Zaimovic, A., Avanzini, P., Chittolini, B., Giucastro, G., Caccavari, R., Palladino, M., Maestri, D., Monica, C., Delsignore, R., & Brambilla, F. (1997). Neurotransmitter-neuroendocrine responses to experimentally induced aggression in humans: Influence of personality variables. *Psychiatry Research*, *66*, 33–43.

Gerra, G., Zaimovic, A., Franchini, D., Palladino, M., Giucastro, G., & Reali, N. (1998a). Neuroendocrine responses of healthy volunteers to 'techno-music': Relationships with personality traits and emotional state. *International Journal of Psychophysiology*, *28*, 99–111.

Gerra, G., Zaimovic, A., Giucastro, G., Folli, F., Maestri, D., Tessoni, A., Avanzini, P., Caccavari, S., Bernasconi, S., & Brambilla, F. (1998b). Neurotransmitter-hormonal responses to psychological stress in peripubertal subjects: Relationship to aggressive behavior. *Life Sciences*, *62*, 617–625.

Gerra, G., Zaimovic, A., Raggi, M. A., Giusti, F., Delsignore, R., & Bertacca, S. (2001). Aggressive responding of male heroin addicts under methadone treatment: Psychometric and neuroendocrine correlates. *Drug and Alcohol Dependence*, *65*, 85–95.

van Goozen, S. H., Matthys, W., Cohen-Kettenis, P. T., Gispen-de Wied, C., Wiegant, V. M., & van Engeland, H. (1998). Salivary cortisol and cardiovascular activity during stress in oppositional-defiant disorder boys and normal controls. *Biological Psychiatry*, *43*, 531–539.

Gotthardt, U., Schweiger, U., Fahrenberg, J., Lauer, C. J., Holsboer, F., & Heusser, I. (1995). Cortisol, ACTH, and cardiovascular response to a cognitive challenge paradigm in aging and depression. *American Journal of Physiology*, *268*, R865–873.

Gunnar, M. R., Tout, K., de Haan, M., Pierce, S., & Stansbury, K. (1997). Temperament, social competence, and adrenocortical activity in preschoolers. *Developmental Psychobiology*, *31*, 65–85.

Hare, R. D. (1972). Psychopathy and physiological responses to adrenalin. *Journal of Abnormal Psychology*, *79*, 138–147.

Harris, B., Cook, N. J., Walker, R. F., Read, G. F., & Riad-Fahmy, D. (1989). Salivary steroids and psychometric parameters in male marathon runners. *British Journal of Sports Medicine*, *23*, 89–93.

Harris, J. A., Rushton, J. P., Hampson, E., & Jackson, D. N. (1996). Salivary testosterone and self-report aggressive and pro-social personality characteristics in men and women. *Aggressive Behavior*, *22*, 321–331.

Hemmeter, U. (2000). *Der Einfluß der Persönlichkeitsdimension auf die Cortisolreaktion nach experimentellem Streß und Fasten* [The influence of personality dimensions on the cortisol response after experimental stress and fasting]. Hamburg: Kovac.

Hemmeter, U. M., Burkhardt, H., & Netter, P. (1991). Der Einfluß depressions-assoziierter Persönlichkeitsmerkmale auf die Cortisolwerte unter experimentellem Streß und Fastenbedingung [The influence of depression associated personality traits on cortisol values obtained under conditions of experimental stress and fasting]. *Zeitschrift für Klinische Psychologie, 10*, 166–176.

Hennig, J., Kieferdorf, P., Moritz, C., Huwe, S., & Netter, P. (1998). Changes in cortisol secretion during shiftwork: Implications for tolerance to shift work? *Ergonomics, 41*, 610–621.

Henry, J. P., & Stephens, P. M. (1977). *Stress, health, and the social environment*. Berlin: Springer.

Henry, J. P., & Wang, S. (1998). Effects of early stress on adult affiliative behavior. *Psychoneuroendocrinology, 23*, 863–875.

Hermans, H., Petermann, F., & Zielinski, W. (1978). *LMT – Leistungsmotivationstest*. Amsterdam: Swets & Zeitlinger.

Hippocrates (1978). On the nature of man (J. Chadwick & W. N. Mann, Trans.). In: G. E. R. Lloyd (Ed.), *Hippocratic writings* (pp. 260–271). Harmondsworth: Pelican classics (Original work written ca. 460 BC).

Hubert, W., & de Jong-Meyer, R. (1992). Saliva cortisol responses to unpleasant film stimuli differ between high and low trait anxious subjects. *Neuropsychobiology, 25*, 115–120.

Johansson, G., Frankenhaeuser, M., & Magnusson, D. (1973). Catecholamine output in school children as related to performance and adjustment. *Scandinavian Journal of Psychology, 14*, 20–28.

Jones, K. V., Copolov, D. L., & Outch, K. H. (1986). Type A, test performance, and salivary cortisol. *Journal of Psychosomatic Research, 30*, 699–707.

Kirschbaum, C., Prüssner, J. C., Stone, A. A., Federenko, I., Gaab, J., Lintz, D., Schommer, N., & Hellhammer, D. H. (1995). Persistent high cortisol responses to repeated psychological stress in a subpopulation of healthy men. *Psychosomatic Medicine, 57*, 468–474.

Krohne, H. W. (1996). *Angst und Angstbewältigung* [Anxiety and coping with anxiety]. Stuttgart: Kohlhammer.

Lindfors, P., & Lundberg, U. (2002). Is low cortisol release an indicator of positive health? *Stress and Health, 18*, 153–160.

Mazur, A. (1995). Biosocial models of deviant behavior among male army veterans. *Biological Psychology, 41*, 271–293.

Mazur, A., & Booth, A. (1998). Testosterone and dominance in men. *Behavioral and Brain Sciences, 21*, 353–397.

McCleery, J. M., & Goodwin, G. M. (2001). High and low neuroticism predict different cortisol responses to the combined dexamethasone-CRH test. *Biological Psychiatry, 49*, 410–415.

Meyer-Bahlburg, H. F., & Strobach, H. (1971). Katecholaminausscheidung in Beziehung zu Persönlichkeits- und Leistungsvariablen [Catecholamine production in relation to personality and performance]. *Zeitschrift für Psychologie, 179*, 331–367.

Miller, G. E., Cohen, S., Rabin, B. S., Skoner, D. P., & Doyl, W. J. (1999). Personality and tonic cardiovascular, neuroendocrine, and immune parameters. *Brain, Behavior and Immunity, 13*, 109–123.

Müller, M. J., & Netter, P. (1992). Unkontrollierbarkeit und Leistungsmotivation — Einflusse auf Cortisol- und Testosteronkonzentrationsänderungen während einer mental- leistungsbezogenen und einer physisch-aversiven Belastungssituation [Uncontrollable stress and achievement motivation — Influences on changes in cortisol and testosterone concentrations in a mental performance and a physical stress condition]. *Zeitschrift für Medizinische Psychologie, 1*, 103–113.

Munck, A., Guyre, P., & Holbrook, N. (1984). Physiological functions of glucocorticoids in stress and their relations to pharmacological actions. *Endocrinological Research*, *5*, 25–44.

Murphy, D. L., & Redmond, J. R. (1975). The catecholamines: Possible role in affect, mood, and emotional behavior in man and animals. In: A. J. Friedhoff (Ed.), *Catecholamines and behavior* (Vol. 2, pp. 73–117). New York: Plenum Press.

Netter, P. (1983). Activation and anxiety as represented by patterns of catecholamine levels in hyper- and normotensives. *Neuropsychobiology*, *10*, 148–155.

Netter, P. (1991). Do biochemical response patterns tell us anything about trait anxiety? In: C. D. Spielberger, I. G. Sarason, S. Kulcsar, & G. van Heck (Eds), *Stress and anxiety* (Vol. 14, pp. 187–214). Washington: Hemisphere.

Netter, P., Croes, S., Merz, P., & Müller, M. (1991). Emotional and cortisol response to uncontrollable stress. In: C. D. Spielberger, J. G. Sarason, J. Strelau, & J. Brebner (Eds), *Stress and anxiety* (Vol. 13, pp. 193–208). Washington: Hemisphere.

Netter, P., Hennig, J., Huwe, S., & Daume, E. (1998a). Disturbed behavioral adaptability as related to reproductive hormones and emotional states during the menstrual cycle. *European Journal of Personality Psychology*, *12*, 287–300.

Netter, P., Hennig, J., Rohrmann, S., Wyhlidal, K., & Hain-Hermann, M. (1998b). Modification of experimentally induced aggression by temperament dimensions. *Personality and Individual Differences*, *25*, 873–887.

Netter, P., Hennig, J., & Toll, C. (2001). Temperament, hormones, and transmitters. In: R. Riemann, F. Spinath, & F. Ostendorf (Eds), *Personality and temperament: Genetics, evolution, and structure* (pp. 80–104). Lengerich: Pabst Science Publishers.

Netter, P., & Neuhäuser-Metternich, S. (1991). Types of aggressiveness and catecholamine response in essential hypertensives and healthy controls. *Journal of Psychosomatic Research*, *35*, 409–419.

Netter, P., Vogel, W., & Rammsayer, T. (1994). Extraversion as a modifying factor in catecholamine and behavioral responses to ethanol. *Psychopharmacology*, *115*, 206–212.

Netter, P., & Vogel, W. H. (1991). The effect of drinking habit on catecholamine and behavioral responses to stress and ethanol. *Neuropsychobiology*, *24*, 149–158.

O'Connor, D. B., Archer, J., Hair, W. M., & Wu, F. C. (2002). Exogenous testosterone, aggression, and mood in eugonadal and hypogonadal men. *Physiology and Behavior*, *75*, 557–566.

O'Hanlon, J. F., & Beatty, J. (1976). Catecholamine correlates of radar monitoring performance. *Biological Psychology*, *4*, 293–304.

Olweus, D., Mattsson, A., Schalling, D., & Loew, H. (1988). Circulating testosterone levels and aggression in adolescent males: A causal analysis. *Psychosomatic Medicine*, *50*, 261–272.

Rauste-von-Wright, M., von-Wright, J., & Frankenhaeuser, M. (1981). Relationships between sex-related psychological characteristics during adolescence and catecholamine excretion during achievement stress. *Psychophysiology*, *18*, 362–370.

Ravindran, A. V., Griffiths, J., Merali, Z., & Anisman, H. (1996). Primary dysthymia: A study of several psychosocial, endocrine and immune correlates. *Journal of Affective Disorders*, *40*, 73–84.

Reinisch, J. M., & Sanders, S. A. (1987). Behavioral influences of prenatal hormones. In: C. B. Nemeroff, & P. Loosen (Eds), *Handbook of clinical psychoneuroendocrinology* (pp. 431–459). New York: Guilford Press.

Rohrmann, S. (1998). *Manipulation der Streßreaktion von Repressern und Sensitizern: Das Angstbewältigungskonstrukt Repression/Sensitization und "Belastungsfeedback" als Moderatoren psychobiologischer Belastungsreaktionen* [Manipulation of stress reactions of repressors and sensitizers: The coping style of repression/sensitization and feedback of stress responses as moderators of psychobiological stress responses]. Hamburg: Kovac.

Rose, R. M., Poe, R. O., & Mason, J. W. (1968). Psychological state and body size as determinants of 17-OHCS excretion. *Archives of Internal Medicine*, *121*, 406–413.

Rosenblitt, J. C., Soler, H., Johnson, S. E., & Quadagno, D. M. (2001). Sensation seeking and hormones in men and women: Exploring the link. *Hormones and Behavior, 40*, 396–402.

Scerbo, A. S., & Kolko, D. J. (1994). Salivary testosterone and cortisol in disruptive children: Relationship to aggressive, hyperactive, and internalizing behaviors. *Journal of the American Academy of Child and Adolescent Psychiatry, 33*, 1174–1184.

Schaal, B., Tremblay, R. E., Soussignan, R., & Susman, E. J. (1996). Male testosterone linked to high social dominance but low physical aggression in early adolescence. *Journal of the American Academy of Child and Adolescent Psychiatry, 35*, 1322–1330.

Schildkraut, J. J. (1965). The catecholamine hypothesis of affective disorders: A review of supporting evidence. *American Journal of Psychiatry, 122*, 509–522.

Schneider, R. H. (1994). Adrenergic mechanisms in type A behavior. In: O. G. Cameron (Ed.), *Adrenergic dysfunction and psychobiology* (pp. 275–297). Washington, DC: American Psychiatric Press.

Schultheiss, O. C., Campbell, K. L., & McCleland, D. C. (1999). Implicit power motivation moderates men's testosterone responses to imagined and real dominance success. *Hormones and Behavior, 36*, 234–241.

Seeber, A., Gutewort, T., Richter, J., & Struemper, R. (1985). Judgments of stress by mental work, type A behavior patterns and catecholamines. In: F. Klix, R. Nataänen, & K. Zimmer (Eds), *Psychophysiological approaches to human information processing* (pp. 401–410). Amsterdam: North Holland.

Seligman, M. E. P. (1975). *Helplessness: On depression, development, and death.* San Francisco: Freeman.

Selye, H. (1936). A syndrome produced by nocuous agents. *Nature, 138*, 32.

Selye, H. (1946). The general adaptation syndrome and the diseases of adaptation. *The Journal of Clinical Endocrinology, 6*, 117–231.

Spangler, G. (1995). School performance, Type A behavior and adrenocortical activity in primary school children. *Anxiety, Stress, and Coping, 8*, 299–310.

Spielberger, C., Gorsuch, R., & Lushene, R. (1970). *Manual for the state-trait anxiety inventory.* Palo Alto, CA: Consulting Psychologists Press.

Suarez, E. C., Kuhn, C. M., Schanberg, S. M., Williams, R. B., Jr., & Zimmermann, E. A. (1998). Neuroendocrine, cardiovascular, and emotional response of hostile men: The role of interpersonal challenge. *Psychosomatic Medicine, 60*, 78–88.

Trestman, R. L., Coccaro, E. F., Bernstein, D., Lawrence, T., Gabriel, S. M., Horvath, T. B., & Siever, L. J. (1991). Cortisol responses to mental arithmetic in acute and remitted depression. *Biological Psychiatry, 29*, 1051–1054.

Udry, J. R., & Talbert, L. M. (1988). Sex hormone effects on personality at puberty. *Journal of Personality and Social Psychology, 54*, 291–295.

Villacres, E. C., Hollifield, M., Katon, W. J., & Wilkinson, C. W. (1987). Symathetic nervous system activity in panic disorder. *Psychiatry Research, 21*, 313–321.

Virkkunen, M. (1985). Urinary free cortisol secretion in habitually violent offenders. *Acta Psychiatrica Scandinavica, 72*, 40–44.

Virkkunen, M., Kallio, E., Rawlings, R., Tokola, R., Poland, R. E., Guidotti, A., Nemeroff, C., Bissette, G., Kalogeras, K., & Karonen, S. L. (1994). Personality profiles and state aggressiveness in Finnish alcoholic, violent offenders, fire setters, and healthy volunteers. *Archives of General Psychiatry, 51*, 28–33.

Vogel, W. H., & Netter, P. (1989). Effects of ethanol and stress on plasma catecholamines and their relation to changes in emotional state and performance. *Alcoholism: Clinical and Experimental Research, 13*, 284–290.

Wang, S., Mason, J., Charney, D., Yehuda, R., Riney, S., & Southwich, S. (1997). Relationship between hormonal profile and novelty seeking in combat related posttraumatic stress disorder. *Biological Psychiatry*, *41*, 145–151.

Weinberger, D. A., Schwartz, G. E., & Davidson, R. J. (1979). Low-anxious, high-anxious, and repressive coping styles: Psychometric patterns and behavioral and physiological responses to stress. *Journal of Abnormal Psychology*, *88*, 369–380.

Westrin, A., Engstom, G., Ekman, R., & Traskman-Bendz, L. (1998). Correlations between plasma-neuropeptides and temperament dimensions differ between suicidal patients and healthy controls. *Journal of Affective Disorders*, *49*, 45–54.

Windle, M. (1994). Temperamental inhibition and activation: Hormonal and psychosocial correlates and associated psychiatry disorders. *Personality and Individual Differences*, *17*, 61–70.

Wüst, S., Federenko, I., Hellhammer, D., & Kirschbaum, C. (2000). Genetic factors, perceived chronic stress, and the free cortisol response to awakening. *Psychoneuroendocrinology*, *25*, 707–720.

Zuckerman, M. (1983). A biological theory of sensation seeking. In: M. Zuckerman (Ed.), *Biological basis of sensation seeking, impulsivity, and anxiety* (pp. 37–76). Hillsdale, NJ: Lawrence Erlbaum.

Zuckerman, M., Kolin, E. A., Price, L., & Zoob, I. (1964). Development of a sensation seeking scale. *Journal of Consulting Psychology*, *28*, 477–482.

Zumoff, B., Rosenfeld, R. S., Friedman, M., Byers, S. O., Rosenman, R. H., & Hellman, L. (1984). Elevated daytime urinary excretion of testosterone glucuronide in men with the type A behavior pattern. *Psychosomatic Medicine*, *46*, 223–225.

Chapter 20

Personality, Serotonin, and Noradrenaline

J. Hennig

1. Serotonin

1.1. Biological Basis

1.1.1. Historical background Serotonin was first discovered by Page and co-workers (Twarog & Page 1953) as a substance involved in blood clotting. It derived its name from the term *serum* factor influencing blood vessel *tonus*. At the same time, an Italian group isolated enteroamine, a substance produced in the enterochromaffine cells of the gut that contracted smooth muscles. In 1952, it was determined that serotonin and enteroamine were identical. One year later serotonin was discovered as a transmitter in the brain (Twarog & Page 1953; Amin *et al.* 1954). This was also the period when LSD was discovered and identified as acting on the serotonergic system.

Furthermore, it was found that reserpin was able to reduce serotonin concentrations in the brain, and that monoamine oxidase (MAO) inhibitors were able to reduce the metabolism and, as a consequence, increase the bioavailability of serotonin in the brain. In addition, it was discovered that serotonin was synthesized from the amino-acid tryptophan. These discoveries shifted the interest in serotonin as related to causes and treatment of hypertension into the direction of serotonin as a brain neurotransmitter. This was supported by the important findings provided by Fuxe (1965) that the origin of serotonin production is located in the raphé nuclei of the brain stem. Another important discovery was that the serotonin precursors L-tryptophan and 5-hydroxy-tryptophan had antidepressant effects (Quabeck *et al.* 1984). The development of reuptake inhibitors promoted the interest in serotonin (Carlsson *et al.* 1969) and the growing knowledge about different types of serotonin receptors (Peroutka & Snyder 1979).

1.1.2. Biosynthesis and metabolism Serotonin is synthesized from the amino-acid tryptophan which is transformed into 5-hydroxytryptophan (5-HTP) by tryptophan hydroxylase. 5-HTP in turn is decarboxylated into 5-hydroxytryptamin (= 5-HT = serotonin) by the enzyme L-amino-decarboxylase.

On the Psychobiology of Personality
Edited by R. M. Stelmack

ISBN: 0-08-044209-9

Tryptophan hydroxylase is found in almost all tissues except in platelets which also contain serotonin. The intake of 5-HTP, the precursor of serotonin, is capable of increasing serotonin synthesis, and since the amino-acid tryptophan is essential for the synthesis of serotonin, variations of tryptophan content in food are capable of increasing or decreasing serotonin synthesis. Serotonin is metabolized by MAO, particularly by the variant MAO-A that also metabolizes noradrenaline. In contrast, MAO-B, which is usually the enzyme for the breakdown of dopamine, is found in platelets only. The major metabolite of serotonin is 5-hydroxyindoleacetic acid (5-HIAA) that is found in the cerebrospinal fluid (CSF). This is a better indicator of serotonin content in the brain than serotonin found in the periphery. In plasma, serotonin is taken up by platelets that protect it from rapid degradation. The half-life of serotonin in the granula of the platelets is several days.

An essential step in serotonin turnover in the brain is its reuptake into the presynaptic neuron which is mediated by the serotonin transporter (SERT). The structure of the SERT is similar to that of the dopamine and noradrenaline transporter, and it is identical with the SERT found in platelets. The SERT is the target protein for effects of antidepressants and, like a receptor, it is adaptive with respect to sensitivity, density, kinetics of transduction, and localization. Considering that regulation processes of the transporter (e.g. desensitization) only need milliseconds, it may be conceived that these processes of neurotransmission are more essential at the synapse than the transport of neurotransmitters themselves (Blakely & Baumann 2000).

1.1.3. Neuroanatomical aspects Although serotonergic nuclei are restricted to a few areas of the brain, there are numerous projections to almost all areas of the cortex (about 500,000 terminals are estimated to project to the cortex). This is certainly a larger number than that of dopaminergic and noradrenergic projections.

The major location of serotonergic nuclei is the brain stem where they have been divided into clusters B1–B9 (Dahlström & Fuxe 1964). More important than the localization of the nuclei are their projections to certain brain areas. Ascending projections of the nucleus raphae dorsalis and raphae medianus run to the cerebral cortex, to the basal ganglia, to the limbic system, and to the diencephalon. The density of these neurons differs between brain areas and they also differ morphologically and functionally. They are also differently susceptible to neurotoxins and respond differently to different dosages of serotonergic substances. This means that different doses are required to obtain similar effects, for instance, in neurons of the raphae medianus, and in neurons of the nucleus raphae dorsalis. Figure 1 shows the projections of the serotonergic system in the brain. As previously noted, serotonin is not only produced in the brain, but also in the periphery. For this reason, serotonin in plasma is not a valid indicator of serotonergic activity in the brain.

1.1.4. Receptors Like other neurotransmitter systems (dopamine, noradrenaline, histamine, acetylcholin), serotonin has many different subtypes of receptors that serve different functions. Figure 2 shows the receptor families and how they relate to each other. The nomenclature is based on the fact that receptors are defined by their response to selective agonists and antagonists and by their different mechanisms of signal transduction. The two major families are those coupled to G-proteins, i.e.: (1) those working by activating adeylcyclase (5-HT1 and 5-HT4); and (2) those that rely on phospholipase (5-HT2) and the

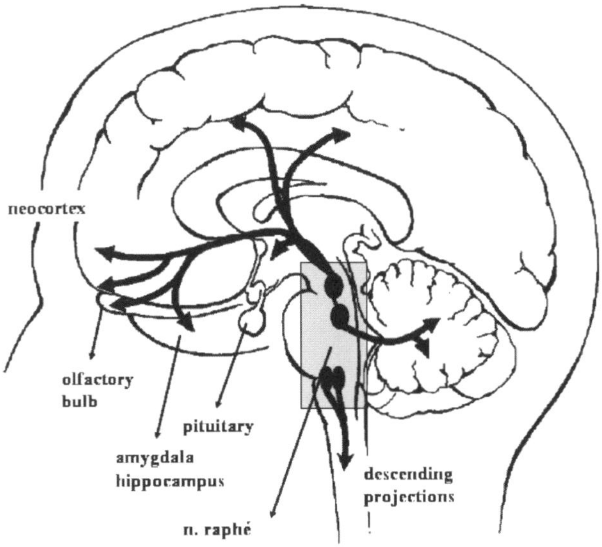

Figure 1: Projections of the serotonergic neurotransmitter system.

other big group of receptors functioning via ligand gated ion channels (5-HT3). So receptors are defined not only by their specific agonists and antagonists, but also by their affinity to ligands, by their molecular structure, and by their transduction mechanisms.

Furthermore, the serotonin receptors differ in localization. The 5-HT1a receptor, for instance, is a somatodentritic autoreceptor which reduces further output of serotonin when stimulated. 5-HT1b receptors found in rodents resemble the 5-HT1d receptors in humans. This latter receptor has been found as a heteroreceptor located on cholinergic, noradrenergic, and glutamatergic neurons where it exerts an inhibitory effect. Also, the 5-HT2 family is composed of different subtypes, of which the 5-HT2a and 2c are the most relevant. They all have partly overlapping and partly different functions. 5-HT4, 5, 6, and 7 are not yet well explored with respect to their functional relevance. Most receptors respond to specific agonists and antagonists, but there are also a number of nonspecific substances that stimulate

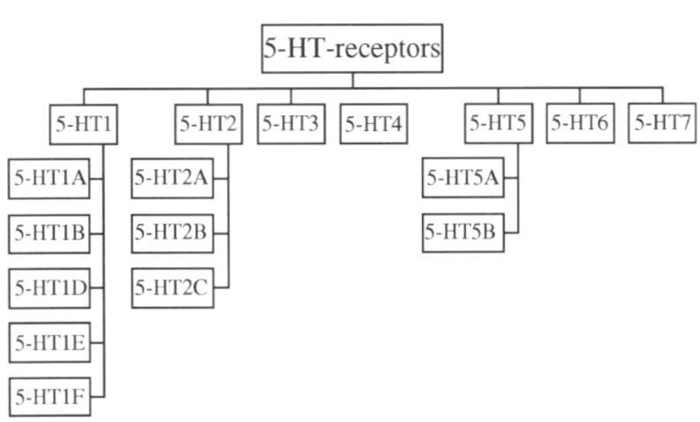

Figure 2: Serotonin-5-HT-receptors.

Table 1: Functional effects in the brain of different serotonin (5-HT) receptors upon stimulation.

Behavioral Function	**1a**	**1b**	**1d**	**2a**	**2b**	**2c**	**3**	**4**	**7**
Feeding	↑	↓		↓		↓	↑		
Nausea							↓		
Core temperature	↓								
Sleep	sws ↑			↑					
Sexual behavior	↓	erection ↑							
Anxiety	↓			↓		↓			
Depression	↓			(↓)					
Aggression			↓						
Motor activity	↓					↓			
Regulation of biological rhythms	+								+
Migraine			+			+			
Drug dependence				(↓)			↓		
Pain				↓			↓		

Notes: ↓ = Decrease upon stimulation; ↑ = Increase upon stimulation; + = Effect present; sws = Slow wave sleep; ( ) = Weak effect.

all receptors in a similar way. Serotonin is perhaps the most diversified transmitter with respect to different types of behavior and physiological functions. Table 1 summarizes some central nervous biological functions of the major 5-HT receptor subtypes.

It must be emphasized that some of these receptors, like 5-HT1a, 2a, 3, and 4 are also active in the periphery. They have a role in the contraction of smooth muscles of the arteries, permeability of the vessels, and platelet aggregation. They are widely distributed in many tissues, in particular, in the gut.

1.1.5. Clinical significance of the serotonergic system and serotonergic drugs As shown in Table 1, serotonin serves many diverse functions. Many of these functions have a significant clinical relevance. More than 20 years ago, van Praag *et al.* (1973) and Asberg *et al.* (1976) demonstrated that the serotonergic neurotransmitter system has an essential role in the regulation of affective states. It was observed that the concentration of the serotonergic metabolite 5-HIAA was particularly low in those patients who had used dramatic methods for committing suicide. Subsequent studies confirmed that this finding was specifically related to impulsive and aggressive behavior.

A second step was the development of the selective 5-HT reuptake inhibitors that were used for treatment of depression. Many of these substances, like fluoxetine, paroxetine, fluvoxamine, citalopram are still effective antidepressants that only affect the serotonergic system. Older substances, such as amitriptylin, affected both the serotonergic and the noradrenergic systems. These novel substances, in particular fluvoxamine, were also successfully applied to panic disorders. The effects of serotonergic substances on feeding behavior were also exploited to treat eating disorders, because they reduce appetite and usually induce some kind of weight loss during long-term treatment.

Specific agonists, like buspirone, ipsapirone and gepirone, partial 5-HT1a agonists, showed anti-anxiety effects. Their action is mediated by stimulation of serotonergic autoreceptors that lead to a reduction in firing rate of the raphé nuclei and a reduction in 5-HT release. Because of the reduction of sensitivity of these autoreceptors, however, these substances need a longer period before their effects become manifest and the full functionality of the system is restored (Blier & de Montigny 1990). A very relevant clinical effect of the 5-HT1a receptor seems to be that adaptive behavior is maintained in aversively experienced situations (Deakin & Crow 1986). The specific effects on body temperature, sleep, and pain were revealed by the discovery that +/− pindolol, a beta-receptor blocker, worked as a 5-HT1a antagonist. However, it could not be decided whether the hypothermic effect was pre- or postsynaptically mediated.

The role of 5-HT1b receptors for aggressive behavior was explicated in animal studies. 5-HT1b agonists, like eltoprazine, were applied and resulted in taming of aggressive animals. These effects, however, had not been found in humans. The equivalence of 5-HT1b with 1d suggests a similar role, but so far the specific anti-aggressive effects of these substances could not be transferred to the treatment of humans.

A large body of knowledge has developed on the 5-HT2 receptor which plays a salient role in anti-anxiety and anti-depressant effects of serotonergic drugs. These drugs are all 5-HT2 antagonists. This effect also plays a part in modern neuroleptics for the treatment of schizophrenia. The combination of dopamine blockade and 5-HT2 blockade results in antipsychotic effects and a reduction of dopamine-induced side effects (Parkinson-like symptoms).

All of these drugs that act on the serotonergic system (uptake inhibitors, 5-HT1a agonists, and 5-HT2 antagonists) exert their anti-anxiety and antidepressant effects by down-regulation of supersensitive receptors. A further principal to increase serotonergic action is the use of releasers. Their most prominent representative is fenfluramine which facilitates the serotonergic output into the synaptic cleft (with an additional but weak reuptake-inhibition). This has not only been used as an anorectic in overweight or bulimic persons, but also as a specific challenge test, because it induces prolactin (PRL) increases. The amount of changes in hormone concentrations indicates the state of the serotonergic system.

1.1.6. Peripheral indicators of serotonergic activity As mentioned above, serotonin is produced in cells of the gut that are capable of synthesizing serotonin just like the cells in the brain. Peripheral 5-HT levels depend to a large extent on the intake of the serotonin precursor amino acid tryptophan. There is, however, a peripheral indicator of serotonergic activity that resembles that of brain serotonin. This is serotonin in the blood platelets. Its synthesis, storage, release, and reuptake resemble those in the central nervous system. Platelets react to selective 5-HT reuptake inhibitors just like the brain, even indicating the therapeutic effect of these substances (Flament *et al.* 1987). The receptors on platelets are of the 5-HT2 type. Platelets of different density and size contain different amounts of serotonin and are suitable for the investigation of individual differences in serotonergic responses.

Although behavioral measures could serve as indicators of serotonergic function, these are governed by very complex systems. Therefore, a less complicated measure of serotonergic activity, hormone response after treatment with specific drugs, has been used as a peripheral indicator of serotonergic activity (neuroendocrine challenge test). The following principals and substances have been used for this purpose:

(1) precursors (L-tryptophan, 5-hydroxytryptophan);
(2) releaser (fenfluramine);
(3) reuptake-inhibitors (flovoxamine, fluoxetine, clomipramine, citalopram); and
(4) agonists (m-CPP, buspirone, gepirone, ipsapirone, MK-212, quipazine).

The following criteria must be met to qualify as a challenge test in this pharmacological approach (Yatham & Steiner 1993):

(1) the hormone response has to be sufficiently large, robust, and consistent;
(2) dose response relations should be observable;
(3) the hormone response has to be unambiguously identifiable as a serotonergic response;
(4) the hormone responses have to be inhibited by nonspecific agonists or antagonists; and
(5) the substance should not induce any stress reactions or side effects obscuring the hormone responses.

The hormones most frequently used in challenge tests for studying the function of the serotonergic system are: growth hormone (GH); prolactin (PRL); and cortisol (Cort). In Table 2, the most frequently used substances, their mechanisms of action, and the most reliably observed hormone responses are listed. GH responses may only be elicited by the precursors when they are given by intravenous injections. The same holds for the reuptake inhibitor clomipramin. It must be emphasized, however, that for most of the substances criteria 2, 3, and 4 are not met for GH responses.

The PRL response has been a subject of debate. Because dopamine is a potent inhibitor of PRL by direct neurons ending in the pituitary where PRL is released, it has frequently been argued that the interaction between the serotonergic and dopaminergic systems may be relevant to the response. Further, PRL responses, in particular after the precursors, only become evident after intravenous injections. In the studies with fenfluramine, which is available in two biochemically different forms (d- and dl-fenfluramine), it must be emphasized that only the d-isomere leads to a serotonergic effect, so if the dl-form is used, a double dose is necessary for a response. But some authors (e.g. Storlien & Smythe 1992) have argued that d-fenfluramine also induces noradrenaline release while others claim that fenfluramine also has an antagonistic effect on the 5-HT2a and 2c receptor.

5-HT1a agonists do not all yield reliable effects. Gepirone and buspirone seem to be better PRL releasers than ipsapirone, whereas the nonspecific agonists mCPP and MK 212 show PRL effects.

Changes in the concentrations of cortisol and ACTH after treatment with serotonergic drugs may be explained by the direct action of 5-HT on the corticotropin-releasing factor (CRF) in the hypothalamus. Overall, however, the 5-HT precursors are not reliable challenge substances for cortisol and ACTH (Yatham & Steiner 1993). Fenfluramine only seems to lead to cortisol increases if given in higher dosages, whereas the 5-HT1a partial agonists seem suitable tools to release ACTH and cortisol. These responses are probably mediated

Table 2: Most commonly used serotonergic challenge tests and respective hormone responses (after Yatham & Steiner 1993).

Principle of action	Substance	Hormone responses GH	PRL	ACTH (A) Cortisol (C)	Remarks
Precursors	L-Tryptophan				for GH no clear dose response relationships
	10 mg i.v.	Ø	↑	Ø	
	200 mg i.v.	↑	↑		
	10 p.o.	↑	↑↓	A ↑ C ↑ A ↓ C ↓	
	5-Hydroxytryptophan 150-200 g p.o.	↑	Ø	↑	
Reuptake inhibitors	Clomipramin	↑ (> 20 mg p.o.)	↑ (i.v.)	C ↑	
	Zimelidine	Ø	Ø	C Ø	
	Fluvoxamine	Ø	Ø	C Ø	
Nonspecific agonists	Quipazine	Ø (↑)	Ø	C ↑	
	mCPP	↑↓	↑	A ↑ C ↑	
	MK 212	↑↓	↑	A ↑ C ↑	
5-HT 1a partial agonists	Ipsapirone	Ø	Ø	C ↑ (≥ 10 mg)	
	Gepirone	↑	↑	A ↑ C ↑	
	Buspirone	↑	↑	A (↑) C (↑)	
Releaser + uptake inhibitor	Fenfluramine	Ø	↑	C ↑ (> 30 mg p.o.)	
5-HT 2a antagonist	Cyproheptadine	inhib. of ↑		C ↓	
5-HT 2ac antagonists	Ketanserin		Ø	C Ø	
	Methysergide			C ↓	
	Metergolin			C ↓	

Notes: ↑ = Increase, ( ) Weak or blunted response, ↓ = Decrease, i.v. Intravenous application, Ø = No change, p.o. oral application.

by axodentritic, somatic synapses with serotonergic neurons providing the neuroanatomical basis for this hormone response.

1.2. Serotonin and Personality

1.2.1. Aggression and personality Considering that the application of 5-HT1a agonists (e.g. ipsapirone, buspirone, and gepirone) exert an aggression-reducing effect in animals (elicited, for instance, by isolation or shock), it appears that low availability of serotonin elicits behavior which is normally suppressed. Within the serotonergic system the 5-HT1a and 5-HT1b receptors seem to be associated with overt aggression, whereas 5-HT2 receptors are rather related to indirect or covert aggression. This suggests that aggression is by no means a unitary construct, but is composed of different subcomponents of aggression.

In animal studies, measurements of serotonin in the mid-brain and the hypothalamus obtained in foxes were significantly higher in domesticated animals than in less tamed controls in the same environment. The negative correlation between 5-HIAA in the CSF and aggression or risky behavior is observed in rhesus monkeys in their natural habitat. These few examples suggest that aggression and serotonin are probably also associated in humans too.

Observations of this relation were first obtained in patients who had committed suicide. Although this kind of self-aggression is certainly not identical with aggression directed to others, a certain amount of common variance exists between suicidal and external aggressive behavior. In particular, patients who endured an exceptionally cruel method of suicide had very low serotonin levels in their CSF, in presynaptic binding sites (for instance, at the transporter), and also in orbito-prefrontal areas of the neocortex. The observation that these patients exhibited a reduced number and sensitivity of postsynaptic 5-HT1a and 5-HT2a receptors in the frontal cortex is consistent with the view that low production of serotonin leads to a super sensitivity of postsynaptic receptors. This was confirmed by studies finding very low post-mortem levels of 5-HIAA in the CSF in these patients. This only became evident when considering the method used for suicide. Only those who used very cruel methods for suicide displayed these very low levels of serotonin (Asberg *et al.* 1976).

This is important to note because depression, which by itself may lead to suicide, is not the essential correlate in this analysis. Rather, it is the impulsive aggressive act that becomes evident in the cruel method of suicide. And it is probably only this aspect that is associated with low serotonin production and turnover. This was confirmed in studies of murderers (Roy & Linnoila 1988, 1989; Roy *et al.* 1988). More recent studies confirmed that the type of aggression has to be taken into account when analyzing biopsychological associations between serotonin and personality. While overt external aggression is positively correlated with 5-HIIA in the CSF, aggression directed against oneself, as in the research on suicide, is negatively correlated to this metabolite (Möller *et al.* 1996).

Evidently there is a genetic disposition for this relation. This is suggested by studies on neonates who showed low CSF 5-HIIA values if they were born in families in which forms of aggressive-impulsive personality disorders were frequently observed when compared to neonates of non-affected families.

Many studies have been performed at the Karolinska Institute in Stockholm relating impulsivity to the enzyme MAO-B in platelets. This relation was reported consistently, although it is still debated whether MAO activity in platelets may be regarded as a representative of MAO in the brain (Winblad *et al.* 1979; Young *et al.* 1986). In one of their studies, af Klinteberg *et al.* (1987) demonstrated that MAO activity measured with different substrates was negatively correlated to different scales of impulsivity. However, this relation was only statistically significant in males. Moreover, this relation is not specific to impulsivity. Other traits were also correlated with MAO activity. Further, subjects with low MAO-B activity also showed high levels of neuroticism and anxiety.

The lack of specificity with respect to MAO-B and personality may be explained by the fact that MAO-B in the central nervous system (CNS) is predominantly engaged in the metabolism of dopamine and is therefore not specific for serotonin. Differences in techniques of measurement, MAO-B substrates, techniques of platelet separation, and differences in composition of samples may be further reasons for the non-specific association between MAO-B and personality dimensions (Stahl 1985). The absence of a relation in female samples has been replicated. The reason for the absence of a relation could not be attributed to neglect of the menstrual cycle phases (Calhoon-La Grange *et al.* 1993). In summary, the relation between neurotransmitters and personality has not been investigated as often with female subjects as with males. There are very few studies that explicitly consider gender differences in this field.

It is supposed that different mediators influence the relation between personality and neurotransmitters in males. From this perspective, it must be considered that neurotransmitters are not only signals elicited into the periphery, but are also themselves targets of hormonal influences. From animal studies, it is well known that steroid hormones (including testosterone) may influence the expression and distribution of 5-HT receptors in the brain in the early stages of life (Sumner & Fink 1998). In this context, a conclusion drawn by Higley *et al.* (1996) may be relevant. They claimed that the combined analysis of testosterone and 5-HIAA in the CSF is essential for discriminating between different types of aggression. Testosterone-associated aggression is related to dominance and activity, whereas the serotonergic component is related to the impulsive disinhibited type of aggression (see chapter on hormones by Netter in this book). It may be assumed that the 5-HT1a receptor has a salient role in these relations. Knock-out mice lacking the 5-HT1a receptor are not active or aggressive. Rather, they show high levels of anxiety. Animals with a high density of 5-HT1a receptors in the limbic system and in the cortex exhibit high aggressiveness (For more detailed analyses of the molecular biological bases of aggression see Nelson & Chiavegatto 2001).

In a study by Wingrove *et al.* (1999), tryptophan-rich and tryptophan-depleted drinks were used to manipulate serotonin availability and applied to subjects whose PRL serum levels were measured before and $4\frac{1}{2}$ hours after the drink. The results are accumulated in Table 3.

Table 3: Correlations between several traits and changes in prolactin levels after tryptophan-enriched and tryptophan-depleted food respectively.

Trait	**Tryptophan Enriched ($n = 14$)**	**Tryptophan Depleted ($n = 13$)**
Hostility (BDHI)	−0.46	0.32
Motor aggression (BDH)	−0.34	0.68^{**}
Total aggression score (BDHI)	-21^{**}	0.62^{*}
Depression (BDI)	−0.27	0.17
Impulsiveness (I 7)	−0.01	0.18

Notes: BDHI = Buss-Durkee Hostility Inventory; BDI = Beck Depression Inventory; I 7 = Impulsivity Scale.

$^{*}p < 0.05$.

$^{**}p < 0.01$.

The results show that the PRL response is consistently negatively correlated to different measures of aggression as indicated by a blunted PRL response to a tryptophan-enriched drink and a positive relation with the tryptophan-depleted drink. Since tryptophan depletion in the diet leads to a reduction of the PRL level, the positive correlation between PRL increase and aggression upon tryptophan depletion indicates low responsivity of the serotonergic system in aggressive subjects. This confirms the results obtained with tryptophan-enriched food or drinks that were previously reported. This result is even more important since neither depression nor impulsivity show a similar correlation pattern with the PRL responses to tryptophan manipulation. Many studies in biological psychiatry provided evidence for altered hormone responses to serotonergic challenge tests (for review see Power & Cowen 1992). In particular, the application of the 5-HT releaser d-fenfluramine consistently leads to a clear increase of PRL that is clearly reduced in subjects with aggressive impulsive personality disorders (Coccaro 1992; Siever *et al.* 1987). In these experiments, it was also evident that the healthy control group showed a negative correlation between the maximal PRL response and the questionnaire score of impulsivity. This finding justifies the extrapolation of the psychopathological findings to normal behavior.

Suicidal depressive patients are also characterized by a blunted PRL response in these kinds of serotonergic challenge tests performed by d-fenfluramine. This effect was interpreted as indicating lack of serotonin production (Coccaro *et al.* 1989; Lopez *et al.* 1988; Malone *et al.* 1993).

Depue and Collins (1999) consider the personality dimension of constraint as the opposite of impulsivity. Depue defines constraint as an affectively neutral dimension that moderates the sensitivity towards positive and negative affective or motivational stimuli. According to Depue, this dimension is predominantly governed by the serotonergic system.

Depue tried to investigate whether changes in PRL concentration upon application of d-fenfluramine are related to the personality dimensions of constraint and negative emotionality and their subfactors (Depue 1995). It can be seen from Figure 3 that the PRL response to d-fenfluramine is negatively correlated with the subscales control (i.e. lack of control) and aggression. This demonstrates that the serotonergic responsivity is not exclusively related to the dimension of constraint. Moreover, aggression is a subfactor of negative emotionality, i.e. equivalent to neuroticism (Tellegen 1985). Thus, the neurotic component of aggression is also related to a blunted PRL response, although aggression in most scales is counted as belonging to the psychoticism factor. These two forms of aggression usually differ in that neurotic aggression is highly related to feelings of guilt, whereas the more psychoticism-like aggression is not.

A closer analysis of relations between impulsivity and challenge responses indicates that it is mainly the motor, cognitive, and social impulsivity that is associated with a blunted serotonergic response. Impulsivity, which is related to risk taking as in the Sensation Seeking scales (Zuckerman *et al.* 1964) or the Novelty Seeking scales (Cloninger *et al.* 1994) is related to the dopaminergic neurotransmitter system (see chapter on dopamine by Rammsayer in this book). Since novelty seeking and impulsivity are usually highly correlated, it is possible to separate them by using a biological approach.

According to Depue, serotonin has a modulating influence on reactions to negative as well as to positive stimuli. This implies that low serotonin levels would lead to a stronger relation between dopaminergic activity and motivation, emotion, and behavior. However, at present,

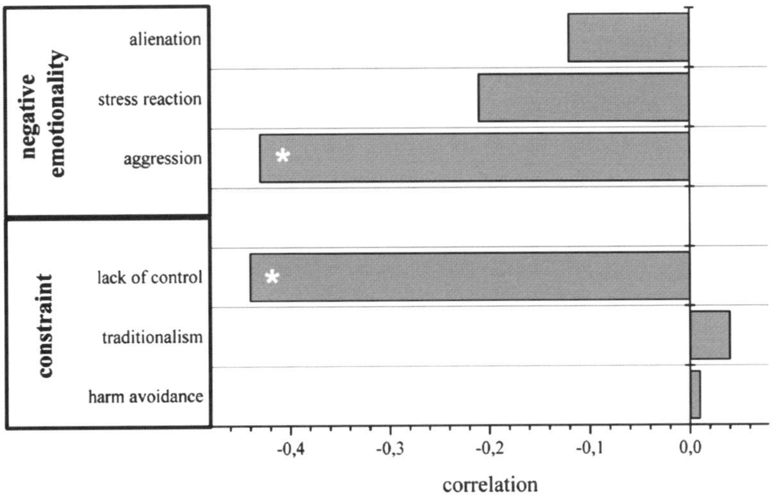

Figure 3: Correlations between personality traits and prolactin responses after treatment with fenfluramine (after Depue 1995).

there is no evidence provided by experiments that this assumption is correct. Depue and co-workers have, however, shown that a single PRL response to the d-fenfluramine challenge test can predict emotional states measured across a longer period of time. This comprises positive (joy) as well as negative (anger) emotions (Zald & Depue 2001). It is doubtful, however, that this gives clear proof for the view that serotonin exerts an affectively neutral function. Depue himself weakens this case in the following statement: "None of the amines appear to serve primarily a mediating role influencing the flow of information in neutral networks . . . Therefore simplistic amine models of behavior may be viewed as important building blocks for more complex future modeling of personality traits" (Depue 1995: 429–430).

The studies reported thus far clearly demonstrate that the serotonergic system is associated with impulsivity and its subfactors. Of course the question must be raised: Are the many different receptors subdividing the serotonergic system, as outlined above, of specific importance for these relations? Unfortunately, in the human field, the possibility of investigating this question is very restricted due to a lack of selective substances for research. The 5-HT1a agonist ipsapirone is a good example. This drug, originally designed as an anti-anxiety and anti-depressant treatment, was never effective enough to be marketed. Yet some studies were performed before it was withdrawn from the test phase. Ten mg of ipsapirone led to a reliable increase of cortisol and decrease of core body temperature, both effects could be antagonized by prior application of the 5-HT1a antagonist +/−pindolol (Lesch *et al.* 1989, 1990).

In several studies with healthy subjects, it was demonstrated that high levels of impulsivity are related to higher cortisol responses to ipsapirone. In addition to greater cortisol responses, greater decreases in body core temperature could also be established (Hennig *et al.* 1993, 1996, 1997). With respect to ipsapirone, it should be kept in mind that it preferentially stimulates 5-HT somatodendritic autoreceptors that further reduce 5-HT release. Therefore, a positive correlation between responses and impulsivity confirm the negative relations frequently observed after d-fenfluramine. According to Lesch *et al.* (1990) this substance is predominantly suitable to test presynaptic 5-HT1a receptor functions which may be hypersensitive in high-impulsive subjects resulting in low 5-HT-release.

1.2.2. Sensation Seeking Although Zuckerman regards catecholamines as the more salient basis of the trait of Sensation Seeking, the involvement of the neurotransmitter serotonin was incorporated into his model of Sensation Seeking (Zuckerman 1991). This is supported by a study performed by Schalling and Asberg (1985) that reports a negative correlation between 5-HIAA levels and the Psychoticism scale of the Eysenck Personality Questionnaire (Eysenck & Eysenck 1975). Although Psychoticism and Sensation Seeking are correlated, there is no relation between the total Sensation Seeking score and HIAA (Ballenger 1983). Two challenge studies measuring cortisol responses to ipsapirone and PRL responses to d-fenfluramine, respectively, related blunted responses to high scores on the Experience Seeking (ES) subscale of the Sensation Seeking Scale (Netter *et al.* 1996). In this respect, high-ES subjects differ from those high in impulsive aggression who also had low PRL responses to d-fenfluramine, but high cortisol responses to ipsapirone (see Section 2.1). This may indicate that in ES, as opposed to impulsive aggressives, presynaptic 5-HT1a receptors are hypersensitive.

Zuckerman provides evidence from the literature that low MAO activity in platelets, which he relates to serotonin, may be conceived as a trait marker for Sensation Seeking (Murphy *et al.* 1977). In a study by Schooler *et al.* (1978), MAO activity was negatively correlated with Sensation Seeking in males and females The finding that males showed generally lower MAO baseline levels than females is consistent with the sex differences in Sensation Seeking (males scoring higher). It was further observed that daily activities, such as engaging in new experiences, e.g. museums and concerts, were associated with low MAO activity, whereas high MAO activity was associated with sleeping, watching television, etc. It must be remembered, however, that MAO activity in platelets is only a very weak representative of MAO activity in the CNS. Furthermore, the greater incidence of substance abuse associated with sensation seekers may influence MAO activity, as suggested by an investigation in which low MAO activities were found in alcoholics (von Knorring *et al.* 1991). Considering that MAO-B is an indicator of dopamine rather than of serotonin metabolism, the relation between Sensation Seeking and serotonin is probably not as prominent as that with dopamine (see chapter by Rammsayer in this book).

1.2.3. Neuroticism/anxiety The construct of Harm Avoidance (HA), which is closely related to Neuroticism, was hypothesized to be positively associated with high serotonin release leading to postsynaptic subsensitivity caused by down-regulation (Cloninger *et al.* 1993).

Although Neuroticism is mainly associated with polymorphisms of the serotonin transporter, findings relating serotonergic challenge tests to Anxiety and HA have also been published (Katsuragi *et al.* 1999; Mazzanti *et al.* 1998; Ricketts *et al.* 1998).

Gerra *et al.* (2000) showed that the application of d-fenfluramine as a challenge substance led to a positive correlation between the elicited PRL response and HA. This would indicate that high scores on HA are associated with high availability of serotonin (it must be remembered that d-fenfluramine is a 5-HT releaser and high hormone concentration increases would indicate high release). The problem, however, is that d-fenfluramine is not very specific for the serotonergic system, so that the involvement of dopamine and noradrenaline in changes of hormone concentrations cannot be ruled out (Rowland & Carlton 1986; Storlien & Smythe 1992). Furthermore, it is surprising that highly specific serotonergic substances, like ipsapirone (Lesch *et al.* 1989) or citalopram (Hennig & Netter 2002), are not able to induce reliable PRL responses.

Gerra *et al.* (2000) also showed that d-fenfluramine could elicit cortisol responses that were significantly correlated with HA. It must be considered, however, that the type of sample and the dosage of the drug may have been the reason for these differences. It seems that higher dose levels (they used 30 mg of d-fenfluramine) are more likely to elicit cortisol responses. But cortisol responses are not usually observed when using 30 mg of the dl substance of which only the d-fraction is effective (Goodwin *et al.* 1994).

Ruegg *et al.* (1997) measured cortisol and PRL responses by perfoming a challenge test with clomipramine, a selective 5-HT uptake inhibitor. Clomipramine was applied intravenously, which has some advantages when compared to the application of tablets, i.e. avoiding first pass effects. These authors demonstrated a positive correlation between the maximal increase of cortisol (Δ-max) and HA which was close to significance ($p = 0.08$). This study, however, deserves to be reported with respect to some other interesting findings. Figure 4 shows that there are not only tentatively positive correlations between HA and Δ-max of the cortisol response to clomipramin, but that there is also a significant positive correlation with baseline values of the PRL concentration and not with the clomipramin-induced PRL production. The latter was also negatively correlated with Novelty Seeking ($r = 0.40$, $p < 0.05$). This again demonstrates that PRL changes are not necessarily indicative of the relation between serotonin and HA, but that changes in cortisol may be specific for this relation. The authors did not comment on the association between baseline

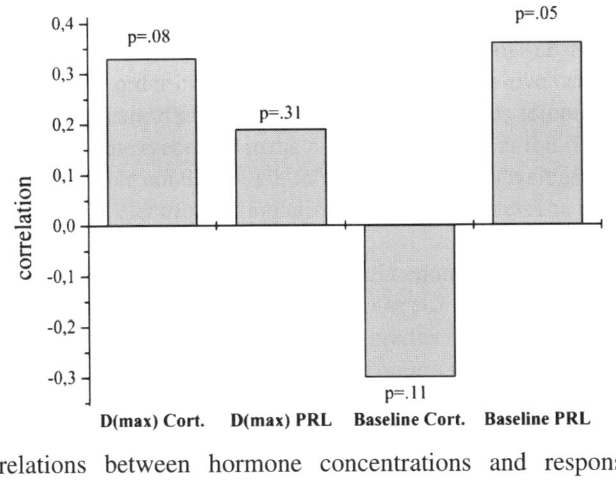

Figure 4: Correlations between hormone concentrations and responses and Harm Avoidance (after Ruegg *et al.* 1997).

PRL levels and HA. One may speculate that this relation may be mediated by mechanisms other than the serotonergic.

A combined challenge test was used to investigate whether HA is consistently related to cortisol responses to d-fenfluramine and to ipsapirone (Hennig *et al.* 2000b). In a multiple crossover design, subjects received placebo, d-fenfluramine, and ipsapirone. With d-fenfluramine, an association was observed between HA and cortisol changes, whereas this was not established for ipsapirone. The combination of the responses to the two drugs, however, demonstrated that those subjects who had a weak response to both substances (−/−) had higher HA scores, in particular on the Fatigue and Asthenia subscales, than all the other types and constellations of reactivity (−/+; +/−; +/+). This not only underlines the significance of serotonin for HA, but also of the 5-HT1a subtype which, in addition to its postsynaptic function, regulates serotonin release by somatodentritic autoreceptors.

Basically, it is reasonable to use substances of high specificity, in particular if the researcher is interested in receptor specificity. It is debatable, however, whether conclusions about the activity of the system may be drawn from this specificity. Hansenne and Ansseau (1999) used the specific 5-HT1a agonist flesinoxan. According to Cloninger's theory (Cloninger *et al.* 1993), they expected that HA would be associated with greater reactions to flesinoxan. They indeed found a positive correlation of $r = 0.46$. It is not clear, however, that the increase in PRL is due solely to the effect of flesinoxan. First, flesinoxan was applied intravenously and there is evidence that intravenous application is not comparable to oral ingestion (Hennig & Netter 2002). Second, highly selective 5-HT agonists applied orally would not elicit a PRL response (Lesch *et al.* 1989). Third, no placebo control was run in this study. It is plausible that PRL release is due to the stress of the venipuncture and that HA is more susceptible to that stress.

In the Temperament and Character Inventory (Cloninger *et al.* 1994), there are some modifications and additions to the previous Temperament and Personality Inventory (Cloninger *et al.* 1991). The original scale of Reward Dependence is divided into the scales of Reward Dependence and Persistence. In addition, character dimensions are included which, in contrast to temperament factors, are more subject to socialization processes (Cloninger *et al.* 1994). Peirson *et al.* (1999) show that not only HA, but also the character dimension Self-Directiveness is associated with receptor sensitivity of the 5-HT2a receptor on platelets. While HA is positively associated with sensitization of receptors, self-directiveness shows an inverse relation. This might suggest that for high-HA subjects there is a low serotonin availability associated, as a consequence, with postsynaptic supersensitivity. This contradicts Cloninger's original idea. The relations between serotonin and character dimensions were evaluated in the context of social behavior in a review article presented by Bond (2001). This paper proposes that serotonergic activity mediates processes that facilitate adaptation to the social environment.

Reward Dependence and HA can significantly predict therapeutic effects of nefazodone, a serotonin reuptake inhibitor and postsynaptic antagonist. HA by itself discriminates between responders and nonresponders (Nelson & Cloninger 1997). This finding suggests that differential responsivity to neurotransmitter-related substances may not only serve basic research but may also help to identify predictors of therapeutic responsiveness.

If the assumption of a continuum between psychopathology and traits in the normal range is valid, it should be possible to change high levels on the trait of Harm Avoidance into a less

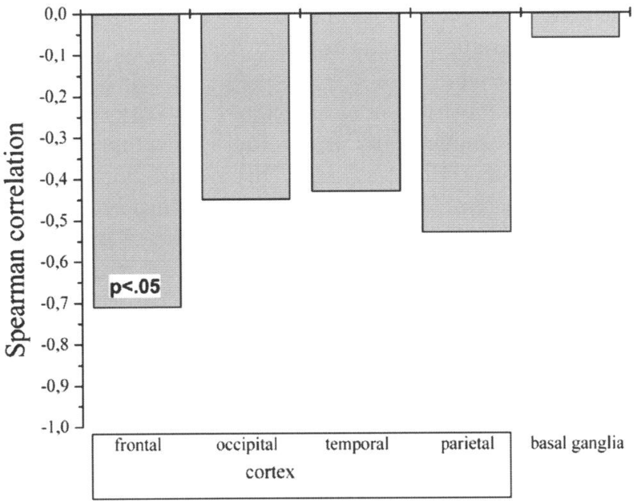

Figure 5: Correlations between harm avoidance and 5-HT-receptor binding in different brain areas as indicated by positron emission tomography (after Moresco *et al.* 2002).

pathological direction in healthy subjects after therapeutic application of serotonergic drugs. In a study by Knutson *et al.* (1998), 20 mg of paroxetin, a reuptake inhibitor, or placebo was given to healthy subjects for a lengthy period. The drug-treated group showed a reduction in hostility and negative affect and an increase in affiliation. More recent investigations address the question of which area of the brain is the serotonergic activity most closely related to Harm Avoidance? In a positron emission tomography study, Moresco *et al.* (2002) demonstrated that HA was negatively correlated with the tracer (18 F) fluorethylspiperon in the frontal cortex. This tracer specifically binds to 5-HT2 receptors. The TCI dimensions, Reward Dependence and Novelty Seeking, were not associated with serotonergic activity in this area (see Figure 5). At this time, however, it is not clear whether low binding is related to 5-HT availability. The negative relation between availability of substrate and postsynaptic receptor sensitivity, which is frequently observed in transmitter processes, may not be valid for the 5-HT2 receptor.

Furthermore, it is doubtful that HA is exclusively related to serotonin. These doubts are based not only on molecular genetic research, but also on neuroimaging studies.

By analyzing experiments from the challenge paradigms, a helpful perspective may be derived that leads to the development of new psychological constructs. The traditional psychometric factors may be replaced by indicator items that are specifically associated with responsiveness to a certain substance. This may lead to a change of concepts about factor structures. This approach was followed in a study by Hennig (2000). Indicator items derived from several subscales of the Freiburg Personality Inventory had very little in common with respect to psychometric factor structure, but they were all associated with high responsiveness of the PRL response to d-fenfluramine. This newly constructed scale correlated with different subscales of neuroticism and would best be termed maladaptability. It may be concluded that the general incapacity to adapt to biological and social requirements is the common denominator which relates this construct to serotonin. Animal studies seem to corroborate this view (Baumgarten & Grozdanovic 1995a, b).

1.2.4. Summary The papers examining the relation between serotonin and personality suggest that a cluster of traits (impulsivity, aggression, and depression) are salient correlates of the serotonergic neurotransmitter system. This is corroborated by observations in psychiatric patients (Apter *et al.* 1993; van Praag 1996). It does not seem reasonable to relate a specific personality dimension to serotonergic activity. Rather, it is more promising to relate processes of adaptation to the serotonergic system (e.g. Baumgarten & Grozdanovic 1995a; Bond 2001; Hennig 2000; Wingrove *et al.* 1999). These adaptation processes may relate to social challenges. So far, however, it cannot be decided if serotonin can be judged as affectively neutral, as Depue argues. This would imply that affective changes achieved by serotonergic treatment in psychiatry would be based on neurotransmitters other than serotonin, with serotonin only having a mediating or modulating role in therapy. Some theories propose, however, that noradrenaline is the modulator of a serotonin deficiency syndrome (e.g. Mongeau *et al.* 1997). These authors claim that the α2-heteroreceptor located on serotonergic neurons inhibits serotonin release after noradrenergic stimulation. Future research might be interested in discriminating modulators and mediators that are not only relevant to psychopathology, but also to personality psychology.

2. Noradrenaline

2.1. Biological Basis

2.1.1. Historical background Like dopamine and adrenaline, noradrenaline belongs to the catecholamines that, together with serotonin, make up the family of the monoamines. Walter Cannon was the first to discover catecholamines in the autonomic nervous system. They were called *sympathin*, because they were considered a product produced by stimulation of sympathetic nerves (Cannon & Uridil 1921). Adrenaline itself was discovered even earlier by the pharmacologist Otto Loewi. He classified it as a substance released from sympathetic ganglia into the blood upon stimulation leading to acceleration of heart rate. This gave rise to calling the sympathetic nerve *nervus accelerans*. At that time, it was supposed that noradrenaline was just an active precursor of adrenaline. Ulf von Euler (1940) discovered that noradrenaline was involved in the effects of the sympathetic nervous system. About 10 years later, the substance was identified as noradrenaline in the brain (Holtz 1950). Because central nervous concentrations were different from those in the periphery, noradrenaline was classified as a neurotransmitter (Vogt 1954).

2.1.2. Biosynthesis and metabolism It was already known in 1939 that noradrenaline and its derivative adrenaline are both synthesized from dopamine (Blaschko 1939). Synthesis takes its origin from the aromatic amino acid tyrosin which is hydroxylated to DOPA by tyrosin hydroxylase (TH). Therefore, availability of all catecholamines can be manipulated by inhibition of TH, e.g. α-methyl-paratyrosin. Dopamine is derived by the activity of L-amino-acid-decarboxilase. Dopamine β-hydroxylase converts dopamine to noradrenaline which again is metabolized to adrenaline. This section will not be concerned with adrenaline, because it is primarily produced in the adrenal medulla and has only a very limited concentration and function in the brain as a neurotransmitter.

Because neurotransmitter activity is frequently judged by its metabolites, degradation of catecholamines has to be briefly mentioned. Degradation is mainly mediated by two enzymes: catechol-O-methyltransferase (COMT) and monoamineoxidase (MAO). An increase of catecholamines in the CNS can therefore be achieved by inhibition of COMT (which has recently been used in the treatment of Parkinsonism), or by MAO inhibitors. MAO metabolizes the monoamines inside the cell. MAO exists in its form MAO B which catabolizes dopamine, and in its form MAO A which is more involved in the metabolism of noradrenaline and serotonin, but partly also of dopamine. Stimulation of catecholamines in the brain only leads to very slight changes of catecholamine levels, since reuptake and metabolism are increased by stimulation. Therefore, metabolites of catecholamines are more relevant as indicators of neurotransmitter activity.

In addition to the metabolism by enzymes, the action of noradrenaline can be limited by reuptake mechanisms. Like serotonin, noradrenaline has a transporter that mediates the reuptake of noradrenaline from the synaptic cleft. This process is energy-dependent and similar to that of serotonin, but it is not specific for noradrenaline. The transporter also acts as a reuptake mechanism for dopamine to which it has an even higher affinity. The noradrenaline transporter (NET) is the target of tricyclic antidepressants. Newly developed substances, like the reuptake-inhibitor reboxetin, are highly specific for noradrenalin.

In summary, noradrenergic activity may be mediated by the following processes:

(1) Rate of synthesis (determined mainly by tyrosin hydroxylase);
(2) Firing rate of the noradrenergic neurons (which depends on afferent stimuli);
(3) Release of noradrenaline (which is mainly governed by presynaptic autoreceptors of the type $\alpha 2$;
(4) Rate of reuptake (depending on the transporter);
(5) Intracellular degradation by MAO and extracellular metabolism by COMT; and
(6) Responsivity of postsynaptic receptors.

2.1.3. Indicators of neurotransmitter activity Metabolites in the cerebrospinal fluid that mainly serve as indicators of dopaminergic activity are 3,4-dihydroxyphenylacetic acid (DOPAC) and homovanillic acid (HVA). Noradrenaline is metabolized into 3-methoxy-4-hydroxyphenylglycol (MHPG) and, to a lesser extent, to vanillylmandelic acid (VMA) which is the major metabolite in urine. However, MHPG is also produced in peripheral nerves (Izzo *et al.* 1979) and is partly converted into VMA (Blombery *et al.* 1980). MHPG is only of limited value as an indicator of central nervous noradrenergic activity. In psychiatry, challenge tests with noradrenergic substances were most frequently performed with amphetamine, which not only stimulates the noradrenergic system, but also the dopaminergic system. The response to amphetamine is mainly an increase of GH and cortisol. In some studies, depressive patients react with blunted responses.

Clonidine is another substance used in challenge paradigms. This is an α_2 agonist which stimulates presynaptic α-receptors and by this leads to: (1) a reduced noradrenaline release and a reduced level of MHPG in urine; and (2) a strong response of GH, but no changes

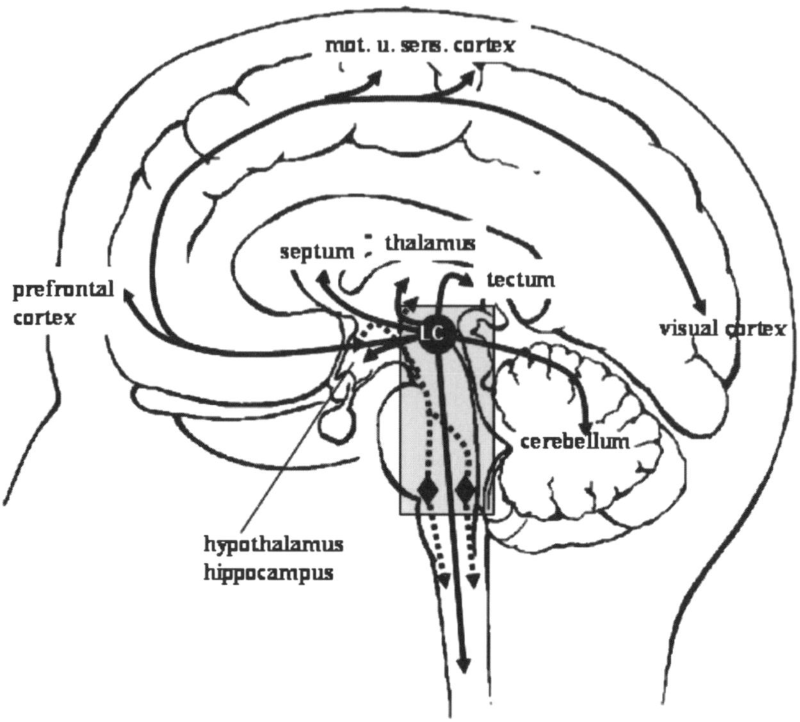

Figure 6: Projections of the noradrenergic neurotransmitter system (LC = locus coeruleus).

in cortisol and PRL (Lai *et al.* 1975). It is primarily used for therapy of hypertension and induces extreme sedation. It also has anxiolytic properties. With this challenge test, many studies report a reduced GH response in depressive patients.

2.1.4. Neuroanatomical aspects Noradrenergic pathways have been traced by histochemical methods, showing that there are two major areas with a very high density of noradrenergic neurons: (1) the locus coeruleus in the upper pons, also called area A6 by Dahlström and Fuxe (1964); and (2) areas A1 and A2 which mainly regulate autonomic and endocrine functions (see Figure 6).

The dorsal noradrenergic bundle projects to the amygdala, the bulbus olfactorius, the septum, hippocampus, neucortex, thalamus, and hypothalamus. The rostral part of the periventricular system projects to the cerebellum, spinal cord, and the medulla oblongata.

Catecholamines act on membrane bound adrenoreceptors which are also expressed on non-neuronal tissues. They all transfer signals by activating second messenger systems. Receptors may be subdivided into α- and β-receptors that form families of subclasses, like the serotonin receptors, as depicted in Figure 7. The major division into α1- and α2-receptors was conceived as indicating that α2 are mainly located presynaptically, as opposed to α1, but this division is not completely valid any more, since α2 can also be found postsynaptically. Subtypes of α1-receptors could be identified by pharmacological binding studies and by

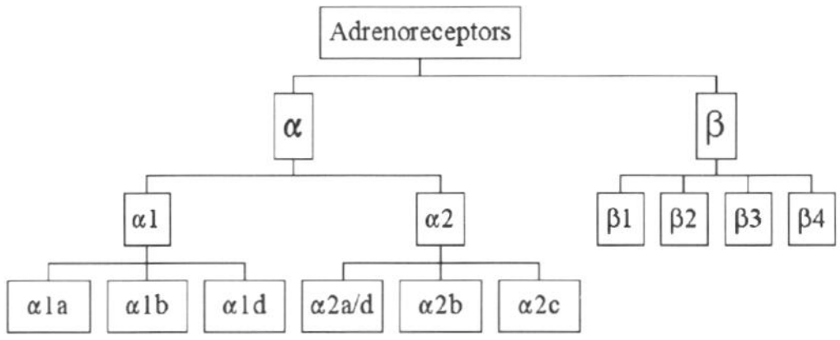

Figure 7: Schema of noradrenalin receptors.

molecular genetic studies that discovered three different genes that are responsible for three receptor subtypes. α1-receptors may not only be found in the CNS, but also in the peripheral nervous system, as in smooth muscle, heart, or liver (Wilson & Minneman 1989). The postsynaptic α1-receptors in the CNS have excitatory effects. α2-receptors exert inhibitory effects. Also, α2-receptors have different subtypes and, as outlined above, by their primary location on the presynaptic neuron, inhibit further release of noradrenaline (Farnebo *et al.* 1971). Autoreceptors may also be subdivided into the somatodentritic, which have been consistently identified, and the presynaptic autoreceptors that are still questionable.

β-receptors are subdivided according to their affinity for different adrenergic agonists (β1 and β2). β1-receptors are mainly located in the heart and fatty tissue. They have a similar affinity for adrenaline and noradrenaline. β2-receptors are located on vessels and the bronchial system. They have a far higher affinity for adrenaline than for noradrenaline. Subtypes β3 and β4 cannot be stimulated by the same antagonists as β1 and β2, but they do not have a central role in the CNS. β1-receptors are primarily located in the striatum, cortex, and in the nuclei of the thalamus, hippocampus, and globus pallidus. β2-receptors are located in the cerebellum and in the nuclei of the thalamus (Rainbow *et al.* 1984).

It is assumed that noradrenaline in the CNS increases general arousal. This is supported by the observation that the firing rate of neurons in the locus coeruleus is reduced during certain stages of sleep. Because this effect is also observed in the waking state, during grooming or feeding in animals, the noradrenergic system is considered responsible for moderating vigilance (Aston-Jones 1985). This is corroborated by findings that noradrenaline has a major role in attention, learning, and memory, in particular in long-term potentiation in areas of the hippocampus. This means that irrelevant, distracting, and interfering stimuli can be neglected during learning on the basis of noradrenergic activity (Berridge *et al.* 1993). Noradrenaline can therefore be conceived as having a "gating" effect which adds salience to certain stimuli from the environment and is therefore responsible for a better signal to noise ratio. Furthermore, noradrenaline seems to be involved in mechanisms that control level of arousal and consciousness, regulate sleep, appetite, sexual behavior, aggression, anxiety, panic disorders, depression, and, in part, control the reward system.

2.1.5. The noradrenergic synapse We have briefly to refer to the most important agonists and antagonists relevant to the salient receptors α1, α2, and β1, β2. The α1 antagonist terazosin reduces locomotor behavior in a dose-dependent manner in animals. This effect is not observed with substances influencing the β-receptors. Consequently, α1 agonists lead to an increase of activity. This is also seen after an amphetamine application that can be antagonized by α1-antagonists. These concomitantly lead to a reduced dopamine release in subcortical areas indicating the interaction between noradenaline and dopamine. Similarly, there are interactions between noradrenaline and serotonin that differ according to brain area.

The inhibition of noradrenergic activity induced by stimulation of α2-receptors, as described above, can be antagonized by yohimbin, an α2-antagonist. This also leads to exploratory behavior and increased motor activity. In low doses, this is accompanied by an increase in learning capacity and adaptability to changing tasks. A very high dose of yohimbin may produce opposite effects.

The appetite-inhibiting effects of amphetamine frequently described cannot be antagonized by clonidine. Clonidine mainly elicits a reduction in exploration of new situations which is relevant when discussing the biological basis of Sensation Seeking and Novelty Seeking.

For β-receptors a mechanism in consolidation of memory content in the hippocampus and amygdala was discussed above. β-blockers seem to reduce conditioned reactions if the substance is applied after the acquisition of learning material, so that an influence on learning can be excluded. On the other hand, stimulation of neurons in the locus coeruleus (noradrenergic activity) potentiates memory functions. β-receptors are also known to have a role in goal-directed motivational behavior, in particular in situations involving novelty.

2.1.6. Clinical significance of noradrenaline It must be remembered that in Parkinson patients not only dopamine neurons in the substantia nigra may be degenerated, but also noradrenergic neurons in the locus coeruleus. This may explain symptoms of depression, dementia, and endocrine disturbances in these patients.

More important are noradrenergic disturbances in psychiatric diseases, derived mostly from observations of changes in metabolites (e.g. MHPG). However, these studies suffer from the fact that peripheral sympathetic activity and central nervous noradrenergic activation cannot be easily separated when analyzing metabolites. On the other hand, studies using specific centrally acting noradrenergic drugs yield fairly unambiguous effects. Noradrenaline clearly seems to be associated with anxiety. In particular, panic disorders and the posttraumatic stress syndrome are characterized by an excess of noradrenaline, while the generalized anxiety syndrome and obsessional disturbances are not associated with noradrenaline.

The role of noradrenaline in depressive disorders is particularly well documented. The first observations were obtained in hypertensives who were treated with the antihypertensive substance reserpin, which depletes the presynaptic neuron from its noradrenergic supplies. This led to depression in these patients. This observation gave rise to Schildkraut's hypothesis of depression resulting from a catecholamine deficit (Schildkraut 1965). The development of tricyclic antidepressants (inhibiting reuptake) and monoamine inhibitors (preventing degradation of noradrenaline) was the outcome of this work. The successful application of tricyclic antidepressants and monoamine inhibitors for depression seems to support this idea. However, it must be emphasized that this monocausal idea is by no means valid any longer considering what has been said about the role of serotonin in depression. Rather, it seems that noradrenaline has a moderating role in serotonergic mechanisms involved in depression (Mongeau *et al.* 1997).

In summary, one might follow the concept put forward by Aston-Jones *et al.* (1986) that sympathetically induced noradrenaline release serves quick adaptation to sudden events of the environment, whereas noradrenaline associated with the locus coeruleus mediates the mental component of adaptability and guides vigilance, attention, and related cognitive processes.

2.2. Noradrenaline and Personality

2.2.1. Neuroticism/depression The catecholamine hypothesis of depression put forward by Schildkraut (1965) would suggest relating noradenaline to gloominess or low satisfaction with life. So far, this has not been done extensively in personality research. However, a study using a challenge paradigm with the very specific noradrenergic challenge substance, reboxetin, was conducted by Hennig *et al.* (2000a). They measured cortisol responses to indicate noradrenergic responsiveness in healthy subjects who were classified on depression-related personality dimensions. Subjects with high scores on the depression scale showed more pronounced increases of cortisol than low scorers. This effect was dependent on the dosage of reboxetin. The 2 mg dosage (given orally) was effective in discriminating between high and low scorers, but the 4 mg dosage was not. These effects are shown in Figure 8.

There is also evidence that the noradrenergic system is implicated in individual differences in anxiety. In an experiment performed by Abelson *et al.* (1992), the α2-agonist clonidine was administered to patients with panic disorders. Compared to a control group, patients responded with a smaller increase of GH, indicating a subsensitivity of receptors due to chronic, excessive supply of noradrenaline. Patients also had higher responses to the α2-antagonist yohimbin as determined from their MHPG levels. These two findings support the idea that the noradrenergic system shows a greater responsiveness in traits or states

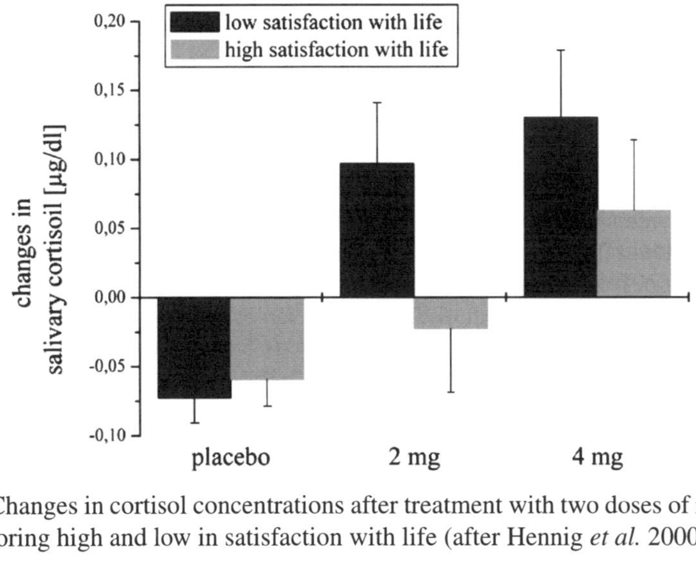

Figure 8: Changes in cortisol concentrations after treatment with two doses of reboxetin in subjects scoring high and low in satisfaction with life (after Hennig *et al.* 2000a).

associated with anxiety (Bremner *et al.* 1996; Seibyl *et al.* 1991). Also, for healthy subjects, a negative correlation between the GH response to clonidine and the Irritability scale of the Buss-Durkey Hostility Inventory was demonstrated (Coccaro *et al.* 1991). It must be remembered that irritability is not only a subscale of aggression, but also a salient subfactor of neuroticism. These findings support the view that Negative Emotionality is noradrenergically mediated (Depue 1995).

The dimension of neuroticism has rarely been investigated with central nervous noradrenergic procedures. Depue and Collins (1999) provided indirect evidence of a relation between neuroticism and noradrenergic mechanisms. A high positive correlation was reported between neuroticism and pupillary dilation during adaptation to the dark, which is noradrenergically mediated (also see Plouffe & Stelmack 1979). The association between neuroticism and noradrenergic tone was assumed because the pupillary muscle is governed by a tonic noradrenergic mechanism. Phasic changes (in pupil size) were not relevant because there was no correlation between neuroticism and changes in pupillary diameter (induced by the application of an $\alpha 1$-agonist). In their view, noradrenaline determines stress reactivity that is typically high for high scorers on neuroticism.

In animal models, negative affect is related to noradrenergic activity in the locus coeruleus (Blizzard 1988). Also, consider the hypothesis that noradrenalin modulates the signal to noise ratio of incoming stimuli. This leads to the view that low noradrenergic activity may be associated with a dispositional super demand to interpret internal noradrenaline-mediated signals as external stimuli. This would lead to worry, pessimism, and anxiety, i.e. neuroticism. Moreover, this relation is modulated by serotonergic activity. This concept seems attractive, although an empirical basis is still missing.

2.2.2. Extraversion/Reward dependence Cloninger's assumption that Reward Dependence is associated with low noradrenaline levels seems to be confirmed by experiments in which high Reward Dependence was found to be associated with low levels of MHPG in urine (Garvey *et al.* 1996). Results also point to a certain specificity because the other questionnaire dimensions, Harm Avoidance and Novelty Seeking, do not correlate with MHPG levels.

In a larger subsequent study, Curtin *et al.* (1997) reported opposite findings, i.e. a positive correlation between Reward Dependence and MHPG levels. There is a notable difference between the two studies. Garvey *et al.* collected the urine during a 24-hour period, whereas Curtin *et al.* only collected nocturnal urine (8 p.m. to 7 a.m.). The nocturnal period is not influenced by exogenous stimuli, nor by motor activity that has a strong influence on noradrenaline release. The study by Curtin also shows that the different metabolites measured in this study, i.e. VMA, HVA, 5-HIAA, and dopamine and noradrenaline levels, were all positively correlated, indicating a lack of specificity of these monoamines. It is surprising that very different amines, like the serotonin metabolite 5-HIAA, and DA or NE are positively related. From these findings it must be concluded that peripheral metabolites are not only fairly unreliable indicators of CNS activity, but are not independent from one another.

Gerra *et al.* (2000) used clonidine in a challenge study testing noradrenergic responsiveness for individuals who varied in Reward Dependence. The $\alpha 2$-agonist clonidine leads to robust increases of GH. The authors considered that high increases in GH would indicate postsynaptic supersensitivity (upregulation) resulting from low availability of noradrenaline. The amount of GH increase, measured as area under the curve, was significantly correlated with Reward Dependence ($r = 0.55, p < 0.01$).

Thus, several studies report associations between Reward Dependence and noradrenaline, but the direction of the association is not consistent. While Gerra *et al.* used an area measure of GH as the dependent variable, another study, using a quite similar approach, classified subjects according to their maximal amplitude of hormone concentrations (Tancer *et al.* 1994). They used the questionnaire scores as the dependent variable. Although the approach is different, the two measures are usually correlated and cannot explain the opposite results. A further problem in this study is that Reward Dependence was also correlated with a bromocriptine-induced decrease of PRL indicating dopaminergic activity, so that it may be assumed that Reward Dependence is not only related to noradrenaline, but also to other neurotransmitters.

Genetic studies performed by Ebstein *et al.* (1997) revealed that Reward Dependence is associated with a polymorphism of the 5-HT2c receptor gene. The subfactor Persistence, which was later defined as a separate dimension by Cloninger *et al.* (1994), was characterized by a combination of the 5-HT2c receptor gene polymorphism and the polymorphism of the dopamine receptor D4. This combination was able to explain 30% of the variance of Persistence (Ebstein *et al.* 1997).

2.2.3. Sensation Seeking Results relating the noradrenergic system to Psychoticism and/or Sensation Seeking are somewhat contradictory. Studies relating the metabolite MHPG to these personality dimensions report both positive (Zuckerman 1993) and negative (Ballenger 1983) results. The inconsistency may depend on whether MHPG is measured in plasma or in CSF. Considering that CSF-MHPG is probably more relevant for central nervous noradrenergic activity, one has to accept that high Sensation Seeking is associated with low levels of the metabolite (Zuckerman 1990). Gerra *et al.* (1999), however, come to a different conclusion. They found that noradrenaline concentrations were positively correlated with Novelty Seeking. But it must be remembered that the peripheral noradrenaline level is most probably an unreliable indicator of the locus coerulus-associated noradrenaline activity in the brain. They speculate that hypersecretion of peripheral noradrenaline is not the cause but the consequence of the chronic stress reaction induced by problems encountered due to Sensation Seeking.

2.2.4. Aggression Peripherally injected noradrenaline induces an increase in aggression in rats. The same effect is obtained when administering α1-agonists, whereas clonidine, the α2-agonist, leads to a reduction of aggressive behavior. β-receptor blockers also reduce aggression in animals. These findings are corroborated by a positive correlation between aggression and noradrenaline and/or MHPG levels in the CSF. In this effect, it is understood that the neurons of the locus coeruleus exert a tonic influence on the behavioral inhibition systems located in the hippocampus, the septum, and the frontal cortex. When noradrenergic activity is stimulated, impulsive and aggressive acts are the consequence.

In their comprehensive review, Haller *et al.* (1998) assume that all noradrenergic systems (not only those associated with the locus coerulus, but also with the sympathicus and the adrenal medulla) synergistically serve the preparation of aggressive behavior (at least in animals). This view is mainly derived from pharmacological experiments with

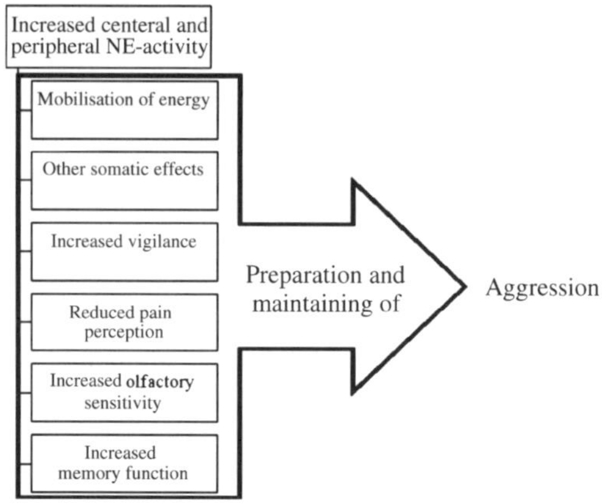

Figure 9: A model concerning the involvement of noradrenaline in preparing and maintaining aggressive behavior (after Haller *et al.* 1998).

substances acting on α2- and β2-receptors. Figure 9 depicts the noradrenergically mediated psychological and physical processes that serve the preparation of aggressive acts.

Experiments relating dimensions of aggression to noradrenaline or indirect indicators of neurotransmitter availability in humans are rare. In a report by Gerra *et al.* (1994), siblings of heroin addicts who exhibited aggressive behavior presented reduced responses of GH to clonidine. Those siblings who did not exhibit aggressive behavior presented greater hormone responses.

2.2.5. Summary Taken together, results relating personality to noradrenaline remain somewhat unsatisfying. The most consistent findings relate to the field of aggression. The notion that norepinephrine mainly mediates the "signal-to-noise-ratio" may be a more promising perspective for future research. Individual differences in the ability to discriminate "signal" and "noise" may provide different behavioural patterns that reflect individual styles of adaptation (stress load, depression, irritability, etc.). This view is consistent with the hypothesis that norepinephrine mediates negative emotionality (Depue 1995). However, allocating this function to noradrenaline strongly reminds us of the central function of serotonin, which was characterized as a neurotransmitter that facilitates adaptation. In fact, there is little doubt that both systems closely work together. This is nicely demonstrated by the therapeutic effectiveness of tricyclic antidepressants or by the well-known interaction between noradrenergic and serotonergic neurons via the α2-heteroreceptor on serotonergic neurons in the brain stem (see Mongeau *et al.* 1997).

Given these interactions, it is definitively more promising to consider interactions of neurotransmitter activity to personality instead of investigating relations between traits and isolated neurotransmitter systems. This idea is not new. However, data are rare and should be obtained in the future to get more insight on the interdependencies of neurotransmitter systems. Individual patterns of configurations of neurotransmitter activity may explain variance in personality more unambiguously than most of the recent approaches.

References

Abelson, J. L., Glitz, D., Cameron, O. G., Lee, M. A., Bronzo, M., & Curtis, G. C. (1992). Endocrine, cardiovascular and behavioural responses to clonidine in patients with panic disorder. *Biological Psychiatry, 32*, 18–25.

Amin, A. H., Crawford, B. B., & Gaddum, J. H. (1954). Distribution of 5-hydroxytryptamine and substance P in central nervous system. *Journal of Physiology, London, 126*, 596–618.

Apter, A., Plutchik, R., & van Praag, H. M. (1993). Anxiety, impulsivity and depressed mood in relation to suicidal and violent behavior. *Acta Psychiatrica Scandinavica, 87*, 1–5.

Asberg, M., Traskman, L., & Thoren, P. (1976). 5-HIAA in the cerebrospinal fluid: A biochemical suicide predictor? *Archives of General Psychiatry, 33*, 1193–1197.

Aston-Jones, G. (1985). Behavioral functions of locus coeruleus derived from cellular attributes. *Physiological Psychology, 13*, 118–126.

Aston-Jones, G., Ennis, M., Pieribone, V. A., Nickell, W. T., & Shipley, M. T. (1986). The brain nucleus locus coeruleus: Restricted afferent control of a broad efferent network. *Science, 234*, 734–737.

Ballenger, J. C. (1983). Biochemical correlates of personality traits in normals: An exploratory study. *Personality and Individual Differences, 4*, 615–625.

Baumgarten, H. G., & Grozdanovic, Z. (1995a). Die Rolle des Serotonins in der Verhaltensmodulation [The role of serotonin in the modulation of behavioral problems]. *Fortschritte der Neurologie-Psychiatrie [Advances of Neuropsychiatry], 63*, 3–8.

Baumgarten, H. G., & Grozdanovic, Z. (1995b). Psychopharmacology of central serotonergic systems. *Pharmacopsychiatry, 28*, 73–79.

Berridge, C. W., Arnsten, A. F. T., & Foote, S. L. (1993). Noradrenergic modulation of cognitive function: Clinical implications of anatomical, electrophysiological and behavioral studies in animal models. *Psychological Medicine, 23*, 557–564.

Blakely, R. D., & Baumann, A. L. (2000). Biogenic amine transporters: Regulation in flux. *Current Opinion in Neurobiology, 10*, 328–336.

Blaschko, H. (1939). The specific action of L-dopa carboxylase. *Journal of Physiology, 96*, 50–51.

Blier, P., & de Montigny, C. (1990). Differential effect of gepirone on presynaptic and postsynaptic serotonin receptors; single cell recording studies. *Journal of Clinical Psychopharmacology, 10*, 13–20.

Blizzard, D. (1988). The locus coeruleus: A possible neural focus for genetic differences in emotionality. *Experientia, 44*, 491–495.

Blombery, P. A., Kopin, I. J., Gordon, E. K., Markey, S. P., & Ebert, M. H. (1980). Conversion of MHPG to vanillylmandelic acid: Implications for the importance of urinary MHPG. *Archives of General Psychiatry, 37*, 1095–1098.

Bond, A. J. (2001). Neurotransmitters, temperament and social functioning. *European Neuropsychopharmacoly, 11*, 261–274.

Bremner, J. D., Krystal, J. H., Southwick, S. M., & Charney, D. S. (1996). Noradrenergic mechanisms in stress and anxiety: II. Clinical studies. *Synapse, 23*, 39–51.

Calhoon-La Grange, L. L., Don Jones, T., Reyes, E., & Ott, S. (1993). Monoamine oxidase levels in females: Relationships to sensation seeking, alcohol misuse, physical fitness, and menstrual cycle. *Personality and Individual Differences, 14*, 439–446.

Cannon, W. B., & Uridil, J. E. (1921). Studies on the conditions of activity in endocrine glands. VIII. Some effects on the denervated heart of stimulating the nerves of the liver. *American Journal of Physiology, 58*, 353–354.

Carlsson, A., Corrodi, H., Fuxe, K., & Hokfelt, T. (1969). Effect of antidepressant drugs on the depletion of intraneural brain 5-hydroxytryptamine stores caused by 4-methyl-a-ethyl-meta-tyramine. *European Journal of Pharmacology, 5*, 357–366.

Cloninger, C. R., Przybeck, T. R., & Svrakic, D. M. (1991). The Tridimensional Personality questionnaire: U.S. normative data. *Psychological Reports*, *69*, 1047–1057.

Cloninger, C. R., Przybeck, T. R., Svrakic, D. M., & Wetzel, R. D. (1994). *The temperament and character inventory (TCI): A guide to its development and use*. St. Louis, MO: Center for Psychobiology and Personality.

Cloninger, C. R., Svrakic, D. M., & Przybeck, T. R. (1993). A psychobiological model of temperament and character. *Archives of General Psychiatry*, *50*, 975–990.

Coccaro, E. F. (1992). Impulsive aggression and central serotonergic system function in humans: An example of a dimensional brain-behavior relationship. *International Journal of Clinical Psychopharmacology*, *7*, 3–12.

Coccaro, E. F., Lawrence, T., Trestman, R., Gabriel, S., Klar, H. M., & Siever, L. J. (1991). Growth hormone responses to intravenous clonidine challenge correlate with behavioral irritability in psychiatric patients and healthy volunteers. *Psychiatry Research*, *39*, 129–139.

Coccaro, E. F., Siever, L. J., Klar, H. M., Maurer, G., Cochrane, K., Cooper, T. B., Mohs, R. C., & Davis, K. L. (1989). Serotonergic studies in patients with affective and personality disorders. Correlates with suicidal and impulsive aggressive behavior. *Archives of General Psychiatry*, *46*, 587–599.

Curtin, F., Walker, J.-P., Peyrin, L., Sulier, V., Badan, M., & Schulz, P. (1997). Reward Dependence is positively related to urinary monoamines in normal men. *Biological Psychiatry*, *42*, 275–281.

Dahlström, A., & Fuxe, K. (1964). Evidence for the existence of monoamine neurons in the central nervous system. I. Demonstration of monoamines in cell bodies of brain stem neurons. *Acta Physiologica Scandinavia, Supplement*, *232*, 1–55.

Deakin, J. F. W., & Crow, T. J. (1986). Monoamines, reward and punishment – the anatomy and physiology of the affective disorders. In: J. F. W. Deakin (Ed.), *The biology of depression* (pp. 1–25). London: Gaskell Press.

Depue, R. A. (1995). Neurobiological factors in personality and depression. *European Journal of Personality*, *9*, 439.

Depue, R. A., & Collins, P. F. (1999). Neurobiology of the structure of personality: Dopamine, facilitation of incentive motivation, and extraversion. *Behavioral Brain Sciences*, *22*, 491–517.

Ebstein, R. P., Segman, R., Benjamin, J., Osher, Y., Nemanov, L., & Belmaker, R. H. (1997). 5-HT2C (HTR2C) serotonin receptor gene polymorphism associated with the human personality trait of reward dependence: Interaction with dopamine D4 receptor (D4DR) and dopamine D3 receptor (D3DR) polymorphisms. *American Journal of Medical Genetics*, *74*, 65–72.

Eysenck, H. J., & Eysenck, S. B. G. (1975). *Manual of the Eysenck Personality Questionnaire*. London: Hodder & Stoughton.

Farnebo, L. O., Hamberger, B., & Jonsson, G. (1971). Release of (3 H)noradrenaline and (3 H)dopamine from field stimulated cerebral cortex slices. Effect of tyrosine hydroxylase and dopamine-hydroxylase inhibition. *Journal of Neurochemistry*, *18*, 2491–2500.

Flament, M. F., Rapoport, J. L., Murphy, D. L., Berg, C. J., & Lake, C. R. (1987). Biochemical changes during clomipramine treatment of childhood obsessive-compulsive disorder. *Archives of General Psychiatry*, *44*, 219–255.

Fuxe, K. (1965). Evidence for the existence of monoamine neurons in the central nervous system. IV. The distribution of monoamine terminals in the central nervous system. *Acta Physiologica Scandinavia*, *Supplement 247*, 41–85.

Garvey, M. J., Noyes, R., Jr., Cook, B., & Blum, N. (1996). Preliminary confirmation of the proposed link between reward-dependence traits and norepinephrine. *Psychiatry Research*, *65*, 64.

Gerra, G., Avanzini, P., Zaimovic, A., Sartori, R., Bocchi, C., Timpano, M., Zambelli, U., Delsignore, R., Gardini, F., Talarico, E., & Brambilla, F. (1999). Neurotransmitters, neuroendocrine correlates of sensation seeking temperament in normal humans. *Neuropsychobiology*, *39*, 207–213.

Gerra, G., Caccavari, R., Marcato, A., Zaimovic, A., Avanzini, P., Monica, C., Mutti, A., Fontanesi, B., Delsignore, R., & Brambilla, F. (1994). Alpha-1- and -2-adrenoceptor subsensitivity in siblings of opioid addicts with personality disorders and depression. *Acta Psychiatrica Scandinavia, 90*, 269–273.

Gerra, G., Zaimovic, A., Timpano, M., Zambelli, U., Delsignore, R., & Brambilla, F. (2000). Neuroendocrine correlates of temperamental traits in humans. *Psychoneuroendocrinology, 25*, 479–496.

Goodwin, G. M., Murray, C. L., & Bancroft, J. (1994). Oral d-fenfluramine and neuroendocrine challenge: Problems with the 30 mg dose in men. *Journal of Affective Disorders, 30*, 117–122.

Haller, J., Makara, G. B., & Kruk, M. R. (1998). Catecholaminergic involvement in the control of aggression: Hormones, the peripheral sympathetic and central noradrenergic systems. *Neurosciences and Biobehavioral Reviews, 22*, 85–97.

Hansenne, M., & Ansseau, M. (1999). Harm avoidance and serotonin. *Biological Psychology, 51*, 77–81.

Hennig, J. (2000). Serotonin und Persönlichkeit [Serotonin and personality]. *Zeitschrift für Differentielle und Diagnostische Psychologie [Periodical for differential and diagnostic psychology], 21*, 226–234.

Hennig, J., Becker, H., & Netter, P. (1996). 5-HT agonist-induced changes in peripheral immune cells in healthy volunteers: The impact of personality. *Behavioral Brain Research, 73*, 359–363.

Hennig, J., Lange, N., Haag, A., Rohrmann, S., & Netter, P. (2000a). Reboxetine in a neuroendocrine challenge paradigm: Evidence for high cortisol responses in healthy volunteers scoring high on subclinical depression. *International Journal of Neuropsychopharmacology, 3*, 193–201.

Hennig, J., Laschefski, U., Becker, H., Rammsayer, T., & Netter, P. (1993). Immune cell and cortisol responses to physically and pharmacologically induced lowering of body core temperature. *Neuropsychobiology, 28*, 82–86.

Hennig, J., & Netter, P. (2002). Oral application of citalopram (20mg) and its usefulness for neuroendocrine challenge tests. *International Journal of Neuropsychopharmacology, 5*, 67–71.

Hennig, J., Opper, C., Huwe, S., & Netter, P. (1997). The antagonism of ipsapirone induced biobehavioral responses by +/- pindolol in high and low impulsives. *Journal of Neural Transmission, 104*, 1027–1035.

Hennig, J., Toll, C., Schonlau, P., Rohrmann, S., & Netter, P. (2000b). Endocrine responses after d-fenfluramine and ipsapirone challenge: Further support for Cloninger's tridimensional model of personality. *Neuropsychobiology, 41*, 38–47.

Higley, J. D., Mehlman, P. T., Poland, R. E., Taub, D. M., Vickers, J. H., Suomi, S. J., & Linnoila, M. (1996). CSF testosterone and 5-HIAA correlate with different types of aggressive behaviors. *Biological Psychiatry, 40*, 1067–1082.

Holtz, P. (1950). Über die sympathikomimetische Wirksamkeit von Gehirnextrakten. *Acta Physiologica Scandinavia, 20*, 354–362.

Izzo, J. L., Horwitz, D., & Keiser, H. R. (1979). Reduction of human urinary MHPG excretion by guanethidine: Urinary MHPG as index of sympathetic nervous activity. *Life Sciences, 24*, 1403–1406.

Katsuragi, S., Kunugi, H., Sano, A., Tsutsumi, T., Isogawa, K., Nanko, S., & Akiyoshi, J. (1999). Association between serotonin transporter gene polymorphism and anxiety-related traits. *Biological Psychiatry, 45*, 368–370.

af Klinteberg, B., Schalling, D., Edman, G., Oreland, L., & Asberg, M. (1987). Personality correlates of platelet monoamine oxidase (MAO) activity in female and male subjects. *Neuropsychobiology, 18*, 89–96.

von Knorring, A., Hallman, J., von Knorring, L., & Oreland, L. (1991). Platelet monoamine oxidase activity in type 1 and type 2 alcoholism. *Alcohol and Alcoholism, 26*, 409–416.

Knutson, B., Wolkowitz, O. M., Cole, S. W., Chan, T., Moore, E. A., Johnson, R. C., Terpstra, J., Turner, R. A., & Reus, V. L. (1998). Selective alteration of personality and social behavior by serotonergic intervention. *American Journal of Psychiatry, 155*, 373–379.

Lai, S., Tolis, G., Martin, J. B., Brown, G. M., & Guyda, H. (1975). Effect of Clonidin on growth hormone, prolactin, luteinizing hormone, follicle-stimulating hormone and thyroid stimulating hormone in the serum of normal men. *Journal of Clinical Endocrinology and Metabolism, 41*, 827–832.

Lesch, K.-P., Poten, B., Söhnle, K., & Schulte, H. M. (1990). Pharmacology of the hypothermic response to 5-HT_{1A} receptor activation in humans. *European Journal of Clinical Pharmacology, 39*, 17–19.

Lesch, K. P., Rupprecht, R., Poten, B., Muller, U., Sohnle, K., Fritze, J., & Schulte, H. M. (1989). Endocrine responses to 5-hydroxytryptamine-1A receptor activation by ipsapirone in humans. *Biological Psychiatry, 26*, 203–205.

Lopez, I. J. J., Saiz, R. J., & Iglesias, L. M. (1988). The fenfluramine challenge test in the affective spectrum: A possible marker of endogeneity and severity. *Pharmacopsychiatry, 21*, 9–14.

Malone, K. M., Thase, M. E., Mieczkowski, T., Myers, J. E., Stull, S. D., Cooper, T. B., & Mann, J. J. (1993). Fenfluramine challenge test as a predictor of outcome in major depression. *Psychopharmacology Bulletin, 29*, 155–161.

Mazzanti, C. M., Lappalainen, J., Long, J. C., Bengel, D., Naukkarinen, A., Eggert, M., Virkkunen, M., Linnoila, M., & Goldmann, D. (1998). Role of the serotonin transporter promotor polymorphism in anxiety related traits. *Archives of General Psychiatry, 55*, 940.

Möller, S. E., Mortensen, E. L., Breum, L., Alling, C., Larsen, O. G., Boge-Rasmussen, T., Jensen, C., & Bennicke, K. (1996). Aggression and personality: Association with amino acids and monoamine metabolites. *Psychological Medicine, 26*, 323–331.

Mongeau, R., Blier, P., & de Montigny, C. (1997). The serotonergic and noradrenergic systems of the hippocampus: Their interactions and the effects of antidepressant treatments. *Brain Research and Brain Research Reviews, 23*, 145–195.

Moresco, F. M., Dieci, M., Vita, A., Messa, C., Gobbo, C., Galli, L., Rizzo, C., Panzacchi, A., De Peri, L., Invernizzi, G., & Fazio, F. (2002). In vivo serotonin 5-HT2a receptor binding and personality traits in healthy subjects: A positron emission tomography study. *Neuroimage, 17*, 1470–1478.

Murphy, D. L., Belmaker, R. H., Buchsbaum, M. S., Martin, N. F., Ciaranello, R., & Wyatt, R. J. (1977). Biogenic amine related enzymes and personality variations in normals. *Psychological Medicine, 7*, 149–157.

Nelson, E., & Cloninger, C. R. (1997). Exploring the TPQ as a possible predictor of antidepressant response to nefazodone in a large multi-site study. *Journal of Affective Disorders, 44*, 197–200.

Nelson, R. J., & Chiavegatto, S. (2001). Molecular basis of aggression. *Trends in Neuroscience, 24*, 713–719.

Netter, P., Hennig, J., & Roed, S. (1996). Serotonin and dopamine as mediators of sensation seeking. *Neuropsychobiology, 34*, 155–165.

Peirson, A. R., Heuchert, J. W., Thomala, L., Berk, M., Plein, H., & Cloninger, C. R. (1999). Relationship between serotonin and the temperament and character inventory. *Psychiatry Research, 89*, 29–37.

Peroutka, S. J., & Snyder, S. H. (1979). Multiple serotonin receptors: Differential binding of [^{3}H]5-hydroxytryptamine, [^{3}H]-spiroperidol. *Molecular Pharmacology, 16*, 687–699.

Plouffe, L., & Stelmack, R. M. (1979). Neuroticism and the effect of stress on the pupillary light reflex. *Perceptual and Motor Skills, 49*, 635–642.

Power, A. C., & Cowen, P. J. (1992). Neuroendocrine challenge tests: Assessment of 5-HT function in anxiety and depression. *Molecular Aspects in Medicine, 13*, 205–220.

van Praag, H. M. (1996). Faulty cortisol/serotonin interplay. Psychopathological and biological characterisation of a new, hypothetical depression subtype (SeCA depression). *Psychiatry Research*, *65*, 143–157.

van Praag, H. M., Korf, J., & Schut, D. (1973). Cerebral monoamines and depression. *Archives of General Psychiatry*, *28*, 827–831.

Quabeck, M., Lehmann, E., & Tegeler, J. (1984). Comparison of the antidepressant action of tryptophan, tryptophan/5-Hydroxytryptophan combination and nomifensine. *Neuropsychobiology*, *11*, 111–115.

Rainbow, T. C., Parsons, B., & Wolfe, B. B. (1984). Quantitative autoradiography of beta 1- and beta 2-adrenergic receptors in rat brain. *Proceedings of the National Academy of Sciences, U.S.A*, *81*, 1585–1589.

Ricketts, M. H., Hamer, R. M., Sage, I. J., Manowitz, P., Feng, F., & Menza, M. A. (1998). Association of a serotonin transporter gene promotor polymorphism with harm avoidance behaviour in an elderly population. *Psychiatry Genetics*, *42*, 1129.

Rowland, N. E., & Carlton, J. (1986). Neurobiology of an anoretic drug: Fenfluramine. *Progress in Neurobiology*, *27*, 62.

Roy, A., Adinoff, B., Roehrich, L., Lamparski, D., Custer, R., Lorenz, V., Barbaccia, M., Guidotti, A., Costa, E., & Linnoila, M. (1988). Pathological gambling. A psychobiological study. *Archives of General Psychiatry*, *45*, 369–373.

Roy, A., & Linnoila, M. (1988). Suicidal behavior, impulsiveness and serotonin. *Acta Psychiatrica Scandinavia*, *78*, 529–535.

Roy, A., & Linnoila, M. (1989). CSF studies on alcoholism and related behaviours. *Progress in Neuropsychopharmacology and Biological Psychiatry*, *13*, 505–511.

Ruegg, R. G., Gilmore, J., Ekstrom, R. D., Corrigan, M., Knight, B., Tancer, M., Leatherman, M. E., Carson, S. W., & Golden, R. N. (1997). Clomipramine challenge responses covary with tridimensional personality questionnaire scores in healthy subjects. *Biological Psychiatry*, *42*, 1129.

Schalling, D., & Asberg, M. (1985). Biological and psychological correlates of impulsiveness and monotony avoidance. In: J. Strelau, F. H. Farley, & A. Gale (Eds), *The biological bases of personality and behavior: Theories, measurement techniques, and development* (Vol. 1, pp. 181–194). Washington, DC: Hemisphere Publishing.

Schildkraut, J. J. (1965). The catecholamine hypothesis of affective disorders: A review of supporting evidence. *American Journal of Psychiatry*, *122*, 509–522.

Schooler, C., Zahn, T. P., Murphy, D. L., & Buchsbaum, M. S. (1978). Psychological correlates of monoamine oxidase in normals. *Journal of Nervous and Mental Diseases*, *166*, 177–186.

Seibyl, J. P., Krystal, J. H., Price, L. H., Woods, S. W., D'Amico, C., Heninger, G. R., & Charney, D. E. (1991). Effects of Ritanserin on the behavioral, neuroendocrine, and cardiovascular responses to meta-chlorophenyl-piperanzine in healthy human subjects. *Psychiatry Research*, *38*, 227–236.

Siever, L. J., Coccaro, E. F., Zemishlany, Z., Silverman, J., Klar, H., Losonczy, M. F., Davidson, M., Friedman, R., Mohs, R. C., & Davis, K. L. (1987). Psychobiology of personality disorders: Pharmacologic implications. *Psychopharmacology Bulletin*, *23*, 333–336.

Stahl, S. M. (1985). Platelets as pharmacological models for the receptors and biochemistry of monoaminergic neurons. In: G. L. Longenecker (Ed.), *The platelets: Physiology and pharmacology* (pp. 307–340). New York: Academic Press.

Storlien, L. H., & Smythe, G. A. (1992). D-fenfluramine effects on hypothalamic monoamine activities and their hormonal correlates. *Brain Research*, *597*, 60–65.

Sumner, B. E., & Fink, G. (1998). Testosterone as well as estrogen increases serotonin 2A receptor mRNA and binding site densities in the male rat brain. *Brain Research and Molecular Brain Research*, *59*, 205–214.

Tancer, M. E., Ranc, J., & Golden, R. N. (1994). Pharmacological challenge test of the Tridimensional Personality Questionnaire in patients with social phobia and normal volunteers. *Anxiety*, *1*, 224–226.

Tellegen, A. (1985). Structures of mood and personality and their relevance to assessing anxiety, with an emphasis on self-report. In: A. H. Tuma, & J. D. Maser (Eds), *Anxiety and anxiety disorders* (pp. 681–706). Hillsdale, NJ: Erlbaum.

Twarog, B. M., & Page, I. H. (1953). Serotonin content of some mamalian tissues and urine and an method for its determination. *American Journal of Physiology*, *175*, 157–161.

Vogt, M. (1954). The concentration of sympathin in different parts of the central nervous system under normal conditions and after the administration of drugs. *Journal of Physiology*, *123*, 451–481.

Wilson, K. M., & Minneman, K. P. (1989). Regional variations in alpha 1-adrenergic receptor subtypes in rat brain. *Journal of Neurochemistry*, *53*, 1782–1786.

Winblad, B., Gottfries, C.-G., Oreland, L., & Wilberg, A. (1979). Monoamine oxidase in human platelets and brain of non-neurological geriatric patients. *Medical Biology*, *57*, 129–132.

Wingrove, J., Bond, A. J., Cleare, A. J., & Sherwood, R. (1999). Trait hostility and prolactin response to tryptophan enhancement/depletion. *Neuropsychobiology*, *40*, 202–206.

Yatham, L. N., & Steiner, M. (1993). Neuroendocrine probes of serotonergic function: A critical review. *Life Sciences*, *53*, 447–463.

Young, W., Laws, E., Sharbrough, F., & Weinshilboum, R. M. (1986). Human monoamine oxidase. Lack of brain and platelet correlation. *Archives of General Psychiatry*, *43*, 604–609.

Zald, D. H., & Depue, R. A. (2001). Serotonergic modulation of positive and negative affect in psychiatrically healthy males. *Personality and Individual Differences*, *30*, 71–86.

Zuckerman, M. (1990). The psychophysiology of sensation seeking. *Journal of Personality*, *58*, 313–358.

Zuckerman, M. (1991). *Psychobiology of personality*. Cambridge: Cambridge University Press.

Zuckerman, M. (1993). P-impulsive sensation seeking and its behavioral, psychophysiological and biochemical correlates. *Neuropsychobiology*, *28*, 30–36.

Zuckerman, M., Kolin, E. A., Price, L., & Zoob, I. (1964). Development of a sensation seeking scale. *Journal of Consulting Psychology*, *28*, 477–482.

Chapter 21

Extraversion and the Dopamine Hypothesis

T. H. Rammsayer

1. Introduction

According to Eysenck's (1967, 1981, 1994) biological theory of personality, the personality dimension of extraversion (E) is related to the ascending reticular activating system (ARAS). The ARAS represents a neuroanatomical structure ascending from the brain stem to cortical regions. Collaterals from the ascending sensory pathways elicit neuronal activity in the ARAS, which subsequently induces enhanced excitation in various sites dispersed throughout the cerebral cortex. More specifically, introverts and extraverts should differ in their general levels of activity in this corticoreticular loop, with introverts being chronically more aroused than extraverts. Obviously, this theory has been based on physiological and psychological concepts of arousal common at the time it was first presented in 1967.

Over the last three decades, however, distinct arousal-related neuroanatomical regions were identified that are characterized neurochemically by different neurotransmitter systems (e.g. Fallon & Loughlin 1987; Robbins & Everitt 1987; Shepherd 1988). The reticular norepinephrine system originates in the locus coeruleus, and dopaminergic cell bodies are present in the substantia nigra and the ventral tegmental area, whereas mesencephalic 5-hydroxytryptamine cell bodies originate in the raphe nuclei and cholinergic projections from the nucleus basalis of Meynert. This suggests that these regions have different functions, even when projecting into the same terminal area (Robbins & Everitt 1995).

Since a general biological theory of E cannot account for the large number of supposedly contradictory findings, Lieberman and Rosenthal (2001) proposed to develop more specific theories of particular neurocognitive systems to explain E-related individual differences rather than a single comprehensive biological theory of E. Following this approach in the present chapter, converging evidence from human studies will be provided for the notion that E-related individual differences in some psychological functions may reflect individual differences in dopaminergic neurotransmission in the brain.

On the Psychobiology of Personality
Edited by R. M. Stelmack

ISBN: 0-08-044209-9

2. Major Dopaminergic Systems in the Brain

Dopaminergic projections from mesencephalic cell groups can be divided into two major subsystems: the mesostriatal system, consisting of dopamine (DA) neurons projecting from the substantia nigra and the ventral tegmental area to the striatal complex, and the mesolimbocortical system, containing DA neurons also originating in the ventral tegmental area and the medial substantia nigra and primarily projecting to limbic, allocortical, and neocortical areas (Björklund & Lindvall 1986). While the mesolimbocortical DA neurons play a crucial role in functions such as locomotor activity, active avoidance, incentive-reward motivation, associative learning, or cognitive processes (Kimberg *et al.* 1997; Müller *et al.* 1998; Robinson & Berridge 2000; Salamone 1994; Sokolowski *et al.* 1994; Tzschentke 2001), the mesostriatal DA system is primarily involved in motor-response activation, execution of learned motor programs, sequencing and timing of behavior (Dunnett & Robbins 1992; Harrington *et al.* 1998; Koob 1992; Le Moal & Simon 1991; Rammsayer 1997; Sander & Schmidt 1994).

Thus, the two major DA systems in the brain appear to mediate distinct classes of behavior. Unlike neurons characterized by other neurotransmitters, however, DA neurons do not have highly specific functions (Le Moal & Simon 1991; Robbins & Everitt 1987). Rather, DA neurons play a more general regulatory role in different aspects of activation, which increases the probability and strength of an appropriate behavioral response (Le Moal & Simon 1991).

3. Indirect Evidence for an Association Between Extraversion and Mesostriatal Dopaminergic Activity

Mesostriatal DA neurons appear to act as an inhibitory system on the striatum (Björklund & Lindvall 1986), which in turn exerts a powerful inhibitory effect on the thalamus and the reticular formation (Carlsson & Carlsson 1990). Therefore, any increase in mesostriatal DA activity will counteract the inhibitory effect of the striatum and, thus, result in increased reticular arousal. As a consequence, sensory reactivity to punctate physical stimulation should be enhanced.

Similarly, Stricker and Zigmond (1986), Heffner *et al.* (1977), Zigmond *et al.* (1980) put forward the idea that mesostriatal DA neurons modulate the threshold for behavioral responses to sensory input. In this respect, the mesostriatal DA system acts as a tonic regulatory system. Each sensory input triggers two processes: a specific process to activate neuronal assemblies necessary for eliciting an appropriate response; and a nonspecific DA process that reduces existing striatal inhibition. Within the framework of this account, higher sensitivity of the mesostriatal DA system should also result in lower sensory thresholds.

From this perspective, the finding of superior sensory sensitivity in introverts compared to extraverts would support the view that E-related functional differences may exist in the mesostriatal DA system. Indeed, E-related individual differences in sensory reactivity has been observed with a large range of different psychophysical and psychophysiological methods. For example, there are numerous reports of greater sensory reactivity to physical stimulation for introverts than extraverts, including lower auditory thresholds (e.g. Shigehisa & Symons 1973; Smith 1968; Stelmack & Campbell 1974), lower noise thresholds (e.g. Dornic & Ekehammar 1990; Elliott 1971; Geen 1984; Weinstein 1978), and lower pain thresholds (e.g. Bartol & Costello 1976; Haslam 1967; Lynn & Eysenck 1961; Petrie 1967; Schalling 1971). These findings are paralleled by the outcome of psychophysiological studies showing larger early event-related potential amplitudes (i.e. N1 amplitudes) for introverts than extraverts in response to auditory tones (e.g. Doucet & Stelmack 2000; Rammsayer & Stahl 2004; Stelmack *et al.* 1977; Stelmack & Michaud-Achorn 1985). These latter results also affirm the enhanced sensory reactivity of introverts to punctate physical stimulation.

There is also a good deal of empirical evidence that suggests differences between introverts and extraverts in tasks that assess speed of responding and motor control (for reviews see Brebner 1990; Eysenck 1971; Stelmack 1985). Nevertheless, the large bulk of research examining E-related differences by means of response-time measures based on the time from stimulus onset to the press of a target button presents a rather puzzling picture of positive, negative, and neutral results (for reviews see Bullock & Gilliland 1993; Doucet & Stelmack 1997; Rammsayer 1998). To more specifically elucidate E-related differences in response times, reaction time (RT) can be measured independently of movement time (MT) by means of a response panel that makes use of a "home" button. With this paradigm, the time required from stimulus onset to the release of the home button is scored as RT, and the time required from this release to the subsequent press of a target button is measured separately as MT. While RT is useful as an index of central processing speed, MT appears to be largely independent of cognitive task requirements and can be considered a valid indicator of speed of response execution (Doucet & Stelmack 1997, 2000; Frewer & Hindmarch 1988).

Only very few studies on E (Doucet & Stelmack 1997; Muniz-Fernandez & Paz-Caballero 1984; Rammsayer 1995, 1998; Rammsayer *et al.* 1993; Stelmack *et al.* 1993) obtained RT and MT as separate response-time measures. While none of these studies reported overall differences between introverts and extraverts in RT, three studies (Doucet & Stelmack 1997; Rammsayer 1995; Stelmack *et al.* 1993) found that extraverts showed faster MTs than introverts. In a pioneering study, Doucet and Stelmack (1997) applied a simple auditory RT task with three different distances (7, 15, and 23 cm) between the home button and the target button. This procedure enabled the authors to distinguish E-related differences in the initial acceleration phase from possible differences in ballistic movement. If differences between introverts and extraverts depend on processes associated with ballistic movement, differences in MT between groups would be expected to increase with increasing distance. Since the magnitude of the difference in MT between both groups remained constant in spite of the increasing distance of the response button, Doucet and Stelmack (1997, 2000) concluded that it is the initial acceleration phase of MT, rather than the later ballistic phase, that is associated with E-related individual differences. Most interestingly, initiation of voluntary movement is mediated by the mesostriatal DA system (Amalric *et al.* 1993; Dunnett & Robbins 1992; Salamone *et al.* 1993). Thus, extraverts' faster initiation of movement compared to introverts suggests E-related differences in mesostriatal DA neurotransmission.

4. Direct Evidence for an Association Between Extraversion and Mesostriatal Dopaminergic Activity

There are at least three major approaches to more directly examine the assumed association between E and DA: the pharmacopsychological approach, molecular-genetics strategies, and neuroimaging techniques. The ultimate aim of the pharmacopsychological approach is to discover neurochemical brain systems that are mediating specific E-related individual differences. This can be achieved by utilizing the specific pharmacological actions and action mechanisms of drugs for a better understanding of the biological basis of E (Eysenck 1983; Janke 1988; Russell 1987). With molecular-genetics strategies, specific information about genotypes can be used to test the importance of individual genes on behavior and complex personality traits in healthy human individuals (Bouchard & Loehlin 2001; Dick & Rose 2002). Neuroimaging techniques make it possible to visualize the anatomy of the living human brain and regional differences in brain activation using external monitoring devices. These techniques include computerized axial tomography, single photon emission tomography, positron emission tomography (PET), magnetic resonance imaging, and functional magnetic resonance imaging. To date, most of the existing data on DA and E are based on the pharmacopsychological and the molecular-genetics approach.

4.1. Pharmacopsychological Evidence

In a pharmacopsychological study, Rammsayer *et al.* (1993) provided the first evidence for a DA-related neural process that appears to be implicated in the mediation of both the sensory and the motor effects that distinguish introverts and extraverts. Rammsayer *et al.* (1993) addressed the question of whether pharmacologically induced decreases in DA activity in the brain would differentially affect RT and MT of extraverts and introverts. Pharmacologic blockade of DA synthesis by means of alpha-methyl-para-tyrosine (AMPT), an inhibitor of tyrosine hydroxylase (Brodie *et al.* 1971; Carlsson *et al.* 1973), resulted in a pronounced reduction in DA activity of more than 60% in both introverts and extraverts, but did not interact with the personality dimension of E. Furthermore, biochemical analyses also revealed that, under physiological conditions, DA turnover is the same in introverts and extraverts.

The most intriguing finding of this study, however, was that performance on RT and MT was markedly impaired in introverts but not in extraverts as compared to the respective placebo groups. This finding leads to the conclusion that introverts are more responsive to pharmacologically induced changes in DA activity than extraverts. In other words, rather than simple hyper- or hypo-DA states, responsiveness to alterations from the physiological range of DA activity may be indicative of biological differences between introverts and extraverts.

Since AMPT produces a nonspecific decrease in brain DA activity, the DA type 2 (D2) receptor blocker remoxipride was chosen to more specifically affect homeostasis of DA neurotransmission in a subsequent study (Rammsayer 1998). Remoxipride primarily inhibits DA neurons of the ventral tegmental area that project to limbic and cortical regions

(Köhler *et al.* 1990; Seeman 1990) and has a low propensity to block striatal D2-receptors (Westlind-Danielsson *et al.* 1994). In introverts, remoxipride caused a pronounced increase in RT compared to extraverts while MT was not affected in either group.

With the experimental paradigm applied by Rammsayer (1998), RT primarily reflects speed of cognitive processes such as stimulus identification, stimulus recognition, and stimulus evaluation (Frewer & Hindmarch 1988; Sanders 1998; Sternberg 1969, 1998; Theios 1975). Several behavioral studies have shown that cognitive processes are more likely mediated by the mesolimbocortical rather than by the mesostriatal DA system (e.g. Brozoski *et al.* 1979; Cohen & Servan-Schreiber 1992; Luciana *et al.* 1992; Sawaguchi *et al.* 1988, 1990). Therefore, from a neurobiological point of view, the impairing effect of remoxipride on RT in introverts has most likely been brought about by blockade of postsynaptic receptors in the mesolimbocortical DA system. This is a very likely interpretation given the high potency of remoxipride to block D2 receptors of mesolimbocortical DA neurons. In this respect, the finding of a pronounced increase in RT of introverts under remoxipride suggests that, in introverts, cognitive mechanisms involved in RT are more responsive to decreases in mesolimbocortical D2 receptor activity than in extraverts. Furthermore, the absence of a remoxipride-induced effect on MT, is in line with the relatively weak effect of remoxipride on mesostriatal compared to mesolimbocortical DA activity (Ögren *et al.* 1990; Westlind-Danielsson *et al.* 1994). Therefore, it is not surprising that MT, primarily mediated by the mesostriatal DA system, was not affected in either introverts or extraverts.

Taken together, there is converging pharmacopsychological evidence for E-related differences in responsivity to deviations from the physiological level of both mesostriatal and mesolimbocortical D2 receptor activity.

Evidence for E-related differences in DA responsiveness has also been provided for other DA systems in the brain. Depue *et al.* (1994) reported a significant positive correlation between individual scores on positive emotionality (PE) of the Multidimensional Personality Questionnaire (Tellegen 1995) and the inhibitory effect of the D2/D3 sub-receptor agonist bromocriptine on prolactin secretion. The PE dimension is highly correlated with the E scale of Eysenck's Personality Questionnaire (Depue *et al.* 1994) and inhibition of prolactin secretion represents a peripheral indicator of brain DA activity. Inhibition of prolactin secretion is mediated by the tuberoinfundibular and tuberohypophysial DA systems (Ben-Jonathan 1985). The observed positive correlation between individual PE scores and the inhibitory effect of bromocriptine on prolactin secretion may indicate that DA activity is positively related to PE (cf. Depue *et al.* 1994). Animal studies, however, have shown that agonistic drugs are strongly effective at low values of fractional occupancy of receptors by the endogenous agonist (Jaspers *et al.* 1984; Jaspers & Cools 1985; Weiss 1988). Therefore, subjects showing a strong response to a DA agonist, such as bromocriptine, should be characterized by a functionally low activity of DA, while the reverse applies to subjects showing a weak response to DA agonists. Accordingly, high DA reactivity in rats is associated with a reduced prolactin response to stress (Rots *et al.* 1996). From this perspective, the positive correlation between PE scores and the inhibitory effect of bromocriptine on prolactin secretion points to a higher DA responsiveness in low PE than in high PE subjects. This conclusion is in line with the general notion of higher DA responsiveness in introverts compared to extraverts.

Depue *et al.* (1994) also found a highly significant correlation between PE scores and time after bromocriptine administration to reach the maximum spontaneous blink rate. Spontaneous blink rate in non-human primates and humans has been considered to be positively related to activity of the mesostriatal DA system (Hallett 2000; Sandyk 1990; Taylor *et al.* 1999). Thus, the shorter time to maximum spontaneous blink rate for introverted than for extraverted subjects is also indicative of more pronounced DA sensitivity in the former group. This is because a more responsive DA system is better adapted to more quickly and more efficiently initiate neuronal processes, such as receptor down-regulation, to compensate for the pharmacologically induced hyperdopaminergic state. As a result, maximum spontaneous blink rate could be expected to be lower and time to blink maximum should be shorter for introverts (due to their higher DA responsiveness) than for extraverts. Exactly this predicted pattern of bromocriptine-induced DA agonistic effects is reflected by Depue *et al.*'s (1994) finding of positive correlations between E and time to reach maximum spontaneous blink rate and maximum spontaneous blink rate, although the latter correlation failed to reach the 5% level of statistical significance.

Finally, it should be noted that in several studies on E and DA, measures of critical flicker fusion frequency (CFF) have been obtained (e.g. Corr & Kumari 1997; Rammsayer 1998, 2003; Rammsayer *et al.* 1993). CFF represents a highly reliable psychophysical indicator of unspecific cortical arousal and, therefore, a widely used method for demonstrating sedative drug effects (Hindmarch 1982; Smith & Misiak 1976). Within the framework of pharmacological interventions with DA drugs, however, CFF cannot be considered a valid indicator of brain DA activity (cf. Rammsayer 2003). Specific DA-induced effects on CFF appear to be mediated by peripheral DA receptors at the retinal level rather than by central DA mechanisms (van Duijn *et al.* 1985; Gottlob *et al.* 1987). This may account for the highly inconsistent results observed in the studies cited above.

4.1.1. Dopaminergic interactions with other neurotransmitter systems A given neurotransmitter may interact with other neurotransmitter systems. For example, there are well-documented interactions between glutamatergic N-methyl-D-aspartic acid (NMDA) receptor activity and DA release in the brain. Imaging studies in healthy human subjects revealed an increase in DA activity after acute administration of NMDA receptor antagonists (e.g. Breier *et al.* 1998a; Smith *et al.* 1998; Vollenweider *et al.* 2000). Hence, enhanced DA activity in the brain can be produced by acute systemic administration of NMDA receptor antagonists. A recent study (Rammsayer 2003) addressed the question of whether a pharmacologically induced change in the glutamatergic neurotransmitter system would also differentially affect the transmission of sensory input into motor output in introverts and extraverts. For this purpose, the effect of the NMDA receptor antagonistic memantine was investigated in introverts and extraverts.

Memantine produced a significant increase in RT of introverts but not of extraverts. This differential effects of memantine on RT in introverts and extraverts paralleled the effects observed with the DA antagonists remoxipride and AMPT in the two previous studies (Rammsayer *et al.* 1993; Rammsayer 1998). Several studies showed that systemic administration of NMDA receptor antagonists increased DA activity in the human prefrontal cortex (Breier *et al.* 1998a; Smith *et al.* 1998). This well-established interaction between NMDA receptor activity and DA release in the prefrontal cortex suggests that the E-related differential effects of memantine were primarily mediated by enhanced DA activity in the prefrontal cortex. From this perspective, the differential effects of memantine on RT in introverts and extraverts may indicate that introverts are more responsive to enhanced levels of prefrontal DA activity than extraverts. Together with the outcome of previous studies demonstrating introverts' higher responsiveness to pharmacologically induced decreases in prefrontal DA activity (Rammsayer 1998; Rammsayer *et al.* 1993), this finding provides converging evidence for the general notion that introverts are more susceptible than extraverts to any deviation from the physiological level of mesolimbocortical DA activity due to less effective compensatory mechanisms.

Although there was no significant interaction between NMDA antagonistic treatment and E, memantine caused a significant decrease in MT in both introverts and extraverts. Unlike RT, MT represents an indicator of performance on motor execution, a function primarily associated with the mesostriatal DA system (e.g. DeLong 1990; Graybiel *et al.* 1994; Mink 1999). It is important to note, that there is no evidence for a clear functional relationship between NMDA and DA in the mesostriatal DA system (Betarbet & Greenamyre 1999; Carlsson *et al.* 2000; Castro & Zigmond 2001; Kretschmer 2000; Kretschmer *et al.* 2000; Waters *et al.* 1996). Furthermore, NMDA receptor antagonists are capable of inducing motor activity in animals completely depleted of DA (Carlsson & Carlsson 1989; Svensson & Carlsson 1992). Therefore, it appears reasonable to assume that the faster MT observed with memantine resulted from a non-DA, memantine-induced decrease of excitatory glutamatergic effects on striatopallidal neurons which exert an inhibitory influence on the motor nuclei of the thalamus (Pollack 2001).

If the performance increment in MT after treatment with memantine represents a pure glutamatergic effect, rather than a secondary effect due to NMDA-DA interactions, the present findings would support the following hypothesis: E-related differential behavioral responsiveness to pharmacologically induced changes in NMDA receptor activity is limited to functions that involve an interaction between the glutamatergic and DA systems. Thus, differences between introverts and extraverts in the transmission of sensory input into motor output seem to be a genuine function of DA modulation.

4.2. DA and Extraversion from a Molecular-Genetics Point of View

It is well-established that genetic variation represents a major factor in causing individual differences in E (e.g. Carey *et al.* 1978; Eysenck 1990; Floderus-Myrhed *et al.* 1980; Pedersen *et al.* 1988; Tellegen *et al.* 1988). Although these findings do not suggest that the differential sensitivity to changes in DA activity between introverts and extraverts may be due to genetic factors, more recently, first reports were published that specific polymorphisms of DA receptor genes might influence E-related personality dimensions in healthy humans.

In 1996, Ebstein *et al.* found an association between the type 4 DA receptor (DRD4) gene and the personality trait of novelty seeking. At the same time, Benjamin *et al.* (1996) reported an association between the same DRD4 polymorphism and individual scores on the Excitement Seeking scale of the Neuroticism Extraversion Openness to experience Personality Inventory-Revised questionnaire (NEO PI-R; Costa & McCrae

1992). Subsequent studies, using different psychometric measures of novelty seeking and E, have both supported (Benjamin *et al.* 2000; Ekelund *et al.* 1999; Noble *et al.* 1998; Okuyama *et al.* 2000; Ono *et al.* 1997; Strobel *et al.* 1999; Tomitaka *et al.* 1999) and refuted (Burt *et al.* 2002; Gebhardt *et al.* 2000; Jönsson *et al.* 1997, 1998, 2002; Mitsuyasu *et al.* 2001; Persson *et al.* 2000; Pogue-Geile *et al.* 1998; Vandenbergh *et al.* 1997) these findings. It should be noted that several of the studies that confirmed an association between DRD4 polymorphism and novelty seeking also provided evidence that this polymorphism affects exploratory, extravagant, and extraverted aspects of novelty seeking rather than impulsive, disorderly, and monotony-avoidant ones (Ono *et al.* 1997; Strobel *et al.* 1999; Tomitaka *et al.* 1999).

Several possible reasons for the failure to replicate the association between DRD4 polymorphism and E/novelty seeking have been discussed: the use of different questionnaires for personality assessment, methods that inflate the potential for false positive results, lack of statictical power, lack of control for ethnic variability, or demographic differences among participants in the studies (cf. Burt *et al.* 2002; Malhotra & Goldman 2000; Strobel *et al.* 1999). Neither of these possible reasons, however, seems to account for the failure to replicate the positive findings (e.g. Burt *et al.* 2002; Pogue-Geile *et al.* 1998). Thus, the relatively large number of null results argues against the generality of the positive findings.

Although there is one study (Noble *et al.* 1998) reporting a positive association between the D2 dopamine receptor (DRD2) gene and high novelty seeking, subsequent attempts to replicate this finding were not successful (de Brettes *et al.* 1998; Burt *et al.* 2002; Gebhardt *et al.* 2000).

At present, the general assumption of a functional role of the DRD4 and DRD2 polymorphisms in the personality dimension of E appears to be highly questionable. This, however, does not preclude other DA influences as a possible biological basis of E. A genetic basis for individual differences in sensitivity to changes in DA activity has been demonstrated in several animal studies. Cools *et al.* (1990) achieved differences in DA receptor sensitivity by selective breeding or choosing different strains. In subsequent experiments, these authors found that different genetically determined sensitivity to the DA receptor agonist apomorphine was associated with differential behavioral changes in apomorphine susceptible and non-susceptible rats. The rats also showed differences in behaviors not related to drug application (Ellenbroek *et al.* 1995; Rots *et al.* 1996). Similarly, Glick *et al.* (1988) reported behavioral differences in rats in response to 6-hydroxydopamine lesions of the substantia nigra and various DA drugs suggesting the existence of two distinct populations which differ with respect to compensatory mechanisms for maintaining homeostasis in DA neurotransmission. Thus, there is at least indirect evidence for the assumption that the higher responsiveness of introverts to experimentally induced alterations from the physiological range of DA activity is genetically determined.

4.3. Evidence from Neuroimaging Studies

Although a relatively large number of neuroimaging studies report differences in patterns of brain activation for introverts and extraverts (e.g. Ebmeier *et al.* 1994; Johnson *et al.* 1999;

Mathew *et al.* 1984; Stenberg *et al.* 1990; Stenberg *et al.* 1993), very few studies allow for inferences with regard to specific E-related individual differences in brain DA activity.

Using single photon emission tomography, Gray *et al.* (1994) found significant negative correlations between Psychoticism (P) scores on the Eysenck Personality Questionnaire (EPQ; Eysenck & Eysenck 1975) and D2-receptor binding in the basal ganglia. No association, however, could be shown between D2 receptor binding and EPQ-E scores. In two more recent PET studies (Breier *et al.* 1998b; Farde *et al.* 1997), a positive correlation was reported between D2 receptor density and E-related personal detachment as measured by the Karolinska Scales of Personality (Schalling *et al.* 1987). Similar studies (Breier *et al.* 1998a; Kestler *et al.* 2000), using the Tridimensional Personality Questionnaire (Cloninger *et al.* 1991) and the NEO PI-R, however, failed to detect a relation between D2 receptor density and E-related aspects of personality such as personal detachment, warmth, gregariousness, and positive emotions, or the NEO PI-R dimension of E as a whole. These findings may suggest a highly complex relationship between E-related aspects of personality and D2 receptor density. Furthermore, the choice of the personality scale used may be critical in determining this relationship (cf. Kestler *et al.* 2000).

Fischer *et al.* (1997) also used PET measures of regional cerebral blood flow to investigate central neural activity in introverts and extraverts. Their data indicate significantly increased activity in DA-related brain areas such as the caudate nucleus and the putamen in introverts compared to extraverts. This finding not only suggests a DA basis for individual differences in E, it is also in accordance with the idea of more pronounced DA responsivity in introverts than in extraverts as put forward by (Rammsayer 1998, 2003; Rammsayer *et al.* 1993). While in the other PET studies on E, participants were instructed just to lie still and were not required to perform any tasks, Fischer *et al.* (1997) presented their subjects with videotaped scenes of individuals walking in a park as a visual stimulation during the PET recordings. This visual stimulation may have been critical for elicting increased neural activity in the mesostriatal DA system in introverts as compared to extraverts. Such an interpretation would be consistent with Rammsayer *et al.*'s (1993) conclusion that under normal condidtions (i.e. without any experimentally or pharmacologically induced stimulation) mesostriatal DA activity in introverts and extraverts is within a similar range, and, therefore, no E-related differences are to be expected.

5. Dopamine, Extraversion, and Other Higher-Order Personality Traits

In a commendable effort, Depue and Collins (1999) were the first who developed a highly sophisticated neurobiological model of E. In their model, Depue and Collins (1999) put forward the idea that DA projections from the ventral tegmental area to the nucleus accumbens represent the neurobiological substrate of E-related individual differences in incentive-facilitated behavior. Although this model is based on an integration of behavior, affect, and both cortical and subcortical neural mechanisms, it still suffers from at least two major short-comings.

First, Depue and Collins' (1999) basic assumption that a DA-dependent positive incentive motivational system is responsible for E-related individual differences is debatable.

Although Lucas and Diener (2001; Lucas *et al.* 2000) also arrived at the conclusion that sensitivity to rewards rather than sociability forms the core of E, Ashton *et al.* (2002) hold the view that social attention, not reward sensitivity, is the central feature of E. As an additional alternative theoretical account, for example Brebner's (1983, 1985) motor theory of E proposes individual differences in stimulus analysis and response organization as a general explanation of behavioral differences between extraverts and introverts. Secondly, Depue and Collins' (1999) model lacks corroborative evidence from human pharmacopsychological studies (cf., Lawrence *et al.* 1999) and does not take into account the role of the mesostriatal DA system to explain E-related individual differences in sensory and motor functions.

The association between brain DA activity and basic personality traits is not limited to the personality dimension of E but also holds for other higher-order personality traits. For example, an increasing number of studies support the notion of a functional relationship between DA neurotransmission and the personality dimensions of P and impulsive antisocial sensation seeking (P-ImpUSS) (cf. Eysenck 1995; Gray 1999; Pickering & Gray 2001; Zuckerman 1991). Although it seems premature to make a final statement whether measures of E are more strongly related to brain DA functioning than measures of P-ImpUSS (cf. Pickering & Gray 2001), a large number of studies provided converging evidence for an association between DA activity and P. For example, latent inhibition (Baruch *et al.* 1988; Kumari *et al.* 1999; Lubow *et al.* 1992; Lubow & Gewirtz 1995), negative priming (Beech & Claridge 1987; Beech *et al.* 1990; David 1995; Swerdlow *et al.* 1995; Williams 1995), and pre-pulse inhibition (Simons & Giardina 1992; Swerdlow *et al.* 1995; Kumari *et al.* 1997) represent DA-mediated phenomena that are unrelated to E, but reduced in normal individuals scoring high on psychometric measures of P or psychosis proneness.

Furthermore, precision of timing of brief intervals in the range of milliseconds has been shown to be dependent on the effective level of DA activity in the mesostriatal system (Rammsayer 1997, 1999) but was found to be unrelated to both the personality dimensions of E and P (Rammsayer 1995; Lienert & Rammsayer 1998). All these findings point to the conclusion that the association between E and DA is not a general one but appears to be restricted to some specific E-related behaviors. Thus, only a limited number of DA-mediated functions seem to be associated with the personality dimension of E. Furthermore, it appears unlikely to assume that all E-related individual differences can be accounted for by brain DA activity. For example, differences between introverts and extraverts have been observed at the level of the peripheral nervous system that cannot be explained in terms of central DA mechanisms (Pivik *et al.* 1988; Stelmack & Pivik 1996). All these considerations support Pickering and Gray's (2001) notion of more than one dimension of personality that is associated with variations in DA brain mechanisms.

6. Summary

Converging evidence has been provided for a functional relationship between E and DA mechanisms in the brain. Rather than simple hyper- or hypo-DA states, responsiveness to naturally occurring or experimentally induced alterations from the physiological range of dopamineregic activity may be indicative of biological differences between introverts and extraverts. Peripheral physiological responses mediated by the tuberoinfundibular and tuberohypophysial DA systems as well as behavioral responses primarily mediated by mesostriatal and mesolimbocortical DA systems support the view that DA responsiveness is higher in introverts than in extraverts. Since behavioral data after systemic drug treatment may not yield highly conclusive information about the involvement of specific neurotransmitter systems in the brain, additional indirect evidence have been discussed for an association between E and brain DA activity as well as possible evidence from molecular genetics and neuroimaging studies.

References

Amalric, M., Berhow, M., Polis, I., & Koob, G. F. (1993). Selective effects of low-dose D2 dopamine receptor antagonism in a reaction-time task in rats. *Neuropsychopharmacology*, *8*, 195–200.

Ashton, M. C., Lee, K., & Paunonen, S. V. (2002). What is the central feature of extraversion? Social attention vs. reward sensitivity. *Journal of Personality and Social Psychology*, *83*, 245–252.

Bartol, C. R., & Costello, N. (1976). Extraversion as a function of temporal duration of electrical shock: An exploratory study. *Perceptual and Motor Skills*, *42*, 1174.

Baruch, I., Hemsley, D. R., & Gray, J. A. (1988). Latent inhibition and "psychotic proneness" on normal subjects. *Personality and Individual Differences*, *9*, 777–783.

Beech, A., & Claridge, G. (1987). Individual differences in negative priming: Relations with schizotypal personality traits. *British Journal of Psychology*, *78*, 349–356.

Beech, A., Powell, T. J., McWilliam, J., & Claridge, G. S. (1990). The effect of a small dose of chlorpromazine on a measure of 'cognitive inhibition'. *Personality and Individual Differences*, *11*, 1141–1145.

Benjamin, J., Li, L., Patterson, C., Greenberg, B. D., Murphy, D. L., & Hamer, D. H. (1996). Population and familial association between the D4 dopamine receptor gene and measures of novelty seeking. *Nature Genetics*, *12*, 81–84.

Benjamin, J., Osher, Y., Kotler, M., Gritsenko, I., Nemanov, L., Belmaker, R. H., & Ebstein, R. P. (2000). Association between tridimensional personality questionnaire (TPQ) and three functional polymorphisms: Dopamine receptor D4 (DRD4), serotonin transporter promoter region (5-HTTLPR) and catechol O-methyltransferase (COMT). *Molecular Psychiatry*, *5*, 96–100.

Ben-Jonathan, N. (1985). Dopamine: A prolactin-inhibiting hormone. *Endocrinology Review*, *6*, 564–589.

Betarbet, R., & Greenamyre, T. J. (1999). Differential expression of glutamate receptors by the DA neurons of the primate striatum. *Experimental Neurology*, *159*, 401–408.

Björklund, A., & Lindvall, O. (1986). Catecholaminergic brain stem regulatory systems. In: American Physiological Society (Ed.), *Handbook of physiology. Section 1. The nervous system. Vol. IV. Intrinsic regulatory systems of the brain* (pp. 155–235). Bethesda, MD: American Physiological Society.

Bouchard, T. J., Jr., & Loehlin, J. C. (2001). Genes, evolution, and personality. *Behavior Genetics*, *31*, 243–273.

Brebner, J. (1983). A model of extraversion. *Australian Journal of Psychology*, *35*, 349–359.

Brebner, J. (1985). Personality theory and movement. In: B. D. Kirkcaldy (Ed.), *Individual differences in movement* (pp. 27–41). Lancaster, England: MTP Press Limited.

Brebner, J. (1990). Psychological and neurophysiological factors in stimulus-response compatibility. In: R. W. Proctor, & T. G. Reeve (Eds), *Stimulus-response compatibility: An integrated perspective* (pp. 241–260). Amsterdam: Elsevier.

Breier, A., Adler, C. M., Weisenfeld, N., Su, T. P., Elman, I., Picken, L., Malhotra, A. K., & Pickar, D. (1998a). Effects of NMDA antagonism on striatal dopamine release in healthy subjects: Application of a novel PET approach. *Synapse*, *29*, 142–147.

Breier, A., Kestler, L., Adler, C., Elman, I., Wiesenfeld, N., Malhotra, A., & Pickar, D. (1998b). Dopamine D2 receptor density and personal detachment in healthy subjects. *American Journal of Psychiatry*, *155*, 1440–1442.

de Brettes, B., Laurent, C., Lepine, J. P., Mallet, J., Puech, A. J., & Berlin, I. (1998). The dopamine D2 receptor gene Taq I A polymorphism is not associated with novelty seeking, harm avoidance and reward dependence in healthy subjects. *European Psychiatry*, *13*, 427–430.

Brodie, H. K. H., Murphy, D. L., Goodwin, F. K., & Bunney, W. E. (1971). Catecholamines and mania: The effect of Ó-methyl-para-tyrosine on manic behavior and catecholamine metabolism. *Clinical Pharmacolgy and Therapeutics*, *12*, 218–224.

Brozoski, T. J., Brown, R. M., Rosvold, H. E., & Goldman, P. (1979). Cognitive deficit caused by regional depletion of dopamine in prefrontal cortex of rhesus monkey. *Science*, *205*, 929–931.

Bullock, W. A., & Gilliland, K. (1993). Eysenck's arousal theory of introversion-extraversion: A converging measures investigation. *Journal of Personality and Social Psychology*, *64*, 113–123.

Burt, S. A., McGue, M., Iacono, W., Comings, D., & MacMurray, J. (2002). An examination of the association between DRD4 and DRD2 polymorphisms and personality traits. *Personality and Individual Differences*, *33*, 849–859.

Carey, G., Goldsmith, H. H., Tellegen, A., & Gottesman, I. I. (1978). Genetics and personality inventories: The limits of replication with twin data. *Behavior Genetics*, *8*, 299–313.

Carlsson, A., Roos, B. E., Wålinder, J., & Skott, A. (1973). Further studies on the mechanism of antipsychotic action: Potentiation by Ó-Methyltyrosine of thioridazine effects in chronic schizophrenics. *Journal of Neural Transmission*, *34*, 125–132.

Carlsson, A., Waters, N., Waters, S., & Carlsson, M. L. (2000). Network interactions in schizophrenia — therapeutic implications. *Brain Research Reviews*, *31*, 342–349.

Carlsson, M. L., & Carlsson, A. (1989). The NMDA antagonist MK-801 causes marked locomotor stimulation in monoamine-depleted mice. *Journal of Neural Transmission*, *75*, 221–226.

Carlsson, M., & Carlsson, A. (1990). Schizophrenia: A subcortical neurotransmitter imbalance syndrome? *Schizophrenia Bulletin*, *16*, 425–432.

Castro, S. L., & Zigmond, M. J. (2001). Stress-induced increase in extracellular dopamine in striatum: Role of glutamatergic action via N-methyl-D-aspartate receptors in substantia nigra. *Brain Research*, *901*, 47–54.

Cloninger, C. R., Przybeck, T. R., & Svrakic, D. M. (1991). The Tridimensional Personality Questionnaire: U.S. normative data. *Psychological Reports*, *69*, 1047–1057.

Cohen, J. D., & Servan-Schreiber, D. (1992). Context, cortex, and dopamine: A connectionist approach to behavior and biology in schizophrenia. *Psychological Review*, *99*, 45–77.

Cools, A. R., Brachten, R., Heeren, D., Willemen, A., & Ellenbroek, B. (1990). Search after neurobiologic profile of individual-specific features of Witstar rats. *Brain Research Bulletin*, *24*, 49–69.

Corr, P. J., & Kumari, V. (1997). Sociability/impulsivity and attenuated dopaminergic arousal: Critical flicker/fusion frequency and procedural learning. *Personality and Individual Differences*, *22*, 805–815.

Costa, P. T., Jr., & McCrae, R. R. (1992). *NEO PI-R. Professional manual*. Odessa, Fl.: Psychological Assessments Ressources.

David, A. S. (1995). Negative priming (cognitive inhibition) in psychiatric patients: Effect of neuroleptics. *Journal of Nervous and Mental Disease*, *183*, 337–339.

DeLong, M. R. (1990). Primate models of movement disorders of basal ganglia origin. *Trends in Neurosciences*, *13*, 281–285.

Depue, R. A., & Collins, P. F. (1999). Neurobiology of the structure of personality: Dopamine, facilitation of incentive motivation, and extraversion. *Behavioral and Brain Sciences*, *22*, 491–569.
Depue, R. A., Luciana, M., Arbisi, P., Collins, P., & Leon, A. (1994). Dopamine and the structure of personality: Relation of agonist-induced dopamine activity to positive emotionality. *Journal of Personality and Social Psychology*, *67*, 485–498.
Dick, D. M., & Rose, R. J. (2002). Behavior genetics: What's new? What's next? *Current Directions in Psychological Science*, *11*, 70–74.
Dornic, S., & Ekehammar, B. (1990). Extraversion, neuroticism, and noise sensitivity. *Personality and Individual Differences*, *11*, 989–992.
Doucet, C., & Stelmack, R. M. (1997). Movement time differentiates extraverts from introverts. *Personality and Individual Differences*, *23*, 775–786.
Doucet, C., & Stelmack, R. M. (2000). An event-related potential analysis of extraversion and individual differences in cognitive processing speed and response execution. *Journal of Personality and Social Psychology*, *78*, 956–964.
van Duijn, H., Beckmann, M. K. F., & Stoof, J. C. (1985). VEP latency delay by a single dose of haloperidol. *Electroencephalography and Clinical Neurophysiology*, *61*, 172–173.
Dunnett, S. B., & Robbins, T. W. (1992). The functional role of the mesotelencephalic dopamine systems. *Biological Review*, *67*, 491–518.
Ebmeier, K. P., Deary, I. J., O'Carrol, R. E., Prentice, N., Moffoot, A. P. R., & Goodwin, G. M. (1994). Personality associations with the uptake of the cerebral blood flow marker ^{99m}Tc-Exametazime estimated with single photon emmission tomography. *Personality and Individual Differences*, *17*, 587–595.
Ebstein, R. P., Novick, O., Umansky, R., Priel, B., Osher, Y., Blaine, D., Bennett, E. R., Nemanov, L., Katz, M., & Belmaker, R. H. (1996). Dopamine D4 receptor (DRD4) exon III polymorphism associated with the human personality trait of novelty seeking. *Nature Genetics*, *12*, 78–80.
Ekelund, J., Lichtermann, D., Jarvelin, M. R., & Peltonen, L. (1999). Association between novelty seeking and type 4-dopamine receptor gene in a large Finnish cohort sample. *American Journal of Psychiatry*, *156*, 1453–1455.
Ellenbroek, B. A., Geyer, M. A., & Cools, A. R. (1995). The behavior of APO-SUS rats in animal models with construct validity for schizophrenia. *Journal of Neuroscience*, *15*, 7604–7611.
Elliott, C. D. (1971). Noise tolerance and extraversion in children. *British Journal of Psychology*, *62*, 375–380.
Eysenck, H. J. (1967). *The biological basis of personality*. Springfield, Illinois: Thomas.
Eysenck, H. J. (1971). *Readings in extraversion-introversion. 3. Bearings on basic psychological processes*. London: Staples.
Eysenck, H. J. (1981). *A model for personality*. New York: Springer.
Eysenck, H. J. (1983). Drugs as research tools in psychology: Experiments with drugs in personality research. *Neuropsychobiology*, *10*, 29–43.
Eysenck, H. J. (1990). Genetic and environmental contributions to individual differences: The three major dimensions of personality. *Journal of Personality*, *58*, 245–261.
Eysenck, H. J. (1994). Personality: Biological foundations. In: P. A. Vernon (Ed.), *The neuropsychology of individual differences* (pp. 151–207). San Diego: Academic Press.
Eysenck, H. J. (1995). Creativity as a product of intelligence and personality. In: D. H. Saklofske, & M. Zeidner (Eds), *International handbook of personality and intelligence* (pp. 231–247). New York: Plenum Press.
Eysenck, H. J., & Eysenck, S. B. G. (1975). *Manual of the Eysenck Personality Questionnaire* (EPQ). London: Hodder & Stoughton.
Fallon, J. H., & Loughlin, S. E. (1987). Monoamine innervation of the cerebral cortex and a theory of the role of monoamines in cerebral cortex and basal ganglia. In: E. G. Jones, & A. Peters (Eds),

Cerebral cortex. Vol. 6. Further aspects of cortical function, including hippocampus (pp. 41–127). New York: Plenum Press.

Farde, L., Gustavsson, J. P., & Jonsson, E. (1997). D2 dopamine receptors and personality traits. *Nature*, *385*, 590.

Fischer, H., Wik, G., & Fredrikson, M. (1997). Extraversion, neuroticism and brain function: A PET study of personality. *Personality and Individual Differences*, *23*, 345–352.

Floderus-Myrhed, B., Pedersen, N., & Rasmuson, I. (1980). Assessment of heritability for personality, based on a short-form of the Eysenck Personality Inventory: A study of 12,898 twin pairs. *Behavior Genetics*, *10*, 153–162.

Frewer, L. J., & Hindmarch, I. (1988). The effect of time of day, age, and anxiety on a choice reaction task. In: I. Hindmarch, B. Aufdembrinke, & H. Ott (Eds), *Psychopharmacology and reaction time* (pp. 103–114). Chichester: Wiley.

Gebhardt, C., Schüssler, P., Fuchs, K., Stompe, T., Sieghart, W., Hornik, K., Kasper, S., Aschauer, H. N., & Leisch, F. (2000). Non-association of dopamine D4 and D2 receptor genes with personality in healthy individuals. *Psychiatric Genetics*, *10*, 131–137.

Geen, R. G. (1984). Preferred stimulation levels in introverts and extraverts: Effects on arousal and performance. *Journal of Personality and Social Psychology*, *46*, 1303–1312.

Glick, S. D., Hinds, P. A., & Baird, J. L. (1988). Two kinds of nigrostriatal asymmetry: Relationship to dopaminergic drug sensitivity and 6-hydroxydopamine lesion effects in Long-Evans rats. *Brain Research*, *450*, 334–341.

Gottlob, I., Schneider, E., Heider, W., & Skrandies, W. (1987). Alteration of visual evoked potentials and electroretinograms in Parkinson's disease. *Electroencephalography and Clinical Neurophysiology*, *66*, 349–357.

Gray, J. A. (1999). But the schizophrenia connection.... *Behavioral and Brain Sciences*, *22*, 523–524.

Gray, N. S., Pickering, A. D., & Gray, J. A. (1994). Psychoticism and dopamine D2 binding in the basal ganglia using single photon emission tomography. *Personality and Individual Differences*, *17*, 431–434.

Graybiel, A. M., Aosaki, T., Flaherty, A. W., & Kimura, M. (1994). The basal ganglia and adaptive motor control. *Science*, *265*, 1826–1831.

Hallett, M. (2000). Clinical physiology of dopa dyskinesia. *Annals of Neurology*, *47*(Suppl. 1), 147–153.

Harrington, D. L., Haaland, K. Y., & Hermanowicz, N. (1998). Temporal processing in the basal ganglia. *Neuropsychology*, *12*, 3–12.

Haslam, D. R. (1967). Individual differences in pain threshold and level of arousal. *British Journal of Psychology*, *58*, 139–142.

Heffner, T. G., Zigmond, M. J., & Stricker, E. M. (1977). Effects of dopaminergic agonists and antagonists on feeding in intact and 6-hydroxydopamine-treated rats. *Journal of Pharmacology and Experimental Therapeutics*, *14*, 380–399.

Hindmarch, I. (1982). Critical flicker fusion frequency (CFF): The effects of psychotropic compounds. *Pharmacopsychiatry*, *15*(Suppl. 1), 44–48.

Janke, W. (1988). Drugs as research tools in achievement research: Heinrich Düker's importance to pharmacopsychology. *Archives of Psychology*, *140*, 223–245.

Jaspers, R., & Cools, A. R. (1985). GABA-specificity of behaviour responses to picrotoxin injected into the colliculus superior of cats. *Behavioural Brain Research*, *18*, 63–69.

Jaspers, R., Schwarz, M., Sontag, K. H., & Cools, A. R. (1984). Caudate nucleus and programming behaviour in cats: Role of dopamine in switching motor patterns. *Behavioural Brain Research*, *14*, 17–28.

Johnson, D. L., Wiebe, J. S., Gold, S. M., Andreasen, N. C., Hichwa, R. D., Watkins, G. L., & Boles Ponta, L. L. (1999). Cerebral blood flow and personality: A positron emission tomography study. *American Journal of Psychiatry, 156*, 252–257.

Jönsson, E. G., Ivo, R., Gustavsson, J. P., Geijer, T., Forslund, K., Mattila-Evenden, M., Rylander, G., Cichon, S., Propping, P., Bergman, H., Asberg, M., & Nöthen, M. M. (2002). No association between dopamine D4 receptor gene variants and novelty seeking. *Molecular Psychiatry, 7*, 18–20.

Jönsson, E. G., Nöthen, M. M., Gustavsson, J. P., Neidt, H., Brené, S., Tylec, A., Propping, P., & Sedvall, G. C. (1997). Lack of evidence for allelic association between personality traits and the dopamine D4 receptor gene polymorphisms. *American Journal of Psychiatry, 154*, 697–699.

Jönsson, E. G., Nöthen, M. M., Gustavsson, J. P., Neidt, H., Forslund, K., Mattila-Evenden, M., Rylander, G., Propping, P., & Asberg, M. (1998). Lack of association between dopamine D4 receptor gene and personality traits. *Psychological Medicine, 28*, 985–989.

Kestler, L. P., Malhotra, A. K., Finch, C., Adler, C., & Breier, A. (2000). The relation between dopamine D2 receptor density and personality: Preliminary evidence from the NEO Personality Inventory-Revised. *Neuropsychiatry, Neuropsychology, and Behavioral Neurology, 13*, 48–52.

Kimberg, D. Y., D'Esposito, M., & Farah, M. J. (1997). Effects of bromocriptine on human subjects depend on working memory capacity. *Neuroreport, 8*, 3581–3585.

Köhler, C., Hall, H., Magnusson, O., Lewander, T., & Gustafsson, K. (1990). Biochemical pharmacology of the atypical neuroleptic remoxipride. *Acta Psychiatrica Scandinavica, 82*(Suppl.), 27–36.

Koob, G. F. (1992). Dopamine, addiction and reward. *Seminars in the Neurosciences, 4*, 139–148.

Kretschmer, B. (2000). NMDA receptor antagonist-induced dopamine release in the ventral pallidum does not correlate with motor activation. *Brain Research, 859*, 147–156.

Kretschmer, B. D., Goiny, M., & Herrera-Marschitz, M. (2000). Effect of intracerebral administration of NMDA and AMPA on dopamine and glutamate release in the ventral pallidum and on motor behavior. *Journal of Neurochemistry, 74*, 2049–2057.

Kumari, V., Cotter, P. A., Mulligan, O. F., Checkley, S. A., Gray, N. S., Hemsley, D. R., Thornton, J. C., Corr, P. J., Toone, B. K., & Gray, J. A. (1999). Effects of d-amphetamine and haloperidol on latent inhibition in healthy male volunteers. *Journal of Psychopharmacology, 13*, 398–405.

Kumari, V., Toone, B., & Gray, J. A. (1997). Habituation and prepulse inhibition of the acoustic startle reflex: Effects of smoking status and psychosis-proneness. *Personality and Individual Differences, 23*, 183–191.

Lawrence, A. D., Koepp, M. J., Gunn, R. N., Cunningham, V. J., & Grasby, P. M. (1999). Steps to a neurochemistry of personality. *Behavioral and Brain Sciences, 22*, 528–529.

Le Moal, M., & Simon, H. (1991). Mesocorticolimbic dopaminergic network: Functional and regulatory roles. *Physiological Reviews, 71*, 155–234.

Lieberman, M. D., & Rosenthal, R. (2001). Why introverts can't always tell who likes them: Multitasking and nonverbal decoding. *Journal of Personality and Social Psychology, 80*, 294–310.

Lienert, G. A., & Rammsayer, T. H. (1998). Relating precision of time estimation to Eysenck personality patterns by stepwise configural frequency analysis. *Studia Psychologica, 40*, 5–16.

Lubow, R. E., & Gewirtz, J. C. (1995). Latent inhibition in humans: Data, theory and implications for schizophrenia. *Psychological Bulletin, 117*, 87–103.

Lubow, R. E., Ingberg-Sachs, Y., Zalstein-Orda, N., & Gewirtz, J. C. (1992). Latent inhibition in low and high 'psychotic-prone' normal subjects. *Personality and Individual Differences, 13*, 563–572.

Lucas, R. E., & Diener, E. (2001). Understanding extraverts' enjoyment of social situations: The importance of pleasantness. *Journal of Personality and Social Psychology, 81*, 343–356.

Lucas, R. E., Diener, E., Grob, A., Suh, E. M., & Shao, L. (2000). Cross-cultural evidence for the fundamental features of extraversion. *Journal of Personality and Social Psychology, 79*, 452–468.

Luciana, M., Depue, R. A., Arbisi, P., & Leon, A. (1992). Facilitation of working memory in humans by a D2 dopamine receptor agonist. *Journal of Cognitive Neuroscience*, *4*, 58–68.

Lynn, R., & Eysenck, H. J. (1961). Tolerance for pain, extraversion and neuroticism. *Perceptual and Motor Skills*, *12*, 161–162.

Malhotra, A. K., & Goldman, D. (2000). The dopamine D-sub-4 receptor gene and novelty seeking. *American Journal of Psychiatry*, *157*, 1885–1886.

Mathew, R. J., Weinman, M. L., & Barr, D. L. (1984). Personality and regional cerebral blood flow. *British Journal of Psychiatry*, *144*, 529–532.

Mink, J. W. (1999). Basal ganglia. In: M. J. Zigmond, F. E. Bloom, S. C. Landis, J. L. Roberts, & L. R. Squire (Eds), *Fundamental neuroscience* (pp. 951–972). San Diego: Academic Press.

Mitsuyasu, H., Hirata, N., Sakai, Y., Shibata, H., Takeda, K., Ninomiya, H., Kawasaki, H., Tashiro, N., & Fukumaki, Y. (2001). Association analysis of polymorphisms in the upstream region of the human dopamine D4 receptor gene (DRD4) with schizophrenia and personality traits. *Journal of Human Genetics*, *46*, 26–31.

Müller, U., von Cramon, D. Y., & Pollmann, S. (1998). D1- vs. D2-receptor modulation of visuospatial working memory in humans. *Journal of Neuroscience*, *18*, 2720–2728.

Muniz-Fernandez, J., & Paz-Caballero, M. D. (1984). Tiempo de reaccion y personalidad [Reaction time and personality]. *Informes de Psicologia*, *3*, 153–161.

Noble, E. P., Ozkaragoz, T. Z., Ritchie, T. L., Zhang, X., Belin, T. R., & Sparkes, R. S. (1998). D2 and D4 dopamine receptor polymorphisms and personality. *American Journal of Medical Genetics*, *81*, 257–267.

Ögren, S.-O., Florvall, L., Hall, H., Magnusson, O., & Ängeby-Möller, K. (1990). Neuropharmacological and behavioural properties of remoxipride in the rat. *Acta Psychiatrica Scandinavica*, *82*(Suppl.), 21–26.

Okuyama, Y., Ishiguro, H., Nankai, M., Shibuya, H., Watanabe, A., & Arinami, T. (2000). Identification of a polymorphism in the promoter region of DRD4 associated with the human novelty seeking personality trait. *Molecular Psychiatry*, *5*, 64–69.

Ono, Y., Manki, H., Yoshimura, K., Muramatsu, T., Mizushima, H., Higuchi, S., Yagi, G., Kanba, S., & Asai, M. (1997). Association between dopamine D4 receptor (D4DR) exon III polymorphism and novelty seeking in Japanese subjects. *American Journal of Medical Genetics*, *74*, 501–503.

Pedersen, N. L., Plomin, R., McClearn, G. E., & Friberg, L. (1988). Neuroticism, extraversion, and related traits in adult twins reared apart and reared together. *Journal of Personality and Social Psychology*, *55*, 950–957.

Persson, M. L., Wasserman, D., Geijer, T., Frisch, A., Rockah, R., Michaelovski, E., Apter, A., Weizman, A., Joensson, E. G., & Bergman, H. (2000). Dopamine D4 receptor gene polymorphism and personality traits in healthy volunteers. *European Archives of Psychiatry and Clinical Neuroscience*, *250*, 203–206.

Petrie, A. (1967). *Individuality in pain and suffering*. Chicago: University of Chicago Press.

Pickering, A. D., & Gray, J. A. (2001). Dopamine, appetitive reinforcement, and the neuropsychology of human learning: An individual differences approach. In: A. Eliasz, & A. Angleitner (Eds), *Advances in research on temperament* (pp. 111–149). Lengerich, Germany: Pabst Science Publishers.

Pivik, R. T., Stelmack, R. M., & Bylsma, F. W. (1988). Personality and individual differences in spinal motoneuronal excitability. *Psychophysiology*, *25*, 16–24.

Pogue-Geile, M., Ferrell, R., Deka, R., Debski, T., & Manuck, S. (1998). Human novelty-seeking personality traits and dopamine D4 receptor polymorphisms: A twin and genetic association study. *American Journal of Medical Genetics*, *81*, 44–48.

Pollack, A. E. (2001). Anatomy, physiology, and pharmacology of the basal ganglia. *Neurologic Clinics*, *19*, 523–534.

Rammsayer, T. (1995). Extraversion and alcohol: Eysenck's drug postulate revisited. *Neuropsychobiology*, *32*, 197–207.
Rammsayer, T. (1997). Are there dissociable roles of the mesostriatal and mesolimbocortical dopamine systems on temporal information processing in humans? *Neuropsychobiology*, *35*, 36–45.
Rammsayer, T. (1998). Extraversion and dopamine: Individual differences in responsiveness to changes in dopaminergic activity as a possible biological basis of extraversion. *European Psychologist*, *3*, 37–50.
Rammsayer, T. (1999). Neuropharmacological evidence for different timing mechanisms in humans. *Quarterly Journal of Experimental Psychology, Section B: Comparative and Physiological Psychology*, *52*, 273–286.
Rammsayer, T. (2003). NMDA receptor activity and the transmission of sensory input into motor output in introverts and extraverts. *Quarterly Journal of Experimental Psychology, Section B: Comparative and Physiological Psychology*, *56B*, 207–221.
Rammsayer, T., & Stahl, J. (2004). Extraversion-related differences in response organization: Evidence from lateralized readiness potentials. *Biological Psychology*, *66*, 35–49.
Rammsayer, T., Netter, P., & Vogel, W. H. (1993). A neurochemical model underlying differences in reaction times between introverts and extraverts. *Personality and Individual Differences*, *14*, 701–712.
Robbins, T. W., & Everitt, B. J. (1987). Psychopharmacological studies of arousal and attention. In: S. M. Stahl, S. D. Iversen, & E. C. Goodman (Eds), *Cognitive neurochemistry* (pp.135–170). Oxford: Oxford University Press.
Robbins, T. W., & Everitt, B. J. (1995). Arousal systems and attention. In: M. S. Gazzaniga (Ed.), *The cognitive neurosciences* (pp. 703–720). Cambridge, MA: MIT Press.
Robinson, T. E., & Berridge, K. C. (2000). The psychology and neurobiology of addiction: An incentive-sensitization view. *Addiction*, *95*(Suppl. 2), 91–117.
Rots, N. Y., Cools, A. R., Oitzl, M. S., de Jong, J., Sutanto, W., & de Kloet, E. R. (1996). Divergent prolactin and pituitary-adrenal activity in rats selectively bred for different dopamine responsiveness. *Endocrinology*, *137*, 1678–1686.
Russell, R. W. (1987). Drugs as tools for research in neuropsychobiology: A historical perspective. *Neuropsychobiology*, *18*, 134–143.
Salamone, J. D. (1994). The involvement of nucleus accumbens dopamine in appetitive and aversive motivation. *Behavioural Brain Research*, *61*, 117–133.
Salamone, J. D., Kurth, P. A., McCullough, L. D., Sokolowski, J. D., & Cousins, M. S. (1993). The role of brain dopamine in response initiation: Effects of haloperidol and regionally specific dopamine depletion on the local rate of instrumental responding. *Brain Research*, *628*, 218–226.
Sander, T., & Schmidt, L. G. (1994). Molecular biological perspectives in treating neuropsychiatric disorders with dopaminergic drugs. *Pharmacopsychiatry*, *27*(Suppl.), 11–14.
Sanders, A. F. (1998). *Elements of human performance: Reaction processes and attention in human skill*. Hillsdale, NJ: Lawrence Erlbaum Associates.
Sandyk, R. (1990). The significance of eye blink rate in Parkinsonism: A hypothesis. *International Journal of Neuroscience*, *51*, 99–103.
Sawaguchi, T., Matsumura, M., & Kubota, K. (1988). Dopamine enhances the neuronal activity of spatial short-term memory task in the primate prefrontal cortex. *Neuroscience Research*, *5*, 465–473.
Sawaguchi, T., Matsumura, M., & Kubota, K. (1990). Effects of dopamine antagonists on neuronal activity related to a delayed response task in monkey prefrontal cortex. *Journal of Neurophysiology*, *63*, 1401–1412.
Schalling, D. (1971). Tolerance for experimentally induced pain as related to personality. *Scandinavian Journal of Psychology*, *12*, 271–281.

Schalling, D., Asberg, M., Edman, G., & Oreland, L. (1987). Markers for vulnerability to psychopathology: Temperament traits associated with platelet MAO activity. *Acta Psychiatrica Scandinavica, 76*, 172–182.

Seeman, P. (1990). Atypical neuroleptics: Role of multiple receptors, endogenous dopamine, and receptor linkage. *Acta Psychiatrica Scandinavica, 82*(Suppl.), 14–20.

Shepherd, G. M. (1988). *Neurobiology*. New York: Oxford University Press.

Shigehisa, T., & Symons, J. R. (1973). Effect of intensity of visual stimulation on auditory sensitivity in relation to personality. *British Journal of Psychology, 64*, 205–213.

Simons, R. F., & Giardina, B. D. (1992). Reflex modification in psychosis-prone young adults. *Psychophysiology, 29*, 8–16.

Smith, G. S., Schloesser, R., Brodie, J. D., Dewey, S. L., Logan, J., Vitkun, S. A., Simkowitz, P., Hurley, A., Cooper, T., Volkow, N. D., & Cancro, R. (1998). Glutamate modulation of dopamine measured in vivo with positron emission tomography (PET) and ^{11}C-raclopride in normal human subjects. *Neuropsychopharmacology, 18*, 18–25.

Smith, J. M., & Misiak, H. (1976). Critical flicker frequency (CFF) and psychotropic drugs in normal human subjects. *Psychopharmacology, 47*, 175–182.

Smith, S. L. (1968). Extraversion and sensory threshold. *Psychophysiology, 5*, 293–299.

Sokolowski, J. D., McCullough, L. D., & Salamone, J. D. (1994). Effects of dopamine depletion in the medial prefrontal cortex on active avoidance and escape in the rat. *Brain Research, 651*, 293–299.

Stelmack, R. M. (1985). Personality and motor activity: A psychophysiological perspective. In: B. D. Kirkcaldy (Ed.), *Individual differences in movement* (pp. 192–213). Lancaster, England: MTP Press Limited.

Stelmack, R. M., Achorn, E., & Michaud, A. (1977). Extraversion and individual differences in auditory evoked responses. *Psychophysiology, 14*, 368–374.

Stelmack, R. M., & Campbell, K. B. (1974). Extraversion and auditory sensitivity to high and low frequency. *Perceptual and Motor Skills, 38*, 875–879.

Stelmack, R. M., Houlihan, M., & McGarry-Roberts, P. A. (1993). Personality, reaction time, and event-related potentials. *Journal of Personality and Social Psychology, 65*, 399–409.

Stelmack, R. M., & Michaud-Achorn, A. (1985). Extraversion, attention, and habituation of the auditory evoked response. *Journal of Research in Personality, 19*, 416–428.

Stelmack, R. M., & Pivik, R. T. (1996). Extraversion and the effects of exercise on spinal motoneuronal excitability. *Personality and Individual Differences, 21*, 69–76.

Stenberg, G., Risberg, J., Warkentin, S., & Rosen, I. (1990). Regional patterns of cortical blood flow distinguish extraverts from introverts. *Personality and Individual Differences, 11*, 663–673.

Stenberg, G., Wendt, P. E., & Risberg, J. (1993). Regional cerebral blood flow and extraversion. *Personality and Individual Differences, 15*, 547–554.

Sternberg, S. (1969). The discovery of processing stages: Extensions to Donder's method. *Acta Psychologica, 30*, 276–315.

Sternberg, S. (1998). Discovering mental processing stages: The method of additive factors. In: D. Scarborough, & S. Sternberg (Eds), *Methods, models, and conceptual issues* (Vol. 4, pp. 703–863). Cambridge, Massachusetts: MIT Press.

Stricker, E. M., & Zigmond, M. J. (1986). Brain monoamines, homeostasis, and adaptive behavior. In: American Physiological Society (Ed.), *Handbook of physiology. Section 1. The nervous system. Vol. IV. Intrinsic regulatory systems of the brain* (pp. 677–700). Bethesda, MD: American Physiological Society.

Strobel, A., Wehr, A., Michel, A., & Brocke, B. (1999). Association between the dopamine D4 receptor (DRD4) exon III polymorphism and measures of novelty seeking in a German population. *Molecular Psychiatry, 4*, 378–384.

Svensson, K., & Carlsson, M. L. (1992). Injection of the competitive NMDA receptor antagonist AP-5 into the nucleus accumbens of monoamine-depleted mice induces pronounced locomotor stimulation. *Neuropharmacology*, *31*, 513–518.

Swerdlow, N. R., Filion, D., Geyer, M. A., & Braff, D. L. (1995). "Normal" personality correlates of sensorimotor, cognitive, and visuospatial gating. *Biological Psychiatry*, *37*, 286–299.

Taylor, J. R., Elsworth, J. D., Lawrence, M. S., Sladek, J. R., Roth, R. H., & Redmond, D. E., Jr. (1999). Spontaneous blink rates correlate with dopamine levels in the caudate nucleus of MPTP-treated monkeys. *Experimental Neurology*, *158*, 214–220.

Tellegen, A. (1995). *Manual for Multidimensional Personality Questionnaire*. Minneapolis: University of Minnesota Press.

Tellegen, A., Lykken, D. T., Bouchard, T. J., Wilcox, K., Segal, N., & Rich, S. (1988). Personality similarity in twins reared apart and together. *Journal of Personality and Social Psychology*, *54*, 1031–1039.

Theios, J. (1975). The comparison of response latency in simple human information processing tasks. In: P. M. A. Rabbitt, & S. Dornic (Eds), *Attention and performance* (Vol. 5, pp. 418–440). London: Academic Press.

Tomitaka, M., Tomitaka, S., Otuka, Y., Kim, K., Matuki, H., Sakamoto, K., & Tanaka, A. (1999). Association between novelty seeking and dopamine receptor D4 (DRD4) exon III polymorphism in Japanese subjects. *American Journal of Medical Genetics*, *88*, 469–471.

Tzschentke, T. M. (2001). Pharmacology and behavioral pharmacology of the mesostriatal dopamine system. *Progress in Neurobiology*, *63*, 241–320.

Vandenbergh, D. J., Zonderman, A. B., Wang, J., Uhl, G. R., & Costa, P. T., Jr. (1997). No association between novelty seeking and dopamine D4 receptor (D4DR) exon III seven repeat alleles in the Baltimore longitudinal study of aging participants. *Molecular Psychiatry*, *2*, 417–419.

Vollenweider, F. X., Vontobel, P., Oye, I., Hell, D., & Leenders, K. L. (2000). Effects of (S)-ketamine on striatal dopamine: A [^{11}C]raclopride PET study of a model psychosis in humans. *Journal of Psychiatric Research*, *34*, 35–43.

Waters, N., Lundgren, C., Hansson, L. O., & Carlsson, M. L. (1996). Concurrent locomotor stimulation and decrease in dopamine in rats and mice after treatment with the competitive NMDA receptor antagonists D-CPPene and CGS 19755. *Journal of Neural Transmission*, *103*, 117–129.

Weinstein, N. D. (1978). Individual differences in reactions to noise: A longitudinal study in a college dormitory. *Journal of Applied Psychology*, *63*, 458–466.

Weiss, B. (1988). Modulation of adrenergic receptors during aging. *Neurobiology of Aging*, *9*, 61–62.

Westlind-Danielsson, A., Gustafsson, K., & Andersson, I. (1994). Remoxipride shows low propensity to block functional striatal dopamine D2 receptors in vitro. *European Journal of Pharmacology*, *288*, 89–95.

Williams, L. M. (1995). Further evidence for a multidimensional personality disposition to schizophrenia in terms of cognitive inhibition. *British Journal of Clinical Psychology*, *34*, 193–213.

Zigmond, M. J., Heffner, T. G., & Stricker, E. M. (1980). The effect of altered dopaminergic activity on food intake in the rat: Evidence for an optimal level of dopaminergic activity for behavior. *Progress in Neuro-Psychopharmacology and Biological Psychiatry*, *4*, 351–362.

Zuckerman, M. (1991). *Psychobiology of personality*. Cambridge: Cambridge University Press.

Chapter 22

On the Psychobiology of Impulsivity

B. af Klinteberg, L. von Knorring and L. Oreland

1. Introduction

Impulsivity seems to be a very basic personality trait, both in psychiatric syndromes and personality disorders, with a high genetic component. Impulsive personality/behavior has therefore become an interesting area for both geneticists and researchers in the psychological field. There is strong support for the view that genetic factors interact with the environment in influencing and contributing to the development of impulsive personality/behavior. This, in turn, indicates an enhanced risk to develop different forms of psychosocial disturbances. In this chapter, some perspectives on the complexity of psychosocial and psychogenetic associations with impulsivity will be illustrated, as well as the possible nature of some biological factors underlying personality/behavior.

2. Psychological Aspects of Impulsivity

2.1. Impulsivity as a Personality Trait: Its Role in Different Models of Personality

Impulsivity is a prominent personality trait both in healthy subjects, psychiatric syndromes and personality disorders. According to the theoretical formulations by Eysenck and Eysenck (1975), impulsivity was originally part of the extraversion concept based on an optimal level of arousal theory. However, it was repeatedly pointed out by Schalling (1978) that Extraversion (E) in the Eysenck Personality Inventory (EPI; Eysenck & Eysenck 1964) was composed of both Sociability and Impulsiveness. Later, when the Eysenck Personality Questionnaire (EPQ; Eysenck & Eysenck 1975) was introduced, impulsiveness was included in the Psychoticism dimension, while sociability was kept in the E scale (Schalling 1978). These changes gave rise to the results that tobacco smoking, strongly related to impulsivity, correlated with E on the EPI (e.g. Eysenck *et al.* 1960), while in the EPQ a stronger relation was demonstrated between tobacco smoking and Psychoticism (von Knorring & Oreland 1985; McManus & Weeks 1982), indicating the importance

On the Psychobiology of Personality
Edited by R. M. Stelmack

ISBN: 0-08-044209-9

of impulsivity as a personality trait. Additional findings suggested that the Psychoticism dimension, including impulsivity, is associated with psychopathy and lack of conformity to social norms (Robinson & Zahn 1985). Gray *et al.* (1983) included susceptibility to signals of reward and punishment into his model of impulsivity/anxiety in describing the dimensions of introversion-extraversion. Zuckerman (1979, 1991) also developed a psychobiological approach to impulsivity. He developed an optimal level of arousal theory of sensation seeking as a main component in disinhibitory behavior (Zuckerman 1994). In his model, impulsivity is mainly related to the Disinhibition subscale of the Sensation Seeking Scale (SSS) while Sociability and Novelty Seeking is included in the Thrill and Adventure Seeking and Experience Seeking scales. In the Karolinska Scales of Personality (KSP) constructed during the 1970s by Schalling, the dimensions of impulsivity and novelty seeking are included in the impulsiveness and monotony avoidance scales (Schalling *et al.* 1987). The latter scale is closely related to the SSS. The Impulsiveness scale is related to "subsolidity" in the personality dimensional system described by the Swedish psychiatrist Sjöbring (Essen-Möller 1980).

Impulsivity seems to be a very basic trait with a high genetic component (Seroczynski *et al.* 1999). It has been suggested that impulsivity may eventually be a more productive target for study than any of the currently available personality disorders (Ruegg & Frances 1995), and there is an ongoing discussion on impulsivity, its multidisciplinary characteristics and its psychiatric and social consequences (Barratt & Slaughter 1998; Ruegg & Frances 1995). In the present chapter, results from different research groups on the issue of impulsivity will be reviewed and related to psychosocial disturbances. However, different research groups define impulsivity differently, and impulsivity scales load on different parts of the personality spectrum. The impulsiveness scale as used in the KSP is, according to a factor analytical study reported by Zuckerman, closely related to the Psychoticism-Unsocialized Sensation Seeking factor (Figure 1).

2.2. Impulsivity in a Longitudinal Perspective

It is of interest to note that results from previous studies report that the most important indicators for the development of various aspects of psychosocial disturbance is childhood hyperactive behavior, early impulsivity and antisocial behavior. These predictors overlap somewhat with the vulnerabilities that have been found in studies of antisocial personality disorder (APD). According to the Diagnostic and Statistical Manual of Mental Disorder, 4th ed. (DSM-IV; Americam Psychiatric Association, 1994), APD emerged from the early research of Robins (1966) who described a disturbance featuring irresponsibility and antisocial behavior, an inability to feel guilt, and evidence that the disturbance was present during adolescence.

Another form of APD is psychopathic personality, originally described by Cleckley (1976) and later by Hare in the Psychopathy Check List (PCL; Hare 1985). This is a personality disturbance that through psychiatric diagnosis can be compared to APD, but is better defined in terms of personality characteristics and behaviors, i.e, high impulsivity, constant seeking of new and powerful experiences, disinhibitory disturbances, lack of responsibility, incapability of empathy and an unstable emotional life. These features are

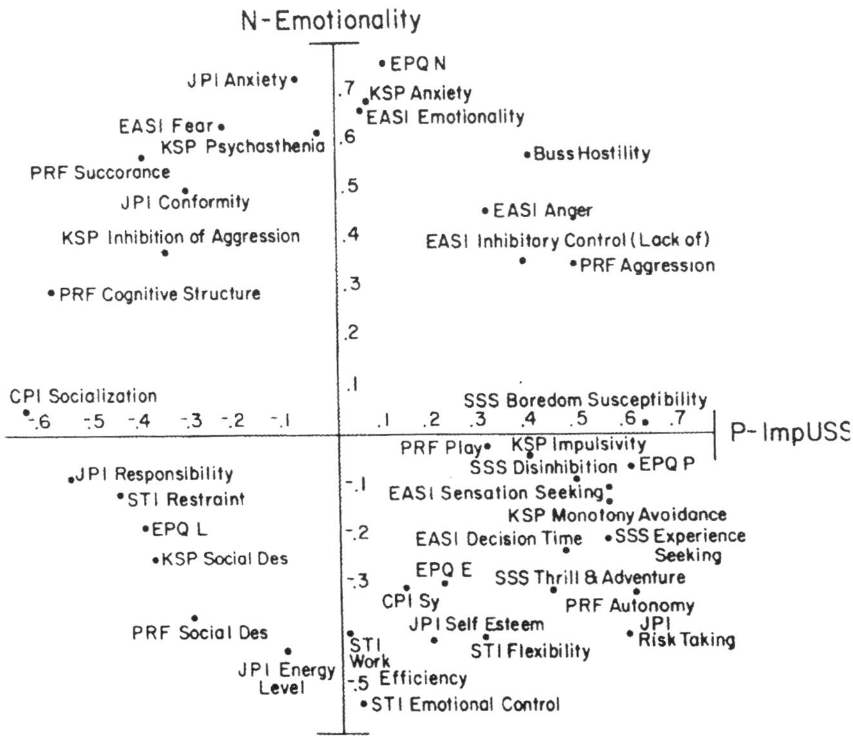

Figure 1: Factor loadings of personality scales plotted on the neuroticism (N) emotionality, and psychcotism unsocialized sensation seeking (P-ImpUSS) dimensions. *Note:* Reprinted from M. Zuckerman (1989), Personality in the third dimension: A psychobiological approach, *Personality and Individual Differences, 10*, p. 397 with permission from Pergamon Press Plc.

manifested in lack of respect for others and, when the social network is weak, in an inability to empathize with others. Later factor analyses of the PCL construct on adolescent and adult samples indicated three-factor solutions of the PCL that underscored the importance of the impulsivity dimension (Cooke & Michie 2001; Frick *et al.* 2000; af Klinteberg *et al.* 1992). The following were identified as vulnerable dispositions to the development of APD disturbances: (1) indications of childhood hyperactive behavior; (2) early impulsivity; and (3) deficient impulse control.

In further studies, subgroups among children with hyperactivity were found to display a certain vulnerability to develop APD, psychopathic behaviors and substance abuse as adults. They were also found to have greater difficulties with school and in their workplace (Mannuzza *et al.* 1993). In addition, findings suggest a higher prevalence of psychopathy within these families (Pfiffner *et al.* 1999). Results in a number of studies also demonstrate specific polygenetic characteristics in the dopaminergic system for different behavior disturbances. Hyperactive behavior is one example of this (Comings *et al.* 1996). This is important for the development of future support systems needed by these children.

During childhood development, the hyperactive syndrome complicates a child's working interaction with the environment and becomes a fundamental disturbance by which other kinds of problems arise. The disturbances are evident within three areas: social relations, personality and emotional well-being, and behavior.

Findings supporting the notion that childhood hyperactive behavior is a precursor of adult antisocial behavior were replicated in numerous internationally known longitudinal programs (Farrington 1995; Loeber & Farrington 2000; Magnusson *et al.* 1994; Satterfield & Schell 1997). Similarly, it was reported that hyperactive behaviors increase the risk for future alcohol dependence (Cloninger *et al.* 1988; Comings *et al.* 1996; Mannuzza *et al.* 1993). Models that attempt to explain the origin of antisocial behavior and alcohol dependence emphasize either psychosocial or genetic factors. Currently, it is well known that these two perspectives complement each other, especially when individual development is studied from an interactionistic perspective. Through empirical research, a common psychobiological basis has been found between substance abuse, hyperactive behavior, and antisocial behavior, especially with regard to the personality characteristic impulsivity and its biological indicators. Moreover, results showed that impulsivity is associated with both alcohol problems and antisocial behavior. Similarly, hyperactivity is associated with both of these psychosocial disturbances. Biological determinants are of major importance regarding the aspects of antisocial behavior that are related to aggression and violent behavior (see below).

2.3. *Age as a Pathoplastic Factor in the Expression of Impulsivity*

Impulsivity tends to decrease with increasing age. This was demonstrated, for example, by a negative correlation between age and the impulsiveness scale in the KSP as well as in the later Swedish universities Scales of Personality (Gustavsson *et al.* 2000). Furthermore, in children with Attention Deficit Hyperactivity Disorders (ADHD) who were followed from childhood to adult life, the impulsive, hyperactive behavior seems to decline over time, while the attention deficit tends to remain in about 25% of the subjects (Socialstyrelsen 2002).

2.4. *Sex Differences in the Expression of Impulsivity*

Although impulsivity is evident in both men and women, the phenotypic expression might differ. In the Stockholm adoption study, it was demonstrated that there are at least two types of alcoholism (Cloninger *et al.* 1981). Type I alcoholism was observed in both men and women. Type II alcoholism was only observed in males. It was characterized by early onset and an increased frequency of social difficulties. When the clinical characteristics were defined (von Knorring *et al.* 1985), it was found that Type II alcoholism was strongly related to impulsivity. It was previously found that females with a genetic predisposition for Type II alcoholism had no increased risk of alcoholism or criminality (von Knorring 1983). Instead, they had an increased risk of somatization disorder. Later, von Knorring *et al.* (1986) demonstrated a similar biological basis for males with Type II alcoholism and females with somatization disorder. Furthermore, it is well known that the personality disorders in the DSM system related to impulsivity have pronounced sex differences (Ekselius *et al.* 1996). Thus, APD is much more common among males, while borderline personality disorder is more common among females.

2.5. Other Factors Influencing the Expression of Impulsivity

In a large sample of young adult males, it was demonstrated that impulsivity and sensation seeking personality traits, notably Thrill and Adventure Seeking and Experience Seeking, in subjects with high intellectual level and with good social resources, are related to high achievement in the military services (von Knorring *et al.* 1984). Impulsivity and sensation seeking in subjects with lower intellectual level and with fewer social resources are related to use and abuse of alcohol and illegal drugs.

2.6. Normal and Abnormal Aspects of Impulsivity

The degree to which impulsivity might be the underlying factor to the susceptibility of comorbidity of drug abuse and violence appears to be high. Extreme levels of impulsivity imply an inability to comprehend the consequences of one's own actions. Some studies suggest that impulsivity is closely related to the expression of aggression, especially the destructive aspects of violent behavior that are fostered by alcohol or drug use. This means that persons who score high on impulsivity and, in addition, are vulnerable to disinhibitory tendencies, often act destructively in stressful situations. They also display lack of patience and are unable to structure their tasks at work effectively.

Patterns of hyperactivity and later social misbehaviors, such as alcohol dependency and violent crimes, were investigated (af Klinteberg *et al.* 1993). The results suggested that childhood hyperactive behaviors are related to alcohol problems later in life. Further, childhood hyperactive behavior was related to violence against another person. In order to determine if these adaptation problems occurred within the same individual more often than by chance, pattern analysis was used, specifically configural frequency analysis (Krauth & Lienert 1982). Two significant types emerged. One type showed that hyperactivity is closely related to alcohol problems and crimes of violence in adulthood. The other type exhibited the common combination of low display of hyperactive behavior in childhood, no problems with alcohol, and no violent crimes.

It may be of interest to note, that in this study of hyperactivity in normal adolescents, the occurrence of violence together with alcohol dependency and early hyperactive behaviors in the same individual occurred ten times as often as expected by chance. If viewed from a problem perspective, it is even more interesting to note that violent criminality without alcohol problems, as well as violent criminality without hyperactivity, occurred in only one out of three individuals as expected by chance. These results were recently replicated in another longitudinal program on juvenile delinquents and controls (Eklund & af Klinteberg 2003). Additional aggressiveness worsened the outcome. This is consistent with findings by Biederman *et al.* (1996) that comorbid ADHD and conduct disorder are associated with an enhanced risk for alcohol and drug dependence at follow-up.

Biological deviances are found in highly impulsive persons, not only within groups of patients and criminals but also within normal groups (Barratt & Patton 1983; Schalling 1993). The finding of a connection between impulsivity and biological indicators even in normal adolescents and adults support the hypothesis that a biological vulnerability can be present within an individual without the expresson of a psychosocial disturbance if protective resources are available within the individual or in the individual's surrounding environment.

3. Impulsivity in Specific Psychological States

3.1. Personality Disorders: Focusing on the DSM — Cluster B Disorders

The impulse control disorders in the DSM include several rather separate disorders both on Axis I and Axis II. On Axis I, these impulse control disorders include intermittent explosive disorder, kleptomania, pathological gambling, pyromania, trichotillomania (compulsion to pull out one's hair), repetitive self-mutilation, compulsive shopping, and compulsive sexual behavior. On Axis II the impulse control disorders include borderline personality disorder and APD. However, within Axis II a considerable comorbidity has been demonstrated both within Cluster B and between the three Clusters A, B, and C (Ekselius *et al.* 1994).

By means of the subgrouping definition of alcoholism into Type I and Type II, Type II alcoholics are characterized by early onset, use and abuse not only of alcohol, but also of glue, cannabis, amphetamine and opioids together with several social complications. The subjects with Type II alcoholism also have more alcoholism and depression among their first-degree relatives than the subjects with Type I alcoholism. The Type II alcoholics have increased scores in the SSS and the E scale in the EPI as well as low levels of platelet monoamine oxidase (MAO) activity. Low platelet MAO activity is considered a biological marker of vulnerability for disinhibition and psychosocial deviances, and is repeatedly shown to be associated with high impulsivity (Oreland *et al.* 2002a, and below). Impulsivity, in turn, is a major predictor of adult antisocial and delinquent behaviors as demonstrated in a series of prospective studies (Farrington 1995; af Klinteberg 1996; Tremblay & LeMarquand 2001; White *et al.* 1994).

3.2. Use and Abuse of Alcohol and Drugs

From a social point of view, findings in studies of impulsive aggression indicate an accepting attitude to various actions and behaviors in certain situations. One such situation is when alcohol is involved. This means that if society accepts a certain degree of violence as a normal concomitant of alcohol consumption, there may be an increase in the risk that alcohol may lead to aggressive and violent behavior. The support for a link between alcohol and violence is of major importance. Multiple studies in several countries suggest that from 65 to 80% of all violent crimes are committed under the influence of alcohol. Current studies are focussing on identifying the factors that determine this link in order to improve our understanding of what initiates the process. Within the interactive-based personality psychology, there is an assumption that individuals who are at risk for developing disinhibitory tendencies become extremely vulnerable to situations that evoke aggression when under the influence of alcohol. Moreover, under this influence, these individuals tend to lower their already weak inhibition functioning. Thus, they are at great risk to act violently when under the influence of alcohol. Early behavioral manifestations of adaptation disturbances are closely related to the development of disinhibitory symptoms.

3.3. Disinhibitory Syndromes — Imbalanced Biological Systems?

Impulsivity is a differential characteristic in individuals with disinhibitory syndromes, such as alcohol dependence, and suicidal, hyperactive and psychopathic tendencies. More precisely, impulsivity takes on different expressions in the lifestyles of these individuals, i.e. they talk and act before they think; they make decisions on a whim; they do not learn from their mistakes; and they lack well-functioning inhibitory mechanisms, which theoretically has been linked to a disturbance of the frontal lobes. Thus, the concept of impulsivity is connected to both motor (motor disinhibition) and cognitive functions (non-planning style).

Research has shown that indicators of a weak or an unstable serotonin system are related to aggressive behavior and lack of inhibitory control. Disinhibitory syndromes are mainly characterized by deficient control of impulses (Bongioanni 1991; Gorenstein & Newman 1980; Schalling *et al.* 1988; Soubrié 1986). Further, a strong association appears to exist between actions based on impulsivity and aggression and low serotonin activity, as well as a specific link between the impulsivity aspect and different kinds of violence (Lidberg *et al.* 1985; Linnoila *et al.* 1983; Virkkunen & Linnoila 1993; Virkkunen *et al.* 1994). When groups of persons with this form of disturbance are studied (e.g. hyperactive children and psychopaths), not only are discrepancies found in the development of the neuro-chemical functions of the central nervous system, as indicated, for example, by the biological marker platelet MAO (see below), but there are also various forms of imbalance in the autonomic and the endocrine systems (Zuckerman 2003). These results are also consistent with findings of work conducted with normal populations (Braun & Hodgins 1995; af Klinteberg 2000; LaPierre *et al.* 1995; Lewis 1991; Satterfield 1987; Schalling 1978, 1993).

It is worth noting that seven out of ten persons who were characterized by both alcohol and violence problems in the study by af Klinteberg *et al.* (1993) were also rated high in hyperactive components such as motor restlessness and concentration problems by the age of 13 years. These findings support previous results reported from the same longitudinal program (Magnusson 1988) indicating that hyperactive behavior in childhood is an important precursor to impulsivity in adulthood (af Klinteberg *et al.* 1989). Because biological measures, such as MAO activity, are relatively stable over time, it was assumed that only the impulsivity aspect of hyperactivity would be related to biological indicators. In additional studies, impulsivity was consistently related to substance abuse, criminal behavior and psychopathic characteristics (Blackburn 1969; Cloninger *et al.* 1988; af Klinteberg *et al.* 1992; von Knorring *et al.* 1987; Rydelius 1983).

4. Neurobiological Aspects on Impulsivity and Psychosocial Disturbances

4.1. Platelet MAO Activity as a Marker for Impulsivity and Sensation Seeking

As noted above, enzyme platelet MAO activity is of particular interest in understanding the biological bases for disinhibited personality traits and different forms of psychosocial disturbances (for reviews, see Oreland 1993; Oreland *et al.* 2002a). There are two different MAO proteins, MAO-A and MAO-B. However, in human platelets only MAO-B is extant. Platelet MAO activity is expressed in a stable fashion over several decades, with a small increase after the age of 40 (Bridge *et al.* 1985; Murphy 1976; Robinson *et al.* 1972). Several reports have shown a high degree of heritability for MAO activity, e.g. Nies *et al.* (1973). In two studies on twins, a heritability factor of about 0.75 was found for MAO activity in both males and females (Oxenstierna *et al.* 1986; Pedersen *et al.* 1993). The associations between personality/behavior and platelet MAO-B, although confirmed in numerous ways, seem to be of a subtle nature. Our present notion is that these associations reflect common transcriptional regulation mechanisms of this enzyme and of specific brain structures, rather than a direct causal relationship.

Thus, no associations with personality/behavior have so far involved polymorphisms of the MAO-B gene. Not even a complete inactivation of the gene in MAO-B knock-out mice induces any easily observed changes in behavior (Garpenstrand *et al.* 2000; Holschneider *et al.* 2001). Furthermore, MAO-B activity was almost completely inhibited in a large number of patients with Parkinson's disease who received the irreversible and selective MAO-B inhibitor selegiline. Again, there were no obvious changes in personality. For these reasons, it seems unlikely that the associations between platelet MAO-B and personality could be explained by a parallelism between brain and platelet MAO-B activities. This notion is supported by results where no such parallelism could be demonstrated in a study, which directly addressed that question (Winblad *et al.* 1979).

4.2. Platelet MAO and the Vulnerability Hypothesis

There is good support for the finding that alcoholics exhibit low levels of platelet MAO (for a review, see von Knorring & Oreland 1996). This low activity appears to be constitutional rather than an effect of alcohol consumption (Wiberg *et al.* 1977). It was also speculated that platelet MAO could act as a genetic marker for the central serotonin system, a hypothesis which is still consistent with current research. Concerning the concept of Type I and Type II alcoholism, Type I alcoholics have, in principle, a low degree of heretability (genetic load) for alcoholism, a late debut of the abuse and few coinciding social complications. Type II alcoholics, on the other hand, have a strong genetic load, and as noted above an early debut of the abuse and several social complications. In line with expectations, it was found that low platelet MAO activity was mainly confined to Type II alcoholics.

The vulnerability hypothesis (Buchsbaum *et al.* 1976; Murphy 1976) proposed that low platelet MAO activity is associated with personality traits that increase the vulnerability for drug abuse and social maladaptation. It was found that the Type II alcoholics were characterized by a personality pattern of Impulsiveness, Sensation Seeking and E (von Knorring *et al.* 1986). In this way, the Type I/II concept for alcoholism, in combination with results with platelet MAO, both demonstrated the clinical usefulness of the vulnerability hypothesis of Buchsbaum *et al.* (1976) and envisaged a link between biology and disposition for alcoholism. The connection between low activity of platelet MAO and personality characteristics, such as sensation seeking, impulsiveness, monotony avoidance, and to some degree, aggression, was later replicated in several studies on healthy controls (af Klinteberg *et al.* 1987; von Knorring *et al.* 1984; Oreland 1993). Recently, the personality trait of Novelty Seeking in the Temperament and Character Inventory (TCI; Cloninger *et al.* 1994) was reported to be a powerful mediator between platelet MAO and externalizing psychopathology (Ruchkin *et al.* 2003).

There is also an association between platelet MAO activity and neuro-psychological measures (af Klinteberg *et al.* 1991). Response time in a computerized test was found to be significantly associated with platelet MAO activity. In a perceptual maze test, there was a significant relationship between low platelet MAO activity and shorter check times after completing the problem. In addition, there was a significant correlation with failed inhibition, a measure of how many mistakes the persons make when shown a visual sign indicating, "press the button," and at the same time, given an auditory signal cancelling this order. A simple way to describe those results is that persons with low platelet MAO prefer speed to accuracy. These results with the neuropsychological tests are consistent with expectations for high scorers on the SSS and the impulsiveness scale on the KSP (cf. Schalling 1977).

One factor, which seems to be involved in both the expression of platelet MAO and of monoaminergic components in the brain, is the transcription factor Activating Protein-2 (AP-2; Oreland *et al.* 2002a). The association between platelet MAO activity and personality will indirectly result in an association between this enzyme activity and behavioral disturbances, such as drug abuse and other forms of psychosocial disturbances. However, since compounds in cigarette smoke have an inhibitory effect on platelet MAO, and smoking is connected both with personality and alcoholism, smoking is an important confounding factor (see below).

4.3. Platelet MAO is Inhibited by Cigarette Smoke

Oreland *et al.* (1981) demonstrated that cigarette smokers had lower platelet MAO activity than non-smokers. Also, persons who had stopped smoking exhibited platelet MAO activity similar to the non-smokers. In a study on college students by Propping *et al.* (1981), it was shown that persons with very low MAO activity smoked more than those with very high activity. This was later confirmed several times in studies both on males and females (Berlin & Anthenelli 2001).

It was shown, in vitro, that nicotine does not inhibit platelet MAO activity (Oreland *et al.* 1981). More recently, Fowler *et al.* (1998), using positron emission tomography (PET) on the baboon brain, also demonstrated the lack of an acute inhibiting effect of nicotine on MAO-B. In contrast, however, Yu and Boulton (1987) and Norman *et al.* (1982) demonstrated that cigarette smoke has inhibiting properties on platelet MAO activity. The inhibition seems to be irreversible (Yu & Boulton 1987). Evidence for an inhibiting effect of smoking on platelet MAO was also presented by Berlin *et al.* (1995), who suggested the possibility that this might have an antidepressive effect. In the human brain, a considerable inhibiting effect of cigarette smoke ($\approx 40\%$) on both MAO-A and MAO-B was demonstrated using PET (Fowler *et al.*, 1996a, b). Furthermore, it was shown that brain MAO-B inhibition in smokers remained at the same low level both 10 minutes after smoking a cigarette and 11 hours later, indicating a long-lasting effect (Fowler *et al.* 2000).

In a number of studies, a similar pattern of personality traits was observed in smokers as in persons with low platelet MAO activity, i.e. Impulsiveness (Reuter & Netter 2001), E (Spielberger & Jacobs 1982), Sensation Seeking (Kopstein *et al.* 2001; Perkins *et al.* 2000; Zuckerman 1979) and Novelty Seeking (Ravaja & Keltikangas-Jarvinen 2001). In 1985, it was observed that regular smokers were extraverts, sensation seekers, easily bored, and with a strong tendency to avoid monotony (von Knorring & Oreland 1985). Thus, the question can be raised to what extent does the inhibitory effect of cigarette smoke contribute to the association between personality and platelet MAO activity?

Personality and platelet MAO was studied in a sample of over 1000 recruits, 229 non-smokers, 252 ex-smokers, 388 irregular smokers and 213 regular smokers (von Knorring *et al.* 1984). Platelet MAO activity differed only for one group. The regular smokers had significantly lower mean platelet MAO activity compared to the other groups. Analyses of personality traits in each of the groups were conducted. Results revealed significant Pearson correlation coefficients of the same order between platelet MAO activity and Thrill and Adventure Seeking and a modified version of the SSS Experience Seeking scale in both the smoking and the non-smoking groups (see also Oreland *et al.* 1999). Ward *et al.* (1987) conducted another study addressing the same question using a smaller sample. They reported a similar correlation between platelet MAO and disinhibition and total scores of the SSS in smoking and non-smoking persons. The obvious interpretation of these results is that there is an association between platelet MAO activity and personality traits, such as those mentioned above, which is independent of the effect of smoking.

In support of the notion of a true association between platelet MAO activity and personality/behavior, there are a number of studies that show a relationship where the effect of smoking can be excluded for natural reasons. In early studies on monkeys, associations between platelet MAO and behavior were found, which, in essence, confirm the findings in humans (Redmond *et al.* 1979). Also, the same associations were found in newborn babies. Specifically, Sostek *et al.* (1981) reported that newborn babies with low platelet MAO activity exhibited greater screaming and motor activity and lower consolability than newborns with higher MAO activity. Harro *et al.* (2004) reported low platelet MAO activity to be a predictor of regular smoking, and it was recently suggested that even among non-smoking humans, low platelet MAO activity is associated with excessive alcohol use combined with antisocial behavior/drunk driving (Eensoo *et al.* 2004). In a sample of forensic psychiatric patients, where all persons were heavy smokers, strong associations between platelet MAO activity and personality traits (KSP scales: Impulsiveness, Monotony avoidance, Psychasthenia, Verbal aggression, Irritability) were found (Stålenheim *et al.* 1997). Similar results were obtained for a sample of convicted criminals who were matched in smoking behavior with a control group (Garpenstrand *et al.* 2002).

In a study on persistent criminals (juvenile delinquents continuing their criminal activity in adult life) and controls, platelet MAO activity in the whole sample was highly negatively correlated with smoking. In a two-way analysis of variance, significant effects of both smoking and adult criminality were shown, with smoking subjects as well as subjects characterized by adult criminality displaying the lower platelet MAO activity (Oreland *et al.* 1999). Additional analyses showed that the subjects with a continued/persistent criminal career had lower platelet MAO activity than those who did not commit any crime from 15 years of age, even when persons were matched for similar smoking habits (for a review, see Oreland *et al.* 2002b).

4.4. Platelet MAO and Early Onset alcoholism: Current Status

The notion that there is an association between low platelet MAO activity and Type II alcoholism has been challenged. There are several reports where no association between alcoholism and platelet MAO was found when smoking was taken into account (Anthenelli *et al.* 1998; Farren *et al.* 1998; Whitfield *et al.* 2000). Recent publications, however, present what should be considered conclusive evidence for an association between low platelet MAO activity and vulnerability for alcohol abuse. In a study of free-living Rhesus monkeys (Higley *et al.* 1996b), primates with low platelet MAO activity exhibited both significantly excessive alcohol consumption and the Type II-like alcohol features previously described (Fahlke *et al.* 2002).

In a clinical sample, male Type II alcoholism was linked to low levels of cerebrospinal fluid (CSF) 5-hydroxyindoleacetic acid (5-HIAA; Virkkunen *et al.* 1994). In a study on non-human primates, platelet MAO activity was linked both to low levels of 5-HIAA in the CSF and to a high voluntary ethanol intake (Fahlke *et al.* 2002). This is consistent with recent indications that the genes involved in the serotonergic pathways are involved in the development of Type II alcoholism, although at a low level (Parsian & Cloninger 2001).

Furthermore, low platelet MAO for Type II alcoholics (von Knorring *et al.* 1985) was also reported in two recently published studies. Demir *et al.* (2002) observed surprisingly similar effects when smoking was controlled. In another recent study involving a large international population of male subjects, Snell *et al.* (2002) reported that cigarette smoking, as well as lifetime history of alcohol dependence, were associated with low platelet MAO activity. MAO differences associated with gender and lifetime alcohol dependence were largely attributed to differences in MAO-B protein concentration, whereas those associated with smoking behavior appeared to be the result of binding of an inhibitor at the catalytic site of MAO. This result is exactly what should be expected if low platelet MAO activity in a subgroup of alcoholics is genetically determined, while compounds in cigarette smoke merely inhibit the enzyme.

An important difference between the study of Snell *et al.* (2002) and those of Anthenelli *et al.* (1998) and Whitfield *et al.* (2000) was that in the former study approximately twice as many of the alcoholics met the criteria for lifetime alcohol dependence. This was not the case in the other studies. There are reasons to believe that subjects in studies from Sweden (Hallman *et al.* 1996; Sherif *et al.* 1992) were usually even more heavily alcohol dependent than those in the report by Snell *et al.* (2002). It should be mentioned, however, that Snell *et al.* (2002) were cautious in interpreting their results. Because they did not observe a relation between low MAO activity and a family history of alcohol dependence, they did not claim that MAO-B concentration represents a trait marker of vulnerability for alcohol abuse.

4.5. Short Notes on Possible Mechanisms Behind the Association Between Platelet MAO Activity and Impulsivity/Sensation Seeking

Oreland and Hallman (1995) discussed several possibile explanations for the association between platelet MAO activity and personality/behavior. One possibility is that platelet MAO is correlated with brain MAO-B. MAO-B then would contribute to the expression of the personality traits of interest as a result of an effect on the rate of monoamine neurotransmitter degradation, and subsequently, on monoaminergic activity.

A second possibility is that platelet MAO directly influences the level of some trace amine that might be of importance for behavior. A third possibility is that platelet MAO is regulated together with other mitochondrial enzymes. Low platelet MAO might indicate generally low mitochondrial function (or number), which might result in lower efficiency in a particularly vulnerable transmitter system, e.g. the serotonin system. Lastly, platelet MAO activity might be a genetic marker, for example, of the capacity of some central transmitter system. Such a common genetic control could occur via common gene promoter sequences and co-regulation of platelet MAO and monoamine transmitter genes. At present, this last possibility seems to be the most likely. According to this hypothesis, platelet MAO can be considered a genetic marker that is regulated by mechanisms that are also important in regulating some brain function for personality.

In healthy persons, there is a significant correlation between CSF levels of the serotonin metabolite 5-HIAA and platelet MAO activity (Fahlke *et al.* 2002; Oreland *et al.* 1981). This is good agreement with the finding that human as well as nonhuman primates with a tendency for aggressive behavior, have low levels of 5-HIAA in the CSF (Brown *et al.* 1979; Higley *et al.* 1996a; Kruesi *et al.* 1990) and that aggressiveness in children is associated with low platelet MAO activity (af Klinteberg & Oreland 1995). Low levels of CSF 5-HIAA have also been linked to Type II alcoholics (Virkkunen & Linnoila 1993), who in several studies have been found to have low platelet MAO activity (von Knorring & Oreland 1996). Of great interest in this regard are also strong indications of a low density or a low activity genotype of the serotonin transporter (5-HT) in persons from clinical samples, expressing behavior concordant with Type II alcoholism (Hallikainen *et al.* 1999; Mantere *et al.* 2002). Furthermore, Novelty Seeking and APD correlate negatively to prefrontal 5-HT transporter density in alcoholics using single photon emission tomography (Laine *et al.* 2003).

4.6. Is Transcription Factor Family AP-2 a Link Between Platelet MAO Activity and Certain Personality Traits Associated with Psychosocial Disturbances?

AP-2 is a cell type-specific DNA-binding transcription factor family. It is one of several critical factors for neural gene expression (Mitchell *et al.* 1991). Moreover,

AP-2 gene expression is subject to positive autoregulatory mechanisms with its own gene product (Bauer *et al.* 1994). Several genes in the monoaminergic systems display multiple binding sites for AP-2 in their regulatory regions and some studies indicate a functional role for AP-2 in the regulation of monoaminergic genes. It is well known that transcriptional control is a critical mechanism for specification of neurotransmitter phenotypes. Brainstem levels of transcription factor AP-2 are correlated to monoamine metabolism in the forebrain (Damberg *et al.* 2001a). Thus, the results suggest a role of AP-2 in regulating the expression of monoaminergic genes, which affects the turnover of 5-HT and possibly also the catecholamines in the nerve terminals. This, in turn, is likely to exert a great influence on personality traits such as impulsivity and sensation seeking (see Figure 2).

Recently, significant associations were found between genotype of AP-2 (its ß form) and personality variables, as estimated by several personality inventories including the KSP and the TCI (Damberg *et al.*, 2000a, 2003). Furthermore, a similar association was found with binge eating disorder in females, another psychosocial disorder with impulsivity as a prominent feature (Damberg *et al.* 2001b).

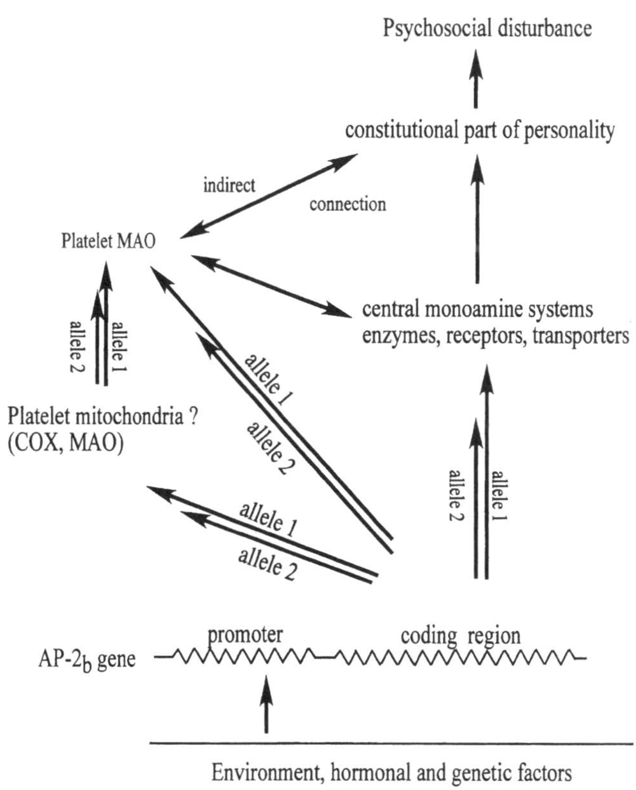

Figure 2: Possible mechanisms behind the associations between platelet MAO activity and personality traits related to different forms of psychosocial disturbances.

The association of both platelet MAO and genotype of AP-2ß with personality characteristics suggest that these two biological markers in some way are linked to each other. In a recent study, Damberg *et al.* (2000b) tested the hypothesis that transcription factor AP-2ß is connected to the expression of the human MAO-B gene in platelets as estimated by platelet MAO activity. Male and female subjects were analyzed with regard to an AP-2ß intron 2 genotype and platelet MAO activity. Males homozygous for the long allele displayed significantly lower platelet MAO activity as compared to those with one or two short alleles. Similarly, women homozygous for the long allele had lower platelet MAO activity than those with one or two short alleles.

4.7. Genes, Platelet MAO Activity, Impulsivity and Sensations Seeking: Future Perspectives

It seems obvious that not a single gene, but a particular genetic combination is crucial in the determination of such a complex phenotype as personality (Benjamin & Belmaker 2000; Damberg *et al.* 2001b; Ebstein *et al.* 2000; Reif & Lesch 2003). One way of explaining such a complex phenotype, without presuming a specific combination of gene alleles, would be that a set of relevant genes are regulated by a common transcriptional mechanism, such as sharing a common transcription factor. One common transcription factor is likely to be AP-2. Interestingly, it has been reported that the expression of the 5-HT transporter is reduced in women with binge eating disorder (Kuikka *et al.* 2001), but that the density of this transporter protein is normalized by reduced body weight (Tammela *et al.* 2003), indicating regulation on a transcriptional level. The 5-HT transporter gene is one example of genes with multiple binding sites for AP-2. It was previously reported that, among binge eating women, there is an over-representation of persons carrying that particular AP-2ß gene allele, which is connected with low platelet MAO activity (Damberg *et al.* 2001b). Personality is connected with both 5-HT transporter (Murphy *et al.* 2001) and AP-2 genotype.

A simple explanation for the association between platelet MAO and personality would be that platelet MAO is included among the set of proteins within the monoamine field for which AP-2 is a regulatory factor. Another important piece of information, in finding an explanation, might be the strong correlation between MAO and other mitochondrial membrane enzymes in platelets, e.g. cytochrome oxidase (COX) (Prince *et al.* 1994). This correlation could be the result of a transcriptional regulation by a common transcription factor, but it could also be that the common denominator is a transcriptional regulation of the density of mitochondria per cell, or the size of the mitochondrial membrane. If this latter explanation is true, platelet MAO would merely play the role of being a marker for platelet mitochondria, as well as for some central monoamine system properties, consistent with one of the possible hypotheses presented earlier (Oreland & Hallman 1995). In any explanation, there should be a role for AP-2. The exploration of such basic issues are currently under way, as well as continued studies on AP-2 genotype in relation to impulse control disorders and disturbed behavior with impulsivity and sensation seeking as prominent components, e.g. Type II alcoholism, criminal/violent behavior and eating disorders.

5. An Integrated Summary

Interdisciplinary cooperation is necessary to continue the research on impulsive behavior and personality, as well as the biological factors associated with disinhibitory syndromes. Studies regarding early vulnerabilities for substance abuse, violence and psychopathic tendencies are of specific interest. This direction of research, that is, the combination of neuropsychological and psychobiological aspects, is motivated by the continuous progress and contribution of findings within the borderline of psychology and neurobiology. We understand that these are the origins of the psychosocial disturbance phenomenon.

Acknowledgments

The present research was financially supported by grants from the Ministry of Health and Social Affairs, Sweden (Dnr S2001/7781/FH, BaK), the Alcohol Research Council of the Swedish Alcohol Retailing Monopoly (Dnr 286/01, BaK), the Mobilizing against Drugs Committee, Sweden (Dnr 20/2003:9, BaK/LO), the Swedish Science Foundation (no 4145, LO), and the Söderström-König Foundation (LO). Special thanks are forwarded to M. Vaefors for editing the work.

References

American Psychiatric Association (1994). *Diagnostic and statistical manual of mental disorders* (4th ed.). Washington, DC: American Psychiatric Association.

Anthenelli, R. M., Tipp, J., Li, T. K., Magnes, L., Schuckit, M. A., Rice, J., Daw, W., & Nurnberger, J. I., Jr. (1998). Platelet monoamine oxidase activity in subgroups of alcoholics and controls: Results from the Collaborative Study on the Genetics of Alcoholism. *Alcoholism: Clinical and Experimental Research*, *22*, 598–604.

Barratt, E. S., & Patton, J. H. (1983). Impulsivity: Cognitive, behavioral, and psychophysiological correlates. In: M. Zuckerman (Ed.), *Biological bases of sensation seeking, impulsivity and anxiety* (pp. 77–122). Hillsdale: Erlbaum.

Barratt, E. S., & Slaughter, L. (1998). Defining, measuring, and predicting impulsive aggression: A heuristic model. *Behavioral Sciences and the Law*, *16*, 285–302.

Bauer, R., Imhof, A., Pscherer, A., Kopp, H., Moser, M., Seegers, S., Kerscher, M., Tainsky, M. A., Hofstaedter, F., & Buettner, R. (1994). The genomic structure of the human AP-2 transcription factor. *Nucleic Acids Research*, *22*, 1413–1420.

Berlin, I., & Anthenelli, R. M. (2001). Monoamine oxidases and tobacco smoking. *International Journal of Neuropsychopharmacology*, *4*, 33–42.

Berlin, I., Said, S., Spreux-Varoquaux, O., Olivares, R., Launay, J. M., & Puech, A. J. (1995). Monoamine oxidase A and B activities in heavy smokers. *Biological Psychiatry*, *38*, 756–761.

Biederman, J., Faraone, S., Milberger, S., Guite, J., Mick, E., Chen, L., Mennin, D., Marrs, A., Quellette, C., Moore, P., Spencer, T., Norman, D., Kraus, I., & Perrin, J. (1996). A prospective 4-year follow-up study of attention-deficit hyperactivity and related disorders. *Archives of General Psychiatry*, *53*, 437–446.

Blackburn, R. (1969). Sensation seeking, impulsivity and psychopathic personality. *Journal of Consulting and Clinical Psychology*, *33*, 571–574.

Bongioanni, P. (1991). Platelet MAO activity and personality: An overview. *New Trends in Experimental and Clinical Psychiatry*, *7*, 17–28.

Bridge, T. P., Soldo, B. J., Phelps, B. H., Wise, C. D., Francak, M. J., & Wyatt, R. J. (1985). Platelet monoamine oxidase activity: Demographic characteristics contribute to enzyme activity variability. *Journal of Gerontology*, *40*, 23–28.

Brown, G. L., Goodwin, F. K., Ballenger, J. C., Goyer, P. F., & Major, L. F. (1979). Aggression in humans correlates with cerebrospinal fluid amine metabolites. *Psychiatry Research*, *1*, 131–139.

Buchsbaum, M. S., Coursey, R. D., & Murphy, D. L. (1976). The biochemical high-risk paradigm: Behavioral and familial correlates of low platelet monoamine oxidase activity. *Science*, *194*, 339–341.

Cleckley, H. (1976). *The mask of sanity* (5th ed.). St. Louis, MO: Mosby.

Cloninger, C. R., Bohman, M., & Sigvardsson, S. (1981). Inheritance of alcohol abuse. *Archives of General Psychiatry*, *38*, 861–868.

Cloninger, C. R., Przybeck, T. R., Svrakic, D. M., & Wetzel, R. D. (1994). *The temperament and Character Inventory (TCI): A guide to its development and use*. St. Louis, MO: Center for Psychobiology of Personality.

Cloninger, C. R., Sigvardsson, S., & Bohman, M. (1988). Childhood personality predicts alcohol abuse in young adults. *Alcoholism: Clinical and Experimental Research*, *12*, 494–505.

Comings, D. E., Wu, S., Chiu, C., Ring, R. H., Gade, R., Ahn, C., MacMurray, J. P., Dietz, G., & Muhleman, D. (1996). Polygenic inheritance of Tourette syndrome, stuttering, attention deficit hyperactivity, conduct, and oppositional defiant disorder: The additive and subtractive effect of the three dopaminergic genes — DRD2, DßH, and DAT1. *American Journal of Medical Genetics (Neuropsychiatric Genetics)*, *67*, 264–288.

Cooke, C. D., & Michie, C. (2001). Refining the construct of psychopathy: Towards a hierarchical model. *Psychological Assessment*, *13*, 171–188.

Damberg, M., Eller, M., Tonissaar, M., Oreland, L., & Harro, J. (2001a). Levels of transcription factors AP-2alpha and AP-2beta in the brainstem are correlated to monoamine turnover in the rat forebrain. *Neuroscience Letters*, *313*, 102–104.

Damberg, M., Garpenstrand, H., Alfredsson, J., Ekblom, J., Forslund, K., Rylander, G., & Oreland, L. (2000a). A polymorphic region in the human transcription factor AP-2beta gene is associated with specific personality traits. *Molecular Psychiatry*, *5*, 220–224.

Damberg, M., Garpenstrand, H., Berggård, C., Asberg, M., Hallman, J., & Oreland, L. (2000b). The genotype of human transcription factor AP-2beta is associated with platelet monoamine oxidase B activity. *Neuroscience Letters*, *291*, 204–206.

Damberg, M., Garpenstrand, H., Hallman, J., & Oreland, L. (2001b). Genetic mechanisms of behavior — don't forget about the transcription factors. *Molecular Psychiatry*, *6*, 503–510.

Demir, B., Ucar, G., Ulug, B., Ulusoy, S., Sevinc, I., & Batur, S. (2002). Platelet monoamine oxidase activity in alcoholism subtypes: Relationship to personality traits and executive functions. *Alcohol and Alcoholism*, *37*, 597–602.

Ebstein, R. P., Benjamin, J., & Belmaker, R. H. (2000). Personality and polymorphisms of genes involved in aminergic neurotransmission. *European Journal of Pharmacology*, *410*, 205–214.

Eensoo, D., Paaver, M., Pulver, A., Harro, M., & Harro, J. (2004). Low platelet MAO activity associated with high dysfunctional impulsivity and antisocial behavior: Evidence from drunk drivers. *Psychopharmacology*, *172*, 356–358.

Eklund, J., & af Klinteberg, B. (2003). Child behavior as related to subsequent drinking offences and violent offending: A prospective study of 11–14 year old youths into their fourth decade. *Criminal Behaviour and Mental Health*, *13*, 294–309.

Ekselius, L., Bodlund, O., von Knorring, L., Lindström, E., & Kullgren, G. (1996). Sex differences in DSM-III-R, Axis II-Personality disorders. *Personality and Individual Differences*, *20*, 457–461.

Ekselius, L., Hetta, J., & von Knorring, L. (1994). Relationship between personality traits as determined by means of the Karolinska scales of personality (KSP) and personality disorders according to DSM-3-R. *Personality and Individual Differences*, *16*, 589–595.

Essen-Möller, E. (1980). The psychology and psychiatry of Henrik Sjobring (1879–1956). *Psychological Medicine*, *10*, 201–210.

Eysenck, H. J., & Eysenck, S. B. G. (1964). *Manual of the Eysenck Personality Inventory*. London: University of London Press.

Eysenck, H. J., Tarrant, M., Woolf, M., & England, L. (1960). Smoking and personality. *British Medical Journal*, *1*, 1456–1460.

Eysenck, S. B. G., & Eysenck, H. J. (1975). *Manual of the Eysenck Personality Questionnaire*. London: Hodder & Stoughton.

Fahlke, C., Garpenstrand, H., Oreland, L., Suomi, S. J., & Higley, J. D. (2002). Platelet Monoamine Oxidase Activity in a nonhuman primate model of type 2 excessive alcohol consumption. *American Journal of Psychiatry*, *159*, 2107–2109.

Farren, C. K., Clare, A. W., Tipton, K. F., & Dinan, T. G. (1998). Platelet MAO activity in subtypes of alcoholics and controls in a homogenous population. *Journal of Psychiatric Research*, *32*, 49–54.

Farrington, D. (1995). The development of offending and antisocial behavior from childhood: Key findings from the Cambridge study in delinquent development. *Journal of Child Psychology and Psychiatry*, *360*, 920–964.

Fowler, J. S., Volkow, N. D., Logan, J., Pappas, N., King, P., MacGregor, R., Shea, C., Garza, V., & Gatley, S. J. (1998). An acute dose of nicotine does not inhibit MAO B in baboon brain in vivo. *Life Sciences*, *63*, 19–23.

Fowler, J. S., Volkow, N. D., Wang, G. J., Pappas, N., Logan, J., MacGregor, R., Alexoff, D., Shea, C., Schlyer, D., Wolf, A. P., Warner, D., Zezulkova, I., & Cilento, R. (1996a). Inhibition of monoamine oxidase B in the brains of smokers. *Nature*, *379*, 733–736.

Fowler, J. S., Volkow, N. D., Wang, G. J., Pappas, N., Logan, J., Shea, C., Alexoff, D., MacGregor, R. R., Schlyer, D. J., Zezulkova, I., & Wolf, A. P. (1996b). Brain monoamine oxidase A inhibition in cigarette smokers. *Proceedings of the National Academy of Sciences USA*, *93*, 14065–14069.

Fowler, J. S., Wang, G. J., Volkow, N. D., Franceschi, D., Logan, J., Pappas, N., Shea, C., MacGregor, R. R., & Garza, V. (2000). Maintenance of brain monoamine oxidase B inhibition in smokers after overnight cigarette abstinence. *American Journal of Psychiatry*, *157*, 1864–1866.

Frick, P. J., Bodin, S. D., & Barry, C. T. (2000). Psychopathic traits and conduct problems in community and clinic-referred samples of children: Further development of the psychopathy screening devise. *Psychological Assessment*, *12*, 382–393.

Garpenstrand, H., Ekblom, J., Forslund, K., Rylander, G., & Oreland, L. (2000). Platelet monoamine oxidase activity is related to MAO-B intron 13 genotype. *Journal of Neural Transmission*, *107*, 523–530.

Garpenstrand, H., Longato-Stadler, E., af Klinteberg, B., Grigorenko, E., Damberg, M., Oreland, L., & Hallman, J. (2002). Low platelet monoamine oxidase activity in Swedish imprisoned criminal offenders. *European Neuropsychopharmacology*, *12*, 135–140.

Gorenstein, E. E., & Newman, J. P. (1980). Disinhibitory psychopathology: A new perspective and a model for research. *Psychological Review*, *87*, 301–315.

Gray, J. A., Owen, S., Davis, N., & Tsaltas, E. (1983). Psychological and physiological relations between anxiety and impulsivity. In: M. Zuckerman (Ed.), *Biological bases of sensation seeking, impulsivity, and anxiety* (pp. 181–217). Hillsdale, NJ: Erlbaum.

Gustavsson, J. P., Bergman, H., Edman, G., Ekselius, L., von Knorring, L., & Linder, J. (2000). Swedish Universities Scales of Personality (SSP): Construction, internal consistency and normative data. *Acta Psychiatrica Scandinavica*, *102*, 217–225.

Hallikainen, T., Saito, T., Lachman, H. M., Volavka, J., Pohjalainen, T., Ryynanen, O. P., Kauhanen, J., Syvalahti, E., Hietala, J., & Tiihonen, J. (1999). Association between low activity serotonin transporter promoter genotype and early onset alcoholism with habitual impulsive violent behavior. *Molecular Psychiatry*, *4*, 385–388.

Hallman, J., von Knorring, L., & Oreland, L. (1996). Personality disorders according to DSM-III-R and thrombocyte monoamine oxidase activity in type 1 and type 2 alcoholics. *Journal of Studies on Alcohol*, *57*, 155–161.

Hare, R. (1985). A comparison of procedures for the assessment of psychopathy. *Journal of Consulting and Clinical Psychology*, *53*, 7–16.

Harro, J., Fischer, K., Vansteelandt, S., & Harro, M. (2004). Both low and high activities of platelet monoamine oxidase increase the probability of becoming a smoker. *European Neuropsychopharmacology*, *14*, 65–69.

Higley, J. D., Mehlman, P. T., Poland, R. E., Taub, D. M., Vickers, J., Suomi, S. J., & Linnoila, M. (1996a). CSF testosterone and 5-HIAA correlate with different types of aggressive behaviors. *Biological Psychiatry*, *40*, 1067–1082.

Higley, J. D., Suomi, S. J., & Linnoila, M. (1996b). A nonhuman primate model of type II excessive alcohol consumption? Part 1. Low cerebrospinal fluid 5-hydroxyindoleacetic acid concentrations and diminished social competence correlate with excessive alcohol consumption. *Alcoholism: Clinical and Experimental Research*, *20*, 629–642.

Holschneider, D. P., Chen, K., Seif, I., & Shih, J. C. (2001). Biochemical, behavioral, physiologic, and neurodevelopmental changes in mice deficient in monoamine oxidase A or B. *Brain Research Bulletin*, *56*, 453–462.

af Klinteberg, B. (1996). Biology, norms, and personality: A developmental perspective. *Neuropsychobiology*, *34*, 146–154.

af Klinteberg, B. (2000). Psychobiological patterns at adult age: Relationships to personality and early behavior. In: L. R. Bergman, R. B. Cairns, L.-G. Nilsson, & L. Nystedt (Eds), *Developmental science and the holistic approach* (pp. 209–228). Mahwah, NJ: Erlbaum.

af Klinteberg, B., Andersson, T., Magnusson, D., & Stattin, H. (1993). Hyperactive behavior in childhood as related to subsequent alcohol problems and violent offending: A longitudinal study of male subjects. *Personality and Individual Differences*, *15*, 381–388.

af Klinteberg, B., Humble, K., & Schalling, D. (1992). Personality and psychopathy of males with a history of early criminal behavior. *European Journal of Personality*, *6*, 245–266.

af Klinteberg, B., Magnusson, D., & Schalling, D. (1989). Hyperactive behavior in childhood and adult impulsivity: A longitudinal study of male subjects. *Personality and Individual Differences*, *10*, 43–50.

af Klinteberg, B., & Oreland, L. (1995). Hyperactive and aggressive behaviors in childhood as related to low platelet monoamine oxidase (MAO) activity at adult age: A longitudinal study of male subjects. *Personality and Individual Differences*, *19*, 373–383.

af Klinteberg, B., Oreland, L., Hallman, J., Wirsén, A., Levander, S. E., & Schalling, D. (1991). Exploring the connections between platelet mono-amine oxidase activity and behavior: Relationships with performance in neuropsychological tasks. *Neuropsychobiology*, *23*, 188–196.

af Klinteberg, B., Schalling, D., Edman, G., Oreland, L., & Åsberg, M. (1987). Personality correlates of platelet monoamine oxidase (MAO) activity in female and male subjects. *Neuropsychobiology*, *18*, 89–96.

von Knorring, A.-L. (1983). *Adoption studies on psychiatric illness. Epidemiological, environmental and genetic aspects*. Unpublished Doctoral dissertation, Umeå University, Umeå, Sweden.

von Knorring, A.-L., Bohman, M., von Knorring, L., & Oreland, L. (1985). Platelet MAO activity as a biological marker in subgroups of alcoholism. *Acta Psychiatrica Scandinavica*, *72*, 51–58.

von Knorring, L., von Knorring, A.-L., Smigan, L., Lindberg, U., & Edholm, M. (1987). Personality traits in subtypes of alcoholics. *Journal of Studies on Alcohol*, *48*, 523–527.

von Knorring, L., & Oreland, L. (1985). Personality traits and platelet monoamine oxidase in tobacco smokers. *Psychological Medicine*, *15*, 327–334.

von Knorring, L., & Oreland, L. (1996). Platelet MAO activity in type I/type II alcoholics (From the ISBRA/RSA James B. Isacson Memorial Award Lecture, Washington, 1996). *Alcoholism: Clinical and Experimental Research*, *20*, 224–230.

von Knorring, L., Oreland, L., & von Knorring, A.-L. (1986). Personality traits and psychopathology related to platelet MAO activity. In: C. Shagass, R. C. Josiassen, W. H. Bridger, K. J. Weiss, D. Stoff, & G. Simpson (Eds), *Biological psychiatry* (pp. 530–532). Amsterdam: Elsevier.

von Knorring, L., Oreland, L., & Winblad, B. (1984). Personality traits related to monoamine oxidase activity in platelets. *Psychiatry Research*, *12*, 11–26.

Kopstein, A. N., Crum, R. M., Celentano, D. D., & Martin, S. S. (2001). Sensation seeking needs among 8th and 11th graders: Characteristics associated with cigarette and marijuana use. *Drug and Alcohol Dependence*, *62*, 195–203.

Krauth, J., & Lienert, G. A. (1982). Fundamentals and modifications of configural frequency analysis (CFA). *Interdisciplinaria*, *3*, 1–14.

Kruesi, M. J., Rapoport, J. L., Hamburger, S., Hibbs, E., Potter, W. Z., Lenane, M., & Brown, G. L. (1990). Cerebrospinal fluid monoamine metabolites, aggression, and impulsivity in disruptive behavior disorders of children and adolescents. *Archives of General Psychiatry*, *47*, 419–426.

Kuikka, J. T., Tammela, L., Karhunen, L., Rissanen, A., Bergstrom, K. A., Naukkarinen, H., Vanninen, E., Karhu, J., Lappalainen, R., Repo-Tiihonen, E., Tiihonen, J., & Uusitupa, M. (2001). Reduced serotonin transporter binding in binge eating women. *Psychopharmacology (Berl)*, *155*, 310–314.

Laine, T. P. J., Ahonen, A., Räsänen, P., & Tiihonen, J. (2003). Novelty seeking correlates negatively to prefrontal monoaminergic activity among alcoholics. *The Islandic Medical Journal*, *48*, 30.

LaPierre, D., Braun, C. M. J., & Hodgins, S. (1995). Ventral frontal deficits in psychopathy: Neuropsychological test findings. *Neuropsychologia*, *33*, 139–151.

Lewis, C. E. (1991). Neurochemical mechanisms of chronic antisocial behavior (psychopathy): A literature review. *Journal of Nervous and Mental Disease*, *179*, 720–727.

Lidberg, L., Modin, I., Oreland, L., Tuck, J. R., & Gillner, A. (1985). Platelet monoamine oxidase activity and psychopathy. *Psychiatry Research*, *16*, 339–343.

Linnoila, M., Virkkunen, M., Scheinin, M., Nuutila, A., Rimon, R., & Goodwin, F. K. (1983). Low cerebrospinal fluid 5-hydroxyindoleacetic acid concentration differentiates impulsive from nonimpulsive violent behavior. *Life Sciences*, *33*, 2609–2614.

Loeber, R., & Farrington, D. P. (2000). Young children who commit crime: Epidemiology, developmental origins, risk factors, early interventions, and policy implications. *Development and Psychopathology*, *12*, 737–762.

Magnusson, D. (1988). Individual development from an interactional perspective: A longitudinal study. In: D. Magnusson (Ed.), *Paths through life* (Vol. 1, pp. 1–226). Hillsdale, NJ: Erlbaum.

Magnusson, D., af Klinteberg, B., & Stattin, H. (1994). Juvenile and persistent offenders: Behavioral and physiological characteristics. In: R. D. Ketterlinus, & M. E. Lamb (Eds), *Adolescent problem behaviors: Issues and research* (pp. 81–91). Hillsdale, NJ: Erlbaum.

Mannuzza, S., Klein, R. G., Bessler, A., Malloy, P., & LaPadula, M. (1993). Adult outcome of hyperactive boys. Educational achievement, occupational rank, and psychiatric status. *Archives of General Psychiatry*, *50*, 565–576.

Mantere, T., Tupala, E., Hall, H., Sarkioja, T., Rasanen, P., Bergstrom, K., Callaway, J., & Tiihonen, J. (2002). Serotonin transporter distribution and density in the cerebral cortex of alcoholic and nonalcoholic comparison subjects: A whole-hemisphere autoradiography study. *American Journal of Psychiatry*, *159*, 599–606.

McManus, I. C., & Weeks, S. J. (1982). Smoking, personality and reasons for smoking. *Psychological Medicine*, *12*, 349–356.

Mitchell, P. J., Timmons, P. M., Hebert, J. M., Rigby, P. W., & Tjian, R. (1991). Transcription factor AP-2 is expressed in neural crest cell lineages during mouse embryogenesis. *Genes and Development*, *5*, 105–119.

Murphy, D. L. (1976). Clinical, genetic, hormonal and drug influences on the activity of human platelet monoamine oxidase. In: Ciba Foundation Symposium, *Monoamine oxidase and its inhibition*, *39*, 341–351. Amsterdam: Elsevier.

Murphy, D. L., Li, Q., Engel, S., Wichems, C., Andrews, A., Lesch, K. P., & Uhl, G. (2001). Genetic perspectives on the serotonin transporter. *Brain Research Bulletin*, *56*, 487–494.

Nies, A., Robinson, D. S., Lamborn, K. R., & Lampert, R. P. (1973). Genetic control of platelet and plasma monoamine oxidase activity. *Archives of General Psychiatry*, *28*, 834–838.

Norman, T. R., Chamberlain, K. G., French, M. A., & Burrows, G. D. (1982). Platelet monoamine oxidase activity and cigarette smoking. *Journal of Affective Disorders*, *4*, 73–77.

Oreland, L. (1993). Monoamine oxidase in neuropsychiatric disorders. In: H. Yasuhara, S. H. Parvez, K. Ogushi, & M. Sandler (Eds), *Monoamine oxidase: Basic and clinical aspects* (pp. 219–247). Utrecht: VSP Press.

Oreland, L., Fowler, C. J., & Schalling, D. (1981). Low platelet monoamine oxidase activity in cigarette smokers. *Life Sciences*, *29*, 2511–2518.

Oreland, L., Damberg, M., Hallman, J., Berggård, C., & Garpenstrand, H. (2002a). Risk factors for the neurohumoral alterations underlying personality disturbances. *Neurotoxicity Research*, *4*, 421–426.

Oreland, L., Damberg, M., Hallman, J., & Garpenstrand, H. (2002b). Smoking only explains part of the associations between platelet monoamine oxidase activity and personality. *Journal of Neural Transmission*, *109*, 963–975.

Oreland, L., Garpenstrand, H., Damberg, M., Alm, P. O., Thorell, L.-H., af Klinteberg, B., & Ekblom, J. (1999). The correlation between platelet MAO activity and personality: The effect of smoking and possible mechanisms behind the correlation. *Neurobiology*, *7*, 191–203.

Oreland, L., & Hallman, J. (1995). The correlation between platelet MAO activity and personality: Short review of findings and a discussion on possible mechanisms. *Progress in Brain Research*, *106*, 77–84.

Oreland, L., Wiberg, A., Asberg, M., Traskman, L., Sjostrand, L., Thorén, P., Bertilsson, L., & Tybring, G. (1981). Platelet MAO activity and monoamine metabolites in cerebrospinal fluid in depressed and suicidal patients and in healthy controls. *Psychiatry Research*, *4*, 21–29.

Oxenstierna, G., Edman, G., Iselius, L., Oreland, L., Ross, S. B., & Sedvall, G. (1986). Concentrations of monoamine metabolites in the cerebrospinal fluid of twins and unrelated individuals: A genetic study. *Journal of Psychiatry Research*, *20*, 19–29.

Parsian, A., & Cloninger, C. R. (2001). Serotonergic pathway genes and subtypes of alcoholism: Association studies. *Psychiatric Genetics*, *11*, 89–94.

Pedersen, N. L., Oreland, L., Reynolds, C., & McClearn, G. E. (1993). Importance of genetic effects for monoamine oxidase activity in thrombocytes in twins reared apart and twins reared together. *Psychiatry Research*, *46*, 239–251.

Perkins, K. A., Gerlach, D., Broge, M., Grobe, J. E., & Wilson, A. (2000). Greater sensitivity to subjective effects of nicotine in nonsmokers high in sensation seeking. *Experimental and Clinical Psychopharmacology*, *8*, 462–471.

Pfiffner, L. J., McBurnett, K., Lahey, B., Loeber, R., Green, S., Frick, P. J., & Rathouz, P. J. (1999). Association of parental psychopathology to the comorbid disorders of boys with Attention Deficit-Hyperactivity Disorder. *Journal of Consulting and Clinical Psychology*, *67*, 881–893.

Prince, J., Jia, S., Bave, U., Anneren, G., & Oreland, L. (1994). Mitochondrial enzyme deficiencies in Down's syndrome. *Journal of Neural Transmission: Parkinson's Disease and Dementia Section, 8*, 171–181.

Propping, P., Rey, E. R., Friedl, W., & Beckmann, H. (1981). Platelet monoamine oxidase in healthy subjects: The "biochemical high-risk paradigm" revisited. *Archiv der Psychiatrische Nervenkr, 230*, 209–219.

Ravaja, N., & Keltikangas-Jarvinen, K. (2001). Cloninger's temperament and character dimensions in young adulthood and their relation to characteristics of parental alcohol use and smoking. *Journal of Studies on Alcohol, 62*, 98–104.

Redmond, D. E., Jr., Murphy, D. L., & Baulu, J. (1979). Platelet monoamine oxidase activity correlates with social affiliative and agonistic behaviors in normal rhesus monkeys. *Psychosomatic Medicine, 41*, 87–100.

Reif, A., & Lesch, K. P. (2003). Toward a molecular architecture of personality. *Behavioral Brain Research, 139*, 1–20.

Reuter, M., & Netter, P. (2001). The influence of personality on nicotine craving: A hierarchical multivariate statistical prediction model. *Neuropsychobiology, 44*, 47–53.

Robins, L. (1966). *Deviant children grown up: A sociological and psychiatric study of sociopathic personality*. Baltimore: William & Wilkins.

Robinson, D. S., Nies, A., Davis, J. N., Bunney, W. E., Davis, J. M., Colburn, R. W., Davis, J. N., Bourne, H. R., Bunney, W. E., Shaw, D. M., & Coppen, A. J. (1972). Ageing, monoamines, and monoamine-oxidase levels. *Lancet, 1*, 290–291.

Robinson, T. N., & Zahn, T. P. (1985). Psychoticism and arousal: Possible evidence for a linkage of P and psychopathy. *Personality and Individual Differences, 6*, 46–66.

Ruegg, R., & Frances, A. (1995). New research in personality disorders. *Journal of Personality Disorders, 9*, 1–48.

Ruchkin, V. V., Koposov, R. A., af Klinteberg, B., Oreland, L., & Grigorenko, E. (2003). *Platelet MAO, personality, and psychopathology in juvenile delinquents*. Manuscript submitted for publication.

Rydelius, P.-A. (1983). Alcohol-abusing teenage boys. *Acta Psychiatrica Scandinavica, 68*, 381–385.

Satterfield, J. H. (1987). Childhood diagnostic and neurophysiological predictors of teenage arrest rates: An eight-year prospective study. In: S. A. Mednick, T. E., Moffitt, & S. A. Stack (Eds), *The causes of crime* (pp. 199–207). Cambridge: Cambridge University Press.

Satterfield, J. H., & Schell, A. (1997). A prospective study of hyperactive boys with conduct problems and normal boys: Adolescent and adult criminality. *Journal of American Academy of Child and Adolescent Psychiatry, 36*, 1726–1735.

Schalling, D. (1977). The trait-situation and the physiological correlates of behavior. In: D. Magnusson, & N. S. Endler (Eds), *Personality at the cross-roads*. Hillsdale, NJ: Erlbaum.

Schalling, D. (1978). Psychopathy-related personality variables and the psychophysiology of socialization. In: R. D. Hare, & D. Schalling (Eds), *Psychopathic behavior: Approaches to research* (pp. 85–106). Chichester: Wiley.

Schalling, D. (1993). Neurochemical correlates of personality, impulsivity and disinhibitory suicidality. In: S. Hodgins (Ed.), *Mental disorder and crime* (pp. 208–226). Newbury Park, CA: Sage.

Schalling, D., Åsberg, M., Edman, G., & Oreland, L. (1987). Markers for vulnerability to psychopathology: Temperament traits associated with platelet MAO activity. *Acta Psychiatrica Scandinavica, 76*, 172–182.

Schalling, D., Edman, G., Åsberg, M., & Oreland, L. (1988). Platelet MAO activity associated with impulsivity and aggressivity. *Personality and Individual Differences, 9*, 597–605.

Seroczynski, A. D., Bergeman, C. S., & Coccaro, E. F. (1999). Etiology of the impulsivity/aggression relationship: Genes or environment? *Psychiatry Research*, *86*, 41–57.

Sherif, F., Hallman, J., & Oreland, L. (1992). Low platelet gamma-aminobutyrate aminotransferase and monoamine oxidase activities in chronic alcoholic patients. *Alcoholism: Clinical and Experimental Research*, *16*, 1014–1020.

Sjöbring, H. (1913). *Den individualpsykologiska frågeställning en inom psykiatrin*. Unpublished doctoral dissertation, Uppsala University, Sweden.

Snell, L. D., Glanz, J., & Tabakoff, B. (2002). Relationships between effects of smoking, gender, and alcohol dependence on platelet monoamine oxidase-B: Activity, affinity labeling, and protein measurements. *Alcoholism: Clinical and Experimental Research*, *26*, 1105–1113.

Socialstyrelsen (2002). *ADHD hos barn och vuxna* (ADHD in children and adults). Stockholm, Sweden: Socialstyrelsen.

Sostek, A. J., Sostek, A. M., Murphy, D. L., Martin, E. B., & Born, W. S. (1981). Cord blood amine oxidase activities relate to arousal and motor functioning in human newborns. *Life Sciences*, *28*, 2561–2568.

Soubrié, P. H. (1986). Reconciling the role of central serotonin neurons in human and animal behavior. *Behavioral and Brain Science*, *9*, 319–363.

Spielberger, C. D., & Jacobs, G. A. (1982). Personality and smoking behavior. *Journal of Personality Assessment*, *46*, 396–403.

Stålenheim, E. G., von Knorring, L., & Oreland, L. (1997). Platelet monoamine oxidase activity as a biological marker in a Swedish forensic psychiatric population. *Psychiatry Research*, *69*, 79–87.

Tammela, L. I., Rissanen, A., Kuikka, J. T., Karhunen, L. J., Bergstrom, K. A., Repo-Tiihonen, E., Naukkarinen, H., Vanninen, E., Tiihonen, J., & Uusitupa, M. (2003). Treatment improves serotonin transporter binding and reduces binge eating. *Psychopharmacology (Berl)*, *170*, 89–93.

Tremblay, R. E., & LeMarquand, D. (2001). Individual risk and protective factors. In: R. Loeber, & D. P. Farrington (Eds), *Child delinquents: Development, intervention, and service needs* (pp. 137–164). Thousand Oaks: Sage.

Virkkunen, M., & Linnoila, M. (1993). Brain serotonin, type II alcoholism and impulsive violence. *Journal of Studies on Alcohol Suppl.*, *11*, 163–169.

Virkkunen, M., Rawlings, R., Tokala, R., Poland, R. E., Guidotti, A., Nemeroff, C., Bissette, G., Kalogeras, K., Karonen, S.-L., & Linnoila, M. (1994). CSF biochemistry, glucose metabolism, and diurnal activity rhythms in alcoholic, violent offenders, fire setters, and healthy volunteers. *Archives of General Psychiatry*, *51*, 20–27.

Ward, P. B., Catts, S. V., Norman, T. R., Burrows, G. D., & McConaghy, N. (1987). Low platelet monoamine oxidase and sensation seeking in males: An established relationship? *Acta Psychiatrica Scandinavica*, *75*, 86–90.

White, J. L., Moffitt, T. E., Caspi, A., Bartusch, D. J., Needles, D. J., & Stouthamer-Loeber, M. (1994). Measuring impulsivity and examining its relationship to delinquency. *Journal of Abnormal Psychology*, *103*, 192–205.

Whitfield, J. B., Pang, D., Bucholz, K. K., Madden, P. A., Heath, A. C., Statham, D. J., & Martin, N. G. (2000). Monoamine oxidase: Associations with alcohol dependence, smoking and other measures of psychopathology. *Psychogical Medicine*, *30*, 443–454.

Wiberg, A., Gottfries, C. G., & Oreland, L. (1977). Low platelet monoamine oxidase activity in human alcoholics. *Medical Biology*, *55*, 181–186.

Winblad, B., Gottfries, C. G., Oreland, L., & Wiberg, A. (1979). Monoamine oxidase in platelets and brains of non-psychiatric and non-neurological geriatric patients. *Medical Biology*, *57*, 129–132.

Yu, P. H., & Boulton, A. A. (1987). Irreversible inhibition of monoamine oxidase by some components of cigarette smoke. *Life Sciences*, *41*, 675–682.

Zuckerman, M. (1979). *Sensation seeking. Beyond the optimal level of arousal*. Hillsdale, NJ: Erlbaum.

Zuckerman, M. (1991). *Psychobiology of personality*. Cambridge: Cambridge University Press.

Zuckerman, M. (1994). *Behavioral expressions and biosocial bases of sensation seeking*. Cambridge: Cambridge University Press.

Zuckerman, M. (2003). Biological bases of personality. In: T. Millon, & M. J. Lerner (Eds), *Handbook of psychology* (pp. 85–116). Hoboken, NJ: Wiley.

Chapter 23

The Neuropsychology of Impulsive Antisocial Sensation Seeking Personality Traits: From Dopamine to Hippocampal Function?

A. D. Pickering

1. Introduction: Terminology Issues

This chapter describes the first steps on my search to understand the neuropsychological foundations of a specific cluster of personality traits which I refer to as impulsive antisocial sensation seeking (ImpASS). This search is very much a work in progress. Nonetheless, for a number of reasons, which I will note up as the chapter proceeds, it seems entirely appropriate as part of this tribute to the career of Marvin Zuckerman. First, Zuckerman has stressed the importance of this trait cluster by claiming (Zuckerman 1993) that it is a basic personality dimension, although he has often referred to it as Psychoticism-Impulsive Unsocialised Sensation Seeking (P-ImpUSS). In making this claim, Zuckerman took a position at odds with the growing dominance of the Big Five approach, including P-ImpUSS as part of his alternative Five-Factor Model (Zuckerman 1992; Zuckerman *et al.* 1993).

An obvious question emerges from the opening paragraph: why, apart from the neater acronym, would I want to retitle this cluster of personality traits slightly? There are two main reasons. First, I prefer antisocial to unsocialised on the grounds that the latter carries more of an implication that environmental-developmental processes have gone awry during the normal process of socialization. I feel that such unintended suggestions of causal mechanisms should probably be avoided, given our current lack of understanding of the complex pathways leading an individual to have an antisocial, unsocialised personality.

More importantly, I removed the Psychoticism part of Zuckerman's label. I believe that Zuckerman included this because the Psychoticism (P) scale, from the Eysenck Personality Questionnaire (EPQ; Eysenck & Eysenck 1975) is a strong and well-known marker of the personality dimension which Zuckerman was describing. I have no difficulty with this. As I will illustrate below, in my studies EPQ-P is one of the most interesting measures of

On the Psychobiology of Personality
Edited by R. M. Stelmack

ISBN: 0-08-044209-9

ImpASS traits. My difficulty with including P in the label for ImpASS traits is that the term also suggests a set of schizotypal personality traits. I believe that schizotypal and ImpASS traits are likely to be distinct in their neuropsychology and yet they have sometimes been confused and conflated in research. In my view, part of this confusion is because measures of the two types of trait usually show modest positive intercorrelations, and because there has been a lack of clarity over terminology. The following paragraphs will, I hope, offer a logical position over terminology.

Schizotypal personality traits, as I define them, are tendencies to behave and think in ways that are qualitatively similar to features seen in schizophrenia, although we consider alternative definitions briefly below. These traits are readily measured by self-report questionnaires and show considerable variation within samples of healthy individuals.

There is now quite strong evidence that healthy individuals, scoring highly on schizotypal personality questionnaires, also perform similar to schizophrenic patients on a number of information-processing tasks (e.g. Baruch *et al.* 1988; Broks 1984; Bullen & Hemsley 1984). However, it is clear that schizotypal personality is a multidimensional construct, as is schizophrenia itself. Vollema and van den Bosch (1995) reviewed the evidence from several factor analytic studies with healthy participants and concluded there were four schizotypal personality factors which they termed Positive Schizotypy, Negative Schizotypy, Cognitive Disorganization/Social Anxiety, and Nonconformity. Following Mason *et al.* (1995), I prefer to refer to this latter factor of schizotypal personality as Impulsive Nonconformity (ImpNon) in keeping with the impulsive content of some of the items on the scales that measure this factor.

It is particularly illuminating, in the present context, to consider the ImpNon factor in relation to the definition of schizotypal personality. In my definition offered above, ImpNon does not qualify as a genuinely schizotypal factor. This follows because the trait does not reflect cognitions or behaviours that are similar to those of schizophrenics. In fact, it relates to mild versions of the impulsive, antisocial and sensation seeking behaviours seen in specific personality disorders, e.g. borderline, schizoid, or antisocial personality disorder. Having said that, the first scale which deliberately attempted to assess the ImpNon factor, the Impulsive Nonconformity scale of Chapman *et al.* (1984), was expressly constructed to measure "impulsive antisocial behaviour of the sort often reported in the premorbid adjustment of some psychotics" (p. 681).

Alternative definitions of schizotypal personality emphasize the increased presence of high scores on such traits in the close relatives of schizophrenic individuals, or suggest that high scores on such traits are an index of proneness to schizophrenia or psychosis. There is weak evidence of higher scores on the ImpNon factor in the relatives of schizophrenic individuals (Claridge *et al.* 1983; although see Thaker *et al.* 1993). The necessary follow-up studies to determine schizophrenia-proneness in high trait scorers are obviously difficult to undertake. The only study of which I am aware did not show a significantly increased risk of psychosis or proneness to psychosis in high ImpNon scorers, indexed by the EPQ-P scale or the Chapman ImpNon scale, over a 10-year follow-up (Chapman *et al.*, 1994a, b). In the same sample, high ImpNon scorers showed increased rates of substance use disorders 10 years later, particularly if the individuals had also been high scorers 10 years earlier on positive schizotypy measures (Kwapil 1996). In a final study with this sample, subjects with high scores on a hypomania scale were particularly prone to bipolar mood disorders, poor overall adjustment and higher rates of arrest if they also had high ImpNon scale scores (Kwapil *et al.* 2000). In sum, the ImpNon factor does not seem to qualify as a true schizotypal factor on any definitional grounds. Its inclusion in inventories of schizotypal personality scales is thus largely historical and adds to the confusion between ImpASS and schizotypal personality traits.

In contrast with the above, my view would be to consider measures of the ImpNon factor to be possible indices of ImpASS traits central to this chapter. Note that the ImpNon measure from the Mason *et al.* (1995) Oxford-Liverpool Inventory of Feelings and Experiences (OLIFE) battery includes eight EPQ-P items; if the EPQ-P is a good measure of certain aspects of the ImpASS trait cluster, then so is the ImpNon scale.

Is there any cognitive-behavioural evidence for a distinction between ImpASS and schizotypal personality traits? In various studies of healthy participants in my laboratory — some described later in this chapter — I have found that measures of ImpASS and measures of schizotypal personality dissociate in their relationships with specific behavioural measures. In another study carried out by Harry Pidd, a student in my laboratory, we used a latent inhibition (LI) task. LI refers to the retardation in learning that develops following non-reinforced pre-exposure of the conditioned stimulus. We found that schizotypal personality and ImpASS scales each made significant, but statistically independent, contributions to task performance (Pickering 2002). This result is consistent with the idea that LI tasks involve multiple psychological processes, some of which are associated with ImpASS traits while others are associated with schizotypal personality traits.

As reviewed elsewhere (Pickering & Gray 2001), LI tasks have previously revealed relationships with either ImpASS or schizotypal personality measures (in separate studies) but our study looked at both types of trait simultaneously. Another study also did this using different personality scales (Gray *et al.* 2002). They found a significant association of schizotypal personality and LI that was independent of the contribution of their ImpASS score; however, the significant relation between LI and ImpASS, which they also found, was not statistically independent of the contribution of schizotypal personality. From the study of Gray *et al.* (2002), one might conclude that some of the processes involved in LI are associated with schizotypal personality. But the apparent relationship between LI and ImpASS traits may be spurious and arise because ImpASS traits are correlated with schizotypal personality traits that are associated with LI. Whatever relations between LI, schizotypal personality and ImpASS traits turn out to be correct, these studies illustrate the need to look at the influence of other, correlated personality traits when studying the links between ImpASS and specific behaviours. These issues resurface at several points later in the text when we consider the joint influence of ImpASS and other traits, i.e. extraversion, anxiety, plus schizotypal personality, on specific behavioural tasks.

2. Measures of the ImpASS Trait Cluster

There are many different scales that measure elements of the ImpASS personality trait cluster. To investigate the research questions posed in this chapter, there are currently few clues to help determine which measures may provide the strongest correlations with

Table 1: A sample of the scales that measure aspects of the ImpASS personality trait cluster.

Example Measures of the ImpASS Trait Cluster		
Scale	**Originator**	**Inventory**
Novelty seeking	Cloninger	Tridimensional Personality Questionnaire (TPQ; Cloninger 1989)
Psychoticism scale	Eysenck	Eysenck Personality Questionnaire; (EPQ; Eysenck & Eysenck 1975)
Impulsiveness and venturesomeness	Eysenck	The I_7-Impulsiveness Scale (Eysenck *et al.* 1985)
Sensation seeking scale	Zuckerman	Sensation Seeking Scale (SSS; Zuckerman 1979)
Behavioural activation system scale	Carver & White	Behavioural Inhibition System and Behavioural Activation System Scales (BIS-BAS; Carver & White 1994)
Impulsive nonconformity scale	Mason & Claridge	Oxford-Liverpool Inventory of Feelings and Emotions (OLIFE; Mason *et al.* 1995)

Note: Several of the scales have been updated. The versions referenced in the table are those that I tend to use in my laboratory.

the psychological and/or neural measures of interest. Therefore, most research in my lab uses a wide range of measures until a clear pattern starts to emerge as to which are the most relevant. Some examples of scales, along with their originators, are given in Table 1.

The various scales tap the components of the ImpASS cluster to differing degrees; some emphasize the impulsive aspects, e.g. the I_7-Impulsiveness measure; others emphasize the antisocial, e.g. EPQ-P; while others are more focussed on sensation seeking, e.g. the SSS. Naturally, it follows that if one or more of the particular ImpASS components, e.g. impulsiveness, are critical to the neuropsychological processes under investigation, then we would expect the measures that empasize those components to show the strongest and most consistent correlations with neural and behavioural measures. At the moment, I adopt an empirical approach: any possible fractionation of the ImpASS cluster will, in my view, need to be driven by the emerging data. When more data exist, we may be able to describe the neuropsychology of impulsive or antisocial or sensation seeking personality; until then, as noted in the title of this chapter, I am striving to understand the neuropsychology of ImpASS personality traits.

It is important to empasize, once again, a specific contribution from Marvin Zuckerman. His scale, i.e. the various versions of the SSS and its later derivatives, has been a particularly valuable tool for personality researchers. We routinely include the SSS in most studies in my laboratory and, as will be noted later, it was the first ImpASS scale to be related to one of our critical behavioural measures, category learning performance.

3. ImpASS Traits and the Behavioural Approach System

Having sorted out the basic issues above, the search for the neuropsychology of ImpASS traits can begin in earnest. As would be the case for many personality theorists who proposed biological theories, such as Zuckerman, Gray, Cloninger, or Eysenck, my search is predicated on the assumption that variation in ImpASS traits will, in part, relate to some variation in a particular brain-behavioural system or neurochemical pathway. This system or pathway may, of course, affect a large number of psychological functions and involve widespread brain structures. The assumption I am making means simply that these neural variations, whatever they are, are associated with being impulsive and/or antisocial and/or sensation seeking. We might even go further and suggest that these neural variations cause people to vary in the extent of their ImpASS traits, although the correlational nature of our evidence means that we are unlikely to be very confident about making a causal claim such as this.

Let us consider just the impulsive part of the ImpASS cluster of traits. One way to proceed in the search would be to look for evidence about the nature and/or location of an impulse control system in the brain. Such evidence might come from animal studies in which lesions to, or psychopharmacological manipulation of, a particular brain structure, pathway or system, produced an analogue of impulsive behaviour in the experimental animal. From this type of evidence, one might speculate that inter-individual differences in the functioning of this impulse control system were responsible for the trait of impulsivity. One might then complete the circle of evidence by carrying out a study in healthy human participants which demonstrated, in some way, that functional activity in the relevant brain regions was correlated with measured trait impulsivity in the sample. This type of tidy picture has not yet, to my knowledge, emerged in the literature.

In addition, the above sort of direct theoretical account is limited to a fairly coarse level of behavioural analysis; that is, to a description of the impulsive behaviours that are the central part of the personality trait concerned. However, there is a tradition in personality research of proposing a finer-grained, or more fundamental level of psychobiological explanation for trait variations. For example, Eysenck's classic account of extraversion (Eysenck 1967; Eysenck & Eysenck 1985) was couched in terms of a basic psychobiological construct, cortical arousal, which explained the behavioural characteristics of extraverts at a grosser level, e.g. sensation seeking. This might be called an "indirect" account of the trait in question.

In relation to ImpASS traits, a specific indirect psychobiological account was proposed by Jeffrey Gray, and broadly endorsed and elaborated by a number of distinguished biologically inclined personality theorists, including Zuckerman, Cloninger, and Depue. The precise name for the personality trait concerned varies from theorist to theorist, each emphasizing different aspects of the ImpASS cluster; indeed Gray himself originally emphasized the term "impulsivity." At a psychological level, it has been suggested that a subset of ImpASS traits corresponds to variations in the functioning of a behavioural approach system (BAS) which directs responses to rewarding stimuli and stimuli associated with reward (see Pickering & Gray 1999, 2001). The BAS includes the term "approach" in its title because the principal behaviour invoked by this system is to approach any rewards in the environment, or any stimuli associated with reward. Despite having a large number of advocates, the direct evidence from human participants related to this psychological account is very inconsistent (see Pickering & Gray 2001, for a review).

The neural substrate of the BAS is also spelled out, although in fairly broad terms. The BAS is argued to be centred upon the projections of midbrain dopaminergic neurons to limbic structures, e.g. the amygdala, involved in emotions, and to basal ganglia nuclei, ventral striatum (nucleus accumbens) and dorsal striatum (caudate) involved in motivation, and the control of attention and movement. The evidence from animal studies for a BAS-like system, involving dopamine and including these brain structures, has been thoroughly reviewed by Depue and Collins (1999).

There is also a variety of evidence suggesting that ImpASS traits are associated with variations in brain dopamine (DA) function (see Pickering & Gray 1999, 2001, for a review). Some of this evidence relates to the EPQ-P scale, and also finds no relation between DA markers and EPQ-Extraversion (e.g. Gray *et al.* 1994). However, there is a roughly equivalent amount of evidence suggesting that the strongest correlate of DA function is actually Extraversion, with particular emphasis on its sociability features, e.g. as measured by the Positive Emotionality scale (Tellegen 1982; Tellegen & Waller 1992). Based on this evidence, it is argued that any relationship between DA function and ImpASS derives from the fact that ImpASS is correlated with Extraversion. This is the position taken by Depue and colleagues (see Depue & Collins 1999). My view (see Pickering 1999) is that the scales of evidence, regarding correlations with DA markers, are currently not tipped decisively in favour of either Extraversion or ImpASS traits. It is also possible that both Extraversion and ImpASS traits may have independent associations with differing aspects of brain DA function.

Thus far we have mainly been covering old ground. For the rest of this chapter, I will present brief summaries of some recent studies from my laboratory. These studies were conducted within the broad framework set out above and address the general question of whether ImpASS trait measures are associated with behavioural measures of BAS functioning. In doing so, as highlighted earlier, I will also note the relation of the same behavioural measures to schizotypal personality, anxiety or Extraversion. To foreshadow the results, it appears that measures of Extraversion are modestly associated with behavioural indices of BAS functioning.

The second main finding is that ImpASS measures, and perhaps especially those measures emphasizing the antisocial component, e.g. EPQ-P, do not appear to be associated with BAS function. A pattern of correlations between other tasks and EPQ-P did emerge, however. The tasks with which EPQ-P was correlated seemed very likely to involve the functioning of the hippocampal system. Hence, my search for clues as to the neuropsychology of ImpASS traits has taken me from dopamine to hippocampal function.

4. Searching for the Personality Correlates of BAS-Induced Motivational Effects

One recent study attempted to explore the motivational effects of stimuli associated with reward on task performance (Pickering *et al.* 2001). We did so because such motivational effects are part of the function of the BAS. Stimuli associated with reward are supposed to activate the BAS; if the BAS is activated then one effect will be to motivate any ongoing goal-directed behaviour. Thus, a participant performing an experimental task will do so more rapidly in the presence of a BAS-activating stimulus. Moreover, a subject with a high level of a BAS-related personality trait, henceforth referred to as a high BAS individual, should show a stronger motivational effect than a person with a low level of a BAS-related personality trait (low BAS individual).

The study began by training participants to associate a specific visual stimulus, e.g. a filled white triangle, with the presence of reward. Each time the reward stimulus appeared, rather than an alternative shape, this signalled to the participant that he or she had gained 50 UK pence. Training consisted of 7 shape-reward exposures. Next, in the guise of a separate experiment, we familiarized the participants with a choice reaction time (RT) task. We wanted to investigate the effect, on choice RT performance, of presenting the stimulus previously associated with reward. To present the reward stimulus we used an extended warning stimulus on the RT trials. This warning signal consisted of a sequence of 4 coloured circles at successive locations around the central fixation cross (0.25 s per circle, appearing west, north, east and south of the fixation cross). On infrequent reward motivational probe RT trials, the geometric stimulus previously associated with reward was shown instead of the last circle from the warning stimulus (i.e. the reward stimulus was shown for the 0.25 s just prior to the presentation of the choice RT stimulus). The measure of the BAS effect induced by the reward stimulus was the extent to which the choice RT was speeded up on reward motivational probe RT trials relative to standard RT trials. High BAS individuals were predicted to show greater speeding up than low BAS individuals.

Before we began this study, we felt that there was likely to be a major complication: introducing a change to the warning stimulus sequence, even with a familiar neutral stimulus, seemed likely to affect RTs via a mismatch detection process. We confirmed these suspicions in an initial experiment without reward motivational probe trials. Infrequent probe trials were used in which a familiar neutral stimulus was shown instead of the fourth circle from the standard warning sequence. We called these trials associative mismatch (AM) probe trials. The RTs on AM probe trials were very significantly slower than RTs on standard trials. Furthermore, as we predicted from Gray's Reinforcement Sensitivity Theory (Pickering *et al.* 1997), we found that the extent of the slowing on AM trials was correlated with trait anxiety in the first experiment. It seemed likely that the reward motivational stimulus would create slowing due to an anxiety-related mismatch process, in addition to any BAS-related speeding up of RT. The results of the second experiment confirmed these expectations.

Figure 1 shows the results from the reward motivational study. Mean RTs are displayed for the AM probe trials and for the reward motivational probe trials. The mean RTs for each type of probe trial are shown alongside mean RTs from control trials. The control trials were a corresponding subset of standard trials in fact, those standard trials immediately preceding the probe trials concerned. While a strong general mismatch effect was present in the comparison of AM probes and standard trials, around 40 msec on average, there was virtually no difference in RT in the comparison of reward motivational probes and standard trials. This is consistent with the idea that two effects may be cancelling each other out in the reward motivational probe trials: a mismatch effect slowing RT and a reward motivational effect speeding up RT. The question is whether the association with personality measures supported this interpretation?

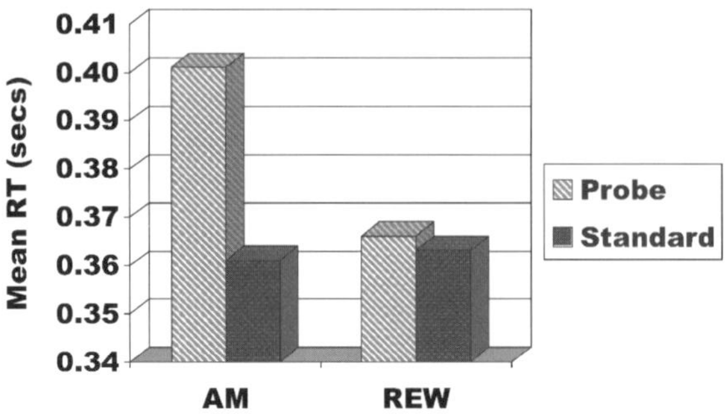

Figure 1: Mean reaction time (RT) for probe trials and their corresponding standard trials. *Note:* AM denotes probe trials were of the associative mismatch type. REW denotes probe trials were of the reward motivational type. The difference between probe and standard trials was highly significant for the AM trials; the probe-standard difference was negligible for the REW trials.

The study tested 40 healthy male medical students and took 4 measures of trait anxiety from each. The study also took 4 possible ImpASS trait measures: EPQ-P; I7-IMP; TPQ Novelty Seeking; the BAS scale. Two Extraversion-Introversion scales, EPQ-Extraversion and the OLIFE Introvertive Anhedonia scale,[1] were also included.

The dependent variable in this study was an RT difference measure: the RT for a particular type of probe trial minus the mean RT for the corresponding standard trials. As expected, based on the first study, anxiety was related to performance on AM probe trials. Analyses revealed that performance was most strongly associated with two of the anxiety measures, TPQ Harm Avoidance and the BIS scale. These two measures were combined into a single trait anxiety index (ANX). The ANX index was negatively correlated, $r = -0.28, p = 0.08$, with the RT difference calculated using AM probe trials minus their corresponding standard trials. This relation was similar when the RT difference was calculated using the reward motivational probe trials minus their corresponding standard trials, $r = -0.27$, $p = 0.09$. Thus, there was a modest tendency for the most trait anxious participants to be the least slowed down by the mismatch effect, with less anxious participants experiencing greater slowing of RT by mismatch.

Therefore, the key question was which, if any, of the possible BAS-related personality traits, from the four ImpASS and two extraversion measures taken, were associated with RT changes on reward motivational probe trials, after partialling out the anxiety-related mismatch effect? This was explored by multiple regression analyses. After partialling out the effect of ANX, EPQ-Extraversion showed a significant negative correlation with the RT difference on reward motivational trials, $\beta = -0.32$, $p < 0.05$; for ANX, $\beta = -0.35$, $p < 0.05$. The extraversion effect remained significant when outliers in the RT difference

[1] Although this scale is drawn from a schizotypal personality battery (Mason *et al.* 1995) its content — concerning an inability to enjoy social and physical pleasures and rewards — strongly suggests that it might be a BAS-related scale (with high scores indicative of low BAS functioning). The measure includes several EPQ-E items (inversely scored) and so I class it as an introversion-extraversion scale.

measure distribution were removed. This indicates that extraverts show a greater degree of speeding up on reward motivational probe trials than introverts, after removing the anxiety-related mismatch effect that is also present. In analogous regression analyses with ANX and each of the other five candidate BAS-related measures none showed a significant effect. Finally, when EPQ-Extraversion and ANX were used to predict the RT difference on AM trials, the regression coefficient for EPQ-Extraversion was small and positive, $\beta = 0.11$, $p > 0.4$. These analyses further confirm a specific association between extraversion, as measured by EPQ-Extraversion, and the motivational effect produced by secondary positive reinforcers.

5. Searching for the Personality Correlates of BAS-Induced Reinforcement Effects

Another series of studies from my lab looked at possible BAS influences on learning, as opposed to the BAS-related motivational influences on task performance that were studied in the research just summarised. Before describing some of the studies, the rationale for the methods used needs to be explained in detail.

It was noted earlier that there is a widespread belief that ascending dopaminergic projections to limbic and basal ganglia structures form an intrinsic part of the neural substrate of the BAS. This encouraged us to look for simple learning tasks that were likely to be dependent upon such dopaminergic projections; such considerations suggested that category learning (CL) tasks might be suitable tools for our research. In CL tasks the participant is presented with a set of novel stimuli and has to learn to categorise each into arbitrary categories. Subjects usually start such tasks by guessing the category assignments, but learning performance is guided by feedback about whether earlier responses were correct or incorrect. In an extensive review of the neuropsychology of CL, Ashby *et al.* (1998) argued that some forms of CL task are dependent on the neural circuitry that personality theorists believe to be linked to the BAS. In particular, performance on some CL tasks is impaired in patients with Parkinson's disease (e.g. Knowlton *et al.* 1996). Parkinson's disease is caused by a severe degeneration of the ascending dopaminergic projections, particularly those from the substantia nigra to the dorsal striatum (Agid 1991). Scanning studies, using fMRI, also show activation of the dorsal striatum (caudate) during CL tasks in healthy subjects (Poldrack *et al.* 1999, 2001).

On this basis, then, CL tasks look as if they may be useful tools for testing the effects of BAS-related personality traits on learning. One might suggest that some CL tasks depend upon the BAS neural circuitry because the feedback about responses acts as a form of reinforcement, rewarding correct responses and/or punishing incorrect responses. Based on many informal debriefings of participants in reinforcement studies, I have gained the clear impression that many of them find the correct/incorrect feedback in such experiments just as strong a reinforcer as the explicit financial rewards/penalties given in such tasks (see Pickering *et al.* 1995). We human beings are social animals and thus social reinforcers are likely to be especially powerful for us; the strong influence of performance feedback seems plausible, therefore, if we consider that feedback is part of the indirect social interaction with the experimenter. Over and above this, neuroimaging studies (e.g. Elliott *et al.* 1997) have shown that the medial caudate is a principal focus for neural activation by positive feedback signals. This confirms that feedback is activating similar neural systems to those activated by explicit rewards.

From the foregoing, we can derive the simple prediction: that the BAS would be more strongly activated during a CL task, by the rewards present in the form of positive feedback after successful responses, for high BAS individuals than for low BAS individuals. What effects would this increased BAS activation have on task performance? First, it seems likely that the motivational effects, discussed earlier, would lead to more rapid responding in high BAS individuals. However, if high BAS individuals are more sensitive to reward stimuli than low BAS individuals, then they might learn more rapidly from the feedback given during the task. In other words, because rewards improve learning partly through reinforcement, then learning should be faster/greater in high BAS (c.f. low BAS) individuals.

The foregoing is a simple, intuitive prediction. However, from what we know about the possible functions of the dopaminergic projections to the striatum and related structures, this prediction can be made with greater confidence. Cell recording studies in monkeys have shown that midbrain dopaminergic cells fire phasically in response both to primary rewards, e.g. an unsignalled drop of fruit juice placed into the animal's mouth, and to conditioned visual or auditory stimuli that have become valid predictors of reward. After learning has established the conditioned stimulus as a reward-predictor, the primary reward no longer elicits phasic firing in the dopaminergic cell (see Brown *et al.* 1999; Schultz *et al.* 1995, for details and references).

Assuming we were able to measure single DA cell firing in humans, the monkey findings cited above might lead us to expect that a high BAS individual would show greater midbrain DA cell firing in response to reward than a low BAS individual. Although such an experiment is not possible, the behavioural effects (whatever they are) of such DA cell firing might well be able to be measured, and these effects should also be greater in high BAS individuals.[2] In fact, there is a considerable consensus about one important function served by the ascending DA cell firing: it is widely believed to be vital for the long-term synaptic changes underpinning learning in the striatum (and elsewhere; see Schultz 1998; Wickens & Kotter 1995, for comprehensive reviews).

We can now summarise our complete set of plausible hypotheses and assumptions: high BAS individuals respond to reward stimuli more strongly than low BAS individuals; reward stimuli act on the BAS by increasing cell firing in ascending midbrain DA neurons and thereby increase DA release in the striatal and other targets of these projections; the neural functions supported by DA cell firing and release in these ascending pathways will differ

[2] The monkey data suggest that an effect of reward, or a conditioned stimulus signalling reward, is to increase midbrain dopamine cell firing. The notion that a high BAS (c.f. low BAS) individual is more sensitive to reward stimuli leads to a prediction of differential reward-induced dopamine cell firing. However, the dopamine cell firing produces its behavioural effects by actions on dopamine receptors at the sites of dopamine release in the striatum and elsewhere. Even if the dopamine cell firing response to reward stimuli were not different between high and low BAS individuals, then a high BAS individual could still be more sensitive to reward stimuli; this could occur, for example, if the receptors stimulated by the reward-induced dopamine release were differentially sensitive to dopamine in high and low BAS individuals. At a behavioural level we would not be able to differentiate the various possible loci of sensitivity differences within the dopamine projection system.

between high and low BAS individuals and are critical for learning to occur within the striatal structures to which the DA neurons project; and, these striatal structures are part of the brain system which supports learning on some forms of CL task. It therefore follows that CL performance is predicted to be associated with BAS personality traits in line with the simple intuitive prediction made above.

At this point, it should be noted that Marvin Zuckerman has made another direct contribution to research in this area, with the only published study of CL and personality (Ball & Zuckerman 1990). I have analysed this study in detail elsewhere (Pickering & Gray 2001), and concluded that it represents one of the best published experiments looking at the influence of BAS-related personality traits on learning. Ball and Zuckerman tested 140 undergraduate subjects who scored either in the upper or lower decile of the SSS. They describe their task as a concept-learning task, in keeping with the previous literature, although it is a type of CL task. At that time, the neuropsychological data suggesting the value of CL tasks in BAS research did not exist; Ball and Zuckerman presumably chose their task because it provided a simple basis upon which to construct a test of the links between personality and reinforcement sensitivities.

The visual stimuli were presented in a pair on each trial, with one stimulus on each trial being the target to which the subject had to respond, with the other stimulus serving as a distractor. This is a forced-choice CL scenario, equivalent to being asked "which of these two stimuli is from category A?" The position of the target stimulus varied from left to right across trials. The stimuli were compounds of elements drawn from eight binary dimensions, e.g. a stimulus contained either a letter T or an X; it had different shaped borders around the letter etc., and the target and distractor had different values on each dimension. Two of the eight dimensions were "critical" as they were reliably associated with target status, e.g. the target stimulus always contained a letter T and a square border, and the distractor stimulus contained the letter X and a circular border. The other 6 dimensions were non-critical as they were uncorrelated with target status.[3]

Ball and Zuckerman (1990) used four different reinforcement conditions, formed by crossing two between-subjects factors: verbal feedback vs. monetary reinforcement; and reward-only vs. punishment-only conditions. No feedback was given for errors during the reward-only condition, or for correct responses in the punishment-only condition. Ball and Zuckerman (1990) reported the number of trials that each subject took to reach a criterion of five consecutive correct responses.

The main finding was that the high sensation seeking group of subjects learned the task significantly faster, i.e. reached the criterion in fewer trials, than the low sensation seeking group. The other key finding was that the effect of sensation seeking group on learning did not interact with reinforcement conditions. There were no effects of verbal feedback vs. monetary reinforcement, or of the reward-only vs. punishment-only manipulation. The lack of difference between verbal feedback and monetary reinforcement can be seen as consistent with the arguments we made earlier about the probable BAS-activating effects of verbal

---

[3] This was true only for the "Random condition" of their experiment; half the subjects were tested in a so-called "Correlated condition" in which the values for one of the six non-critical dimensions had a 75% concordance with the target values from the critical dimensions. This factor did not affect the findings most relevant for the present chapter and so can be ignored.

feedback. However, Ball and Zuckerman (1990) had predicted that the beneficial effects on learning of sensation seeking, and other BAS-related traits, would have been restricted to the reward-only reinforcement conditions. The lack of difference, in terms of the correlations with personality, between reward-only and punishment-only conditions therefore raises the possibility that BAS-related personality traits may affect learning through mechanisms that are not connected with sensitivity to positive reinforcers.

Ball and Zuckerman (1990) offered two alternative explanations for why high sensation seekers might have learned this task faster than low sensation seekers, irrespective of reinforcement condition. First, they suggested that, relative to low sensation seekers, high sensation seekers might have adopted a beneficial risk-taking cognitive strategy during the early trial-and-error stages of the task. Second, they argued that high sensation seekers might have superior selective attention abilities than low sensation seekers, and thus be better able to focus in on the relevant stimulus dimensions rather than the irrelevant ones.

These suggestions bring to mind one of the key points of Ashby *et al.* (2002), about CL: that only some CL tasks are likely to depend critically on BAS-related circuitry. In particular, they argued that the dopaminergic pathways were particularly important for CL tasks where the assignment to categories was learned slowly, and where the category assignment "rule" could not be readily verbalised. They characterised these CL tasks as a form of implicit learning. This was in contrast to rapidly learned CL tasks for which the category assignments can be readily expressed in the form of a verbal rule, e.g. if the stimulus is on a blue background then it is in category A, etc. The neural circuitry proposed by Ashby *et al.* (2002) for these rule-based CL tasks is much less dependent on the brain structures comprising the BAS, and does not involve a critical role for dopaminergic neurotransmission. In addition, the rule-based CL tasks often can be solved by making responses based on values of a single dimension of the multidimensional stimulus. Such tasks benefit from a hypothesis-testing approach by the participant, systematically trying to find stimulus features that predict category membership. Selective attention to relevant stimulus features is thus a key element in performing these tasks. By contrast, the implicit CL tasks typically require the participant to integrate information from more than one stimulus dimension before making a decision on the integrated information. Thus, these tasks are referred to as information-integration CL tasks.

Ball and Zuckerman's (1990) task appears more likely to be of the rule-based type, e.g. "the target stimulus always contained a T." In keeping with this suggestion, successful learning was rapid and only one stimulus dimension needed processing to learn the task. The prediction that an association between sensation seeking and learning would be restricted to the reward-only conditions, which was based on the hypothetical effects of BAS activation, might therefore not be expected to apply to Ball and Zuckerman's (1990) CL task. Furthermore, their alternative suggestions for why high sensation seekers learned their task rapidly assumed a rule-based solution strategy which involved restricting attention to the critical stimulus dimensions. Even if these alternative suggestions prove to be incorrect, it is noteworthy that an ImpASS trait measure was associated with learning performance in this task under conditions where BAS-mediated effects were not very likely to be operating. I shall return later to consider other possible mechanisms which might underlie this relation.

In my lab, we have now carried out a number of studies looking at CL performance and personality trait measures. In two of our initial studies (Pickering *et al.* in preparation), as with Ball and Zuckerman (1990), the CL task used was of the rapidly learned, rule-based type that was based on Kruschke (1993). The visual stimuli had two dimensions: (1) the height of a rectangle; and (2) the position within it of an internal line segment. Only one of these, height of the rectangle, determined category membership. The first small-scale study tested only males ($N = 30$), and used only two personality measures, Novelty Seeking and Harm Avoidance from the TPQ. The former was included as a putatively dopaminergic ImpASS trait (e.g. see Cloninger *et al.* 1993); the latter was a control anxiety trait measure that was not expected to be related to performance. There were eight stimuli, four from each category, and each was presented, and responded to, once in a random order within a "learning epoch." There were six learning epochs, which meant that the index of CL performance was the overall number of correct responses. This score was out of 48 (chance = 24). Within each epoch the CL score, i.e. number correct, was out of 8 (chance = 4).

Novelty Seeking and the four Novelty Seeking subscales, plus Harm Avoidance and the four Harm Avoidance subscales, were correlated with CL performance overall. Neither Harm Avoidance, nor any of the Harm Avoidance subscales, were significantly associated with CL performance, ($-0.22 < r < 0.16$). However, the correlations of overall CL performance with the Novelty Seeking impulsivity subscale and with the Novelty Seeking disorderliness subscale were both positive and significant, $r = 0.41$ and $r = 0.37$, respectively. The relations with the other Novelty Seeking subscales were weaker; with the result that the correlation between CL performance and total Novelty Seeking score was only a positive trend, $r = 0.25, p < 0.18$. We also subdivided the participants into two groups based on the median score on the Novelty Seeking impulsivity subscale. Repeated measures analysis of CL performance in each of the 6 epochs, with the two Novelty Seeking impulsivity subscale groups forming a between-subjects factor, revealed a highly significant main effect of Novelty Seeking impulsivity subscale grouping. The effect is illustrated in Figure 2, and shows that both groups appeared to be performing largely at chance during the first learning epoch. In subsequent epochs the high Novelty Seeking impulsivity subscale group showed superior CL performance relative to the low Novelty Seeking impulsivity subscale group.

Encouraged by the findings from the first study, we carried out several further experiments. In a second study, we used the same task and tested 23 female and 28 male students. In the first phase of the task, the lateral position of the internal line segment determined the category membership and the height of the rectangle was irrelevant. Without explicitly signalling this to the participant, the category assignment rule was changed in a second phase of the task so that the height of the rectangle was relevant and the internal line segment position was irrelevant. For the reasons discussed earlier in the chapter, both ImpASS and schizotypal personality measures were used: the EPQ-P was administered as a measure of ImpASS traits, and the Unusual Experiences scale from the OLIFE battery was given as a measure of positive schizotypal personality.

Four dependent variables were analysed: total CL accuracy over both phases; CL accuracy in phase 1; CL accuracy in phase 2; and CL accuracy in phase 1 minus CL accuracy in phase 2. These dependent variables were predicted using multiple regression analyses with subject gender, EPQ-P and Unusual Experiences scores as predictors. No predictors were associated with the difference in CL accuracy across phases. Gender was not a significant predictor in any analyses. Both personality variables were significantly associated with total CL

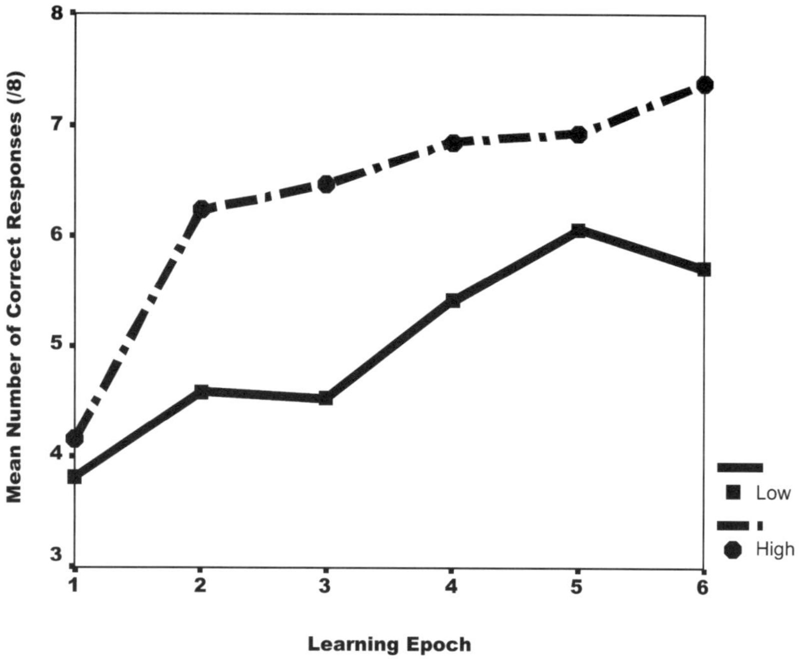

Figure 2: The mean number of correct responses during each epoch of the category learning task. *Note:* The upper dashed line is for participants who scored in the high impulsivity group; the lower solid line is for low impulsivity participants. Impulsivity groupings were based on a median split for the impulsivity subscale of the Novelty Seeking Scale (Cloninger 1989).

performance, EPQ-P: $\beta = 0.29$; UnExp: $\beta = -0.432$. Analyses of CL performance in each phase revealed that the positive association between EPQ-P and learning was significant only in phase 1of the task, $\beta = 0.32, p < 0.05$, whereas in phase 2 $\beta = 0.17, p > 0.25$. In contrast, Unusual Experiences showed a significant negative association with CL performance only in phase 2, $\beta = -0.41, p < 0.01$, whereas in phase 1, $\beta = -0.22, p > 0.15$. These findings were unchanged when Extraversion from the EPQ was added as a further predictor in the regressions.

First, these findings replicated the positive association between an ImpAss trait and CL performance. In addition, they showed that this relationship was independent of a significant negative association between positive schizotypal personality and CL performance. This dissociation between the effects of ImpASS and schizotypal traits is all the more striking because the trait measures concerned were themselves significantly positively associated, $r = 0.43$.

Although we have found replicable evidence of a positive association between CL performance and measures of ImpASS personality, consistent with Ball and Zuckerman (1990), the outcome does not clarify the mechanisms for the association. However, as noted earlier, the use of rule-based CL tasks in the above studies from our lab, and in

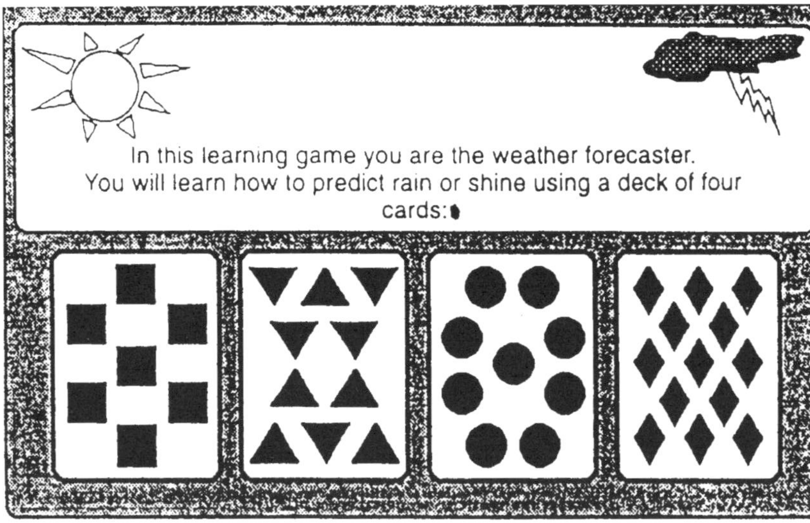

Figure 3: A representation of the computerised stimulus materials used in the weather prediction task.

Ball and Zuckerman (1990), suggests that the ImpASS-CL association might well have been obtained under conditions where the influence of the BAS was minimal. Ashby *et al.* (2002) and Maddox *et al.* (2003) showed that the rule-based CL tasks are insensitive to manipulations affecting the delivery of feedback, whereas matched information-integration CL tasks were highly sensitive to these manipulations. In our next CL study, conducted in collaboration with my student Rozmin Halari, we attempted to test the relations with personality traits under conditions which maximised the likelihood of BAS involvement. In this study (Pickering 2003), we used a probabilistic CL task ("the weather task") which was used in early studies of CL and Parkinson's disease (Knowlton *et al.* 1996). In this computerised task, participants are presented with a subset of four cards each bearing distinct patterns (see Figure 3). The participant has to learn to assign these card combinations to categories, sunshine or rain, based on correct-incorrect feedback given in response to their previous choices.

In the standard version of this task, one of the four cards has a probabilistic association with sunshine, i.e. across the whole task, the probability of sun when that card is present equals 0.76. Another card has the same 0.76 probabilistic association with rain. One of the other cards is weakly associated, 0.58, with sunshine and the remaining card is weakly associated, 0.58, with rain. It is not clear where the standard version of the task sits with respect to the rule-based vs. information-integration distinction discussed above. However, there are a variety of rule-based strategies that healthy subjects appear to adopt when solving this task (see Gluck *et al.* 2002). In order to increase chances of engaging BAS-related mechanisms, we decided to give the task an information-integration structure. We did this by assigning a value for each card, 0.25 for two cards and −0.25 for the other two cards. Across the whole training phase of the task, the probability of sun appearing for a particular combination of cards was given by 0.5 plus the values of the cards present. Thus, two cards increased the chances of sun and two cards increased the chances of rain. The result of this procedure was that, across the whole training phase, each card was modestly associated, 0.64, with one of the two weather categories. We also increased the rewarding nature of the feedback by giving the participants 10 UK pence for each correct response during training. After training, i.e. four runs though all possible stimuli with feedback/reinforcement, the amount learned was assessed by a test phase consisting of single run through the possible stimuli. The responses of the participants during the test phase did not receive any feedback/reinforcement.

We wanted to compare learning of the BAS-engaging, information-integration task described above with a matched control task. For the control task, we devised a paired-associate or observational learning version of the task. In the training phase of a paired-associate task, no feedback or reinforcements are delivered. Participants simply observe the stimuli present on a trial and are informed of the category, i.e. sunshine or rain. There is thus little chance of engaging the BAS during paired-associate tasks. Consistent with this view, Ashby *et al.* (2002) showed that paired-associate training impaired ability of the participants to learn an information-integration category structure, but not a rule-based category structure. Paired-associate training seems likely to be preventing the engagement of the reinforcement-dependent, BAS-related neural system that is necessary for information-integration, but not rule-based, CL tasks.

In our paired-associate task, the assignment of stimulus combinations to categories during training was very similar to that of the standard weather task. The amount learned after paired-associate training was assessed by a test phase consisting of a single run through all the possible stimuli in which participants responded with their category judgements but did not receive feedback or reinforcement.

We wanted to observe the correlations between personality measures and test-phase performance on the rewarded information-integration task. Then, using a within-subjects design, we wanted to compare these correlations with the correlations between personality and test-phase performance on the paired-associate version of the task. To do this we therefore constructed a symptoms and diseases task which was exactly analogous in structure to the weather task. In the disease task the role of the four cards was taken by four symptoms, e.g. bleeding gums, and the two categories were two fictitious diseases, e.g. nermitis and caldosis, rather than weather outcomes. Each participant was assessed using one cards and weather task, and one symptoms and diseases task. In a fully counterbalanced design, one task, i.e. weather or diseases, given first or second, was administered using the rewarded information-integration format. The other task, with the other materials, was given in the paired-associate format.

We tested 40 male participants, mostly students, on the two formats and assessed a variety of ImpAss measures, including EPQ-P, plus measures of extraversion from the EPQ and the Introvertive Anhedonia from the OLIFE, and a measure of positive schizotypal personality, Unusual Experiences from OLIFE. The results were very clear. EPQ-P was significantly correlated in the expected positive direction with the amount of CL but only in the paired-associate task, $r = 0.30, p < 0.05$. In the rewarded information-integration task the EPQ-P relation with CL was close to zero. A combined extraversion score based on Introvertive Anhedonia and EPQ-Extraversion showed the complementary pattern of associations i.e.

rewarded information-integration task: $r = +0.34$, $p < 0.05$; paired-associate task: $r = +0.13$, ns. These relations were maintained when the effect of extraversion was partialled out of the EPQ-P and learning correlations, and when the effect of EPQ-P was partialled out of the extraversion and learning correlations. Positive schizotypy, i.e. Unusual Experiences, had no significant relation with learning. Also, partialling out the influence of positive schizotypy did not affect the relations between learning and EPQ-P or Extraversion.

The results of this experiment show what neuropsychologists would call a "double dissociation." One task, rewarded information-integration CL, is associated with extraversion but not ImpASS (EPQ-P), whereas another task, paired-associate category learning, shows the complementary pattern i.e, associated with ImpAss, but not with extraversion. We can therefore conclude that the effects of extraversion and ImpAss measures on CL tasks are likely to be independent; that is, they relate to distinct mechanisms. The extraversion measures relate to processes at work specifically in the rewarded information-integration task, while ImpAss traits, as measured by EPQ-P, relate to processes specifically at work in the paired-associate task. Because we constructed the tasks so that BAS-mediated processes would be largely limited to the rewarded information-integration task, it seems that extraversion measures, but not ImpASS measures, are tapping into BAS-mediated reinforcement processes. This result confirms the position of researchers such as Depue (e.g. Depue & Collins 1999), rather than the complementary view (e.g. as proposed by Pickering & Gray 1999, 2001). Furthermore, it means that we must still seek a non-BAS explanation for the reliable relations between ImpASS measures and CL.

6. ImpASS Measures and Hippocampal Function

Several possible explanations can be offered for the repeated positive correlations between ImpASS measures and CL from Ball and Zuckerman (1990), plus the three studies from my laboratory. The attention interpretation by Ball and Zuckerman (1990) noted earlier is one candidate. However, a recent fMRI scanning study of CL suggests another serious possibility.

Poldrack *et al.* (2001) carried out an fMRI investigation of the standard version of the weather task and compared the neural activations produced with those obtained from a paired-associate version. Their paired-associate task was similar to the one that we had used. These workers found that the standard task, involving feedback for correct and incorrect responses, activated the basal ganglia (caudate nucleus) and widespread areas of cortex relative to a control task. The medial temporal lobes (MTL), including the hippocampus were deactivated by the standard feedback weather task relative to the control task. These results were consistent with a previous study (Poldrack *et al.* 1999). The novel finding was that the caudate activity was significantly greater for the feedback task than for the paired-associate task, whereas MTL activity was significantly greater in the paired-associate task than in the feedback task. Furthermore, right caudate activity was negatively correlated, across subjects and both tasks, with left MTL activity. This suggests a competition between caudate and MTL during CL tasks.

These results raise the possibility that the correlation between EPQ-P and paired-associate CL performance which we found, might arise in healthy subjects because of a link between

EPQ-P scores and hippocampal-MTL function. This is a novel proposal, as far as I am aware, concerning the neural substrate of ImpASS traits. However, there is some evidence from the study of psychopaths that is broadly consistent with this position. The EPQ-P scale emphasizes the antisocial and tough-minded elements of the ImpASS trait cluster; these same characteristics are present in extreme form in psychopaths or individuals with antisocial personality disorder. It might be reasonably argued that these clinical entities represent one extreme along a continuum with normal variation in EPQ-P scores, or variation in other ImpASS measures. There are a number of studies showing structural and functional hippocampal abnormalities in institutionalised psychopathic and aggressive populations (see Raine *et al.* 2004 for a review). Recently, Raine *et al.* (2004) found significantly greater hippocampal structural asymmetry (R $>$ L) in a non-institutionalised community sample of unsuccessful psychopaths, i.e. individuals with high psychopathy scores and past criminal convictions, relative to either a control sample with low psychopathy scores and no convictions, or a sample of successful psychopaths with high psychopathy scores but no convictions. While I would not want to suggest that our samples of high EPQ-P scoring students contained (m)any psychopaths, the data of Raine *et al.* (2004) at least raises the possibility that hippocampal structure, and perhaps functioning, could vary in the general population in relation to the extent of antisocial traits present.

Other evidence potentially linking EPQ-P, and possibly other ImpASS measures, with variations in hippocampal function comes from studies of latent inhibition (LI). As already noted, a review of the evidence shows that LI task performance was repeatedly correlated with ImpASS measures, especially with EPQ-P (Pickering & Gray 2001). In our research (Pickering 2002), the effect of ImpASS traits on LI was independent of the effect of schizotypal personality traits (but see Gray *et al.* 2002). This is relevant because LI task performance in animals is disrupted by lesions to the hippocampal system (for references, see Gray *et al.* 1991). The effect of the hippocampal lesions is to reduce the magnitude of the LI effect by increasing learning specifically about the so-called pre-exposed stimulus. High ImpASS trait scores also seem to reduce the size of the LI effect, again by increasing learning about the pre-exposed stimulus (Pickering & Gray 2001).

At the start of this chapter, I emphasized the evidence linking ImpASS traits with variations in DA markers in the brain, e.g. a negative correlation between EPQ-P scores and neuroimaging measures of D2 DA receptor binding in the striatum (Gray *et al.* 1994). How can such evidence be reconciled with this new suggestion that ImpASS trait variation might, in part, reflect variations in hippocampal functioning?

First, it should be noted that there are intense dopaminergic projections from midbrain to the hippocampus, especially the CA1 region, where all five types of DA receptors can be found, and where DA enhances synaptic plasticity (see Otmakhova & Lisman 1996). It is possible that a personality-related change in the activity of DA projection cells, and/or alterations in the efficiency of DA receptors at the synapses contacted by these projections, could occur in multiple brain regions and we have obtained direct evidence for this only in the striatal targets of DA projections. However, the changes occurring at some point along the DA projection pathways, could give rise to ImpASS-related changes in tasks sensitive to hippocampal function. Alternatively, overactivity in striatal DA, specifically in the nucleus accumbens, has been proposed to alter the information processing operations, such as mismatch detection, that are thought to depend upon the hippocampal efferents to the nucleus accumbens (Gray *et al.* 1991). A closely related model proposes that novelty/mismatch detection is controlled by a loop: the novelty/mismatch computation is carried out in the CA1 region of the hippocampus and then hippocampal outputs project the outcome of the computation indirectly to the dopaminergic cells in the ventral tegmental area of the midbrain; these cells in turn modulate functioning of CA1 (Lisman & Otmakhova 2001).

If a link between ImpASS traits and variations in hippocampal function were to exist, then one must ask about the nature of information-processing operations that would be expected to covary with ImpASS traits. One possibility, implied in the foregoing paragraph, is that mismatch and novelty detection processes might be involved. Such a possibility would be broadly consistent with the attention account that Ball and Zuckerman (1990) apply to their ImpASS and CL findings. The link between ImpASS traits and LI, a task that involves mismatch/novelty detection, also fits such a suggestion. We are actively trying to investigate this suggestion, and have some preliminary data that is consistent with it (Pickering 2002).

It has long been recognised that the hippocampus and related MTL brain structures play a critical role in explicit episodic memory (see Squire 1992). Therefore, we might expect that ImpASS trait scores would be correlated with measures of episodic memory function. In my lab, we have begun to test this idea directly. Before noting some of our initial results, I should briefly consider how such an idea might account for the positive correlation between ImpASS traits and CL performance. A positive relation might be expected if two conditions were satisfied. First, high-ImpASS subjects would need to have more efficient hippocampus-related episodic memory processes than low-ImpASS subjects; and, second, CL task performance would need to be influenced by a contribution from episodic memory.

A number of years ago, I argued for the influence of episodic memory processes during CL tasks. Therefore, I suggested that amnesic patients, with damage to the hippocampal episodic memory system, might be expected to show impairments in some CL tasks (Pickering 1997). This claim was against the then-prevailing view that CL tasks were mediated by brain systems other than those involved in episodic memory. There is now evidence that hippocampal impaired amnesics do show deficits on some CL tasks (see Hopkins *et al.* 2004), and we have already seen neuroimaging evidence for MTL activity changes during CL tasks (Poldrack *et al.* 2001). In their review of multiple systems at work in CL tasks, Ashby and Ell (2001) suggest that the influence of episodic memory processes might be most marked on CL tasks that have only a few stimulus exemplars per category. In the studies noted above, where ImpASS traits were significantly associated with CL performance, the CL tasks all involved a very small number of exemplars (4–8) per category. Thus, this observation is consistent with the idea that high-ImpASS individuals might be good at some CL tasks because they have good episodic memory relative to low-ImpASS individuals.

There is, however, one complication with this proposal that should be noted. The positive ImpASS-CL correlations may be explained by arguing that above-average hippocampal system functioning occurs in high-ImpASS individuals. However, the high-ImpASS individuals also show reduced LI; that is, they show the same pattern of behaviour found in animals with lesions to the hippocampal system. In LI, then, it seems as if the

Table 2: Correlations between personality measures and recall performance on verbal paired associates (Pickering 2002).

	EPQ-P	EPQ-P*	Intelligence	Unusual Experiences	EPQ Extraversion
Test 1	0.43	0.40	0.26	0.15	0.17
Test 2	0.33	0.29	0.27	0.09	−0.03
Test 3	0.33	0.29	0.28	0.08	−0.10
Delayed test	0.37	0.35	0.15	−0.01	−0.04

Note: Shaded correlations are significant at $p < 0.05$.
* Denotes correlations after partialling out intelligence test score.

performance of high-ImpASS individuals is more likely to reflect impaired hippocampal functioning.[4]

Finally, I will briefly note the results of an initial study, conducted by Lucy Schomberg, when she was a student in my lab (Pickering 2002). We wanted to test the influence of ImpASS traits, specifically EPQ-P, on performance of a classic episodic memory task. We decided to test learning and delayed recall of unrelated verbal paired associates (VPAs). This is a classic task at which patients with hippocampal system lesions are severely impaired and it is incorporated within the standard clinical tool for assessing memory impairments (the Wechsler Memory Scale).

In our study we used a list of 12 unrelated verbal paired associates (e.g. SOIL-MILE; SIDE-BRAVE). The A-B word pairs were presented once each for learning; recall testing followed immediately in which the A word (e.g. SOIL) was presented and the participant had to recall the accompanying B word (e.g. MILE). This cycle of learning plus an immediate cued recall test constituted one trial. Three such trials were given in succession. Then, after a filled delay lasting several minutes, a further surprise delayed cued recall test was given. The number of words recalled correctly was recorded on the three recall tests during learning (tests 1–3), and on the delayed recall test. The participants were 40 healthy medical students who were given the EPQ-P as an ImpASS personality measure, plus measures of positive schizotypal personality, Unusual Experiences, and EPQ Extraversion. We also took a quick measure of intelligence, using a test with a high "g" loading, the Matrices subtest from the Wechsler Adult Intelligence Scale III. If we found the predicted positive correlation between EPQ-P scores and verbal paired associates recall performance, we wanted to demonstrate that this was independent of the expected positive association between intelligence and memory.

The correlations between personality measures and verbal paired associates recall performance are shown in Table 2. They show that EPQ-P scores were significantly

---

[4] It is of interest that the performance of high-ImpASS individuals (and hippocampal-lesioned animals) during LI tasks actually reflects an enhancement of learning relative to low-ImpASS individuals (or intact animals). This enhancement of learning occurs, however, under task conditions that are designed to make learning unusually slow.

positively correlated with performance on all four cued recall tests. The correlations were barely changed when the intelligence measure was partialled out. There were no significant relations between the cued recall performance measures and either EPQ-Extraversion or positive schizotypy (Unusual Experiences). These results are strongly consistent with the hypothesis that high-ImpASS individuals have better episodic memory processes than low-ImpASS individuals, and that this variation in episodic memory ability might derive from ImpASS-related variations in hippocampal system functioning. We have replicated these findings in a second sample of participants.

7. Summary and Conclusions

In this chapter I have sketched some preliminary neuropsychological accounts of ImpASS personality traits. Such traits, according to Marvin Zuckerman and other major personality theorists, form one of the basic personality dimensions on which all human beings vary. One neuropsychological account suggests that ImpASS traits might reflect, in part, variations in functioning of a dopaminergic behavioural approach system (BAS). In studies using behavioural markers of BAS functioning, the evidence did not support this view; in fact, it appeared that extraversion, rather than ImpAss trait measures, was associated with BAS-related task performance.

A novel alternative account, relating to the psychobiological substrate of ImpASS traits, was then outlined. Specifically, it was proposed that variation in ImpASS traits might relate to variation in the functioning of the hippocampal system and related structures. This proposal was more consistent with the evidence presented in this chapter; it offered a plausible account of why ImpASS traits correlated positively with specific learning and memory tasks. It is hoped that this novel hypothesis will stimulate further research into this fascinating cluster of personality traits.

Acknowledgments

I would like to thank the many students in my lab whose research projects have contributed to the findings summarised in this chapter: Wasima Ahmed, Debbie Benson, Rozmin Halari, James Jeffs, Luke Jones, Fiona MacNab, Harry Pidd, and Lucy Schomberg. I'd like to thank Greg Ashby and Todd Maddox for their many insightful contributions during our discussions on category learning. These discussions have been greatly facilitated by our membership of an international research consortium funded by a JS McDonnell Foundation Collaborative Activity Grant held by Mark Gluck. The annual consortium workshop has been very helpful in developing some of the ideas expressed in this chapter.

References

Agid, Y. (1991). Parkinson's disease: Pathophysiology. *Lancet*, *337*, 1321–1324.

Ashby, F. G., Alfonso-Reese, L. A., Turken, A. U., & Waldron, E. M. (1998). A neuropsychological theory of multiple systems in category learning. *Psychological Review*, *105*, 442–481.

Ashby, F. G., & Ell, S. W. (2001). The neurobiology of human category learning. *Trends in Cognitive Sciences*, *5*, 204–210.
Ashby, F. G., Maddox, W. T., & Bohil, C. J. (2002). Observational vs. feedback training in rule-based and information-integration category learning. *Memory & Cognition*, *30*, 666–677.
Ball, S. A., & Zuckerman, M. (1990). Sensation seeking, Eysenck's personality dimensions and reinforcement sensitivity in concept formation. *Personality and Individual Differences*, *11*, 343–353.
Baruch, I., Hemsley, D. R., & Gray, J. A. (1988). Latent inhibition and 'psychotic proneness' in normal subjects. *Personality and Individual Differences*, *9*, 777–783.
Broks, P. (1984). Schizotypy and hemisphere function — II. Performance asymmetry on a verbal divided visual field task. *Personality and Individual Differences*, *5*, 649–656.
Brown, J., Bullock, D., & Grossberg, S. (1999). How the basal ganglia use parallel excitatory and inhibitory learning pathways to selectively respond to unexpected rewarding cues. *The Journal of Neuroscience*, *19*, 10502–10511.
Bullen, J. G., & Hemsley, D. R. (1984). Psychoticism and visual recognition thresholds. *Personality and Individual Differences*, *5*, 735–739.
Carver, C. S., & White, T. L. (1994). Behavioural inhibition, behavioural activation, and affective responses to impending reward and punishment: The BIS/BAS scales. *Journal of Personality and Social Psychology*, *67*, 319–333.
Chapman, L. J., Chapman, J. P., & Kwapil, T. R. (1994a). Does the Eysenck psychoticism scale predict psychosis? A ten year longitudinal study. *Personality and Individual Differences*, *17*, 369–375.
Chapman, L. J., Chapman, J. P., Kwapil, T. R., Eckblad, M., & Zinser, M. C. (1994b). Putatively psychosis-prone subjects 10 years later. *Journal of Abnormal Psychology*, *103*, 171–183.
Chapman, L. J., Chapman, J. P., Numbers, J. S., Edell, W. S., Carpenter, B. N., & Beckfield, D. (1984). Impulsive nonconformity as a trait contributing to the prediction of psychotic-like and schizotypal symptoms. *Journal of Nervous and Mental Disease*, *172*, 681–691.
Claridge, G. S., Robinson, D. L., & Birchall, P. (1983). Characteristics of schizophrenics and neurotics' relatives. *Personality and Individual Differences*, *4*, 651–664.
Cloninger, C. R. (1989). *The Tridimensional Personality Questionnaire*. Department of Psychiatry and Genetics, Washington University School of Medicine.
Cloninger, C. R., Svrakic, D. M., & Przybeck, T. R. (1993). A psychobiological model of temperament and character. *Archives of General Psychiatry*, *50*, 975–990.
Depue, R. A., & Collins, P. F. (1999). Neurobiology of the structure of personality: Dopamine, facilitation of incentive motivation, and extraversion. *Behavioral and Brain Sciences*, *22*, 491–533.
Elliott, R., Frith, C. D., & Dolan, R. J. (1997). Differential neural response to positive and negative feedback in planning and guessing tasks. *Neuropsychologia*, *35*, 1395–1404.
Eysenck, H. J. (1967). *The biological basis of personality*. Springfield: Thomas.
Eysenck, H. J., & Eysenck, M. W. (1985). *Personality and individual differences*. New York: Plenum.
Eysenck, H. J., & Eysenck, S. B. G. (1975). *Manual of the Eysenck Personality Questionnaire*. London: Hodder & Stoughton.
Eysenck, S. B. G., Pearson, P. R., Easting, G., & Allsopp, J. F. (1985). Age norms for impulsiveness, venturesomeness and empathy in adults. *Personality and Individual Differences*, *6*, 613–619.
Gray, J. A., Feldon, J., Rawlins, J. N. P., Hemsley, D. R., & Smith, A. D. (1991). The neuropsychology of schizophrenia. *Behavioral and Brain Sciences*, *14*, 1–84.
Gray, N. S., Fernandez, M., Williams, J., Ruddle, R. A., & Snowden, R. J. (2002). Which schizotypal dimensions abolish latent inhibition? *British Journal of Clinical Psychology*, *41*, 271–284.
Gray, N. S., Pickering, A. D., & Gray, J. A. (1994). Psychoticism and dopamine D2 binding in the basal ganglia using SPET. *Personality and Individual Differences*, *17*, 431–434.

Gluck, M. A., Shohamy, D., & Myers, C. (2002). How do people solve the "weather prediction" task: Individual variability in strategies for probabilistic category learning. *Learning and Memory*, *9*, 408–418.

Hopkins, R. O., Myers, C. E., Shohamy, D., Grossman, S., & Gluck, M. (2004). Impaired probabilistic category learning in hypoxic subjects with hippocampal damage. *Neuropsychologia*, *42*, 524–535.

Knowlton, B. J., Mangels, J. A., & Squire, L. R. (1996). A neostriatal habit learning system in humans. *Science*, *273*, 1399–1402.

Kruschke, J. (1993). Human category learning: Implications for backpropagation models. *Connection Science*, *5*, 3–36.

Kwapil, T. R. (1996). A longitudinal study of drug and alcohol use by psychosis-prone and impulsive-nonconforming individuals. *Journal of Abnormal Psychology*, *105*, 114–123.

Kwapil, T. R., Miller, M. B., Zinser, M. C., Chapman, L. J., Chapman, J. P., & Eckblad, M. (2000). A longitudinal study of high scorers on the Hypomanic Personality Scale. *Journal of Abnormal Psychology*, *109*, 222–226.

Lisman, J. E., & Otmakhova, N. A. (2001). Storage, recall, and novelty detection of sequences by the hippocampus: Elaborating on the SOCRATIC model to account for normal and aberrant effects of dopamine. *Hippocampus*, *11*, 551–568.

Maddox, W. T., Ashby, F. G., & Bohil, C. J. (2003). Delayed feedback effects on rule-based and information-integration category learning. *Journal of Experimental Psychology: Learning, Memory and Cognition*, *29*, 650–662.

Mason, O., Claridge, G., & Jackson, M. (1995). New scales for the assessment of schizotypy. *Personality and Individual Differences*, *18*, 7–13.

Otmakhova, N. A., & Lisman, J. E. (1996). D1/D5 dopamine receptor activation increases the magnitude of early long-term potentiation at CA1 hippocampal synapses. *Journal of Neuroscience*, *16*, 7478–7486.

Pickering, A. D. (1997). New approaches to the study of amnesic patients: What can a neurofunctional philosophy and neural network methods offer? *Memory*, *5*, 255–300.

Pickering, A. D. (1999). Personality correlates of the dopaminergic facilitation of incentive motivation: Impulsive sensation seeking rather than extraversion? *Behavioral and Brain Sciences*, *22*, 534–535.

Pickering, A. D. (2002). Category learning and 'dopaminergic' personality traits: Evidence for a hippocampal contribution to some task variants? Paper presented at the 1st Annual Cognitive Neuroscience of Category Learning Workshop, New York.

Pickering, A. D. (2003). A framework for constructing neural models of dopaminergic contributions to personality. Paper presented at the 11th Biennial Meeting of the International Society for the Study of Individual Differences (ISSID), Graz, Austria.

Pickering, A., Brady, P., Jeffs, J., & Jones, L. (2001). Personality correlates of the responses to associative mismatch and to stimuli associated with reward or punishment. Paper presented at the January 2001 meeting of the Experimental Psychology Society, London.

Pickering, A. D., Corr, P. J., Powell, J. H., Kumari, J. C., Thornton, J. C., & Gray, J. A. (1997). Individual differences in reactions to reinforcing stimuli are neither black nor white: To what extent are they Gray? In: H. Nyborg (Ed.), *The scientific study of human nature: Tribute to Hans J. Eysenck at eighty* (pp. 36–67). Oxford: Pergamon.

Pickering, A. D., Díaz, A., & Gray, J. A. (1995). Personality and reinforcement: An exploration using a maze-learning task. *Personality and Individual Differences*, *18*, 541–558.

Pickering, A. D., & Gray, J. A. (1999). The neuroscience of personality. In: L. Pervin, & O. John (Eds), *Handbook of personality* (2nd ed., pp. 277–299). New York: Guilford Press.

Pickering, A. D., & Gray, J. A. (2001). Dopamine, appetitive reinforcement, and the neuropsychology of human learning: An individual differences approach. In: A. Eliasz, & A. Angleitner (Eds),

Advances in individual differences research (pp. 113–149). Lengerich, Germany: PABST Science Publishers.

Poldrack, R. A., Prabakharan, V., Seger, C., & Gabrieli, J. D. E. (1999). Striatal activation during cognitive skill learning. *Neuropsychology*, *13*, 564–574.

Poldrack, R. A., Clark, J., Pare-Blagoev, J., Shohamy, D., Creso Moyano, J., Myers, C., & Gluck, M. A. (2001). Interactive memory systems in the human brain. *Nature*, *414*, 546–550.

Raine, A., Ishikawa, S. S., Arce, E., Lencz, T., Knuth, K. H., Birhle, S., LaCasse, L., & Coletti, P. (2004). Hippocampal structural asymmetry in unsuccessful psychopaths. *Biological Psychiatry*, *55*, 185–191.

Schultz, W. (1998). Predictive reward signal of dopamine neurons. *Journal of Neurophysiology*, *80*, 1–27.

Schultz, W., Romo, R., Ljungberg, T., Mirenowicz, J., Hollerman, J. R., & Dickinson, A. (1995). Reward-related signals carried by dopamine neurons. In: J. C. Houk, J. L. Davis, & D. G.Beiser (Eds), *Models of information processing in the basal ganglia* (pp. 233–248). London: MIT Press.

Squire, L. R. (1992). Memory and the hippocampus: A synthesis from findings with rats, monkeys, and humans. *Psychological Review*, *99*, 195–231.

Tellegen, A. (1982). *Multidimensional Personality Questionnaire manual*. Minneapolis, MN: University of Minnesota Press.

Tellegen, A., & Waller, N. G. (1992). Exploring personality through test construction: Development of the multidimensional personality questionnaire. In: S. Briggs, & J. Cheek (Eds), *Personality measures: Development and evaluation* (Vol. 1). Greenwich, CT: JAI Press.

Thaker, G., Moran, M., Adami, H., & Cassady, S. (1993). Psychosis Proneness Scales in schizophrenia spectrum personality disorders: Familial vs. nonfamilial samples. *Psychiatry Research*, *46*, 47–57.

Vollema, M. J., & van den Bosch, R. J. (1995). The multidimensionality of schizotypy. *Schizophrenia Bulletin*, *21*, 19–31.

Wickens, J., & Kotter, R. (1995). Cellular models of reinforcement. In: J. C. Houk, J. L. Davis, & D. G. Beiser (Eds), *Models of information processing in the basal ganglia* (pp. 189–214). London: MIT Press.

Zuckerman, M. (1979). *Sensation-seeking: Beyond the optimal level of arousal*. Hillsdale, NJ: Erlbaum.

Zuckerman, M. (1992). What is a basic factor and which factors are basic? Turtles all the way down. *Personality and Individual Differences*, *13*, 675–681.

Zuckerman, M. (1993). P-impulsive sensation seeking and its behavioural, psychophysiological biochemical correlates. *Neuropsychobiology*, *28*, 30–36.

Zuckerman, M., Kuhlman, D. M., Teta, P., Joireman, J., & Kraft, M. (1993). A comparison of three structural models of personality: The big three, the big five, and the alternative five. *Journal of Personality and Social Psychology*, *65*, 757–768.

Note: Some of my conference presentations cited here can be downloaded from my web-pages as Powerpoint files. The URL is: http://homepages.gold.ac.uk/aphome/talks.html).

Part V

Epilogue

A Postscript on the Psychobiology of Personality

As I noted at the beginning of this text, it was a privilege for me to edit this book to honor Marvin Zuckerman. Through this process, my respect for his work, which has always been high, was elevated to another level. The influence and impact of his research and writing, as evidenced by the authors throughout this book, is substantial and his accomplishments are certainly worthy of this tribute. We can also be certain that this influence will be sustained in future research on personality.

This book, I believe, is testimony to the progress in the scientific study of personality that has been made during the past 50 years. How many would have thought, even 25 years ago, that a lexicon consisting of thousands of adjectives to describe personality could be understood in terms of a handful of basic descriptive constructs. And even more stunning is that the heritability of these personality traits were convincingly demonstrated in behavioral genetic analyses. Similarly, the consistency of these fundamental dispositions across the life span has also been effectively established. On the strength of these three achievements, much of the resistance to biological approaches to understanding personality began to erode. Clearly from this basis, a paradigm for research on personality, i.e. a common frame of reference, is beginning to emerge that will have reciprocal influence across a broad range of social and biological disciplines.

Much has been accomplished but there is a very long way to go before an integrated understanding of personality is achieved. The few gains that have been made through psychophysical and psychophysiological analysis, e.g. the greater sensory sensitivity of introverts or the augmenting of stimulus intensity of sensation seekers, do not seem to have won wide spread acceptance. Certainly, there has not been much effort to date to integrate this knowledge into genetic or biochemical research on personality (but see Rammsayer & Siegel in this book). Similarly, the biochemical research on personality is still struggling to establish compelling profiles of hormones and neurotransmitters that are associated with fundamental personality traits. At the same time there is growing recognition that basic physiological processes contribute to many psychological processes that may serve individual differences in personality. As Zuckerman has argued, different physiological systems can influence variation in a personality trait and at the same time each physiological system can influence different personality traits (see Matthews in this book).

There have been some complaints that the biological approach to personality research has neglected the social and human side of personality. There is some justification for this view, but perhaps less of a complaint today than a few years ago. The integration of biological systems with social and pathological behavior does depend on a foundation of physiological fact, a foundation that remains in the assembly stage. Nevertheless, even within the frameworks and with the facts of personality that are available today, our understanding of participation in everyday activity and of personal problems, such as criminality and substance abuse, is expanding. This research does contribute significantly to personal, social and public life. As Richard Haier noted in regard to his work using imaging technology, personality research is undergoing a slow revolution and a very exiting one at that.

Robert M. Stelmack
University of Ottawa,
Ottawa, Canada

The Shaping of Personality: Genes, Environments, and Chance Encounters

Marvin Zuckerman

Abstract

I started my career as a clinical psychologist with an interest in personality assessment. But a loss of faith in psychoanalytic theory, projective tests, and clinical case-studies in general, led to a shift in my interests to personality research. Subsequent jobs at research institutes and universities allowed me to indulge in science. I developed the trait-state concept and its application in tests for affect measurement. For 10 years I did experimental work in the field of sensory deprivation. The sensation seeking idea and tests evolved from this work but soon expanded to many other areas. Research in the biological basis of sensation seeking started with genetic and psychophysiological research, but research conducted in other laboratories also pointed to a psychopharmacological basis for the trait. Over the last several decades I have formulated a psychobiological model for personality. I have used factor analysis and the biosocial model to develop an "alternative-five" factorial trait structure for personality.

In 1996, Ebstein and his colleagues (Ebstein *et al.* 1996) in Jerusalem reported the first discovery of a major gene associated with a personality trait. The gene was for the dopamine D4 receptor and the personality trait was "Novelty Seeking." Novelty seeking is assessed by a scale devised by Cloninger (1987). The content of Cloninger's scale is closely related to the test for sensation seeking that I first devised in the 1960s. The most current form of the test, Impulsive Sensation Seeking, correlates very highly with Cloininger's Novelty Seeking (Zuckerman & Cloninger 1996). Robert Plomin, one of the primary behavior geneticists, alerted me to Ebstein's pioneering study. Excited by this finding, I decided to spend my last sabbatical before retirement at Plomin's laboratory at the Institute of Psychiatry in London. I wanted to learn more about the new science of molecular genetics and possibly look for other genes associated with sensation seeking (Figure 1).

On the Psychobiology of Personality
Edited by R. M. Stelmack

Reprinted with permission by Lawrence Erlbaum Associates, Inc., from the Journal of Personality Assessment, Volume 82, Issue 1, pp. 11–22
ISBN: 0-08-044209-9

Figure 1: Marvin Zuckerman (2002).

I had spent my first sabbatical at the Institute with Hans Eysenck in 1976. One of our projects was a twin study of sensation seeking and impulsivity to determine the heritability of sensation seeking (Fulker *et al.* 1980). The heritability of sensation seeking was quite high (58%) and at the upper limits of the range found for other personality traits. Since then the genetical findings have been confirmed in a study of twins separated at birth and raised apart (Hur & Bouchard 1997) as well as one using twins raised together (Koopmans *et al.* 1995).

When I was in college at mid-century the gene was still a hypothetical construct, but by the year before I received my doctoral degree, Watson and Crick (1953) had described the structure of the DNA molecule. Over the remaining half century techniques were developed for identifying specific genes and investigating their relationships with disease, psychopathology and biological and psychological traits.

Soon after arriving at the institute in London I asked them to analyze my own DNA for the presence of the form of the D4 gene associated with high or low novelty seeking. For years people have been asking me if I am a high sensation seeker on the assumption that there is a relationship between areas of psychological interest and personality. This is a dubious assumption to begin with. Are all investigators who study schizophrenia schizoid? Are all those who study anxiety, anxious? Are those who do research on aggression, aggressive? My observations of colleagues in these areas revealed no invariable associations of topic with investigator. Nevertheless, I felt I should answer the question. The problem is that the main definition of the trait comes from the scale which I devised. So here was a chance to answer the question in terms of a portion of the genetic basis for the trait.

The D4 receptor gene comes in two primary forms, depending on the number of repeats of the base sequence: a short form and a long form. The long form is associated with high sensation seeking and the short form with average or low sensation seeking. My DNA revealed that I had the long form. This confirmed some of my life-history data when I was younger, but sensation seeking falls with age even though the genes don't change. As I told my colleagues in London, sensation seeking for me at age 70 consisted of riding on the top deck of the double decker bus in London (at the very front seat, though). Genes are not destiny and their influence varies at different ages and in different environments.

Let me begin my personal story with my ancestors who I did not know or only knew when they were older, and my parents who supplied both genes and environment during my formative years. Sensation seeking, like most other personality traits, shows little influence of the shared family environment, but a major influence of the nonshared environment outside of the home. The latter includes the environments we create for ourselves in our choices of friends and activities, and the "chance encounters" which may significantly influence our destinies, like the person who we happen to meet at a party who we become involved with and marry. If we had not gone to that party would we have met and married someone else who would have had the same kind of influence on our personality development? There is an "uncertainty principle" in personality explanation analogous to that in physics (Zuckerman 1979b).

Ancestors

I suspect that most Jewish psychologists who have won some distinction in the clinical or scientific areas have rabbis in their ancestry. What other vocation was there in Russia for a person with a scholarly disposition and an interest in human experience? Secular universities were not open for Jews. My great-grandfather on my father's side was a rabbi. Figure 2 shows him with a flowing and full white beard and yarmulke. His son and my grandfather are pictured in a Russian type cap and military style jacket with a more trimmed beard (something like mine). He was a teacher in a Hebrew school.

Figure 2: Zuckerman ancestors: Left to right, Great-Grandfather, Grandfather, Father.

My father came over from Russia before World War I when he was 17. He wanted to go to a secular college, impossible for a Jew in Russia. He taught himself English out of a Hebrew–English bible. I always wondered why he did not speak in the King James dialect. When they asked him what he wanted to study in college, he said "maybe Engineering." When they told him that there were no Jewish engineers he replied "Now I know that is what I will be." He had neither beard or mustache and dressed in a natty American style with suit and tie. Note the progression in the male line from devoutly religious to secular in both dress and occupation. Even though my father was president of his local synagogue I became a atheist just before my bar mitzvah, although I can remember questioning the existence of an omnipotent god when I was only five years old in Sunday school. At the same time I identify strongly as a Jew. A Jewish atheist (Freud was one) may seem a contradiction to some, but being a Jew means an ethnic identification with the history of a people, a pride in their accomplishments, and a refusal to conform to the mandate of the majority by conversion or denial of one's ethnic background. Other than this there is a taste for pastrami and a special appreciation of Woody Allen's humor.

On my mother's side her father, my grandfather, emigrated from Romania, with a stay in England, to the United States. While in England he met and married my grand-mother (Figure 3). His father, my great-grandfather, was a rabbi, and he left the old country as much to escape from his destiny as a rabbinical student as to escape the Czarist military draft. After he settled in Cincinnati and acquired a dry-goods store he ran for alderman on the socialist ticket and, of course, lost.

My lack of mention of the women in the family, mother and grandmothers, is not due to misogyny. These were strong, loving, and traditional women who held the family together through feuds and fights and made sure everyone was well-fed if not contented. They ruled in the home and in the rearing of the children.

Figure 3: Pilder (maternal) ancestors: Grandfather and Grandmother.

Adolescence

My father gave me two important values: the importance of education and finding a kind of work you really loved. During the late 1960s my son then in high school, asked me how would I feel if he didn't go to college but just wandered around the country for a time earning his "bread" at odd jobs. I replied that first I would cry for a couple of months and then accept it.

He went to college and became a leader in the revolutionary movement on campus, did some drugs, but never missed a class and got top grades. But more on my children later.

Strangely enough I had a similar crisis with my father. Graduating from high school at 16 years of age during the last years of World War II, I wanted to enlist in the Navy rather than go to college. But he would not give his permission insisting that I go at least a year to college before going into the military. I finally gave in and went to the University of Kentucky (my father's college) where I reached my full sensation-seeking potential through drinking, sex, and hitchhiking around the country. My first love affair with an "older" (19 years old) woman lifted me to a state of euphoria only to plunge into the depths of melancholy when the affair ended. In the latter state I wrote a great deal of adolescent mawkish poetry, some of which was actually published in a college magazine. By the time the draft caught me the war was over and at 18 I reluctantly entered the peacetime Army. Several months of basic training in the swamps of Louisiana followed by a long boring year of garrison duty in Texas put an end to any military ambitions I might have had.

Tracing the origins of my interest in psychology I remember coming across a book on graphology while in high school. I went around analyzing the character of friends and family through their handwriting, perhaps a portent of my interest in personality assessment. Nasty questions of reliability and validity did not disturb my confidence in my ability to read character from scrawls. This kind of "faith validity" carried me through my early years of clinical training when we were taught projective techniques.

During my melancholic period at the University of Kentucky I read Freud's great works on *The Interpretation of Dreams* and *The Psychopathology of Everyday Life* (Freud, 1905, 1938). Oddly enough I left the book on the train, but despite this "slip" I overcame my repression and obtained another copy. I began to interpret my own dreams and in an English course I wrote a term paper on "Sexual symbolism in dreams. My prissy instructor told me that this was not a fit topic for an English course, but I went over his head to the chair of the department who gave me permission. Of course I got only a "C" grade for my first paper in psychology. I also took courses in introductory and personality psychology.

After discharge from the Army I returned to college but now at New York University (NYU). In my first year of college, I had majored in journalism with the idea of becoming a writer but earning a living as a reporter. Some years later I actually returned to Kentucky to give a talk on sensation seeking at a conference sponsored by Lew Donohew in the Communications department. Communications is the new term for Journalism, now more broadly defined. My visit was a lesson in the futility of nostalgia. I could not find my old drinking and dancing places or the secluded grassy places where we would make love under the stars. Everything was paved over with housing and highways. Stick with the dreams, time travel is impossible.

Graduate School

I finished my undergraduate work at NYU starting as a major in premed with the ultimate goal of psychiatry. At this time NYU started one of the early Ph.D programs in clinical psychology and I decided to pursue my career in psychology. At this point in my life I married at too young an age for the wrong reasons, such as the need to concentrate on my studies without the distractions of "dating" (the term we used for short-term mating strategies). The marriage lasted 12 years and the marital relationship was not a happy one, but despite the defects in the shared environment it produced two great children and four grandchildren. Who can comprehend the mysteries of assortative mating?

In graduate school I patched together a living from the G.I. Bill educational allotment, a teaching assistantship (TA) in experimental psychology, and research assistantships. The TA under the supervision of Margaret Tresselt was a major influence in my subsequent career. I became interested in experimental methods and theories based on research rather than clinical anecdote. Clinical students like myself had multiple personalities. On the one hand we had Dr. Jekyll: learning theory, logical positivism, comparative and physiological psychology or, in sum, science. Then there was Mr. Hyde: psychoanalytic theory, Rorschach, and other projectives, and insight-oriented psychodynamic psychotherapy. Remember, this was before the alternatives of behavior and cognitive therapy and, except in Minnesota and a few other places, training in objective test assessment. For a time I resolved my cognitive disonance through the book by Dollard and Miller (1950) *Personality and Psychotherapy*. Miller, a learning theorist in the Clark Hull model, translated all of the fuzzy Freudian constructs into the terms of learning theory — no mean trick considering that Hull's theory was entirely behavioristic even when describing mental events as stimuli and responses inside the head. Still, the elegant analogue between conflict behavior in the rat and the human — approach, avoidance, and inhibition — gave the illusion of a scientific basis for psychodynamic theories. But one cannot generalize across species unless there are common methods of investigation and the exploration of conflict in humans happened almost entirely on the couch.

While still in graduate school, I did my first study (Zuckerman 1951) which was published in the *Journal of Abnormal and Social Psychology* and which I presented as a paper at the 1953 meeting of the American Psychological Association. This was the last meeting of the APA held at a college campus (Pennsylvania State University). Presenting a paper before an audience of distinguished psychologists (in those days they actually went to hear the papers) was a highly rewarding experience, much more so than a clinical presentation. Then there were the drinking parties organized by the various university departments. One could wander from party to party with free booze at each. At one point I found myself at a party exchanging dirty jokes with my idol Neal Miller. The campus police eventually came around and closed down the loud, raucous parties bordering on riot. This is one reason the APA stopped having parties on college campuses. The other is that the organization grew too big.

During the third year I went on internship to Wayne County General Hospital outside of Detroit. Wayne County was an old type hospital consisting of an admissions building where most of the evaluation and therapy was done, and a number of custodial buildings where the old chronics were kept for many years. The latter were "snake-pits," where one rarely ventured with one's black box containing Wechsler-Bellevue Intelligence kits and Rorschach cards unless there was a rumor of recovery in one of the chronics. The young residents were all imbued with Freudian psychoanalytic theory and were just putting in their time until they could go into psychoanalytic training and practice. The older staff doctors were a melange of alcoholics, bipolars, and simply apathetic types. The first antipsychotic drugs were just starting to be used. The therapy was largely electric and insulin shock, lobotomy, and hydrotherapy, with a very few patients given some kind of psychotherapy. I couldn't help noticing that it was largely the young attractive women who were selected by the male residents for dynamic therapy that went beyond "so how are you feeling today." Psychological reports at staff meetings were embraced as scientific confirmation if they supported the diagnosis of the chief of staff, and derided as hocus-pocus if they conflicted with his infallible conclusions. The total atmosphere was disillusioning and depressing. I began to question my career goals.

I remember taking a day off to go to the library at the University of Michigan, just down the road, to do some preliminary library research for my dissertation. It was a beautiful, crisp fall day; the leaves had turned to glorious oranges and reds. I could hear the crowd cheering in the football stadium. The thought occured to me that this would be a pleasant place to work as an academic clinical psychologist.

I returned to school and began work on my dissertation. By that time I had two children. Living conditions were difficult. I worked at three part-time jobs, including my TA, attended some classes, and collected the data for my dissertation. My work day went from 8 a.m. to 11 p.m.

My first idea was to work in the area of conflict using human subjects. However, the methodology using the conflict board and reaction times seemed a poor way of testing conflict dispositions. One simply could not develop the kind of strong conflict motivations that were possible using rats. Reward points were not the same as food versus shock for a hungry rat. I then became interested in what was being called the "New Look" in research on perception.

Personality traits and values were associated with perceptual thresholds for words with relevant content. My idea was to measure aggressiveness as a trait, using the Rosenzweig Picture Frustration test, a projective test based on responses to cartoon pictured situations. Aggression or hostility as a state was supposedly induced by a frustration with criticism using manipulated failure on an "intelligence test." After the induction of negative emotion the subject's perceptual thresholds for aggressive and neutral words were measured using a tachistoscope. My hypothesis was that frustration would lower thresholds for aggressive words, particularly in those with high levels of trait aggression. Frustration increased thresholds for all words, but there was no interaction between content of words and the personality of the subject. In retrospect the failure could have been in the measure used for a personality trait and the lack of a state measure of affect. Disappointment in the outcome of this research for a time left me disillusioned with research as well as clinical work. I began to read outside of the field in archeology and anthropology.

Life after Graduate School

My first clinical job during and after the Ph.D work was at Norwich State Hospital in Connecticut. Norwich was another old snake-pit. My only compensation was my delightful colleagues, Bud Orgel and Peggy Scales, and a weekly trip to the outpatient clinic in Hartford. I remember a patient I saw there who raised doubts about the dynamic theories that guided my therapy efforts. He was a depressed middle-aged man who only wanted to talk about his wife's extravagant spending habits and how they angered him, rather than their general relationship dynamics. Finally, I gave up the search for insight and helped him devise a reasonable budget to present to his wife. A week later he showed a dramatic improvement and thanked me for his "cure." In contrast, other patients developed profound insights but remained as depressed as ever. I think dynamic therapists must maintain a great deal of faith in their theories and never ask the question "what really helped this patient to recovery?" A bit of practical suggestion may go a long way even though patients are supposed to develop their own solutions to life problems including the interpersonal ones. Of course this was all before cognitive therapy.

In 1954 I moved to a more modern hospital, Larue D. Carter Memorial Hospital in Indianapolis. Arnold Buss was the chief psychologist and he was the one who decisively turned my interests back to research. Arny ran the psychologist section like a University department, with research seminars and discussions of new techniques. During my orientation with other new employees he appeared (reluctantly) to discuss the role of the clinical psychologist in the hospital. He said: "Clinical psychology is assessment, therapy and research, and other than that it is a black art," and then stalked out of the room.

Arny was an intellectually provocative and skeptical person with an extraordinary level of activity, sociability and enthusiasm. He was always challenging his colleagues to games of tennis, chess, impromptu discussions of current films, books, and even dramatic plays in which we all took parts. Our informal seminars were augmented by trips to Indiana University in Bloomington to attend their seminars. We enjoyed spontaneous parties thrown by Arny and his wife Edith. I began doing research again and conceived of life outside of clinical settings. I realized that I enjoyed doing and talking about research more than testing and treating patients. It is not that I didn't sometimes become engrossed with particular patients or gratified by their improvement, I just did not find the process intellectually satisfying. I became convinced that the answers to basic questions about the sources of behavior must come from controlled research.

In 1956 one of those chance events happened that determine our destinies. An institute for psychiatric research opened in the medical center next door to Carter Hospital. I was hired by the director, John Nurnberger, a research-oriented psychiatrist, to join an interdisciplinary team of biochemists, microbiologists, and experimental psychologists. I trace my interest in psychobiology to these years although it only came to full expression in my theorizing and research years later. However, despite some efforts at collaboration, my four years there were largely spent studying problems in personality assessment including direct (questionnaire) versus indirect (projective) methods in the assessement of dependency, anxiety and affect traits, response set influences in tests, and the measurement of trait and state emotions. Dr. Nurnberger asked my help in developing measures of affect to be used in a study of pregnancy over time. I realized the trait-state problem in such research and developed the first real trait-state test for anxiety (Zuckerman 1960), later expanded into a three factor test (anxiety, depression, hostility), the Multiple Affect Adjective Check List (Zuckerman & Lubin 1965). The current form of this test includes scales for positive affects as well as the three negative affects (Lubin & Zuckerman 1999; Zuckerman & Lubin 1985).

During my last year at the Institute I began doing experimental research in the area of sensory deprivation. In this research, volunteers are placed in dark, soundproof rooms with tactual and movement as well as visual and auditory restriction. The reactions to such deprivation are varied and include anxiety, panic, hallucinations, complaints of cognitive inefficiency, boredom and restlessness. My research in this was primarily directed at finding the sources of these reactions in otherwise normal subjects by experimentally varying the physical components of the complex situation and the expectations induced by different kinds of instructions to the subjects. A group of investigators in Boston had used an iron lung to confine movement in their subjects. We found an old one in the storehouse of the medical center and began to use it for eight hour studies of perceptual isolation. Both sensory deprivation and social isolation without sensory deprivation proved to be significant factors in producing anxiety and stress in subjects (Zuckerman *et al.* 1962). Perceptual deprivation and set interacted to produce hallucinations. Subsequent experiments were done using an ordinary bed in a dark soundproof room. The degree of movement restriction also proved to be a significant source of stress.

I finally made the move to academia in 1959, joining the faculty at Brooklyn College. The move coincided with a drastic change in my life with a divorce, personal therapy, and a period of turmoil and growth. I could not afford a car in New York so I buzzed around town on a Vespa motor scooter (Figure 4). After a period living in the old home with my parents I got my own place in a loft near the beach in Brooklyn. Dating is difficult after a long period of marriage, particularly when one is short on money. It was during this period that I got the idea for the trait called "sensation seeking."

Figure 4: Marvin and his beloved Vespa motor scooter.

I was interested in personality as a predictor of responses to sensory deprivation. Sensory deprivation has been called a "walk-in inkblot," an ambiguous situation in which personality might shape responses. It was clear that persons high on neuroticism or trait anxiety might feel particularly anxious in such an undefined situation, particularly if the procedures and instructions led to an expectation of stress in the situation.

Sensory deprivation is for most persons well below an "optimal level of stimulation" (OLS) at which they feel good and function well. The OLS theory dates back to Wilhelm Wundt, the founder of psychology at the end of the 19th century. Freud, in his early paper with Breuer, had suggested that individuals might vary in their optimal levels of "cerebral excitement." The construct was revived in the early 1950s with the discovery of the reticular activating system, a system for regulating cerebral arousal to keep it within optimal limits for effective functioning. But no one had developed a personality trait measure based on the OLS construct. Because of its possible relevance to reactions to sensory deprivation we developed the first sensation seeking scale in the early 1960s (Zuckerman *et al.* 1964).

The first scale was based on a general factor with items reflecting the need for novel, complex, exciting and intense experience and susceptibility to boredom when stimulation was constant, repetitious, and dull. Later research showed that there were essentially four factors in the total scale: Thrill and Adventure Seeking, Experience Seeking, Disinhibition, and Boredom Susceptibility (see Zuckerman 1971, 1979a, 1994b for descriptions).

The scale was first applied to prediction of responses to sensory deprivation and a study of those volunteering for the experiment. Would the results support an OLS theory of individual differences in response to sensory deprivation? The main difference between high and low sensation seekers in sensory deprivation was that over time, the highs became more bored and restless, as measured by random movements on the mattress to which they were confined. There was no difference in affective responses. Trait anxiety predicted who would have negative affective reactions.

In 1962 I moved to Adelphi University where I continued the sensory deprivation experiments and development of the Sensation Seeking Scale (SSS). During my years in Indianapolis I had become an activist in the Civil Rights movement. The head of the local Civil Liberties Union was a black lawyer who set up his cases for violations of civil rights ordinances with sit-in challenges. Several of us, psychologists from the Indiana University Medical Center went on these sit-ins in restaurants, bars, and even an amusement park. These encounters in the late 1950s were not yet accepted, even in the North and once we were confronted with a pistol by an irate owner of a bar. We left. Letting oneself be arrested is one thing, being shot is another.

When I moved to Adelphi I joined the local chapter of the Congress for Racial Equality (CORE). I got tired of walking a picket line one evening and joined the "lie-in" in the lobby of an apartment house in Long Beach that had refused to rent to African Americans. I spent an evening in the local jail and when the bail money did not arrive the next morning, we were carted off to prison. The bail arrived before I had much time to acclimate myself to my cell or the other inmates who were engaged in a card game of whist (!) when I arrived. The Long Island paper published a picture of me lying prone in the police station with the caption "Adelphi professor arrested in demonstration." There was another picture of me being dragged off to prison in handcuffs looking unshaven and belligerent (Figure 5).

Adelphi Psychology Prof Arrested In Long Beach Sit In Protest

Figure 5: Arrested convicts in long beach.

Needless to say, the administrators of Adelphi were not thrilled with this publicity and I did not have tenure so my stay there was guaranteed to be short.

Fortunately, a colleague from the Institute in Indianapolis, Harold Persky, a biochemist, was in the process of moving to the research laboratories of the Department of Endocrinology and Human Reproduction at Albert Einstein Medical Center in Philadelphia. He invited me to join the group there and collaborate with him in a project on the experimental induction of different emotions using hypnosis and the measurement of psychological, physiological and endocrine reactions which might distinguish one emotion from another. I also was able to move my sound-proof room once again and continue my studies in sensory deprivation with the addition of psychophysiological and endocrine measures of stress. This was a particularly productive period for me during which we managed to identify many of the variables influencing responses to sensory deprivation and further explore the role of personality. One particular finding made us reconsider our conceptions of the sensation seeking. We found that the persons volunteering for the hypnosis and the sensory deprivation studies scored high on the SSS. We could understand why they volunteered for hypnosis, but why were sensation seekers volunteering to be deprived of sensory stimulation and activity for reasons other than the money paid to all participants? During the postexperimental questioning we found that because of media sensationalism they expected to have unusual experiences, including hallucinations without the aid of drugs like LSD. Low sensation seekers regarded the experiment as risky but came just for the money. This led us to amend the definition of the construct: "the need for novel, complex, and intense sensations and experiences *and the willingness to take risks for the sake of such experience*." Not all sensation seeking activities are risky but it takes a great deal of risk appraisal to deter a high sensation seeker from engaging in such activities. We also found that high sensation seekers tend to have lower risk appraisals of activities they have never tried than low sensation seekers. Lows are not necessarily fearful, they just do not see the sense in taking risks they don't have to for the sake of the dubious rewards of novel experiences.

At the end of the decade of the 1960s I faced another work and relationship crisis. Albert Einstein Medical Center was entirely funded on soft money with no institutional back-up. When I started there my salary was funded partly on Persky's grant and partly on my own, but by 1968 my salary was entirely derived from my own grant. After 10 years of support from the National Institute of Mental Health (NIMH) for sensory deprivation research they decided that there was nothing more to be learned about the topic. I wanted to pursue the individual difference aspects. I suddenly realized the difference between "hard" and "soft" money. Looking for an appropriate-level position at the age of 40 can be a demoralizing experience. In addition to my job desperation my second marriage was in trouble.

Fortunately I got a job at the University of Delaware where they were starting a new program in clinical psychology. Once again my massive double-wall sensory deprivation room was disassembled, moved, and reassembled in Delaware. Without a grant, however, sensory deprivation research was too expensive to pursue. One has to pay subjects to spend eight hours in sensory deprivation and one cannot rely on the free participant pool. I decided to concentrate on sensation seeking research to see what else could be predicted other than volunteering and sensory deprivation behaviors. The 1970s were a good time for sensation seeking research using college students. This was the time of the sexual, drug and political (antiwar) revolutions on campuses. People were beginning to engage in extreme sports like parachuting, hang-gliding, and scuba diving. Sexual experience, drug use, liberal beliefs, and participation in extreme sports were all related to sensation seeking. But the phenomenal expressions of sensation seeking were much broader. Tastes in music, art, media, humor, and food were influenced by the trait. Risky driving habits, health risks, and gambling were correlated with sensation seeking. The trait plays a role in vocational preferences and choices; social, premarital and marital relationships, and mate choices. Cognitive styles, fantasy, and creativity are also correlates. Although the SSS was developed with the narrow goal of predictive validity for sensory deprivation, it became apparent that it also had a broad construct validity.

The Biological Roots of Sensation Seeking: I. Psychophysiology

My first sabbatical in 1976 was spent at the Institute of Psychiatry with Hans Eysenck. Eysenck (1967) is regarded as the father of the biological approach to personality. The first time I met him was on the way to the 1966 internatonal psychology conference in Moscow. I wanted to tell him about my idea that sensation seeking was based on individual differences in the optimal level of sensation. He listened quietly to what I had to say. After a long pause, he said "Yes I have already made that the fundamental basis for extraversion." But that was no problem to Hans, he simply regarded sensation seeking as a subtrait of extraversion.

Eysenck described himself as a stable introvert and indeed he was. When asked a question he thought long on it until one began to think that he had not heard the question. But his answer was well framed. He delighted in controvery and was antiauthoritarian, whether of the left or right. He was the opposite of politically correct and incurred a great deal of hostility because of his views on heredity. But he believed in the open marketplace of ideas and that all points of view which had some backing from data deserved to be heard. Science would eventually sort out the incorrect from the correct hypotheses. His faith in data made him gullible to dubious research on pseudoscientific areas such as astrology.

Eysenck pioneered the behavioral genetic approach to personality using identical and fraternal twins. While on the sabbatical we developed a new and shorter form of the SSS (Form V) and with David Fulker and Sybil Eysenck we did a genetical analysis of the SSS using subjects from the Maudsley twin bank (Fulker *et al.* 1980). Our results are described in the early part of this article (p. 11). The high heritability for the trait found in this study convinced me that sensation seeking was not just a minor subtrait of personality but one with a strong evolutionary-biological source. But what was inherited? Genes do not make personality traits. Genes only make proteins, including those that shape neuronal systems and neurotransmitters in the brain.

My first studies of the biological basis of sensation seeking were in psychophysiology. Richard Neary and I found that high sensation seekers had a strong orienting reflex, an indication of interest in novelty features of stimuli. This finding was extended from skin conductance to heart rate responses. When stimuli were novel, high sensation seekers showed greater arousal than lows but as soon as stimuli became familiar their responses did not differ. In collaboration with Jerome Siegel, a colleague, and Thomas Murtaugh, then a graduate student, we found a relationship between the strength of the coritical visually evoked potential (EP) in reaction to increasing intensities of stimulation, and sensation seeking (disinhibition). High sensation seekers were augmenters, that is, their EPs increased in amplitude in proportion to increases in stimulus intensities; low sensation seekers tended to be reducers, that is, their EPs showed little increase in amplitude with increasing stimulus intensity and sometimes showed reduction at the highest stimulus intensities. Some replications and failures of replication by others of these psychophysiological experiments are described in Zuckerman (1990).

I view sensation seeking as a trait with a biological basis and an evolutionary history expressed in other species and human infants in terms of explorativeness and approach responses to novel stimuli (Zuckerman 1984, 1991). It is therefore important to show that the kind of individual differences observed in humans can be seen in other species. If this similarity is only based on behaviors of a like sort then it is only metaphorical and even anthropomorphic. Neal Miller's comparison of experimentally induced conflict in rats and conflict in humans was an example of this kind of comparison. But if we find a common biological link between the differences observed in humans and other species we are on more solid ground.

One of the more gratifying aspects of an academic career is the opportunity to work with colleagues on problems of mutual interest. My work on the biological basis of sensation seeking has been somewhat limited because of the lack of a medical school and the absence of interested biologists at the University of Delaware. However I had the good fortune to have a colleague and close friend who is an outstanding neuroscientist, Jerome Siegel. We recently retired at the same time and now share an office at the University. Jerry extended our work on human augmenting-reducing of the cortical EP first to cats and then to rats (Siegel & Driscoll 1996). In cats, he found that those showing the augmenting EP pattern were more exploratory, active, and aggressive and more likely to approach novel stimuli than the reducer cats, who were more generally passive and avoidant of novel stimuli. In experimental tasks the augmenter cats more easily adapted to the experimental situation and responded more for a simple fixed-interval rewarded bar pressing task. But the reducer cats were superior on a task in which reinforcement was contingent on a slow rate of responding. The augmenter cats were too impulsive and could not adapt to the demand for restraint in responding. At the human level impulsivity as well as sensation seeking has been related to EP augmenting.

Siegel and Driscoll (1996) studied two strain of rats, one actively avoidant and aggressive in response to shock and the other tending to freeze and slow to learn avoidance in the shock situation. Members of the actively avoidant strain were nearly all moderate to strong EP augmenters, whereas nearly all of the fear-inhibited strain were EP reducers or very weak augmenters. The low-avoidant, EP reducer rats are less exploratory and more fearful in the open field test and the females are more nurturing to their pups. The high-avoidant, augmenter rats are more likely to develop a taste for alcohol, and are less nurturing toward their pups. The augmenters are more responsive to high intensity brain stimulation in the "reward centers" of the lateral hypothalamus. Under stress the augmenters show more dopaminergic response in the frontal lobes, whereas the reducers show more endocrine stress response in the hypothalamic-pituitary-cortical pathway.

The Biological Roots of Sensation Seeking: II. Biochemistry

The search for the biological roots of sensation seeking went deeper with the finding of biochemical correlates. The psychophysiology depends upon psychopharmacology because neurons react through chemical mediators and regulators. In the 1970s Reid Daitzman, a former student, undertook studies of sensation seeking in relation to gonadal hormones (e.g. Daitzman & Zuckerman 1980). The fact that males are higher than females on sensation seeking and that the trait declines with age (as does testosterone) suggested the possibility of a hormonal connection. The disinhibitory type of sensation seeking was related to levels of plasma testosterone in males, as were a variety of other personality traits including sociability, dominance, extraversion, and activity. Then an even more exciting finding changed my entire course of theory.

Monte Buchsbaum (1971) developed the EP augmenting-reducing paradigm when he was at the NIMH. In 1974, I received a call from him informing me that investigators, including Dennis Murphy and himself, had discovered a relationship between the enzyme monoamine oxidase (MAO) and sensation seeking in two samples of males (Murphy *et al.* 1977). The correlations were negative: high sensation seekers had low levels of MAO and low sensation seekers had high levels.

Realizing the importance of this finding I began a crash course for myself in psychopharmacology which continues to this day. Most replications in diverse populations (summarized in Zuckerman 1994b) have confirmed the MAO-SSS finding; although the actual relationship is a relatively weak one, it is fairly reliable (9 of 13 studies). MAO, as indicated by its name, regulates the monoamine neurotransmitters. More recently it has been discovered that the type B MAO is a preferential regulator of dopamine, whereas the type A MAO regulates both serotonin and norepinephrine. MAO-B is a reliable biological trait with many correlates in psychopathology and normal behavior extremes, such as drug and alcohol use, and sensation seeking analogous behavior in monkeys (Zuckerman 1979a, 1984, 1994b; Zuckerman *et al.* 1980). Generally, things that are related to MAO are also related to sensation seeking. The convergent validity pointed to further research on the role of the monoamine neurotransmitters in sensation seeking.

Eysenck was an important influence in my research and theory of my earlier years. However with the shift in attention to brain neurotransmitters I looked to another psychologist, and neuroscientist, Jeffrey Gray, at Oxford University. Jeffrey is a "bottom up" theorist in contrast to Hans, who was a "top-down" type. Both believed in the importance of comparative psychology, genetics and neurpsychology, but Jeffrey actually did neuropsychological experiments on rats, whereas Eysenck's work was primarily based on psychophysiological and behavioral research on humans. Jeffrey (Gray 1982, 1987) developed a theory linking brain neuronal systems and neurotransmitters in the brain to motivational mechanism governing sensitivities to signals of reward and punishment. The motivational mechanisms, in turn, affect the basic personality traits: anxiety, impulsivity (approach), and aggression (fight-flight). In 1983 I spent a sabbatical in Oxford with Jeffrey during which I learned a great deal about his theory and its applicability to my own theoretical model.

Oxford is a cloistered, medieval university both architecturally and academically, using the tutorial system instead of regularly scheduled class lectures. I lived with my then partner, Mary Hazard, on the last cobblestone street in Oxford behind the university. I remember one night after dining and drinking at "high table," reeling home through the narrow university streets under the spires of the colleges and thinking of the centuries of drunken scholars who preceded me down these streets. When I got back to the United States I began to work on the book, *Psychobiology of Personality* which was finally published in 1991 in Gray's series with Cambridge University Press, "Problems in the behavioural sciences." Gray's guidance on this book was invaluable.

As I said before my own collaborations in this field were limited by the lack of collaborative opportunities in Delaware. Fortunately, other laboratories began to use sensation seeking as a model for some of their work on individual differences in humans and other species. Murphy, Post, and Ballenger at NIMH studied cerebrospinal fluid monoamine metabolites, personality and psychopathology (Ballenger *et al.* 1983). A group of Swedish psychologists and psychiatrists including Åsberg, Edman, Klinteberg, von Knorring, Oreland, Schalling and Winblad, pursued the personality, MAO and monoamine connections in normal individuals and those with behaviour disorders (Klinteberg *et al.* 1985; von Knorring *et al.* 1987). Petra Netter and her colleagues at the University of Giesen in Germany did research on the effects of monoamine agonists and antagonists on different types of personality including sensation seeking (Netter *et al.* 1996). Dellu, LeMoal, and Simon at the University of Bordeaux in France studied "novelty seeking in rats" with the goal of establishing relationships to sensation seeking in humans (Dellu *et al.* 1996). At the University of Kentucky, Bardo studied the role of dopamine in the preference for novelty in rats while Lewis Donohew has used sensation seeking to design effective advertisements to discourage drug use and encourage safe sex in adolescents (Bardo *et al.* 1996).

It is particularly gratifying at this late stage of my career to see the influence of my work on such an international group of distinguished scientists. It is not exactly immortality but it is more than I anticipated when I ventured into this new world of the "psychobiology of personality" (Zuckerman 1991). My model for impulsive sensation seeking (Zuckerman 1994a, 1995, 1996) may be wrong in most aspects, or at least proven grossly over simplified by future research, but it will have stimulated a great deal of comparative research.

My work has not gone unnoticed in the media and I now find the term "sensation seeking," which I believe I devised, being used in popular publications without attribution. Contributing a new word to the lexicon is a kind of tribute even if the context is not always appropriate.

International Society for the Study of Individual Differences (ISSID)

We all belong to large organizations like American Psychological Association or American Psychological Society, but every psychological scientist needs a smaller group in which he or she can exchange views with others of like interests at paper and symposium sessions and informal chats in restaurants and lounges. As portrayed in David Lodge's (1995) book *Small World*, once or twice every year we leave the small quiet world of our academic homes, flying around the world to meet the same colleagues in varied exotic settings. We are the academic "jet-set."

Hans and Sybil Eysenck founded the journal "Personality and Individual Differences" in 1980. Ernest Barrett, Robert Stelmack and I, at a bar somewhere at some conference, came up with the idea of forming a society for the study of individual differences which could be associated with the journal. We presented the idea to Hans and Sybil and they enthusiastically agreed. Hans asked for my advice about a name for the society. I suggested the "Individual Difference Society." I think he liked it until he realized that the acronym was IDS. Hans had a intense antipathy to Freud and psychoanalysis. We compromised on the name "International Society for the Study of Individual Differences."

It is a truly international society with members from many countries around the world. We decided to hold our meetings alternatively in North American and Europe. Eysenck was acclaimed as the first president in 1983 and I was elected as the second one in 1985. Subsequent presidents include foremost researchers in the field of individual differences: Gordon Claridge, Ernest Barratt, Robert Stelmack, Jan Strelau, Paul Costa, Nathan Brody, Ian Deary, T. Vernon, and Adrian Furnham. The society and its journal have fostered the growth of the science of individual differences. Sadly, its founder Hans Eysenck who led and nurtured the psychobiological approach to individual differences died in 1997. His memory is honored in all of our work.

Personality Structure

During the preparation for my 1991 book *Psychobiology of Personality* I realized I had to construct the book around the scaffolding of some personality trait theory. This was prior to the development of the Big-Five in the Costa and McCrae version. Besides, the early versions were based on lexical analyses of adjectives mostly applicable only to human personality, and my own approach was a comparative one. Factors like "conscientiousness" are not useful in describing non-human species. I decided to do a factor analysis of scales that had been used in psychobiological research with several markers for each of the hypothesized basic personality traits. Several factor analyses of scales yielded five replicable factors: Sociability, Neuroticism-Anxiety, Impulsive Unsocialized Sensation Seeking, Aggression-Hostility, and Activity. We called this the "Alternative Five-Factor Model" (Zuckerman 1994a). Using the items in the tests that were the best factor markers we developed our own five-factor test: the Zuckerman-Kuhlman Personality Questionnaire (ZKPQ). The ZKPQ has been used in our own research and in translated versions around the world (Zuckerman 2002).

Within the ZKPQ is a scale for Impulsive Sensation Seeking (ImpSS). In our factor analytic studies scales for impulsivity and sensation seeking were closely related and always loaded on the same factor if one limited the analysis to the five primary factors. Sensation seeking is a subtrait of extraversion whereas impulsivity is a subtrait of the psychoticism factor in Eysenck's last structural model. In Costa and McCrae's Big-Five, "excitement seeking" is also regarded as a subtrait of extraversion but impulsiveness is considered a subtrait of neuroticism. Of course what you get out of a factor analysis depends on what you put in to it. I included the several subscales of the SSS and several types of impulsivity scales in my analyses, whereas others included only one general scale for each of these factors. If you have only one marker you cannot identify a broader factor. Which are primary and which are secondary factors depends upon both your theory and the number of possible markers included in the analysis. We considered sensation seeking to be an important primary factor because of its high heritability, comparative analogues, and strong biological connections. Our surprise was in how closely it was linked to impulsivity. In actual fact, Buss and Plomin (1975) included sensation seeking as a subtrait of impulsivity in their earlier structural theory. Some of these arguments about which are the primary dimensions of personality may be resolved by research in molecular genetics.

Descendents

I started this chapter with an account of my ancestors. Please indulge me in some words of pride about my children and grandchildren. This section illustrates the problems of applying concepts from population-derived genetics to individual families. My son Steven was a true sensation seeker particularly when he was younger. He was a political rebel in high school and college, an experimenter in the drug and sex scene of the 1970s in college, a world traveller by foot and bicycle, but also a fine student. He studied anthropology in graduate school and with his wife Paula went off to the highlands of New Guinea to live among the Papuan highlanders. His wife, Paula Gorlitz, got her degree in clinical psychology and set up a practice in Chicago. Steve found a position in family practice hospitals training residents and doing psychotherapy. He took further training in family therapy and now has a part-time private practice in addition to his regular hospital job.

Steve and Paula made two extraordinary children: Ariel and Eric. Ariel, the elder, is a superb tennis player and plays the cello, piano, and guitar. She is showing signs of developing the empathy of a "shrink" but who knows where her interests will develop. Like his father and grandfather when they were his age Eric loves to play action and war games. He has an impressive arsenal of toy weapons and soldiers. Unlike his father and grandfather, he is great at sports, particularly soccer. The whole family goes skiing together and they travel together in Europe. Steve goes fly-fishing in Colorado. He has come far from his days as wild-haired revolutionary. When we go out I defer to his choice of wines. He also advises me on my clothes. His ideology is unchanged but his life-style has markedly expanded.

April as a child could be described as a cautious sensation seeker (a rebuke to my linking of the two traits). Steve clamored up the monkey-bars, sometimes slipping and falling. April went up carefully watching her feet placements before going to the next level. During anti-war demonstrations whlle they were in college Steve would be at the front of the demonstration taunting and confronting the police, while April would hang toward the rear of the crowd noting the possible escape routes in case the police should charge.

April had two children by her first marriage. Veronica the oldest, achieved some fame as a child, appearing in a television program on child prodigies. She read at a very early age and wrote adult quality poetry. She is now in graduate school in English literature. Genvieve showed impressive artistic talents. Hanging in my appartment, I have a painting she did of me. She is now going to college and majoring in women's studies.

April was what I used to call a "Jewish dropout," meaning she stopped her education after winning the Bachelor's degree and devoted herself for many years to raising her children. However, after her divorce she decided to get a master's degree in social work and took on a responsible job as the assistant supervisor of a community based center for psychiatrically disturbed individuals. Like my son, she took further training in family therapy and now has a small part-time private practice outside of her job. She is remarried to a great guy, an English professor. He is more of a sensation seeker, a scuba diver. They take trips to the Caribbean where she snorkels or sits under a palm tree while he goes on deep dives. They like to travel in France. She is an experience seeker when it comes to food. We can detect the presence of a genetic taste for chocolate down from father, to mother, to grandaughter. Unlike her parents she is a dedicated exerciser. She gets up at 5 a.m. in order to go for a work-out before she goes to her job. Where does she get this kind of discipline? Not from her parents.

Retirement: On the Beach

In September of 2002 I finally retired. At 74 it was overdue. I had some trepidation about retirement. I have seen some notable psychologists who simply disappeared from the scientific scene after retirement. I am not the type to retire to Florida and play golf. However, I can relax at the beach in Delaware where I have a house (Figure 6). But when I am at the beach, I spend my mornings writing and afternoons on the beach, swimming, reading and just watching the waves.

Retirement is simply an extended sabbatical. I loved my sabbatical years spent in Europe. A major part of this pleasure was the opportunity to write, study, and talk to colleagues,

Figure 6: On the beach contemplating the next book.

freed of the pressures of teaching schedules, boring faculty meetings, and trivial academic politics. Undergraduate teaching has its rewards but I was no "Mr. Chips." What I sometimes regarded as a brilliant digression from the main topic, the students described in evaluations as "rambling." Afterwards they asked that question that infuriates teachers, "Is this going to be on the test?"

When I was a young sensation seeker I imagined that after I retired I would do all kinds of adventurous things like hang gliding, parachute jumping, and learning to fly an airplane. These are the further things from my plans now. But whereas thrill and adventure seeking and disinhibtion fall rapidly with age, experience seeking does not change. I have moved to Philadelphia where there is more social life and cultural opportunities. My apartment is on the 40th floor with great views (not for acrophobics). I have season tickets to the symphony, chamber music groups, and theaters. There is a jazz club nearby and many good restaurants. Most importantly I spend my mornings and even part of the afternoon writing. I am currently revising my 1991 book, *Psychobiology of Personality*. I have kept an office at the University of Delaware where I am still engaged in some research. I also have an appointment as a research professor at the Jefferson Medical University in Philadelphia. I plan to colloborate on some research there. In the summer I will be making short trips to Europe to give talks and visit friends. I have a loving lady friend whom I am with on week-ends.

How long I can keep this up is a question, but for now life is stimulating and productive. I plan to continue writing and I try to keep up with the latest advances in my field. This is an exciting period in psychobiology. The advances in methods such as neuroimaging and molecular genetics have allowed research we never dreamed of in the mid-century. Whereas these methods were once restricted to studies of pathology, they are now starting to be used in the study of personality.

I started my research program in personality assessment. The controversies over response sets, consistency, trait versus state and person versus situation, engaged me for a time, but I always felt that the goal of assessment was to define meaningful personality traits. Reliability is a requisite but construct validity is the goal. Personality traits should define constructs within a theory and should not be mere items in a catalogue of traits.

References

Ballenger, J. C., Post, R. M., Jimerson, D. C., Lake, C. R., Murphy, D. L., Zuckerman, M. *et al.* (1983). Biochemical correlates of personality traits in normals: An exploratory study. *Personality and Individual Differences*, *4*, 615–625.

Bardo, M. T., Donohew, R. L., & Harrington, N. G. (1996). Psychobiology of novelty seeking and drug seeking behavior. *Behavioral Brain Research*, *77*, 23–43.

Buchsbaum, M. S. (1971). Neural events and the psychophysical law. *Science*, *172*, 502.

Buss, A. H., & Plomin, R. (1975). *A temperament theory of personality development*. New York: Wiley.

Cloninger, C. R. (1987). A systematic method for clinical description and classification of personality variants. *Archives of General Psychiatry*, *44*, 573–588.

Daitzman, R. J., & Zuckerman, M. (1980). Disinhibitory sensation seeking, personality and gonadal hormones. *Personality and Individual Differences*, *1*, 103–110.

Dellu, F., Piazza, P. V., Mayo, W., LeMoal, M., & Simon, H. (1996). Novelty seeking in rats and possible relationships with the sensation seeking trait in humans. *Neuropsychobiology*, *34*, 136–145.

Dollard, J., & Miller, N. E. (1950). *Personality and psychotherapy: An analysis in terms of learning, thinking, and culture*. New York: McGraw Hill.

Ebstein, R. P., Novick, O., Umansky, R., Priel, B., Oshyer, Y., Blaine, D. *et al.* (1996). Dopamine D4 receptor (D4DR) exon III polymorphism associated with the human personality trait of novelty seeking. *Nature Genetics*, *12*, 78–80.

Eysenck, H. J. (1967). *The biological basis of personality*. Springfield, IL: Thomas.

Freud, S. (1938). *The basic writings of Sigmund Freud*. A. A. Brill (Ed.). New York: Modern Library, Random House (Original work published 1905).

Fulker, D. W., Eysenck, S. B. G., & Zuckerman, M. (1980). The genetics of sensation seeking. *Journal of Personality Research*, *14*, 261–281.

Gray, J. A. (1982). *An enquiry into the functions of the septohippocampal system*. New York: Oxford University Press.

Gray, J. A. (1987). The neuropsychology of emotion and personality. In: S. M. Stahl, S. D. Iverson, & E. C. Goodman (Eds), *Cognitive neurochemistry* (pp. 171-190). Oxford, England: Oxford University Press.

Hur, Y., & Bouchard, T. J., Jr. (1997). The genetic correlation between impulsivity and sensation seeking traits. *Behavior Genetics*, *27*, 455–463.

Klinteberg, B., Schalling, D., Edman, G., Oreland, L., & Åsberg, M. (1985). Personality correlates of monoamine oxidase (MAO) activity in female and male subjects. *Neuropsychobiology*, *18*, 89–96.

Koopmans, J. R., Boomsa, D. I., Heath, A. C., & Lorenz, J. P. D. (1995). A multivariate genetic analysis of sensation seeking. *Behavior Genetics*, *25*, 349–356.

Lodge, D. (1995). *Small world: An academic romance*. New York: Penguin.

Lubin, B., & Zuckerman, M. (1999). *Manual for the multiple Affect Adjective Check List*. San Diego, CA: Educational and Industrial Testing Service.

Murphy, D. L., Ballenger, R. H., Buchsbaum, M. S., Martin, M. F., Ciaranello, K., & Wyatt, R. J. (1977). Biogenic amine related enzymes and personality variations in normals. *Psychological Medicine*, *7*, 149–157.

Netter, P., Hennig, J., & Roed, I. S. (1996). Serotonin and dopamine as medicators of sensation seeking behavior. *Neuropsychobiology*, *34*, 130–135.

Siegel, J., & Driscoll, P. (1996). Recent developments in an animal model of visual evoked potential augmenting/reducing and sensation seeking behavior. *Neuropsychobiology*, *34*, 130–135.

von Knorring, L., Oreland, L., & von Knorring, A. L. (1987). Personality traits and platelet MAO activity in alcohol and drug abusing teenage boys. *Acta Psychiatrica Scandinavica*, *75*, 164–167.

Watson, J. D., & Crick, F. H. C. (1953). Genetical implications of deoxyribonucleic acid. *Nature*, *171*, 164–167.

Zuckerman, M. (1951). The effect of threat on perceptual affect in a group. *Journal of Abnormal and Social Psychology*, *46*, 529–533.

Zuckerman, M. (1960). The development of an affect adjective check list for the measurement of anxiety. *Journal of Consulting Psychology*, *24*, 457–462.

Zuckerman, M. (1971). Dimensions of sensation seeking. *Journal of Consulting and Clinical Psychology*, *36*, 45–52.

Zuckerman, M. (1979a). *Sensation seeking: Beyond the optimal level of arousal*. Hillsdale, NJ: Lawrence Erlbaum.

Zuckerman, M. (1979b). Traits, states, situations and uncertainty. *Journal of Behavioral Assessment*, *1*, 43–54.

Zuckerman, M. (1984). Sensation seeking: A comparative approach to a human trait. *Behavioral and Brain Sciences*, *7*, 413–471.

Zuckerman, M. (1990). The psychophysiology of sensation seeking. *Journal of Personality*, *58*, 313–345.

Zuckerman, M. (1991). *Psychobiology of Personality*. Cambridge, UK: Cambridge University Press.

Zuckerman, M. (1994a). An alternative five-factor model for personality. In: C. F. Halverson, Jr., & R. P. Martin (Eds), *The developing structure of temperament and personality from infancy to adulthood* (pp. 53–68). Hillsdale, NJ: Lawrence Erlbaum.

Zuckerman, M. (1994b). *Behavioral expressions and biosocial bases of sensation seeking*. New York: Cambridge University Press.

Zuckerman, M. (1995). Good and bad humors: Biochemical bases of personality and its disorders. *Psychological Science*, *6*, 325–332.

Zuckerman, M. (1996). The psychobiological model for impulsive unsocialized sensation seeking: A comparative approach. *Neuropsychobiology*, *34*, 125–129.

Zuckerman, M. (2002). Zuckerman-Kuhlman Personality Questionnaire (ZKPQ): An alternative five-factorial model. In: B. DeRaad, & M. Peruginini (Eds), *Big five assessment* (pp. 377–396). Seattle, WA: Hogrefe & Huber.

Zuckerman, M., Allbright, R. J., Marks, G. S., & Miller, G. L. (1962). Stress and hallucinatory effects of perceptual isolation and confinement. *Psychological Monographs*, *76*(30, Whole No. 549).

Zuckerman, M., Buchsbaum, M. S., & Murphy, D. L. (1980). Sensation seeking and its biological correlates. *Psychological Bulletin*, *88*, 187–214.

Zuckerman, M., & Cloninger, C. R. (1996). Relationships between Cloninger's, Zuckerman's, and Eysenck's dimensions of personality. *Personality and Individual Differences*, *21*, 283–285.

Zuckerman, M., Kolin, E. A., Price, L., & Zoob, I. (1964). Development of a sensation seeking scale. *Journal of Consulting Psychology*, *28*, 477–482.

Zuckerman, M., & Lubin, B. (1965). *Manual for the Multiple Affect Adjective Check List*. San Diego, CA: Educational and Industrial Testing Service.

Zuckerman, M., & Lubin, B. (1985). *Manual for the Multiple Affect Adjective Check List- Revised (MAACL-R)*. San Diego, CA: Educational and Industrial Testing Service.

Bibliography of Marvin Zuckerman

1951–1959

Zuckerman, M. (1951). The effect of threat on perceptual affect in a group. *Journal of Abnormal and Social Psychology*, *46*, 529–533.

Zuckerman, M. (1955). The effect of frustration on the perception of neutral and aggressive words. *Journal of Personality*, *23*, 407–422.

Zuckerman, M., Baer, M., & Monashkin, I. (1956). Acceptance of self, parents, and people in patients and normals. *Journal of Clinical Psychology*, *12*, 327–332.

Zuckerman, M., Izner, S. I., & Leiser, R. (1954). The sodium amytal Rorschach in incipient schizophrenia. *Diseases of the Nervous System*, *15*, 3–8.

Zuckerman, M., & Monashkin, I. (1957). Self-acceptance and psychopathology. *Journal of Consulting Psychology*, *21*, 145–148.

Zuckerman, M., Ribback, B. B., & Monashkin, I. (1958). Normative data and factor analysis on the parental attitude research instrument. *Journal of Consulting Psychology*, *22*, 165–171.

Zuckerman, M., & Tresselt, M. (1953). Objective characteristics of the figure drawing test in a hospital population, *Psychological Newsletter 46*.

1960–1969

Barrows, G. A., & Zuckerman, M. (1960). Construct validity of three masculinity-femininity tests. *Journal of Consulting Psychology*, *24*, 441–445.

Biase, D. V., & Zuckerman, M. (1967). Sex differences in stress responses to total and partial sensory deprivation. *Psychosomatic Medicine*, *24*, 380–390.

Curtis, C., & Zuckerman, M. (1968). A psychopathological reaction precipitated by sensory deprivation. *American Journal of Psychiatry*, *125*, 255–260.

Levitt, E. E., Lubin, B., & Zuckerman, M. (1962). The student nurse, the college woman, and the graduate nurse: A comparative study. *Nursing Research*, *11*, 80–82.

Levitt, E. E., Lubin, B., & Zuckerman, M. (1962). A simplified method for scoring Rorschach content for dependency. *Journal of Projective Techniques*, *22*, 234–236.

Lubin, B., Levitt, E. E., & Zuckerman, M. (1962). Some personality differences between responders and non-responders to a survey questionnaire. *Journal of Consulting Psychology*, *26*, 192.

Lubin, B., & Zuckerman, M. (1967). Affective and perceptual-cognitive patterns in sensitivity training groups. *Psychological Reports*, *21*, 365–376.

Lubin, B., & Zuckerman, M. (1969). Level of emotional arousal in laboratory training. *Journal of Applied Behavioral Sciences*, *5*, 483–490.

Nurnberger, I., Zuckerman, M., Norton, J. A., & Brittain, H. M. (1961). Certain socio-cultural and economic factors influencing utilization of state institutional facilities in Indiana. *American Journal of Psychiatry*, *117*, 1065–1073.

Persky, H., Zuckerman, M., Basu, G. K., & Thornton, D. (1966). Psycho-endocrine effects of perceptual and social isolation. *Archives of General Psychiatry*, *15*, 499–505.

Persky, H., Zuckerman, M., & Curtis, G. (1968). Endocrine function in emotionally disturbed and normal men. *Journal of Nervous and Mental Diseases*, *146*, 488–497.

Zuckerman, M. (1960). The effects of subliminal and supraliminal suggestion on productivity. *Journal of Abnormal and Social Psychology*, *60*, 404–411.

Zuckerman, M. (1960). The development of an affect adjective check list for the measurement of anxiety. *Journal of Consulting Psychology*, *24*, 457–462.

Zuckerman, M. (1964). Perceptual isolation as a stress situation. *Archives of General Psychiatry*, *3*, 255–276.

Zuckerman, M. (1966). Save the pieces! A note on "The role of the family in the development of psychopathology". *Psychological Bulletin*, *68*, 78–80.

Zuckerman, M. (1967). The relations of mood and hypnotizability: An illustration of the importance of the state vs. trait distinction. *Journal of Consulting Psychology*, *31*, 464–470.

Zuckerman, M. (1968). Field dependency as a predictor of responses to sensory and social isolation. *Perceptual and Motor Skills*, *27*, 757–758.

Zuckerman, M. (1969). Variables affecting deprivation results. In: J. P. Zubek (Ed.), *Sensory deprivation: Fifteen years of research* (pp. 47–84). New York: Appleton-Century-Crofts.

Zuckerman, M. (1969). Hallucinations, reported sensations, and images. In: J. P. Zubek (Ed.), *Sensory deprivation: Fifteen years of research* (pp. 85–125). New York: Appleton-Century-Crofts.

Zuckerman, M. (1969). Theories of sensory deprivation: I. In: J. P. Zubek (Ed.), *Sensory deprivation: Fifteen years of research* (pp. 407–432). New York: Appleton-Century-Crofts.

Zuckerman, M. (1969). Response set in a check list test: A sometimes thing. *Psychological Reports*, *25*, 773–774.

Zuckerman, M., Albright, R. J., Marks, C. S., & Miller, G. L. (1962). Stress and hallucinatory effects of perceptual isolation and confinement. *Psychological Monographs*, *76*, 549.

Zuckerman, M., & Biase, V. (1962). Further data relevant to the construct validity of the affect adjective check list measure of anxiety. *Journal of Consulting Psychology*, *26*, 291.

Zuckerman, M., & Cohen, N. (1964). Is suggestion the source of reported visual sensations in perceptual isolation? *Journal of Abnormal and Social Psychology*, *68*, 655–660.

Zuckerman, M., & Cohen, N. (1964). Sources of reported visual and auditory sensations in perceptual isolation. *Psychological Bulletin*, *62*, 1–20. Reprinted. In: *The Bobbs-Merrill reprint series in the social sciences* (pp. 586–606). Indianapolis: Bobbs-Merrill.

Zuckerman, M., & Eisen, B. (1962). Relationship of acquiescence response set to authoritarianism and dependency. *Psychological Reports*, *10*, 95–102.

Zuckerman, M., & Haber, M. M. (1965). Need for stimulation as a source of stress response to perceptual isolation. *Journal of Abnormal and Social Psychology*, *70*, 371–377.

Zuckerman, M., & Hopkins, T. R. (1966). Hallucinations or dreams? A study of arousal levels and reported visual sensations during sensory deprivation. *Perceptual and Motor Skills*, *22*, 447–459.

Zuckerman, M., Kolin, B. A., Price, L., & Zoob, I. (1964). Development of a sensation-seeking scale. *Journal of Consulting Psychology*, 477–482.

Zuckerman, M., Levitt, E. E., & Lubin, B. (1961). Concurrent and construct validity of direct and indirect measures of dependency. *Journal of Consulting Psychology*, *25*, 316–323.

Zuckerman, M., Levine, S., & Biase, D. V. (1964). Stress response in total and partial perceptual isolation. *Psychosomatic Medicine*, *26*, 250–260.

Zuckerman, M., & Link, K. E. (1968). Construct validity data for the sensation seeking scale. *Journal of Consulting and Clinical Psychology*, *32*, 420–426.

Zuckerman, M., & Link, K. E. (1968). Expectancy and birth order as determinants of affective responses to isolation. *Perceptual and Motor Skills*, *27*, 279–286.

Zuckerman, M., Lubin, B., Vogel, L., & Valerius, E. (1964). Measurement of experimentally induced affects. *Journal of Consulting Psychology*, *28*, 418–425.

Zuckerman, M., & Lubin, B. (1965). *Test manual for the Multiple Affect Adjective Check List (MAACL)*. San Diego, CA: Educational and Industrial Testing Service.

Zuckerman, M., Lubin, B., & Robins, S. (1965). Validation of the Multiple Affect Adjective Check List in clinical situations. *Journal of Consulting Psychology*, *29*, 594.

Zuckerman, M., & Lubin, B. (1965). Normative data for the Multiple Affect Adjective Check List. *Psychological Reports*, *16*, 438.

Zuckerman, M., & Norton, J. (1961). Response set and content factors in the California F scale and the parental attitude research instrument. *Journal of Social Psychology*, *53*, 199–201.

Zuckerman, M., Nurnberger, J. I., Gardiner, S. H., Vandiveer, J. M., Barrett, B. H., & den Breeijen, A. (1963). Psychological correlates of somatic complaints in pregnancy and difficulty in childbirth. *Journal of Consulting Psychology*, *27*, 324–329.

Zuckerman, M., Oltean, M., & Monashkin, I. (1960). The parental attitudes of mothers and schizophrenics. *Journal of Consulting Psychology*, *22*, 307–310. Reprinted (1960). In: M. L. Haimowitz, & N. R. Haimowitz (Eds), *Human development: Selected readings* (pp. 426–431). New York: Crowell.

Zuckerman, M., Oppenheimer, C., & Gershowitz, D. (1965). Acquiescence and extreme sets of actors and teachers. *Psychological Reports*, *16*, 168–170.

Zuckerman, M., Persky, H., Hopkins, T. R., Murtaugh, T., Basu, G. K., & Schilling, M. (1966). Comparison of stress effects of perceptual and social isolation. *Archives of General Psychiatry*, *14*, 356–366.

Zuckerman, M., Persky, H., Eckman, K. M., & Hopkins, T. R. (1967). A multi-trait multi-method measurement approach to the traits (or states) of anxiety, depression and hostility. *Journal of Projective Techniques and Personality Assessment*, *31*, 39–48.

Zuckerman, M., Persky, H., & Curtis, G. (1968). Relationships between anxiety, depression, hostility and autonomic variables. *Journal of Nervous and Mental Diseases*, *146*, 481–487.

Zuckerman, M., Persky, H., Link, K. E., & Basu, G. K. (1968). Experimental and subject factors determining responses to sensory deprivation, social isolation, and confinement. *Journal of Abnormal Psychology*, *73*, 183–194.

Zuckerman, M., Persky, H., Link, K. E., & Basu, G. K. (1968). Responses to confinements: An investigation of sensory deprivation, social isolation, movement restriction, and set factors. *Perceptual and Motor Skills*, *27*, 319–334.

Zuckerman, M., Persky, H., Miller, L., & Levin, B. (1969). Contrasting effects of under-stimulation and over-stimulation. *Proceedings of the 77th Annual Convention of the American Psychological Association*, 319–320.

Zuckerman, M., Persky, H., & Link, K. E. (1969). The influence of set and diurnal factors on autonomic responses to sensory deprivation. *Psychophysiology*, *5*, 612–624.

Zuckerman, M., Schultz, D. P., & Hopkins, T. R. (1967). Sensation seeking and volunteering for sensory deprivation and hypnosis experiments. *Journal of Consulting Psychology*, *31*, 358–363.

1970–1979

Carroll, E., & Zuckerman, M. (1977). Psychopathology and sensation seeking in 'downers,' 'speeders,' and 'trippers': A study of the relationship between personality and drug choice. *International Journal of Addiction*, *12*, 591–601.

Daitzman, R. J., Zuckerman, M., Sammelwitz, T., & Ganjam, V. (1978). Sensation seeking and gonadal hormones. *Journal of Biosocial Science*, *10*, 401–408.

Eysenck, S. B. G., & Zuckerman, M. (1978). The relationship between sensation seeking and Eysenck's dimensions of personality. *British Journal of Psychology*, *69*, 483–487.

Kurtz, J. P., & Zuckerman, M. (1978). Race and sex differences on the sensation seeking scales. *Psychological Reports*, *43*, 529–530.

Mangelsdorff, A. D., & Zuckerman, M. (1975). Habituation to scenes of violence. *Psychophysiology*, *12*, 124–129.

Mellmstrom, M., Jr., Cicala, G. A., & Zuckerman, M. (1976). General vs. specific trait anxiety measures in the prediction of fear of snakes, heights, and darkness. *Journal of Consulting and Clinical Psychology*, *44*, 83–91.

Mellstrom, M., Jr., & Zuckerman, M. (1978). General versus specific traits in the assessment of anxiety. *Journal of Consulting and Clinical Psychology*, *46*, 423–431.

Mellstrom, M., Jr., Zuckerman, M., & Cicala, G. A. (1974). Anxiety: General vs. specific trait in the prediction of snake fear. *Psychological Reports*, *35*, 317–318.

Neary, R. S., & Zuckerman, M. (1976). Sensation seeking, trait and state anxiety and the electrodermal orienting response. *Psychophysiology*, *13*, 205–211.

Patrick, S. W., & Zuckerman, M. (1977). An application of the state-trait concept to the need for achievement. *Journal of Research in Personality*, *11*, 459–465.

Patrick, A. W., Zuckerman, M., & Masterson, F. A. (1974). An extension of the trait-state distinction from affects to motive measures. *Psychological Reports*, *34*, 1251–1258.

Skolnick, N., & Zuckerman, M. (1979). Personality change in drug abusers: A comparison of therapeutic community and prison groups. *Journal of Consulting and Clinical Psychology*, *47*, 768–770.

Tushup, R. J., & Zuckerman, M. (1977). The effects of stimulus invariance on daydreaming and divergent thinking. *Journal of Mental Imagery*, *1*, 291–302.

Zuckerman, M. (1970). Sensations and hallucinations in sensory deprivation: Research data pertinent to thirteen hypotheses and a reformulation. In: W. Keup (Ed.), *Origins and mechanisms of hallucinations* (pp. 133–148). New York: Plenum Press.

Zuckerman, M. (1970). *Bibliography for the Multiple Affect Adjective Check List (MAACL)*. San Diego: Educational and Industrial Testing Service.

Zuckerman, M. (1971). Physiological measures of sexual arousal in the human. *Psychological Bulletin*, *75*, 297–329. Reprinted. (1972). In: N. S. Greenfield, & R. A. Sternbach (Eds), *Handbook of psychophysiology* (pp. 709–740). New York: Holt, Rinehart and Winston.

Zuckerman, M. (1971). Dimensions of sensation seeking. *Journal of Consulting and Clinical Psychology*, *36*, 45–72.

Zuckerman, M. (1972). Drug usage as one manifestation of a "sensation-seeking" trait. In: W. Keup (Ed.), *Drug abuse, current concepts and research* (pp. 154–163). Springfield, IL: Charles Thomas.

Zuckerman, M. (1973). Scales for sex experience for males and females. *Journal of Consulting and Clinical Psychology*, *41*, 27–29.

Zuckerman, M. (1974). The sensation seeking motive. In: B. A. Maher (Ed.), *Progress in experimental personality research* (pp. 80–148). New York: Academic Press.

Zuckerman, M. (1976). General and situation-specific traits and states: New approaches to assessment of anxiety and other constructs. In: M. Zuckerman, & C. D. Spielberger (Eds), *Emotions and anxiety: New concepts, methods and applications* (pp. 133–174). Hillsdale, NJ: Erlbaum.

Zuckerman, M. (1976). Sensation seeking and anxiety, traits and states, as determinants of behavior in novel situations. In: I. Sarason, & C. D. Spielberger (Eds), *Stress and anxiety* (pp. 141–170). Washington, DC: Hemisphere.

Zuckerman, M. (1976). Sexual behavior of college students. In: W. W. Oaks, G. A. Melchiode, & I. Ficher (Eds), *Sex and the life cycle: The thirty-fifth Hahnemann symposium* (pp.67–80). New York: Grune & Stratton.

Zuckerman, M. (1976). Research on pornography. In: W. W. Oaks, G. A. Melchiode, & I. Ficher (Eds), *Sex and life cycle: The thirty-fifth Hahnemann symposium* (147–161). New York: Grune & Stratton.

Zuckerman, M. (1977). The development of a situation-specific test for the prediction and assessment of affective responses. *Journal of Consulting and Clinical Psychology*, *45*, 513–523.

Zuckerman, M. (1978). Sensation seeking. *Psychology Today*, *11*, February.

Zuckerman, M. (1978). Sensation seeking and psychopathy. In: R. D. Hare, & D. Schalling (Eds), *Psychopathic behavior: Approaches to research* (pp. 165–185). London: Wiley.

Zuckerman, M. (1978). Sensation seeking. In: H. London, & J. Exner (Eds), *Dimensions of personality* (pp. 487–555). New York: Wiley.

Zuckerman, M. (1979). *Sensation seeking: Beyond the optimal level of arousal*. Hillsdale, NJ: Erlbaum.

Zuckerman, M. (1979). Sensation seeking and risk taking. In: C. E. Izard (Ed.), *Emotions in personality and psychopathology* (pp. 163–197). New York: Plenum.

Zuckerman, M. (1979). Traits, states, situations, and uncertainty. *Journal of Behavioral Assessment*, *1*, 43–54.

Zuckerman, M. (1979). What and where is the unconditioned (or conditioned) stimulus in the conditioning model of neurosis? Comment on "The conditioning model of neurosis" by H. J. Eysenck. *Behavioral and Brain Sciences*, *2*, 187–188.

Zuckerman, M., Bone, R. N., Neary, R., Mangelsdorff, D., & Brustman, B. (1972). What is the sensation seeker? Personality trait and experience correlates of the sensation-seeking scales. *Journal of Consulting and Clinical Psychology*, *39*, 308–321.

Zuckerman, M., Eysenck, S. B. G., & Eysenck, H. J. (1978). Sensation seeking in England and America: Cross-cultural, age, and sex comparisons. *Journal of Consulting and Clinical Psychology*, *46*, 139–149.

Zuckerman, M., Miller, L., & Levin, B. (1970). Sensory deprivation vs. sensory variation. *Journal of Abnormal Psychology*, *76*, 76–82.

Zuckerman, M., & Mellstrom, Jr., M. (1977). The contributions of persons situations, modes of responses, and their interactions in self-reported responses to hypothetical and real anxiety-inducing situations. In: D. Magnussen, & N. S. Endler (Eds), *Personality at the crossroads: Current issues in interactional psychology* (pp. 193–200). Hillsdale, NJ: Erlbaum.

Zuckerman, M., Murtaugh, T., & Siegel, J. (1974). Sensation seeking and cortical augmenting-reducing. *Psychophysiology*, *11*, 535–542.

Zuckerman, M., Neary, R. S., & Brustman, B. A. (1970). Sensation seeking scale correlates in experience (smoking, drugs, alcohol, "hallucinations" and sex) and preference for complexity (designs). *Proceedings, 78th Annual Convention of the American Psychological Association*, 317–318.

Zuckerman, M., & Neeb, M. (1979). Sensation seeking and psychopathology. *Psychiatry Research*, *1*, 255–264.

Zuckerman, M., & Schwartz, L. (1977). *Bibliography for the Multiple Affect Adjective Check List (MAACL)*. San Diego: Educational and Industrial Testing Service.

Zuckerman, M., Sola, S., Masterson, J., & Angelone, J. V. (1975). MMPI patterns in drug abusers before and after treatment in therapeutic communities. *Journal of Consulting and Clinical Psychology*, *43*, 286–296.

Zuckerman, M., & Spielberger, C. D. (Eds) (1976). *Emotions and anxiety: New concepts, methods and applications*. Hillsdale, NJ: Erlbaum.

Zuckerman, M., Tushup, R., & Finner, S. (1976). Sexual attitudes and experience: Attitude and personality correlates and changes produced by a course in sexuality. *Journal of Consulting and Clinical Psychology*, *44*, 7–19.

1980–1989

Ballenger, J. C., Post, R. M., Jimerson, D. C., Lake, C. R., Murphy, D., Zuckerman, M., & Cronin, C. (1983). Biochemical correlates of personality traits. *Personality and Individual Differences*, *4*, 615–625.

Ballenger, J. C., Post, R. M., Jimerson, D. C., Lake, C. R., & Zuckerman, M. (1984). Neurobiological correlates of depression and anxiety in normal individuals. In: R. M. Post, & J. D. Ballenger (Eds), *Neurobiology of mood disorders* (pp. 481–501). Baltimore, MD: Williams & Wilkens.

Carrol, E. N., Zuckerman, M., & Vogel, W. H. (1982). A test of the optimal level of arousal theory of sensation seeking. *Journal of Personality and Social Psychology*, *43*, 572–575.

Daitzman, R., & Zuckerman, M. (1980). Disinhibitory sensation seeking, personality, and gonadal hormones. *Personality and Individual Differences*, *1*, 103–110.

Ficher, M., Neeb, M., Zuckerman, M., Fishkin, R. E., Goldman, A., Cohen, S. N., Jacobs, J. A., Weisberg, M., De Lisser, O., & Fink, P. J. (1984). Study of sexual dysfunction among male diabetics. In: M. Ficher, R. E. Fishkin, & J. A. Jacobs (Eds), *Sexual arousal: New concepts in basic sciences, diagnosis, and treatment* (pp. 159–204). Springfield, IL: Charles C. Thomas.

Ficher, M., Zuckerman, M., Fishkin, R. E. *et al.* (1984). Do endocrines play an etiological role in diabetic and non-diabetic sexual dysfunctions? *Journal of Andrology*, *5*, 8–16.

Ficher, I. V., Zuckerman, M., & Neeb, M. (1981). Marital compatibility and sensation seeking trait as a factor in marital adjustment. *Journal of Sex and Marital Therapy*, *7*, 60–69.

Ficher, I. V., Zuckerman, M., & Steinberg, M. (1988). Sensation seeking congruence in couples as a determinant of marital adjustment: A partial replication and extension. *Journal of Clinical Psychology*, *44*, 803–809.

Fulker, D. W., Eysenck, S. B. G., & Zuckerman, M. (1980). A genetic and environmental analysis of sensation seeking. *Journal of Research in Personality*, *14*, 261–281.

Kozma, C., & Zuckerman, M. (1983). An investigation of some hypotheses concerning rape and murder. *Personality and Individual Differences*, *4*, 23–29.

Litle, P., & Zuckerman, M. (1986). Sensation seeking and music preferences. *Personality and Individual Differences*, *7*, 575–576.

Lubin, B., Zuckerman, M., Breytspraak, L. M., Bull, N. C., Gumbhir, A. K., & Rinck, C. M. (1988). Affects, demographic variables, and health. *Journal of Clinical Psychology*, *44*, 131–141.

Lubin, B., Zuckerman, M., Hanson, P. G., Armstrong, T., Rinck, C. M., & Seever, M. (1986). Reliability and validity of the Multiple Affect Adjective Check List-Revised. *Journal of Psychopathology and Behavioral Assessment*, *8*, 103–117.

Zuckerman, M. (1980). To risk or not to risk: Predicting behavior from negative and positive emotional states. In: K. R. Blanksteen, P. Pliner, & J. Polivy (Eds), *Advances in the study of communications and affect* (pp. 71–94). New York: Plenum Press.

Zuckerman, M. (1982). Leaping up the phylogenetic scale: Perils and possibilities. Comment on "Précis of The neuropsychology of anxiety: An enquiry into the functions of the septo–hippocampal system" by J. A. Gray. *Behavioral and Brain Sciences*, *5*, 505–506.

Zuckerman, M. (1982). Can arousal be pleasurable? Comment on "Toward a general psychobiology of emotions" by J. Panksepp. *Behavioral and Brain Sciences*, *5*, 449.

Zuckerman, M. (1983). Sensation seeking: The initial motive for drug abuse. In: E. Gottheil, K. A. Druley, T. E. Skoloda, & H. M. Waxman (Eds), *Etiologic aspects of alcohol and drug abuse* (pp. 202–220). Springfield, IL: Charles Thomas.

Zuckerman, M. (1983). Preface. In: M. Zuckerman (Ed.), *Biological bases of sensation seeking, impulsivity, and anxiety* (pp. ix–xii). Hillsdale, NJ: Erlbaum.

Zuckerman, M. (1983). A biological theory of sensation seeking. In: M. Zuckerman (Ed.), *Biological bases of sensation seeking, impulsivity, and anxiety* (pp. 37–76). Hillsdale, NJ: Erlbaum.

Zuckerman, M. (1983). A summing up with special sensitivity to the signals of reward in future research. In: M. Zuckerman (Ed.), *Biological bases of sensation seeking, impulsivity, and anxiety* (pp. 249–260). Hillsdale, NJ: Erlbaum.

Zuckerman, M. (1983). Sensation seeking and sports. *Journal of Personality and Individual Differences*, *4*, 285–292.

Zuckerman, M. (1983). The distinction between trait and state scales is not arbitrary: Comment on Allen and Potkay's "On the arbitrary distinction between traits and states". *Journal of Personality and Social Psychology*, *44*, 1083–1086.

Zuckerman, M. (1983). Sensation seeking: A biosocial dimension of personality. In: A. Gale, & J. Edwards (Eds), *Physiological correlates of human behavior, Individual differences and psychopathology* (Vol. 3, pp. 99–115). New York: Academic Press.

Zuckerman, M. (1983). Sexual arousal in the human: Love, chemistry or conditioning? In: A. Gale, & J. Edwards (Eds), *Physiological correlates of human behavior: Basic issues* (Vol. 1, pp. 299–326). New York: Academic Press.

Zuckerman, M. (1983). Biosocial bridges. Book reviews of "Human motivation" by R. E. Franken and "Motivation: Biosocial approaches" by S. B. Klein. *Contemporary Psychology*, *28*, 224–225.

Zuckerman, M. (1983). Sensation seeking: Optimal levels of arousal or reward system neurotransmitters. In: R. Sinz, & M. R. Rosenzweig (Eds), *Psychophysiology: Memory, motivation and event-related potentials in mental operations* (pp. 257–262). Jena, Germany: Fischer-Verlag.

Zuckerman, M. (1983). Sensation seeking and arousal systems. *Personality and Individual Differences*, *4*, 381–386.

Zuckerman, M. (1984). Sensation seeking: A comparative approach to a human trait. *The Behavioral and Brain Sciences*, *7*, 413–471.

Zuckerman, M. (1984). Experience and desire: A new format for sensation seeking scales. *Journal of Behavioral Assessment*, *6*, 101–104.

Zuckerman, M. (1985). Biological foundations of the sensation seeking temperament. In: J. Strelau, F. H. Farley, & A. Gale (Eds), *The biological bases of personality and behavior* (Vol. 1, pp. 97–112). Washington, DC: Hemisphere.

Zuckerman, M. (1985). Sensation seeking, mania, and monoamines. *Neuropsychobiology*, *13*, 121–128.

Zuckerman, M. (1985). Review of sixteen personality factor questionnaire. In: J. V. Mitchell, Jr. (Ed.), *The ninth mental measurements yearbook*, (Vol. 2, pp. 1392–1394). Lincoln, NE: University of Nebraska Press.

Zuckerman, M. (1985). A critical look at three arousal constructs in personality theories: Optimal level of arousal, strength of the nervous system, and sensitivities to signals of reward and punishment. In: J. T. Spence, & C. E. Izard (Eds), *Motivation, emotion, and personality* (pp. 119–136). Amsterdam: Elsevier.

Zuckerman, M. (1985). Book review of "Temperament, personality and activity" by J. Strelau. *Biological Psychology*, *21*, 141–144.

Zuckerman, M. (1986). Sensation seeking and augmenting-reducing. Evoked potentials and/or kinesthetic figural aftereffects. *Behavioral and Brain Sciences*, *9*, 749–754.

Zuckerman, M. (1986). Serotonin, impulsivity and emotionality. Comment on "An essay on circulation as behavior" by B. T. Engel. *Behavioral and Brain Sciences*, *9*, 348–349.

Zuckerman, M. (1986). Sensation seeking and the endogenous deficit theory of drug abuse. In: S. I. Szara (Ed.), *Neurobiology of behavioral control in drug abuse*. NIDA Research Monograph (Vol. 74, pp. 59–70).

Zuckerman, M. (1987). A critical look at three arousal constructs in personality theories. In: J. Strelau, & H. J. Eysenck (Eds), *Personality dimensions and arousal* (pp. 217–231). New York: Plenum Press.

Zuckerman, M. (1987). Biological connection between sensation seeking and drug abuse. In: J. Engel, & L. Oreland (Eds), *Brain reward systems and abuse* (pp. 165–176). New York: Raven.

Zuckerman, M. (1987). All parents are environmentalists until they have their second child. Comment on "Why are children in the same family so different?" by R. Plomin & D. Daniels. *Behavioral and Brain Sciences*, *10*, 42–44.

Zuckerman, M. (1987). Is sensation seeking a predisposing trait for alcoholism? In: E. Gottheil, K. A. Druley, S. Peshko, & S. P. Weinstein (Eds), *Stress and addiction* (pp. 283–301). New York: Bruner/Mazel.

Zuckerman, M. (1988). Behavior and biology: Research on sensation seeking and reactions to the media. In: L. Donhew, H. E. Sypher, & E. T. Higgins (Eds), *Communication, social cognition and affect* (pp. 173–194). Hillsdale, NJ: Erlbaum.

Zuckerman, M. (1988). Brain monoamine systems and personality. In: D. Hellhammer, I. Florin, & H. Weiner (Eds), *Neurobiological approaches to human disease* (pp. 5–14). Toronto: Hans Huber Publishers.

Zuckerman, M. (1988). Sensation seeking, risk taking, and health. In: M. P. Janisse (Ed.), *Individual differences, stress, and health psychology* (pp. 72–88). New York: Springer-Verlag.

Zuckerman, M. (1989). Personality in the third dimension: A psychobiological approach. *Personality and Individual Differences*, *11*, 343–353.

Zuckerman, M., Ballenger, J. C., Jimerson, D. C., Murphy, D. L., & Post, R. M. (1983). A correlational test in humans of the biological models of sensation seeking, impulsivity, and anxiety. In: M. Zuckerman (Ed.), *Biological bases of sensation seeking, impulsivity, and anxiety* (pp. 229–248). Hillsdale, NJ: Erlbaum.

Zuckerman, M., Ballenger, J. C., & Post, R. M. (1984). The neurobiology of some dimensions of personality. In: J. R. Smythies, & R. J. Bradley (Eds), *International Review of Neurobiology* (pp. 391–436). New York: Academic Press.

Zuckerman, M., & Brody, N. (1988). Oysters, rabbits, and people: A critique of "Race differences in behaviour" by J. P. Rushton. *Personality and Individual Differences*, *9*, 1025–1033.

Zuckerman, M., Buchsbaum, M. S., & Murphy, D. L. (1980). Sensation seeking and its biological correlates. *Psychological Bulletin*, *88*, 198–214.

Zuckerman, M., Kuhlman, D. M., & Camac, C. (1988). What lies beyond E and N? Factor analyses of scales believed to measure basic dimensions of personality. *Journal of Personality and Social Psychology*, *54*, 96–107.

Zuckerman, M., & Litle, P. (1986). Personality and curiosity about morbid and sexual events. *Personality and Individual Differences*, *7*, 49–56.

Zuckerman, M., & Lubin, B. (1985). *Manual for the MAACL-R: The Multiple Affect Adjective Check List-Revised*. San Diego, CA: Educational and Industrial Testing Service.

Zuckerman, M., Lubin, B., & Rinck, C. M. (1983). Construction of new scales for the Multiple Affect Adjective Check List. *Journal of Behavioral Assessment*, *5*, 119–129.

Zuckerman, M., Lubin, B., Rinck, C. M., Soliday, S. M., Albott, W. L., & Carlson, K. (1986). Discriminant validity of the Multiple Affect Adjective Check List. *Journal of Psychopathology and Behavioral Assessment*, *8*, 119–128.

Zuckerman, M., & Myers, P. L. (1983). Are homosexuals sensation seekers? *Archives of Sexual Behavior*, *12*, 347–356.

Zuckerman, M., & Neeb, M. (1980). Demographic influences in sensation seeking and expressions of sensation seeking in religion, smoking, and driving habits. *Personality and Individual Differences*, *1*, 197–206.

Zuckerman, M., Neeb, M., Ficher, M. *et al.* (1985). Nocturnal penile tumescence and penile responses in the waking state in diabetic and non-diabetic sexual dysfunctionals. *Archives of Sexual Behavior*, *14*, 109–129.

Zuckerman, M., Simons, R. F., & Como, P. G. (1988). Sensation seeking and stimulus intensity as modulators of cortical cardiovascular and electrodermal response. *Personality and Individual Differences*, *9*, 361–372.

1990–1999

Ball, S. A., & Zuckerman, M. (1990). Sensation seeking, Eysenck's personality dimensions and reinforcement sensitivity in concept formation. *Personality and Individual Differences*, *11*, 343–353.

Ball, S. A., & Zuckerman, M. (1992). Sensation seeking and selective attention. Focused and divided attention on a dichotic listening task. *Journal of Personality and Social Psychology*, *63*, 825–831.

Breen, R. B., & Zuckerman, M. (1999). 'Chasing' in gambling behavior: Personality and cognitive determinants. *Personality and Individual Differences*, *27*, 1097–1111.

Cronin, C., & Zuckerman, M. (1992). Sensation seeking and bipolar disorder. *Personality and Individual Differences*, *13*, 385–387.

Horvath, P., & Zuckerman, M. (1993). Sensation seeking, risk appraisal, and risky behavior. *Personality and Individual Differences*, *14*, 41–52.

Kraft, M. R., Jr., & Zuckerman, M. (1999). Parental behavior and attitudes of their parents reported by young adults from intact and stepparent families and relationships between perceived parenting and personality. *Personality and Individual Differences*, *27*, 453–476.

Lubin, B., Whitlock, R. V., & Zuckerman, M. (1998). Affect traits in differentiation of anxiety, depressive, and schizophrenic disorders using the Multiple Affect Adjective Check List-Revised. *Assessment*, *5*, 309–320.

Lubin, B., & Zuckerman, M. (1999). *Manual for the MAACL-R: Multiple Affect Adjective Check List-Revised.* San Diego, CA: Educational and Industrial Testing Service.

O'Sullivan, D. M., Zuckerman, M., & Kraft, M. (1996). The personality of prostitutes. *Personality and Individual Differences*, *21*, 445–448.

O'Sullivan, D. M., Zuckerman, M., & Kraft, M. (1998). Personality characteristics of male and female participants in team sports. *Personality and Individual Differences*, *25*, 119–128.

Russo, K. R., & Zuckerman, M. (1992). Psychological, physiological and physical characteristics of subjects at risk for essential hypertension. *Personality and Individual Differences*, *13*, 61–68.

Thornquist, M. H., & Zuckerman, M. (1995). Psychopathy, passive-avoidance learning and basic dimensions of personality. *Personality and Individual Differences*, *19*, 525–534.

Thornquist, M. H., Zuckerman, M., & Exline, R. V. (1991). Loving, liking, looking and sensation seeking in unmarried college couples. *Personality and Individual Differences*, *12*, 1283–1292.

Zuckerman, M. (1990). Broad or narrow affect scores for the Multiple Affect Adjective Check List? Comment on Hunsley's "Dimensionality of the Multiple Affect Adjective Check List-Revised". *Journal of Psychopathology and Behavioral Assessment*, *12*, 93–97.

Zuckerman, M. (1990). The psychophysiology of sensation seeking. *Journal of Personality*, *58*, 313–345.

Zuckerman, M. (1990). Some dubious premises in research and theory on racial differences: Scientific, social, and ethical issues. *American Psychologist*, *45*, 1297–1303.

Zuckerman, M. (1990). Still another failure of arousal theory: A critique of "Personality, situation, and physiological arousability" by G. Stemmler, & E. Meinhardt. *Personality and Individual Differences*, *11*, 309–312.

Zuckerman, M. (1991). *Psychobiology of personality*. New York: Cambridge University Press.

Zuckerman, M. (1991). Biotypes for basic personality dimensions? 'The twilight zone' between genotype and social phenotype. In: J. Strelau, & A. Angleitner (Eds), *Explorations in temperament: International perspectives on theory and measurement* (pp. 129–146). New York: Plenum Press.

Zuckerman, M, (1991). One person's stress is another person's pleasure. In: C. D. Spielberger, I. G. Sarason, Z. Kulcsar, & G. L. van Heck (Eds), *Stress and emotion: Anxiety, anger and curiosity* (Vol. 14, pp. 31–45). New York: Hemisphere.

Zuckerman, M. (1991). Sensation seeking trait. In: *Encyclopedia of Human Biology* (Vol. 6, pp. 809–817). New York: Academic Press.

Zuckerman, M. (1991). Sensation seeking: The balance between risk and reward. In: L. P. Lipsit, & L. L. Mitnick (Eds), *Self-regulatory behavior and risk-taking: Causes and consequences* (pp. 143–152). Norwood, NJ: Ablex Publishing Corporation.

Zuckerman, M. (1992). What is a basic factor and which factors are basic? Turtles all the way down. *Personality and Individual Differences*, *13*, 675–681.

Zuckerman, M. (1992). Out of sensory deprivation and into sensation seeking: A personal and scientific journey. In: G. G. Brannigan, & M. R. Merrens (Eds), *The undaunted psychologist: Adventures in research* (pp. 45–57). Philadelphia, PA: Temple University Press.

Zuckerman, M. (1993). Personality from top (traits) to bottom (genetics) with stops at each level between. In: J. Hettema, & I. J. Deary (Eds), *Foundations of personality* (pp. 73–100). Dordrecht, The Netherlands: Kluwer.

Zuckerman, M. (1993). P-impulsive sensation seeking and its behavioral, psychophysiological and biochemical correlates. *Neuropsychobiology*, *28*, 30–36.

Zuckerman, M. (1993). Sensation seeking and impulsivity: A marriage of traits made in biology? In: W. G. McGowan, J. L. Johnson, & M. B. Shure (Eds), *The impulsive client* (pp. 71–91). Washington, DC: American Psychological Association.

Zuckerman, M. (1994). Impulsive unsocialized sensation seeking: The biological foundations of a basic dimension of personality. In: J. E. Bates, & T. D. Wachs (Eds), *Temperament: Individual differences at the interface of biology and behavior* (pp. 219–55). Washington, DC: American Psychological Association.

Zuckerman, M. (1994). *Behavioral expressions and biosocial bases of sensation seeking*. New York: Cambridge University Press.

Zuckerman, M. (1994). Sensation seeking. In: R. J. Corsini (Ed.), *Encyclopedia of psychology* (2nd ed., Vol. 3, pp. 374–377). New York: Wiley.

Zuckerman, M. (1994). An alternative five-factor model for personality. In: C. F. Halverson, Jr., G. A. Kohnstamm, & R. P. Martin (Eds), *The developing structure of temperament and personality from infancy to adulthood* (pp. 53–68). Hillsdale, NJ: Erlbaum.

Zuckerman, M. (1995). Good and bad humors: Biochemical bases of personality and its disorders. *Psychological Science*, *6*, 325–332.

Zuckerman, M. (1995). Is the distinction between primary and secondary sociopaths a matter of degree, secondary traits, or nature vs. nurture? Comment on "The sociobiology of sociopathy: An integrated evolutionary model' by L. Mealey. *Behavioral and Brain Sciences*, *18*, 578–579.

Zuckerman, M. (1996). Sensation seeking. In: C. G. Costello (Ed.), *Personality characteristics of the personality disordered* (pp. 289–316). New York: Wiley.

Zuckerman, M. (1996). Sensation seeking and the taste for vicarious horror. In: J. B. Weaver, & R. Tamborini (Eds), *Horror films: Current research on audience preferences and reactions* (pp. 147–160). Mahwah, NJ: Erlbaum.

Zuckerman, M. (1996). Item revisions in the Sensation Seeking Scale Form-V (SSS-V). *Personality and Individual Differences*, *20*, 515.

Zuckerman, M. (1996). Conceptual clarification or confusion in "The study of sensation seeking" by J. S. H. Jackson, & M. Maraun. *Personality and Individual Differences*, *21*, 111–113.

Zuckerman, M. (1996). The psychobiological model for impulsive unsocialized sensation seeking: A comparative approach. *Neuropsychobiology*, *34*, 125–129.

Zuckerman, M. (1997). The psychobiological basis of personality. In: H. Nyborg (Ed.), *The scientific study of human nature* (pp. 3–16). New York: Elsevier.

Zuckerman, M. (1997). Sensation seeking trait. In: R. Dulbecco (Ed.), *Encyclopedia of human biology* (Vol. 7, pp. 755–763). San Diego: Academic Press.

Zuckerman, M. (1999). *Vulnerability to psychopathology: A biosocial model*. Washington, DC: American Psychological Association.

Zuckerman, M. (1999). Temperament: Humors and genes. Review of "Temperament: A Psychological Perspective" by J. Strelau. *Contemporary Psychology: APA Review of Books*, *44*, 500–501.

Zuckerman, M., Ball, S., & Black, J. (1990). Influences of sensation seeking, gender, risk appraisal, and situational motivation on smoking. *Addictive Behaviors*, *15*, 209–220.

Zuckerman, M., & Cloninger, C. R. (1996). Relationships between Cloninger's, Zuckerman's and Eysenck's dimensions of personality. *Personality and Individual Differences*, *21*, 283–285.

Zuckerman, M., Joireman, J., Kraft, M., & Kuhlman, D. M. (1999). Where do motivational and emotional traits fit within three factor models of personality? *Personality and Individual Differences*, *26*, 487–504.

Zuckerman, M., Kuhlman, D. M., Thornquist, M., & Kiers, H. (1991). Five (or three) robust questionnaire scale factors of personality without culture. *Personality and Individual Differences*, *12*, 929–941.

Zuckerman, M., Kuhlman, D. M., Joireman, J., Teta, P., & Kraft, M. (1993). A comparison of three structural models for personality: The big three, the big five, and the alternative five. *Journal of Personality and Social Psychology*, *65*, 757–768.

Zuckerman, M., & Lubin, B. (1990). A useful measure for state affects [citation classic]. *Current Contents*, *18*, 16.

Zuckerman, M., Ulrich, R. S., & McLaughlin, J. (1993). Sensation seeking and reactions to nature paintings. *Personality and Individual Differences*, *15*, 563–576.

2000–

Breen, R. B., & Zuckerman, M. (2002). 'Chasing' in gambling behavior: Personality and cognitive changes. In: J. J. Marotta, J. A. Cornelius, & W. R. Eadington (Eds), *The downside: Problem and pathological gambling* (pp. 223–241). Reno, NV: Institute for the Study of Gambling and Commercial Gaming Institute.

McDaniel, S. R., & Zuckerman, M. (2003). The relationship of impulsive sensation seeking and gender to interest and participation in gambling activities. *Personality and Individual Differences*, *35*, 1385–1400.

Zuckerman, M. (2000). Sensation seeking, creativity, and psychopathology. *Bulletin of Psychology and the Arts*, *1*, 48–49.

Zuckerman, M. (2000). Are you a risk-taker? *Psychology Today*, *33*(Nov/Dec), 52–57; 82–87.

Zuckerman, M. (2000). Sensation seeking. In: A. E. Kazdin (Ed.), *Encyclopedia of psychology* (Vol. 7, pp. 225–226). Washington, DC: American Psychological Association.

Zuckerman, M. (2000). Sensation seeking. In: W. E. Craighead, & C. B. Nemeroff (Eds), *The Corsini encyclopedia of psychology and social science* (3rd ed., Vol. 4, pp. 1485–1488). New York: Wiley.

Zuckerman, M. (2001). Optimism and pessimism: Biological foundations. In: E. C. Chang (Ed.), *Optimism and pessimism: Implications for theory, research, and practice* (pp. 169–188). Washington, DC: American Psychological Association.

Zuckerman, M. (2001). Adult temperament and its biological basis. In: A. Eliasz, & A. Angleitner (Eds), *Advances in research on temperament* (pp. 42–59). Lengerich, Germany: Pabst Science Publishers.

Zuckerman, M. (2002). Genetics of sensation seeking. In: J. Benjamin, R. P. Epstein, & R. H. Belmaker (Eds), *Molecular genetics and the human personality* (pp. 193–210). Washington, DC: American Psychiatric Association.

Zuckerman, M. (2002). Personality and psychopathy: Shared behavioral and biological traits. In: J. Glicksohn (Ed.), *The neurobiology of criminal behavior* (pp. 27–49). Norwell, MA: Kluwer.

Zuckerman, M. (2002). Zuckerman-Kuhlman Personality Questionnaire (ZKPQ): An alternative five-factorial model. In: B. DeRaad, & M. Perugini (Eds), *Big five assessment* (pp. 377–396). Göttingen: Hogrefe & Huber.

Zuckerman, M. (2003). Biological bases of personality. In: I. B. Weiner, T. Millon, & M. J. Lerner (Eds), *Handbook of psychology, personality and social psychology* (Vol. 5, pp. 85–116). Hoboken, NJ: Wiley.

Zuckerman, M. (2003). Are there racial and ethnic differences in psychopathic personality? A critique of "Racial and ethnic differences in psychopathic personality" by R. Lynn. *Personality and Individual Differences*, *35*, 1463–1469.

Zuckerman, M. (2004). The shaping of personality: Genes, environments, and chance encounters. *Journal of Personality Assessment*, *82*, 11–22.

Zuckerman, M., & Kuhlman, D. M. (2000). Personality and risk-taking: Common biosocial factors. *Journal of Personality*, *68*, 999–1029.

Author Index

Subject Index